For Reference

Not to be taken from this room

Women in American History

Women in American History

A Social, Political, and Cultural Encyclopedia and Document Collection

VOLUME ONE: PRECOLONIAL NORTH AMERICA
TO THE EARLY REPUBLIC

PEG A. LAMPHIER AND ROSANNE WELCH, EDITORS

ABC-CLIO™

An Imprint of ABC-CLIO, LLC
Santa Barbara, California • Denver, Colorado

Library of Congress Cataloging-in-Publication Data

Names: Lamphier, Peg A., editor. | Welch, Rosanne, editor.
Title: Women in American history : a social, political, and cultural encyclopedia
    and document collection / Peg A. Lamphier and Rosanne Welch, editors.
Description: Santa Barbara, California : ABC-CLIO, [2017] Contents:
    Volume 1. Precolonial North America to the Early Republic—
    Volume 2. Antebellum America through the Gilded Age—Volume 3.
    Progressive Era through World War II—Volume 4. Cold War America to today.
    | Includes bibliographical references and index.
Identifiers: LCCN 2016021767 (print) | LCCN 2016036285 (ebook) | ISBN 9781610696029
    (set : alk. paper) | ISBN 9781440846045 (volume 1 : alk. paper) | ISBN 9781440846052
    (volume 2 : alk. paper) | ISBN 9781440846069 (volume 3 : alk. paper) | ISBN 9781440846076
    (volume 4 : alk. paper) | ISBN 9781610696036 (ebook)
Subjects: LCSH: Women—United States—History—Encyclopedias. | Women—
    United States—History—Sources.
Classification: LCC HQ1410 .W6468 2017 (print) | LCC HQ1410 (ebook) | DDC 305.40973–dc23
LC record available at https://lccn.loc.gov/2016021767

ISBN: 978-1-61069-602-9 (set)
       978-1-4408-4604-5 (vol. 1)
       978-1-4408-4605-2 (vol. 2)
       978-1-4408-4606-9 (vol. 3)
       978-1-4408-4607-6 (vol. 4)
EISBN: 978-1-61069-603-6

21 20 19 18 17   1 2 3 4 5

This book is also available as an eBook.

ABC-CLIO
An Imprint of ABC-CLIO, LLC

ABC-CLIO, LLC
130 Cremona Drive, P.O. Box 1911
Santa Barbara, California 93116-1911
www.abc-clio.com

This book is printed on acid-free paper ∞
Manufactured in the United States of America

Contents

VOLUME 2: ANTEBELLUM AMERICA THROUGH THE GILDED AGE

VOLUME 3: PROGRESSIVE ERA THROUGH WORLD WAR II

3. World War II (1939–1945), 297

VOLUME 4: COLD WAR AMERICA TO TODAY

Preface

Choosing the entries for *Women in American History: A Social, Political, and Cultural Encyclopedia and Document Collection* was both a huge task and an immense privilege. The editors understood from the start that the work on these volumes would be largely a labor of love and historical archaeology. Along the way, we have enjoyed envisioning the young people who would first be introduced to these accomplished role models by perusing these volumes. It is for the readers as well as for these historically significant and yet largely unknown women and organizations that we took on this task. Along the way, we made a number of editorial decisions that are explained here.

Containing more than 750 entries and more than 195 primary documents, *Women in American History* is arranged chronologically, with each of the its four volumes divided into three chronological sections:

Volume 1: Precolonial North America to the Early Republic

1. Precolonial North America (Pre-1607)
2. Colonial North America (1607–1754)
3. Revolutionary America and the New Republic (1754–1819)

Volume 2: Antebellum America through the Gilded Age

1. The Antebellum Era (1820–1860)
2. The Civil War and Reconstruction (1861–1877)
3. The Gilded Age (1878–1899)

Volume 3: Progressive Era through World War II

1. The Progressive Era (1900–1929)
2. The Great Depression and the New Deal (1930–1941)
3. World War II (1939–1945)

Volume 4: Cold War America to Today

1. Cold War America (1946–1962)
2. Second-Wave Feminism (1963–1989)
3. Third-Wave Feminism (1990–Present)

Each section has its own primary documents following relevant entries and bibliography as well as a historical overview and thematic issues essays. The historical overview explores the general history of the period, while the thematic issues essays cover the following 10 categories for each section:

Childbirth and child rearing
Clothing and fashion
Courtship, marriage, and divorce
Education
Fertility and fertility control
Gender roles
Immigration and migration
Legal and political power
Violence, domestic and sexual
Work, waged and unwaged

The intention with these essays was to avoid repetition of entries on their broad topics in each section and to instead cover all these categories in one place for each section.

In the entries, the editors decided to use a woman's best-known last name to identify her even if she did not use that name over the course of her entire life. Thus, Abigail Adams is referred to as Adams in her entry before she married John Adams, though her birth name was Abigail Smith. Historians, for example, would never refer to Thomas Jefferson as Thomas or Tom. Women, on the other hand, are commonly referred to by their first names; Abigail Adams, for instance, might be called Abigail in a biography of John Adams. In the case where the woman had a famous husband, as in John and Abigail Adams, we refer to Abigail Adams as Adams and to John Adams either by his full name or by his first name. More problematically, women change their last names, sometimes multiple times, throughout their lives. Using a woman's best-known name consistently throughout an entry, regardless of which name an individual used at an particular time, avoids confusion.

This volume is not a comprehensive biographical encyclopedia but instead is a historical and cultural collection of the history of American women, and as such, some women of note may be missing. Oftentimes the editors chose a representative woman or topic entry and ensured that other women or organizations of note were mentioned in that entry. For example, the encyclopedia has an entry for both the National Association of Colored Women (NACW) and Josephine Ruffin, a founder of the NACW, but no entry for notable NACW founders Margaret Murray Washington and Victoria Earle Matthews.

Also, some fairly obscure women or organizations are included in this encyclopedia so that the editors could include women of all types. Because heterosexual, middle-class, or elite-class white Protestant women are more likely to be well known in American history than non-Protestants, lesbians, or women of color, the editors took great care to be inclusive so as to introduce readers to women who represent a wider spectrum of the American experience. This range of coverage includes women from various ethnic, cultural, economic, and religious backgrounds as well as LGBTQ women. Some might call this being politically correct, but we would argue that the second word

in that phrase—"correct"—is precisely what we are about. Minority women's achievements have been particularly ignored in American history so as to make it seem that they never existed. By bringing them into the story, we are correcting that error.

In most cases, the editors chose traditional scholarly sources for an entry's Further Reading bibliography, but the 21st century has given both historians and students access to comprehensive scholarly online archives. These archives provide readers and students with easy access to primary sources, and so in the cases where the archives are maintained by a university or other institution of long standing, it seemed both safe and prudent to use them.

The "See also" cross-references at the ends of entries are not meant to be complete but rather a guide for what else a reader might enjoy reading, in part because the editors cannot foresee how a reader will use an entry, given readers' varying goals. A "See also" entry should lead readers on a trail, but it is a trail that readers must manage for themselves. The cross-references first list entries found in the same volume and section as the entry being consulted. Related entries found elsewhere in the encyclopedia indicate the particular volume and section where these entries may be found.

The editors have attempted to avoid gendered language wherever possible. Much of this language goes unnoticed and unremarked on in common usage. Take, for example, the term "hunter-gatherer." Recent anthropological studies contend that gathering actually accounted for the vast majority of the calorie intake of indigenous communities. More accurately, we ought to say "gatherer-hunters," thus giving women's gathering work precedence. The word "work," when used in relationship to women, is problematic as well. The editors contend that American women have always worked, though they have not always been paid for that work. Domestic and volunteer work, both types of labor done overwhelmingly by women, is unwaged and undervalued, but it is work. Thus, the editors prefer to refer to women's labor as either waged or unwaged work, as indicated by the thematic issues essay on this topic in each section.

We have also tried to avoid phrasing or ideas reflective of patriarchal, paternalistic, or militaristic ideology. For example, almost all of our contributors used the phrase "broke out" or "outbreak" in reference to war. This kind of passive language construction suggests that war is something that people and countries catch, like the flu, and so desensitizes readers to the violence of war while disguising the human decision making and culpability inherent in military conflict. So, we prefer "The Civil War began in 1861" to "in 1861 the Civil War broke out."

We have also endeavored, when possible, to be clear about our subjects' sexuality. In a homophobic society, readers will assume heterosexuality in the absence of specific language to the contrary. While it is certainly not the editors' job to out anyone, claiming a nonheterosexual woman as a lesbian resists secrecy and shame and encourages our LGBTQ readers to know that people like them exist in American history. The editors also acknowledge that the word "lesbian" is a modern construct, but we have used the word to describe women who lived in time periods that did not use the word or even have a category of sexual

difference for women. We have done so to clarify meaning for our readers, who are not likely to be professional academics but rather high school and college students and interested nonspecialists.

As the lives of our entry subjects changed year by year, so too did the lives of our contributors across the creation of this encyclopedia. Marriages were begun or ended, and some children were born while others left the nest. Writers' lives changed and were not documented in any official way, serving as a reminder that we all have a hand in history, whether it is on the public stage or the private one. History may be the past to us, but it was the present to the people who were there. We hope that it is life-affirming to learn about the lives of America's great women. Remember as you flip the pages of these volumes trying to find someone, maybe for a research paper or school report or just to satisfy your curiosity, that every woman chronicled here was part of someone's life and was once as real as you are now.

Acknowledgments

The editors would like to thank all of our contributors, the writers who researched carefully, wrote thoughtfully, and met their deadlines. Some contributors wrote one or two entries on a subject in their specialty area, while others wrote dozens of entries, using the writing opportunity to learn about women or organizations outside of their narrow specialty. Having contributor writers from all over the country and even some from other nations made this a stronger work. Both editors particularly enjoyed the electronic relationships and even friendships that arose from our work on these volumes.

We are grateful to Michael Millman and John Wagner at ABC-CLIO for offering us this project. Both men are thoughtful, kind, and incredibly pleasant. Our project coordinator, Barbara Patterson, answered every question we had in our early organizational days, and we appreciate both her patience and her attention to detail.

A 2014 grant from the Cal Poly Pomona Center for Professional Development allowed us to hire assistant editors Sarah Nation and Leo Burke Jr. Both Sarah and Leo played an important role in our ability to meet deadlines. They also enhanced our ability to honor the people and organizations in this encyclopedia and did so with humor and patience.

Both Rosanne and Peg would like to thank our students. We both feel immensely lucky to spend our workdays with young people who care about ideas, meaning, and doing the right thing. No one who truly connects with college students ever grows too old, too tired, or too incurious to stop learning.

Both editors owe their deepest debts of gratitude to their husbands, Douglas E. Welch and Leo Burke Sr., and their children, Joseph Welch and Emma Burke, who endured the days, weekends, and evenings we devoted to completing these four volumes. We hope along the way that they learned firsthand about organization, research, and the immense contributions that so many women made to the country in which they live. Peg would also like to thank her parents, Jackie and Paul Lamphier, who encouraged her to read and didn't give her a hard time for staying in college for far too many years. Rosanne would like to thank her mother, Mary Danko, for providing a house full of books and an annual summer historical site vacation on only a secretary's salary.

Finally, as ridiculous as it might sound, the editors would like to thank each other. Each of us said time and again over the three years that this project took to complete that we wouldn't have and probably couldn't have done it with anyone else. We sent what seems like thousands of e-mails to each other and spent countless lunch hours talking about the work and had a lot of fun doing it. Everyone should have someone with whom they work so well.

Introduction

While women's history has expanded exponentially in the last 30 years, most of that scholarship has not translated to high school and college textbooks. This is particularly true for American women's history. Advanced placement courses and tests continue to largely concentrate on an exceedingly old-school version of history, one that is top-down and male-centered. Thus, even the best students may have little or no real knowledge of American women's history. This problem compounds itself when we consider how little students learn about nonwhite, nonelite Americans.

Women in American History: A Social, Political, and Cultural Encyclopedia and Document Collection consists of four volumes that chronologically confront the wealth of women's history available to students and other interested readers.

Volume 1: Precolonial North America to the Early Republic

"Section 1: Precolonial North America (Pre-1607)" focuses on preliterate, preconquest women. Thus, most of the entries in that section are as much anthropology as they are history, in part because history deals with the written word, and North American indigenous peoples had oral cultures. Entries on topics such as the Corn Mother, food production, and Pueblo culture explore the multiplicity of indigenous experiences, emphasizing the complexity of these cultures before the Euro-American conquest. Other entries, such as those on Malinche and La Llorona, remind readers that while American history has a clear East Coast and English colonization bias, much early American history is rooted in what would become the American Southwest.

"Section 2: Colonial North America (1607–1754)" shifts the focus from indigenous women to Euro-American women. Entries on Protestant, Catholic, and Quaker women examine the importance of religion in colonial women's lives, while entries on Puritans and witchcraft cases illustrate the gendered danger of religious intolerance. Entries on Queen Alliquippa and Kateri Tekakwitha suggest that indigenous or Native American women did not simply disappear from American history after European conquest but rather continued to play a significant role in the development of the nation.

"Section 3: Revolutionary America and the New Republic (1754–1819)" focuses on the American Revolutionary War period, from the French and Indian War in 1754 through the New Republic period. While many women in this section, including Abigail Adams and the women who made up the Daughters of Liberty, supported the independence movement, many other women remained loyal to the British government. Entries on Loyalist Women and Peggy Shippen Arnold argue that women who ended up on the losing end of the American Revolution nonetheless have stories significant to American history. Other entries remind us that Native American women played an important role in the American Revolution, while some entries remind us that however much this span of years seems dominated by the revolutionary experience, many women lived lives not centered on the maelstrom of revolutionary politics and the war for independence.

Volume 2: Antebellum America through the Gilded Age

Volume 2 of this encyclopedia covers the antebellum, American Civil War, and Reconstruction periods of

American history. As indicated by "Section 1: The Antebellum Era (1820–1860)," historians of women discovered early on that the 19th century, particularly the decades before the Civil War, provide fertile ground for scholarship. Antebellum women took gendered ideologies of womanhood, commonly known as the "cult of true womanhood," and used them to place themselves at the forefront of the vibrant social and cultural reform movements of the time. Women participated in the temperance movement, often pairing their antialcohol message with protests against family violence. Dress reformers not only sought to rationalize women's fashions to be more comfortable and healthy but often connected the physical limitations of women via clothing with the limitations that women faced in American public life. Some abolition and antislavery organizations allowed for female participation, but many more did not, driving women to form their own associations. Many women learned valuable organizational skills within the abolition movement, which they transferred to the women's rights movement. Indeed, women from all branches of 19th-century reform created the first women's rights movement in the United States when they met at Seneca Falls, New York, in 1848. Their "Declaration of Rights and Sentiments" is the founding document of the first women's rights movement.

Black women played an increasingly significant role in both the women's rights and abolition movements. Some, such as Ellen Craft and Harriet Tubman, resisted slavery by stealing themselves away from their masters and encouraging others to do so as well. Other black women, many of them free blacks, formed their own abolition societies and free produce societies, which encouraged consumers to buy products made by free people, not slaves.

Poor women, both native born and immigrant, created the first labor reform movement in the country. These reforms, though born in the years before the Civil War, continued through the war and well into the later decades of the 19th century. Many women involved themselves in multiple reforms at one time, finding the goals of temperance, dress reform, slavery abolition, and women's rights tied up together in a common desire to expand American liberty.

Considered to be the first total war, the Civil War both disrupted women's reform activities and expanded

opportunity for women. "Section 2: The Civil War and Reconstruction (1861–1877)" explores the immense contribution of both Union and Confederate women to the war effort. Despite common belief, American women did not sit passively by while their men fought in the most destructive and deadly war in American history. They raised money and collected supplies to be sent to the front and often went themselves as nurses, spies, soldiers, and more. Large numbers of women worked as nurses for the first time in the nation's history, beginning the feminization and professionalization of nursing. Other women, black and white, dressed as men and volunteered as soldiers, while others worked as spies.

"Section 3: The Gilded Age (1878–1899)" covers the decades after the Civil War up to the beginning of the 20th century. White women found their demands for equal citizenship and voting rights put aside in favor of the enfranchisement of black men. In fact, one of the important lessons that women's rights organizers learned in these years was that putting their reform demands on hold to meet the needs of war would not be rewarded. When World War I came, suffragettes would remember this lesson. Black women and other women of color faced immense racism in these decades as the nation rebounded from war into conservatism and white supremacy. Working women also struggled to improve poor wages, inhumane working conditions, and long hours at work. They continued to organize and seek reform even while many male-led labor unions ignored or discounted their work.

Volume 3: Progressive Era through World War II

"Section 1: The Progressive Era (1900–1929)" includes entries that one would expect alongside ones that a reader might not expect. Often there is new information about individuals that was discovered while researching them in the course of this project. So, this section covers Jane Addams and her creation of settlement houses, beginning with Hull House in Chicago, and suffragists such as Carrie Chapman Catt, who is known for her presidency of the National American Woman Suffrage Association (NAWSA). But the entries also remind readers that Addams was a pacifist and the vice president of the NAWSA in these crucial years leading up to the vote and that after women won the right to vote, Catt founded the League of Women Voters to help educate women on this new right.

With the focus on culture as well as history, this section also includes writer Anita Loos, who wrote hundreds of early silent films as well as the best-selling novel *Gentlemen Prefer Blondes* and its lesser-known sequel *But Gentlemen Marry Brunettes*. Both the Ziegfeld Follies and Mae West make appearances, powerfully suggesting the rising power of popular entertainments.

While these women were more financially affluent, this section does not ignore those who were less so. The Triangle Shirtwaist Fire of 1911 helped usher women into the protest movement that led to unions, such as the International Women's Garment Workers Union, continuing the labor organizing work that women began in the 19th century.

In "Section 2: The Great Depression and the New Deal (1930–1941)," readers will meet a host of women who survived during the Great Depression and supported the social programs of President Franklin D. Roosevelt's New Deal. Other women and organizations worked for the burgeoning civil rights movement, though their work would not see fruition until several decades later. Dorothea Lange photographed families fleeing the Dust Bowl to expose American poverty, while Frances Perkins, as the first female secretary of labor, helped Roosevelt create the Social Security Administration.

Popular culture served an important role during the Great Depression. Satirist Dorothy Parker became one of the few female members of the elite Algonquin Round Table before moving to Hollywood to write films. Bonnie Parker went on a bank-robbing rampage with partner Clyde Barrow and died beside him in a hail of bullets on a Texas back road. In this era, African American virtuoso Marian Anderson sang on the National Mall thanks to arrangements made by First Lady Eleanor Roosevelt, exemplifying the need for both races to work together to achieve civil rights. Zora Neale Hurston emerged from the Harlem Renaissance as a novelist and playwright, while actress Hattie McDaniel was the first African American, man or woman, to win an Oscar, an award she received for her performance in *Gone with the Wind*.

"Section 3: World War II (1939–1945)" has entries on such women as nurse Laura Cobb, who cared for wounded soldiers before becoming a prisoner of war herself. Jackie Cochran created the Women's Air Force Service Pilots (WASP) to train new male recruits to fly aircraft after being denied the chance to join the military herself. While white women were welcomed to aid the war effort in a variety of women's military auxiliaries, Japanese American women heeded the government's call to move into relocation camps in an attempt to prove that they were not spies or traitors. From those camps these women went into the workforce, welding airplanes and ships together or building tanks, yet they returned each night to the barely furnished barracks until the war was over. Some 30 years later, protesters among them eventually achieved an apology and reparations for their unconstitutional treatment.

Volume 4: Cold War America to Today

In "Section 1: Cold War America (1946–1962)" the postwar United States explodes with new financial stability and personal freedoms. Actress Lucille Ball became the first woman to own her own production company, and former child star Shirley Temple, later Shirley Temple Black, became an ambassador. Mexican American Dolores Huerta helped found the movement for the creation of the United Farm Workers alongside Cesar Chavez. Brownie Wise invented the Tupperware Party as a way for housewives to earn their own money, creating a female entrepreneurship network that empowered countless working-class and middle-class women. Female artists such as Grandma Moses, Helen Frankenthaler, and Georgia O'Keeffe rose to prominence as their work was displayed in museums traditionally heavy on male-created art. This era also saw the invention of computer language, in great part due to Grace Hopper's work.

"Section 2: Second-Wave Feminism (1963–1989)" focuses on the renewed fight for the Equal Rights Amendment. More women moved into politics, including Bella Abzug and Shirley Chisholm. Others such as Betty Friedan, author of *The Feminine Mystique,* led the charge through their writing. First ladies took a page from Eleanor Roosevelt's book and turned the position into a full-time, though unpaid, occupation. Ladybird Johnson's program for beautifying highways and Jacqueline Kennedy's celebration of the arts proved important to the era. The U.S. Supreme Court sanctioned the interracial marriage of Mildred Jeter and Richard Loving, making it the new law of the land. Eunice Kennedy Shriver started the first Special Olympics in honor of her mentally ill and institutionalized sister, and the Women of All Red Nations came together to protest the treatment of Native Americans.

"Section 3: Third-Wave Feminism (1990–Present)" covers a movement more racially, socially, and economically diverse than previous feminist movements. Women of all backgrounds have achieved goals that their grandmothers could only dream of. Attorney Marian Wright Edelman established the Children's Defense Fund to advocate for issues such as providing health care and helping end poverty among children. Scientist Mae Jemison became the first female African American mission specialist to go into space, and Loretta Lynch became the first African American female attorney general of the United States. Sonia Sotomayor was appointed to the U.S. Supreme Court, where she joined Ruth Bader Ginsburg and was later joined by Elena Kagan. Oprah Winfrey owned her own cable network and made the Forbes 500 list of billionaires, while Janet Yellen became the first female chair of the Federal Reserve.

On a lighter note, former 1980s rocker Cyndi Lauper earned the first Tony Award for best original score by a solo female composer, and Lady Gaga harnessed the power of the emerging social media for both career success and promoting her social justice causes. Underground feminist punk rockers created the Riot Grrl movement, which dovetailed with young women's public protests in Take Back the Night and SlutWalk demonstrations.

While the editors hope that all readers will benefit from this encyclopedia, we believe that works such as this one are particularly significant for girls and women. While not all American men are equally privileged, all American men benefit from a culture of male privilege, and nowhere is that more true than in the study of American history. The American education system provides boys and young men with countless examples of male leadership and greatness. American girls and boys grow to maturity knowing few notable women from American history, a reality that creates the fiction that women have contributed little or nothing to their country. Thus, readers of *Women in American History* should find in its volumes not just information but also a deep well of inspiration and revelation.

Chronology

12th–13th centuries: Ancestral Puebloans (Ansazis) migrate from traditional homelands.

1519: Nahuah woman Malinche (Malintzin/Malinalli), sold as a slave to Hernán Cortés, acts as translator, cultural mediator, and the mother of the first mestizo.

1587: Virginia Dare is the first child born to English parents in the New World.

1608: Anne Burras marries John Laydon, becoming the first English woman to marry in the New World.

1613: Pocahontas is kidnapped by English settlers in Jamestown and marries John Rolfe the next year.

1619: The first African women arrive in Jamestown on a Portuguese slave ship.

1638: Anne Hutchinson is banished from Massachusetts Bay Colony for heresy.

1650: Anne Bradstreet publishes the first volume of poetry.

1656: Ann Hibbins is executed for witchcraft in Boston. Nathaniel Hawthorne fictionalized her story in *The Scarlet Letter* (1850).

1692: The Salem Witch Trials are held in Salem, Massachusetts.

1730s–1740s: A series of religious revivals known as the Great Awakening encourages female religious freedom, literacy, and political power.

1754: Seneca leader Queen Alliquippa dies.

1755: Mary Jemison is captured by a Native American raiding party; she assimilates into Seneca culture and resists efforts to return her to Euro-American society.

1766: The Daughters of Liberty is established to organize boycotts of British goods.

1774: Penelope Barker leads 51 women in the Edenton Tea Party to sign a document vowing to boycott tea.

1776: Abigail Adams writes the "Remember the Ladies" letter to her husband.

July 19 and 20, 1848: Three hundred people attend the first women's rights convention, held in Seneca Falls, New York.

1849: Elizabeth Blackwell becomes the first licensed woman physician in the United States.

1850: Harriet Tubman joins the Underground Railroad efforts, leading slaves to freedom.

October 23–24, 1850: The National Woman's Rights Convention is held in Worcester, Massachusetts. Annual national conferences continue to be held through 1860 (except in 1857).

1851: The Bloomer costume is adopted to urge dress reform for women.

May 28 and 29, 1851: Sojourner Truth gives her spontaneous "Ain't I a Woman?" speech at the woman's rights convention in Akron, Ohio.

1855: Lucy Stone marries Henry Blackwell and keeps her birth name.

1866: The Young Women's Christian Association (YWCA) is founded in Boston, Massachusetts.

October 10, 1866: Elizabeth Cady Stanton declares herself a candidate for Congress from the 8th Congressional District of New York and eventually loses.

1869: The Wyoming Territory grants women the vote in all elections.

May 1869: The National Woman Suffrage Association is founded by Susan B. Anthony and Elizabeth Cady Stanton to achieve the vote through a congressional amendment while also addressing other women's rights issues.

November 18, 1869: Lucy Stone, Henry Blackwell, and others break from the National Woman Suffrage Association to form the American Woman's Suffrage Association.

1870: Women in Wyoming become the first to vote following the granting of territorial status.

May 10, 1872: Victoria Woodhull becomes a presidential candidate on her own ticket.

June 17, 1873: Susan B. Anthony is convicted for voting and fined $100, which she refuses to pay.

1876: Susan B. Anthony and Matilda Joslyn Gage disrupt the official centennial program at Independence Hall in Philadelphia and present a "Declaration of Rights for Women."

1889: Jane Addams and Ellen Starr found Hull House in Chicago, Illinois.

March 25, 1911: In the Triangle Shirtwaist Fire in New York City, 123 women and 23 men die.

1913: The National Woman's Party is founded by Alice Paul and Lucy Burns as an auxiliary of the National American Woman Suffrage Association.

March 3, 1913: Organized by Alice Paul for the day preceding President Woodrow Wilson's inauguration, 8,000 suffragists parade in Washington, D.C.

1916: Police close down Margaret Sanger's birth control clinic.

1916: Montanan Jeannette Rankin becomes the first woman elected to Congress.

August 1916: The National American Woman Suffrage Association endorses NAWSA president Carrie Chapman Catt's "Winning Plan" to pass a women's suffrage amendment.

January 10, 1917: National Woman's Party picketers, or Silent Sentinels, appear in front of the White House holding aloft banners demanding the vote for women.

June 22, 1917: Arrests of the National Woman's Party picketers begin on charges of obstructing traffic.

November 27 and 28, 1917: In response to public outcry and jailers' inability to stop the National Woman's Party picketers' hunger strikes, the government unconditionally releases the picketers.

June 4, 1919: The U.S. Senate passes the Nineteenth Amendment.

February 14, 1920: The League of Women Voters is founded.

August 26, 1920: The Nineteenth Amendment granting American women the right to vote is signed into law.

1921: The American Birth Control League is founded by Margaret Sanger.

1923: Alice Paul proposes the Equal Rights Amendment, which is introduced in Congress every year after.

January 5, 1925: Nellie Tayloe Ross of Wyoming is inaugurated as the first woman governor in the United States.

1932: Amelia Earhart makes the first transcontinental nonstop flight by a woman.

March 4, 1933: Frances Perkins is sworn in as secretary of labor and is the first woman in the U.S. cabinet.

May 18, 1953: Jacqueline Cochran becomes the first woman to break the sound barrier.

June 19, 1953: Ethel Greenglass Rosenberg and her husband Julius Rosenberg are executed after being convicted of espionage.

1955: Autherine Lucy wins her case before the U.S. Supreme Court, making her the first black student at the University of Alabama.

December 1, 1955: Rosa Parks is arrested in Montgomery, Alabama, sparking the American civil rights movement.

1961: Enovid, the first birth control pill, goes on the market.

1960: In *Fannie Mae Clackum v. United States,* the Supreme Court overturns Clackum's discharge from the military on the basis of her sexuality.

1962: Rachel Carson's book *Silent Spring* calls attention to the dangers of agricultural pesticides and inspires the modern environmental movement.

February 11, 1963: Julia Child makes her television debut on *The French Chef.*

1963: The Equal Pay Act abolishing pay inequity based on sex is passed by Congress.

1963: Betty Friedan's book *The Feminine Mystique* sparks the contemporary feminist movement.

1964: The Civil Rights Act, Title VII, outlaws employment discrimination based on race, color, religion, sex, or national origin.

1965: The Moynihan Report posits that families headed by black women are a root cause of black poverty; critics suggest that the report is sexist and racist.

1965: In *Griswold v. Connecticut* the U.S. Supreme Court rules that the U.S. Constitution protects the right of privacy, ruling that the state could not make contraceptive drugs illegal. The ruling paves the way for *Roe v. Wade* (1973).

1966: The National Organization for Women (NOW) is organized.

1967: The U.S. Supreme Court case *Loving v. Virginia* makes laws against interracial marriage illegal.

1968: Shirley Chisholm becomes the first black woman elected to the U.S. House of Representatives.

1968: Robin Morgan, Shulamith Firestone, and 400 women organize the Miss America pageant protest in Atlantic City, saying that it objectifies women, supports the Vietnam War, and promotes racism.

1968: Contiguous with the Miss America pageant protest, black women hold the first Miss Black America pageant in resistance to white beauty standards.

August 26, 1970: The Women's Strike for Equality is held in New York to celebrate the 50th anniversary of the Nineteenth Amendment. Over 20,000 women attend, making it the largest women's rights rally in American history.

1971: The National Women's Political Caucus (NWPC) is founded by Bella Abzug, Gloria Steinem, Shirley Chisholm, Betty Friedan, and others to lobby for women's equality.

December 1971: *Ms.* magazine is launched.

1972: Title IX of the Education Amendments prohibits sex discrimination in schools.

January 25, 1972: Shirley Chisholm becomes the first major party black American to run for president as well as the first woman to seek the Democratic Party presidential nomination.

March 22, 1972: The Equal Rights Amendment is passed by Congress and sent to the states for ratification.

1973: *Roe v. Wade* overturns state laws restricting the right to abortion.

1973: Billie Jean King defeats Bobby Riggs in the "Battle of the Sexes" tennis match.

1973: The National Black Feminist Organization (NBFO) is formed.

1974: Women of All Red Nations (WARN) is formed to promote Native American women's rights.

1974: The Equal Credit Opportunity Act is enacted, making it illegal to discriminate based on race, religion, sex, marital status, or age in a credit transaction.

1975: Susan Brownmiller's *Against Our Will* is published and redefines rape as a crime of violence, not lust.

1978: The Pregnancy Discrimination Act makes it illegal to discriminate against pregnant women.

1981: Sandra Day O'Connor becomes the first woman seated on the U.S. Supreme Court.

1982: The Equal Rights Amendment fails ratification by the states.

1983: Sally Ride becomes the first American woman to fly in space.

1983: Dian Fossey publishes *Gorillas in the Mist.* Poachers murder her two years later.

1984: Geraldine Ferraro becomes the first woman nominated for vice president by a major party.

1985: Emily's List, a political action committee to elect pro-choice female Democrats, is founded.

1991: Susan Faludi publishes *Backlash: The Undeclared War against American Women,* counterarguing the idea that feminism has made American women's lives worse.

1993: Janet Reno becomes the first woman attorney general of the United States.

1997: Madeleine Albright is sworn in as the first female secretary of state.

2005: Condoleezza Rice serves as the first female African American secretary of state.

January 2007: Hillary Rodham Clinton announces her candidacy for the Democratic presidential nomination.

June 2008: Hillary Rodham Clinton concedes to Barack Obama, who wins the Democratic nomination and ultimately the 2008 presidential election.

August 2008: Alaska governor Sarah Palin is announced as the vice presidential nominee on the John McCain ticket in the 2008 presidential election.

2009: Hillary Rodham Clinton becomes the third woman to hold the post of secretary of state.

2009: The Lilly Ledbetter Fair Pay Act is the first bill signed into law by President Obama. The law helps protect those who face pay discrimination and was named for an Alabama woman who complained at the end of her 19-year career that discovered she had been paid less than her male coworkers.

2009: Sonia Sotomayor becomes the third female and first Hispanic U.S. Supreme Court justice.

2015: Loretta Lynch becomes first the female and first African American female to serve as attorney general.

2015: The *Obergefell v. Hodges* marriage equality ruling finds same-sex marriage legal according to the U.S. Constitution.

2016: Hillary Clinton becomes the first female major party nominee for president of the United States.

1. Precolonial North America (Pre-1607)

HISTORICAL OVERVIEW

Oral traditions across pre-Columbian North American indigenous cultures recognized the active and complimentary role of female and male forces. Women were honored for being creators and sustainers of life. For many people in the Americas, such as the Dinés (Navajos) and Wyandots, the first grandmothers were made out of maize, while for others in the Southwest it was a woman from whose body corn was produced. In North America, most social scientists asserted that people migrated over the Bering land bridge that connected Siberia to Alaska some 15,000 years ago. In South America, social scientists agree that people reached the Americas in multiple ways and at multiple times. Evidence suggests that people from Africa, Australia, and Polynesia reached the coasts of South America prior to European contact. Oral tradition between the Chumash peoples and Hawaiians still exist that recalls contact between the two peoples long before Europeans came to North America.

Many societies have creation stories that also tell of migrations to the lands they consider their ancestral home, lands intended for their use and gifted by the Creator. Most pre-Columbian American societies tell stories that began with the creation of the universe, Earth, stars, and the sun and moon. Earth spirits then made the first plants and animals and sources of life such as rivers, lakes, thunder, and clouds. Some differ in their account of how humans first came into being and became a part of the present world. For many people, humans originated from the first woman who fell from the sky. Women occupy a central and honored place in the creation and continuation of the people. The name of any given civilization is often translated in the group's distinct language as "the people," or the people of a certain place or direction.

The societies that developed in the Western Hemisphere were diverse and interconnected. They included approximately 17 major language groups, 16 major cultural regions, and hundreds of distinct tribes, bands, nations, communities, and linguistic groups. Regions include the Northwest coast, the Plateau, the Great Basin, the Arctic, the Subarctic, and the Great Plains, as well as the U.S. Northeast, Southeast, and Southwest and California, Mesoamerica, Amazonia, Gran Chaco, the Andes, the Circum-Caribbean, Pampas, Patagonia, and Tierra del Fuego. People of the Americas were advanced in math, physics, astronomy, art, literature, and philosophy. Several civilizations built large agricultural complexes, pyramids, temples, and water systems. All civilizations had calendars including descriptive, based on changing patterns in nature; astronomical, based on people's observance of the sun or moon; and those that list months numerically. World belief systems were most often based on practical systems of knowledge that sought to maintain equilibrium within individuals, and between people, and the large community of beings. Whether the economy was based on seasonal rounds or large agricultural complexes, the people learned how to intensively and sustainably manage their environment and resources. Social scientists estimate the populations prior to contact to be between 65 million and 100 million people dispersed in various types of civilizations throughout the Americas prior to 1492. Women of pre-Columbian societies contributed significantly to the subsistence economies, both plant and protein. Gender was a fluid or flexible concept and did not restrict women to particular roles. Women occupied a variety of leadership roles, including military and civic. They were healers of various kinds and were often honored as the keepers of tradition as well as for their power of creation.

Among the people of the far north (the Inuits and Aleuts of the Arctic), many variations of cultural traditions developed over 18,000 years as a result of successive migrations from Siberia and throughout the Arctic. The Inuit and Aleut cultures became distinct and the most widespread about 2,000–3,000 years ago. The people developed a largely hunting culture and lived in small units of families or family groups. Women contributed to every aspect of life, tending to make decisions surrounding the home and in the repair of clothing. Those who desired to learn hunting skills also contributed in hunting as well as in searching out roots, plant food, and seaweed to supplement the diet. They often lived along the coasts, subsisting on seal, walrus, and whale, as well as caribou and other game (Josephy 1991, 57–64). Ideas of gender relationships imposed by Europeans remained in conflict with previous perceptions that did not recognize gender categories but instead sought balance among all members of society and valued elders for their accumulated wisdom and experience.

Several other cultures that developed and migrated to the Northwest depended more on salmon and shell fishing than those of the far North. Ten thousand to 8,000 years ago people became more dependent on shell fishing, characteristically thought of as women's work, though men have been known to collect shellfish and understand their ecology. Women are credited with manipulating some mollusk species and animals to enhance desirable traits. Salish women, for example, bred dogs, selecting for white hair (Barsh et al. 2002, 1–11). The people have been harvesting and managing the salmon runs for over 7,000 years. Chinook- and Sahaptin-speaking people met to fish and trade and were part of a trade route that extended throughout North America (Calloway 2008, 23). Eighteen communities of the Northwest today include Salish, Makah, Chinook, and Tlingit peoples, while on the Columbia Plateau there are Chinook, Salish, and Sahaptin peoples.

Like many societies, oral tradition constituted common law and legal codes. People owned the right to gift songs and dances, assorted privileges, goods, or land use. Among the Tlingits, clan chiefs possessed the authority to supervise the harvest, recruit a militia, receive a portion of the clan's harvest, subsidize craftspersons, give names, and redistribute wealth. Some of this wealth and production was used in the *patshatl* (potlatch) to perpetuate the authority of the chief and the interests of the clan by giving away wealth to the community. Senior women supervised productivity, and all women maintained control of the resources they processed. Families competed for status or, rather, took turns hosting and giving away their wealth (Johansen 1967, 7–8). Most people of the Northwest were bilateral, or reckoned descent through both parents. For some groups, as among the Mayas, higher rank was achieved through the mother's family.

The people of California collectively spoke approximately 300 dialects, of 100 languages, that originated from three major language families: Penutian, Yukon, Uto-Aztecan. Later immigrants brought Algonquian language and Athapascan speakers such as the Hupas, Totowas, and Mattoles. Over 10,000 years ago the ancestors of historic California nations began harvesting the marine resources of the coast. Hunting, harvesting, and gathering, they lived in permanent independent villages with a population of 50 to 100 people. As early as 7,000 years ago, families harvested acorns, pinon, and mesquite. Homes varied and included the *samat,* a circular dome structure of poles covered with brush or grass, sometimes chinked and plastered with mud or adobe in the Coachella and Borrego areas. In the southern inland valley, homes were made of tule or palm fronds. To the north, large round earth-covered lodges, often semisubterranean, were used. Pit houses were used for sweat baths, centers for purification and ceremony. Between 500 and 1500 CE, growth of population, accommodation to different environments, and independence of various groups led to variations of culture. By 1300 CE, many distinct California groups emerged.

While families often harvested food together, women processed and prepared these staple foods, grinding and cooking them into bread meal or porridge. Most probably women's innovations and technological development led to new subsistence patterns and more sedentary communities. The Chumash traders were part of an extensive trade system and subsistence economy in California that included 48 nations and supported a population up to 1 million people. In 1542, the Spanish explorer Juan Rodriguez Cabrillo reached present-day Santa Barbara. At that time 15,000 Chumashes inhabited the coastal area and islands of the region and had mastered ocean hunting, first using tule canoes and later plank *tomolos* (Calloway 2008, 21–22). 'Antap, the political-religious organization, included local hereditary chiefs, elites, members of specific craft guilds, shamans, and political officers, some likely to be women. These officials were specialists who maintained esoteric knowledge, songs, dances, and language appropriate to specific dances and duties (Schmidt and Voss 2000, 179–187).

For at least 10,000 years the ancestors of today's Paiutes, Shoshones, and Utes lived in the Great Basin region, some 4000,000 square miles between the Rocky Mountains and the Sierra Nevada that included Utah, eastern Nevada, western Colorado, and southern Idaho. The people lived in permanent communities subsisting on a varied diet of fish, game, and plants available in different seasons. For over 7,000 years they were incorporated into a vast trade network in which they obtained shells from the Pacific coast and obsidian from southern Idaho. Archaeologists refer to new developments in this region between 400 and 1300 CE as the Freemont Culture, characterized by the practice of corn horticulture and the development of pottery technology (Calloway 2008, 24). Women enjoyed equal status and considerable economic agency.

On the plains between 12,000 and 8000 BCE, the people hunted mammoths, mastodons, and bison on foot. They used projectile points and later drives and corrals as additional communal hunting techniques. By 8500 BCE, climactic changes led to mass extinction of ice age mammals, and most people were hunting bison. Five thousand to 7,000 years ago, plains culture was dependent primarily on plant products, and women engaged in a seasonal round that was necessary to maintain subsistence levels (Schneider 2002, 33–50). Women as well as men hunted small game to supplement the diet. Habitation sites suggest that women engaged in work central to village life. Between 500 BCE and 1000 CE people were living in

semipermanent farming villages tending corn, beans, squash, and sunflowers. By 1000 CE people throughout the plains and the Arctic were using the bow and arrow, which replaced early spears and projectile points (Calloway 2008, 25). Although hunting contributed to their economy, agriculture was the principal source of food.

In the agricultural societies of the Pawnees and Omahas of Nebraska, women owned the lodge and tipi and all its contents as well as the fields and seeds and implements for production, and they had the right to trade the surplus. While bison hunting, women made the decision where to camp, and the senior wife made the most important decisions. Women were held in high esteem for their craft work, which played an important role in healing and spiritual responsibilities. When the Spanish arrived in the 1520s, they noted an extensive trade network in which they participated by trading buffalo hides. The Spanish introduction of the horse led to horse-centered cultures such as that of the Lakotas and Dakotas. Midwestern groups such as the Chippewas, Sauks, Foxes, Miamis, Potawatomis, and others had economies based on agriculture and were primarily sedentary, though they moved about periodically and hunted and fished. In Hidatsa culture, the division of labor was informed by age and gender, with women producing food and maintaining the home. Society was matrilineal and matrilocal as well as polygamous. Divorce was accomplished by placing the man's things outside the woman's home. Women played key roles in the sun dance and rituals associated with agricultural success (Schmidt and Voss 2000, 203).

In the Southwest, five agriculturally based cultural groups emerged between 3500 and 1500 BCE: the Anasazis or ancient Puebloan peoples, the Mogollons, the Hohokams, the Sinaguas, and the Salados. The Mogollon people of today's northwestern Mexico, Arizona, and New Mexico grew corn and squash, and by 200 CE they were making pottery and became known for their black-on-white mimbre style. Mogollon pit houses were made in 18 different styles originally and gradually became uniform in style until the Mongollons began building masonry pueblos at least 900 years ago. The pit house became the kiva, the ceremonial center and community center for the family. The

Hohokams, ancestors of today's Akimels, O'odhams (Pimas), and Tohono O'odhams (Papagos), constructed a vast irrigation network, primarily along the Salt and Gila Rivers, and established an agricultural economy between 800 and 1,400. Sedentary villages accommodated up to 600 people and were occupied for up to 1,200 years before environmental changes led to decline and eventual abandonment.

The ancient Puebloan peoples of today's Utah, Colorado, Arizona, and New Mexico developed a distinct agriculturally based culture that peaked between 900 and 1300 CE. In addition to domesticating corn, beans, and squash and the American turkey, they also intensely managed and harvested foods such as *Portulaca Sp., Chenopodium,* and cacti. Women engaged in agriculture and harvest and sometimes hunted antelope and small game. Prior to 1492, men and women enjoyed a high degree of mobility and engaged in relationships of reciprocity and exchange between more distant communities (Claasen 1997, 108). With population growth, people built multistoried complexes in over 200 villages that accommodated 5,000–15,000 people (Calloway 2008, 27). Chaco Canyon was the center of trade in the region, with 400 miles of straight roads linking it with other civilizations all over America. The volcanic eruption of Sunset Crater in 1064 led to a diaspora of the people of the Southwest as a result of drastic environmental changes. Some scholars believe that the kachina phenomenon of the Southwest developed from these changes (Calloway 2008, 27). Hopi women, descendants of ancient civilizations of the Southwest, had considerable authority and influence in their society, directly controlling the homes and food sources.

People in Mesoamerica began shifting from seasonal rounds to agricultural-based societies about 9,000 years ago and began domesticating maize (corn) and potatoes between 5000 and 1000 BCE. Complex civilizations of Teotihuacan in central Mexico and Monte Alban in southwestern Mexico, the Mayas and Olmecs (1500–400 BCE), and Toltecs developed and flourished for thousands of years. The Olmec and Mayan civilizations were characterized by ceremonial centers, hieroglyphic writing, ball courts, waterworks, a calendar, and monumental stone sculptures. The center of classic Mayan civilization (200–900 CE) included the Yucatán Peninsula and Guatemala. Mayan city-states were governed by elite families who sometimes ruled for generations and from whom the priests were also drawn. Commoners were artisans, peasants, merchants, and slaves captured in battle. The political structure of decentralized states provided many opportunities for elite Mayan women politically and religiously. At Palenque, women who ruled outright included Kanal-ikal (583–604 CE) and her granddaughter Zac K'uk (612–615 CE). They claimed descent from Lady Beastie, a mythical female ancestor who was the first creator goddess.

At contact, the Spanish encountered the Aztec Empire (1200–1519 CE) developed from previous civilizations. The Mexicas had arrived from the north in the Valley of Mexico in about 1218 BCE. By 1344 they had begun to build the town of Tenochtitlan around Lake Texcoco. Initially they were composed of *calpulli,* or landholding groups based on kinship. Noble women maintained social power and economic opportunities in trade or occupational specialization. Women traders dominated the marketplaces of Tenochtitlan and the villages. A rise in power and wealth in the decades before the Spanish arrived eroded the traditional institutions and women's empowerment as a consequence of empire building.

Hudson Bay divided the subarctic tribes into major families or tribes. Originally, the people of various tribes lived in small independent hunting and fishing groups. For at least 4,000 years, the women of the eastern nations had been domesticating native foods such as sunflowers, squash, and marsh elder. The original people of today's Illinois were growing squash as early as 5000 BCE (Calloway 2008, 29). Cultivation of corn began in Mesoamerica and reached today's Tennessee about 350 BCE, the Ohio Valley about 300 BCE, and the Illinois Valley about 650 CE (Calloway 2008, 29). The Hopewell culture developed around 100–300 CE at the same time the Hohokam were developing irrigation complexes in the Southwest. Hopewell culture included a trade network that reached from the Great Lakes to Yellowstone and the Gulf of Mexico. As the Hopewell civilization seemingly declined around 550 CE, corn agriculture spread throughout the East, and a new culture developed in the lower Mississippi Valley around 700 CE and spread throughout what is today's eastern half of the United states, peaking by 1300 CE.

To the north and prior to European contact, the Mohawk, Oneida, Onondaga, Cayuga, and Seneca tribes met to end intertribal conflict by establishing the Great League of Peace that arrived at decisions through consensus and formed intertribal policies. The villages consisted of longhouses that incorporated matrilineal families, or families related by clan through the maternal side. Women tended the homes; cultivated and harvested the cornfields; gathered berries, fruits, and nuts; made clothing and pottery; engaged in war and trade; and cared for the children. They subsisted on a seasonal round, exploiting the abundant resources by harvesting, hunting, fishing, and engaging in limited agriculture (Calloway 2008, 34–35).

The Southeast was home to several different language families who lived in farming towns, formed a number of strong confederacies, and were matrilineal and hierarchal, with a complex culture very similar to the northeastern woodlands tribes. For 4,000 years, people of the Eastern Woodlands also conducted earthen architecture, leaving 10,000 identified earthen mounds to be studied in the the 19th–21st centuries. Near Watson Brake, Louisiana, there are the remains of 11 major earthen pyramids built between 3400 and 3000 BCE. The earliest cultures in the Eastern Woodlands are referred to as Adena (800–11 BCE), known for their effigy mounds and Serpent Mound (400 BCE). Populations in the Southeast grew, and with that growth came towns and the trade network. Ancient peoples of Florida did not adopt the Mississippian Culture but instead continued to depend on intensive resource management, hunting, fishing, and harvesting. Based on a very rich subsistence economy, 350,000 people lived there at contact (Calloway 2008, 34).

In most North American civilizations that existed prior to contact, people had developed a variety of economies and adapted homes and clothing to their environment. Many created huge ceremonial complexes and a calendaric system that ordered their subsistence and ceremonial lives, and they participated in trade networks that spanned the continent. For most of the history of indigenous North American people, women figured prominently in the worldview, though they experienced a decline in power at the onset of Euro-American conquest and colonization.

Leleua Loupe

Further Reading

Barsh, Russel L., Joan Megan Jones, and Wayne Suttles. 2002. "History, Ethnography, and Archaeology of the Coast Salish Woolly-Dog." In *Dogs and People in Social, Working, Economic or Symbolic Interaction. Proceedings of the 9th Conference of the International Council of Archaeozoology,* edited by L. M. Snyder and E. A. Moore, 1–11. Durham, UK: Oxbow Books.

Beck, Peggy. 1996. *The Sacred: Ways of Knowledge, Sources of Life.* Tasaile, AZ: Navajo Community College Press.

Blackburn, Thomas C., and Kat Anderson. 1993. *Before the Wilderness: Environmental Management by Native Californians.* Menlo Park, CA: Ballena.

Brown, Joseph. 2010. *Understanding Native American Religious Traditions.* Oxford: Oxford University Press.

Calloway, Colin G. 2008. *First Peoples: A Documentary Survey of American Indian History.* Boston: Bedford St. Martin.

Hughes, Sarah Shaver, and Brady Hughes. 1995. *Women in World History,* Vol. 1. London: M. E. Sharpe.

Johansen, Dorothy O. 1967. *Empire of the Columbia: A History of the Pacific Northwest.* New York: Harper and Row.

Josephy, Alvin M., Jr. 1991. *The Indian Heritage of North America.* Boston: Houghton Mifflin.

McMaster, Gerald, and Clifford Trafzer, eds. *Native Universe: Voices of Indian America.* Washington, DC: National Museum of the American Indian, Smithsonian.

Schmidt, Robert A., and Barbara L. Voss, eds. 2000. *Archaeologies of Sexuality.* London: Routledge.

Schneider, Fred. 2002. "Prehistoric Horticulture in the Northeastern Plains." *Plains Anthropologist* 47(180): 33–50.

Amina of Nigeria. *See* Queens, African, Nzinga of Angola and Amina of Nigeria

Anasazi Culture

The Anasazis, also known as Ancestral Puebloans and ancient Pueblo people and by the Hopi word "Hisatsinom," emerged in what is today considered to be the Four Corners, the rugged Mesa and Rio Grande region with canyons crossing Utah, Colorado, New Mexico, and Arizona. This area has been inhabited for at least 6,000 years. Water, tremendous ecological variation, and a vast dramatic landscape shaped the rise of the ancient Anasazi Pueblo culture by about 100 BCE, or what we would call the start of the Common Era. The Anasazis abandoned their homeland in the 1200s, leaving homes, farms, and material goods, for reasons that remain unclear.

The territory of Pueblo people has changed over time as the southwestern landscape has changed. The Anasazis found water and then developed a complex civilization of closely related communities with architecture that included large multilevel apartment-like buildings, walled cities, and cliff dwellings. Anasazi women, like most southwestern people, were responsible for farming, child care, and food preparation. Given the harshness of the climate, Anasazi women were small, averaging under five feet tall, while men were slightly larger.

The Mogollons of the southwestern mountain terrain of New Mexico has been home to a variety of peoples, including the Hohokams of southern Arizona and northern Mexico and the southern Athabascan people consisting of Navajos and Apaches. The evolution of ancestral Pueblo peoples falls into several periods, beginning with the Archaic–Early Basketmaker era, 7000–1500 BCE; Early Basketmaker II, 1500 BCE–50 CE; Late Basketmaker II, 50–500 CE; and Basketmaker III, 500–750 CE. The culture peaked during Pueblo I, 750–900 CE; Pueblo II, 900–1150 CE; and Pueblo III, 1150–1350 CE. Drought and warfare brought about a collapse during Pueblo IV, 1350–1600 CE, and Pueblo V, 1600–present.

These petroglyphs from Colorado's Mesa Verde National Park depict the daily life of the Anasazi people who engraved them. The Anasazi were ancient Native Americans living in the four connecting corners of Utah, Arizona, New Mexico, and Colorado beginning around the 12th century. (Frank Bach/Dreamstime)

Anasazi cultural origins are conveyed with an emergence myth that is derived from archaic Cochise culture that lasted from about 7000 to 500 BCE forged in harsh environmental conditions. Lake Cochise covered a vast portion of the land where Anasazis foraged, and as it dried up, ancient peoples had to adapt to desert and cliff landscapes, taking shelter in caves and under ledges. Men hunted and trapped small limited game, and women gathered edible plants that that they learned to use such as yucca, prickly pear, and juniper.

Animal figurines made from split twigs dating back to the Archaic period have been found near the Grand Canyon in Arizona and are thought to be religious offerings. Stone paintings in southern Utah depicting a shaman with his animal are familiar. Pictographs and petroglyphs found clustered near springs and game trails as well as in caves and canyons suggest that the early communities were based on hunting associations. At around 3500 BCE, the Anasazis experienced contact with Mesoamerican people who brought corn northward from Mexico, which revolutionized Anasazi diets, along with technology for making pit houses. With this cultural exchange came the adoption of agriculture that required a more sedentary lifestyle, longer-lasting dwelling architecture, and the development of tools, arts, and crafts, specifically pottery making. The shift to agriculture would also have radically changed women's roles, as they shifted from being being peripatetic gatherers to farmers with homes to manage.

During the Basketmaker II period, people mastered weaving food containers and sandals and other wears from straw, vines, rushes, and yucca fibers. It is also marked by the addition of pottery making by women. As the ancient Pueblo peoples were settled and began cultivating plants, they would have continued some hunting and gathering. Women would forage for agave, cacti, mesquite, amaranth, minion, grapes, hackberries, walnuts, and yucca along with edible seeds, leaves, bark, and roots. The foundation for Anasazi culture began with small villages with small semipermanent circular pit houses that were used seasonally. Food storage structures help archaeologists mark the Anasazis' population growth. Over the next 1,100 years there was a slow transition from small-room seasonal farmsteads to massive permanent fortress cities.

Pictographs and clay dolls made during the Basketmaker III era depict painted or woven attire. Carved shell bangle bracelets with bird and snake designs made of glycymeris shell dating from the Pueblo I era derived from the Gulf of California suggest that the Anasazi trade networks extended to the Pacific. Many of the roadways were not designed to be connectors for physical locations but were actually cosmological corridors linking ceremonial landmarks to topographic locations, horizon markers, and astronomical orientations used in measuring ceremonial cycles by the sun (Father) and moon (Mother).

After about 750 CE, the Anasazis' semipermanent dwellings were eclipsed by a radical change in architectural technology known as the pueblo. These were homes erected aboveground on mesas or in canyons with stone and adobe mortar. They had beamed roofs that started as single-room dwellings but evolved into multiroomed, multitiered apartment buildings. Portable female-gendered artifacts reflect periods when women were active in ritual trade, politics, and textile production before communities settled into long-term villages.

During the Pueblo II era the Anasazis carved birds to carry prayers as well as animals associated with water, including frogs and dragonflies. Petroglyphs feature figures playing flutes. Cradleboards made of wood found during this period suggest that women carried infants with them while they worked. Women would have used stone hoes and wooden scoops in the cultivation of staple foods, including maize, beans, and squash. Women also grew supplement foods such as sunflowers and gathered prickly pear cactus.

Baskets have been found from this period that contain carved and painted prayer sticks that were used as shrine offerings. There is evidence of ongoing trade with tribes living near the Pacific Ocean. In the Pueblo II period males wove and painted textiles, and women made pottery. Both products were used in trading. Anasazi Pueblo women would have been skilled farmers and artisans as well as ethnobotanists who collected plants for medicinal purposes.

In what is today New Mexico, Chaco Canyon became the location of one of the most elaborate pueblo communities, which was shaped as a semicircular five-story-high complex of over 800 rooms. By the end of the Pueblo II era, the Anasazis had evacuated the aboveground pueblos in favor of homes carved into cliff ledges that offered protection against invaders and cannibalistic neighbors (descendants of the Toltecs from Mesoamerica). Archaeologists speculate that a prolonged drought and excessive reliance on corn crops resulted in soil depletion between 1276 and 1299 that may have caused a mass exodus and relocation of indigenous people. Histories orally transmitted by Acoma, Hopi, Pueblo, and Zuni peoples corroborate that their ancestors left earlier homelands because of disease, extended droughts, famine, and warfare and returned to nomadic ways or merged with groups to the south where the soil had not been depleted.

Ceramics dating back to the Pueblo III era were fired in large open-area kilns with black on white designs. Women would have constructed Pueblo pottery by layering coils of clay that were pressed together and then smoothed with tools made from gourds. Homes had spaces for gendered domestic tasks based on function, often including a pottery studio with bowls, jars, awls, and axes used by female artisans. Food was stored as the population grew.

Unlike Native Americans in other regions who used building materials that would not outlive the builders, the Anasazis were builders on a large and permanent scale. At first contact, the Spanish found multiterraced fortress-like buildings housing communities of about 3,000 residents who were active in religious rituals. Spirituality was reflected in material culture; masked dancers impersonated the deities known as kachinas.

The pueblo of Acoma in New Mexico was established in about 1250 CE on top of a sandstone mesa, which offered protection from violent neighbors. In about 1300 CE there was a vast reorganization of Pueblo peoples that led to several centuries of migration and the introduction of indigenous Mexican culture. Spanish-born Pope Alexander VI decreed on May 4, 1493, in the papal bull *Inter caetera* that lands west of the meridian 100 leagues west of the Cape Verde Islands should belong to Spain. The Vatican wanted to spread the Catholic faith in the New World. Citing the need to overthrow and care for souls in "barbarous nations," Spain was ordered to "instruct the aforesaid inhabitants and dwellers therein in the Catholic faith, and train them in good morals." However, when Spanish missionaries arrived with formulas for conversion, the Pueblo people resisted. Religious conflicts arose when missionaries forbade kachina dances and burned kachina masks that were central to Pueblo social unity. Spanish oppression in the name of Catholicism led to the Pueblo Revolt of 1680, when tribes in Arizona and New Mexico came together to successfully defeat the Spanish on American soil.

Meredith Eliassen

See also Cultural Interaction; Hunter-Gatherers; Religion, Native American

Further Reading

Brody, J. J. 1990. *The Anasazi: Ancient Indian People of the American Southwest.* New York: Rizzoli.

Hays-Gilpin, Kelly. 2000. "Gender Constructs in the Material Culture of Seventeenth-Century Anasazi Farmers in North-Eastern Arizona." In *Representations of Gender from Prehistory to the Present*, 31–44. New York: St. Martin's.

Morro, Baker H., and V. B. Price. 1997. *Anasazi Architecture and American Design.* Albuquerque: University of New Mexico Press.

Berdache/Transgendering

The term "berdache" is used by contemporary anthropologists to identify the spectrum of mixed-gender, cross-gender, and nonbinary persons among Native American tribes. Most commonly a male-bodied individual with a gender-variant identity, berdaches assumed various roles within their tribe ranging from single-gender identities to a mixture of two gender identities and had responsibilities unique to berdaches—such as performing healing or spiritual rites. The majority of tribes in all regions of North America featured berdachism to some degree.

Berdachism manifested in a variety of ways in tribes, ranging from men and women who adopted nontraditional roles or dress, male- and female-bodied individuals who identified more strongly with the opposite sex, and individuals who identified as being neither male nor female but as a mixed or third gender. Typically berdaches were not intersexual, nor did they fit into the contemporary identity of a transgender person, since berdaches maintained a separate social identity from male and female. However, some intersex or hermaphroditic individuals also maintained the status of berdache.

Each tribe had its own terminology to describe berdachism, including the Lakota *winkte*, the Zuni *lhamana*, and the Navajo *nádleehí*. The term "berdache"—adapted from the Persian term for "prisoner" and later appropriated by the French to mean "homosexual," was one of the words used by European colonists to describe gender-variant Native Americans. Anthropologists adopted the term in the 20th century, and in 1990s that usage has partially shifted from berdachism to two-spirit.

Euro-Americans did not distinguish between biological sex and sociocultural gender identity the way that Native Americans did. As a result, early literature describing observations of berdachism tends to misconstrue identification of berdaches in addition to describing them as perverse or deviant. Colonial European accounts conflict about the experiences of berdaches within individual tribes as a result.

Although acceptance varied between tribes, berdaches were not typically viewed as deviant within their culture. In fact, some tribes elevated berdaches as spiritually superior. Since many tribes attributed equal importance to feminine and masculine responsibilities, berdaches who preferred to adopt feminine roles were not subjected to a lower status. Likewise, female-bodied berdaches were permitted to engage in traditionally male roles such as hunter or warrior.

Most American indigenous people did not view gender as a predetermined construct. In fact, children in some tribes were not raised with rigid gender roles and were given the opportunity to explore their preferences; others were raised with one gender in mind but were granted the opportunity to cross gender boundaries as they developed divergent tendencies. In both cases, children were never forced into adopting the role of berdaches, and free exploration of both gender and sexuality were usually encouraged.

During their early years of development, some children may have already begun to display a tendency toward opposite-sex interests and roles. As they neared adulthood, they would undergo a test to confirm their status as a berdache. These tests varied by tribe but typically involved a dream or vision quest. Since these tests were religious in nature, many tribes respected the path that the spirits carved for their offspring.

Once an individual's gender identity choice was confirmed, some tribes would initiate the child as a berdache during a ceremony not unlike the rites of passage attributed to becoming a man or a woman in the tribe. Other tribes tested children at puberty, or the berdache would publicly note his or her identity as an adult. After accepting the status of a berdache, individuals might alter their physical presence according to the opposite-sex, mixed-gender, or androgynous appearance. Berdaches would express their gender through a variety of means, including physical appearance, physical gestures, social roles, and group bonding. While some might choose to wear a mixture of masculine and feminine clothing and adornments, others might choose to exclusively wear those subscribed for the opposite sex.

Some of the roles that the berdaches satisfied included crafts-person, childcare provider (for their own adopted children, extended family, and those of the community), mediator between the sexes, and caretaker for the sick. Although male-bodied berdaches would occasionally adopt warrior roles, they tended to prefer the domestic roles of women. Since berdaches were perceived as being strongly connected to the spiritual world, they were also consulted for education and guidance.

Many berdaches would continue to live with their parents; some, however, chose to live on their own or to marry, usually with a partner of the same biological sex. Those berdaches who continued to live with their biological family may have elected to care for extended family, including the young and elderly. Most berdaches only sought sexual partnerships, both short- and long-term, with members of one sex, typically their own; they did not, however, engage in relationships with other berdaches. Indigenous North American people did not stigmatize same-sex partnerships, but most encouraged berdaches to take a more passive role in the relationship. Although European explorers assumed that berdaches were homosexual, this label does not accurately account for their gender identity.

The number of berdaches decreased over time as a result of European influences—particularly through conquests and missionaries. Similar to other facets of Native American culture that were perceived to be sinful by colonists, berdachism was targeted as morally wrong. Western religion spread throughout the New World as a result of these encounters between Europeans and the tribes, causing a dwindling number of visible gender-variant Native Americans and the traditions associated with them.

Despite these influences, contemporary natives and anthropologists have contributed to the renewed interest in reconnecting and studying two-spirited persons and their social and cultural significance.

Cynthia M. Zavala

See also Sexuality

Further Reading

Lang, Sabine. 1998. *Men as Women, Women as Men: Changing Gender in Native American Cultures.* Austin: University of Texas Press.

Roscoe, Will. 1998. *Changing Ones: Third and Fourth Genders in Native America.* New York: Palgrave Macmillan.

Williams, Walter L. 1992. *The Spirit and the Flesh: Sexual Diversity in American Indian Culture.* Boston: Beacon.

Clothing, Native American Women

Prior to European contact, Native American women held equal status with men because female gender-specific occupational roles included clothing production, a highly skilled craft and source of economic autonomy. Native American societies vary in organization, language, belief systems, and cultural practices; however, most North American societies practiced what anthropologists call gender complementarity. All community members needed and valued clothing; therefore, a woman with garment-making expertise was highly respected.

Women and men complemented each other by doing different jobs and having different expertise. Both women and men combined interdependent skills to gather a variety of natural materials and create complex clothing. Women collected grasses, roots, bark, and animal wool for weaving. They also cultivated plant fibers such as cotton and cornhusks. Men hunted game, which provided pelts, hides, sinew, antler, and bone. Women processed the animal skins, while men carved antler and bone into needles and leather punches (awls). These specialized tools were then used by women to create clothing. When young girls reached eight years of age, their mothers began teaching them gender-specific knowledge regarding clothing production. Most clothing was fabricated during the winter when less time was devoted to food production.

All native clothing had to be handmade or obtained through trade. Even infant diapers were crafted of soft leather and lined with absorbent materials such as moss or rabbit fur.

Tunic-shaped silhouettes for shirts and dresses were somewhat unisex. In warm climates bare chests were common, with women wearing skirts or aprons and men wearing breechcloths. Leggings could be added for warmth or protection. Shawls or wraparound robes provided warmth, while Arctic people wore fur parkas. Footwear varied regionally, but most moccasins were leather.

Across cultures, women and men wore headdresses as distinguishing symbols of individual status or authority, especially during ceremonies. Among California acorn economies, women wore basketry hats as clothing and as an economic standard of value: a measured hatful of acorns was equal to specific quantities of other trade items.

Tanning animal skins transforms stiff hide into soft buckskin. This complex process required detailed knowledge and skillful workmanship. Hides were soaked, stretched, scraped, treated with cooked animal brains, and softened with patient handwork. Most buckskin was smoked to a golden brown, rendering it water resistant. White buckskin was unsmoked and used primarily for ceremonial clothing. Holes were punched in the hide with an awl so pieces could be stitched together. Durable thread was made from animal sinew.

Specific hides had different uses: deer and elk in clothing, thick moose hide in footwear. Bison and carnivore pelts became robes and blankets, while bison hide was used in shelters such as the tipi. Fringe frequently decorated garment edges and served to quickly shed water.

Whether rabbit skin or bison hide, a woman owned the skins she processed. She could barter or sell her tanned hides or finished leather products. Women gained individual status from the quality of their workmanship and were economically autonomous.

Female occupations included weaving and basketry-related technologies. Unfortunately, plant fibers do not preserve well, leaving less documentation of their historical and cultural importance. However, elaborate cloth fragments—dyed bright red, yellow, and black—reveal that the Mississippian Culture wove plant-fiber textiles prior to 1300 CE. In the Southwest, Hohokam people similarly cultivated cotton for woven fabrics.

Cultures in California fabricated minimal clothing employing basketry-like techniques to combine plant materials. Feathers were sometimes twisted with plant fibers for ceremonial garments, while strips of rabbit and squirrel fur were woven into blankets and robes.

Women of the Pacific Northwest collected shed mountain goat wool and raised a special breed of dog (now extinct) for its undercoat. The wool was spun into yarn, dyed, and woven into robes and ceremonial garments.

Most clothing ornamentation represented the wearer as an individual or specific group member. Ceremonial and special-event garments were more highly decorated and were considered valued luxury items.

Women showcased craftsmanship and artistic talent decorating clothing, including feather details, moose-hair tufts shaped as flowers, and porcupine quills dyed, flattened, and appliquéd like embroidery. Elongated fringe enhanced gestures, while applied animal teeth, claws, and hooves made distinctive sounds that accentuated movement, especially during dancing. Ornamentation also displayed wealth, indicating time available to devote to artistic expression and resources available to trade for rarities such as pearls, copper, and shell beads.

Among the Great Plains cultures, women dressed less ostentatiously than men; modesty was regarded as a sign of inner power. Elk Woman was a female spirit who stood up to her husband and his trickster friends, Moose and Crow. Plains women symbolically allied with Elk Woman by wearing elk-hide clothing adorned with elk teeth, moose hooves, and crow feathers. Elk teeth also demonstrated an alliance with a successful hunter. Each elk has only two eyeteeth. From boyhood, a man saved these special teeth from his hunts to present them on a dress to his bride. A man depended on his mother or sister to make the garment. Decoration on clothing provided an artistic canvas for women and a way to honor family with meaningful imagery.

European contact greatly impacted cultural clothing; Native Americans were compelled to wear "civilized" European-style clothing, and mass-produced garments required less work. But when women no longer controlled materials and clothing production, their cultural status, economic autonomy, and political power declined. In the wilderness environment, however, European-made shoes did not wear as well as handmade moccasins. Women who specialized in making footwear maintained higher status longer than other women. The social imbalance created by the loss of complementarity was destructive to Native American societies and caused a decline in female social status within tribal cultures through to the 20th century.

Keri Dearborn

See also Food Production, Native American Women; Great Plains Culture; Hunter-Gatherers; Matrilineal Descent; Mississippian Culture; Polygamy, Native American; Pueblo Culture; Religion, Native American

Further Reading

Adovasio, J. M., Olga Soffer, and Jake Page. 2007. *The Invisible Sex: Uncovering the True Roles of Women in Prehistory*. New York: HarperCollins.

Bruhns, Karen Olsen, and Karen E. Stothert. 1999. *Women in Ancient America*. Norman: University of Oklahoma Press.

Klein, Laura F., and Lillian A. Ackerman. 1995. *Women and Power in Native North America*. Berkeley: University of California Press.

Corn Mother

The Corn Mother is a female deity thought to bring corn or maize to the peoples of the world, specifically the indigenous people of Indonesia, Mexico, and the

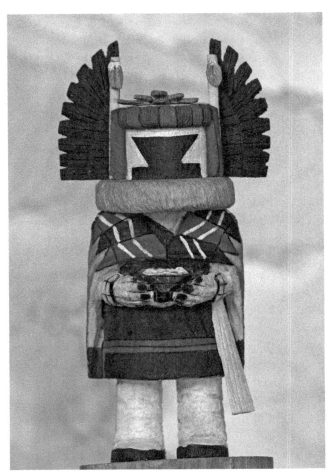

This Hopi Katchina Doll represents the Corn Mother or Mother Nature of the ancient Hopi tribe. Such dolls were made to instruct youngsters about the immortal beings that control the natural world and act as messengers between humans and the spirit world. (Alamy Stock Photo)

United States. The original legends regarding the Corn Mother in North America differ by geographical region: the Southeast, the Eastern Woodlands, and the Pueblo and Plains regions.

The peoples in southeastern America, such as the Cherokee, Creek, and Natchez tribes, follow the same general legend regarding the Corn Mother. In the southeastern legend, the Corn Mother looked after an orphan child while caring for the overall needs of her village. She also created maize by rubbing or shaking her body, an activity that the village called witchcraft. The Corn Mother either committed suicide or was killed by the orphan child she looked after but not before she gave instructions for future maize-growing

techniques. Although this was the general Corn Mother legend of the southeastern region, different groups had their own version.

The Cherokees in southeastern America believed that the Corn Mother, called Selu, was married to the master of hunting game. She also cared for a wild orphan boy known as Blood-clot Boy. As Blood-clot Boy spied on Selu, he found that she produced maize by rubbing her stomach. Blood-clot Boy considered her a witch because of her behavior, and he planned to kill her. When Selu discovered his plot, she told him to drag her body in a circle seven times and then drag her body through the circle seven times. The boy performed this ritual according to her instructions. By the following day, maize had grown in the circle.

The story slightly differs among the southern neighbors of the Cherokees, the southeastern Creek Indians. Instead of being killed by the orphan boy, Corn Mother was ashamed after people found out how she produced maize and killed herself. Before her death, she gave instructions for future maize growing.

The southeastern Natchez Indians believed that Corn Mother cared for twin orphan girls. The girls were disgusted after discovering where the food came from, and they burned the Corn Mother. Maize, beans, and pumpkins sprouted up from where she was killed.

According to Eastern Woodland peoples, the Corn Mother did not care for a specific orphan child but instead cared for her village as a whole. In some versions of the Eastern Woodlands legend, Corn Mother fled the village; in other versions, she was sacrificed. The New England groups such as the Malecites, the Abnakis, and the Penobscots believe in the sacrificial end to Corn Mother. According to the Penobscot legend, she had an affair with a snake and ordered her husband to kill her for her betrayal. The young man killed Corn Mother and dragged her body across a clearing. The clearing was immediately covered in maize, enough to keep the whole town well fed and healthy.

The Seneca and Shawnee peoples primarily tell the other type of Eastern Woodlands legend in which Corn Mother fled instead of being sacrificed. In the Seneca version, Corn Mother married a young man from a famine-stricken area. She brought his village food. She was insulted by her husband's brother and fled to live with her mother. Her husband followed her to her mother's house, and Corn Mother gifted him with many crop seeds for his village. In the Shawnee version, Corn Mother was insulted not by her brother-in-law but by a man who had sex with an ear of corn. Corn Mother fled to a woman known to the Shawnees as "Our Grandmother." A rescuer crossed four oceans to reach Corn Mother and convinced her to return to the village to benefit the Shawnee people with crops and food.

In the Pueblo area, Corn Mother is also referred to as Corn Maiden. She guarded many children and looked after her village by rubbing her body to produce corn. In some Pueblo legends, she married a young man. In these legends Corn Mother was not spied upon, nor was she sacrificed. The Pueblo legends focused primarily on her flight—she was either frightened away by unwanted sexual advances, or her husband was unfaithful. Corn Mother was found hiding beneath a duck's wing. Afterward, she returned to her village to reinitiate corn production.

In the Plains region, the Pawnee, Cheyenne, Mandan, Hidatsa, and Arikara peoples told completely different legends of the Corn Mother. The Plains legends related directly to neither each other nor the legends of the other regions. For example, the Arikara people believe that Corn Mother was formed out of an ear of corn from the heavens. She was sent down to Earth, where she led humankind out of the subterranean levels of earth up to the surface. She initiated food production and became the leader of the peoples of the world.

The Pawnee people also see the Corn Mother as a hero and a leader. In Pawnee culture, she has ties to war and fertility rituals. Another major difference between the legends of the Plains and other regions was the tie between Corn Mother and meat. There are many tales from the Plains region relating the Corn Mother to buffalo, which is different than the Eastern Woodlands, southeastern, and Pueblo regions, which focus more on vegetation.

All of these legends have in common that Corn Mother is a giver of life through food creation and thus not unlike Mother Earth or Mother Nature. She represents growth, life, creativity, and feminine power. Significantly, in many versions of Corn Mother's story

her power is seen as dangerous, and she is destroyed. In her destruction, though, she gives life, suggesting her fundamental immortality. Some Corn Mother legends prophesy that she will return to Earth one day, bringing peace and enlightenment to her believers.

Corn Mother iconography plays an important part in modern southwestern art. Indigenous women artists particularly find representations of Corn Mother meaningful, seeing in her representation an opportunity to celebrate all that is native, feminine, and holy.

B. C. Biggs

See also Creation/Origin Stories; Food Production, Native American Women; Great Plains Culture; Pueblo Culture

Further Reading
Mooney, James. 1902. *Myths of the Cherokee.* Washington, DC: Smithsonian Bureau of American Ethnology.
Swanton, John Reed. 1929. *Myths and Tales of the Southeastern Indians.* Washington, DC: Smithsonian Bureau of American Ethnology.

Creation/Origin Stories

Many scholars assert that Native Americans arrived around 10,000 years ago by crossing the ice bridge that formed in the Bering Strait that linked Asia to the Americas. Archaeologists have challenged this to push the dates back to an era dating to 12,000 to 20,000 years ago prior to the ice bridge. They suggest that Native Americans are indigenous, not immigrants, reflecting great diversity in developing stories of their own genesis. Indigenous creation stories evolved through oral tradition convey primordial symbolic meanings that reflect ancient worldviews as well as indigenous wisdom of life that integrates the individual into society and also integrates the society into its environment. Creation stories always reflect how Native American societies grope to understand existence and are designed to harmonize the culture, putting it in accord with the universe.

The snake, which has negative connotations in the Christian creation story, has different semantics connected to rebirth. Native Americans recognized that life lives off of killing and eating itself (life is sustained by eating other creatures or living things) akin to the way a snake casts off death (its old self) when it sheds its skin; each shedding of skin is a sign of being reborn. The Hopis have a snake dance in which tribal dancers lift snakes to their mouths to make peace with them before returning the snakes to the hill as a symbolic communication between humans and the spirit world. Conversely, some indigenous societies have creation stories that have loose similarities to Genesis in the Bible. For example, Pimas in Arizona believe that originally in the beginning there was only darkness and water everywhere; the darkness was collected and thick in places and then separated, gathered again and then separated, crowded again and separated, and so on.

In the sacrifice of motherhood, or a woman giving her substance for the sake of her progeny, she gives birth, and afterward we are reliant upon her until we are autonomous, which is sometimes portrayed as Mother Earth from whom we find our food subsistence. Some Native American creation stories feature a male savior who brings mankind to life, and then mankind sets out to destroy him, ripping him to shreds, sometimes multiple times, akin to the sentiment that says "saving a man's life, you create an enemy for life."

Northwestern Native Americans have creation stories that delineate their arrival and place them in North America. Many creation stories chronicle the emergence of humans from another world into the one in which they currently inhabit. They describe the creation of people as a staged metamorphosis or ascent from nascent forms. In stories featuring Mother Earth, humans emerge from the womb of Earth, where there is a ladder or rope that the humans use to climb. Sometimes someone grabs the rope and it breaks, depicting the separation of humans from their source, suggesting that there is a challenge to reconnect the rope or means of communication. Often inner forces or extreme emotions and the desire to live without oppression or challenge serve as catalysts for the passage from one stage to the next.

Tricksters appear in many creation stories, providing a dichotomy found within Native American wisdom. The trickster in these stories creates a world, sometimes coming from the sky and sometimes emerging from Earth's center, and later leads his people to their new homeland. Then his people turn against him brutally, not killing him once but sometimes killing him multiple times, yet he always comes back. For example, the Kiowa plains Indians tell of a trickster leading the people out of the lower world and into this world through the hollow of a cottonwood tree log where a pregnant woman got stuck blocking the way for others; this explains the small size of the tribe. In some stories the trickster goes into the mountains, where few humans care to follow because the path is so confused, and only those on a spiritual quest will follow him there.

A composite story of the Pomo Indians of Mendocino County in northern California collected during the summer of 1904 exemplifies how creation stories have been told in areas where indigenous cultures have been endangered by European or American oppression. This story has six components from an informant in Ukiah, California, that consisted of logically connected ideas. A trickster coyote seduces a mate after convincing the women of a village to go on a gathering excursion without two sisters, whom he tricks into having a miraculous birth of four children. Because he used deceit, the sisters killed two of the children, and the others survived but experienced continual abuse from the other villagers. To avenge his children, Coyote employed fire that burned mountaintops and then the world. He managed to escape this world when Spider spun a web that carried Coyote to the sky or heaven. The emergence from a previous world is often likened to the process of being born from the womb of Mother Earth, and many cultures have a female spider that helps in the emergence. Male characters may be part of the story, but they do not serve in the birth process, as women are associated with birth, or giving life, and men are associated with hunting, or taking life.

However, Coyote decides to return to Earth, where he cannot find food or drink with the humans gone. He drinks the ocean down until his stomach explodes, supplying water that collects to form Clear Lake. Coyote misses the humans and begins to erect a small tule dwelling for himself, and then he talks the birds into helping him prepare a small village. While the birds work, Coyote secretly plucks two feathers from each. He retires to rest and talks to himself all night, designating the duties and powers of each feather that is metamorphosed into a human by the next morning. The sun did not appear in the sky as it now does, determined to find out why Coyote gathers his dancing paraphernalia and tricks in his hunting sack and travels east for four days. When he arrives at the home of the Sun People who have visions and can see all that transpires on Earth, he stops and does a dance for them before he steals the sun. Once he returns to his home, his people provoke him, and Coyote transforms them into animals and birds, assigning each creature attributes and habitats.

Iroquois and Algonquin tribes have creation stories centered on the creation of Earth on the back of a giant turtle from which the Pan-Indian term "Turtle Island" is derived. The slow-moving turtle is significant because of its longevity and its ability to dig with its claws, retract into its shell, and be at home both on land and in the water. In the Southeast, Cherokees tell the story that in the beginning all was water, and the animals lived above it so that the sky became crowded and there was no space left. An industrious water beetle named Dayuni'si volunteered to explore but could find no solid ground. He dug and found mud, and it spread and became Earth. An animal attached this land to the sky using four strings. The animals sent a great buzzard to see if Earth was firm enough to inhabit, but by the time he arrived the buzzard was so tired that when his wings touched the ground valleys formed, creating the dramatic landscape where the Cherokees live characterized by mountains and valleys.

In Pueblo architecture the kiva reflects a creation story when a *sipapu* (small round hole in the floor) is present that represents the portal from the underworld through which ancestors first emerged. In the beginning, the Zuni people moved from place to place in search of a homeland and met many dangers from hostile enemies. Father Sun created the War Twins to help the Zunis overcome obstacles and hold a homeland. Winter solstice observances mark a time of world renewal. Newly built homes are blessed, and masked kachinas appear in villages to hear prayers and entertain with dancing. The War Twins are highly revered in Zuni religion, for they can be benevolent or deadly in protecting the Zunis. Their intermediary spirits are kachinas. The War Twins are ceremonially recognized each year at the winter solstice and every four years for members initiated into the tribe.

Meredith Eliassen

See also Anasazi Culture; Corn Mother; Hunter-Gatherers; Religion, Native American

Further Reading

Barnett, S. A. 1906. "A Composite Myth of the Pomo Indians." *Journal of American Folklore* 1972 (January–March): 37–51.

Bastian, Dawn E., and Judy K. Mitchell. 2004. *Handbook of Native American Mythology.* Santa Barbara, CA: ABC-CLIO.

Coffer, William E. 1978. *Spirits of the Sacred Mountains: Creation Stories of the American Indian.* New York: Van Nostrand Reinhold.

Kroeber, A. L. 1976. *Handbook of the Indians of California.* New York: Dover.

Leeming, David, and Jake Page. 1998. *The Mythology of Native North America.* Norman: University of Oklahoma Press.

Waldman, Carl. 2000. *Atlas of the North American Indian.* New York: Checkmark Books.

Native American Creation or Origin Stories

New World indigenous people had, as do all people, a variety of creation stories. Many of these stories feature a goddess-type figure who gives birth to Earth and nourishes the people. The following is a sampling of these stories.

1. IROQUOIS

In the beginning there was no earth to live on, but up above, in the Great Blue, there was a woman who dreamed dreams.

One night she dreamed about a tree covered with white blossoms, a tree that brightened up the sky when its flowers opened but that brought terrible darkness when they closed again. The dream frightened her, so she went and told it to the wise old men who lived with her, in their village in the sky.

"Pull up this tree," she begged them, but they did not understand. All they did was to dig around its roots, to make space for more light. But the tree just fell through the hole they had made and disappeared. After that there was no light at all, only darkness.

The old men grew frightened of the woman and her dreams. It was her fault that the light had gone away forever.

So they dragged her toward the hole and pushed her through as well. Down, down she fell, down toward the great emptiness. There was nothing below her but a heaving waste of water and she would surely have been smashed to pieces, this strange dreaming woman from the Great Blue, had not a fish hawk come to her aid. His feathers made a pillow for her and she drifted gently above the waves.

But the fish hawk could not keep her up all on his own. He needed help. So he called out to the creatures of the deep. "We must find some firm ground for this poor woman to rest on," he said anxiously. But there was no ground, only the swirling, endless waters.

A helldiver went down, down, down to the very bottom of the sea and brought back a little bit of mud in his beak. He found a turtle, smeared the mud onto its back, and dived down again for more.

Then the ducks joined in. They loved getting muddy and they too brought beakfuls of the ocean floor and spread it over the turtle's shell. The beavers helped—they were great builders—and they worked away, making the shell bigger and bigger.

Everybody was very busy now and everybody was excited. This world they were making seemed to be growing enormous! The birds and the animals rushed about building countries, the continents, until, in the end, they had made the whole round earth, while all the time they sky woman was safely sitting on the turtle's back.

And the turtle holds the earth up to this very day.

Source: "Native American Creation Myths," Biblioteca Pleyades, http://www.bibliotecapleyades.net/mitos_creacion/esp _mitoscreacion_13.htm#women.

2. HURON CREATION STORY

In the beginning there was only one water and the water animals that lived in it.

Then a woman fell from a torn place in the sky. She was a divine woman, full of power. Two loons flying over the water saw her falling. They flew under her, close together, making a pillow for her to sit on.

The loons held her up and cried for help. They could be heard for a long way as they called for other animals to come.

The snapping turtle called all the other animals to aid in saving the divine woman's life.

The animals decided the woman needed earth to live on.

Turtle said, "Dive down in the water and bring up some earth."

So they did that, those animals. A beaver went down. A muskrat went down. Others stayed down too long, and they died.

Each time, Turtle looked inside their mouths when they came up, but there was no earth to be found.

Toad went under the water. He stayed too long, and he nearly died. But when Turtle looked inside Toad's mouth, he found a little earth. The woman took it and put it all around on Turtle's shell. That was the start of the earth.

Dry land grew until it formed a country, then another country, and all the earth. To this day, Turtle holds up the earth.

Time passed, and the divine woman had twin boys. They were opposites, her sons. One was good, and one was bad. One was born as children are usually born, in a normal way. But the other one broke out of his mother's side, and she died.

When the divine woman was buried, all of the plants needed for life on earth sprang from the ground above her. From her head came the pumpkin vine. Maize came from her chest. Pole beans grew from her legs.

Source: "Native American Creation Myths," Biblioteca Pleyades, http://www.bibliotecapleyades.net/mitos_creacion/esp _mitoscreacion_13.htm#women.

3. HOPI SPIDER WOMAN CREATION STORY—THE FOUR CREATIONS

The world at first was endless space in which existed only the Creator, Taiowa. This world had no time, no shape, and no life, except in the mind of the Creator.

Eventually the infinite creator created the finite in Sotuknang, whom he called his nephew and whom he created as his agent to establish nine universes. Sotuknang gathered together matter from the endless space to make the nine solid worlds. Then the Creator instructed him to gather together the waters from the endless space and place them on these worlds to make land and sea. When Sotuknang had done that, the Creator instructed him to gather together air to make winds and breezes on these worlds.

The fourth act of creation with which the Creator charged Sotuknang was the creation of life. Sotuknang went to the world that was to first host life and there he created Spider Woman, and he gave her the power to create life. First Spider Woman took some earth and mixed it with saliva to make two beings. Over them she sang the Creation Song, and they came to life. She instructed one of them, Poqanghoya, to go across the earth and solidify it. She instructed the other, Palongawhoya, to send out sound to resonate through the earth, so that the earth vibrated with the energy of the Creator. Poqanghoya and Palongawhoya were despatched to the poles of the earth to keep it rotating.

Then Spider Woman made all the plants, the flowers, the bushes, and the trees. Likewise she made the birds and animals, again using earth and singing the Creation Song. When all this was done, she made human beings, using yellow, red, white, and black earth mixed with her saliva. Singing the Creation Song, she made four men, and then in her own form she made four women. At first they had a soft spot in their foreheads, and although it solidified, it left a space through which they could hear the voice of Sotuknang and their Creator. Because these people could not speak, Spider Woman called on Sotuknang, who gave them four languages. His only instructions were for them to respect their Creator and to live in harmony with him.

These people spread across the earth and multiplied. Despite their four languages, in those days they could understand each other's thoughts anyway, and for many years they and the animals lived together as one. Eventually, however, they began to divide, both the people from the animals and the people from each other, as they focused on their differences rather than their similarities. As division and suspicion became more widespread, only a few people from each of the four groups still remembered

their Creator. Sotuknang appeared before these few and told them that he and the Creator would have to destroy this world, and that these few who remembered the Creator must travel across the land, following a cloud and a star, to find refuge. These people began their treks from the places where they lived, and when they finally converged Sotuknang appeared again. He opened a huge ant mound and told these people to go down in it to live with the ants while he destroyed the world with fire, and he told them to learn from the ants while they were there. The people went down and lived with the ants, who had storerooms of food that they had gathered in the

Spider Rock, Canyon de Chelly National Monument, Arizona, is believed to be the home of Spider Woman. Spider Woman or Spider Grandmother is one of many indigenous North American goddesses. She is signficant in a number of Native American cultures' belief systems, often linked to creation myths that suggest female power. (robertharding/Alamy Stock Photo)

summer, as well as chambers in which the people could live. This went on for quite a while, because after Sotuknang cleansed the world with fire it took a long time for the world to cool off. As the ants' food ran low, the people refused the food, but the ants kept feeding them and only tightened their own belts, which is why ants have such tiny waists today.

Finally Sotuknang was done making the second world, which was not quite as beautiful as the first. Again he admonished the people to remember their Creator as they and the ants that had hosted them spread across the earth. The people multiplied rapidly and soon covered the entire earth. They did not live with the animals, however, because the animals in this second world were wild and unfriendly. Instead the people lived in villages and built roads between these, so that trade sprang up. They stored goods and traded those for goods from elsewhere, and soon they were trading for things they did not need. As their desire to have more and more grew, they began to forget their Creator, and soon wars over resources and trade were breaking out between villages. Finally Sotuknang appeared before the few people who still remembered the Creator, and again he sent them to live with the ants while he destroyed this corrupt world. This time he ordered Poqanghoya and Palongawhoya to abandon their posts at the poles, and soon the world spun out of control and rolled over. Mountains slid and fell, and lakes and rivers splashed across the land as the earth tumbled, and finally the earth froze over into nothing but ice.

This went on for years, and again the people lived with the ants. Finally Sotuknang sent Poqanghoya and Palongawhoya back to the poles to resume the normal rotation of the earth, and soon the ice melted and life returned. Sotuknang called the people up from their refuge, and he introduced them to the third world that he had made. Again he admonished the people to remember their Creator as they spread across the land. As they did so, they multiplied quickly, even more quickly than before, and soon they were living in large cities and developing into separate nations. With so many people and so many nations, soon there was war, and some of the nations made huge shields on which they could fly, and from these flying shields they attacked other cities. When Sotuknang saw all this war and destruction, he resolved to destroy this world quickly before it corrupted the few people who still remembered the Creator. He called on Spider Woman to gather those few and, along the shore, she placed each person with a little food in the hollow stem of a reed. When she had done this, Sotuknang let loose a flood that destroyed the warring cities and the world on which they lived.

Once the rocking of the waves ceased, Spider Woman unsealed the reeds so the people could see. They floated on the water for many days, looking for land, until finally they drifted to an island. On the island they built little reed boats and set sail again to the east. After drifting many days, they came to a larger island, and after many more days to an even larger island. They hoped that this would be the fourth world that Sótuknang had made for them, but Spider Woman assured them that they still had a long and hard journey ahead. They walked across this island and built rafts on the far side, and set sail to the east again. They came to a fourth and still larger island, but again they had to cross it on foot and then build more rafts to continue east. From this island, Spider Woman sent them on alone, and after many days they encountered a vast land. Its shores were so high that they could not find a place to land, and only by opening the doors in their heads did they know where to go to land.

When they finally got ashore, Sotuknang was there waiting for them. As they watched to the west, he made the islands that they had used like stepping stones disappear into the sea. He welcomed them to the fourth world, but he warned them that it was not as beautiful as the previous ones, and that life here would be harder, with heat and cold, and tall mountains and deep valleys. He sent them on their way to migrate across the wild new land in search of the homes for their respective clans. The clans were to migrate across the land to learn its ways, although some grew weak and stopped in the warm climates or rich lands along the way. The Hopi trekked and far and wide, and went through the cold and icy country to the north before finally settling in the arid lands between the Colorado River and Rio Grande River. They chose that place so that the hardship of their life would always remind them of their dependence on, and link to, their Creator.

Source: "The Four Creations," Bruce Railsback's Geoscience Resources, http://www.gly.uga.edu/railsback/CS/CS FourCreations.html.

Cultural Interaction

Anthropologists assert that some Native American tribes, Paleo-Indians, migrated from Asia over a land bridge about 20,000 to 35,000 years ago, and therefore these newcomers share some ancient cultural memories with their Eurasian and African contemporaries, including rituals and healing practices related to shamanism. Intertribal trade shaped the cultural interactions of Native American tribes over time, acting as a catalyst for the diffusion of ideas before European contact. Agriculture was innovated in Mesoamerica and South America, and migration led to the sharing of techniques for seed planting. Southwestern tribes traded in turquoise and textile, tribes of the western Great Lakes traded in copper, California tribes traded with shell beads, northwestern Indians traded in woodwork, and northeastern Indians traded canoes, establishing regular trade routes along rivers and lakes.

In the Atlantic Northeast, the Iroquois League of 50 chiefs (or Haudenosaunee, meaning "People of the Longhouse") consisted of the Mohawks (9 chiefs), Senecas (8 chiefs), Onondagas (14 chiefs), Cayugas (10 chiefs), Oneidas (9 chiefs), and later the Tuscaras. Hiawatha, chief of the Onondagas, established the five-nation Iroquois Confederacy in about 1575 to halt intertribal wars and to strengthen diplomacy and economic stability. In the Iroquois Confederacy women held a high degree of political and ceremonial power, as clans were matrilineal. For instance, clan mothers selected the chiefs of the confederacy and had veto power over legislation and decisions to go to war. Iroquoians innovated agricultural planning with the three-sister crops (corn, beans, and squash) grown in integrated fields to maximize farm yields, so they had less need to augment their diet with extensive trade outside their network.

Religious beliefs, rituals, and myths have evolved out of the diffusion and cross-fertilization of two distinct indigenous cultural traditions: shamanistic (male) northern hunting traditions involving bears and other hunted animals; and southern agricultural traditions related to planting and female fertility. European settlers believed that indigenous women were inferior in status to European women because they worked in the fields doing farmwork. However, with a substantial number of tribes being matrilineal, women actually controlled food supplies, were free to choose husbands within reason, and governed clans and served as chiefs and shamans in some tribes. In some hunter-gatherer societies, women were isolated from men during menstruation. Women's networking centered often on food cultivating, harvesting, and preparation. Women accumulated considerable knowledge of plant life needed to cultivate and prepare raw natural materials to construct practical items for survival. Women were charged throughout the seasons with harvesting, preserving, and cooking food to make the best use of these natural resources.

The Spanish introduced the horse, which was the dominant European mode of land transportation during the 16th century; this formed a new horse culture on the Great Plains. By the later part of the 18th century use of the horse was widespread throughout North America, and many tribes abandoned settlements in favor of migratory hunting. Cultural diversity diminished somewhat as the buffalo became the basis for economic stability on the Great Plains. In California at the time of the American Revolution, Spanish Franciscans operating missions initiated a system to denaturalize and destabilize the aboriginal sense of self-identity, connectivity, and kinship to the spiritual world, reducing all native people from sophisticated land stewards to children, or neophytes. Franciscans established forms of paternal kinship with baptisms of native people, which brought about the demographic collapse of the tribes when Spaniards stood as godparents, undermining the authority of tribal headmen within the new political hierarchy.

At Mission San Francisco de Asis (Mission Dolores), built with Ohlone labor in 1776, entire village communities were moved to different missions to break down existing political structures and dialects. Approximately 1,699 Coast Miwoks between 1783 and 1817 entered Mission Dolores, and by the end of that time only 485 survived. Spanish soldiers raped indigenous women, introducing syphilis into native populations in the missions that were unknowingly carried home to tribal villages.

Mission staff did not use functional aboriginal basketry, which was the basis for indigenous survival and knowledge about the environment, but instead used European pottery. Spanish authorities banned ethnographic burns, disrupting the cultivation of seed crops, forage for wildlife, and reliable food supplies for tribes. When the best basket-making supplies diminished without controlled burns, many Coast Miwoks were subsequently compelled to join the mission system. Neophytes had less varied diets and more sedentary living conditions, and the indigenous population of the San Francisco Bay Area was nearly depleted during the years of Franciscan proselytization. Neophyte women returning to their homelands to gather food and basket-making materials were limited to harvest times to collect acorns from tribal lands, so it was not possible to maintain the land, intertribal relations, or their culture. Within a generation, native peoples on *paseos* (the priest's permission to promenade or leave the mission to visit homelands) were dying at home because they ate bad seafood due to loss of selecting skills. Basket-making materials, which dictated the types of baskets that were constructed, could not be found adjacent to missions, which curtailed construction or influenced some tribal basket design motifs over time.

Meredith Eliassen

See also Hunter-Gatherers; Religion, Native American

Further Reading

Brody, J. J. 1990. *The Anasazi: Ancient Indian People of the American Southwest.* New York: Rizzoli.

Rockwell, David B. 1991. *Giving Voice to the Bear: North American Indian Myths, Rituals, and Images of the Bear.* Lanham, MD: Roberts Rinehart.

Treuer, Anton, et al. 2010. *Indian Nations of North America.* Washington, DC: National Geographic.

Waldman, Carl. 2000. *Atlas of the North American Indian.* New York: Checkmark Books.

Disease, Postconquest Impact on Native Americans

Indigenous America was by no means disease-free prior to contact with Old World populations. Yet because Native Americans lived in isolation from the rest of the world for so long, their immune systems proved ineffective against the strains of disease that Europeans and their African slaves transmitted to them. The highest mortality rates among Native Americans occurred within the first century of contact, reducing American Indian populations in the path of epidemics by as much as 90 percent. The worst killers included smallpox, typhus, plague, and measles.

The diseases that crossed the Atlantic during the 16th century caused what are called virgin-soil epidemics, because every Native American person who came in contact with them was susceptible. Entire families and even villages perished during these epidemics because every member was struck simultaneously, leaving no one to take care of the basic needs for food and water. The elderly and the young were often more likely to succumb to disease. Since the elderly were the keepers of oral traditions, their deaths caused a significant loss of cultural knowledge. Losing the young, on the other hand, affected long-term population recovery.

Disease also had gender-specific consequences. Complications from disease could render a woman infertile or reduce her reproductive capacity, again with long-term effects on population recovery. Venereal diseases also spread among Indian women as they became victims of European sexual violence, leading to reduced birthrates and lower resistance to other illnesses. It is likely that women suffered from rape trauma, as described by modern psychologists, which may have contributed to lower birthrates among victims of rape. This psychological effect remained with communities long past the immediate horror of sexual violence.

While survivors developed immunity to some diseases, they had no protection against other epidemics. Furthermore, survivors most likely experienced severe psychological trauma amid the death and destruction of their communities. Anyone who survived a high mortality rate epidemic suffered from depression, survivor's guilt, and a host of other psychological problems. They also struggled with basic needs such as food, water, and safety because of the physical destruction of their families and communities. Native people's long-term survival also depended on reconstructing identities, political and economic institutions, and cultural traditions when small groups of survivors had to combine resources with each other. This restructuring of the tribal landscape had consequences far into the future of relations between whites and Native Americans.

As European colonies proliferated in the 17th century, so did written records of migrations and epidemics catastrophic to Native Americans. Smallpox, malaria, measles, influenza, and diphtheria decimated Indian populations on the North American frontiers at a time when European colonists began to move inland, giving them a strategic advantage over indigenous peoples, who would have been not only numerically weakened but also psychologically and structurally weakened. Diseases also preceded the arrival of colonists in the interior regions, further facilitating the takeover of Indian land and resources.

Old World diseases continued to reach epidemic proportions in the 18th century: at least 16 major epidemics swept away natives in all or large parts of North America. The 19th century witnessed a new pathogen from Europe when cholera reached North America in 1832, causing widespread mortality among Indians. The old killer smallpox continued to decimate Native Americans populations in a series of epidemics that swept the North American continent from the Southwest all the way to Alaska.

While mortality rates in the 19th-century epidemics varied, demographic and geographic changes were increasingly determined by the expansionist policies of the United States. Americanizing the American Indians became an essential element of this expansion as the nation reached from the Atlantic to the Pacific. Indian tribes were placed on reservations, dependent on government rations while their traditional food sources dwindled. Particularly devastating to the Plains Indian tribes was the federal government's purposeful near extermination of the buffalo, the center of not only their economic system but also their spiritual life. Alcoholism began to reach epidemic proportions among reservation Indians, a symptom of the culture of conquest that defined Indian life.

On reservations, white flour, sugar, milk products, and lard replaced traditional foods of wild game and native plants, with long-term consequences for Indian health. This trend only escalated in the 20th century.

After World War II, when new medicines had been developed to control tuberculosis and trachoma among Indians, diabetes emerged as the major killer of Native Americans in the United States. Other diet-related health issues include a high incidence of obesity and heart disease. Alcoholism continues to plague Indian communities, contributing to high mortality rates from suicide, accidents, and cirrhosis of the liver.

While it is impossible to know exactly how many Indians populated the American continent at the time of European arrival, it is clear that their numbers significantly declined as a result. Using archaeological data and demographic studies, historians believe that there were 50 million to 100 million native people in the Americas before conquest. Diseases that Europeans and Africans brought with them played a significant role in this decline; other reasons included increased warfare, the destruction of Native American ways of life, and expansionist policies that both reduced Indian populations and prevented normal population recovery. Given the extent of native people's population decimation combined with the causes, scholars believe that it can be categorized as a genocide.

Population decline began to reverse around 1900, partly as a result of lower mortality rates and increased life expectancy. Native American birthrates also tended to be higher than those among the general population. Increasingly, while still suffering from certain diseases in higher proportions than the general population, American Indians of the 21st century are susceptible to the same health problems as the rest of the population, including new ones such as HIV-AIDS.

Päivi H. Hoikkala

See also Great Plains Culture; *Vol. 1, Sec. 2:* Slavery, African

Further Reading

Alchon, Suzanne Austin. 2003. *A Pest in the Land: New World Epidemics in a Global Perspective.* Albuquerque: University of New Mexico Press.

Crosby, Alfred W., Jr. 1972. *The Columbian Exchange: Biological and Cultural Consequences of 1492.* Westport, CT: Greenwood.

Elizabeth I of England. *See* Queens, European, Elizabeth I of England and Isabella of Castile

Food Production, Native American Women

In North America prior to European contact, Native American women held equal status with men because gender-specific occupational roles gave women control over food and vital resources. Native American societies varied in organization, language, belief systems, and cultural practices. However, most of these hunter-gather and hunter-agricultural societies practiced what anthropologists call gender complementarity. Women and men complemented each other by doing different jobs, thereby enabling the group to find and process the most available food.

In many cultures, women gathered wild plant foods: leafy plants, seaweed, berries, roots, nuts, and seeds. Successful gathering required botanical knowledge of plant location, collection period, and specific preparation.

Mothers and female relatives began teaching girls gender-specific knowledge when they reached eight years old. Girls learned plant identification and processing: baking and drying roots and drying and grinding grains. Once dried, food staples could be stored and reconstituted in a stew or porridge or baked as a cake or bread. Meat and other vegetables were added to these staples.

Some resources, such as acorns, required skilled preparation to make them safe for eating. The camus bulb, gathered on the northwestern plateau, required expertise to distinguish edible from poisonous bulbs. Among these people, young girls demonstrated advancement into womanhood by successfully collecting edible camus and preparing it for tribal elders, a ceremonial equivalent to a boy's first hunt. Sacagawea's knowledge of camus and other roots saved the Lewis and Clark expedition from deprivation.

Women made tools for their own horticultural use. Digging sticks served to unearth wild roots and plant seeds. Storing and processing food required containers; therefore, girls learned basketry, pottery, and leather working.

Women originated farming technology and typically grew agricultural crops. Gourds, sunflowers, and goosefoot or quinoa were North American crop plants. Women in Mexico and Central America developed melons, chilies, squash, beans, and maize. Prior to European arrival, these crops were grown from the Anasazi and Pueblo cultures of the Southwest to the Iroquois Confederacy in the Northeast. Food surpluses produced by women increased native populations and enabled semipermanent villages and large civic complexes. The women who produced these foods held high or equivalent social positions with men, who provided large-game protein.

The Iroquois identified maize, beans, and squash as distinctively feminine icons, known as the Three Sisters. Eaten together, these staples provided a nutritionally well-balanced diet. The three plants also nurtured each other: the squash shaded the maize's roots, the maize provided a stalk for the beans to climb, and the beans replenished the soil with nitrogen for its sisters.

Women developed maize into a high-yield crop essential to community well-being. Many cultures integrated maize into their religion, celebrating planting and/or harvesting in the Green Corn Ceremony. The Corn Mother and other feminine spirits honored fertility, regeneration, and the vital role of women.

In most cultures, women managed agricultural lands and transferred farming or gathering rights through matrilineal descent (from mother to daughter). Women controlled their harvest and in many cultures could barter or sell excess food they produced. In addition, the tools and containers a woman made were her individual property. Food production provided women with independent economic power within their communities. Contrary to the views of Europeans documenting encounters with native peoples, Native American women were not performing drudgery work for their husbands; they were managing their own agricultural enterprises.

Male occupations included hunting large game and fishing, but women frequently captured small game—voles, prairie dogs, and rabbits—in plant fiber nets or snares. Gender roles did not bar a skilled woman from hunting. Some women's graves within mound-building cultures have been found to contain personal hunting paraphernalia: stone balancing weights for a spear-tossing implement called an *atlatl*.

Similarly, a man could act in a female role. Female and male genders complemented each other, and therefore both were valued.

Men hunted caribou, bison, and deer, while women typically processed the carcasses—skinning, cutting up the flesh, and drying or smoking the meat. Prey such as salmon and bison were harvested in vast quantities in short bursts of time. In such situations community members worked together to secure the greatest resource abundance. Women with expertise fished, and men assisted women in smoking salmon and butchering bison.

Women did not prepare or process food during their menstrual cycle. Menses was a time of spiritual introspection; other family members handled the woman's everyday tasks.

Among the Iroquois, the clan mother made sure clan members (extended matrilineal relatives) received enough food. Even in cultures where women did not butcher meat, they typically distributed meat resources. Control over food gave women social and economic power. Among the Senecas of the Iroquois Confederacy, women provisioned warriors. They could not stop male warfare, but they could refuse to provide food supplies, effectively curtailing a war party.

Management of food resources yielded personal autonomy. Women who controlled their own resources were independent and usually free to divorce. Some female English captives, such as Mary Jemison, stayed within Native American societies because they experienced greater personal autonomy.

When Europeans influenced Native American men to become farmers or imposed food resources on native societies, they changed the economic status of women within these societies. Without control over food resources, women's political power diminished. The social imbalance, created by the loss of complementarity, was destructive to Native American societies and caused a decline in female social status within tribal cultures through the 20th century.

Keri Dearborn

See also Anasazi Culture; Clothing, Native American Women; Corn Mother; Disease, Postconquest Impact on Native Americans; Hunter-Gatherers; Iroquois Confederacy; Matrilineal Descent; Mound-Building Cultures; Pueblo Culture; Religion, Native American; *Vol. 1, Sec. 2:* Captives, English; Jemison, Mary; *Vol. 1, Sec. 3:* Sacagawea

Further Reading

Adovasio, J. M., Olga Soffer, and Jake Page. 2007. *The Invisible Sex: Uncovering the True Roles of Women in Prehistory.* New York: HarperCollins.

Bruhns, Karen Olsen, and Karen E. Stothert. 1999. *Women in Ancient America.* Norman: University of Oklahoma Press.

Klein, Laura F., and Lillian A. Ackerman. 1995. *Women and Power in Native North America.* Berkeley: University of California Press.

Great Plains Culture

Using the boundaries of the present-day United States, the Great Plains encompasses all or part of the states of Colorado, Kansas, Montana, Nebraska, New Mexico, North Dakota, Oklahoma, South Dakota, Texas, and Wyoming. Native peoples who practiced a variety of cultures shaped by their diverse environments have resided on the Great Plains for more than 18,000 years. Contemporary Americans often regard Great Plains Indians as the archetypal American Indians, in great part because of their portrayal in TV and film westerns.

Paleo-Indians first arrived on the Great Plains during the Pleistocene epoch. The region received much more precipitation than it does today, which supported a great variety of vegetation. The plants also provided food for many types of megafauna, such as mammoths, horses, camels, and musk oxen. With such a variety of vegetation and fauna, the area was enticing to the Native Americans who were primarily hunter-gatherers. Women collected fruits, nuts, and edible plants, while men hunted large game using spears. Modern archaeological studies have begun to show that the population survived largely on a diet of the vegetation collected and cultivated by the women more than the rare acquisition of hunted meat. This reality would lead to the creation of matriarchal and/or matrilineal tribal practices in which native women had much more social and political power than their European counterparts.

Approximately 10,000 years ago, conditions on the Plains began to change as the precipitation declined and conditions warmed. During this period, the megafauna became extinct. Two causes have been posited for their extinction. The climate change, especially the severe decline in rainfall, resulted in the vegetation they depended on for sustenance disappearing. The other reason may have been overhunting by Native American populations. The onset of the Holocene epoch, the period we are still in today, saw great environmental changes on the Great Plains. Grass became the dominant form of vegetation. This allowed for bison (incorrectly known as buffalo) to thrive so that eventually the region came to be dominated by large herds of the animals. Other large herbivores, such as elk, also thrived. All of the changes required the cultures of the region's native peoples to adapt to their new reality, particularly because given their immense size, bison were extremely difficult to kill before the advent of the horse. Native peoples probably continued to exist primarily on diets of foods gathered by women rather than on meat hunted by men.

One common feature of most of the residents of the Great Plains, even during the Pleistocene, was that people migrated constantly, following the demands of a gathering culture. Some of the migration was seasonal in that bands lived in one locale during warm weather and another during the winter. Other peoples were constantly on the move due to factors such as warfare or trade. The ancestors of the Apaches originated in present-day Canada and began their southward migration in waves beginning around 2,000 years ago. By 1100 CE, some of the Apaches had settled in today's Colorado and New Mexico. At the time the Spanish arrived in the Southwest, Apaches were also in Texas. The Comanches could originally be found in parts or all of the present-day states of Idaho, Montana, Nebraska, and Wyoming. They too gradually migrated southward. During the 18th century, the Comanches acquired their first horses and quickly became horse breeders. They were drawn southward by the opportunity to trade with both the Spanish and the French. The Comanches traded horses for the weaponry necessary to fight the Apache peoples whose lands they desired. The Comanches eventually established a new homeland, known as Comancheria, that encompassed portions of Colorado, Kansas, New Mexico, Oklahoma, and Texas, as well as territory in northern Mexico.

Not all of the migration was to the south. The Lakotas, for example, came to the Plains from the Great Lakes region, particularly after the introduction of horses to their culture. Horses allowed the Lakota people to more effectively hunt bison, a reality that undermined the position of Lakota women. As hunting became more important to the culture, men's power rose. And because women had been in charge of the butchering and drying of bison meat, men who could kill multiple bison began to acquire multiple wives. Though Lakota and other Great Plains women continued to have more power than their Euro-American counterparts, polygamy eroded some of their traditional power base.

Prior to the arrival of Europeans on the North American continent, some Native American societies on the Great Plains, such as the Mandans, Omahas, Osages, and Pawnees, were agriculturalists, or people who grew food rather than gathering it. These groups established their farms on the floodplains of rivers, growing beans, maize, and squash. It was the women in these groups who were responsible for growing and harvesting crops. These crops not only provided sustenance for the community but also provided a surplus that was used to trade for meat and hides from other native peoples residing on untillable land who were dependent on hunting game. The meat obtained through trade supplemented the game provided by the men of the tribe. In farming, though, women experienced economic power that transferred to other areas of tribal life.

Although women provided more than their share of the food required for the survival of the community, they wielded very little formal political or ceremonial authority. Their power in the community came through the ownership of most of the material goods they produced. Since they provided the surplus agricultural goods, women made the decisions about how the goods were exchanged. Females were responsible for the manufacturing of household items such as clothing and pottery. Their duties also included the erecting or dismantling of their lodging whenever the band was migrating to a new locale, establishing the women as owners of their homes. Through the ownership of key physical resources, most notably vegetables and the home, women had immense power that ensured spousal respect. If a man mistreated his wife, he faced the real possibility of homelessness. While owning the domicile gave women practical authority, it was by no means an easy life. They often carried water and firewood long distances to their community. When migrating, they often hauled much of what they owned by foot. Those realities combined with childbirth meant that most native women of the Great Plains did not live to an advanced age.

Life on the Great Plains experienced a cultural revolution during the early 1700s with the introduction of horses. Horses had been in the region during the late Pleistocene epoch but had become extinct. When the Spanish made their entrance into North American in the late 16th century, they brought horses with them from Europe. The descendants of those horses arrived onto the plains just over a century later. Lifestyles changed when the native peoples adapted their cultures to the horses. Suddenly they could travel long distances fairly quickly, trading at much more distant markets for what they required. Since the agriculturalists could no longer depend on their nomadic neighbors as trading partners, many abandoned agriculture and became bison hunters.

This overdependence on bison created problems for native people in the 19th century. The bison herds slowly disappeared as the U.S. government undertook a program of purposeful eradication of the species so as to disempower native people. The need to hunt required native peoples to move farther afield to locate their prey, which resulted in warfare between groups competing for bison-rich territory. Increasing encroachment by citizens of the United States throughout the 1800s resulted in Native American groups banding together to fight a common enemy. Many of the wars saw all Native American groups suffering the loss not only of men but also of women and children. Eventually, the U.S. government forced all of the native peoples of the Great Plains onto reservations.

The transition to reservations caused yet another restructuring of Native American cultures that saw women come to the fore as the primary supporters of their respective families. This was due to two factors.

First, the male Native American population had been decimated by warfare, and thus many families were led by women. Second, women had always been responsible for the home and its related work. These responsibilities were still in existence, so their cultural role changed very little. For men, their primary responsibilities of hunting and warfare were gone, resulting in the practical disappearance of their cultural function. They subsequently adopted the lifestyle of their American neighbors, as much as they were allowed by the federal government's policies.

John R. Burch Jr.

See also Hunter-Gatherers; Matrilineal Descent

Further Reading

Albers, Patricia, and Beatrice Medicine. 1983. *The Hidden Half: Studies of Plains Indian Women.* Washington, DC: University Press of America.

Calloway, Colin G. 2003. *One Vast Winter Count: The Native American West before Lewis and Clark.* Lincoln: University of Nebraska Press.

DeMallie, Raymond J., ed. 2001. *Handbook of North American Indians,* Vol. 13, *Plains.* Washington, DC: Smithsonian Institution Press.

Wishart, David J., ed. 2007. *Encyclopedia of the Great Plains Indians.* Lincoln: University of Nebraska Press.

Hinestrosa, Francisca (d. 1541)

When she purportedly disguised herself as a man to accompany her husband on Hernando de Soto's 1539 expedition to what is now the southeastern United States, Francisca Hinestrosa became one of the first European females to step onto the North American continent.

Very little is known about Hinestrosa. Some sources say that she was the wife of Luis de Inostrosa (Ynistrosa) of Seville. Others say that she was married to Hernando Bautista of Seville or one of de Soto's soldiers. Spanish historian Rene Leon's account indicates that she was from a prominent family in Havana and that one of her relatives had served as lieutenant governor of Cuba in 1530. Because de Soto's expedition stopped in Cuba before going on to present-day Florida, this is another possibility.

By 1539, de Soto had considerable experience in the New World. He had already been in Central and South America and had participated in Francisco Pizarro's subjugation of the Incas in the early 1530s. On April 6, 1538, de Soto left Sanlucar, Spain, with 10 ships and 700 fighting men, hoping to find gold and silver and perhaps a hospitable place to settle in North America. After a year's delay in Cuba, he departed for present-day Florida on May 18, 1539, with about 600 men as well as horses, equipment, and pigs for food. When de Soto landed near Tampa Bay on May 25, Hinestrosa was apparently part of the company. This is another reason the Cuba connection makes sense. There was one other woman with the group, Ana Mendez, who was the servant of de Soto's wife, Isabel de Bobadilla. Sources differ on how long it took to discover that Francisca was not, in fact, a male soldier. Some say that she managed to maintain the disguise for only a month, while others say that the deception was not discovered until after her death. Those who maintain that she was discovered early in the expedition report that after her discovery, she worked as a nurse and a cook.

After landing in Florida, de Soto embarked on a meandering route through the Southeast. His method was to travel during the warm months and then establish a camp, sometimes in a deserted or commandeered Native American village, for the winter. He was probably in present-day Florida in 1539 and the early part of 1540. Later in 1540 he traveled through Georgia, the Carolinas, Tennessee, Alabama, and Mississippi. Francisca Hinestrosa would have been in the company through all these travels working alongside male soldiers, though it is impossible to know what exactly she did or experienced.

In 1540–1541, de Soto established his winter camp in a Chicasa (Chickasaw) village in the northwestern part of present-day Mississippi. In March, according to his usual practice, de Soto asked the local Chickasaw leader for women and 100 porters to accompany him on his way. De Soto undoubtedly wanted the women to do both domestic and sexual work for his soldiers. In essence he was asking the Chickasaws to turn over women to be raped. Chickasaw women

would not have looked kindly on this request. On the night before his scheduled departure, the Chickasaws attacked de Soto's camp, shooting arrows to set the huts on fire. Sources say that Hinestrosa was either unable to leave her hut because she was pregnant and about to give birth or that she escaped and then ran back in to retrieve her pearls. In any case, she died in the burning hut. The Spanish lost a dozen other people during the attack as well as a large quantity of weapons, gear, and clothing.

De Soto and his remaining men went on through Arkansas, Oklahoma, and Texas in 1541. By this time almost half of his men had died from wounds or disease, most of the horses had been killed or lost, and the remaining soldiers were in poor health. They had found no gold or silver and no good place for a settlement. They turned back east, and on May 21, 1542, de Soto died in either present-day Arkansas or Louisiana. Luis de Moscoso Alvarado took over the expedition, and it was abandoned the following year.

As the first exploration of the interior southeastern United States, de Soto's expedition vastly increased the Europeans' knowledge of the New World and its inhabitants. It also set a standard for the Spanish conquest in that it did not seek understanding of the native peoples or attempt to create any meaningful trading partnerships. Rather, de Soto's expedition left chaos and destruction in its path. Written accounts of the expedition provide modern scholars with invaluable information on the Native American tribes of the Mississippian period, which by the time they were encountered by later explorers had either disappeared or changed radically, perhaps in part because of their initial encounters with de Soto.

The difficulty in knowing anything concrete about Francisca Hinestrosa's part in the de Soto expedition is suggestive of one of the main challenges of women's history: a paucity of written sources about a group considered not worthy of recording or not engaged in the public sphere makes women's history profoundly difficult. Because most women lived their lives in the private sphere, in homes and families, their lives and work escape the public record. Even when women do make an appearance outside of the private sphere, as did Francisca Hinestrosa, they tend to elude the public record, leaving women historically invisible as a result of a patriarchal value system that marks their lives as unimportant.

Nancy Snell Griffith

See also Mississippian Culture; Slavery, Native Americans

Further Reading

Clayton, Lawrence A. et al., eds. 1993. *The De Soto Chronicles: The Expedition of Hernando de Soto to North America in 1539–1543.* Tuscaloosa: University of Alabama Press.

Duncan, David Ewing. 1996. *Hernando De Soto: A Savage Quest in the Americas.* New York: Crown.

Hunter-Gatherers

Though generally called hunter-gathering, scientists speculate that between two-thirds to three-quarters of indigenous people's food sources came from foraging plant material, a task done most often by women. The term "hunter-gatherer" stems from modern and inaccurate ideas about the primacy of hunting, a primarily male occupation.

Anthropologists speculate that Paleo-Indians who crossed the ice bridge made up of the Bering Strait from Siberia were big-game hunters following herds of mammals to the grassland interiors of North America. Many hunting techniques where derived from when hunters preyed on foot, utilizing a spear used by Native Americans dating back to Paleo-Indians. The hunting of large game, including bighorn bison and musk oxen, required collaboration of multiple hunters, including women, that became models for social bonding and coordination to drive herds into traps or over cliffs. Big-game hunters supplemented their diets by foraging for seeds, berries, roots, bulbs, and other edible plants. Control of fire utilized for big-game drives was adapted for other purposes, including clearing grasslands and cultivating wild food plants, which led to the first human modifications of the landscape.

With climate changes, Native Americans adapted cultures that developed into sophisticated subsistence patterns. California Indians were mostly peaceful hunter-gatherer tribes living in verdant environments.

Baskets were essential to economic stability, diplomatic intertribal relationships, and sacred harmony. Spirit imbued the creation of baskets from the basket-making materials to their eventual contents. Oak trees were central to life for northern California tribes. Stewardship of oak groves passed through matrilineal family lines. Acorns, which can be stored for two years or more, were the most important seeds for life, contributing carbohydrates, protein, fiber, and fat to the diet. Indigenous women were sophisticated in cultivating the land. Women engineered a diverse variety of baskets that were functional. Spirituality and thanksgiving were reflected in seedbeaters used only to harvest only mature seeds, leaving immature seeds to propagate later.

Coiled basketry requires a form of sewing done with bone awls. Basket makers observed plants and animals like ethnobotanists and practiced controlled burns in gathering areas a year prior to gathering materials in order to harvest young shoots. The strength of tule fibers, grasslike sedges of the genus *Scirpus* growing along rivers and by wetlands, was identified for manufacturing water-resistant products. Sedge beds along streams under the shade of oak trees were carefully cultivated using digging stick to expose the rhizomes for selecting the best rhizomes for baskets. Rainfall patterns, soil types, and growth characteristics of regional plants from their roots to shoots were observed throughout the year, with each season unfolding changes in pliability and hues, and basket makers knew the best spots for gathering. Women pruned wild plants throughout the year to eliminate knobs and lateral branches and cultivate only straight rhizomes and branches.

Specific geographic locations fostered the development of distinct stylistic basket motifs. Generic baskets were not produced; names were assigned to baskets in relation to function. Tightly woven storage baskets constructed of hazel with straight sides were traditionally hung in structures. Working mothers safely carried infants in tule shade cradles. Acorn baskets featured an open stitch to allow air to move through the seeds in a coastal climate where fog supported mold growth. Parching trays were round and flat, close-woven water-resistant conical burden baskets held seeds, course-woven conical burden baskets constructed of hazel were used to gather foodstuffs, and coiled basket hoppers were used for grinding acorns. California Indians used baskets to gather, prepare, store, and serve food. Large tightly woven cooking baskets made from roots efficiently held water that could be heated to boiling in order to cook acorn mush. The hopper basket was placed on the ground, water and acorn meal were placed into the basket, and then hot rocks were dropped in, bringing the contents to a boil within minutes.

During the California Gold Rush (1848–1855), many indigenous women gathering food and materials for basket making were placed in mortal danger of being kidnapped, raped, or sold into involuntary servitude (which was legal until the start of the Civil War) by miners. Today Native Americans living on reservations are challenged to resurrect nurturing cultural traditions destroyed by dominant and aggressive colonizers.

Meredith Eliassen

See also Religion, Native American

Further Reading

Brody, J. J. 1990. *The Anasazi: Ancient Indian People of the American Southwest.* New York: Rizzoli.

Kroeber, A. L. 1976. *Handbook of the Indians of California.* New York: Dover.

Shanks, Ralph, and Lisa Woo Shanks. 2006. *Indian Baskets of Central California: Art Culture, and History; Native American Basketry from San Francisco Bay and Monterey Bay North to Mendocino and East to the Sierras.* Seattle: University of Washington Press.

Waldman, Carl. 2000. *Atlas of the North American Indian.* New York: Checkmark Books.

Iroquois Confederacy

The Iroquois Confederacy, known to its members as the Haudenosaunee, was founded in present-day New York sometime during the 15th or 16th centuries. The confederacy consisted of the Cayuga, Mohawk, Oneida, Onondaga, and Seneca tribes, all of whom spoke Iroquoian dialects. The respective groups were divided into clans. Each clan had specific social, political, and ritualistic responsibilities within Iroquois society. Since the Iroquois were matrilineal, children were members of their mother's clan, and women had considerable cultural power.

Clan mothers were responsible for selecting the peace chiefs within the clan and were led by a clan matron, who was the most influential woman in the group. When the League Council met, the respective clans were represented by an equal number of clan mothers, peace chiefs, pine tree chiefs, and war chiefs, although the pine tree and war chiefs could not vote. The Tuscaroras joined the confederacy around 1722 after migrating from North Carolina. Together, the six nations of the Iroquois Confederacy formed one of the most influential and formidable Native American groups in North America during the colonial period.

Because Iroquois women were in charge of farming, particularly the cultivation of corn and squash, this created a kind of economic power for Iroquois women. Because agriculture accounted for well over 50 percent of the people's calorie intake, women were the main providers of food. Women were also in charge of longhouse construction, family matters, and child rearing. While Iroquois men sat on tribal councils, women advised men at those councils, determined who could be chief, and had the power to call for war.

The Iroquois first encountered the French during the early 17th century, and shortly thereafter warfare ensued. Intermittent warfare between the two groups continued until 1624, when the respective parties signed their first peace treaty. By that time, the Iroquois had also forged a relationship with the Dutch from the New Netherland colony. The British replaced the Dutch as trade partners when they assumed control of the New Netherland colony, which they renamed New York. The Iroquois took advantage of the imperial competition between the French and English and began playing the European powers against each other to advance the interests of the confederacy.

The troubles with New France were related to the Beaver Wars, which raged from 1641 to 1701. The Iroquois endeavored to become the primary trading partner with both the French and English and thus began warring with other native groups to control trade routes. The wars proved devastating to the Iroquois, as the combination of endemic diseases and warriors

Before it was purchased by the Dutch, Manhattan belonged to the Iroquois Confederacy. This photo shows the Iroquois communal dwellings known as longhouses that housed several families. (North Wind Picture Archives)

killed in battle greatly reduced their population and destabilized their culture. To rebuild their numbers, the Iroquois began adopting some of the natives they captured while on the warpath, such as Eunice Williams, who was kidnapped from the English and learned to enjoy her life among the native people so much that she refused to be returned to her English family.

When the French and Indian War began in 1754, the Iroquois decided on neutrality, although some Senecas joined the French cause. To entice the Iroquois to join the English war effort, the English convened the Albany Congress in 1754. They only joined the war effort after it was apparent that Britain was going to win. Iroquois women undoubtedly played an important role in the decision to finally join the war.

The relationship between Britain and the Iroquois strengthened during this period by Mohawk Clan matron Degonwadonti, better known as Molly Brant. From 1759 to 1776 she was the mistress of Sir William Johnson,

who served as British superintendent of Indian affairs for the northern district and was the mother of several of his children. She became one of Johnson's primary intermediaries with the Iroquois, representing British interests. At the same time, she was able to gain special considerations for the Iroquois from Johnson to which the English otherwise would not have agreed. She also advanced the career of her brother Thayendanegea, also known as Joseph Brant, who became a respected war chief and a close ally of the British.

When the American Revolution began, Molly Brant convinced the Cayugas, Mohawks, Senecas, and most of the Onondagas to ally themselves with the British. The Oneidas and some Onondagas and Tuscaroras joined the Americans. With combatants on both sides, Iroquoia became a war zone. Attacks by American generals in 1779 resulted in many towns being razed and the destruction of agricultural crops that were needed for sustenance. This resulted in many of the elderly, women, and children starving to death. Pro-British Iroquois were led by Joseph Brant on retaliatory raids on Oneida and Tuscarora communities. The end of the American Revolution left the Iroquois Confederacy shattered. The British endeavored to care for their allies by establishing reserves for them in Canada. The Iroquois who opted to remain in the United States were forced by the new nation to move to reservations.

In time, the Iroquois Confederacy rebuilt itself culturally and politically. The effort began in 1799 when Handsome Lake, a Seneca, established the Church of Handsome Lake. Among other things, Handsome Lake encouraged his people to reject Euro-American–inspired disrespect for women. Also known as the Longhouse Religion, it first spread to the Onondagas and then to the other members of the confederacy. Its teachings and traditions continue to inspire the Iroquois today.

John R. Burch Jr.

See also Matrilineal Descent; *Vol. 1, Sec. 3:* Brant, Molly; Williams, Eunice

Further Reading

Fenton, William N. 1998. *The Great Law and the Longhouse: A Political History of the Iroquois Confederacy.* Norman: University of Oklahoma Press.

Jennings, Francis. 1984. *The Ambiguous Iroquois Empire: The Covenant Chain Confederation of Indian Tribes with English Colonies, from its Beginnings to the Lancaster Treaty of 1744.* New York: Norton.

Richter, Daniel K. 1992. *The Ordeal of the Longhouse: The Peoples of the Iroquois League in the Era of European Colonization.* Chapel Hill: University of North Carolina Press.

Isabella of Castile. *See* Queens, European, Elizabeth I of England and Isabella of Castile

Jamestown

Jamestown was founded on May 13, 1607, by an all-male contingent of settlers. A commercial venture by London's Virginia Company, the colony became the first permanent English settlement in North America. The first women arrived in the second wave of settlers in October 1608: Anne Forrest (wife of Thomas Forrest) and her 14-year-old maid, Anne Buras. Within a year Buras would marry a carpenter named James Layton in the first European marriage held in Virginia and shortly thereafter give birth to a daughter named Virginia in honor of her new home.

Named after King James I, Jamestown was located on an island on the James River in present-day Virginia. The location was selected as a defendable position from attack by Spanish ships but was not conducive to practical habitation. The land was swampy and infested with disease-bearing mosquitoes. Water was often brackish due to its proximity to the Chesapeake Bay, and the colonists compounded their water problems by dumping their waste into the James River, their main water source. The resulting pollution caused diseases such as dysentery. Just as problematic was the colony's location in the midst of the Powhatan Confederacy's heartland.

The company's investors had instructed the colony's first 104 settlers to befriend the local natives in hopes of making them trade partners. Relations between the colonists and Powhatan were initially cordial, so the Englishmen could search for gold and precious gems. They did not begin by building a fort, which proved disastrous when warfare erupted between the colonists and the natives. Despite advice from the Powhatan people, the colonists did not plant gardens or hunt for the food required to subsist through the winter. Only 38 of the initial 104 colonists survived the first nine months of the colony's existence. Despite the high rate of death, settlers continued migrating to the colony.

Some of the struggles faced by the settlers were the result of poor timing, as one of the worst droughts in centuries gripped Virginia from 1606 to 1613. Jamestown's inhabitants were in such poor health by June 1607 that only 10 men were fit enough to work. The men were subsisting on a pint of wheat and barley each day. Due to their weakened condition, they did not tend the crops they had planted, which only exacerbated their plight. Captain John Smith had not been present during this period and was outraged when he returned from a reconnaissance mission in September 1607 and found the fort in disrepair and the crops gone. He seized control of the colony's leadership and instituted a rule that anyone who did not work did not eat.

Conditions improved gradually as the few women began migrating in 1608. In 1609 there was once again insufficient food to meet needs. The colony did receive much-needed staples from a supply flotilla from the Caribbean during the summer of 1609, but there was not enough to last through the winter, as some of the supply ships had not completed the trip. One of the ships that did arrive had approximately 20 women on board who joined 2 other English women who were already living in Jamestown. Another 100 women, including Thomasine Causey, sailed to Jamestown a few months later. They arrived just in time to experience the winter of 1609–1610, which became known as the Starving Time. According to John Smith, the colony's population of approximately 500 was whittled down to just over 60 in a span of months. Apparently most of the women did not survive, as there is little mention of them in later accounts. One who did live was Temperance Flowerdew Yeardley, whose husband George eventually became the colony's colonial governor. Joan Pierce and her daughter Jane also made it through the winter. Pierce later became John Rolfe's second wife.

Most of the English viewed the Powhatans as savages and would not treat them humanely. The one exception was John Smith. Wahunsunacock, the Powhatan paramount chief better known as Powhatan, even tried to symbolically adopt Smith into his family, using his daughter Pocahontas as intermediary, but the effort resulted in the onset of the First Anglo-Powhatan War in 1610 due to English intransigence.

John Smith had made it clear to the Powhatans that the English were only interested in using Jamestown as a trading community, but the sudden presence of so many women indicated another agenda. The presence of families was a necessary step in creating a permanent settlement that promised growth over time. The expansion of Jamestown was guaranteed in 1612 when John Rolfe began developing a form of tobacco that would become the colony's most profitable export. The discovery was accompanied by a renewed effort to recruit unmarried English women to migrate to the colony and marry settlers.

The Virginia Company believed that the ability to marry and have children would entice the women in the colony to become permanent residents. The creation of a tobacco-based economy required the expansion of the colony, as its citizens left Jamestown and began constructing farms on Powhatan territory. The expansion infuriated the Powhatans, and the war begun in 1610 continued. It ended with the marriage of Pocahontas to John Rolfe in 1614. Since the Powhatans were matrilineal, Rolfe joined Wahunsunacock's family, who hoped that the marriage would be followed by other marriages to forge further kinship ties. The majority of the Englishmen refused to marry "savages," and while the marriage between Rolfe and Pocahontas secured peace between the two groups, the English continued seizing Powhatan lands for the growth of tobacco. The Powhatans struggled to combat English imperialism in the face of disastrous disease mortality rates. Contact with European diseases killed more native peoples than did war.

Jamestown continued to play a significant role in Virginia's history despite the colony's expansion. It served as the capital of Virginia until 1699, but its last decades were fraught with difficulties. During Bacon's Rebellion in 1676, Jamestown was put to the torch. The town was gradually rebuilt, but tragedy struck during October 1698 as the town was once again set ablaze. Rather than expending the resources to rebuild Jamestown again, the Virginia General Assembly opted to relocate the capital to Williamsburg, and Jamestown ceased to exist.

John R. Burch Jr.

See also Pocahontas; Powhatan People; *Vol. 1, Sec. 2:* Laydon, Anne Burras

Further Reading

Horn, James. 2005. *A Land as God Made It: Jamestown and the Birth of America.* New York: Basic Books.

Kelso, William M. 2006. *Jamestown: The Buried Truth.* Charlottesville: University of Virginia Press.

Smith, John. 2007. *Captain John Smith with Other Narratives.* New York: Library of America.

La Llorona

La Llorona, also known as "The Weeping Woman," is a folktale originating in the Mexican central highlands that has spread throughout North and South America. There are two versions of the story: La Llorona as a murderer of children and as a seducer of men. The first part is typically told to children to keep them from venturing out after dark, and the second part is a warning to men to keep them faithful to their wives.

The legend began in Mexico in approximately 1550. Elements of the legend have been drawn from Aztec lore. The Aztecs told many tales about feminine spirits and also placed importance on water, which is present in most La Llorona tales. Many versions also point out a husband's responsibility to care for and tend to his family and use female spirits to threaten men who fail in their domestic responsibilities. There are three types of women identified as La Llorona: the siren, who seduces men; the grieving woman, who lost her children and wails in anguish; and the dangerous woman, who kidnaps children and takes them into the night to some dire fate.

Over time, these different elements have mingled and spread over North and South America. Although many versions of the story exist, there is one two-part legend that is the most popular. The first part of the legend tells of a young girl named Maria. Maria was a beautiful girl from a small village, and all of the villagers knew of her beauty. As Maria grew up, she too became aware of her beauty and thought herself better than everyone else in the village. She refused to look for a husband in her hometown because she thought she deserved the most handsome man in the world.

One day, a man rode into Maria's village. He was the most handsome man Maria had ever seen. She fell in love with him, but she did not let it show. The man eventually softened Maria's heart, and the two were soon engaged and eventually married. They had children together and Maria loved him deeply, but the man seemed disengaged from his family responsibilities. He would leave the family for long periods of time to return to the previous wild life he once led. When he did come home it was only to visit his children, not his wife. He did not care much for Maria and even spoke of divorcing her to marry a wealthier woman. Maria eventually became jealous not just of her husband but also of her own children.

One night when Maria was out walking with her children, she saw her husband in a carriage with an elegant woman. Her husband stopped to talk to the children but did not even acknowledge Maria before he rode off with the elegant other woman. Maria became angry, and in a fit of rage she threw her own children into the river to drown. Only after they had long been floating down the river did she realize what she had done and regret her impulsive behavior. In her remorse she killed herself. The next day, the villagers discovered Maria's beautiful body dead on the bank of the river. The night after Maria was buried, the villagers heard the sound of La Llorona, the weeping woman, crying out for her children.

Those who pay heed to the tale believe that God refused to take Maria's soul to heaven because of her horrible wrongdoings; her punishment is to walk the earth forevermore. She cannot atone or repent for her sins. Children are warned not to go out after dark because La Llorona might snatch them up, never to be heard from again. Since La Llorona was deprived, she feels that it is her right to deprive others more fortunate than herself. Therefore, she aims to harm not only the hearts of those with children but also of those with husbands as well.

The second part of the legend tells of Maria as a seducer of men. La Llorona is said to be invisible until she chooses to reveal herself to her victims, which she does only to deceive them. She typically reveals herself in her former beautiful glory. The legend claims that she wears a white dress and has long dark hair. As she walks around searching for her long-lost children, men are attracted to her and follow her around. She then leads them away to dangerous places, where they are typically injured or killed.

The legend claims that La Llorona usually targets men unable to defend themselves, such as men who are intoxicated or otherwise not thinking clearly. She tends to target men out on the town late at night. Thus, La Llorona punishes men who are unfaithful to their wives and failing their children. She aims to hurt men in the same way she has been hurt—she tries to tear apart families by seducing men and killing them or by ripping apart marriages by causing quarrels.

The legend of La Llorona skyrocketed in popularity in southwestern America due to the direct contact with Mexico. There have been many reports regarding supposed sightings of La Llorona, which authorities have been unable to confirm or deny. La Llorona victims range in age. Many people continue to believe that she continues to target very young children and elderly men. La Llorona is also sometimes identified with or confused with the Malinche story, in part because as Hernán Cortés's translator and the mother of at least one of his children, Malinche's tale is one of woe and betrayal. The La Llorona story is culturally interesting for a number of reasons, primarily because it disempowers women by making them bad, and because of the danger she represents, La Llorona symbolizes the female power.

B. C. Biggs

See also Cultural Interaction; Malinche

Further Reading

Kearney, Michael. 1969. "La Llorona as a Social Symbol." *Western Folklore* 28(3): 199–206.

Leddy, Betty. 1948. "La Llorona in Southern Arizona." *Western Folklore* 7(3): 272–277.

Malinche (ca. 1496–ca. 1505)

Malinche does not fit easily into Mexican, Spanish, or American history. She, like innumerable other Mexican women who came after her, was a translator who made possible the communication between Spaniards and Mexican Amerindians. Few of these women have been as prominent as Malinche, chiefly because she was Spanish conquistador Hernán Cortés's (1485–1547) mouthpiece but also because she was the first of her kind. Also, not unlike Pocahontas, Malinche's story has been used as myth, though in Malinche's case her story has devolved into a cautionary tale of the dangers of Euro-American and Native American contact.

Malinche might have been of royal lineage in her native Mexico. She was also a slave and, like other slaves, had no control over how her body was used. Stories told about her portray her as a sexual aggressor, one who used her body to climb the social ladder.

In this mythic tradition she was the seducer who made men do her bidding. This story makes her victimization by both native people and the Spanish invisible. Conversely, the Spanish thought of her as a hero for forsaking her people and taking up with Euro-Americans, not unlike the Euro-American take on Pocahontas. In another version of Malinche's story called the "Black Legend," Mexican nationalists thought (and still think) of her as a traitor for abetting Cortés's conquest. In this context Malinche has been called the Mexican Eve for betraying her people. She is also seen as the mother of mestizos, or mixed-race people, because she gave birth to two children whose father was most likely Cortés.

Historians know little about Malinche's early years, not even her birth name. She is also known as La Malinche or Malintzin. One of Cortés's men called her Doña Marina. Cortés called her simply Marina, shunning the honorific "doña." Some scholars believe that her birth name was Malinalli, suggesting that she had been a rebellious child. Historian Gloria Duran admits, because of the paucity of evidence, that the way to approach Malinche's early years is to construct a plausible fiction. Duran assumes that Malinche was the firstborn of Mexican Amerindian nobles. Malinche was born in the Yucatán Peninsula, the place where Mayan and Aztec worlds converged.

Malinche became a slave within her first decade of life. One account holds that after her father's death, her mother, jealous of the bond between father and daughter, sold Malinche into slavery. Another account holds that her mother's new lover resented Malinche and wanted her killed. Her mother placated him by selling Malinche into slavery. A third account holds that her mother sold Malinche so she could not inherit any of her mother's wealth. What most of the accounts of Malinche's enslavement have in common is that they blame a woman, Malinche's mother, for her bondage. Thus, each of these stories may be more a product of sexism than reality.

Whatever the truth, one must recognize the ubiquity of slavery in Latin America throughout time. The Mayas, Aztecs, Incas, and many less well-known peoples all practiced slavery well before Euro-Americans began enslaving native people and importing African slaves. As a slave, Malinche had no control over her

Often considered synonymous with "traitor" in Mexico, Malinche was also the mother of mestizo culture. She was less traitor than powerless young woman, handed from man to man, forced by the Spanish to act as interpreter during the early conquest. (Universal History Archive/Getty Images)

body or her destiny. She must have been the repeated victim of rape. She would also have prepared food and made clothes for her owner. Her first owner was the wife of an aristocrat who rented Malinche to other men, whose motives were surely sexual.

When Cortés arrived in the New World, he and his men gradually moved inland. When they reached Pontonchan, Mexico, the inhabitants offered him 20 women, among them Malinche. Cortés parceled out the women, some of whom would have been quite young, to his men. He assigned Malinche to the soldier Portocarrero. Cortés soon found Malinche indispensable because of her fluency in languages: she could speak both Yucatec and Nahua. Cortés had with him a Spanish soldier who spoke Nahua and Spanish, so the two interpreters could together bridge the language divide between the native peoples and the Spanish.

Because of her importance as in interpreter, Cortés took Malinche from Portocarrero.

Malinche apparently had an unerring understanding of the motives of the peoples of Mesoamerica. She is said to have warned Cortés that the Aztec ambassadors who greeted him were also spies. Through Malinche, Cortés lectured the Aztecs on the superiority of Christianity. The Spanish, like most Euro-American conquerors, had no sympathy for notions of cultural relativism and failed to recognize not only that the natives had religion but also that their religions were as legitimate as any other. Cortés soon angered the Aztecs. Realizing the error of proselytizing, Cortés asked Malinche to soften the effect of his words on the Aztec ambassadors. Over time, the Aztecs came to know the Spanish through Malinche. She acted as intermediary between two peoples, bridging the native and Spanish worlds.

Malinche endeavored to learn Spanish quickly so she could translate directly to Cortés. She aided him in the search for allies who chafed under Aztec rule. These allies were not hard to find because the Aztecs imposed a heavy tribute on their subjects, requiring them to provide hundreds and even thousands of sacrificial victims. The practice of human sacrifice appears to have been common in Mesoamerica. With Malinche as translator, Cortés promised defectors that they would be free of Aztec oppression. When she was not with Cortés, Malinche, still a slave, ground corn and prepared other food. She endured the hardship of the long march inland toward Tenoctitlan, including a battle with the Tlaxcalan Amerindians.

It is easy in hindsight to suppose that the conquest of Mexico was inevitable. After all, Europeans thought they were superior to the indigenous peoples of the Americas and of Africa as well. Nonetheless, a belief in cultural superiority would not have been enough to conquer Mexico, particularly given the fact that the native peoples had developed quite complicated and technologically advanced cultures. Rather, the attempt to conquer Mexico might have failed but for the fact that the Amerindians, having been separated from Eurasia and Africa for at least 12,000 years, had no immunity to European diseases. Smallpox, plague, tuberculosis, and other scourges killed more people than guns. Smallpox, for example, had a 75–90 percent mortality rate among natives and appears to have decimated the Aztec capital city just before Cortés arrived (the disease having traveled faster than the Spanish army).

Cortés was wounded in the battle with the Tlaxcalans, and Malinche nursed him back to health. After the battle Montezuma and Cortés met, and Malinche translated. Though a slave, she had status at these conferences. Montezuma's death left the Aztec Empire in shambles. In addition to Malinche, Cortés took Montezuma's daughters as his concubines. His sexual appetite must have been insatiable and led to an inquiry by Spanish authorities.

In 1522, Malinche gave birth to a son. Cortés named him Martin. Fearing censure from the Spanish authorities, Cortés sought the advice of a priest, who counseled Cortés to rid himself of Malinche. He publicly questioned whether Martin was really his son, implying that Malinche was promiscuous. This assumption was common among Europeans. They believed that indigenous women, whether from the Americas or Africa, had an inordinate sex drive. This was convenient ideology because it justified white men's sexual predation of native and slave women.

Cortés's relationship with Malinche also created a scandal because Cortés was married. With his wife Catalina scheduled to arrive in Mexico soon, Cortés had to act. He decided to house Malinche in Vera Cruz. When Catalina died, one account holds that Malinche wished to marry Cortés. If true, Cortés surely did not wish to marry Malinche. He needed to marry a Spanish noblewoman, one whose family could represent him before the Spanish Crown. Cortés seems to have regarded Malinche as little more than a possession convenient to his sexual and professional needs.

Malinche had a second child with Cortés, this one a daughter, Maria. Cortés assigned her to one of his governors. Malinche contracted malaria, as did Cortés, but Cortés survived the disease. Malinche died at age 28. Her place of burial is unknown.

All of the stories told about Malinche, including this one, depend more on cultural needs than historical facts. Indeed, Malinche's story is sometimes conflated with La Llorona, or the legend of the Weeping Woman. The folktale has many functions and a varied history but does serve as a cautionary tale told to children to warn them of the consequences of bad behavior. In either victimizing and scapegoating Malinche, she slips from real woman to symbol, and in her symbolic meaning she becomes mythic.

Christopher Cumo

See also Disease, Postconquest Impact on Native Americans; La Llorona; Pocahontas; Sexuality

Further Reading
Cypress, Sandra Messinger. 1991. *La Malinche in Mexican Literature: From History to Myth.* Austin: University of Texas Press.
Duran, Gloria. 1993. *Malinche: Slave Princess of Cortez.* Hamden, CT: Linnet Books.
Esquivel, Laura. 2006. *Malinche.* New York: Atria Books.

Bernal Diaz del Castillo Describes Malinche in His Memoirs (1517–1518)

Because she was an indigenous woman caught in the Spanish conquest, we have no words from Malinche, the Nahua-speaking woman who acted as translator for Hernán Cortés. Bernal Diaz del Castillo, one of Cortés's men, did write about her. The following excerpt comes from his memoirs, The Discovery and Conquest of Mexico, 1517–1521, *published in 1585.*

Early the next morning many Caciques and chiefs of Tabasco and the neighbouring towns arrived and paid great respect to us all, and they brought a present of gold, consisting of four diadems and some gold lizards, and two [ornaments] like little dogs, and earrings and five ducks, and two masks with Indian faces and two gold soles for sandals, and some other things of little value. I do not remember how much the things were worth; and they brought cloth, such as they make and wear, which was quilted stuff.

This present, however, was worth nothing in comparison with the twenty women that were given us, among them one very excellent woman called Doña Marina, for so she was named when she became a Christian. Cortés received this present with pleasure and went aside with all the Caciques, and with Aguilar, the interpreter, to hold converse, and he told them that he gave them thanks for what they had brought with them, but there was one thing that he must ask of them, namely, that they should re-occupy the town with all their people, women and children, and he wished to see it repeopled within two days, for he would recognize that as a sign of true peace. The Caciques sent at once to summon all the inhabitants with their women and children and within two days they were again settled in the town.

One other thing Cortés asked of the chiefs and that was to give up their idols and sacrifices, and this they said they would do, and, through Aguilar, Cortés told them as well as he was able about matters concerning our holy faith, how we were Christians and worshipped one true and only God, and he showed them an image of Our Lady with her precious Son in her arms and explained to them that we paid the greatest reverence to it as it was the image of the Mother of our Lord God who was in heaven. The Caciques replied that they liked the look of the great Teleciguata

(for in their language great ladies are called Teleciguatas) and [begged] that she might be given them to keep in their town, and Cortés said that the image should be given to them, and ordered them to make a well-constructed altar, and this they did at once.

The next morning, Cortés ordered two of our carpenters, named Alonzo Yañez and Alvaro López, to make a very tall cross.

When all this had been settled Cortés asked the Caciques what was their reason for attacking us three times when we had asked them to keep the peace; the chief replied that he had already asked pardon for their acts and had been forgiven, that the Cacique of Champoton, his brother, had advised it, and that he feared to be accused of cowardice, for he had already been reproached and dishonoured for not having attacked the other captain who had come with four ships (he must have meant Juan de Grijalva) and he also said that the Indian whom we had brought as an Interpreter, who escaped in the night, had advised them to attack us both by day and night.

Cortés then ordered this man to be brought before him without fail, but they replied that when he saw that the battle was going against them, he had taken to flight, and they knew not where he was although search had been made for him; but we came to know that they had offered him as a sacrifice because his counsel had cost them so dear.

Cortés also asked them where they procured their gold and jewels, and they replied, from the direction of the setting sun, and said "Culua" and "Mexico," and as we did not know what Mexico and Culua meant we paid little attention to it.

Then we brought another interpreter named Francisco, whom we had captured during Grijalva's expedition, who has already been mentioned by me but he understood nothing of the Tabasco language only that of Culua which is the Mexican tongue. By means of signs he told Cortés that Culua was far ahead, and he repeated "Mexico" which we did not understand.

So the talk ceased until the next day when the sacred image of Our Lady and the Cross were set up on the altar and we all paid reverence to them, and Padre Fray Bartolomé de Olmedo said mass and all the Caciques and chiefs were present and we gave the name of Santa Maria de la Victoria to the town, and by this name the town of Tabasco is now called. The same friar, with Aguilar as interpreter, preached many good things about our holy faith to the twenty Indian women who had been given us, and immediately afterwards they were baptized. One Indian lady, who was given to us here was christened Doña Marina, and she was truly a great chieftainess and the daughter of great Caciques and the mistress of vassals, and this her appearance clearly showed. Later on I will relate why it was and in what manner she was brought here.

Cortés allotted one of the women to each of his captains and Doña Marina, as she was good looking and intelligent and without embarrassment, he gave to Alonzo Hernández Puertocarrero. When Puertocarrero went to Spain, Doña Marina lived with Cortés, and bore him a son named Don Martin Cortés.

We remained five days in this town, to look after the wounded and those who were suffering from pain in the loins, from which they all recovered. Furthermore, Cortés drew the Caciques to him by kindly converse, and told them how our master the Emperor, whose vassals we were, had under his orders many to render him obedience, and that then, whatever they might be in need of, whether it was our protection or any other necessity, if they would make it known to him, no matter where he might be, he would come to their assistance.

The Caciques all thanked him for this, and thereupon all declared themselves the vassals of our great Emperor. These were the first vassals to render submission to His Majesty in New Spain.

Cortés then ordered the Caciques to come with their women and children early the next day, which was Palm Sunday, to the altar, to pay homage to the holy image of Our Lady and to the Cross, and at the same time Cortés ordered them to send six Indian carpenters to accompany our carpenters to the town of Cintla, there to cut a cross on a great tree called a Ceiba, which grew there, and they did it so that it might last a long time, for as the bark is renewed the cross will show there for ever. When this was done he ordered the Indians to get ready all the canoes that they owned to help us to embark, for we wished to set sail on that holy day because the pilots had come to tell Cortés that the ships ran a great risk from a Norther which is a dangerous gale.

The next day, early in the morning, all the Caciques and chiefs came in their canoes with all their women and children and stood in the court where we had placed the church and cross, and many branches of trees had already been cut ready to be carried in the procession. Then the Caciques beheld us all, Cortés, as well as the captains, and every one of us marching together with the greatest reverence in a devout procession, and the Padre de la Merced and the priest Juan Díaz, clad in their vestments, said mass, and we paid reverence to and kissed the Holy Cross, while the Caciques and Indians stood looking on at us.

When our solemn festival was over the chiefs approached and offered Cortés ten fowls and baked fish and vegetables, and we took leave of them, and Cortés again commended to their care the Holy image and the sacred crosses and told them always to keep the place clean and well swept, and to deck the cross with garlands and to reverence it and then they would enjoy good health and bountiful harvests.

It was growing late when we got on board ship and the next day, Monday, we set sail in the morning and with a fair wind laid our course for San Juan de Ulua, keeping close in shore all the time.

As we sailed along in fine weather, we soldiers who knew the coast would say to Cortés, "Señor, over there is La Rambla, which the Indians call Ayagualulco," and soon afterwards we arrived off Tonalá which we called San Antonio, and we pointed it out to him. Further on we showed him the great river of Coatzacoalcos, and he saw the lofty snow capped mountains, and then the Sierra of San Martin, and further on we pointed out the split rock, which is a great rock standing out in the sea with a mark on the top of it which gives it the appearance of a seat. Again further on we showed him the Rio de Alvarado, which Pedro de Alvarado entered when we were with Grijalva, and then we came in sight of the Rio de Banderas, where we had gained in barter the sixteen thousand dollars, then we showed him the Isla Blanca, and told him where lay the Isla Verde, and close in shore we saw the Isla de Sacrificios, where we found the altars and the Indian victims in Grijalva's time; and at last our good fortune brought us to San Juan de Ulúa soon after midday on Holy Thursday.

XXIII

Before telling about the great Montezuma and his famous City of Mexico and the Mexicans, I wish to give some account of Doña Marina, who from her childhood had been the mistress and Cacica of towns and vassals. It happened in this way:

Her father and mother were chiefs and Caciques of a town called Paynala, which had other towns subject to it, and stood about eight leagues from the town of Coatzacoalcos. Her father died while she was still a little child, and her mother married another Cacique, a young man, and bore him a son. It seems that the father and mother had a great affection for this son and it was agreed between them that he should succeed to their honours when their days were done. So that there should be no impediment to this, they gave the little girl, Doña Marina, to some Indians from Xicalango, and this they did by night so as to escape observation, and they then spread the report that she had died, and as it happened at this time that a child of one of their Indian slaves died they gave out that it was their daughter and the heiress who was dead.

The Indians of Xicalango gave the child to the people of Tabasco and the Tabasco people gave her to Cortés. I myself knew her mother, and the old woman's son and her half-brother, when he was already grown up and ruled the town jointly with his mother, for the second husband of the old lady was dead. When they became Christians, the old lady was called Marta and the son Lázaro. I knew all this very well because in the year 1523 after the conquest of Mexico and the other provinces, when Crist'obal de Olid revolted in Honduras, and Cortés was on his way there, he passed through Coatzacoalcos and I and the greater number of the settlers of that town accompanied him on that expedition as I shall relate in the proper time and place. As Doña Marina proved herself such an excellent woman and good interpreter throughout the wars in New Spain, Tlaxcala and Mexico (as I shall show later on) Cortés always took her with him, and during that expedition she was married to a gentleman named Juan Jaramillo at the town of Orizaba.

Doña Marina was a person of the greatest importance and was obeyed without question by the Indians throughout New Spain.

When Cortés was in the town of Coatzacoalcos he sent to summon to his presence all the Caciques of that province in order to make them a speech about our holy religion, and about their good treatment, and among the Caciques who assembled was the mother of Doña Marina and her half-brother, Lázaro.

Some time before this Doña Marina had told me that she belonged to that province and that she was the mistress of vassals, and Cortés also knew it well, as did Aguilar, the interpreter. In such a manner it was that mother, daughter and son came together, and it was easy enough to see that she was the daughter from the strong likeness she bore to her mother.

These relations were in great fear of Doña Marina, for they thought that she had sent for them to put them to death, and they were weeping.

When Doña Marina saw them in tears, she consoled them and told them to have no fear, that when they had given her over to the men from Xicalango, they knew not what they were doing, and she forgave them for doing it, and she gave them many jewels of gold and raiment, and told them to return to their town, and said that God had been very gracious to her in freeing her from the worship of idols and making her a Christian, and letting her bear a son to her lord and master Cortés and in marrying her to such a gentleman as Juan Jaramillo, who was now her husband. That she would rather serve her husband and Cortés than anything else in the world, and would not exchange her place to be Cacica of all the provinces in New Spain.

Doña Marina knew the language of Coatzacoalcos, which is that common to Mexico, and she knew the language of Tabasco, as did also Jerónimo de Aguilar, who spoke the language of Yucatan and Tabasco, which is one and the same. So that these two could understand one another clearly, and Aguilar translated into Castilian for Cortés.

This was the great beginning of our conquests and thus, thanks be to God, things prospered with us. I have made a point of explaining this matter, because without the help of Doña Marina we could not have understood the language of New Spain and Mexico.

Source: Bernal Diaz del Castillo, *The Memoirs of the Conquistador Bernal Diaz del Castillo Written by Himself Containing a True and Full Account of the Discovery and Conquest of Mexico and New Spain,* Vol. 1, translated by John Ingram Lockhart (London: J. Hatchard and Son, 1844), 77–80.

Matrilineal Descent

Matrilineal descent refers to a kinship system in which ancestry from the mother's lineage is the primary means of establishing ownership of property and power in a society, in terms of ordering one's position in contemporary society and also in the generational transfer of power from generation to generation. There are three options for determining lineage: patrilineal (through the father), matrilineal (through the mother), and ambilineal (through both). All social institutions (family, economy, education, government, and religion) are affected by a society's kinship system. Native Americans tended to favor matrilineal, while Euro-Americans tended to favor patrilineal. This became one of many sources of conflict in the course of the Columbian exchange.

Matrilineality points to higher status for women. A society that includes matrilocality (that newly married couples reside with the mother's kin group) can mean more status for the woman. It certainly means that the physical abuse of the woman is likely to be better contained by her kin group than in a patrilocal system. If the society engages in foraging (hunting and gathering) or engages in horticulture (no plows, no animal husbandry, and smaller plots), then the women's status is elevated compared to agricultural societies (such as those in Europe). Thus, the combination of a matrilineal, matrilocal horticultural or foraging society typically results in the highest status that women achieved in the world prior to the 20th century.

Matrilineality was common among Native American tribes, with estimates running as high as 80 percent across the continent. It was ubiquitous in every ecological niche from New England to the Pacific Northwest and from the southern woodlands (virtually all societies were in this region) through the Southwest. Worldwide, only about 14 percent of societies are matrilineal. Early European settlers were confused by the emphasis on female lineages, as evidenced in

The Five Tribes of the Iroquois, including the Seneca people pictured here, lived in matrilineal communities. This familial and social arrangement made women the head of families. Naming also followed the female line. (Getty Images)

John Smith's account of his first foray up the James River when he met Pocahontas's chieftan father: "Powhatan hath three brethren, and two sisters. . . . For the Crowne, their heyres inherite not, but the first heyres of the Sisters, and so successively the weomens heires." There are numerous examples of European culture shock and confusion about this societal structure.

The best-known example of matrilineality is the Iroquois Confederacy. This was a matrilocal, matrilineal kinship system in which the women had considerable power. Descent was ordered through mothers. Women negotiated the marriages; upon marriage, the groom moved into the longhouse of his bride's kin. The primary male in the lives of children here (and in most matrilineal, matrilocal Native American tribes) was the eldest maternal brother. The longhouse could be more than 328 feet (100 meters) long. It was subdivided into nuclear family areas, with two nuclear families sharing a hearth. A passageway the length of the longhouse at one side connected all the inhabitants. Female elders also distributed land. All land was held in common, but *usufruct* (the ability to create and keep wealth using resources you do not own) was determined by the elder women of the tribes.

Female elders of the longhouse would choose a *sachem*, the male who possessed political and military power over her kin group. Males were subject to recall (literally "dehorning") if they did not adequately reflect the desires of their kin group. The Iroquois Confederacy had a representative government consisting of 50 sachems who passed laws on matters pertaining to the five tribes as a whole, such as warfare.

In societies in which women selected men to rule, the status of the men in council with other clans or tribes (in the case of the Iroquois) was based on female lineage, war prowess, age, male ancestors, and wisdom, among other things. Thus, the entry to power for males in these societies was through women, but qualification was also determined by gendered male accomplishments. Yet in matrilineal societies, women held other roles of power not yet acceptable to Euro-Americans. An example of this was Toypurina, medicine woman to the Tongva tribe, located in what is today southern California. In 1785 tribal males asked her to lead a revolt against the Spanish soldiers at

Mission San Gabriel. On her word other local tribal chiefs joined the rebellion, though they were ultimately thwarted, and Toypurina was banished to a mission in northern California to destroy her power.

The Hopis had a matrilineal and matrilocal culture. Since war was rare, there was less of a demand for males to exert military or political leadership. Theoretically, egalitarianism was the rule for all regardless of gender. Indeed, theologically, the power of women was compared to the generative power of the earth.

Lineages need not be literal tracings of descent to the beginning of society. Fictive kinship exists to supply the necessary authority and order to the world. For example, among the Choctaws all outsiders were interpreted as either distant kin or foes.

Women did have comparatively more power in Iroquois and other Native American societies than perhaps any other society on Earth at the time. According to anecdotal records and captivity narratives, more than a third of European women kidnapped chose to remain with Native American cultures, in no small part in accord with the relative status that women possessed compared to European societies.

The matrilineal systems of Native Americans offered women dramatically more freedom and power than one could find in agricultural societies. Only in the 20th century did Western civilization strive to catch up with Native American cultures in this regard.

Mark Anthony Phelps

See also Iroquois Confederacy; Pocahontas; *Vol. 1, Sec. 2:* Captivity Narratives; *Vol. 1, Sec. 3:* Toypurina

Further Reading

Jacobs, Margaret. 1991. *Engendered Encounters: Feminism and Pueblo Cultures, 1879–1934.* Women in the West Series. Lincoln: University of Nebraska.

Oberg, Kalervo. 1973. *The Social Economy of the Tlingit Indians.* Seattle: University of Washington Press.

Pesantubbee, Michelene. 2005. *Choctaw Women in a Chaotic World: The Clash of Cultures in the Colonial Southeast.* Albuquerque: University of New Mexico Press.

Richter, Daniel. 1992. *The Ordeal of the Longhouse: The Peoples of the Iroquois League in the Era of European Colonization.* Chapel Hill: University of North Carolina Press.

Mississippian Culture

Mississippian Culture is a term used to collectively identify the mound-building peoples who resided in the Eastern Woodlands from approximately 1000 CE to the arrival of the Spanish conquistadors in North America. Although the respective Mississippian peoples spoke different languages and had distinct social customs, they shared cultural traits as agriculturalists primarily residing in river valleys along the banks of the Mississippi River or its tributaries. Their primary crops were maize, an easily stored and highly productive crop, and beans. The abundance of food allowed large communities to develop, which provided the labor force required to construct large earthen platform mounds. Mississippian mounds were generally rectangular with a flat tier at the top. On the mounds were structures that served either as temples or as residences for the ruling elites. The mounds were often arranged to mark the boundaries of a central plaza and were protected by defensive fortifications that often included bastions.

Whether elites or commoners, Mississippian families were matrilocal. This means that when a man and woman married they lived with the wife's family. The male children resulting from the union were taught their gender role by their uncles on their mother's side. Among a man's duties was hunting for game animals, primarily bear, deer, and turkeys. Hunting expeditions lasted for weeks at a time, and among the accompanying responsibilities were meat preservation and the collection of hides. Males were also fishermen, but women assisted in the preservation of the catch. Training their nephews to become warriors was also a major responsibility, as warfare between polities was constant. Since male duties often resulted in being outside their home community, they were the ones who primarily interacted with traders from other Mississippian communities or with Europeans. Their access to goods enabled men to raise their prestige within Mississippian society by using what they acquired to both enrich their families and endear themselves to the ruling caste through tributes.

Although men assisted women in the clearing of fields for planting, agriculture was primarily the domain of women. In addition to maize and beans, they planted sunflowers and squash. Women also helped provide food for the community by gathering foods growing wild such as fruits and nuts. These staples were often cooked by the women in the form of stews, in which they combined the vegetables they grew with the meat and fish provided by their male counterparts. The responsibility of providing foodstuffs provided women influence in decision making. It also helped women elevate the prestige of their respective families through tributes paid to elites in the form of foodstuffs. Other female duties included making baskets and pottery, tanning the hides provided by hunters, and helping raise both male and female children during the times when the men were on the warpath.

Mississippian communities were organized as chiefdoms, whose leaders in the matrilineal societies inherited their positions through their mother. The chief's blood relatives helped him rule over commoners. When members of the elite class of either gender died, they were buried in mortuary mounds with appropriate symbols of their status within the community, such as flint swords and intricately carved shells. Many of the items buried in their graves were constructed of exotic materials, such as copper and mica, obtained from locales throughout North America through continent-wide trade networks. Most chiefdoms during the Mississippian era were tributary parts of a paramount chiefdom. The paramount chief gained power and status over his rivals through warfare, and thus the composition of paramount chiefdoms was often in flux due to one's fortunes on the battlefield. If a paramount chief died during peacetime, he was succeeded by a male relative from his mother's family.

Despite the impressive fortifications constructed by the respective chiefdoms, the concentration of their populations proved to be a common weakness. The need to feed people through primarily agricultural foodstuffs made chiefdoms susceptible to natural events such as droughts. When communities were unable to meet the dietary needs of their respective populations and people began to starve, they often resorted to warfare to seize what they required. The combination of natural disasters and the ensuing warfare resulted in the destruction of many Mississippian communities. The communities that still existed when the Spanish arrived in the 16th century proved susceptible to biological agents such as smallpox. This can be illustrated by the Spanish accounts on the town of Coosa, in present-day northwestern Georgia. The accounts written by members of Hernando De Soto's expedition in 1540 described a densely populated large community that was rich in fruits and vegetables, due to the region's fertile soils. Twenty years later, accounts from Tristán de Luna's expedition described Coosa as having no more than 30 residences surrounded by uncultivated fields overrun by forests with little fruit to be found. Coosa's rapid decline was symptomatic of what was occurring throughout the Mississippian world, as the outbreak of virulent diseases brought from Europe caused the surviving natives to abandon the major mound centers, which resulted in the complete collapse of most Mississippian sociopolitical societies.

The end of the Mississippian era affected the respective mound-building Native American groups differently. Although the Cherokees quit building mounds, they remained a distinct people and were able to expand their territory from present-day northwestern Georgia and western North Carolina to portions of Tennessee. In contrast, the Muskogean peoples of the Southeast who had inhabited such large mound centers as Moundville, in present-day Alabama, and Coosa dispersed and reemerged as the Chickasaws, Choctaws, and Creeks.

John R. Burch Jr.

See also Mound-Building Cultures

Further Reading

Bowne, Eric E. 2013. *Mound Sites of the Ancient South: A Guide to the Mississippian Chiefdoms.* Athens: University of Georgia Press.

Eastman, Jane M., and Christopher B. Rodning, eds. 2001. *Archaeological Studies of Gender in the Southeastern United States.* Gainesville: University Press of Florida.

Smith, Marvin T. 2000. *Coosa: The Rise and Fall of a Southeastern Mississippian Chiefdom.* Gainesville: University Press of Florida.

Townsend, Richard F. 2004. *Hero, Hawk, and Open Hand: American Indian Art of the Ancient Midwest and South.* New Haven, CT: Yale University Press.

Mound-Building Cultures

"Mound-building cultures" is a phrase used to collectively identify groups that spoke different languages and had distinct social customs but constructed earthen works in North America in the pre-Columbian period. Mound building may have begun as early as 6,000 years ago, with individual groups constructing small earthworks. Due to their size, those structures would have eroded over time. The first mound-building culture whose earthworks still exist emerged in the lower Mississippi Valley around 3500 BCE. It was followed by numerous different mound-building cultures throughout the Southeast and Midwest until approximately 1600 CE. The increasing complexity of the respective mound-builder societies accompanied a gradual change in the Native American lifestyle from hunting and gathering to large-scale agriculture. The increasing emphasis on agriculture accompanied a corresponding elevation of the status of women both socially and politically, as they were responsible for growing crops.

The oldest known earthwork can be found in the present-day state of Louisiana. Dating to approximately 3500 BCE, Watson Brake consists of one large mound surrounded by 10 much smaller mounds connected by an earthen ring. It is believed that Watson Brake represented a sacred site where several hunter-gatherer groups would congregate at certain times of the year, thereby sharing a sense of community.

By 1600 BCE, earthen constructions were not just ceremonial sites. The largest earthworks from that era could be found at Poverty Point in present-day Louisiana. The people there constructed six mounds, some conical and others shaped like animals, and six rings. Construction of the earthworks took place over several centuries. It is estimated that hundreds of people lived there. Although most native peoples of that era still subsisted as hunter-gatherers, it is believed that the area around Poverty Point was so abundant in natural resources that its population did not need to migrate to find the foodstuffs they required.

The earthen constructions at both Watson Brake and Poverty Point were largely devoid of material goods related to the people who constructed them. By 1000 BCE, the cultures that created mounds were using many of them for burials, accompanied by mortuary rituals. The Adena culture is the best-known mound-building culture from this period, which ranged from 1000 BCE to 500 BCE. Adena mounds can be found in the present-day states of Indiana, Kentucky, Ohio, Pennsylvania, and West Virginia. Although Adena communities showed some characteristics of hunter-gather cultures, the people had become somewhat sedentary. Their diets included gourds, sumpweed, and sunflowers, which were grown locally by the women in the community.

Around 100 BCE, mound-building cultures commonly described as Hopewellian societies emerged. The Hopewell societies tended to live in dispersed settlements that were associated with centralized ceremonial centers, where they constructed mounds and other earthen structures. Hopewell constructions were significantly larger and more complex than those constructed by their predecessors. Hopewell cultures encompassed a wide geographical area, ranging east to west from present-day New York to Kansas and south to north from the Gulf Coast to the Great Lakes. Mortuary ritual was a central feature of all Hopewell cultures, which is evidenced particularly by the graves of the elites. Elites were buried with material goods such as shell necklaces, copper items, and ceremonial weaponry. Many of these items were constructed of materials that were not locally available. The Hopewell people acquired goods from throughout North America through their extensive trade network centered around access to the Ohio and Mississippi Rivers. In present-day Ohio, elites were found buried with grave goods made of mica from western North Carolina, copper from the Great Lakes region, carved conch shells from the Gulf of Mexico, and obsidian extracted from the Rocky Mountains. The Hopewell era lasted approximately 500 years. By 450 CE, the trade net-

works and the mortuary rituals that connected these peoples had disappeared. Mound building was still occurring but at a much smaller scale.

Mound building reached its zenith with the emergence of the Mississippian Culture around 1000 CE. The Mississippians were agriculturalists who resided along the Mississippi River or its many tributaries. The culture's rise accompanied the adoption of maize as a primary agricultural crop. Maize was highly productive, had a high caloric content, and was easily storable and carried in the baskets and pottery constructed by the women in the community. Other agricultural crops were also grown, such as beans, squash, and sunflowers. These were used to supplement the fish, deer, and bear that were provided by the male members of these respective groups together with meat and vegetables prepared as a stew.

The Mississippian Culture was adopted by peoples from throughout the southern part of the country. The Muskogean ancestors of the present-day Creeks resided in communities such as Moundville in present-day Alabama and Ocmulgee in Georgia. The Cherokees could be found in Etowah, in northern Georgia. The Caddos resided in Spiro, located in present-day Oklahoma. The largest Mississippian community was Cahokia, which is located at the same site as present-day St. Louis, Missouri. Although these were distinctly different peoples, they resided in similar communities with large rectangular mounds containing a flat-tier top arranged around a central plaza. The homes of chiefs and shamans were found on top of the respective mounds. When elites died, they were buried in the mound they had occupied. Like the Hopewell culture that preceded them, the Mississippians developed a continent-wide trading network, which resulted in Mississippian elites buried with exotic materials such as mica and copper.

The mound-building cultures disintegrated with the arrival of Europeans in the South. When the Spanish arrived in the Southeast in the 16th century, they brought with them pathogens such as smallpox. The heavily populated Mississippian centers proved especially susceptible to the pathogens. The survivors abandoned the Mississippian cities and after a few centuries emerged as different groups, most notably the Caddos, Cherokees, Chickasaws, Choctaws, and

Creeks. Diseases were not the only cause of the Mississippian decline. Climate change also played a role. Extended periods of drought led to crop failures. This plunged the Mississippian world into constant conflict as groups attacked others to seize foodstuffs. Weakened by warfare with their neighbors and decimated by disease, people ceased to build mounds.

John R. Burch Jr.

See also Mississippian Culture

Further Reading

Bowne, Eric E. 2013. *Mound Sites of the Ancient South: A Guide to the Mississippian Chiefdoms.* Athens: University of Georgia Press.

Gibson, Jon L. 2001. *The Ancient Mounds of Poverty Point: Place of Rings.* Gainesville: University Press of Florida

Townsend, Richard F. 2004. *Hero, Hawk, and Open Hand: American Indian Art of the Ancient Midwest and South.* New Haven, CT: Yale University Press.

New France, Women in

Empowered by French civic law and culture, independent women and women representing Catholic institutions played an active role in the French colonization of North America. New France (Nouvelle France) offered women positions of power and influence greater than what was found in the British colonies. French settlements were eventually absorbed into a larger English society, but the women of New France had a long-term cultural and political influence on the eventual United States.

Beginning in 1541, French outposts were short-lived all-male ventures. In 1608, only a year after the ill-fated British settlement at Jamestown, Samuel de Champlain established Quebec, the military and government center of New France. The first surviving female colonists arrived in 1613 and with nine families in 1636. By 1750 New France encompassed three times the territory held by Britain, yet the population of approximately 55,000 was a fraction of the 1.25 million British colonists. Women in New France, however, enjoyed heightened social and economic power because there was only 1 woman to every 5 men.

New France was a network of towns and Catholic missions primarily along waterways from the Hudson Bay, along the coast of Acadia, through the Saint Lawrence River Valley to the Great Lakes, down the Mississippi Valley to the Gulf of Mexico, and west to the Rocky Mountains.

While a few French Protestants (Huguenots) settled in French colonies, the primary motive for immigrating to North America was economic opportunity, not religious freedom. New France was a speculative financial investment, and disbursement of land was based on a feudal model. The French king owned the land and granted chosen individuals the right to harvest resources. The grant holder, or seigneur, profited from lumber, fur trapping, and leasing tracts of land to tenants, called habitants, for a rental fee or a percentage of annual agricultural profits.

The majority of French tenants were farmers and skilled craftspeople. They earned additional nontaxed income from fishing, woodworking, and other trades. French inheritance laws divided property equally among heirs, allowing widows and female children to inherit. Unlike under British law, French women owned and managed property. Industrious tenants strived to become seigneurs, and by 1663 half of the individuals managing property in the French colonies were women.

While the British subjugated Native Americans, the French actively developed trade partnerships with native people. Champlain, the first governor of Quebec, promoted cultural and lingual exchange and cemented intercultural relationships with the Huron and Algonquin peoples by encouraging his men to marry Native American women. Mixed-blood children, called métis, became important cultural and economic intermediaries.

Inspired by Jesuit priests who had accompanied French explorers and called for missionaries to convert the native North Americans, wealthy widow Marie-Madeleine de Chauvigny de la Peltrie financed the emigration of six nuns from two Catholic orders. Arriving in Quebec in 1639, Peltrie and three Augustinian sisters established Hôtel-Dieu—the first hospital in North America, outside Mexico. Nursing and apothecary care were provided to both settlers and Native

Americans. Peltrie and other noblewomen financed a second hospital in the mission town of Montreal operated by Jeanne Mance, an early settler.

The Ursuline nuns accompanying Peltrie founded the first convent and girls' school in North America. They were an order of teachers and taught literacy to both French and Native American girls. Their first mother superior, Mother Marie de l'Incarnation, immersed herself in native languages and created the first dictionary and Christian books in the Huron, Algonquian, Montagnais, and Iroquois languages. In New Orleans, the sisters extended education to African girls and managed the military hospital.

Under the Ursulines, women in New France became more educated than men and extended influence over trade and diplomacy. Madame Montour, a mixed-race woman educated by the sisters, employed her multilingual skills as a translator for the governor of New York during the negotiations with the five nations of the Iroquois Confederacy (1709–1719) and participated in talks between native peoples and the Pennsylvania colony.

In 1665, there were only 70 families in Quebec. Over a seven-year period during Louis XIV's reign, the government sent nearly 1,000 marriageable-age women to the colony in an attempt to increase the population. The Filles du Roi (King's Daughters), as they were known, were allegedly orphans recruited primarily from Paris and cities in northern France. They were provided passage and a dowry. Opponents insinuated that the women were poor or were prostitutes. Marriages were conducted under contract, and a waiting period allowed the woman and the prospective husband to change their minds. Some historians believe that Parisian brides brought cultivated tastes in music and the arts to New France.

To further increase the population, families with 10 or more living children received financial rewards. Women bore the burden of bearing an average of 12 children. Incentive money was also paid to men and women who married young.

Some women came to New France as indentured domestic servants. Most signed a 36-month contract to work in a household or for a business or a religious order. They received transportation to New France, lodging, and food in exchange for their labor. Some

Marie-Madeleine de Chauvigny de la Peltrie founded the Order of Ursulines in Quebec in New France in the early 1600s. (BLM Collection/Alamy Stock Photo)

also received an annual wage and specific supplies for their new life.

An estimated 1,100 slaves were distributed throughout northern New France. Northeastern native cultures enslaved individuals captured from enemy cultures. Most house slaves in settlement towns were Native Americans, captured by warring tribes and sold to the French. A few female African slaves from the Caribbean served in wealthy households in Montreal and Quebec.

New Orleans and its surrounding territory had difficulty attracting marriageable women, and the economy was heavily invested in slave labor. In a total population of 14,000, half were enslaved Africans, primarily from the Caribbean. A large percentage of the women in New Orleans were mixed race.

Throughout New France large extended families lived together, with men and women working the fields and minding livestock. Women tended household vegetable gardens, prepared food, cleaned, and typically handled business matters because they were more likely to be literate. As the merchant class grew, women established themselves as managers of trading posts, businesses, and tanneries. Women were entrusted with educating children. Self-sufficient children who could participate in economic ventures were regarded as the family's primary asset.

As in New England, women grew flax and tended sheep for textiles. Clothing imports from France were few; sewing and weaving skills were highly valued. Cultural clothing such as knitted hats (called *tuques*) and braided sashes with family-specific color patterns identified family members even from a distance.

Women's clothing reflected their active lifestyle. As with Native American women, skirts were only midcalf in length. Pockets were not sewn into clothing; satchels were tied on at the waist. English Puritans shunned frivolity, but French Catholicism embraced decorative embroidery and color. Women wore a bonnet or cap to cover the head, but their linen undergarments were trimmed with lace. They wore a cross pendant, but it often hung on a colorful ribbon.

Following the 1763 Treaty of Paris ending the French and Indian War, France ceded all territory east of the Mississippi River to Great Britain. The British expelled the Jesuit priests, but the Ursuline sisters took in the daughters of British officers and kept their schools open. The Quebec Act of 1774 allowed French descendants to retain their inheritance laws and Catholic religion.

Extensive landownership and established business networks enabled French descendants to become leading merchant, banking, and railroad families. They started the Bank of Missouri, the Bank of Michigan, and the Farmers' and Mechanics Bank. Family matriarchs founded theaters, museums, schools, and cathedrals. In St. Louis, Julia Soulard provided two square blocks of land for an open-air marketplace; Soulard Market continues to be one of the country's largest farmer's markets.

In 1804 the founding families of St. Louis petitioned for bilingual courts and schools, but English became the official language. In Detroit legal documents were printed bilingually until 1827, and French was spoken throughout the Midwest into the 1830s. Women retained property rights in Missouri and Illinois into the 19th century, but gradually French inheritance laws were overturned. French civic law prevailed only in New Orleans.

Many French descendants, especially in New Orleans, sided with the Confederacy during the American Civil War in an attempt to preserve both French culture and slave ownership. Though influential French families supported the Union, bigotry labeled all French speakers as secessionists. When the Confederacy lost the war, French American society quietly assimilated.

Some French families continued to wield political power through ownership of English-language newspapers. They influenced Wyoming to become the first state to give women equal voting rights. The first female vote cast in a general election occurred in Laramie, a former French trading post. Cities throughout the United States and Canada continue to benefit from the civic institutions founded by the women of New France.

Keri Dearborn

See also Clothing, Native American Women; Cultural Interaction; Food Production, Native American Women; Sexuality; Slavery, Native Americans; *Vol. 1, Sec. 2:* Catholic Women; Indentured Servants; Inheritance Laws; Mestiza; Protestant Women; Slavery, African; *Vol. 1, Sec. 3:* Ballard, Martha; Dower Rights; Ursuline Nuns

Further Reading

Gitlin, Jay. 2010. *Bourgeois Frontier: French Towns, French Traders, & American Expansion.* New Haven, CT: Yale University Press.

Holbrook, Sabra. 1976. *The French Founders of North America and Their Heritage.* New York: Atheneum.

"Virtual Museum of New France." 2013. Canadian Museum of Civilization, http://www.civilization .ca/virtual-museum-of-new-france/.

New Spain, Women in

Spanish settlement in New Spain began with the fall of Tenochtitlan (Mexico City) in 1521. The Spanish empire integrated the Nahua people native to the region with Euro-Americans and forever altered indigenous society. The Spanish brought with them a system of patriarchy, which enforced the role of the man as head of the household. Families of one sort or another were essential elements of identity and survival. For women unwilling or unable to marry, life in a convent was a viable option.

The most dominant cultural group in central Mexico was the Nahuas, or speakers of Nahuatl, which by the 15th century was the language of the majority of the people living in this region. Nahua morality emphasized moderation in all things, from personal appearance to expressions of sexuality. The primary duties of men and women were clearly defined and set from the time of birth: a boy's umbilical cord was buried on the battlefield, while a girl's was buried near the hearth. Women did the household work, including performing the sacred art of weaving, but they also worked outside the home in markets and temples. They were autonomous beings and, unlike their counterparts in Iberia, were not considered to be the dependents of men.

The Nahuas who survived the conquest were forced to adapt to the imposition of a Spanish political regime as well as the arrival of a new spiritual doctrine transmitted by Catholic missionaries. In colonial Mexico it was not the Virgin Mary but the Virgin of Guadalupe who served as a model to be emulated. She first appeared on the Mexican countryside in 1531 near the former sanctuary of the Nahua goddess of fertility, Tonantzin. Guadalupe, however, was a dark-skinned virgin, an interesting blend of Nahua and Catholicism. The syncretic Virgin, however, ultimately spelled the demise of women's participation in Church leadership as native religious institutions were closed or destroyed and given over to the control of male Catholic missionaries.

Family history was an important indicator of status in colonial Mexico. In the early days of Spanish conquest, marriage in New Spain was premised on the idea of free will, and love was believed to be an expression of free will. In the 16th century, young men and women who were denied the opportunity to marry their beloved could petition the Church for support. In many of these cases, both the Church and the community strongly disapproved of parental coercion, and the parties were allowed to marry. Family honor in this period was closely tied to virtue, especially women's virtue. Maintaining honor became a useful tool in forcing parents to consent to an otherwise undesirable marriage. Families were a mechanism of social control that required constant maintenance and monitoring. This was particularly true in the 17th century, when capitalism began to significantly alter families' material prospects. Thanks in part to the rise of merchant capitalism, marriages arranged in the pursuit of money or material goods were no longer considered uncouth. Parents, especially fathers who controlled the family purse, thus gained more influence over the marriage choices of their sons and daughters. In 1776, a royal pragmatic sanction issued by the king of Spain decreed that all persons under the age of 25 had to obtain parental consent before marriage. The law spread to New Spain in 1778, essentially nullifying women's freedom to create families of their own choosing, a freedom granted to the earliest settlers of New Spain. At the same time, an increase in interracial marriages also threatened the prestige of Spanish families as a distinct racial category. Maintaining completely Spanish bloodlines became more and more of a challenge as the society of New Spain matured through its first few generations.

Euro-American women in New Spain had different life experiences depending on their class location. Elite women had servants, often women, to do household work but were under the strict control of first fathers and then husbands. Poorer women often worked at both waged and unwaged labor. They worked in homes and on farms. Mixed-blood (mestizo) women generally fell into the lowest and most vulnerable class because they were not pure-blood Spanish. Nonetheless, women in New Spain had more political and social power than did their counterparts in the English colonies. They were allowed to own property after marriage and thus to own and operate businesses and farms of their own, a privilege that many women lost when Mexico ceded its northern territory to the United States under the Treaty of Guadalupe-Hidalgo in 1848.

Women in the Spanish Empire also had mixed access to education, with elite-class women far more likely to be literate than poor and mestizo women. Many women published their writings, which often focused on gender inequalities and class hierarchies.

Sor Juana Inés de la Cruz was a nun, scholar, and poet in colonial Mexico in the mid-1600s. De la Cruz wrote a public letter in favor of female education that caused the Catholic hierarchy to condemn and silence her, but today her work is considered foundational in Mexican literature.

Convents offered women an opportunity to create households free from patriarchy, at least on a day-to-day level. These all-female families played a key role in reproducing patriarchal Spanish life by teaching young women the domestic arts and customs of "proper" Spanish ladies. With their ever-increasing dowry pools, the convents became a major source of credit in the 16th and 17th centuries. In addition to the nuns, many laywomen lived in convents, including girls deposited for safekeeping, girls enrolled in the convent school, orphaned children, servants, and slaves. Nuns essentially functioned as adoptive mothers, and their role was clear: to inculcate young women with the values of Spanish religion and culture.

Kathleen Barker

See also Mississippian Culture; Mound-Building Cultures; Sexuality; *Vol. 1, Sec. 2:* Catholic Women

Further Reading

Gutierrez, Ramon. 1991. *When Jesus Came the Corn Mothers Went Away: Marriage, Sexuality, and Power in New Mexico, 1500–1846.* Stanford, CA: Stanford University Press.

Twinam, Ann. *Public Lives, Private Secrets: Gender, Honor, Sexuality, and Illegitimacy in Colonial Spanish America.* Stanford, CA: Stanford University Press, 1999.

Nzinga of Angola. *See* Queens, African, Nzinga of Angola and Amina of Nigeria

Pocahontas (ca. 1595–1617)

Disney has honored Pocahontas in film, and she is a staple of the public school curriculum and a symbol of a good Native American. We think we know her, but the events of her life have grown beyond the bounds of

Pocahontas was a Powhatan woman who served as an intermediary between her people and English colonists. The famous story told by John Smith is largely fictional, as are movies made about her story. (Library of Congress)

history. She has become a myth, one useful in telling a particular version of the American past. Even historians cannot always be sure what is true and what is not when it comes to Pocahontas. In many ways she is the American version of Eve, the progenitor of a new race of humans and a new destiny for her people and for Euro-Americans. Because much of what is known about Pocahontas came from the writings of Europeans, her story is often couched in the bias that Native Americans were primitive and godless savages grateful for the civilizing influence of Euro-Americans. The Pocahontas story also works to redeem Anglo–Native Americans relations by representing the belief that Euro-Americans and Native Americans could co-exist peacefully in a racial hierarchy that embraced white superiority.

Pocahontas belonged to a group of people who lived in the deciduous forests that once covered Virginia. The chief of this region, Powhatan, may have had more than 100 wives and dozens of children, among them Pocahontas. It is difficult to pinpoint her birth. Historians tend to fix it in 1595, though the day and month are almost certainly lost. At least one historian believes that Pocahontas was Powhatan's favorite child. Historians appear to know nothing about her mother, suggesting that Euro-Americans largely ignored Powhatan women. Powhatan apparently named her Matoake or Matowaka, meaning "Little Snow Feather." Historians are not sure why the father chose this name. Perhaps the name signified that Pocahontas had been born in winter. The name Pocahontas means "playful and mischievous." She was likely born at her father's chief estate, Wenowocomoco, meaning "royal."

As a girl, Pocahontas may have tended a garden to supplement a diet of meat, fish, marine invertebrates, roots, nuts, and berries. Powhatan's wives likely cared for Pocahontas as she grew into adolescence. She probably learned to swim at an early age and bathed at dawn and dusk. Along with other girls, Pocahontas may have gathered wood, made pottery, wove baskets, made clothes, and helped raise younger children. It is possible, however, that Pocahontas's status elevated her above mundane chores.

Pocahontas was about 12 years old when Europeans settled Virginia in 1607. In the tense relations between the two peoples, the Powhatan Native Americans captured one of the leaders of the European colonists, John Smith. When they brought Smith to Powhatan, Pocahontas had her first glimpse of a European. According to Smith's account, Powhatan, conferring with his lieutenants, decided to kill the Englishman, but Pocahontas intervened to save him. Herein lies the source of the romantic view of Pocahontas that has eclipsed all other interpretations of her: that Pocohantas instantly fell in love with Smith when she saw him and begged her father not to kill him.

Because this story comes from Smith's own recollections, one might be tempted to believe it. Smith, however, wrote other accounts in which beautiful women rescued him from death, leaving his story about Pocahontas in doubt. Moreover, Smith waited 17 years to write this account, leaving historians perplexed by the delay. Pocahontas was 12 years old when the event occurred and thus unlikely to fall instantly in love with any middle-aged Englishman. According to historians, it is more likely that Pocahontas acted as part of a ritual acceptance or adoption of Smith in her embrace of him. Smith may have been mistaken to think his life in danger. Pocahontas's actions may have signified that Powhatan royalty, of which she was a member, had embraced Smith as a friend of the tribe. Even if some Native Americans were suspicious of Smith, they would have recognized the political advantages of adopting an Englishman. Certainly, in ensuing decades the story has played an important part in the racist notion that Indians recognized their own inferiority when faced with the greatness of Euro-Americans.

Smith temporarily settled in a hut near Powhatan's palace, and in the ensuing weeks Pocahontas befriended him. Smith was not free to return to Jamestown, but neither did he appear to have been Pocahontas's slave. In January 1608 Powhatan freed Smith, though the chief expected tribute from him in gratitude for his freedom. Pocahontas, surely with her father's blessing, brought food to the colonists, saving them from starvation. She also served as Powhatan's mouthpiece, carrying messages from the chief to the Englishmen. The frequency of her visits and her gifts led the colonists to esteem her. She was a symbol of peace and prosperity.

When relations between the settlers and Native Americans deteriorated, Smith took several of the latter as captives. Powhatan sent Pocahontas to secure their release, believing that Smith would not ignore her either because of his friendly relationship with her or because of her status as Powhatan's favored daughter. As the chief had foreseen, Smith relented and released the captives, undoubtedly recognizing that the English were in no position to fight a war with Powhatan's people.

Throughout 1608 Pocahontas continued to visit Smith and his men, but because the natives had a poor harvest, she could not provide them a steady supply of food as they had come to expect. That winter Powhatan invited Smith to his palace on the pretext of dining with him. In truth, Powhatan had apparently decided to kill Smith and his retainers. When Pocahontas learned the truth, she warned Smith to leave his encampment. It is impossible to know why Pocahontas did this or how much Powhatan knew. She may have been saving Smith and his men from violence or acting so as to trick the English into leaving the area, thus avoiding armed conflict. Whether Smith ever showed appropriate gratitude for the risks Pocahontas had taken for him is also unclear.

In about 1610, Pocahontas may have married Native American warrior Kocoum. Certainly by 1613, in her next encounter with the English, no husband accompanied her, leading historians to believe that Kocoum died, that the marriage had dissolved, or that he never existed in the first place. In 1613 the English, who owed so much to Pocahontas, captured her. During her imprisonment with the English, she adopted European customs. She converted to Anglicanism; adopted European habits, manners, and clothes; and learned the English language. Powhatan was unable to buy his daughter's freedom, though he made every effort to secure her release.

As a native princess, Pocahontas retained her status as a noblewoman in European society. In 1614, she married tobacco baron John Rolfe. Powhatan did not attend his daughter's wedding to Rolfe. In English society, Pocahontas took the name Rebecca. Between 1614 and 1622 Jamestown enjoyed the Peace of Pocahontas, so named to honor the woman who had brought peace to the colony. In 1615 Pocahontas gave birth to a son, Thomas. At the invitation of investors in London, Rolfe, Pocahontas, and Thomas crossed the Atlantic Ocean to meet King James I. English nobility held parties in her honor and found her a fascinating, charming woman. While in London, Pocahontas expected to be reunited with her friend John Smith. In January or February 1617 near the end of her life, Smith at last visited Pocahontas, though by that time she may already have contracted tuberculosis, a disease to which Native Americans had no immunity. His visit did not cheer her.

On a return voyage to Virginia, Pocahontas fell gravely ill. Some suspect that tuberculosis was causing her lungs to bleed. The ship turned away from the Atlantic Ocean and took her back to England. She died there on March 21, 1617. Rolfe arranged a Christian mass and burial, perhaps at St. George's Church in Gravesend. Fire destroyed the cemetery, so no one now knows where Pocahontas is buried. Two statues, one in England and the other in the United States, commemorate her.

Today the myth of Pocahontas, exacerbated by the inaccuracies of the Disney animated movie, overshadow the real woman whose life was both interesting and tragic. Her power appears to lie more in the stories that Americans tell that reassure them of their cultural superiority than in any real lessons about the conquest of North America, the genocide of native peoples, and the costs of colonialism.

Christopher Cumo

See also Jamestown; Malinche; Slavery, Native Americans; Virginia Company

Further Reading

Allen, Paula Gunn. 2003. *Pocahontas: Medicine Woman, Spy, Entrepreneur, Diplomat.* San Francisco: HarperSanFrancisco.

Custalow, Linwood, and Angela Daniel. 2001. *The True Story of Pocahontas: The Other Side of History.* Golden, CO: Fulcrum.

Jones, Victoria Garrett. 1996. *Pocahontas: A Life in Two Worlds.* New York: Sterling.

Mossiker, Frances. 1976. *Pocahontas: The Life and the Legend.* New York: Da Capo.

Turner, Erin, ed. 2009. *Wise Women: From Pocahontas to Sarah Winnemucca; Remarkable Stories of Native American Trailblazers.* Guilford, CT: Twodot.

Letter of John Rolfe, Husband of Pocahontas, to Sir Thomas Dale (1614)

In the following 1614 letter to Sir Thomas Dale, governor of Virginia, Englishman and Virginia settler John Rolfe explained his reasons for marrying Pocahontas, daughter of the powerful local chief Powhatan.

Let therefore this my well advised protestation . . . condemn me herein, if my chiefest intent and purpose be not, to strive with all my power of body and mind, in the undertaking of so mighty a matter, no way led (so far forth as man's weakness may permit) with the unbridled desire of carnal affection: but for the good of this plantation, for the honour of our country, for the glory of God, for my own salvation, and for the converting to the true knowledge of God and Jesus Christ, an unbelieving creature, namely Pokahuntas. . . .

Shall I be of so untoward a disposition, as to refuse to lead the blind into the right way? Shall I be so unnatural, as not to give bread to the hungry? or uncharitable, as not to cover the naked? Shall I despise to actuate these pious duties of a Christian? Shall the base fears of displeasing the world, overpower and withhold me from revealing unto man these spiritual works

of the Lord, which in my meditations and prayers, I have daily made known unto him? God forbid. . . .

Now if the vulgar sort, who square all men's actions by the base rule of their own filthiness, shall tax or taunt me in this my godly labour: let them know, it is not any hungry appetite, to gorge my self with incontinency; sure (if I would, and were so sensually inclined) I might satisfy such desire, though not without a seared conscience, yet with Christians more pleasing to the eye, and less fearful in the offence unlawfully committed.

Source: Lyon Gardiner Tyler, ed., *Narratives of Early Virginia, 1606–1625* (New York: Scribner, 1907), 237–244.

Polygamy, Native American

Native Americans practiced polygamy, or the practice of being married to two or more people at the same time, across the continent up until the early 20th century. Specifically, polygyny, the practice of a man married to two or more women at the same time, was found in nearly all Native American societies. However, the practice was usually limited to a small number of men, because the number of members of each sex was roughly equal in a tribe. Women marrying at younger ages and males having high mortality rates offset any disparity in the numbers between marriage partners. This form of marriage was not sexually motivated. Instead, it was a logical solution for forming a larger household, having more children in a family group, increasing wealth and status in a community, cementing kinships, or settling possible tribal disputes.

Polygyny was seen as necessary when there was a mutual dependency between demographic location and kinship ties. This was especially evident among the Plains Indians, where these bonds were necessitated by the trade of buffalo robes. Native American men killed buffalo faster than women could process them. Therefore, polygamy resulted from female labor contributing to household production and requiring men to seek additional wives.

For women, polygyny could be beneficial as well. Sororal polygamy, in which sisters were typically married to the same husband, was typical in New World hunter-gatherer societies. Women could continue to cohabit with family members, receiving help with child care and household chores. They tended to have fewer children, while men had more than those in monogamous marriages because of the Native American practice of abstinence following the birth of a child.

Jealousy among married adults did not appear to be of great concern. Among the Blackfeet, adultery by younger wives was generally tolerated by older husbands. However, the young wives were severely punished if they eloped with a younger man, because this represented a decrease in domestic wealth for the husband. The pursuit of domestic wealth shifted polygamy from sororal to economically based polygamy as the demand for hides increased from the mid to late 19th century.

In tribes of the coastal Northwest, polygyny occurred up until the mid-19th century between high-status men and women, increasing as the demand for furs grew. Because polygynous wives were responsible for increasing wealth, managing potlatches, and cementing social relations, they could expect better treatment from their husbands. First wives had the most prestigious position and could devote themselves to ceremonial matters more so than monogamous women, because housekeeping duties were shared by lesser wives.

Westerners such as the missionaries in California did not understand Native American polygamy. They considered the practice against the laws of God. Their cultural assumptions led many Euro-Americans to believe that Native American men had no real attachment to their families and could take sisters and mothers-in-law as wives with little regard for the sanctity of marriage. Also, Catholic priests sometimes failed to see polygamy in native cultures, leading them to believe that it was not practiced. California missionaries, for example, thought that the Chumash peoples did not practice polygamy, when in fact they did practice sororal polygyny commonly. Women came from multiple families or villages as well to consolidate social positions, foster trade relations, and end feuds between groups.

After conversion to Christianity, Native American men were forced to choose one wife, usually the youngest one because she was considered more fertile and able to care for an older husband when he became sick. Despite Euro-American disapproval, polygamy did not immediately disappear from indigenous cultures. The high number of unmarried women in their 40s and regular visitations by men to tribe members outside the mission suggest that it continued despite the Catholic Church's efforts.

Sarah Nation

See also Sexuality; *Vol. 2, Sec. 1:* Mormon Polygamy

Further Reading

Newell, Quincy D. 2005. "The Indians Generally Love Their Wives and Children: Native American Marriage and Sexual Practices in Missions San Francisco, Santa Clara, and San José." *Catholic Historical Review* 91(1) (January): 60–82.

Perkins, Stephen M., Susan C. Vehik, and Richard R. Drass. 2008. "The Hide Trade and Wichita Social Organization: An Assessment of Ethnological Hypotheses Concerning Polygyny." *Plains Anthropologist* 53(208), *Memoir 40: Land of Our Ancestors; Studies in Protohistoric and Historic Wichita Cultures* (November): 431–443.

Walter, Susan M. 2006. "Polygyny, Rank, and Resources in Northwest Coast Foraging Societies." *Ethnology* 45(1) (Winter): 41–57.

Powhatan People

A matrilineal tribe, the Powhatans were the dominant people of a paramount chiefdom that consisted of approximately 14,000 Algonquian-speaking peoples from more than 30 tribes, including the Appamattuck, Chickahominy, Kecoughtan, Pamunkey, and Potomac tribes that resided in the Chesapeake Bay area of present-day Virginia. The Powhatan Confederacy was at the apex of its power under the leadership of paramount chief Wahunsunacock when the English first arrived in 1607. He became known to Europeans as Powhatan. Since the Powhatans were matrilineal, Wahunsunacock inherited his chieftaincy through his mother's family. He consolidated his power within the confederacy by appointing both male and female kinfolk to serve as subchieftains of the principal towns inhabited by subject peoples.

Men and women in Powhatan society had distinct roles that provided both groups power. Men were responsible for hunting, fishing, and warfare. Women were responsible for maintaining the homes. Their tasks included making basketry and pottery, gathering firewood, cooking, and raising the children. The women were also responsible for raising agricultural crops, most notably corn. In Powhatan society corn was a representation of wealth, so it gave women economic and political authority within the community. Although men and women had distinct gender roles, this did not mean that they led separate lives. Both genders shared in foraging expeditions during the harvests and also cleared land together for the establishment of gardens.

The arrival of the English in 1607 and the subsequent establishment of Jamestown put pressure on the Powhatans, especially women, that had never been there before. The English were primarily interested in finding gold and jewels, and thus they did not spend the necessary time and effort to grow crops. They expected the Powhatans to provide them with the necessary agricultural foodstuffs. Since the English did not understand Powhatan matriarchy or gender roles, they turned to Powhatan men to request food. When the native men deferred to the women, the British became confused and angry. In Europe, the men owned and worked agricultural fields. Among the Powhatans, the women controlled agriculture and would only grow the food-stuffs required for their community. The Powhatan women refused to grow corn for the English despite their constant demands. Native American women's repeated rejections helped lead to violence between the Powhatans and the English.

Between 1607 and 1610 the Powhatans and the English tried to coexist, with Wahunsunacock even trying to symbolically adopt John Smith into his family using his daughter Pocahontas, but the effort ended when open warfare broke out between the parties. The war, which lasted from 1610 to 1614, ended with the marriage of Pocahontas to John Rolfe. Although the Powhatans wanted more intermarriage between the groups to forge family ties, the English did not wish to marry "savages."

A major sea change in the balance of power between the Powhatans and the English came about in 1612, when Rolfe began experimenting with tobacco as a cash crop. He succeeded in developing a form of smoking tobacco with seeds from the West Indies that became greatly desired in Europe. Tobacco's establishment as a staple crop caused Englishmen to flood into Virginia, resulting in the seizure of thousands of acres of Indian lands by settlers. Although there was great anger among the Powhatans, Wahunsunacock endeavored to keep the peace.

Following Wahunsunacock's death, Opechancanough replaced his brother as the paramount chief. He had long advocated to his brother a military response to English depredations, but his brother had refused to act. In 1622 Opechancanough began the Second Anglo-Powhatan War, which lasted from 1622 to 1632. Although the Powhatans lost the conflict, Opechancanough was determined to preserve what remained of the Powhatan homeland. In 1644, he launched yet another war against the English but was soundly defeated in 1646 and executed. His successor, Necotowance, surrendered most of the Powhatan homeland to Virginia in exchange for some land on the York River. From that point on the Powhatans functionally ceased to exist, as the respective peoples who had comprised the confederacy began relations with the English, who endeavored to move the respective groups onto small reservations.

The move to reservations completely changed the gender roles for women, as the men were forced by the English to become "civilized," which to the English meant that the men become agriculturalists. The loss of economic and political power that came with women's agricultural work shifted matriarchal native societies to a European-style patriarchy.

John R. Burch Jr.

See also Jamestown; Pocahontas

Further Reading
Gleach, Frederic W. 1997. *Powhatan's World and Colonial Virginia: A Conflict of Cultures.* Lincoln: University of Nebraska Press.
Rountree, Helen C. 1988. *The Powhatan Indians of Virginia: Their Traditional Culture.* Norman: University of Oklahoma Press.

Two Accounts of John Smith's Meeting with Powhatan (1608, 1624)

The dramatic story of John Smith's near death and reprieve by Pocahontas comes from Smith's 1624 General History of Virginia. It does not appear in his 1608 book A True Relation of Virginia, *written the year after the events supposedly occurred. This discrepancy, among other things, suggests that the story is a fabrication. The two versions of Smith's meeting with Powhatan are reproduced here.*

1. ACCOUNT FROM *A TRUE RELATION* (1608)

Arriving at Weramocomoco [? On or about 5 January 1608], their Emperor proudly lying upon a Bedstead a foot high, upon ten or twelves Mats, richly hung with many chains of great pearls about his neck, and covered with a great Covering of Rahaughcums. At head sat a woman, at his feet another; on each side sitting upon a mat uppon the ground, were ranged his chief men on each side of the fire, ten in a rank, and behind them as many young women, each a great Chain of white Beads over their shoulders, their heads painted in red: and with such a grave and Magestic countenance, as draw me into admiration to see such state in a naked Savage.

He kindly welcomed me with such good words, and great Platters of sundry Victuals, assuring me his friendship, and my liberty within four days. . . . He asked me the cause of our coming. . . . He demanded why we went further with our Boat. . . . He promised to give me Corn, Venison, or what I wanted to feed us: Hatchets and Copper we should make him, and none should disturb us.

This request I promised to perform: and thus, having with all the kindness he could devise, sought to content me, he sent me home, with 4 men: one that usually carried my Gown and Knapsack after me, two other loaded with bread, and one to accompany me.

2. ACCOUNT FROM *GENERAL HISTORY OF VIRGINIA* (1624)

At last they brought him [Smith] to Meronocomoco, where was Powhatan their Emperor. . . . [T]wo great stones were brought before Powhatan: then as many as could laid hands on him [Smith], dragged him to them, and thereon laid his head, and being ready with their clubs, to beat out his brains, *Pocahontas* the Kings dearest daughter, when no entreaty could prevail, got his head in her arms, and laid her own upon his to save him from death: whereat the Emperor was contented he should live. . . .

Two days after, Powhatan having disguised himself in the most fearefullest manner he could, caused Capt. Smith to be brought forth to a great house in the woods . . . then Powhatan . . . came unto him and told him now they were friends, and presently he should go to Jamestown, to send him two great guns, and a grindstone, for which he would give him the Country of Capahowosick, and forever esteem him as his son *Nantaquoud*.

Source: John Smith, *A True Relation of Such Occurrences and Accidents of Note as Hath Hapned in Virginia since the First Planting of That Colony, Which Is Now Resident in the South Part Thereof, till the Last Returne from Thence* (London: Printed for John Tappe, 1608). Available at http://www.virtualjamestown.org/exist/cocoon/jamestown/fha/J1007.

Pueblo Culture

Sixteenth-century Spanish explorers used the word "pueblo," meaning "town" or "village" as well as "nation" or "people," to refer to the Native American communities they discovered in what is now the American Southwest. By the time of Spanish arrival in 1540, these villages numbered between 100 and 200 in the Rio Grande Valley in present-day New Mexico and northeastern Arizona. They typically consisted of multilevel adobe or stone dwellings clustered around a central plaza. Even though they spoke different languages, Pueblo Indians displayed similar cultural traits.

Creation stories lay at the center of Pueblo life. Most Pueblos believe that they entered this world through a hole in the roof of the world below, using a ladder. The underground ceremonial chambers, or kivas, often include a ceremonial hole, or *sipapu*, in the floor to symbolize this entrance place. The kiva was used for ceremonies and rituals in which only men participated. They also used the kiva for councils and social gatherings.

Spirituality permeated all Pueblo social structures and cultural traditions. There were fixed rituals and prayers for each ceremonial occasion, performed in the kiva by the men and followed by a ritualistic public dance in the plaza. These dances often featured representations of the spiritual messengers known as *katsinas*. They helped create harmony and balance, values at the core of Pueblo belief systems. The universe itself embodied these principles, with Earth as the personification of the female, while the rain and the sky represented male qualities. From the union of the two came the corn and other crops to sustain human life.

Gender roles reflected this complementarity of male and female. As givers of life, women tended to the young and nurtured all members of the household.

Pueblo culture was highly organized and sophisticated. The Cliff Palace at Mesa Verde National Park illustrates the Peublo people's complex building skills, as well as their talent for successful, high density living. (Corel)

They ground corn, cut and dried meat, and prepared food for family consumption. The Pueblo household revolved around senior women, who owned most family property and controlled its use. Women also built and maintained housing and supervised family affairs. Village business, on the other hand, lay in the male domain. Pueblo men tended the cornfields, attended to spiritual and political matters, conducted trade, and defended the village against attack.

Pueblo tradition permitted some flexibility within these strictly defined gender roles. A socially recognized third gender allowed for an individual to take on the tasks, rituals, and sometimes also dress and hairstyle of the other sex. These two-spirit people, historically called berdaches, were seen as embodiments of both the male and the female. They often held honored and influential positions in Pueblo life.

The balance of the Pueblo universe was thrown off kilter with the arrival of the Spanish. Disease epidemics and trade items preceded the establishment of the first Spanish settlement in 1598. With the settlement came Spanish friars, and by 1630 most pueblos in the region had a priest and a church. New draft animals, crops, and metal tools enriched Pueblo material culture, while the Spaniards benefited from the Pueblo Indians' labor. Pueblo women's blankets and textiles proved useful to Spanish colonists. Pottery made by women also entered the cycle of colonial trade. In the process, Pueblo women served as agents of change in their own communities as they adopted new materials and methods from the colonists to diversify their crafts.

Pueblos tolerated the intrusion until 1680, when they rebelled against their mistreatment by the Spanish, including sexual violence against Pueblo women. The rebels desecrated churches and killed 21 of the province's 33 priests and over 400 of the fewer than 3,000 Spaniards in the colony. The Indian leaders then restored their own religious institutions. This Pueblo renaissance lasted until 1692, when the Spanish reimposed their rule. However, Spanish authorities decided to tolerate Pueblo ceremonies. What emerged was a religious syncretism among the Pueblos that combined Catholic ritual with Pueblo ritual.

Women continued to play an important mediating role on the cultural frontiers of the Southwest. Some Pueblo women married settlers looking for female companionship in a predominantly male world, while other women became concubines. These unions altered perceptions about gender on both sides of the frontier. They also produced a mixed-blood (mestizo) population that eventually dominated Hispanic settlements. The mestizos created a new cultural expression on the Spanish colonial frontier, combining features of both the colonized and the colonizer.

Päivi H. Hoikkala

See also Berdache/Transgendering; Creation/Origin Stories; Disease, Postconquest Impact on Native Americans

Further Reading

Brown, Tracy. 2013. *Pueblo Indians and Spanish Colonial Authority in Eighteenth-Century New Mexico.* Tucson: University of Arizona Press.

Dozier, Edward. 1970. *Pueblo Indians of North America.* New York: Holt, Rinehart and Winston.

Gutiérrez, Ramón. 1991. *When Jesus Came, the Corn Mothers Went Away: Marriage, Sexuality, and Power in New Mexico, 1500–1846.* Stanford, CA: Stanford University Press.

Queens, African, Nzinga of Angola (1581/83–ca. 1663) and Amina of Nigeria (d. 1610)

Nzinga Mbande (ca. 1581/1583–ca. 1663) was a 17th-century African ruler of the Ndongo and Matamba Kingdoms of modern-day Angola. She came of age and ruled Ndongo at a time when merchants of the Netherlands, France, and Britain had begun to challenge the monopoly of Portuguese merchants in the traffic of humans across the Atlantic. Across the course of her reign, she negotiated treaties that kept her people safe.

Amina, or Aminatu (d. 1610), was a leader of Hausaland in present-day Nigeria, remembered particularly

for her military prowess and subsequent expansion of the political and economic power of her state. Prior to Western and Islamic influences, the women of Hausaland played an important political role as ministers, counselors, and ambassadors.

In the late 16th and early 17th centuries, the economic power and territorial control of African states on the Central African coast became threatened by Portuguese attempts to establish a colony at Luanda. Many of these states had become regional powers through their early participation in human trafficking. Portuguese encroachment and the attempt by some rulers to end their participation in the trade created conflict between African states and European business interests.

West African cultures were egalitarian societies: gender complementarity was based on sacred principles and secular laws. The largely matrilineal descent systems and matriarchal philosophies of West Africa were accepted and defended by men. Nzinga and Amina governed peoples who were soon to become entangled in the slave trade. As they were kidnapped and brought to the New World, they carried their culture with them, and in turn it became the basis for African American culture.

Between 1621 and 1622 Portuguese governor Joao Corria de Sousa invited Ngola, or King Mbande, to attend a peace conference to end the hostilities with the Mbundus. Mbande sent his half sister Nzinga to negotiate, and she repositioned Ndongo as an intermediary rather than a supply zone in the slave trade. She achieved an alliance between Ndongo and Portugal, and in doing so she ended Portuguese slave raiding in the kingdom.

Between 1623 and 1624, Nzinga assumed the throne. As queen her objectives were to end human trafficking in her region, end war with the Portuguese, achieve diplomatic recognition, and establish profitable trading relationship with Luanda. Oral history claims that she insisted on being called king and that when leading her army in battle, she dressed in men's clothing.

Nzinga converted to Christianity in an effort to strengthen her ties with Portugal and was baptized Dona Anna de Sousa in honor of Governor Sousa's wife. By 1626 Sousa, representative of the Portuguese trade industry, had betrayed the alliance as the demand for labor in the Americas increased, as did potential

Queen Anna Nzinga led the Ndongo and Matamba Kingdoms of southwest Africa in the early 1600s. She negotiated with Portugal in an attempt to limit the Africans being sold to the New World. She is remembered as a talented political and military tactician. (Fotosearch/Getty Images)

profit. Nzinga strengthened her military power through marriage with a Jaga chief in 1630.

When Nzinga would not hand over escaped slaves, the Portuguese occupied Ndongo, made it a vassal state, and appointed Ari Kiluanji as a puppet or proxy Ngola. Militarily overwhelmed, Nzinga led her people west and founded a new state at Matamba. To further bolster Matamba's military strength, Nzinga offered sanctuary to runaway slaves and Portuguese-trained African slave-soldiers. She adopted a form of military organization known as *kilombo,* in which youths renounced family ties and were raised communally in militias in a continuing effort to become free of Portuguese colonialism. In 1627 Nzinga led forces from Matamba against the Portuguese, initiating a 30-year guerrilla war following their attack on settlements of Ngola Ari.

The Netherlands seized Luanda for its own mercantile purposes in 1641. Nzinga created an alliance with the Dutch just as she broke with the Jaga chief following his plunder of the Mbundu capital of

Matamba. The Jagas then joined the Portuguese. Nzinga requested a detachment of Dutch soldiers to fight with her. Within a year of initially defeating Portuguese forces, they were again forced to retreat to Matamba, where Nzinga capitalized on its position as the gateway to the Central African interior to develop it as a trading power.

By 1659 Nzinga had signed a treaty with the Portuguese negotiating an exchange for the freedom of her sister, Dona Barbara, a captive for 11 years who succeeded Nzinga as ruler of the new settlement of Matamba.

Nzinga reconverted to Christianity before she died on December 17, 1663. Her death accelerated Portuguese occupation and expansion of the slave trade as they moved quickly to occupy the interior of Southwest Africa. Angola remained under Portuguese control until independence in 1975.

Amina/Aminatu descended from a long line of female leaders. Her mother, Queen Bakwa Turunda, is credited with the rise of the Hausa States. She named the capital of the state Zazzau, in northern Nigeria, for her youngest daughter, Zaria. Amina became a famous leader and military commander through annexation of lands and kingdoms. Between 1536 and 1573, she expanded Hausaland economically and politically, leading to its dominance in the regions of the trans-Saharan and east-west trade routes. Amina subjected or subdued states as far away as Kwararafa and Nupe.

Amina is credited with the construction of cities throughout her kingdom and is remembered in the Songhai language in a phrase that is used when speaking of something wise and respected. "As proud and old as the walls of Amina" refers to the defensive fortifications built under her reign that demonstrated the advanced technological development of the ancient Hausa people.

Amina died in Atagrar to the south. The power of the state of Zaria declined and in 1734 it was conquered by Bornu. In 1975, Nigeria issued a 30k stamp depicting Queen Amina riding a white horse in honor of the International Women's Year.

Leleua Loupe

See also Queens, European, Elizabeth I of England and Isabella of Castile

Further Reading

Alou, Antoinette Tidjani. 2009. "Nigher and Sarraounia: One Hundred Years of Forgetting Female Leadership." *Research in African Literatures* 40(1) (Spring): 42–56.
Sweetman, David. 1984. *Women Leaders in African History.* Oxford, UK: Heinemann Educational Books.
Van Sertima, Ivan. 1988. *Black Women in Antiquity.* Rutgers, NJ: Transaction Publishers.

Queens, European, Elizabeth I of England (1533–1603) and Isabella of Castile (1451–1504)

Elizabeth Tudor assumed the throne of England as Queen Elizabeth I in 1558, and Isabella of Castile inherited the Castilian throne in 1474. Although Isabella ruled a united Spain alongside her husband, Ferdinand of Aragon, they maintained separate rule over the individual territories of their family Crowns.

Both Renaissance queens contributed to the colonization of the New World, paving the way for future rulers and explorers to form what would later become the American colonies. Queen Isabella and King Ferdinand provided Christopher Columbus, a Genoese privateer and explorer, with their royal blessing and financial backing to embark on an expedition to locate a passage to the Indies. During her own attempts to fund exploration and colonization, Queen Elizabeth supported expeditions for several men of her court, including Humphrey Gilbert and Walter Raleigh.

Columbus's plan was to establish a financially lucrative route to the Indies via the Atlantic Ocean, but he initially had difficulty earning patronage for his proposal. Although he successfully impressed the Count of Medinaceli, who was willing to finance an expedition, they were wary of potentially violating the Spanish-Portuguese peace treaty restricting international exploration. As a result, they needed an official blessing, with its attendant protection, from one of the European monarchs to proceed. Columbus approached several monarchies, including France and England, unsuccessfully before Medinaceli turned to Spain for advice.

Queen Isabella was impressed by Columbus's proposal and summoned him directly to her court for further discussion. During this meeting, he appealed to Isabella by noting that he hoped to discover unexplored territory, convert natives to Catholicism, and bring wealth to Spain. The queen, whose primary focus fell in line with these goals, desired to support the expedition. However, even though she was intrigued by Columbus's proposition, she acknowledged that she was unfamiliar with the logistics of the voyage and wished to consult with a professional committee who could discern the feasibility of the expedition.

The deliberation process extended for long periods of time during Spain's war against Muslims, who had once controlled Spain but had been pushed south to Granada. As the war raged on, the colonization plan became less and less of a priority; Columbus continued to present his ideas to other monarchs in the hopes that someone else might finance his journey.

In January 1492 Muslim Granada surrendered to Spain, ending the Reconquista. Months later Columbus received Spanish approval and funding for his exploration. All of Columbus's funds did not come from Isabella, but his contract obligated him to claim any conquered territories in the name of Spain for Isabella and Ferdinand. In exchange, Columbus was given the title admiral of the ocean sea.

As pursuit of the New World continued, Isabella grew wary of the conquerors' actions. Although she continued to stress the importance of converting the natives, she was against enslaving and physically harming them. The Spanish conquerors went against her protests during their interactions with the natives and attempted to bring slaves back to Spain. Thus, Isabella played a prominent role in establishing the Spanish connection with the New World, including its native populations, when she provided Christopher Columbus with official support from the Castilian Crown.

England also maintained an interest in territorial expansion under Queen Elizabeth's reign. Although Elizabeth's primary interests during the expansion centered on colonizing the Irish, she granted private licenses to several courtiers interested in exploring and profiting from North America. Humphrey Gilbert's involvement in the efforts to acquire Irish territory led to both his knighthood and an early license to colonize additional territories.

Richard Hakluyt authored two major publications advocating the establishment of an English colony in the New World and pursuit of a northwest passage, a route whereby ships could travel West to Asia rather than south around Africa before turning east to compete with Spanish-Asia trades. In 1584, Hakluyt presented his argument to Elizabeth. Early in her reign Elizabeth could not afford, both literally and metaphorically, to support imperialist voyages to the New World. Her claim to the throne, both as a woman and through her mother Anne Boleyn, was not strong enough to allow for much risk taking. The ongoing struggles between English Catholics and Protestants further complicated Elizabeth's early years. In the third decade of her reign she had considerably more power and security, so she could afford to listen to colonization schemes. Hakluyt's efforts contributed to Elizabeth's decision to grant Raleigh, Gilbert's half brother and another knight of her court, permission to pursue territory in North America.

Raleigh's expedition brought him to the eastern coast of North America, where he founded the Virginia territory in honor of the Virgin Queen and established the Roanoke colony, with Ralph Lane appointed as governor. In addition to establishing a colony, Elizabeth desired to create a base for privateers to raid Spanish settlements and ships. Raleigh also led expeditions to other North American territories, including Florida and North Carolina, to prospect for materials and observe the natives.

As time passed, the Roanoke colony failed to provide the geographical and financial support that the explorers had hoped it would. As supplies were scarce, those stationed in the colony desired to return to England. Ultimately, the initial attempts to colonize Virginia proved unsuccessful. While the fort at Roanoke failed, it would not be the last attempt by the English to establish a prominent colony. Elizabeth's role in granting permission and providing funds for colonial expeditions contributed to future efforts in establishing longer-lasting North American colonies, such as Jamestown.

Cynthia M. Zavala

See also Jamestown; Queens, African, Nzinga of Angola and Amina of Nigeria; Roanoke; Virginia Company

Further Reading

Fitzmaurice, Andrew. 2003. *Humanism and America: An Intellectual History of English Colonisation, 1500–1625*. New York: Cambridge University Press.

Mancall, Peter C. 1995. *Envisioning America: English Plans for the Colonization of North America, 1580–1640*. New York: Palgrave Macmillan.

Rubin, Nancy. 1991. *Isabella of Castile: The First Renaissance Queen*. New York: St. Martin's.

Weissberger, Barbara F. 2008. *Queen Isabel I of Castile: Power, Patronage, Persona*. New York: Boydell and Brewer.

Religion, Native American

Spirituality pervades Native American life. Indigenous people have traditionally been reverent, holding a holistic worldview of themselves within their environment. Native peoples have seen themselves as being in relationship with a spiritual universe where nature was considered a being and humans were part of nature. Kinship is a reflection of the intimate relationship and recognition that plants, animals, inanimate objects, and natural phenomena reflect the Great Spirit. Indigenous belief systems reflect sensibilities whereby the universe is suffused with preternatural forces and powerful spiritual beings that human must be in harmony with. Religion and spiritual rituals were infused inro all activities, including food gathering and hunting, social and political organization, and, when necessary, war. Some indigenous people use psychotropic plants to induce visions. Music and dance along with sacrifices are part of many religious practices.

Indigenous individuals traditionally go through gender-delineated rites of passage when they reach puberty; the individual endures a period of isolation and fasting to experience visions and engagement with the spirit world that takes various forms. Through this passage the individual endures hardship necessary to learn his or her life purpose, power, and character traits. Shamanism is a common belief and is connected to healing and seeing into the future whereby individuals seek to control aspects of the spiritual world through magic. A shaman (or medicine man or woman) is believed to have contact with the spirit or supernatural world. In Pueblo Indian cosmology and religious practices, kachinas (masked dancers), believed to embody a particular ancestral spirit, performed during ceremonies to communicate kinship with powerful ancestral beings.

An important aspect of giving thanks comes from the indigenous appreciation for being blessed with a bountiful environment that is a spiritual world. Many tribes ceremonially honor the first harvest and catch of the season to ensure that prosperity continues for posterity. Native American spirituality reflects the connection between the natural and the supernatural, with myth explaining reality in diverse ways. For instance, California Indians performed gendered tasks essential to economic stability, diplomatic intertribal relationships, and a sacred harmony. Spirit imbued the creation of baskets, from the basket-making materials to their eventual contents.

When Sir Francis Drake, in command of the *Golden Hind,* made the first European contact with Coast Miwoks in June 1579, the ship's chaplain and diarist Francis Fletcher described them as "of a tractable, free and loving nature, without guile or treachery." At the passing of a relative or loved one, aboriginal Californians wailed; ethnographers referred to this practice as a "cry." Coast Miwoks living in Marin County believed that the spirits of their ancestors traveled beyond Point Reyes, California, over the water west toward the setting sun. The setting sun created a line over the surf that was thought to lead the way to the home of the dead. Olompali was the site for annual mourning ceremonies and had a traditional burning ground near the village for cremations. When the English presented Coast Miwok leaders with shirts and linen cloth, the tribe presented the visitors with feathers, net caps, quivers for arrows, and animal skins. Fletcher chronicled how they returned to their homes and commenced with horrifying cries of lament, as if they were mourning the dead. Two days later a larger procession came to the invaders with more offerings. The men left gifts of bows, and women and children followed with additional gifts. The women displayed violent physical expressions of mourning to the point of inflicting bodily self-injury.

Anthropologists speculated that when the Coast Miwoks met the Europeans they believed they were meeting people returning from the dead. American anthropologist Alfred L. Kroeber (1876–1960) asserted that the baskets historically made only by the Coast Miwok, Pomo, Lake Miwok, and Wappo societies, were constructed and then destroyed to honor the dead. After first meeting Europeans Miwok women gave them a round basket filled with offerings. Women made elaborate baskets for rituals, both diplomatic and sacred. Sacred mourning baskets were filled with what the deceased would need for the journey to the land of the dead, and the baskets were destroyed to release the spirit of the basket contents and the natural materials used to make the baskets. Thus, at the conclusion of the diplomatic ceremonies with the first group of Europeans, Coast Miwoks destroyed the very baskets they had given as gifts, intending a benevolent release of the dead spirits for their journey back to the afterlife. Europeans saw the basket destruction not as a positive gesture, but as a hostile act.

The U.S. government historically wanted to open up tribal lands for settlement. Throughout the 19th century, the federal military, state militias, and citizen vigilantes forcibly removed tribes from ancestral lands, which contributed to the destruction of some indigenous belief systems. The Dawson Act of 1887 allowed for the division of shared community-held reservation lands into 160-acre allotments as a means to get Native Americans to forsake traditional tribal ways and relationships in order to become farmers. In the absence of traditional religion, indigenous women today experience a very high rate of domestic violence, rape, and gang rape in comparison to the broader population. They have little support and experience retaliation because tribal police are overwhelmed, and federal investigators are not local and are not engaged with immediate tribal issues. Women sometimes become double victims when they report assaults, first by the investigators and second by tribal males who see them as not loyal to tribal unity. The violence toward women is not part of traditional religion but instead is a symptom of the epidemic of alcohol and substance abuse, sustained poverty whereby the masculine balance is undermined, and a subversion of traditional indigenous diets that continues to challenge Native American populations.

Meredith Eliassen

See also Creation/Origin Stories; Hunter-Gatherers; *Vol. 4, Sec. 2:* Women of All Red Nations

Further Reading

Brody, J. J. 1990. *The Anasazi: Ancient Indian People of the American Southwest.* New York: Rizzoli.

Kroeber, A. L. 1976. *Handbook of the Indians of California.* New York: Dover.

Treuer, Anton, et al. 2010. *Indian Nations of North America.* Washington, DC: National Geographic.

Waldman, Carl. 2000. *Atlas of the North American Indian.* New York: Checkmark Books.

Roanoke

Roanoke Island, located between present-day North Carolina's shore and its Outer Banks, was the site of England's first attempt at establishing a permanent settlement in North America in 1585. The colony

disappeared three years later. One of the notable events that occurred in the colony's brief history was the birth of Virginia Dare on August 18, 1587, the first child of English parentage born in the New World. Women in the Roanoke colony as well as other early English communities in colonial Virginia struggled with difficult living conditions and high mortality rates.

The Roanoke colony had its origins in 1584, when Sir Walter Raleigh obtained permission to establish a base in North America that could be used to launch privateers to raid Spanish shipping. Raleigh sent two ships to scout for suitable locations. Roanoke Island proved ideal, since the islands on North Carolina's Outer Banks blocked it from view from Spanish ships. The tribal Roanoke *werowance* (leader) met with the English, who reported that they received his assurance that the natives supported the establishment of an English settlement on the island.

To facilitate relations between the Roanoke and English people, two Native Americans accompanied the English on their return to England. During the trip, the natives learned English and taught their Algonquian dialect to Thomas Harriot, a scientist on the expedition. Harriot would become famous for *a Briefe and True Report of the New Found Land of Virginia,* the book about Roanoke he published in 1588. The trip had a profound effect on the two native observers. Manteo, one of the two native men, saw great promise in a partnership with the English and would later serve as an interpreter for the last attempt to colonize Roanoke Island.

In 1585 a fleet of seven ships, commanded by Richard Grenville and containing roughly 600 men, arrived at Roanoke Island. Grenville's forces constructed a fort that became the site of the British colony of Virginia, named in honor of Queen Elizabeth I. Grenville returned to England a short time later, leaving 108 soldiers at the fort under the command of Ralph Lane. Thus, this first attempt at a colony was more a military outpost than a real community, and as such no English women were present. Lane believed in the use of force to settle disputes, a tactic that caused war between the natives and the English during the winter of 1585–1586. Sir Francis Drake, a privateer, passed Roanoke Island in June 1856 and found the Englishmen in desperate straits, and he took them

Eleanor White Dare gave birth to the first white, Christian child in the British colonies in 1587. Baptized Virginia, after the colony where she was born, the baby disappeared with other Roanoke colonists sometime in the three years after her birth. (Library of Congress)

back to England. An all-male military-style colony had spectacularly failed.

Determined to establish a permanent settlement in Virginia, Elizabeth I appointed John White governor of a new colony. Unlike the previous all-male settlement efforts, White brought with him some women, including 14 separate families. His pregnant daughter Eleanor and her husband Ananias Dare joined the party, and their child, Virginia, became the first European child born in the Americas. This new group settled at the site of Grenville's fort but had little contact with the local natives, with the exception of the Croatoans.

The English female colonists would have encountered shockingly difficult conditions. Homes were rude shelters that barely kept out the elements, and food was always in short supply. Basic domestic responsibilities such as food preparation and laundry would have been exceedingly difficult to accomplish. Female colonists were vastly outnumbered by men, a fact that would have increased each woman's workload. Eleanor Dare

gave birth to the first English child born in the New World in 1587. Happily, both mother and baby survived the birth, an accomplishment that should not be underestimated given the low standards of hygiene and nutrition in the colony.

In August, the Roanokes killed one of the colonists, who retaliated by attacking a Croatoan village, mistaking them for Roanokes. With supplies running dangerously low, John White, baby Virginia Dare's grandfather, shipped out for England in hopes of resupplying the colony. He was unable to return until 1590 due to England's war with Spain. When he arrived at Roanoke Island, aside from the cryptic message "Croatoan" carved on a post there was no sign as to the fate of the colonists who at that time had included 17 women and 9 children. Roanoke became the "Lost Colony" and its fate an unsolved mystery. Most probably colonists were killed or captured by the Crotoans.

The history of the English occupation of Roanoke Island from 1585 to 1587 had ramifications for the

English for decades to come. Word of the atrocities committed by Lane, most notably the decapitation of Wingina, spread far from the coast of present-day North Carolina. The Powhatan Confederacy, which dominated the Chesapeake Bay area of present-day Virginia, likely knew the reputation of the English before they arrived to establish the Jamestown colony and thus interacted with them more cautiously. England also discovered that colonists better negotiated the rigors of establishing new colonies if they had some women among them, though in the case of Roanoke women did little to ameliorate the English's poor relationships with local native people.

In 1937 a tourist claimed to have found a stone carved by Eleanor Dare. Before 1940 nearly 48 stones were subsequently found. One of the stones purported to call for revenge upon the native people who had kidnapped the Roanoke colonists. Another claimed that Eleanor had married into the local tribe and had a daughter. All but the first stone were later proven to be a hoax, but they suggest how interested Americans are in the fate of the lost Roanoke colonists.

John R. Burch Jr.

See also Jamestown; Powhatan People; Queens, European, Elizabeth I of England and Isabella of Castile; *Vol. 1, Sec. 2:* Dare, Eleanor and Virginia

Further Reading

Horn, James. 2010. *A Kingdom Strange: The Brief and Tragic History of the Lost Colony of Roanoke.* New York: Basic Books.

Kupperman, Karen Ordahl. 2007. *Roanoke: The Abandoned Colony.* 2nd ed. Lanham, MD: Rowman and Littlefield.

Oberg, Michael Leroy. 2008. *The Head in Edward Nugent's Hand: Roanoke's Forgotten Indians.* Philadelphia: University of Pennsylvania Press.

Sexuality

Sexuality in early America varied as a result of cultural, religious, social, and economic perspectives and expectations of men and women. Both precolonial and colonial Euro-Americans subscribed to a patriarchal gender hierarchy in which men were dominant over women. A woman's sexual purity or loyalty was used to establish her worth: she must remain chaste until marriage and remain monogamous until her death, complying with the sexual will of her partner. In contrast, the majority of Native American tribes did not have an established gender hierarchy. Men, women, and berdaches—the third gender of the majority of tribes—were treated as equal in society and in partnerships, and as a consequence indigenous people were significantly less rigid about sexuality than their Euro-American counterparts.

Sexual encounters between European conquerors and Native American women ranged from violent subjugation to willing compliance. The reports of many early explorers throughout the Americas heavily eroticize both the land and women; due to the intimate connection between the two, conquest of land and sexual congress of natives intertwined. Although some accounts implied that native women had voracious sexual appetites that led them to compliance in all sexual matters, coercion and fear certainly played a role in many of these encounters, many of which could best be described as rape. Conquering Euro-Americans engaged in both short- and long-term sexual connections with native women, much as Hernán Cortés took the native woman Malinche as his sexual concubine before passing her to another soldier.

It is difficult to decipher instances of sexual assault and rape in colonial America, because the majority of historical accounts are from the perspective of European males. For European women, sexual violation physically and spiritually affected not only the victim but also her family and community due to the concepts of integrity and dignity embedded in the woman's honor code, and thus incidents were not readily discussed. Native American women, however, were not held to this standard; as a result, there are more accounts of their subjugation in sexual encounters. While some of these women may have received mutual satisfaction from these experiences, others may have complied only out of fear and situational factors or unsuccessfully resisted repeated assault from their captors.

Not all European conquerors engaged in sexual activity with the natives. Some colonizers disapproved of interracial couplings and adopted antimiscegenation practices as a result. Some religious figures, such as missionaries, condemned both the sexuality of the tribes and the intermingling of Europeans with natives. Other missionaries, however, encouraged miscegenation (interracial sex) as a means to religious and cultural conversion over time.

The Native American tribes maintained a distinct perspective on sexuality from Europeans and colonial America that was generally more open to sexual exploration and less connected to marriage and religion. Unlike the European colonists, some Native American tribes did not reproach premarital sex; it was even encouraged that both young men and young women explore their sexuality. Furthermore, sex in general was not an activity exclusively reserved for reproductive purposes. Both men and women could have multiple partners (polygyny and polyandry, respectively) and easily separate or divorce. Same-sex marriages, usually between a male or female and a berdache of the same biological sex, were also socially accepted in most tribes. These marriages were not utilized as the same lifetime-binding contract between husband and wife in European society.

Another element of Native American sexuality often misinterpreted by European explorers and colonizers was the distinction between gender and biological sex. The majority of tribes had three genders: male, female, and a third, sometimes called berdache, that invoked mixed-gender spirits or a nonbinary person. Sexually active berdaches usually engaged in sexual intercourse with same-sex partners in the passive position. To Europeans, this appeared to be a homosexual relationship and therefore was shameful and emasculating, particularly for the male-male sexed partnerships. This perspective, however, was not maintained by the individual tribes who did not view relationships with berdaches as lesser than heterosexual couplings.

For colonial Euro-Americans, sentiments toward sexuality were largely influenced by cultural and religious perspectives. Based on the honor code, a woman was expected to abstain from sexual activity until marriage and remain faithful to her husband until death. In New England premarital sex was not permitted, but marital sex played an important role in society to promote familial stability, especially to determine legitimacy and transfer of property. Although Puritan society limited sex for the purposes of procreation, a healthy and mutually satisfying sex life was encouraged to better guarantee conception. Protestants, likewise, adopted a similar view of encouraging marital sex to combat extramarital sexual deviancy.

The emphasis of discussion and understanding of same-sex pairings was not driven by sexual orientation as an identity but instead by the action of sodomy. As such, legislation passed in the New Haven colony was phrased to condemn the act of sexual transgressions with specific reference to the "misuse of genital organs" and not to the gender of the participants. In general, extramarital sexual activities were illegal in New England, including same-sex practices and masturbation. A woman bearing an illegitimate child was considered both a shameful and punishable offense.

Throughout these societies, the convergence of diverse cultural perspectives shaped early American sentiments toward sexuality. The presence of Judeo-Christian European colonizers diminished the fluid sexual practices of Native American tribes. The establishment of Anglo-Christian colonies shaped colonial American perspectives and laws regarding sex as intimately connected to religion. As a result, the sexuality of women was bound to the patriarchal honor code imported from the colonizers to the New World.

Cynthia M. Zavala

See also Berdache/Transgendering; Malinche; Polygamy, Native American

Further Reading

Foster, Thomas A. 2007. *Long before Stonewall: Histories of Same-Sex Sexuality in Early America.* New York: New York University Press.

Ryan, Mary P. 2006. *Mysteries of Sex: Tracing Women and Men through American History.* Chapel Hill: University of North Carolina Press.

Smith, Merril D., ed. 1998. *Sex and Sexuality in Early America.* New York: New York University Press.

Slavery, Native Americans

Different forms of captivity existed among Native American societies long before the arrival of Europeans. How that captivity manifested itself varied widely across the continent. Among the Iroquois, captives were sometimes adopted into families to fill the roles of deceased relatives. Some groups exchanged members of their communities while negotiating trade agreements as an expression of trust and goodwill. Others utilized captives for diplomatic exchanges. One type of captivity that was not native to the Americas was chattel slavery, which was introduced into the New World by Europeans. This new form of captivity put an economic value on slaves, which completely destabilized native societies. Peoples victimized by slavers also went on the warpath, seeking to free their kinsmen and women. Migration became an alternative for those who did not wish to go to war. The escalating cycles of violence benefited the respective European powers, as they not only gained slaves but also gained access to land due to native depopulation.

The Spanish were the first to enslave the natives they encountered. Hernán Cortés's expedition used a native slave woman named Malinche as a translator on several expeditions. When Hernando de Soto's expedition explored the Southeast, the explorers used their captives to serve as guides. The Spanish treated many of their native slaves with such brutality that the Spanish Crown officially outlawed the practice before the end of the 16th century. As a replacement for the newly freed natives, the Spanish began importing African slaves. In the eyes of the Spanish, it was acceptable to enslave Africans because, unlike Native Americans, the Spanish believed that it was not possible for them to become Catholic. Despite the royal decree, the enslavement of native peoples still continued in Spanish-held areas. To foster the practice, the Spanish held fairs every year to exchange slaves with both Spaniards and Native American traders. Native American women were often purchased for use as concubines or sex slaves, making their enslavement doubly horrifying.

The French did not initially accept slaves into their midst when they were establishing New France. This changed in 1709 when slavery was legalized by their ruler in the New World. French citizens embraced the new institution, which resulted in a significant increase in the demand for native captives. During the Fox Wars, the French found native allies by promising them that they could enslave any Fox they encountered. Although the French, like their European counterparts, used slaves as currency, they did not value them so highly that they became more profitable than trading in furs.

Since the early English settlements were business ventures, slave labor promised larger profits for investors. This was especially true as agricultural products, such as tobacco, proved to be the most profitable commodities. Enslaving natives posed several problems for the English. The natives did not prove to be hearty, as many died from diseases such as smallpox. There was always the possibility that they would run away and try to rejoin their people. The consequence of enslaving local natives was the possibility of war. In many tribes it was the women who called for war in these situations. Enslavement of native children was a significant factor in the Tuscarora War in North Carolina. By the mid-18th century, African slavery had supplanted the enslavement of Native Americans.

In general, Europeans preferred to enslave women and children because they believed that they were less likely to try to escape. Since most of the slaveholders were men, they also wanted the females so they could sexually exploit them. This was especially true of the Spanish- and French-inhabited locales, as men made up a majority of the European populations of those areas. Over time, the Spanish and French began marrying native women instead of enslaving them. This change not only improved relations between the Europeans and the natives but also allowed for the formation of kinship relationships that proved beneficial for both cultures. Native American wives subsequently became cultural brokers who were valued within both of the societies they inhabited.

Although evidence exists that some native slaves were still being taken by the descendants of the Spanish conquistadors into the mid-19th century, the practice had ceased in the other parts of North America by the early 18th century. Around 1790 in the South, some Native American elites began emulating their American neighbors and adopted plantation agriculture, including the use of Africans as slave labor. This proved destabilizing to native societies, as it reflected a change in how elites used the wealth they accumulated. A cultural norm that could be seen across native societies throughout North America was the distribution of wealth from the chiefs to their followers. Generosity was a gauge to demonstrate one's effectiveness as a leader. This changed with the arrival of plantation agriculture. Suddenly elites, most notably among the Creek Confederacy, quit sharing their wealth and began amassing large fortunes, including many slaves.

This created not just a growing economic divide but also a racial divide. Many Creek communities welcomed escaped slaves and made them kin through either adoption or marriage. Creeks with African-descended relatives rightfully saw slaveholding elites as a threat. This division was one of the causes of the Creek War of 1813–1814, a civil war among the Creeks. The protection of African Seminoles was one of the reasons that the Seminoles fought three wars with the United States. Some Native Americans continued to hold African and African American slaves until the conclusion of the American Civil War, when the practice was outlawed by the United States.

John R. Burch Jr.

See also Iroquois Confederacy; *Vol. 1, Sec. 2:* Slavery, African

Further Reading

Brooks, James F. 2002. *Captives & Cousins: Slavery, Kinship, and Community in the Southwest Borderlands.* Chapel Hill: University of North Carolina Press.
Gallay, Alan. 2002. *The Indian Slave Trade: The Rise of the English Empire in the American South, 1670–1717.* New Haven, CT: Yale University Press.
Gallay, Alan, ed. 2009. *Indian Slavery in Colonial America.* Lincoln: University of Nebraska Press.
Snyder, Christina. 2010. *Slavery in Indian Country: The Changing Face of Captivity in Early America.* Cambridge, MA: Harvard University Press.

Spider Woman

The idea or philosophy of Spider Woman, or Grandmother Spider, is something many pre-Christian civilizations throughout the Americas share for teaching about creation and the creative process. The Huichols of western Mexico call her Takutsi Nakawe, the Navajo call her Sus-Sistinnako and also Changing Woman, and the Hopis call her Kokyangwuti, the grandmother of the sun and the great medicine power who sang people into the fourth and present world. The Kiowas call her Konatasohi, and the Cherokees call her Kanane'ski Amai'yehi. The Keres of the Pueblo call her Cochito, or Thought Woman.

The spider defined the world by stretching its legs from the place of emergence and by partitioning Earth into four parts. Among the Lagunas, Grandmother Spider, or Old Spider Woman, brought the light, weaving, medicine, and life. Among the Keres she was known as Thought Woman who created humans and keeps them in creation even now. Spider Woman, Ts'its'tsi'nako, or Thought Woman created through her thinking mind. She also created the Kacina, or spirit messengers and protectors.

These women, through their changing nature and creative thought, teach several fundamental principles that seek to guide the development of balanced relationships and keep humans in harmony with the rest of the world. The intricate patterns of the web that Spider Woman weaves teaches followers to look for the patterns in the world, the power of connection, and that all beings are creations and therefore relatives, making survival tied to respect for all life. Her web forms a medicine wheel, a way of discovering oneself and one's place in the world by learning how to perceive the proper balance of relationships among all creation. The gifts of medicine that she teaches take infinite forms of knowledge and understanding and are gained through seeking life in all its infinite forms.

Spider Woman also reflects the recognition of many civilizations that female creativity is central to the universe and finds balance with male forces. Concepts of masculinity and femininity, such as sexuality, were unlike those introduced with European Christianity. The creator was most often identified as female though at times transformed into male. In the Southwest, spider webs along with vulvas were incised into rocks about 7500 to 600–900 BCE. In circular or polygonal houses and temples throughout the Americas, symbols of this understanding or perception of creation include the full moon; the spider web; the womb, or place of emergence into the present world; and a multilayered vertical universe or cosmic egg.

These perceptions not only informed gender relationships and promoted complementary and equal relationships between men and women but also respected and allowed space for all expressions and variations of gender and sexuality. Women were valued in their role as vitalizers and not just child bearers. The feminine is also recognized as being both creative and destructive, with destruction being a force that allows for regeneration and recreation rather than brute or unnecessary force. The Lakotas also understood all of Earth and its creatures as being intelligent, alive, and intricately and inherently connected. Mothers and mother goddesses are all an aspect of Grandmother Spider, or Thought Woman.

The universal characteristics of life are embodied in the oral tradition, composed of rituals and narratives that begin with Grandmother Spider, or aspects of creation. With the social transformation from egalitarian to patriarchal systems caused by European conquest, mother creators were masculinized. The primacy of female as creator was displaced with ideas such as the Great Spirit. The Hopi goddess of Spider Woman became Maseo or Tawa, referred to in the masculine. Among the Cherokees, the goddess of the River Foam was replaced by thunder in many tales. Among the Iroquois, Sky Woman often gathered her ideas from her dead father or her monstrous grandson. This was the first step in replacing a gender-complementary system with masculine deities. Scholars and activists believe that recovering imagery of mother creators is crucial to Indian resistance to cultural and spiritual genocide.

Leleua Loupe

See also Matrilineal Descent

Further Reading

Carmean, Kelli. 2002. *Spider Woman Walks This Land: Traditional Cultural Properties and the Navajo Nation.* Walnut Creek, CA: Altamira.

Gunn-Allen, Paula. 1986. *The Sacred Hoop: Recovering the Feminine in American Indian Traditions.* Boston: Beacon.

Shuetz-Miller, Mardith K. 2012. "Spider Grandmother and Other Avatars of the Moon Goddess in New World Sacred Architecture." *Journal of the Southwest* 54(2) (Summer): 283–295.

Transatlantic Slave Trade, Women

The transatlantic slave trade refers to the enslavement and transportation of people from Central and West Africa to the plantations of North and South America beginning in the 16th century. African scholars refer to it as the Maafa, which is Swahili for "holocaust," because the term "trade" denotes commercial transactions that benefit, or have the possibility of benefiting, both sides.

In addition to being enslaved for labor, women, and to a lesser extent men, were exploited sexually, establishing a sex trade. Coming mostly from the west coast of Africa and representing diverse ethnic groups, African women arrived at the slave ports after being torn from their families, where they had been agriculturalists, weavers, warriors, and leaders. They were often kept naked in subterranean dungeons and then exposed again naked to European buyers who inspected their eyes, ears, mouths, legs, rectum, and genitalia before they were shipped to the Caribbean and North America. Businessmen branded and shackled women, children, and men and forced them to huddle naked aboard ships. Women joined in acts of resistance against traders and crews in at least 55 mutinies between 1699 and 1845.

The progression in slave trading from the eastern Atlantic to the western Atlantic coincided with the voyages of Christopher Columbus, under the patronage of the Spanish Crown. Columbus introduced sugarcane to the Caribbean and ushered in the development of the indigenous holocaust, the transatlantic slave system, and the sex trade in the Americas. The demographic disaster of the Amerindians served to expand and perpetuate the transatlantic dimension of the slave trade. Women's skills in agriculture and domestic services were crucial to any enterprise, and women were additionally exploited later for their reproductive value.

The official launch of the Middle Passage began when Spain issued the *asiento* in 1518 to supply laborers directly from Africa to satisfy the new demand for labor created by the commercialization of the

Caribbean sugar industry. The first voyage from Africa directly to the Americas destined for the Caribbean occurred in 1525. Over the whole period of the transatlantic slave trade, 36 percent of people transported were women, and they were used primarily as field hands, domestics, and sources for sexual gratification or partnership.

The trade became a commercial highway that interconnected all the continents and their kin. Sugar plantations, particularly in the Caribbean and Latin America, absorbed over two-thirds of those transported. The English dominated the North European slave trade and supplied the English and Spanish colonies and plantations with labor. The Portuguese dominated the southern slave trade and supplied the plantations in Brazil.

Initially, Europeans and then Indigenous peoples of the Americas supplied the bulk of labor in the early years. But by the 1560s, the enslavement of Africans for labor increased in the Spanish Empire due to the declining availability of indigenous peoples and the lowering of duties on Africans.

Historians estimated that between 1450 and 1850 up to 15.4 million people survived their kidnapping in Africa to be brought to labor in the Americas. Less than 5 percent came to the United States. Though the U.S. Congress outlawed the transatlantic slave trade in 1807, the law did not entirely stop the flow of Africans into the country. By 1825 the southern states had the largest enslaved population in the world.

The population of Africa stagnated at 100 million between 1650 and 1850, while that of Europe and Asia doubled and tripled. Fertile and productive areas of West Africa were left empty as people were stolen and killed through military devastation. Consequently, development in science and technology and medical knowledge stagnated. The economic system that developed became distorted, violent, legalistic, and entangled in the traffic of humans. Wars were fought to enlarge empires that would supply humans to European slavers. The creation of larger states and empires enlarged the ruling classes' control over political, economic, and social resources to the detriment of most Africans.

Women, central to many West African communities, became those most likely to be enslaved. The main victims were the healthy robust population ages 15 to 30, the strongest of the community and the next generation of leaders, scientists, nation builders, healers, and teachers, impacting the development of African society and its continent. This process also began the devaluation and exploitation of women in African societies. As Europeans enforced a new capitalist system, they also enforced a new gender and status system.

In the Americas, enslaved women were doubly burdened. By 1662 black African slavery was firmly established in Virginia, with other colonies to follow. There the nature of slavery in America was distinctly gendered, and that year all children, regardless of patrimony, born to enslaved women were declared, held in bondage, or free only according to the conditions of the mother.

In the middle and northern colonies, the economy was diversified. Women lived on smaller farms and engaged in a wide range of tasks that were not necessarily gendered. They cared for children and the elderly, butchered livestock, and farmed. Some worked as midwives, seamstresses, or weavers, and sometimes masters permitted them to hire themselves out to earn extra money. In the South most worked in agriculture, something they were familiar with from Africa. West Africans introduced and allowed for a successful rice crop in the Carolinas. Most tended tobacco, rice, or indigo crops.

Some women earned freedom by pleasing their masters, developing familial relationships, performing exceptional acts, or buying their freedom. Freedwomen managed to earn a living, establish families, build community institutions, and possess private property.

Leleua Loupe

See also *Vol. 1, Sec. 2:* Free Blacks, Colonial, Revolutionary War, and New Republic Periods; Slavery, African; *Vol. 2, Sec. 1:* Free Black Women; Miscegenation

Further Reading

Hagemann, K., and J. Rendall. 2010. *Gender, War and Politics: Transatlantic Perspectives on the Wars of Revolution and Liberation, 1775–1830.* London: Palgrave Macmillan.

Sheffer, J. A. 2012. *The Romance of Race: Incest, Miscegenation, and Multiculturalism in the United States, 1880–1930.* New Brunswick, NJ: Rutgers University Press.

Thompson, A. O. 2008. "The African Maafa: The Impact of the Transatlantic Slave Trade on Western Africa." *Journal of Caribbean History* 41(1): 67–92.

Transgendering. *See* Berdache/ Transgendering

Virginia Company

The Virginia Company was two competing branches of a commercial enterprise supported by investors and granted a charter by King James I of England in 1606 to establish settlements on the East Coast of North America. The most successful of these was Jamestown, which became a stable self-sustaining enterprise when a good working relationship with the local Native Americans was achieved, when tobacco became a profitable export, and when women were recruited to give the colony permanence and stability. Though the types of women ranged from genteel to slave labor, their presence and contributions to the Virginia Company were vital.

The English laid claim to the area known collectively as Virginia, which at that time encompassed the entire Eastern Seaboard of today's United States from Canada southward to the present-day North Carolina. The joint-stock ventures were called the Virginia Company of London (or London Company) and the Virginia Company of Plymouth (or Plymouth Company). Their charter provided the rights of trade, exploration, settlement, and self-government.

To counter the Roman Catholic Spaniards in North America, the Protestant English were determined that their own colonies would thrive. The charters of the Virginia Company branches were the same, but their territories were different. The more northward area that eventually became New England was to be developed by the Virginia Company of Plymouth but did not succeed. Its colony in Maine was abandoned in 1607 after about a year. With the arrival of religious pilgrims aboard the *Mayflower* in 1620, a subsequent Plymouth Company established a permanent settlement in Massachusetts.

When the original Virginia Company of Plymouth was officially declared a failure, its grant of self-government was not formally revoked, either intentionally or otherwise. This principle of self-government became a cornerstone for the concept of democracy in the American colonies.

In 1607 the Virginia Company of London, the more southerly branch, founded the first English settlement in North America to become permanent. It was in today's state of Virginia, with the community and waterway on which it stood named Jamestown and the James River, respectively, in honor of the king. Almost immediately, sickness, starvation, and strife with local Native American tribes under the Powhatan Confederacy brought the colony to the edge of collapse.

However, a Native American woman was the catalyst in its salvation. Pocahontas (ca. 1595–1617) was the daughter of Chief Powhatan. Captain John Smith, president of the Jamestown Council, was a strong leader who was able to forge a working relationship with the Native Americans. In what may have been a ceremonial tribal membership ritual, Pocahontas saved Smith from execution. Smith later recounted the incident as an example of Native American cooperation, thus safeguarding potential investments.

After suffering an injury, Smith returned to England. On April 5, 1614, Pocahontas married colonist John Rolfe, who successfully cultivated a new strain of tobacco that became the colony's extremely profitable export. Pocahontas adopted the English religion and took an English education. This time of harmony between the Native Americans and English colonists became known as the Peace of Pocahontas. Pocahontas and Rolfe lived on Rolfe's plantation, Varina Farms, on the James River and later in England. They had a child, Thomas Rolfe, born on January 30, 1615. With peace foreseeable through the union with Pocahontas and a cash crop nurtured by her husband, the settlement showed every prospect of being a secure destination for colonists. This meant recruiting women.

Many of the early colonists were male adventurers who had visions of soon finding gold or silver, then returning to England as rich men. This turned out not to be the case, and with males outnumbering English females by a ratio of six to one, they had little incentive to stay. Deteriorating relations with the Native Americans did not encourage unions with native women by either the English or the tribes themselves.

In 1619, the Virginia Company began recruiting English women as marriage prospects for Jamestown settlers in the belief that only through the presence of family units with wives and children could the settlement flourish. Women could apply to be sponsored by the Virginia Company by providing a reference attesting that they were respectable as well as being "young" and "handsome." The Virginia Company provided basic bedding and one set of clothes for the women, most of whom were married soon after arrival.

With the economic boom that same year in the high-grade tobacco successfully developed by John Rolfe, the Jamestown settlers scurried to find land to cultivate. When they did, hard labor followed. From 1619 onward, time and energy had to be devoted to planting, hoeing, tilling, weeding, and harvesting the inedible crop. The domestic skills of women in England generally included producing butter, cheese, beer, and homespun fabric, not constant agricultural toil. In America, they now had to work in the fields in addition to cooking, cleaning, and other domestic labor to keep the home running.

With the convergence of these factors, the year 1619 brought forth an event that would change American history forever. A ship bearing 20 kidnapped Africans appeared on the James River. With the human cargo enslaved to labor in the tobacco fields, the era of a plantation-based economy and the African slave trade had begun. Enslaved African woman were valued commodities for both their ability to work hard in homes and fields and their ability to breed more slave labor. Children born to enslaved African women inherited slave status through their mother regardless of paternity. The Virginia Company succeeded but at a great cost.

Nancy Hendricks

See also Pocahontas; Powhatan People; Transatlantic Slave Trade, Women

Further Reading

Bernhard, Virginia. 2011. *A Tale of Two Colonies: What Really Happened in Virginia and Bermuda?* Columbia: University of Missouri Press.

Brown, Kathleen M. 1996. *Good Wives, Nasty Wenches, and Anxious Patriarchs: Gender, Race, and Power in Colonial Virginia.* Chapel Hill: University of North Carolina Press.

McCartney, Martha W. 2007. *Virginia Immigrants and Adventurers: A Biographical Dictionary, 1607–1635.* Baltimore: Genealogical Publishing.

THEMATIC ISSUES ESSAY

Fertility and Fertility Control

Women's ability to create and sustain life was recognized, honored, and celebrated throughout the Americas. Women's phases of fertility, pregnancy, childbirth, motherhood, and marriage, important life-cycle phases, were recognized as providing particular status and empowerment. In Pueblo society, sexuality was recognized and celebrated as the source of life and a means of taming negative spirits in nature and of integrating outsiders into the nation. Pueblo ideology recognized women's sexual power, and like their role in food production, they contributed to egalitarian relationships between the sexes. The existence of many goddesses, often referred to as mother or grandmother, indicated a sacred reverence for female fertility and women as creative agents. Earth mothers and corn goddesses ordered the worldview, and effigies, abundant in the archaeological record throughout the Americas, are believed to be associated with fertility and fruitfulness (Claasen and Rosemary 1997, 77–79).

During menstruation and childbirth, periods of great transformation, women were perceived as being increasingly powerful. The Mayas credited the moon with governing women's menstrual cycles and the planting of maize. Oral traditions tell of women who had the power to transform into different beings, such as deer; copulate with different beings, such as panthers and earthworms; and deliver mixed babies. At contact, people throughout eastern North America, such as Acadians and Malecites, built separate cabins for menstruating women. The Narragansetts called the houses *weuomemese,* meaning "little house." Women of the Great Basin, such as among the Paiutes, also spent their menses separated and observed food and body taboos. It is likely that these houses were associated with female ritual and ceremony that was conducted on a monthly basis and associated with pregnancy and childbirth. In addition to simple biological concerns or observances, postpartum and menstruating women were recognized as conduits of change for good or ill. Due to the phenomenon of menstrual synchrony, when females who live together sync their menstrual cycles, it is likely that women of the same house spent time together doing ceremonial or ritual activities. They probably spent time resting, talking, telling stories, gambling, engaging in ritual purification at the end to burn blood-stained supplies, and bathing to practice good hygiene. Contrary to the interpretations of women's rituals and practices from early Europeans at contact, studies suggest that they were advantageous to women. Such practices were also characteristic of precontact American societies where husbands and males were not particularly dominant, especially in matrilineal and matrilocal societies.

In addition to valuing women for their reproductive powers, women also had knowledge of how to control them. According to the archaeological record, women in semisedentary societies in California spaced their births further apart, and later as permanent villages replaced seasonal rounds (ca. 1300 CE), birth spacing decreased. Comparatively, Native American women had fewer children than Europeans, nursing for three years and using herbs to induce abortion or practicing abortion to space births. In Ohio during the Hopewell culture, the archaeological record reveals an increase on reliance on local seeds for weaning foods that shortened the nursing period and eliminated it as a contraceptive (Claasen and Rosemary 1997, 72). Mississippian women of the East in the 1300s had high life expectancy and generally waited until their 20s to bear children. They practiced birth control through abstinence or taboos or had knowledge of plants to control their fertility (Claasen and Rosemary 1997, 125–126). Among the Cherokees, *Datura stramonium* may have been used to induce abortion or treat difficult childbirth, and in the East blue cohosh was used (Claasen and Rosemary 1997, 60).

Courtship, Marriage, and Divorce

The women of eastern cultures, such as the Natchezes of the Southeast, arranged marriages. Illiniwek women carried kettles, animal skins, buffalo meat, and clothing as gifts from the prospective male spouse in their lineage to the cabin of the woman he wished to wed. In Mayan marriage negotiations cloth was associated with women, while chocolate was associated with men. There was a reciprocal obligation for the bride's father to provide a dowry to the wife receivers, paid in cacao beans, and the wedding feast. During the feast, the husband provided raw food to the woman for her to cook and present to him as a sign of their union. This exchange symbolized their reciprocal obligations to each other for their life.

Prior to contact, most people traced their ancestry through the mother or both parents. In the Southwest, many people recognized matrilineal descent. Women's control of land and its produce ensured their economic agency and empowerment. Pueblos in the Southwest were also matrilocal, where the husband accompanied his wife to her family's home. A woman's identity therefore rested with her family and not with her husband. Women dissolved a marriage by placing a husband's belongings outside of the home.

For many societies, women's maturity was associated with marriage rather than the onset of menses. In the East this phase was marked partially by the wearing of an apron or skirt. For the Mayas, marriage was essential for both men and women to fulfill their potential for mutual independence. Both, however, could easily divorce, and Mayan women retained control over their home and agricultural fields. Mayan aristocratic men could have wives and concubines, but the general population practiced monogamy. Mayan women typically married between the ages of 14 and 15, while men married around the age of 18.

The economic systems that prevailed in the Americas were often based not on the accumulation of wealth but rather on the communal use and distribution of land and resources, most often managed by the woman's family. Concepts of bastardy or illegitimacy did not exist due to the nonexistent practice of wealth accumulation and male inheritance. Divorce was equally a simple process for both men and women, and there was no stigma associated with breaking a union. For most women of Mesoamerica, the Southwestern and Eastern Woodlands, they would simply put the men's belongings outside of the family's house to signify the end of the relationship. Because women maintained the home and food production, the children were always provided for.

Marriage customs differed in the Northwest from one group to another. Central coast Salish women tended to marry outside of their kin group and move to the residence of the husband. Arranged marriages often ensured economic security for the children by creating alliances and access to more resources through a complex system of reciprocity and exchange. Children obtained the privileges and wealth associated with both the mother and father. In wealthy families, members claimed their privileges and rights to resources from their heritage of a certain ancestral "house" (Kennedy 2007, 6, 28). The Eyaks, Tlingits, Tsimshians, Haidas, and Haislas were matrilineal, while most tribes on the southern Northwest coast traced descent through both the mother and father (Walter 2006, 42). Chiefs were polygynous, or married several women, representing up to 25 percent of married men at contact. Most men and women were monogamous (Walter 2006, 42). Senior wives supervised the labor of junior wives and slaves and had time to manufacture ceremonial and trade items important in potlaching and trade. Studies of the coastal Salishes suggest that separation through divorce or death of the male spouse meant that the wife would likely return to her natal family. Babies would go with the mother in cases of divorce, and older children would go with the husband or his family.

Childbirth and Child Rearing

Birthing practices were not widely studied or recorded at contact but must have varied between groups and probably depended on the economy and structure of society; however, little ethnographic evidence exists to make a distinction. According to ethnographic records, pregnant women followed diets, often interpreted as food taboos, and usually continued normal daily routines until the onset of active labor. As birth time neared, the mother often left her village alone or in the care of one or two older women, destined for a special house separate from the village. Women sometimes remained in a vertical posture, hanging, standing, kneeling, or squatting to facilitate birth (Plane 1999). Some accounts report that in Canadian communities younger members aided the mother in making startling noises

While anthropologists and historians generally focus on the activities of men by focusing on politics and war, indigenous women played a central role in their often matriarchal and matrilineal communities, powers granted to them by their combined activities in food production and child birth and child rearing. Indigenous peoples particularly recognized the importance of these spheres of activity. (Library of Congress)

to procure an immediate delivery. Among the Micmacs and Cherokees, women's arms were sometimes attached above to a pole, with their nose, ears, and mouth stopped up while pressing on the belly of the mother to hasten delivery. Medicine people were also called upon to provide external applications of herbs and roots and conduct sweat baths. Tinctures of herbs hastened delivery or eased the pain. Tobacco may have been used as an offering to spirits during labor.

Ideas about childbirth pain probably varied as much with indigenous women then as they do now. However, Algonquian people valued emotional control, self-reliance, and reticence and recognized the value of decreasing fear and discomfort to encourage a successful birth. Cree women and their attendants minimized the moments in which fear or pain interfered with self-control. For the Mayas and later the Aztecs, birth was seen as a battle in which an infant could kill its mother, and therefore pregnancy and labor were equated with sacred blood sacrifice. This view conferred great honor upon the mother. During labor the Mayan midwife placed an image of Ix Chel, the goddess of childbirth, under a laboring woman's bed. The Aztec midwives were renowned for their professional training.

In most societies, once birthed the baby was washed and then wrapped in soft animal skins, often of beaver, and placed on a cradleboard. Among some peoples the baby was fed some oil of seal, bear, or other respected animals. Some kept the naval cord in a bag that was kept around the baby's neck to signify their desire that the newborn develop as a balanced or centered being. Some women returned to normal activities following recovery, while others stayed in the birth house for a month or more. Like during their menses, pregnant and postpartum women were perceived as being especially powerful, and special precautions were taken to maintain balance. In one account a pregnant woman's presence was required to make a certain root effective in removing an arrow from a wounded man. European perceptions of these taboos as demeaning women long skewed historians' ability to understand native childbirth practices.

Just as women were valued in most American societies precontact, children were cherished. The birth of a child represented personal wealth and good fortune. The caring for and guiding of children to maturity and responsible citizenship was the most important obligation of the family and the community. Mothers and fathers shared in the responsibility of providing for children, while older children and elders assisted in their care and guidance. There were no orphans among most pre-Columbian societies; children were welcomed in by extended family and relatives. Elders instructed youths in laws and traditions of the people designed to foster a balanced social, political, economic, and spiritual world. Children were encouraged to seek the advice of elders and learn from their

experience (Costo and Costo 1995). Oral tradition instructed parents on how to raise healthy and functional adults. Stories that feature trickster characters such as the coyote as a father warn parents against negative consequences of sexual abuse and incest. Rituals and ceremonies marked phases of maturity that honored the children for their development and instructed them in their new responsibilities or obligations.

Violence, Domestic and Sexual

High rates of female- and child-targeted aggression are most commonly found in patriarchal and hierarchical societies where there is an imbalance of power across sex, gender, and class. These imbalances did not occur in pre-Columbian indigenous societies, and thus there was much less domestic violence than in Euro-American cultures. In California the ultimate penalty exacted in cases of family murder or rape was execution. The Spanish mission system, established in 1769, imposed a patriarchal and hierarchical order that allowed the Spanish soldiers and priests to systematically sexually and physically abuse women and children, introducing violence into a culture that previously had little. Conversely, archaeological studies of the ancient Pueblo people of the La Plata River Valley in northwestern New Mexico show a high frequency of female head injuries, and women were five times more likely to have evidence of infection and a shorter life expectancy (Claasen and Rosemary 1997, 76). Mayan royal women would be tortured and buried ritually by their enemies in the course of a takeover, while the male ruler would simply be decapitated, denoting an enemy's fear and respect of elite women.

Ethnographic records among eastern tribes indicate some violence aimed at women, usually as a result of extramarital relations. Among the Cenis and Illiniwek peoples, adultery may have been punished by cutting the wife's nose. Among the Alabamus, the wife and lover were whipped with a wooden switch on their back and stomach, had their hair cut off, and were exiled from the village. Elite husbands were often polygynous, while monogamy or serial monogamy tended to be preferred. The sexual double standard known in European society was not likely applicable to precontact societies. Among the Plains tribes, an unkind husband could find himself homeless.

Generally domestic violence was discouraged, and men and women were encouraged to find new partners rather than continue abusive patterns. Ideally, families spent a great deal of time conducting rituals and ceremonies intended to keep relationships among each other in equilibrium. Women often had a strong role in marriage negotiations throughout the Americas, a reality that would have mitigated the occurrence of violent marriages.

Education

The way of knowing, or of seeking knowledge, was similar among the various peoples of the Americas. The belief in the sacred was a commonality among most native communities. Those people who lived in a sacred manner were the most respected in the community and were sought after for advice and guidance. Indigenous American cultures were rooted in and transmitted through oral tradition. Stories, songs, chants, art, prayers, and poems were conducted with social, ceremonial, and ritual significance detail specific cultures and languages and are central to understanding the distinctiveness of each community. Rituals and ceremonies were conducted to initiate people into different phases of their lives. From birth, children were given the knowledge that guided them to be successful contributors to their partners and families and the larger community. Generally, people were taught to be responsible citizens and to keep the world in balance by holding all forms of life in reverence and not exploiting or taking for granted relationships between people and the nonhuman world.

Two mythical figures, the culture hero and trickster, are widespread in the Americas but take different forms or expression depending on the community. The culture hero was regarded as the person who had taught the members of the tribe their way of life in a distant past. The trickster, such as the raven in the North, the coyote in the Southwest, and rabbits or Iktomi, the spider, taught morals to people by behaving badly. They represented all human capacity and often took on undesirable characteristics to illustrate to people why they should live morally. When several

groups of the Southwest said that someone went the way of the coyote, this suggested that a person had followed a negative path or did something against the group's rules. Many of the groups encouraged their young people to embark on a vision quest or perceiving quest. Under hardship, meditation, and prayer, it was a journey to discover oneself (Storm 1972). Some questers would be awarded a mystical experience that could convey to them the connection with all people or empower the individual with new knowledge.

Through dance, song, music, and theater, social relationships were renewed, and all things were maintained in the sacred way. Knowledge about the world around them, material and spiritual, was transmitted through oral tradition, singing, and dancing. Women were the keepers of tradition and played key roles in every aspect of society, including leadership and healing. People had great faith in shamans, both women and men, to cure the sick and restore balance and harmony to the world. Psychiatry or psychosomatic medicine, such as in the Navajo medicine way, was designed to restore patients' health by ministering to their mental state and bringing them back into harmony, or *hozo,* with the universe. Midwives were especially important, given their sacred and learned roles of bringing babies safely into the world while ensuring mothers' health and longevity. In agricultural complexes of the Southeast and Mesoamerica, healers became members of a hierarchy of trained priests. Medicine people often learned their stories and songs by dreaming and being taught by spirits. Indian doctors received spiritual power and/or instruction to diagnose and locate illness in the body and remove it. Women had a significant voice in religious activities and worked as doctors, artisans, and priests, all of whom had educational responsibilities in indigenous cultures.

Gender Roles

In many indigenous societies, the creator or major aspects of the creator were recognized as woman or as having both male and female qualities necessary in creation and maintaining equilibrium. In the Mayan creation myth *Popul Vuh,* women are honored as the sources of life. The female character's name is "blood," and she represents all subsequent wives and mothers. The Tzotzil

Maya word *me'* for "mother" carries a meaning associated with the origins of all things (Claasen and Rosemary 1997, 199). The people believed that the creator had made all beings, and therefore all beings deserved respect and had the right to exist without prejudice or mistreatment. Nisenan culture recognized a spirit that is both male and female, and the Kamia or Tipai culture heroine/hero was a transvestite and admired for introducing many aspects of the culture, including agriculture. In a Kamia origin myth, the people were said to have dispersed from their ancestral Salton Sea territory because they were afraid of him/her. Pre-Columbian societies throughout the Americas recognized and accepted the existence of multiple genders, and in some cases that gender identity was fluid, changing under different circumstance or periods in one's life. Among the Chukchis of Siberia, seven gender categories were identified "including those that could be considered 'intermediate' between male/man and female/woman in a binary gender system . . . and any could be adopted at any time during the individuals life, and transformation need not be permanent" (Claasen and Rosemary 1997, 182). Most creation stories of the people of the Americas acknowledged women as productive, generative, powerful, and highly valued community members.

Many societies also recognized the existence of several genders or perhaps did not perceive sexual differences in the same way as Euro-Americans did at contact. Modern gender systems identify sex and gender based on external genitalia, while many traditional American societies placed more emphasis on supernatural endowment, preferences for types of work, temperament, and other attributes (Schmidt and Voss 2000, 181). Two-spirits are those men recognized as transvestites or homosexuals, though this may be a misunderstanding. Called Berdache by the Lakotas, 'Aqi (Fancy Ones) by the Chumashes, and Joyas (Jewels) by the Spanish, they have been associated with supernatural power in native societies throughout North America. The intermediate gender position they held was a reflection of their spiritual position between the earthly realm and the supernatural. Transgendered people acted as spiritual intermediaries during birth, marriage, and death, and their purpose was to maintain order and continuity (Claasen and Rosemary 1997, 183). For the people of California, including the

Yakuts, Monos, and Tubatulaabals, transgendered or multigendered people are thought to have been part of the guilds who conducted all the ceremonies related to death and mourning (Claasen and Rosemary 1997, 172–188). They wore the women's apron, prepared acorns and tobacco, and made baskets and pottery with the other women. There were also female berdavche shamans, representing a fourth gender, among many northern California groups who were variant females and were allowed to participate in the otherwise male Kuksu cult rituals among the Maidus. Western concepts of two rigidly separated genders may have retarded a genuine understanding of indigenous gender ideologies. Thus, in most societies in the Americas there were at the very least gender-complementary societies where men and women were recognized and valued for their contributions, but multiple-gendered people were also respected for their unique roles.

Clothing and Fashion

Indigenous clothing varied from people to people depending on climate and available materials. The people of the Arctic wore loose-fitting pants and shirts of caribou hide, polar bear, or other fur. Hooded parkas were used during winter, and women's parkas were cut larger to be able to carry a baby inside the garment or within the hood. Stockings, boots, and mittens were made from fur, and sinew was used for stitching. Aleuts also wore carved hats. In the Northwest, people often wore clothing of shredded cedar bark as well as animal skins and cone-shaped basket hats. In California, the favorable climate allowed men to go naked or with skin loincloths, while women wore short skirts, basketry hats, and cloaks of rushes or skins. In cold weather people wore moccasins, skin robes, and leggings. Women and men wore shell necklaces, earrings, and hair nets with shells woven into them. In the southern bayou, women wove skirts of what is today called Spanish moss. Clothing in the Plains cultures was elaborate and was fashioned from skins and ornamented with quills and animal teeth. In many cultures of the Plains and the East clothing was made from skins, and men wore breechcloths, shirts, leggings, and moccasins. Women's garments included a skirt and jacket, and in cold weather both sexes wore skin robes. Figurines in the Cahokia site in Illinois show women with elongated noses, flattened foreheads, prominent chins, and wraparound skirts rolled and fastened at the waist. Long straight hair was pulled back to expose the ears. Other figurines indicated that women wore moccasins and a pelt or small animal skin over the right shoulder (Claasen and Rosemary 1997, 211–213).

Many men and women throughout the Americas tattooed permanently or decorated their bodies with different colors. Cenis women tattooed with bone splinters and charcoal—a streak down their faces and figures on the corners of their eyes and bosoms. Cenis men placed leaf, flower, and creature tattoos on their shoulders, thighs, and other places. Illiniwek, Natchez, Tunica, Timucua, and Houma women tattooed their cheeks, breasts, and arms. Cahuilla women tattooed dots and stripes on their faces, often to indicate their clan or moiety. Ideals of Mayan elite female beauty were often shared with men and included sloping foreheads (newborns were bound to wooden boards), crossed eyes (a small bead was tied to children's bangs), tattoos, bodies painted red, hair ornaments resembling sprouting plants, and ear and neck jewelry of jade, shell, or precious jewels. Some filed their teeth to points and inlaid them with iron, fool's gold, obsidian, jade, or shell. Tattoos and piercings signified many things cross-culturally. Most often they demonstrated accomplishments, bestowed protections, signified honor, or indicated kinship to a particular group.

Legal and Political Power

In many societies precontact, political and economic power was shared between men and women. Creation stories and oral tradition acknowledged the contributions of both men and women and instructed people to share responsibilities and respect each other. The order of the world depended on balance between the male and female and between constructive and destructive forces. The idea of reciprocity governed most societies. Even in the hierarchal societies that developed in eastern North America among the Mayas and Aztecs, the balance between men and women continued to be honored even when a sexual division of labor developed. In matrilineal matrilocal societies women were the primary food providers, a reality that created significant legal and political power for them.

In California, the heads of families or clans and a principal leader constituted the recognized governing body of the tribe. Leadership was accorded to the best man or woman; the better hunter, fisherman, or fisherwoman; a more generous person; or a wiser person in the laws and traditions. While leadership could be considered hereditary, leaders would name someone else if they did not think their offspring would make a good leader. If someone violated the moral code, the involved parties would negotiate restitution or be arbitrated. Offenders who did not provide restitution became the targets of gossip and ridicule and were refused consideration in events, feasts, and ceremonies. Major crimes were trespass and use of land and resources without permission and would be considered offenses against the entire community affected. Stealing food in time of famine would mean ostracism from the tribe (Costo and Costo 1995, 43–46).

Societies in eastern North America were most often matrilineal (lineage established through the mother's line) and matrilocal (spouses moved to the wife's community); women were empowered politically and economically. Identity and land use were established through the mother's line. Among the Haudenosaunees, or the People of the Longhouse (Iroquois), senior women selected and removed the hereditary peace chiefs of their lineage. Women did not speak at the men's councils but could select an orator to speak on their behalf and depose council members if they did not act in the interest of the community. They urged or prohibited raids by providing or withholding supplies or by controlling the actions of the young warriors of their lineage. Women held their own council meetings, held power in the public sphere, traveled extensively outside of the village, and associated with men in all activities.

During the 1000s CE, warfare, population, village size, and agricultural subsistence increased in eastern North America leading to the formation of several pan-tribal confederacies and institutions. The most well known is the five nations of the Iroquois Confederacy that united the Onondaga, Cayuga, Oneida, Seneca, and Mohawk tribes (Claasen and Rosemary 1997, 92). The foundation of Iroquois society was the "fireside," consisting of a mother and all her children. All authority stemmed from the *Ohwachira*, which was headed by women. They named the delegates and Ohwachira representatives in clan and tribal councils as well as the 50 *sachems* or peace chiefs who made up the ruling council of the five nations. A sachem was appointed for life and was chosen from specific families but could be deposed by the clan mother and removed if he acted contrary to the community's best interests (Josephy 1961, 95). A priesthood of 3 men and 3 women, "keepers of the faith," supervised religious ceremonies, and various secret societies performed curing and other ceremonies. Each society had its own officers, masks, songs, dances, and rituals. When a person died, the spirit of the tribe was reduced, and prisoners were adopted into the Ohwachira to recover that spiritual power (Josephy 1961, 15).

In the Southeast, brother-sister rulerships were preferred to maintain the world in balance. French ethnographic records tell of brother-sister chiefs whereby women garnered considerable respect and had a place in all the councils, and several Houma women led war parties (Claasen and Rosemary 1997, 220). Seneca women controlled the food supply, provisioned warriors for raids and wars, and determined adoptions in the clans. Women of the eastern tribes were arbitrators of peace and of war. Southeastern women of the Catawba, Chickasaw, Tuscarora, Choctaw, Cherokee, Timucua, and Creek nations shot arrows over their husbands' shoulders in battle, accompanied husbands in warfare, carried military supplies into war along with male two-spirits, carried medicine bundles into battle, and danced in victory celebrations with enemy scalps. Women also participated in war and decided the fate of captives. Among the Mayas, daughters could inherit property of their families, and textile work gave them an important position in their society and city-state. Women's domain was often the home, though both spouses occasionally worked together in the home or the fields. Women could also be matchmakers, artists, craftspeople, or scribes (Claasen and Rosemary 1997, 45).

Work, Waged and Unwaged

In most American societies precontact, the economies were subsistence based and relied on a combination of horticulture and agriculture, intensive management of uncultivated crops such as cacti and pinon, the hunting of small and large game, and the harvesting of river and ocean resources. Societies ranged from semisedentary seasonal rounds such as those in California to the sedentary agricultural societies in the Southwest. In all cases women contributed significantly to the diet and overall economy, often up to 60–80 percent of the resources of a family. For most of American prehistory, sex did not determine gendered work roles or hinder anyone, male or female, from choosing their work. Sexed work roles took place with the rise of agricultural societies, beginning with the development of more productive maize strains in Mexico 4,500 years ago, in the Southwest 2,000 years ago, possibly with the Adena-Hopewell exchange or of local domesticates and cultigens of the Mississippi–Ohio River drainages 2,000 years ago, and probably with the move to acorn dependence in California. In the nonhierarchal and horticultural or seasonal round communities, sexed roles may not have developed prior to European influence (Claasen and Rosemary 1997, 83).

In California, there was no formal division of labor; individuals did what they did best or in times of stress or catastrophe what was needed. There were no classes and thus no exploitation of women's labor. Men and women worked together to procure subsistence and intensively manage the landscape and resources in a sustainable way. In the Southwest, families often worked together in the agricultural fields and on a variety of activities. Men tended to participate more heavily in trade, defense, and the collection and placement of timbers for construction of the home. Women's work focused on what went on within the community. Grinding dried corn was women's work and was perceived as vital to the people. Women also made moccasins, blankets, and pottery, the latter being an important trade item. Women produced rabbit-skin clothing in the Mogollon highlands and generally hunted small game throughout the Southwest. Among the Fremont, Pueblo, and Hohokam cultures both women and men hunted antelope (Claasen and Rosemary 1997, 77). Hopi women commonly controlled most of the activities in and around the home, such as food processing, storage, and manufacture of goods. Men commonly worked in the fields, hunted, participated in war, and made cloth. Women controlled the production of finished products such as ground maize and pottery and traded with other villages.

In Mississippian Cultures of the East, archaeological studies suggest a hierarchal society but not one characterized as male dominant. Women engaged in agricultural activities, paddled boats, and engaged in trade. In the Eastern Woodlands the entire family would turn out to help in the fields, managed by an elder woman. Men prepared fields for planting, while women and children sowed and raised the crops. Women gathered mushrooms, berries, and nuts; prepared food; and distributed game that the men hunted. Women also made baskets, pottery, and other implements (Claasen and Rosemary 1997, 67–71).

Women in coastal Algonquian communities tended crops, fished, and constructed mats and baskets. Among the Ojibwes of the Great Lakes and the Apaches of the southern plains, men hunted, and women processed the kill. Women gathered feathers from birds, fashioned moccasins, and bartered in the fur trade. In the Southeast, women and families traded with the French and the Spanish and were mobile throughout the territory, using canoes to trade. Women adopted and adapted pottery to both hot rock steaming and direct heat cooking and were responsible for the diffusion of technology across North America. Among the Hidatsas of the Great Plains, the division of labor was informed by age and gender. Women were responsible for agricultural and food production, maintaining the homes, and much of the ceremony associated with agriculture, birds, and healing.

In Mesoamerican societies, spinning and weaving were stereotypically female tasks. When Mayan women wove, they were following the lead of the Moon Goddess, the inventor of weaving and the special patron of women. Until 700 CE women, men, and children worked outdoors in the same space and in the fields until farming methods turned to terracing. Women assisted men in producing pots and clay products, sculpting stucco, and creating latticework on rooftops. While the division of labor was gendered, it did not detract from women's status in society. Women were not restricted by sex but were the complement to men, and often they worked together at various tasks (Claasen and Rosemary 1997, 37–42).

Immigration and Migration

In California, population determined when tribes would break apart to become separate communities, with one group moving away to establish a new city center. People of California have their own creation stories and migration stories that place them here since the beginning of time. Social scientists claim that they share ancestry from both Mesoamerican and northwestern societies (Costo and Costo 1995). The Iroquois may have immigrated to the Eastern Woodlands beginning in about 800 CE and merged with the Algonquian people to create a new syncretic society. At Euro-American contact, captives were taken in warfare and absorbed into society, often with the opportunity to become full citizens within the nation (Claasen and Rosemary 1997, 97–98).

From about 800 CE, the woodland cultures who had possibly blended with, replaced, or developed in the plains, were succeeded by a lifeway that placed more reliance on agriculture and a more settled way of life. In the North, woodland Siouan speakers with strong Mississippian influences moved to the middle Missouri Valley; from the Southeast, Caddoan speakers moved onto the central plains; farther south, a third stream also advanced west from the Caddoan culture area. For centuries these people blended with plains woodland groups already in the area and developed an agricultural economy. By 1500 CE western farms were abandoned, and people returned to hunting and gathering seasonal rounds. The Dakota federation halted its westward migration in the seventh century in Minnesota and settled into a semiagricultural society. The second subculture included the Blackfeet and Hidatsas, who dwelt to the west and after the introduction of horses during the mid-1600s became the plains horse culture that lived primarily from buffalo products. By the 1400s Athabascans, ancestors of the Apaches and Navajos, had reached the Southwest, having migrated from northwestern Canada. By the time the Spanish arrived in the Southwest in 1582, the people of that region had been living there for thousands of years and intermarried among the earlier migrants of the North and later migrants of the Northwest. When the Spanish began invading the Southeast, chiefdoms and earthen temple pyramids were still common. Moundville in Alabama, Etowah in Georgia, and

Spiro in the Arkansas Valley of eastern Oklahoma were centers of population, trade, and artistic and ceremonial life. In Florida, the nations of the Apalachees and Timucuas lived in sedentary agricultural communities. Due to Spanish invasion and the subsequent theft of resources, war, and introduction of European disease, the chiefdoms collapsed, and from that emerged the historic peoples of the Caddos, Choctaws, Chickasaws, Cherokees, and Creeks.

Over the millennia, indigenous peoples separated and joined together enough times to create "universal truths" that helped govern international and intertribal relationships. Eastern and Plains cultures recognized their first social principle as that of a circle of life, a principle that all beings are related and interdependent. Native American cultures and societies have never been static. Native peoples have responded to changes in the environment and the greater political and economic world using the universal and unchanging principles of a belief system that incorporates and considers the existence of all beings, animate and inanimate.

Leleua Loupe

Further Reading

Claassen, Cheryl, and Joyce A. Rosemary, eds. 1997. *Women in Prehistory: North America and Mesoamerica.* Philadelphia: University of Pennsylvania Press.

Clay, Catherine, Paul Chandrika, and Christine Senecal. 2009. *Envisioning Women in World History,* Vol. 1. Boston: McGraw-Hill.

Costo, Rupert, and Jeannette Henry Costo. 1995. *Natives of the Golden State: The California Indians.* San Francisco: Indian Historian Press.

Josephy, Alvin M. 1961. *The Patriot Chiefs.* Toronto, Canada: Macmillan.

Kennedy, Dorothy. 2007. "Quantifying 'Two Sides of a Coin': A Statistical Examination of the Central Coast Salish Social Network." *BC Studies,* no. 153 (Spring): 3–34.

Klein, Laura F., and Lillian A. Ackerman. 1995. *Women and Power in Native North America.* Norman: University of Oklahoma Press.

Olsen Bruhns, Karen, and Karen Stothert. 1999. *Women in Ancient America.* Norman: University of Oklahoma Press.

Plane, Anne Marie. 1999. "Child Birth Practices among Native American Women." In *Women and Health in America of New England and Canada, 1600–1800,* edited by Judith Walzer Leavitt, 38–42. Madison: University of Wisconsin Press.

Schmidt, Robert A., and Barbara L. Voss. 2000. *Archaeologies of Sexuality.* London: Routledge.

Sioui, Georges E. 1999. *Huron Wendot: The Heritage of the Circle.* East Lansing: Michigan State University Press.

Storm, Hyemeyohsts. 1972. *Seven Arrows.* New York: Ballantine Books.

Thom, Brian. 2003. "The Anthropology of Northwest Coast Oral Traditions." *Arctic Anthropology* 40(1): 1–28.

Tollefson, Kenneth D. 1995. "Potlatching and Political Organization among the Northwest Coast Indians." *Ethnology* 34(1) (Winter): 53–73.

Walter, Susan M. 2006. "Polygyny, Rank and Resources in Northwest Coast Foraging Societies." *Ethnology* 45(1) (Winter): 41–47.

BIBLIOGRAPHY

Abrams, Ann Uhry. 1999. *The Pilgrims and Pocahontas: Rival Myths of American Origin.* Boulder, CO: Westview.

Adovasio, J. M., Olga Soffer, and Jake Page. 2007. *The Invisible Sex: Uncovering the True Roles of Women in Prehistory.* New York: Harper-Collins.

Albers, Patricia, and Beatrice Medicine. 1983. *The Hidden Half: Studies of Plains Indian Women.* Washington, DC: University Press of America.

Alchon, Suzanne Austin. 2003. *A Pest in the Land: New World Epidemics in a Global Perspective.* Albuquerque: University of New Mexico Press.

Allen, Paula Gunn. 1990. *Spider Woman's Granddaughters: Traditional Tales and Contemporary Writing by Native American Women.* New York: Ballantine Books.

Allen, Paula Gunn. 2003. *Pocahontas: Medicine Woman, Spy, Entrepreneur, Diplomat.* San Francisco: Harper.

Auslander, Leora. 2009. *Cultural Revolutions: Everyday Life and Politics in Britain, North America, and France.* Los Angeles: University of California Press.

Baumgarten, Linda. 2002. *What Clothes Reveal: The Language of Clothing in Colonial and Federal America.* New Haven, CT: Yale University Press.

Bernhard, Virginia. 2011. *A Tale of Two Colonies: What Really Happened in Virginia and Bermuda?* Columbia: University of Missouri Press.

Brody, J. J. 1990. *The Anasazi: Ancient Indian People of the American Southwest.* New York: Rizzoli.

Brooks, James F. 2002. *Captives & Cousins: Slavery, Kinship, and Community in the Southwest Borderlands.* Chapel Hill: University of North Carolina Press.

Brown, Tracy. 2013. *Pueblo Indians and Spanish Colonial Authority in Eighteenth-Century New Mexico.* Tucson: University of Arizona Press.

Bruhns, Karen Olsen, and Karen E. Stothert. 1999. *Women in Ancient America.* Norman: University of Oklahoma Press.

Calloway, Colin G. 2003. *One Vast Winter Count: The Native American West before Lewis and Clark.* Lincoln: University of Nebraska Press.

Claassen, Cheryl, and Joyce A. Rosemary, eds. 1997. *Women in Prehistory: North America and Mesoamerica.* Philadelphia: University of Pennsylvania Press.

Cotton, Sallie Southall. 2010. *The White Doe: The Fate of Virginia Dare.* New York: FQ Books.

Crosby, Alfred W., Jr. 1972. *The Columbian Exchange: Biological and Cultural Consequences of 1492.* Westport, CT: Greenwood.

Custalow, Linwood, and Angela Daniel. 2001. *The True Story of Pocahontas: The Other Side of History.* Golden, CO: Fulcrum.

Cypress, Sandra Messinger. 1991. *La Malinche in Mexican Literature: From History to Myth.* Austin: University of Texas Press.

Deloria, Philip J. *1998. Playing Indian.* New Haven, CT: Yale University Press.

Dobyns, Henry F. 1983. *Their Number Became Thinned: Native American Population Dynamics in Eastern North America.* Knoxville: University of Tennessee Press.

Donald, Moira, and Linda Hurcombe, eds. 2000. *Representations of Gender from Prehistory to the Present.* New York: Palgrave Macmillan.

Dozier, Edward. 1970. *Pueblo Indians of North America.* New York: Holt, Rinehart and Winston.

Duncan, David Ewing. 1996. *Hernando De Soto: A Savage Quest in the Americas.* New York: Crown.

Esquivel, Laura. 2006. *Malinche.* New York: Atria Books.

Fenton, William N. 1998. *The Great Law and the Longhouse: A Political History of the Iroquois Confederacy.* Norman: University of Oklahoma Press.

Gallay, Alan. 2002. *The Indian Slave Trade: The Rise of the English Empire in the American South, 1670–1717.* New Haven, CT: Yale University Press.

Gitlin, Jay. 2010. *Bourgeois Frontier: French Towns, French Traders & American Expansion.* New Haven, CT: Yale University Press.

Gleach, Frederic W. *Powhatan's World and Colonial Virginia: A Conflict of Cultures.* Lincoln: University of Nebraska Press, 1997.

Gutierrez, Ramon A. 1991. *When Jesus Came, the Corn Mothers Went Away: Marriage, Sexuality, and Power in New Mexico, 1500–1846.* Stanford, CA: Stanford University Press.

Haas, Lisbeth. 1995. *Conquests and Historical Identities in California.* Berkeley: University of California Press.

Horn, James. 2005. *A Land as God Made It: Jamestown and the Birth of America.* New York: Basic Books.

Horn, James. 2010. *A Kingdom Strange: The Brief and Tragic History of the Lost Colony of Roanoke.* New York: Basic Books.

Hudson, Marjorie. 2007. *Searching for Virginia Dare.* Winston-Salem, NC: Press 53 Books.

Iliffe, John. 2007. *Africans: A History of a Continent.* Cambridge: Cambridge University Press.

Jennings, Francis. 1984. *The Ambiguous Iroquois Empire: The Covenant Chain Confederation of Indian Tribes with English Colonies, from Its Beginnings to the Lancaster Treaty of 1744.* New York: Norton.

Kellogg, Susan. 2005. *Weaving the Past: A History of Latin America's Indigenous Women from the Prehispanic Period to the Present.* New York: Oxford University Press.

Kelso, William M. 2006. *Jamestown: The Buried Truth.* Charlottesville: University of Virginia Press.

Klein, Cecelia F., ed. 2001. *Gender in Pre-Hispanic America.* Washington, DC: Dumbarton Oaks Research Library and Collection.

Klein, Laura F., and Lillian A. Ackerman. 1995. *Women and Power in Native North America.* Norman: University of Oklahoma Press.

Knaster, Meri. 1977. *Women in Spanish America: An Annotated Bibliography from Pre-Conquest to Contemporary Times.* Boston: G. K. Hall.

Lavrin, Asunción, ed. 1978. *Latin American Women: Historical Perspectives.* Westport, CT: Greenwood.

McCartney, Martha W. 2007. *Virginia Immigrants and Adventurers: A Biographical Dictionary, 1607–1635.* Baltimore: Genealogical Publishing.

Mooney, James. 1902. *Myths of the Cherokee.* Washington, DC: Smithsonian Bureau of American Ethnology.

Morro, Baker H., and V. B. Price. 1997. *Anasazi Architecture and American Design.* Albuquerque: University of New Mexico.

Ogbomo, Onaiwu. 1997. *When Women and Men Mattered: A History of Gender Relations among the Owan of Nigeria.* Rochester, NY: University of Rochester Press.

Olsen Bruhns, Karen, and Karen Stothert. 1999. *Women in Ancient America.* Norman: University of Oklahoma Press.

Powers, Karen Vieira. 2005. *Women in the Crucible of Conquest: The Gendered Genesis of Spanish America Society, 1500–1600.* Albuquerque: University of New Mexico Press.

Restall, Matthew. 2003. *Seven Myths of the Spanish Conquest.* Oxford: Oxford University Press.

Richter, Daniel. 2003. *Facing East from Indian Country: A Native History of Early America.* Cambridge, MA: Harvard University Press.

Robertson, Claire C., and Martin Kline, eds. 1997. *Women and Slavery in Africa.* Portsmouth, NH: Reed Elsevier.

Rountree, Helen C. 1988. *The Powhatan Indians of Virginia: Their Traditional Culture.* Norman: University of Oklahoma Press.

Shoemaker, Nancy, ed. 1995. *Negotiators of Change: Historical Perspectives on Native American Women.* New York: Routledge.

Snyder, Christina. 2010. *Slavery in Indian Country: The Changing Face of Captivity in Early America.* Cambridge, MA: Harvard University Press.

Swanton, John Reed. 1929. *Myths and Tales of the Southeastern Indians.* Washington, DC: Smithsonian Bureau of American Ethnology.

Terborg-Penn, Rosalyn. 1986. "Women and Slavery in the African Diaspora: A Cross-Cultural Approach to Historical Analysis." *Sage: A Scholarly Journal on Black Women* (Fall): 11–15.

Todorov, Tzetan. 1982. *The Conquest of America: The Question of the Other.* New York: Harper Perennial.

Townsend, Camilla. 2004. *Pocahontas and the Powhatan Dilemma.* New York: Hill and Wang.

Townsend, Camilla. 2006. *Malintzin's Choices: An Indian Woman in the Conquest of Mexico.* Albuquerque: University of New Mexico Press.

Turner, Erin, ed. 2009. *Wise Women: From Pocahontas to Sarah Winnemucca; Remarkable Stories of Native American Trailblazers.* Guilford, CT: TwoDot.

2. Colonial North America (1607–1754)

HISTORICAL OVERVIEW

The establishment of colonies on the North American continent represented one of the major goals for the European powers that sent colonists to the New World. In acquiring such far-flung territory, these nations intended to amass wealth and political power. From the arrival of the Spanish in the early 16th century to the arrival of the French and English in the early 17th century, these three nations vied for occupation of the land, its inhabitants, and its bounty. Although European nations each went about colonization in its own way—with some methods proving much more effective than others—the primary goal of the English, French, and Spanish monarchies was the acquisition and control of what each hoped would be a critical foothold in an economically promising part of the world.

Most scholarship regarding initial colonization centers on the English settlement of what eventually became the 13 colonies. Less information exists for the French and Spanish settlements and their influence on the history of North America. However, it is important to understand that while some significant differences in culture and practice existed, the dominant culture that emerged in America by the late 18th century was clearly English and resulted from the early settlement of those seaboard colonies established in the early 1600s.

Historians sometimes delineate between the characteristics and subsequent social and economic behaviors of the American colonies by describing them as either purifying or profit-making colonies. These two categories involve the primary reason for settlement, whether for religious or moral (purifying) reasons,

such as Massachusetts Bay and Plymouth, or for profit-making motives, the foremost example of which is Virginia. These motivations had profound implications for the ways in which these colonies were structured and functioned and the timelines upon which they developed. It is important to remember, however, that regardless of whether a colony could be described as profit-making or purifying in its primary character, all colonies contained at least some elements of the religious and/or economic in its environment.

Spain established the first colonial settlements in the so-called New World, first in Hispaniola under Christopher Columbus and later spreading to the other Caribbean islands, Latin America, Mexico, and the southern regions of North America. What Spain called "La Florida" encompassed present-day Florida and parts of Georgia, Mississippi, Alabama, and Louisiana. Juan Ponce de Leon attempted the first North American Spanish colony in Florida in 1521, but hostile indigenous peoples forced the expedition to return to Cuba. Other expeditions followed, though Spain did not establish a permanent colony until 1565 at St. Augustine, Florida, the oldest continually occupied city in the United States.

In 1602 the Dutch claimed territory around present-day New York state and in 1615 established Fort Nassau near present-day Albany. In 1621 the Dutch West India Company claimed parts of present-day New York, New Jersey, and western Massachusetts and in 1626 established New Amsterdam on Manhattan Island.

The French also colonized North America, establishing forts and settlements in the north at Quebec and Montreal and in the south at Mobile, Biloxi, Baton Rouge, and New Orleans. France's earliest colonization expeditions date from 1534, when Jacques Cartier explored Newfoundland and the Saint Lawrence River. The French struggled to establish permanent colonies, and as a result fewer French women were likely to immigrate to French colonies. French men often intermarried with indigenous women, creating a mixed, or métis, culture.

The first permanent British settlement in what would eventually become the United States appeared in 1607 in Jamestown, Virginia. A similar attempt had been made in 1584 when Sir Walter Raleigh established a colony at what would be called Roanoke. Three years elapsed between resupply expeditions because of the war between England and Spain. In 1587 Raleigh returned to Roanoke with 115 new colonists and supplies and found the colony in Virginia abandoned. Much has been made of the supposed Lost Colony of Roanoke, but it is likely that colonists ran afoul of local native peoples and were either captured and absorbed into native culture or eradicated in retaliation for their own violent behavior.

The Virginia Company, a joint stock company, established Jamestown in 1607, England's first permanent colony, for the express purpose of finding a marketable product and making money for its stockholders. To that end, the company's initial group of settlers was exclusively male; no women arrived in the colony until 1608, and men continued to outnumber women in Virginia for most of the 17th century.

English Pilgrims established Plymouth Colony in 1620, and English Puritans established Massachusetts Bay Colony in 1630. The Puritans broke from Henry VIII's Church of England when they could not reform it, and the Pilgrims separated from the Puritans and decided to leave England and form their own churches. Both of these colonies were strongly religious in nature, based on their goal of founding Protestant utopian commonwealths in America. Northeastern New England settlers were more likely to arrive in family units, in great part because they intended to stay and make a life in New England. This provided a critical difference from Virginia's almost exclusively male population, where the goal was more generally profit rather than resettlement.

By 1682, 12 of the 13 colonies had been established; with the founding of Georgia in 1732, the process was complete. These colonies can be divided into four separate sections with roughly defined unifying characteristics. New England contained Massachusetts, Connecticut, New Hampshire, and Rhode Island. The unifying factor among the New England Colonies was religion, as all were settled by Puritans or sects that split off from the original Puritan influence. The Middle Colonies consisted of New York, New Jersey, Pennsylvania, and Delaware. These four colonies are the most disparate of the four groups, as they shared no real common characteristics with each other or any of the other sections. Virginia and Maryland made up the Chesapeake Colonies. These 2 colonies shared in common their agricultural economy, climate, geography, dependence on enslaved labor, and the presence of organized settlements, towns, and considerable wealth. Finally, the Southern Colonies were North Carolina, South Carolina, and Georgia. Like the Chesapeake Colonies, these colonies had an agricultural economic base, a similar climate and geography, and a slave labor force, but they were less settled and more rustic than the Chesapeake Colonies. In fact, the Chesapeake Colonies are sometimes considered southern, the only major difference between the two sections being density of settlement.

One of the most important ideological factors present in all of colonial society was the understanding of its hierarchical and patriarchal system of governance. Based on the Great Chain of Being, the concept that every living thing in the universe has a prescribed level of importance that is ordained by God, the idea of hierarchy structured colonial society. This deferential patriarchal society placed elite-class white men at the top of the power structure, with women and nonwhites below them. This system resulted from a rapid population rise in early 16th-century England that altered the economy, stratified society more definitively, and instituted political change. The ruling elites saw chaos everywhere and struggled to keep society under control. At the same time, the previously powerful network of familial and collateral kin gave way to a more nuclear, patriarchal form of family organization. Power gravitated to the husband and away from the community, giving men more personal control of women, children, servants, and any other residents of his household.

At the same time that family organization was undergoing change, the rise of Protestantism—and specifically Puritanism—exerted forces that further reinforced the patriarchy. Removal of the once ubiquitous influence of the Catholic Church resulted in the decrease of influence in the cult of the Virgin Mary and simultaneously limited the option of the convent life as a suitable option to marriage and motherhood. Puritanism likewise stressed the role of the father as the spiritual leader of the household.

Migration to the New World and isolation in the colonies encouraged the settlers' self-sufficiency, which increased colonial leaders' concern for social order. Therefore, instead of providing a release from the tensions mounting in the Old World, migration to America in many ways intensified the social and cultural processes going on in England.

While all the North American colonies depended on this paternalistic, hierarchical structure, regional differences did exist depending on the reasons for settlement and the demographic makeup of the settlers. Vast differences existed early on between the two oldest areas of New England and the Chesapeake region. Environmental factors of the Chesapeake, along with limited religious influence, high mortality rates, and the immigration of few women, prevented the creation of a strong patriarchal system early in the area's settlement. In contrast, Puritanism, low mortality rates, and the migration of families—and therefore the presence of more women—created a very strong patriarchal system in New England from the very beginning.

The colonial period can be divided into two separate periods of development, the migration period of 1620–1660 and the transition (or middle) period of 1660–1750. Widespread rural settlement patterns, limited market involvement, and an increased level of household involvement for women characterized the migration period. Simultaneously, the transition period was characterized by the rise of a predominantly native-born, or Euro-American, population; a change in the ethnic composition of some colonies due to the arrival of Scottish, Dutch, German, and African immigrants; changes in mortality rates; the stabilization of sex ratios; and a solidification of economic opportunities. In the northern colonies the maritime industries became more important, while agriculture and an increase in slave labor became more prevalent in the Chesapeake and Southern Colonies.

The migration period of 1620–1660 was marked by the transplantation of English values and ideologies, many of which required adjustment in the colonies. In this early period colonists struggled not only to feed themselves but also to find marketable resources in order to build their embryonic economies. Scarcity of manufactured goods in these early years forced settlers to do without the basic tools needed for maintenance of their homes and farms. With the pre-existing patriarchal view and the almost constant scramble to feed, clothe, and raise their family without proper resources, women stayed particularly close to home. Indentured servants sometimes lightened a family's burden in these early years, but as time went by, conditions improved in England, and the lure of America became less strong, so enslaved Africans began to replace them as a labor source.

New England had a head start on the Chesapeake in terms of its creation of family units and the stability that came from a family-centered society. Puritans and Pilgrims migrated primarily in family groups, unlike the single male immigrant pattern of the older, more southern colony of Virginia. These groups also brought with them more firmly entrenched English sensibilities regarding the "little commonwealth" ideology, and while they still had to deal with differing conditions in America, New England residents found it much easier to replicate and maintain a patriarchal society when there were women and children around.

Everything happened faster in New England than in the Chesapeake region. Thicker settlement meant more social cohesion and control and the faster development of domestic manufactures and a market economy. Early records indicate that urban areas of Massachusetts produced more home manufactures than rural areas but that the situation had almost reversed by 1700. By that time urban access to the tools of manufacture had been replaced by access to finished goods. The presence of a strong patriarchal and religious component in Puritan society kept the real social chaos to a minimum, although imagined social chaos, as illustrated in witchcraft trials, remained a threat to Puritan Americans well into the 1700s.

The transition or middle years of settlement between 1660 and 1750 brought additional changes in the colonial environment. By the late 17th century the native-born population began to replace migrants in New England. In the Chesapeake region this demographic change did not emerge until approximately 1720. New colonies with new ethnic compositions such as those of Scottish, Dutch, and German descent began to form, and the increase in slave importation, particularly in the South, introduced Africans who replaced the indentured servants brought from England in the early years of settlement. Maritime trades began to take hold in the northern colonies, introducing a new commercial element to the economy, while westward expansion into the interior of the continent increased the tension between colonists and the Native Americans already in residence.

At the same time that the colonies were becoming more ethnically diverse they were becoming more demographically similar. For reasons that are still unclear, mortality rates began to drop in the South. Northern mortality rates began to rise, however, due to exposure to epidemic diseases brought in by the maritime trade. In a complete switch from the patterns of the migrating generation, northern women began to be widowed earlier, while southern women lost their husbands later. By the late 1700s the sex ratio had begun to stabilize, the majority of the colonial population was native born, and the wide divergence in women's experience had begun to equalize. The family still functioned as the center of colonial life. This "little commonwealth" was still considered the glue that held society together and maintained social order.

The gendered hierarchy developed somewhat differently in the less religiously demanding areas of the colonies. The Virginia colony, although founded decades before the Puritan settlements in New England, had experienced a shortage of women since the initial founding of Jamestown in 1607. Legislation proposed throughout the early settlement period attempted to address the shortage of women but to little avail. From 1620 to 1622 only 147 English women were transported to Virginia, and by 1624 fewer than 230 of the 1,250 Europeans in Virginia were female. By 1625, men outnumbered women four to one. The major cause of this demographic imbalance was the tobacco culture and its centrality to the Virginia economy. Although enslaved women regularly worked alongside men in the tobacco fields, male laborers were simply in higher demand than women.

Overemphasis on tobacco culture resulted in minimized subsistence agriculture and slow development of internal markets. This lag in the development of a domestic economy in the early Chesapeake stunted material life; little or no domestic manufactures emerged, which prevented the creation of local markets. This environment was perpetuated by the high market price of tobacco, which encouraged still more focus on that crop to the exclusion of more consumable local crops. The "all hands on deck" nature of tobacco culture precluded many women from entering the marketplace with goods and services due to the need for their labor in the fields. Lacking the proper equipment and products for the usual housewifely chores, many women entered the tobacco fields as laborers in order to have the purchasing power to acquire the few finished goods that were available.

When Virginia became a royal colony in 1624, the lack of visible signs of authority such as manor houses, imported clothing, and horses and carriages made it difficult for those in charge to maintain that power. Sumptuary and slander laws were enacted in order to curb the practices of the lower classes, who challenged the social order by dressing above their station and verbally attacking their betters. Clearly some moral authority needed to be instituted, and gender relations became one way to accomplish the task.

Lacking ecclesiastical courts like the ones in New England, Chesapeake leaders enjoined local ministers to assist in their efforts to rein in the community. The result was an increase in the regulation of marriage, particularly where female servants were concerned. While a 1619 law had required women to get permission to marry from those in power over her, subsequent legislation eventually resulted in more strict laws for all women, including licensing of marriages and the posting of banns prior to marriage. Married women were often treated better by the courts than unmarried women to maintain the defense of marriage as a common good, and married women became an important link between local authorities and female offenders. This partnership depended on married

Tobacco, more so than any other crop in North America, shaped the economic landscape of the English colonies. Women, both white and black, free and enslaved, worked in tobacco production, planting, tending, and harvesting valuable crops. (Library of Congress)

women's help in examining accused females and generally monitoring the social environment when necessary. However, this was not an evenhanded, egalitarian society; differences in the treatment of women depended on their level of servility, motherhood, age, and the position of their husbands or fathers in the community. For better or worse, women were a critical part of the legal system in Virginia and similar colonies.

By the 1720s, the native-born population had replaced immigrants in the Chesapeake. Slaves had replaced indentured servants as a labor force as well, as indentured servants were becoming increasingly scarce, and Africans were now considered slaves for life, making them a better economic investment. The colonial mercantile system also began to take hold, having a positive effect on the domestic economy. While women's diaries continued to record the drudgery of everyday tasks, the region had finally begun to

enjoy an increase in the quality and quantity of material possessions and more time to expand personal horizons in terms of writing, reading, music, and dancing, all of which became valuable social attributes considered crucial to proper behavior in the early 18th-century Chesapeake.

By the mid-1700s society had begun to stabilize in all parts of the British seaboard colonies in terms of settlement patterns, demographics, and the economy. France and Spain still occupied the central part of North America, the West, and the Gulf of Mexico region in the South, all with different colonization strategies and varying degrees of success. By the mid-1760s France would withdraw from North America, and the continent would be split down the middle between Spain and England. The colonial period would draw to an end for British America as the colonies entered into the era of the American Revolution.

Lee Davis Smith

Further Reading

Bailyn, Bernard. 2012. *The Barbarous Years: The Peopling of British North America: The Conflict of Civilizations, 1600–1675*. New York: Knopf.

Brown, Katheleen. 1996. *Good Wives, Nasty Wenches, and Anxious Patriarchs: Gender, Race, and Power in Colonial Virginia*. Chapel Hill: University of North Carolina Press.

Greene, Jack P. 2013. *Creating the British Atlantic: Essays on Transplantation, Adaptation, and Continuity*. Charlottesville: University of Virginia Press.

Hawke, David E. 1989. *Everyday Life in Early America*. New York: HarperCollins.

Taylor, Alan. 2002. *American Colonies*. New York: Penguin.

Bastardy

Bastardy or illegitimacy occurs when a child is born to parents who are not legally married to each other. Before 1235, a child could be considered a bastard if the father had abandoned the child, regardless if he was married to the mother. After this time it meant that the parents were not married before the child's birth, and therefore the child was not entitled to inherit property from the father. Historical attitudes toward children born outside of wedlock illustrate fluctuating social and financial realities.

As Europe and England grew focused on the issues of private property and their economies grew during the High Middle Ages (1100–1200), the issue of illegitimate children became more focused. In England the land barons were concerned with limiting the power of Henry III, and so in a negotiation with the monarch they created the Statute of Merton in 1235. This was the basis of English common law. Among many declarations, the statute declared that a child was considered a bastard if he or she was born before the parents' marriage or to parents who could not marry because of prior marriage or incestuous relationships.

The Middle Ages also saw power struggles between civil authority and church authority. Illegitimacy increasingly became an issue of morality, specifically as it related to fornication. The Catholic Church presided over the establishment of paternity and punishment for offenders. However, in the civil courts, jurisdiction was over real property and inheritance issues. If a person was born outside of marriage, that person could not inherit family or parental property. By the late 14th century, civil courts in most European countries recognized the ecclesiastical courts' jurisdiction over bastardy.

The issue of children born outside of wedlock became less of a moral affront and more of a financial problem in England during the Renaissance. As a result, a series of Poor Acts were passed between 1575 and 1609 that established bastardy laws in an effort to limit economically vulnerable children and mothers. These laws set guidelines for the care of bastard children, establishing the responsibilities of both parents. Problems arose when ecclesiastical courts enacted corporal punishment for fornication, including whippings or imprisonment. Many parents abandoned or killed bastard infants to avoid harsh punishments. Additional acts then made it illegal to commit infanticide or abandon a baby, though predictably these laws were difficult to enforce. In reality, Renaissance England proved relatively tolerant of sexual misdeeds, particularly if bastard children proved to be no burden to the government.

As the 17th century saw the rise of Puritanism and religious conservatism, the public outcry to punish crimes of fornication and adultery grew. The cost to incarcerate immoral parents was significant; prisons filled quickly, and parishes became responsible for providing care for the children of illicit unions. Therefore, punishment began to fall out of favor as taxpayers discovered the high cost of rigid sexual morality. When punishment occurred, mothers were more likely to be sent to prison or whipped, leaving children in parish care or relying on taxpayer support. Fathers were more likely to be ordered to pay financial support of their offspring. If the parents had money, they were not likely to be punished because they could afford to pay for their children.

In the American colonies, bastardy became the jurisdiction of the courts. Once paternity was established by witness testimony, fathers were ordered to pay financial support. Almshouses were established for mothers who had no money or children who had no relatives. As the colonial period progressed, courts and communities placed less focus on the punishment of sexual activity and more on support of the child. By the time of the American Revolution, bastardy had become almost entirely an issue for common law. After independence, the issue of illegitimacy became an issue of support laws and social stigma.

In the 19th century, social attitudes toward illegitimacy became morally conservative again. As the middle class expanded, social propriety became a priority, in part because an expanding and urbanizing population could not control parents of illegitimate children as it could when almost everyone lived in a small town. Bastard children came to represent an affront to patriarchal authority and the control of women's bodies. These children were also a drain on financial resources and a complication to property inheritance. Though systems of establishing paternity and financial support were still in place from previous generations, laws were invoked less often as families tried to avoid the shame related to the loss of premarital female virginity. For this reason, families sent unwed pregnant women away to have their children, and the children were either adopted or quietly kept by a relative. When men were held accountable for paternity, marriage was the preferred option. However, the 1800s were a transient era because of shifting employment opportunities and a boom-and-bust economy, and many times the men could not be located.

By the 1920s, progressive legislators focused on the child and not the mother's morality. They believed that the child had earned undeserved stigma by the nature of his or her birth. Thus, progressives pushed for uniform birth registration, a formalized system of establishing paternity allowing illegitimate children inheritance and their father's name and, the establishment of standards for adoption and guardianship. By the 1970s all states had adopted uniform codes to ensure mutual responsibility by both parents. The social disability of illegitimacy was ruled legally invalid as a result of the equal protection clause of the Fourteenth Amendment, though some stigma is still attached to unwed births among some Americans.

Sarah Nation

See also Infanticide; Inheritance Laws; *Vol. 1, Sec. 1:* Sexuality

Further Reading

Brumberg, Joan Jacobs. 1984. "'Ruined' Girls: Changing Community Responses to Illegitimacy in Upstate New York, 1890–1920." *Journal of Social History* 18(2) (Winter): 247–272.

Solinger, Ricki, and Elaine Tyler May. 1992. *Wake Up Little Suzie: Single Pregnancy and Race before Roe v. Wade.* New York: Routledge.

Stone, Lawrence. 1977. *The Family, Sex and Marriage in England, 1500–1800.* New York: Harper and Row.

Bishop, Bridget (ca. 1630–1692)

The religious passion and antiwoman sentiment of 17th-century colonial North America reached its apogee in Salem, Massachusetts, during the infamous Salem Witch Trials. One victim of the trials, Bridget Playfer Waselby Oliver Bishop, was accused three times of being a witch and was hanged in 1692, the first victim of the Salem hysteria. The vast majority of people executed for witchcraft were women. Eighteen other women followed Bishop to the hangman's noose before the governor put a stop to it a few months later.

Bishop was born Bridget Playfer around 1630, most probably in Norwich, Norfolk County, England, and married Samuel Waselby on April 13, 1660, as per parish records of St. Mary in the Marsh, Norwich. They baptized their first son, Benjamin, on October 6, 1663, and immigrated to America around 1665. She and her husband would have come as part of the Puritan immigration movement in which religious dissenters fled England for less hostile lands. Historians believe that Bishop gave birth to a daughter in Boston, as the record commissioner's report of the town mentions a baby daughter, Mary, born to Bishop and her deceased husband, Samuel, on January 10, 1665.

Bishop married again on July 26, 1666, to Thomas Oliver, a widower with three children who had come from Norwich to America around 1637. Both Bishop and Oliver were emblematic of the problem that Puritans and other early colonists had with marriages—they were often dissolved by death. A daughter named Christian was born to the couple on May 8, 1667. Their married life was not smooth. They came before

This picture illustrates the hanging of accused witch Bridget Bishop in 1692. Bishop was the first of over 70 accusations and 20 executions before the Salem Witch Trials ended a year later. (Bettmann/Getty)

a public hearing with allegations of violent quarreling and physical injury to both. Bishop did not tolerate physical abuse from her husband, and she retaliated. In January 1669, both were fined and whipped in public. Seven years later the couple again came to a public hearing and received the punishment of having their mouths gagged in a public place. Bishop's past is also emblematic of women accused of witchcraft, for Puritan church authorities often sought to use witchcraft accusations and trials to rid themselves of troublesome community members.

When Oliver died on April 24, 1679, Bishop became the administrator of his estate, which included two stores of liquor. The community did not look kindly on her, and when a neighbor accused her of

being a witch, a rumor circulated that she had bewitched her two husbands and caused their deaths. On December 25, 1679, she was accused of witchcraft for the first time, but the charges were dropped after Reverend John Hale testified on her behalf.

Bishop married for the third time around 1685–1687 to Edward Bishop, a leader in the shipbuilding industry. In March 1687 Bridget Bishop was accused of stealing. She denied the charge, pleading that it was an act of borrowing. She was also indicted for witchcraft for the second time because of a neighbor suffering from fits but was again acquitted. In January 1692, the Salem witch paranoia began when some young girls exhibited bizarre behavior, including fainting spells, trancelike conditions, and yelling blasphemy.

The number of accusers increased, as did the accused. It was a question of time before Bishop would be charged with witchcraft for the third time. She was a likely target because of her history, style of living, poor reputation among the community, and independent spirit.

Bishop was arrested on April 18, 1692, after a maid named Mercy Lewis accused her of witchcraft two days previously. Bishop had a harrowing time in a Boston jail from May 12 until May 31. She was brought back to Salem and stood trial on June 2, 1692. Although she was not the first woman to be accused, she would be the first to be charged in a court. Accusers such as Lewis and other women began having fits, confirming that they had been under the spell of witchcraft. Many went against Bishop, mentioning that they had been haunted by her at night; some claimed that they had fallen sick, and one told that he had seen dolls with pins in Bishop's house. Even her own brother-in-law claimed that Bishop was having a dialogue with the devil at night.

It seemed that the whole of Salem was against Bishop. She appealed, pleading innocence by saying "I have no familiarity with the devil. I am as innocent as the child unborn. I am innocent of a witch." Still, she was pronounced guilty. On June 10, 1692, with a large crowd watching, she was taken to Gallows Hill and hanged from the branches of a great oak tree. Bishop became the first hanging victim of the Salem Witch Trials. Unlike many others victims of witchcraft hysteria, Bishop claimed her innocence to the end. Other women confessed to being witches to evade capital punishment, though some women confessed and were executed nonetheless. Puritan authorities reasoned that a penitent witch might live if her crimes were not too severe and she was deemed truly sorry for her sins.

Eventually the court declared that the witch trials were unlawful, and the government of Massachusetts formally apologized in 1692 for the trials. Contemporary observers can see Bishop's story play out through mock witch trials held each day. Her wax figure is kept in the Salem Wax Museum, where she is depicted as serving alcohol in her shop while being arrested. The Bishop House is still in existence.

Patit Paban Mishra

See also Hibbins, Ann; Witchcraft in New England; Witch Trials, Salem, Massachusetts

Further Reading

Foulds, Diane E. 2010. *Death in Salem: The Private Lives behind the 1692 Witch Hunt.* Guilford, CT: Globe Pequot.
Hall, David D. 1991. *Witch-Hunting in Seventeenth-Century New England.* Boston: Northeastern University Press.
Roach, Marilynne K. 2013. *Six Women of Salem: The Untold Story of the Accused and Their Accusers in the Salem Witch Trials.* New York: Da Capo.
Rosenthal, Bernard, ed. 2009. *Records of the Salem Witch-Hunt.* New York: Cambridge University Press.

Bradstreet, Anne (1612–1672)

The first English woman to publish a book of poetry and the first one to do so while living in the New World, Anne Bradstreet came to America with John Winthrop's company of the founders of the Massachusetts Bay Colony in 1630. Her poetry reflects the experiences she had while living in the rugged landscape of New England. Her words grant us insight into what life was like for a woman and a mother in early America.

Bradstreet was born into a Puritan family in Northampton, England, in 1612. Her parents, Thomas Dudley and Dorothy Yorke Dudley, were part of England's gentry, or upper middle class. Bradstreet's father accepted a position as steward for the Earl of Lincoln, which meant that the family held close ties with the English aristocracy. This also meant that Anne Bradstreet and her siblings grew up on the earl's estates. In addition to substantial material comforts, the children had access to an education rich in literature, music, and art.

In 1628 when Anne Bradstreet was approximately 16 years old, she met and married Simon Bradstreet, a graduate of Cambridge who worked for Thomas Dudley. Their marriage would last until her death 44 years later. As the English Crown increased its persecution of Puritans, many felt compelled to leave England to settle in the New World. In 1630 Bradstreet, her husband, and her parents arrived in America, where life proved difficult for them and many other Puritans. Bradstreet suffered from chronic illnesses (most scholars agree that a childhood bout with small-pox left her physically frail and susceptible to illness). Despite these setbacks, she was able to bear eight children, all of whom lived to adulthood, no small feat given that childhood mortality rates approached 50 percent at the time.

The Puritans were a variety of Protestant Christianity that emphasized plainness of worship. They did not appreciate or encourage excessive imagery or anything they viewed as extra adornment. This rejection of overt decoration carried over to their attitudes toward literature. Puritans were suspicious of art whose only value was aesthetic and not didactic. In other words, they believed that the motivation for art should be the desire to teach a lesson, specifically a lesson on morality or ethics. Art created solely for its own sake was not encouraged, because Puritans believed that it took people's attention away from God.

Despite their aversion to aesthetic art, Puritans did produce poetry. However, this writing typically concerned expressing their relationship toward God. Puritans such as Bradstreet wrote verses expressing their search for meaning, their intense desire for grace, and their belief in religious piety. These writings were often intended to be shared with others to encourage or facilitate their journey toward salvation, as this was the Puritan's greatest concern. Puritans believed that God was present in every aspect of their lives, and they would often seek connections between everyday events and God's providence. Because of the supreme importance they applied to their faith, Puritans felt that they had to constantly work to become more righteous. They believed that if they succeeded, they would achieve salvation after death.

Bradstreet's poetry stands out from most Puritan poetry in that it concerned itself with all elements of her daily life, from the love she felt toward her husband to the joys that her children brought her. Bradstreet's strong religious beliefs were also reflected in her work, much as was the norm for poetry produced by Puritans. However, her poetry differs from other Puritan poetry because of how it pushed the limits of stylistic conventions. Bradstreet's sophisticated writing style reveals an extremely learned mind, one that had clearly been steeped in English literature. Her natural wit and love of language (in the guise of word-play) come through even in her earliest poems. It is fair to say that her poems do contain what many Puritans would have considered excessive adornment. At the same time, Bradstreet is successful in integrating these adornments with genuine Puritan piety.

Bradstreet is typically categorized as one of America's early poets, despite the fact that her work, as a whole, does not concern itself with America. She was fascinated by the political situation in England and in particular by Queen Elizabeth, even going so far as to dedicate a poem to the queen titled "In Honour of That High and Mighty Princess Queen Elizabeth of Happy Memory." Scholars have also noted that Bradstreet seemed to hope to return to Britain one day. Poems such as her "Dialogue between Old England and New" implies that she hoped for a true English religious reformation, one that would finally expunge Catholic influence. The fact that this poem was written in 1643, after Bradstreet had been in America for 13 years, serves to highlight the strength of her commitment to her native country.

Bradstreet's poetic aim was never notoriety. She did not have her poetry published. It was done without her knowledge by her brother-in-law. Her aims can be summed up as an ongoing struggle for connection to God, her loved ones, and England. Many of her poems address these concerns simultaneously, such as her poems to her husband expressing the Puritan view that marriage is directly linked to one's relationship with God. For example, in the poem "To My Dear and Loving Husband," Bradstreet writes "Then while we live, in love let's so persevere / That when we live no more, we may live ever" (Bradstreet 1981, 180). What ostensibly appears to be a love poem is in fact a reminder of the faith they share and a reminder that this faith compels them to live in a way that will eventually lead them toward eternal salvation.

Alberta M. Miranda

See also Protestant Women; *Vol. 1, Sec. 1:* Queens, European, Elizabeth I of England and Isabella of Castile

Further Reading

Bradstreet, Anne. 1981. *The Complete Works of Anne Bradstreet.* Edited by Joseph R. McElrath and Allan P. Robb. Boston: Twayne Publishers.

Furey, Constance. 2012. "Relational Virtue: Anne Bradstreet, Edward Taylor, and Puritan Marriage." *Journal of Medieval and Early Modern Studies* 42(1): 201–224.

Two Poems of Anne Bradstreet (1678)

Anne Bradstreet (1612–1672) was the first woman to be published as a poet in colonial British America. Although she also wrote on politics and history, she is best known for her religious- and domestic-themed poems, two of which are reproduced here.

To My Dear and Loving Husband

If ever two were one, then surely we.
If ever man were lov'd by wife, then thee.
If ever wife was happy in a man,
Compare with me, ye women, if you can.
I prize thy love more than whole Mines of gold
Or all the riches that the East doth hold.
My love is such that Rivers cannot quench,
Nor ought but love from thee give recompetence.
Thy love is such I can no way repay.
The heavens reward thee manifold, I pray.
Then while we live, in love let's so persever
That when we live no more, we may live ever.

By Night When Others Soundly Slept

By night when others soundly slept
And hath at once both ease and Rest,
My waking eyes were open kept
And so to lie I found it best.

I sought him whom my Soul did Love,
With tears I sought him earnestly.
He bow'd his ear down from Above.
In vain I did not seek or cry.

My hungry Soul he fill'd with Good;
He in his Bottle put my tears,
My smarting wounds washt in his blood,
And banisht thence my Doubts and fears.

What to my Saviour shall I give
Who freely hath done this for me?
I'll serve him here whilst I shall live
And Love him to Eternity.

Source: Anne Dudley Bradstreet, *Several Poems, Compiled with Great Variety of Wit and Learning . . .* (Boston: Printed by John Foster, 1678). Available at University of Virginia, http://xroads.virginia.edu/~hyper/bradstreet/bradstreet.html.

Brent, Margaret (1601–1671)

A rare female landholder of colonial Maryland, Margaret Brent became the first woman in an English North American colony to demand voting rights.

Brent was born in Gloucester, England, to Lord Admington and Lady Elizabeth. As English law did not entitle females to inherit property and she was prohibited from practicing Roman Catholicism there, Brent left her mother country after the death of her parents. She immigrated to Maryland in November 1639 along with her siblings Mary, Giles, and Fulke. Gradually they carved a niche in the colony and became rich planters. Brent devoted herself to business ventures in St. Mary's City. She also brought nine servants from England with her and went into business bringing indentured laborers from England and selling them to colonists. Brent and her sister received the first land grant of St. Mary's City and founded the Sister's Freehold. Afterward she expanded her entitlement of land to about 1,800 acres. Brent did not hesitate to go to court to claim her properly owed debts. In a span of eight years she was involved in 124 court cases, winning all. She also became guardian, along with Governor Leonard Calvert, of Mary Kitomaquund, the daughter of the chief of the Piscataway tribe. Later on Brent's brother Giles married Kitomaquund and, because women could not own property, became owner of what had been his father-in-law's land.

The English Civil War spilled over to Maryland in 1645, with Protestants rising up against Catholics. The Catholic governor had to flee to Virginia after an attack by supporters of the Protestant English Parliament. Brent's Catholic brother was sent back to England as a prisoner along with two Jesuits. Protestants destroyed Catholic property, but the fortunes of Brent and her clan again rose after Governor Calvert and his army reclaimed Maryland in 1646. Governor Calvert died in 1647 and left Brent, his close confidant, as executor of his will. In that position, she also held power over the property of Calvert's brother, Lord Baltimore, who was in London at that time. Because her first duty was to pay Calvert's troops, she sold the brother's property. The soldiers had been poised to revolt if their payments were delayed, and Brent's bold actions helped ensure the survival of the Catholic colony.

Afterward, Brent appealed to the General Assembly of Maryland in January 1648 to grant her voting rights because she was the executor of an important will and also a woman of independent wealth. She became the first woman in an English colony to demand voting rights, but such rights for women were unheard of in 17th-century England. The General Assembly did praise her work for Lord Baltimore but denied her petition.

About 1650 the Brent family decided to shift to Virginia, where Brent purchased property, including a plantation named Peace. She remained unmarried her entire life and died around 1671. After a century her land investments became the basis of the towns of Alexandria and Fredericksburg.

Brent's legacy as an adventurous and independent woman in the male-dominated society of colonial America has survived the centuries. Brent stood for the rights of her sex and was an early advocate of gender empowerment. She was also responsible for preserving the stability of Catholic government in Maryland in the mid-1640s. To commemorate Brent's memory, a garden in St. Mary's City grounds, a street near St. Mary's College, and several local schools are named after her. In Virginia her memory lingers on in a marker at Jones Point Park and several highway markers. The American Bar Association Commission on Women in the Profession instituted the Margaret Brent Women Lawyers of Achievement Award in 1991 for achievements by female attorneys.

Patit Paban Mishra

See also Catholic Women; Kittamaquund, Mary; *Vol. 2, Sec. 1:* Suffrage Movement

Further Reading

Bernhardt, Marie Frances. 1925. *Mistress Margaret Brent.* Richmond, VA: Catholic Women's Club.

Land, Aubrey C. 1981. *Colonial Maryland: A History.* Millwood, NY: KTO Press.

Mays, Dorothy A. 2004. *Women in Early America: Struggle, Survival, and Freedom in a New World.* Santa Barbara, CA: ABC-CLIO.

Brothels

The brothels of the colonial and antebellum eras of the United States first took root in specific areas to serve a transient population of sailors and soldiers. As settlers arrived and the population of the country increased, the numbers, types, and locations of brothels increased throughout the 18th and 19th centuries.

The practice of prostitution in the New World has been recorded as early as 1721, when King Louis XIV of France emptied La Salpetriere prison and sent 88 of its inmates to his country's colonial territory in Louisiana, where they disembarked in New Orleans. The prostitutes among them were some of the first female settlers in the area, and they continued to ply their trade there. This is not to say that there was no prostitution in the colonies before 1721 but only that it was not officially recorded.

Prior to and shortly after the American Revolutionary War, brothels were found mainly in eastern port cities, such as New York City, Boston, Philadelphia,

New Orleans, and Charleston, South Carolina. Houses were generally found near the docks, and typical customers would be men temporarily stationed at or passing through the city, as opposed to permanent residents. While some cities adopted laws making prostitution illegal, such laws were not always enforced, in part because even large cities such as New York had no municipal police force until the 1840s and relied on citizens to initiate most criminal charges. This lack of enforcement, along with a burgeoning population, led to an expansion of the sex trade in general, resulting in a larger variety of brothels and a wider clientele.

Some brothel owners specialized in certain types of girls or women. Hannah Lewis, a free African American madam, kept only white employees and servants at her Anthony Street establishment in New York City in the 1820s. Some brothels emphasized youth, keeping mainly teenagers, though girls as young as 8 years of age have been recorded in city records at a time when the age of consent in New York was 10. Most prostitutes of the time tended to be teenagers, typically 15 or 16 years old.

Larry Whiteaker, in his book *Seduction, Prostitution, and Moral Reform in New York, 1830–1860*, details several economic classes of brothels found during that period, from the parlor house that catered to elite class men to the slum disorderly house or bawdy house visited by working-class men. The women of the parlor houses were usually young, attractive, and often educated. Working afternoons and early evenings, a woman could earn $50 to $100 a week. She would pay a set amount of money every week to the madam who ran the establishment, and the rest of the money was hers. The police rarely bothered elite-class brothels because their clientele included the city's most powerful men. Even brothels in the slums faced little harassment by the police because the public did not perceive them as threatening civil order.

The next level down was the most common— women who would work in comfortable but not luxurious brothels and would walk the streets or go to local theaters to pick up men if business at the brothel was slow. These women were usually fashionably dressed and could pass for ordinary citizens. Many of these women were former seamstresses or servants who found prostitution much more lucrative. In the 1830s a seamstress typically made between 75 cents and $1.50 a week, and a factory worker made not much more.

The lowest level was the slum brothel, often associated with saloons or gambling establishments and catering to transients and the poorest segment of male society. These girls and women were more likely to be foreign-born and from poor families themselves, with little in the way of prospects. Even here, a prostitute could make up to $20 or $30 a week, though the areas in which they worked were often crime-ridden and garnered much more attention from civil authorities as a result, making the occupation even more risky.

While for most girls and women entering into prostitution was a matter of economic necessity, it was not unusual to find women from wealthier households in brothels, many attempting to escape stultifying or abusive family lives. Women drifted in and out of brothels, only resorting to them when needing money, and most women stayed in the business for only a few years. However, there were also those who saw the business of prostitution as a viable career move in a time when economic independence and a chance to own property were rare for women. Some madams, such as Julia Brown in New York City, were celebrated members of society and stayed in the business for years.

While working from a brothel was considered safer than streetwalking, violence against the brothels themselves was still a risk. There was the phenomenon of brothel riots. Typically this involved a group of men—dissatisfied customers, men who resented the independence shown by the madams (some of whom had the means to pick and choose customers for their establishments), or angry neighbors who wanted the brothel put out of business. Often emboldened by drink, they would smash windows, furniture, and crockery. If the attackers met with resistance from the madam or her employees, the women could be beaten or stabbed as well.

As time passed, social reforms combined with improved law enforcement and the founding of charities to help poor women and children led to a decline in the number of brothels and made the remaining ones much harder to find.

Nancy Beach

See also Free Blacks, Colonial, Revolutionary War, and New Republic Periods; *Vol. 2, Sec. 1:* Free Black Women

Further Reading

Gilfoyle, Timothy J. 1992. *City of Eros: New York City, Prostitution, and the Commercialization of Sex, 1790–1920.* New York: Norton.

Schafer, Judith Kelleher. 2009. *Brothels, Depravity, and Abandoned Women: Illegal Sex in Antebellum New Orleans.* Baton Rouge: Louisiana State University Press.

Whiteaker, Larry. 1997. *Seduction, Prostitution, and Moral Reform in New York, 1830–1860.* New York: Garland Publishing.

New Haven Colony Sodomy Statutes (1655)

These mid-17th-century sodomy statutes from the New Haven Colony are unique because of their inclusion of lesbians.

If any man lyeth with mankinde, as a man lyeth with a woman, both of them have committed abomination, they both shall surely be put to death. Levit. 20. 13. And if any woman change the naturall use into that which is against nature, as Rom. 1. 26. she shall be liable to the same sentence, and punishment, or if any person, or persons, shall commit any other kinde of unnaturall and shame full filthines, called in Scripture the going after strange flesh, or other flesh then God alloweth, by carnall knowledge of another vessel then God in nature hath appointed to become one flesh, whether it be by abusing the contrary part of a grown woman, or child of either sex, or unripe vessel of a girle, wherein the natural use of the woman is left, which God hath ordained for the propagation of posterity, and Sodomiticall filthinesse (tending to the destruction of the race of mankind) is committed by a kind of rape, nature being forced, though the will were inticed, every such person shall be put to death. Or if any man shall act upon himself; and in the sight of others spill his owne seed, by example, or counsel, or both, corrupting or tempting others to doe the like, which tends to the sin of Sodomy, if it be not one kind of it; or shall defile, or corrupt himself and others, by any kind of sinfull filthinesse, he shall be punished according to the nature of the offence; or if the case considered with the aggravating circumstances, shall according to the mind of God revealed in his word require it, he shall be put to death, as the court of magistrates shall determine.

Source: Louis Crompton, "Homosexuals and the Death Penalty in Colonial America," *Journal of Homosexuality* 1(3) (June 20, 1976): 277–293. Copyright © 1976 Routledge, Taylor, & Francis Ltd.

Captives, English

In the 17th, 18th, and 19th centuries Native Americans in New France and New England captured and held as hostage thousands of North American colonists in raids and wars, generally on the frontier where colonial and indigenous peoples clashed over land. Native Americans took hostages in part because it was many tribal people's customs to do so to replace warriors killed in battle or to demonstrate superiority over the group from which the hostages were taken. Native American cultures varied in their treatment of captives. Some tribes ritually killed captives, while others traded them as slaves or adopted and assimilated them into their culture. Euro-Americans found the stories that captives had to tell fascinating, creating a market for captivity tales. No one knows how many English colonists were captured and then ransomed. Colonists used captivity stories as part of a cultural discourse of the "savage Other" to justify the extermination of Native Americans.

Indigenous Americans captured both Native American and European American children, women, and men. Female and male captives were treated differently and expected to act differently. Northeastern Native Americans expected captured men to act honorably and bravely under torture, which was generally a public and group activity. Torture could be extended my rest periods, where captives were revived before undergoing additional torture. Some tribes tortured prisoners to death, while others engaged in ritual torture meant as a painful and difficult test that would do no lasting damage. Both men and women who passed these kinds of trials were often adopted into the tribal group. Indigenous Plains people also engaged in torture, both as a means to murder and as a ritual test, but southwestern and northwestern indigenous peoples were more likely to enslave captives and trade them for profit than they were to kill them. Native people used captive-taking strategies to resist colonial encroachment onto their lands, replace lost family members, and economically profit from ransom.

English captives who were returned or "redeemed" to their families were often part of some kind of peace accord. For example, 1764 treaties between English forces and Ohio peoples included the return of more than 200 captives, some of whom had been held long enough to have been adopted and assimilated into Ohio family groups. Sometimes entire or partial families were captured, and only some of the family members returned either because the capturing parties wanted to keep the captives or because the captives were unwilling to return to their English families. Elizabeth Hanson's family farm in Dover, New Hampshire, was attacked in 1724. Native Americans killed two of Hanson's sons but took Hanson, four of her children (three girls and one boy), and a female servant captive. The Hansons were tortured by mutilation and starvation before female members of the village helped them. Later Hanson would write about how grateful she was to the native women who befriended her and her children. In 1725 Hanson's husband ransomed Elizabeth and all but one of the girl children, Sarah, who had been promised in marriage to one of the native men. Sarah was released in 1727.

One of the most famous English captives, Mary Rowlandson, was returned to her family after 11 weeks of captivity. A Narragansett and Wampanoag raiding party captured Rowlandson and 3 of her children in a raid that killed at least 13 people and captured 24, including Rowlandson and 3 of her children. A daughter died one week after being captured, but the rest of the captives spent 11 weeks on the run with their captors before being ransomed and returned. Six years later Rowlandson wrote a book in which she emphasized the heathen or barbaric nature of her captors, particularly in comparison to Euro-American colonial Christians. *A True History of the Captivity and Restoration of Mrs. Mary Rowlandson* demonizes and denigrates her captors in a way that many colonial Americans found deeply gratifying. Rowlandson's book became the standard for captivity narratives, emphasizing as it did the dangers of wilderness, the inhumanity of native peoples, and the moral superiority of English Christians.

Susannah Johnson's captivity narrative played much the same cultural role as did Rowlandson's. Johnson and her family were captured by an Abenaki raiding party in 1754 from their New Hampshire home, the sortie part of the ongoing French and Indian War that pitted French and English colonists against each other. The Johnsons were taken to Quebec and sold to the French, who jailed the family. The family suffered from smallpox in jail, and Johnson's infant son died. In 1757 they were ransomed and returned to Plymouth, Massachusetts. Four decades later in 1796, Susannah Johnson dictated her story to a local lawyer, who published it as *A Selection of Some of the Most Interesting Narratives of Outrages Committed by the Indians*. Her story, which emphasized Indian cruelty and barbarism, became a best seller.

While many English captives were ransomed for their return, some notable few escaped or were rescued. Jemima Boone, daughter of frontiersman Daniel Boone, and two teenage friends were captured in the summer of 1776. Daniel Boone organized a rescue party, found the raiders three days later, killed two natives, scared off the rest, and rescued the girls. Jemima Boone later reported that the Indians had been kind to their captives.

Some of the most famous English female captives were not really captives at all. In 1777 Native Americans, probably Wyandots in the employ of the British Army, held Jane McCrea for one day before murdering her. Her story, which functioned like a captivity narrative, served as propaganda for colonials who wanted to demonize British Loyalists. Her story is less about her treatment at the hands of native people than it is about her murder by Loyalist forces.

A significant number of English women captured by native people were never ransomed or returned to their birth families but instead chose to stay with native people. Eunice Williams, for example, was seven years old when she was captured by a Mohawk and French raid on Deerfield, Massachusetts, in 1704. She assimilated into a subgroup of Mohawks living at Kahnawake and was adopted by a woman whose daughter had died and was renamed Waongote. She converted to Catholicism, was baptized Marguerite, and eventually married a Catholic Mohawk man named Aronsen. Her father tried on numerous occasions to ransom her and return her to Puritan Deerfield, but Eunice Williams existed more in her family's memory than in reality. She had become Kanenstenhawi Aronsen and wanted nothing to do with Puritan English life, though she did on occasion visit the Williams with her native family.

Eunice Williams/Kanenstenhawi Aronsen was not alone in her preference for life as a Native American. In the 1750s Mary Jemison was captured as a 12-year-old and eventually adopted into the Seneca people. She married a Delaware man and had children. When her first husband died Jemison married again, this time to a Seneca man with whom she had six children. Jemison later told her story to a minister, who published it. In contrast to captivity narratives such as Mary Rowlandson's, Jemison's story suggested that not everything about English colonial life was superior to Seneca culture.

While English women who preferred life with Native Americans baffled colonists, historians note that Native American culture was significantly more empowering for women than colonial European culture. Colonial Americans, buttressed by Christianity, were firm believers in patriarchy. English colonial women had few rights and little power. Coverture, the legal principle that women belonged to men, meant that women were considered property, first of their fathers and of their husbands. Thus, colonial English women had no right to own their own property, sign contracts, or divorce. Indeed, women's names changed upon marriage, from their father's last name to their husband's name, which was meant to signify their change in ownership.

Native American women, on the other hand, had considerably more cultural, legal, and economic power. They generally controlled their families through matrilineal descent, took ownership of stuffs, and had varying degrees of input into political and military matters. Native American women were also more empowered by their sexuality, particularly in comparison to the repressive colonials. Thus, it is less surprising that some English female captives became "white Indians" than it is that female captives wanted to be returned.

Peg A. Lamphier

See also Captivity Narratives; Jemison, Mary; *Vol. 1, Sec. 1:* Matrilineal Descent; New France, Women in; Sexuality; *Vol. 1, Sec. 3:* Boone, Jemima; McCrea, Jane; Rowlandson, Mary; Rowson, Susannah Haswell; Williams, Eunice

Further Reading

Demos, John. 1995. *The Unredeemed Captive: A Family Story from Early America.* New York: Vintage.

Derounian-Stodola, Kathryn Zabelle, ed. 1998. *Women's Indian Captivity Narratives.* New York: Penguin Classics.

Drimmer, Frederick, ed. 1961. *Captured by the Indians: 15 Firsthand Accounts, 1750–1870.* New York: Dover.

Namias, June. 1993. *White Captives: Gender and Ethnicity on the American Frontier.* Chapel Hill: University of North Carolina Press.

Captivity Narratives (1655–1797)

Captivity narratives were accounts of European settlers being abducted by Native American tribes. Popular reading in the colonies, they continued being written through the 19th century. These narratives at times convey real information about the experiences one could have among the tribe in question, but often they were filled with wildly skewed descriptions and events. These accounts are valuable for scholars, as they reveal aspects of Native American societies, but primarily they reveal how the settlers perceived the Native Americans.

Native Americans did indeed take European settlers as captives. In the century or so between King Philip's War (1655) and the Seven Years' War (1763), more than 1,600 colonists were captured. Hundreds were taken captive during the 19th century. Typically these captives were women and children. Motivations for these abductions included assimilating the captives into a tribe that needed more females and selling them to other tribes for ransom. For women, there was an enormous amount of empowerment in Native American societies compared to European ones. Benjamin Franklin opined in a letter that "most" wanted to return after being repatriated.

Generally, the treatment of captives was not horrid, aside from minimal food allowances and constant movement. Rape was rare, as was ongoing violence. Interaction with Native American women was generally depicted as neutral or pleasant.

The narratives often took a form that went beyond merely recounting details. Often, the stories were written by others or greatly influenced by outsiders. For example, the involvement of Cotton Mather with Mary Rowlandson's (1637–1711) account, *The Sovereignty and Goodness of God,* which was later changed to *A True History of the Captivity and Restoration of Mrs. Mary Rowlandson,* is unmistakable. For the Puritans, the captivity narratives became a paradigm for the temptations and dangers of the flesh as opposed to life in God. Rowlandson's depiction of the Native Americans was filled with images such as "ravenous beasts," "hell hounds," "barbarous creatures," and "murderous wretches." Many, if not most, accounts generally demonize the Native Americans, regardless of their actions. Her "restoration" to European society is a metaphor for conquering the flesh and being restored to God.

The popularity of these works increased during times of animosity with Native Americans. The classic example is that of Hannah Dunstan (1657–1736). Her captivity occurred near the end of King William's War in 1697, as the French-allied Abenakis raided Haverhill, Massachusetts, taking her, her newborn daughter, and her maid captive along with 10 others who were segregated from these 3. The newborn was murdered

During King Philip's War several European settlers were taken captive. Six years later Mary Rowlandson published the story of her 11 week ordeal. Captivity Narratives became a popular literary genre to settlers by demonizing Native American cultures. (Fotosearch/ Getty Images)

early in the captivity. Dunstan was held captive by a family unit, consisting of 2 adult males, 3 women, and 7 children. A 14-year-old captive boy from Worchester also accompanied them. One night as the Native Americans were sleeping, Dunstan encouraged the other 2 women to aid her in killing their captors. Only 1 badly injured woman and a child escaped. Dunstan scalped the dead and earned a bounty in Boston. Her story became popular as the country pushed west, encountering the Plains indigenous groups in a genocidal push to possess the land.

In Dunstan's story, the murder of her newborn before her eyes and the murder of 27 others during the raid establishes the inhumanity of the Native

Americans for the reader. She becomes a heroine by killing her captors, this innocent forced into this uncivilized gender-bending role of killer. Safety comes by eliminating the Native Americans. Thus, the moral of the story is that obliterating Native Americans is necessary and righteous. Nathaniel Hawthorne was the first to object to her account as heroic, declaring that her actions were neither virtuous nor innocent nor in self-defense. Few shared his opinion.

The heavily embellished account of Fanny Kelley, ambushed in Kansas on the way to settling in Idaho, is the embodiment of prejudice. The diabolical nature of the Native Americans thoroughly imbues the narrative, as does the good faith and desperation of the white protagonists. The lesson of the encounter at the beginning of her captivity is that one cannot negotiate with the insatiable, dishonest, and homicidal Native Americans.

Another image emerges in some narratives. Elizabeth Hanson (1682–1737) was captured in 1724 by a tribe allied with the French. Her account is found in *God's Mercy Surmounting Man's Cruelty*. She was held captive with four children and a maid for 22 months. Two of Hanson's children were killed in the initial raid. A daughter could not be ransomed initially, as the Native American family that was in control of them wanted the daughter to marry into the tribe. This was circumvented by having her marry a Frenchman. Despite this and the book's title, Hanson spoke thankfully of how the Native American women taught her a number of skills for living in the wilderness.

Abigail Willey was among those captured during a raid in 1689 in New Hampshire, along with two daughters, by Native Americans allied with the French. She refused to return, eventually marrying a French man and living out her life in Quebec.

The best-attested case of a woman choosing to live with Native Americans is found in the account of Mary Jemison (1743–1833). During the Seven Years' War, she was taken after the rest of her family was killed on their way to Fort Duquesne. Jemison married a Delaware man and bore six children. She aided Loyalists during the American Revolution and helped the Senecas negotiate the Treaty of Big Tree (1797), ensuring a better outcome as the tribe sold its land.

Captivity narratives comprise a genre of highly fictionalized accounts of very real events. What they lack in veracity is offset by the adventure they provide both casual readers and historians.

Mark Anthony Phelps

See also Jemison, Mary; *Vol. 1, Sec. 3:* Boone, Jemima; Rowlandson, Mary

Further Reading

Derounian-Stodola, Kathryn, and James Levernier. 1993. *The Indian Captivity Narrative, 1550–1900*. Twayne's United States Authors Series. New York: Macmillan.

The Garland Library of Narratives of North American Indian Captivities at Cornell. http://olinuris .library.cornell.edu/ref/garland.html.

Strong, Paula Turner. 1999. *Captive Selves, Captivating Others: The Politics and Poetics of Colonial American Captivity Narratives*. Boulder, CO: Westview/Perseus Books.

Catholic Women

Catholic presence in colonial America was relatively small. By the turn of the 19th century, America's population was still composed primarily of Protestants of English descent. The same colonists who arrived in America in the 17th century seeking religious freedom often denied that same freedom to members of non-Protestant faiths. As a result, Catholic women were responsible for maintaining and perpetuating their faith at home.

Protestant settlers in colonial America brought with them anti-Catholic sentiments. Each of the 13 colonies limited the presence of Catholics, or their ability to practice their religion, at some point in the colonial era. For example, Virginia exacted a law prohibiting Catholic settlers in 1642, and Massachusetts banned priests from taking up residence there through laws passed in 1647 and 1770. Other colonies, such as Delaware and Rhode Island, recorded few, if any, Catholics during the colonial period.

The primary exception to this anti-Catholic bias was in Maryland, which from the time of its founding in 1634 was intended to be a colony that welcomed Catholics. Even here, however, Catholics made up only a small percentage of the population. In 1634, Maryland recorded fewer than 3,000 Catholics out of a population of 34,000. The English Civil War brought tensions to Maryland's Catholic and Protest communities, and Governor Leonard Calvert's support of the deposed (and beheaded) King James I led to the deportation of Jesuit priests and the destruction of Catholic property in St. Mary's City. The Maryland Toleration Act of 1649 was designed to prevent future violence against persons of any faith, although such toleration was to be short-lived. Catholic domination in Maryland came to an end in 1654 with the passage of discriminatory laws. By 1692 Anglicanism was the established church in Maryland, and in 1704 the Maryland Assembly ordered Catholic churches closed and declared that Mass could only be said in private homes.

Even in colonies where Catholicism was not outlawed, Protestant distrust and a scarcity of priests forced women to make accommodations for their faith. Women would lead prayers and devotions at home and were responsible for their children's religious education. As the primary meal planners, women were also responsible for managing the observance of feasts and fasts. Private chapels were established in the homes of wealthy Catholic families, further elevating the status of the women who maintained them. Women became central figures in their church communities and the perpetuation of rituals associated with events such as marriages, baptisms, and funerals.

The conventional theology that Catholic women carried with them from England, France, and Spain declared that women were subordinate to men, although many Catholic women made significant contributions to their church and their colony (and later nation) in the years before 1800. Women such as Margaret Brent, the largest landowner in 17th-century Maryland, and Mary Digges Lee, who with her husband founded Saint Mary's Roman Catholic Church in Petersville, Maryland, defied the submissive picture of women painted in Catholic advice literature of the day. Very few advice manuals for Catholic girls were available in England and the colonies until after the French (and Catholic) threat had been eliminated in 1763 by the conclusion of the French and Indian War.

Works such as the 1759 French manual *The Lady's Preceptor: Or, a Letter to a Young Lady of Distinction* by the Abbe d'Ancourt encouraged women to behave in ways that ensured their spiritual salvation as well as their eventual role as wives and mothers. Works published in America late in the 18th century continued to focus on women as subservient wives. Historians have suggested, however, that freed from church hierarchy, American Catholic women began to expand the boundaries of traditional gender roles assigned to them by their religion. Works such as the *Manual of Catholic Prayer,* published in Philadelphia in 1774, included specific reminders aimed at women about the sins of lust, abortion, and adultery.

After the American Revolution, John Carroll's appointment as the first bishop of the United States in 1790 brought more formal structure to the Catholic Church in America, but it did little to immediately change American Catholic practices or Protestant attitude toward Catholics. Women did not hold formal leadership positions within the Church. The number of Catholic communities began to multiply after the Revolution as Catholic immigrants from Germany and Ireland came to the United States and established churches in cities such as New York and Philadelphia. Converts from older established American families also helped to increase the influence and prestige of the Church. Perhaps the most influential Catholic person of this postrevolutionary period was Elizabeth Bayley Seton, who in 1806 founded a girls' school in Baltimore that became the forerunner of the parochial school system in the United States.

Catholic women who were not interested in becoming wives and mothers had another option: the convent. French Ursulines established a convent in New Orleans in 1727 (although that particular region would not become part of the United States until the Louisiana Purchase in 1803). The sisters established a model that would be replicated in other parts of the United States in the 19th century by establishing a school that served both Protestants and Catholic daughters of the gentry while also offering educational programs for free African Americans and slaves. The first convent established on American soil was founded in Port Tobacco, Maryland, in 1790 by four sisters from the English Community of Carmelites in

Hoogstraet, Belgium. Unlike their European counterparts, American convents often had few wealthy novitiates, or their dowries, to support the house. American nuns resorted to more creative ways to sustain themselves, including taking on tasks for the local community such as sewing and farming, charging tuition for their schools, and even slaveholding.

Kathleen Barker

See also Protestant Women; *Vol. 1, Sec. 3:* Seton, Elizabeth Ann

Further Reading

Clark, Emily. 2007. *Masterless Mistresses: The New Orleans Ursulines and the Establishment of a New World Society, 1727–1834.* Chapel Hill: University of North Carolina Press.

Kenneally, James J. 1990. *The History of American Catholic Women.* New York: Crossroad.

Chilton, Mary (1607–1679)

The life experiences of Mary Chilton, the first female to arrive at Plymouth Rock on the *Mayflower*'s original voyage, suggest that early North American Puritan colonial life was a complex and dangerous endeavor.

Chilton was born to James Chilton and his stepsister Susanna Furner sometime in 1607. Records show that Chilton was baptized on May 31, 1607, at St. Peter's Church, Sandwich, in Kent, England. Her family joined a growing group of dissenters from the Church of England, known as separatists, and moved to Leiden, Holland, to avoid harassment in England. Unsatisfied with life there and worried that their children were losing their connection to their English heritage, Chilton's family joined the Pilgrims in search of a new homeland. Chilton and her parents boarded the *Mayflower* in September 1620 when she was 13 years old. The immigrants suffered numerous problems, including seasickness, scurvy, and sometimes pneumonia, during 66 days crossing the Atlantic Ocean. James Chilton died in December while the ship was anchored off Provincetown harbor and his wife Susanna died six weeks afterward, leaving their daughter to continue the journey as an orphan. At the sight of the New World on December 21, 1620, Chilton waded ashore onto Plymouth Rock, the first English woman to arrive there. Artist Henry Bacon commemorated the event in an 1877 painting permanently on exhibit at the Pilgrim Hall Museum in Plymouth, Massachusetts.

The Puritan colonists established their first settlement in Plymouth, but out of the original 102 pilgrims only 50 survived the harsh first winter, largely due to the assistance of Native American chief Massasoit and the people of the Wampanaog Confederacy. Along with Chilton there were five adolescent girls among the survivors, including Constance Hopkins, Priscilla Mullins, Elizabeth Tilley, and an unnamed servant. Chilton became a ward of the household of either Myles Standish or John Alden. In the land division of 1623, Chilton was given three acres of land (one for herself and one each for deceased parents) situated between portions of Standish and Alden. In the same month another ship, the *Fortune,* arrived at the colony. Among its 35 passengers was yeoman John Winslow, son of Edward Winslow Sr. and Magdalene Oliver and brother of *Mayflower* passengers Gilbert and Edward Winslow.

By 1625, Chilton was considered a well-off woman of the colony. She married John Winslow in 1624. Chilton and her husband, along with other Puritan settlers, did well harvesting crops and maintained good relations with Massasoit and his people. Apart from fishing and farming, the other sources of food included wild turkey and venison. Both Chilton and Winslow received their shares of a cattle division in May 1627, a black cow and two goats. In that same year their first child, John, was born. He would be followed by nine others: Susanna, Mary, Edward, Sarah, Samuel, Joseph, Isaac, Benjamin, and an unnamed child who died in infancy. Winslow steadily rose in Plymouth colony, especially after his brother, Edward Winslow, became the governor of Plymouth colony and put him in charge of the Kennebec Trading Post in 1651. John Winslow also served the Council of War in 1653.

In 1655 Chilton and her family relocated to Boston and became wealthy through shipping and land speculation. Winslow died in 1674. Two years afterward, Chilton made a will on July 31, probably the only woman of the original *Mayflower* passengers to make a will. The executor of it was her friend, Boston merchant William Tailer. Her estate, containing crockery, furniture, and dresses amounting to 212 pounds, 11 shillings, and 9 pence was divided among her sons, daughters, and grandchildren. Chilton died on May 1, 1679, and was buried in King's Chapel of Boston.

In 1924 descendants of the family placed a plaque on the Chilton house commemorating their residency. Prominent descendants of the couple include actress Jane Wyatt, Ambassador Pamela Harriman, singer Pete Seeger, poet Robert Lowell, and Attorney General Elliot Richardson.

Patit Paban Mishra

See also Protestant Women

Further Reading

Chilton, Ann. 1930. "Chilton and Shelton: Two Distinct Virginia Families." *William and Mary Quarterly* 10(1): 56–63.

Lawton, Wendy. 2003. *Almost Home: A Story Based on the Life of the Mayflower's Mary Chilton.* Chicago: Moody Publishers.

Morison, Samuel M. 1991. *William Bradford, of Plymouth Plantation, 1620–1647.* New York: Knopf.

Philbrick, Nathaniel. 2006. *Mayflower: A Story of Courage, Community, and War.* New York: Penguin Group.

Thacher, James. 1991 [1835]. *History of the Town of Plymouth: From Its First Settlement in 1620, to the Year 1832.* Salem, MA: Higginson.

Coverture

Coverture is a legal principle that subsumes women's legal rights to her husband. Coverture meant that married women could not legally own property or make contracts and did not have any legal rights to their own children in the case of marital dissolution or any right to divorce. When a woman married, she was called a *feme covert.*

The legal doctrine of coverture declared that a husband and wife became one person in marriage, and that person was the husband. By law, a married woman was considered to be *sub potestati viri* (under the power of her husband), and therefore she was unable to make contracts or establish credit without her husband's consent. In practice, everything beyond the

wife's basic maintenance was dependent upon her husband's sense of propriety or generosity, because husbands were legally liable for their wives' support. Nonetheless, a husband's legal obligations to his wife extended only to what she needed to survive.

While historically married women had some protection against adversity from their husbands, single and widowed women had no safety nets even though they were most vulnerable to financial ruin. While the status of *feme covert* was limited and protected by law, the *feme sole,* a single, widowed, or divorced woman, handled the affairs of her estate without the protection that a husband offered. Thus, the status of *feme sole* offered women one area of relative legal equality in that she was as liable for debts as a man. The *feme sole* inherited and purchased property equal to a man under both common and civil law. In the workplace, the *feme sole* was hard-pressed if her debts grew; she was often the first to be fired and the last to be paid. When marriage was terminated by death of the husband, the most important right of the widow was dower rights: the right of a wife upon her husband's death to inherit a life estate of one-third of the land that her husband owned.

By the time of the American Revolution, so-called republican womanhood reconciled politics and domesticity and justified the status quo of coverture. For instance, P. J. Boudier de Villemert in his *The Ladies' Friend* (1781), a typical piece of advice literature, asserted that the mother was the ideal parent to rule the "gentle empire" of the home. The "cult of true womanhood" describes an antebellum ideology that American women were expected to pursue lives of sheltered passivity and ennobled domesticity. In a separate "private" sphere, women had authority over moral and family issues. Women created an "antimaterialistic" world within the home that balanced the "sordid world of men and public life." Women might have no official or legal power, but theoretically they traded that power for influence in the domestic sphere.

Lydia Maria Child (1802–1880) wrote from experience in *The American Frugal Housewife* (1829), offering practical knowledge for women with husbands who could not provide for families, and observed that the great challenges within the American home were derived from the consequence of domestic slavery. She made the case that dependents (wives, children, and servants) were legally slaves and treated as slaves. On the other hand, Reverend Daniel Smith in his book *The Parent's Friend, or Letters on the Government and Education of Children and Youth* (1845) taught that female subordination within the family led to subordination to civil law and divine government. Smith supported the patriarchal hierarchy of coverture that asserted "Influence by reason when you can, by authority when you must." Like so much advice literature, Smith sought to reinforce coverture by convincing women that their authority was in the home, not in the public sphere.

Legal discourses on married women's property rights also addressed concepts of dower rights. Dower rights provided widows with property, money, and agency. Widows cultivated their inheritances to support families or to subsist independently. Wealthy widows with status and resources commonly assisted other women by loaning money, offering board, or providing employment referrals. While the New York legislature modeled its 1848 Married Woman's Property Act after a Texas law, the New York legislation, sponsored by wealthy men, was chiefly concerned with how women's property rights could narrowly be applied to their daughters' inheritance rights. Texas and California, both annexed into the United States under terms dictated by the Treaty of Guadalupe Hidalgo (1848), were mandated to respect elements of Spanish/Mexican civil law. California, in its haste to be admitted to the union after gold discovery, adopted the New York model for married women's property rights, then passed legislation in 1852 encouraging married women to establish small businesses as sole traders so that families had some kind of buffer during the economic fluctuations of the gold rush.

Catharine Beecher (1800–1896) and sister Harriet Beecher Stowe (1811–1896) in their *American Woman's Home* (1869) observed that "The chief cause of woman's disabilities and sufferings, [is] that women are not trained, as men are, for their peculiar duties." Women's voices in regard to coverture shifted radically as they fought for and obtained the vote. Elizabeth Cady Stanton (1815–1902) was 77 years old when she wrote *The Solitude of Self* (1892). Stanton recognized the political ramifications and psychological resources of "self," or a woman having an individual life: "Whatever theories may be on woman's dependence on man, in the supreme moments of her life, he cannot bear her burdens." Later Betty Friedan (1921–2006), a journalist for popular women's magazines, in *The Feminine Mystique* (1963) called on women to seek satisfying and intellectually stimulating careers in public life without renouncing their roles within the home.

Meredith Eliassen

See also *Vol. 1, Sec. 3:* Advice Literature; Dower Rights; *Vol. 2, Sec. 1:* Beecher, Catharine Esther; Cult of True Womanhood; Separation of Spheres; *Vol. 4, Sec. 2:* Friedan, Betty

Further Reading

Cott, Nancy F. 1977. *Bonds of Womanhood: Woman's Sphere in New England, 1780–1835.* New Haven, CT: Yale University Press.

Hemphill, C. Dollett. 1999. *Bowing to Necessities: A History of Manners in America, 1620–1860.* New York: Oxford University Press.

Lasch, Christopher. 1997. *Women and the Common Life: Love, Marriage and Feminism.* New York: Norton.

Law Clarifying Property Rights in the Colony of New York (1710)

Enacted on October 30, 1710, "An act for the better settlm't and assureing of lands in this colony," Chapter 216 of the Laws of New York, more clearly defined property rights in the colony. Among its provisions, the act places married women in the same category as minors, prisoners, individuals not of sound mind, and those overseas in terms of their ability to make claims to land in New York.

AN ACT for the better Settlem't and Assureing Of Lands in this Colony

[Passed October 30, 1710.]

BE IT ENACTED by the Governr, Council and Assembly, and by the Authority of the Same, That every person or persons Bodys Politick and Corporate, Citys or

Towns, who by Themselves, their Tennants or Servants, or his or their Assignee or Assigns, Grantees Their Ancestors, Predecessors or others under whome they Claime, have been Seized to their owne use or uses, or taken the Rents, Issues and proffits of any Messuages, Houses Tenem'ts Lands and Hereditaments Whatsoever in this Colony and Plantation in his or their own proper Right, for the Term and Space of Ten Years now last past, & Shall so Continue whether in their own persons, their heirs, successors or Assigns, or by any other person or persons under them, in possession, as aforesaid, without any Claime either by Actual Entry and possession thereupon Continued, or Suite to be prossecuted to Effect untill the first day of September in the year of our Lord Seventeen hundred & Thirteen Shall from and after the Said first day of September, and forever be Adjudged, Deemed and taken to be the True, Rightfull and Lawfull Owner of Such Messuages, Houses, Lands, Tenements and hereditaments Respectively, and Shall and may have, hold and Enjoy the Same, any Claime, Right, Title, Demand or Pretence to the Contrary thereof by or from any person or persons, Bodys Politick and Corporate Whatsoever, in Any Wise Notwithstanding. Provided, That Niether this Act nor any thing therein contained shall Extend or be Construed to the prejudice or Barr of any person or persons who shall before the said first day of September Seventeen hundred and thirteen, Commence any suit for any Lands, houses, Tenements or hereditaments in this Colony, and afterwards prosecute the same to Effect, Nor to the Prejudice of any Mortgagee or Lessee, whose Mortgage or Lease shall be Recorded in the Secretary's office of this Colony before the said first day of September Seventeen hundred and thirteen

Provided also That neither this Act nor any thing therein Contained, shall be Extended or Construed to the prejudice or hindrance of any person or persons under Age of One and Twenty years, Marryed Women, not of Sound mind, Imprisoned, or beyond the Seas. Provided Such person or persons within Three years after his or their Coming to the Age of One and Twenty years, being unmarryed, becoming of Sound mind, Liberty, or Return into this Plantation and Colony, do make their Actual Entry, or bring their Suite, as aforesaid, otherwise to be utterly debar'd, and Excluded from any Entry, Claime, Suite or Demand Whatsoever.

AND whereas by many Accidents the Deeds and Writings relating to Estates Some 'time have been and may hereafter be Destroyed, Consumed, and Lost Whereby The Lawful and Rightfull Owner of any Lands, Messuages, Houses, Tenements, and Hereditaments may be Exposed to many doubtful, Expensive and Vexatious Suits, and other Inconveniences, for the Preventing Whereof BE IT ENACTED by the Authority aforesaid, That all and every Deed or Deeds, Conveyance or Conveyances and Writings relating to the Title or Property of any Lands, Messuages, Tenements or hereditaments within this Colony which have been already or Shall be hereafter Executed, being Duly Acknowledged & Recorded in the Secretarys office of the Said Colony, or in the County Records where Such Lands are Scituate and being, Such Deed or Writing so Recorded, or Transcript Thereof, shall be good and Effectual Evidence in any Court of Record within This Colony, to all Intents and purposes as if the Original Deed or Deeds, Conveyance or Conveyances and Writings was or Were produced and proved in Court.

AND be it further Enacted by the Authority aforesaid, That the Dutch Word Onroerende, and the Word Vaste Staat, which are Commonly Rendred into English by the Words Immovable and fast Estate, by which in the Dutch Language is understood a Real Estate, houses, Lands and Tenements, and other Real Estate of Inheritance, And are used in any Dutch Antenuptial Contract or Law Will & Testament, or Deed or Deeds made in this Colony, and Duly Executed before Two or More Credible Witnesses at any time before The Publication of this Act, Ought therefore to be Understood of A Real Estate, And That the Parties Who have Or Claime any Right to any Real Estate or part thereof within this Colony, by Virtue of the aforesaid Dutch Words, or either of them used in Such Dutch Antenuptial Contracts, or Wills and Testaments, Or Deed or Deeds, as aforesaid, Shall and may Enjoy the Same to his or their Heirs and Assigns for Ever, in as full And Ample Manner as if the Devise, Deed, Grant or Conveyance was made by the Words Real Estate, Lands or Tenements, and Sue for the Same, in her Majesties Courts within this Colony, and Recover Possession Accordingly, any Law Usage or Custome to the Contrary hereof in any Wise notwithstanding.

Source: "Women's Rights in Early New York: Document 3, Chapter 216 of the Colonial Laws," New York State Archives, http://nysa32.nysed.gov/education/showcase/201001women/activities_dbq3.shtml#translation.

Description of Coverture from
William Blackstone's *Commentaries on the Laws of England* (1765)

Coverture is the legal principle whereby women cede their legal rights to their husbands at marriage. Though coverture had a long history in common-law practice, English jurist William Blackstone codified the principle in his 1765 Commentaries on the Laws of England.

By marriage, the husband and wife are one person in law: that is, the very being or legal existence of the woman is suspended during the marriage, or at least is incorporated and consolidated into that of the husband; under whose wing, protection, and *cover,* she performs every thing; and is therefore called in our law-French a *feme-covert, foemina viro co-operta;* is said to be *covert-baron,* or under the protection and influence of her husband, her *baron,* or lord; and her condition during her marriage is called her *coverture.* Upon this principle, of a union of person in husband and wife, depend almost all the legal rights, duties, and disabilities, that either of them acquire by the marriage. I speak not at present of the rights of property, but of such as are merely *personal.* For this reason, a man cannot grant anything to his wife, or enter into covenant with her: for the grant would be to suppose her separate existence; and to covenant with her, would be only to covenant with himself: and therefore it is also generally true, that all compacts made between husband and wife, when single, are voided by the intermarriage. A woman indeed may be attorney for her husband; for that implies no separation from, but is rather a representation of, her lord. And a husband may also bequeath any thing to his wife by will; for that cannot take effect till the coverture is determined by his death. The husband is bound to provide his wife with necessaries by law, as much as himself; and, if she contracts debts for them, he is obliged to pay them; but for anything besides necessaries he is not chargeable. Also if a wife elopes, and lives with another man, the husband is not chargeable even for necessaries; at least if the person who furnishes them is sufficiently apprized of her elopement. If the wife be indebted before marriage, the husband is bound afterwards to pay the debt; for he has adopted her

and her circumstances together. If the wife be injured in her person or her property, she can bring no action for redress without her husband's concurrence, and in his name, as well as her own: neither can she be sued without making the husband a defendant. There is indeed one case where the wife shall sue and be sued as a feme sole, viz. where the husband has abjured the realm, or is banished, for then he is dead in law; and the husband being thus disabled to sue for or defend the wife, it would be most unreasonable if she had no remedy, or could make no defence at all. In criminal prosecutions, it is true, the wife may be indicted and punished separately; for the union is only a civil union. But in trials of any sort they are not allowed to be evidence for, or against, each other: partly because it is impossible their testimony should be indifferent, but principally because of the union of person; and therefore, if they were admitted to be witness *for* each other, they would contradict one maxim of law, *"nemo in propria causa testis esse debet"*; and if *against* each other, they would contradict another maxim, *"nemo tenetur seipsum accusare."* But, where the offence is directly against the person of the wife, this rule has been usually dispensed with; and therefore, by statute 3 Hen. VII, c. 2, in case a woman be forcibly taken away, and married, she may be a witness against such her husband, in order to convict him of felony. For in this case she can with no propriety be reckoned his wife; because a main ingredient, her consent, was wanting to the contract: and also there is another maxim of law, that no man shall take advantage of his own wrong; which the ravisher here would do, if, by forcibly marrying a woman, he could prevent her from being a witness, who is perhaps the only witness to that very fact.

In the civil law the husband and the wife are considered as two distinct persons, and may have separate estates, contracts, debts, and injuries; and therefore in our ecclesiastical courts, a woman may sue and be sued without her husband.

But though our law in general considers man and wife as one person, yet there are some instances in which she is separately considered; as inferior to him, and acting by his compulsion. And therefore any deeds executed, and acts done, by her, during her coverture, are void; except it be a fine, or the like manner of record, in which case she must be solely and secretly examined, to learn if her act be voluntary. She cannot by will devise lands to her husband, unless under special circumstances; for at the time of making it she is supposed to be under his coercion. And in some felonies, and other inferior crimes, committed by her through constraint of her husband, the law excuses her: but this extends not to treason or murder.

The husband also, by the old law, might give his wife moderate correction. For, as he is to answer for her misbehaviour, the law thought it reasonable to intrust him with this power of restraining her, by domestic chastisement, in the same moderation that a man is allowed to correct his apprentices or children; for whom the master or parent is also liable in some cases to answer. But this power of correction was confined within reasonable bounds, and the husband was prohibited from using any violence to his wife, *aliter quam ad virum, ex causa regiminis et castigationis uxoris suae, licite et rationabiliter*

pertinet. The civil law gave the husband the same, or a larger, authority over his wife: allowing him, for some misdemeanors, *flagellis et fustibus acriter verberare uxorem;* for others, only *modicam castigationem adhibere.* But with us, in the politer reign of Charles the second, this power of correction began to be doubted; and a wife may now have security of the peace against her husband; or, in return, a husband against his wife. Yet the lower rank of people, who were always fond of the old common law, still claim and exert their ancient privilege: and the courts of law will still permit a husband to restrain a wife of her liberty, in the case of any gross misbehaviour.

These are the chief legal effects of marriage during the coverture; upon which we may observe, that even the disabilities which the wife lies under are for the most part intended for her protection and benefit: so great a favourite is the female sex of the laws of England.

Source: William Blackstone, *Commentaries on the Laws of England,* Vol. 1 (London, 1765), 442–445. Available at Blackstone Commentaries: Women and the Law, http:// womenshistory.about.com/cs/lives19th/a/blackstone_law .htm.

Dare, Eleanor (ca. 1563–Unknown) and Virginia (1587–Unknown)

Eleanor White Dare was the mother of Virginia Dare, the first child born to English parents in what is today the United States. Eleanor Dare's husband was Ananias Dare, and her father was John White, governor of the ill-fated Roanoke Colony that completely vanished. For more than 400 years, Eleanor Dare and Virginia Dare have had a place at the center of America's longest-running unsolved mystery, haunting American myth and legend.

Under Queen Elizabeth I, England set out to establish what were intended to be profitable colonies in the New World, today's continents of North America and South America. An early expedition in 1584 was sponsored by the adventuresome Sir Walter Raleigh, who sent a group of men to explore the coastal region of today's North Carolina. Raleigh and Elizabeth agreed that the region would be called Virginia after their monarch's sobriquet, the Virgin Queen.

With disagreements among themselves, conflicts with the Native Americans, a lack of food, and a harsh winter, remnants of this early group of men returned to England in 1586. Raleigh then determined that instead of an all-male group, family groups—men, women, and children—would stand a better chance of establishing a permanent settlement. On April 26, 1587, a small fleet of ships sailed from England with 150 men, women, and children aboard. They hoped to establish the first permanent English colony in the New World. With them were 2 Native Americans, Manteo and

Wanchese, who were returning home after traveling to England with Raleigh's failed expedition in 1586.

The governor of the new colony was John White, a friend of Raleigh who shared his vision for a permanent English settlement. White was an artist, explorer, mapmaker, and surveyor. His faith in the venture was so strong that he brought along his daughter Eleanor and her husband, Ananias Dare.

Eleanor (also recorded variously as Elenora, Ellinor, or Elyonor) was born in London around 1563 and married Ananias Dare, born around 1560, who was a bricklayer. They were wed at St. Bride's Church on London's Fleet Street. For John White's American expedition, Ananias Dare was named an assistant.

While the voyage to the New World usually took about six weeks, this one did not arrive off Roanoke Island until July 22, having taken almost three months. The settlers immediately had to start building shelters. For protection, they constructed a fort by enclosing the settlement with a palisade, or wooden wall of pointed stakes.

Less than a month after enduring the perilous voyage and the flurry of construction, Eleanor White Dare gave birth to a baby girl on August 18, 1587. The child was named Virginia after the region, which contains today's North Carolina. Virginia Dare became the first English child born in America. Records show that the baby was healthy and was baptized on the Sunday following her birth.

Governor White's enjoyment of his infant grandchild was short-lived. Supplies ran out more quickly than expected, and the colonists implored him to return at once to England for more. On August 27, a little over a week after his granddaughter's birth, White set sail. His plan was to obtain supplies, gather more English colonists, and return to the desperate Roanoke Island colony as soon as possible.

However, at that time Spain sent its fleet of warships, the Spanish Armada, to attack England. All seagoing vessels were commandeered to fight the invasion. This was followed by an upsurge of French pirate attacks on the high seas plus unusually bad weather. White was unable to return to America for three years. He was finally able to reach Roanoke Island on his granddaughter Virginia Dare's third birthday, August 18, 1590, but the 90 men, 17 women, and 11 children of the colony had vanished without a trace.

They were gone long enough for some buildings to collapse; others had been dismantled, a sign that they did not leave hurriedly. The fort was overgrown with weeds, but there was no evidence of a battle. In his log book, Governor White reported finding the letters "CRO" carved on a tree near the shore. Near the entrance of the palisade, White found the word "CROATOAN" carved on a post "without any cross or sign of distress," as had been agreed upon if there was trouble. He took this to mean that they had gone to nearby Croatoan Island or were with the friendly Croatan tribe.

Another agreed-upon plan was for the colonists to move 50 miles inland when White returned. He and the landing party embarked on a search but never found so much as a trace of the lost colony. The search party was forced to give up due to massive storms, loss of supplies, and their boats running aground in the tricky channels. In his log, White expressed hope that the colonists, including his daughter Eleanor and his three-year-old grandchild Virginia, were safe with Manteo and the friendly Croatan tribe. White eventually returned to England.

White's lost daughter Eleanor White Dare came to the forefront several centuries later as the so-called Dare Stones received great publicity between 1937 and 1941. Allegedly discovered in northern Georgia and the Carolinas, the 48 carved stones were addressed to John White and signed with Eleanor's name. They allegedly gave clues as to the colony's fate. While some historians believed that the artifacts were genuine, most scholars believe that the Dare Stones are an elaborate hoax.

Throughout the past four centuries, the ghosts of Eleanor Dare and Virginia Dare have been evoked through the many sites in today's North Carolina named in their honor.

Nancy Hendricks

See also *Vol. 1, Sec. 1:* Queens, European, Elizabeth I of England and Isabella of Castile; Roanoke; Virginia Company

Further Reading
Cotton, Sallie Southall. 2010. *The White Doe: The Fate of Virginia Dare.* New York: FQ Books.

Horn, James. 2010. *A Kingdom Strange: The Brief and Tragic History of the Lost Colony of Roanoke.* New York: Basic Books.

Hudson, Marjorie. 2007. *Searching for Virginia Dare.* Winston-Salem, NC: Press 53 Books.

De Jesús de Agreda, María (1602–1655)

María de Jesús de Agreda was a 17th-century Spanish nun who claimed that her spirit traveled to the American Southwest, where she discussed Christianity with Native Americans. Southwestern Native Americans said that they had meetings with the "Lady in Blue," the name by which María de Jesús de Agreda became known. As a result of the Lady in Blue stories, missionaries made inroads into the conversion of Native Americans in Texas and New Mexico, spurring Spanish colonization of the region.

María de Jesús de Agreda lived from 1602 to 1655. She was born in Agreda, a small Spanish town close to Navarro and Aragon. Her parents named her María Coronel. At a young age she showed religious devotion and worked to convert her family home into a Franciscan convent. In 1620, she took her vows to become a nun and took the name María de Jesús. Her mother and father took religious vows as well. The family home convent continued to grow and eventually moved to the Immaculate Conception convent in town, a Poor Clares of St. Francis convent. As a young woman María de Jesús made her mark on the town of Agreda, and as an adult she became well known throughout the Spanish and Catholic world.

María de Jesús experienced religious trances in which her spirit traveled to other places. She claimed to have traveled to New Spain, specifically Texas and eastern New Mexico, and visited with Native Americans who had not been exposed to Christianity. A group of Indians called Jumanos, who lived in New Mexico and Texas but primarily in central Texas, traveled to a Franciscan settlement called Old Isleta, which was located south of Albuquerque. They told the Franciscans that a lady in blue visited them and spoke to them in their own language. From this lady the Native Americans had some basic ideas about Christianity. As a result, an expedition led by Fray Juan de Salas in 1629 traveled to southwestern Texas. The expedition encountered a group of Indians who also claimed that they had met with the Lady in Blue. As a result of the lady's visits, Spanish encouragement, and indigenous interest, around 2,000 Indians agreed to baptism.

The fact that María de Jesús wore a brown Franciscan robe with a blue cloak helped confirm her claims that she was the Lady in Blue. She told her confessor that she had made numerous spiritual journeys to New Spain and had introduced Christianity to Native Americans. Her confessor relayed her accounts to his superiors, who then sent the story on to the archbishop of New Mexico. Her story arrived in New Mexico just before the Jumanos arrived with their similar story.

As a nun, María de Jesús de Ágreda wrote books about the Virgin Mary, corresponded with King Philip IV of Spain, and reportedly appeared to the Jumano Indians in the New World, though she never physically left the monastery she founded in Spain. (DeAgostini/Getty Images)

Fray Alonso de Benavides, a Franciscan missionary who worked in New Mexico, left for Mexico City and then Spain in 1629. He spread word of the work and success of the Franciscans in New Mexico. He asked the king of Spain to encourage the push for the conversion of all the native New Mexicans. While in Spain, Benavides heard the story of María de Jesús and traveled to meet with her. María de Jesús told Benavides that she had made numerous spiritual trips to New Spain and urged natives to seek out missionaries for conversion. She also told Benavides that she recognized him from her travels to New Mexico, and she described the Jumano Indians, including a chief. She said that she helped lead missionaries on their trips into native lands in New Mexico. Benavides encouraged María de Jesús to send a letter to the Franciscans in New Mexico, which she did. Her stories encouraged New Mexican missionaries to travel to new areas and seek new converts. Also, she exchanged letters with the king of Spain, Philip IV, likely encouraging his support for missionization.

In the 1650s María de Jesús changed her story somewhat, saying that Fray Alonso had pressured her into confirming the story and that she did not believe her body traveled to the New World. She thought that maybe an angel using her form appeared to the Native Americans. She changed some of the dates of her travels and said that other priests had embellished some parts of her story. Despite this change, her original story stuck and continued to resonate in the Spanish colonies.

Noted borderlands historian David J. Weber suggests that a possible explanation for the journeys of María de Jesús and her possible confusion over the travels is that she fasted and ate so little that she suffered from trances or hallucinations. Whether this theory explains her supposed travels or not, many people continue to believe in the miracles of María de Jesús.

María de Jesús died in Agreda in 1655, and a story of her life and journeys was published two years later. Soon after her death, religious officials in Spain considered her for beatification and canonization, also known as sainthood. The Catholic Church declared her venerable, and efforts to continue the canonization process remained in the 20th century. Her influence on 17th-century interactions between Spanish and indigenous people was tremendous. The Lady in Blue legend has been powerful for centuries. While male missionaries traveled to the New World to work to convert Native Americans to Christianity, many of those men credited a woman, María de Jesús, with paving their way to success.

Amy M. Porter

See also Catholic Women; *Vol. 1, Sec. 1:* Religion, Native American

Further Reading

Chipman, Donald E., and Harriett Denise Joseph. 1999. *Notable Men and Women in Spanish Texas.* Austin: University of Texas Press.

Kessell, John L. 2002. *Spain in the Southwest: A Narrative History of Colonial New Mexico, Arizona, Texas, and California.* Norman: University of Oklahoma Press.

Weber, David J. 1992. *The Spanish Frontier in North America.* New Haven, CT: Yale University Press.

Dyer, Mary (1611–1660)

Mary Dyer was an English Quaker who was one of four Boston martyrs hanged for breaking a Puritan law that banned Quakers from Boston, Massachusetts. She resisted Massachusetts authorities who sought to tell her how to behave and what to believe. Her life provides a model for the importance of religious tolerance in American democracy.

Mary Dyer was born Mary Barrett in 1611 in England. She married William Dyer in 1633 and moved to Massachusetts in 1635. Both Mary and William Dyer were respectable and well liked. They joined the Boston Puritan church and became good friends with a woman named Anne Hutchinson (1591–1643), who preached religious beliefs different than those of mainstream Puritans. When Dyer was pregnant, Hutchinson, who was an experienced midwife, helped deliver a premature baby girl. Unfortunately, the baby was stillborn and horribly deformed. Dyer requested that the baby be privately buried to prevent the church from blaming the child's deformities and stillbirth on the sins of her and her husband. Back in Dyer's hometown in England stillborn children could be buried privately, but that was not the law in Boston.

Eventually the church discovered Anne Hutchinson's radical political beliefs, among which was the belief that the Holy Spirit or grace dwelt inside people and that only the individual could determine whether or not he or she was saved, or in a state of grace. Grace, Hutchinson contended, could not be determined by religious authorities or by a person's deeds or socioeconomic success. Puritan authorities considered Hutchinson's beliefs blasphemous, or antinomian. Hutchinson was exiled from the Puritan church, and Dyer was excommunicated and banned for following Hutchinson's beliefs. When Dyer left the church, the stillbirth was discovered by John Winthrop, governor of the Massachusetts Bay Colony. He ordered the baby dug up to see its deformities. Just as Dyer feared, she was blamed for her "monster" daughter's deformities, which were seen as part of Satan's work. Both women moved away from Massachusetts and settled in Rhode Island.

Mary Dyer returned to England with her husband in 1652 on a political mission. She stayed in England for five years, but William returned to America to be with their children. Dyer often was away from the family for extended periods to seek religious enlightenment or to share her political beliefs. During her journey in England she met the founders of the Quaker religion, also known as the Society of Friends.

The Society of Friends and its founder, George Fox, preached beliefs similar to Anne Hutchinson's antinomianism. As a result, Dyer became a fervent supporter. She was drawn to the religion's radical belief that men and women should be treated equally, a belief entirely absent in the Puritan religion. Dyer returned to Massachusetts in 1657 and brought her new Quaker beliefs with her. When she refused to repudiate her Quaker beliefs, Boston Puritans threw her in jail. She was released from prison on the condition that she remain quiet about her beliefs and leave Massachusetts. Dyer departed from Massachusetts, but she had no intention of remaining quiet.

Governor Winthrop fell out of power, and Governor John Endicott succeeded him. Unfortunately, Endicott was even more religiously intolerant than Winthrop had been. Endicott tried to stop English Quakers from entering the colony by checking immigrants' papers at the harbor. Anyone with a "Q" for Quaker by his or her name was immediately thrown in jail or sent back to England. When people protested that Endicott's actions were illegal, Massachusetts passed a law banning all Quakers from the colony. Punishments for breaking this law included prison, fines, whipping, banishment, cutting off ears and tongues, and execution.

Two of Dyer's friends were jailed under this new law. She traveled to Boston to visit her friends and was thrown in jail as well. She took the opportunity to minister to her Quaker friends in prison. Dyer and her friends were released later that year and left Boston. Despite warnings of death if they ever returned, Dyer and her friends returned to Boston and again were jailed. Dyer's husband and children worked tirelessly to keep her out of prison, despite her desire to make a stand against religious intolerance.

Eventually Dyer's friends were hanged while she watched, thinking she was next. Unknown to Dyer, Boston lawmakers wanted to teach her a lesson and did not plan to execute her at that time. Her family had prearranged a reprieve for her. Officials proved reluctant to publicly execute a woman. As the noose was slipped around Dyer's neck and she prepared herself for death, she was reprieved and allowed to return to Rhode Island.

Despite the close call Dyer had experienced and the pleas from her family, she decided to give up her own life to make a stand against the religious intolerance in Boston. She returned to Boston one last time. She was caught and hanged for being a Quaker.

Dyer's execution and the execution of other religious dissenters gradually led colonists to question Puritan authority and eventually led to religious tolerance in Boston and the repeal of the anti-Quaker law. Her life story is important in understanding that however much history books may say that Puritans desired religious liberty, they desired it only for themselves. Colonial Puritans sought the liberty to practice their faith and force others to do so as well. The anti-Quaker laws and executions point to a culture of deep religious intolerance. Mary Dyer is now considered a religious martyr.

B. C. Biggs

See also Excommunication; Hutchinson, Anne Marbury; Midwives; Protestant Women; Quakers

Further Reading

Dunn, Mary Maples. 1978. "Saints and Sisters: Congregational and Quaker Women in the Early Colonial Period." *Women and Religion,* special issue of *American Quarterly* 30(5): 582–601.

Myles, Anne G. 2001. "From Monster to Martyr: Re-Presenting Mary Dyer." *Early American Literature* 36: 1–30.

Plimpton, Ruth. 1994. *Mary Dyer: Biography of a Rebel Quaker.* Boston: Branden Publishing.

Excommunication

Religion was exceedingly important to the British North American Puritan colonists. In fact, it was central to their culture. According to Puritan interpretation of the scriptures, God had placed women in subjection to men. When women defied these social conventions in some way they were often punished with excommunication, meaning they were barred from the church and forbidden communion with its members. Most of the time church leaders employed excommunication to convince erring members to repent and return to the church. In rare instances, excommunication was used in purely punitive ways. The different roles that excommunication played in historical events such as the persecution of Anne Hutchinson (1591–1643) and the inquisition during the Salem Witch Trials (1692–1693) must be understood in a larger cultural context.

Puritan leaders used the New Testament as their source for excommunication precepts. They said that the Bible instructed Christians to first confront a sinning believer in private. However, if the person refused to repent, then two or three believers were to confront the transgressor. If the person still refused to repent, then the matter was to be turned over to the church and thus become public. Once reaching this stage, if the sinner still refused to repent, he or she had to be excommunicated or removed from the church. Church leaders also relied on New Testament lists of various transgressions for which a church member should be

excommunicated, including sexual immorality, greed, idolatry, abusive language, drunkenness, fraud, defying church doctrine, and a variety of other private and public behaviors interpreted as sinful.

Opposed to the Catholic tradition of excommunication, which barred members from certain rites but allowed excommunicated people to continue to attend church, the Puritan tradition of excommunication was used more as a spiritual tool of coercive correction. Thus, excommunicated Puritans were barred from the entire church experience and community. The idea was to break off complete fellowship with the transgressor so that the shunned person's pain of separation from the church would motivate him or her to repent and behave as church authorities desired. Puritan church authorities particularly used excommunication or the threat of excommunication to compel women to behave in prescribed ways, force more rebellious women to accept their status as inferior, and disempower community members.

Most excommunicates were eventually restored, but some refused to repent and remained forever outside the Puritan church. Unless people were banished by the civil courts, excommunicates were usually free to remain in their colony for the rest of their lives if they chose to do so, though occasionally an excommunicate was also banished from the community.

Puritans' gender ideology, or ideas they had about men and women, had a direct bearing on the practice of religious punishments, including excommunication. Unlike the Quakers, who regarded women as equal, Puritans viewed women as "weaker vessels." Puritan women were expected to remain silent in the congregation and passive in their homes. Legally, under the principle of coverture women could not vote, own property, or hold political office. Women were expected to be submissive to first their fathers and later their husbands. Widows were expected to remarry. In short, women were expected to submit to male authority their entire lives.

In 1637, Anne Hutchinson defied these norms and was brought to trial by John Winthrop (1588–1649), a church and community leader who accused her of holding Bible classes in her home in which she taught both women and men. Winthrop declared that her practice of teaching men was not "fitting" for a woman.

During the trial, Hutchinson also challenged the Puritan tradition of basing faith on the Bible alone by claiming that she received direct revelation from God. The court found Hutchinson guilty of heresy and threatened to censure her unless she recanted. Refusing to repent, in 1638 Hutchinson was excommunicated from the church and in a separate civil trial was banished from the colony.

In 1692 Cotton Mather (1663–1728), a prominent minister, encouraged the witch-hunting that swept over a Salem village in Massachusetts, which led to the incarceration of more than 100 people and claimed the lives of at least 19, by encouraging the judges to consider spectral (ghost) evidence during the trials. During the witch hunt, excommunication took on an entirely different and punitive dimension. Instead of being used as a spiritual tool to bring sinners back to the fold, it was used as a weapon to drive accused witches out of the community. Thus, in the guise of religious belief, Puritans used excommunication as a tool to rid themselves of rebellious or difficult women.

Puritans believed that the devil preferred to possess women because they were weaker than men. Puritans also thought that women were likely to collude with Satan because they were frustrated with their social limitations and willing to sell their souls to gain power. In fact, most of the people accused of being witches were women who had defied the traditional roles assigned to females. Most of the women were middle-aged or older living independently. For example, in spite of declaring her innocence, elderly Rebecca Nurse was tried as a witch. Friends and neighbors collected a large number of petitions declaring her innocence, and the jury originally found her innocent. However, the judge ordered the jury to reconsider their decision, and the jury changed the verdict to guilty. The governor of Massachusetts issued a pardon, but some Salem residents convinced the governor to rescind it. In the end, Nurse was found guilty, expeditiously excommunicated from the Salem church, and hanged.

Rolando Avila

See also Hibbins, Ann; Hutchinson, Anne Marbury; Protestant Women; Witch Trials, Salem, Massachusetts

Further Reading

Bonomi, Patricia U. 2003. *Under the Cope of Heaven: Religion, Society, and Politics in Colonial America.* New York: Oxford University Press.

Hall, David D. 1989. *Worlds of Wonder, Days of Judgment: Popular Religious Belief in Early New England.* New York: Knopf.

Juster, Susan. 1994. *Disorderly Women: Sexual Politics and Evangelicalism in Revolutionary New England.* Ithaca, NY: Cornell University Press.

Free Blacks, Colonial, Revolutionary War, and New Republic Periods

Colonial North America as well as the French and Spanish colonies had significant numbers of free blacks in both the northern and southern colonies. While all colonists of African descent originally came to the colonies as either indentured servants or slaves, those who were freed created communities, traditions, and folkways based on their shared experience. The American Revolution offered some opportunities for slaves to find freedom. At the founding of the new nation the northern states either immediately or gradually abolished slavery, thus increasing populations of free blacks. In all of this, free black women played an important role in free black culture.

When Africans first arrived in the English colonies in 1619, England did not have slavery laws. Africans were introduced to the colonies, first in Virginia, as indentured servants. By 1650 there were about 300 Africans living in Virginia. A small number of these servants were women. The disease mortality rate for Africans, as with all colonists, was high, but some black servants worked their terms of labor and became free persons. Mary Johnson was imported to Virginia in 1623, but sometime after 1635 she and her husband Anthony became free people. They had a 250-acre farm and had five indentured servants, four white and one black.

By the 1660s English colonists began passing laws about Africans that shifted their status from indentured servant to slave. New World slave laws made human beings property for life and made slavery perpetual in that it was a condition handed down to children through the mother's line. Thus, the free black population gradually shifted from people who had earned their way to freedom to people who were manumitted by masters or had run away. Escaped or fugitive slaves created free African or Maroon communities throughout the slave colonies. Many women of African descent joined indigenous nations such as the Seminoles. By the 1700s one-third to half of all forced African immigrants were women, most from West Africa, where cultural traditions gave women considerable power. As women of West African descent found freedom, they relied on their African roots in creating an identity for themselves as free black women.

The American Revolution

The American Revolution began to transform the North to a society with little or no slavery. Free black women were crucial to the growing communities of free blacks in most colonial towns, north and south, because their children were born free as well. During the American Revolutionary War, British, French, and then colonial Americans mustered black slaves, male and female, into their armies by offering freedom in exchange for their services. Some historians estimate that during the wars for independence 80,000–100,000 slaves escaped hoping to gain freedom on the British side. Loyalists offered liberty to slaves who would work in combat and noncombat positions. While men fought, armies generally assigned black women to nursing, cooking, and washing duties. Also, some masters, inspired by revolutionary ideology, freed their slaves during the war. First a slave and then a free woman, Phillis Wheatley began publishing poetry during the Revolution that attracted the attention of both George Washington and Thomas Paine.

The New Republic

Following the Revolution, different patterns of emancipation and manumission and diverse social, economic, and racial circumstances created several additional distinct groups of free blacks in the North and the upper and lower South. In 1790 the U.S. population was just under 4 million people, with the black population at 757,000.

The American Revolution left the institution of slavery largely intact in southern states, while northern states began a gradual approach to abolition such that 30,000 people remained enslaved in the North by 1810, declining to 20,000 by 1820 and over 1,000 by 1840. The northern free black population was urban and largely unskilled. Thus, free black women did much the same labor as did slave women, including domestic work, laundry, and fieldwork. Nonetheless, free black women had significantly different lives than female slaves, in part because they had choices, however limited.

Southern states passed discriminatory laws against both slaves and free blacks. By 1810 there were 100,000 free blacks in the upper South. Free people of color in the upper South were selective smaller rural populations whose freedom originated from personal relationships with masters, either as female concubines or as the children of master/slave sexual relationships. Masters who freed their female slaves for personal or paternal reasons frequently trained them in a trade, such as dressmaking or cooking. Free black women also worked as domestics, cooks, laundresses, and field hands.

What is today the southwestern portion of the United States was from the sixteenth century to 1821 the northernmost part of New Spain. Centered on Mexico, this colony reached into Texas, California, New Mexico, and Arizona. The first people of African descent were members of the Spanish expeditions. Africans participated in numerous expeditions and assisted in the Spanish conquest of the Pueblo Indians. Some black or mulatto women also joined in the expeditions. Isabel de Olvena traveled in one through New Mexico in 1600. Free women of color played an important role as midwives, nurses, and apothecaries as well as domestics. Through favorable marriages and unions, some women of African descent became "respectable" women in part because there was more racial fluidity in French and Spanish colonies.

Leleua Loupe

See also Free Blacks, Colonial, Revolutionary War, and New Republic Periods; Indentured Servants; Slavery, African; *Vol. 1, Sec. 1:* Transatlantic Slave Trade, Women; *Vol. 1, Sec. 3:* Wheatley, Phillis

Further Reading

Breen, T. H., and Stephen Innes. 1980. *Myne Owne Ground: Race and Freedom on Virginia's Eastern Shore, 1640–1676.* Oxford: Oxford University Press.

Clark, Emily. 2013. *The Strange History of the American Quadroon: Free Women of Color in the Revolutionary Atlantic World.* Chapel Hill: University of North Carolina Press.

Curry, Leonard P. 1986. *The Free Black in Urban America, 1800–1850: The Shadow of a Dream.* Chicago: University of Chicago Press.

Goode, Sarah (1653–1692)

In 1692, Sarah Solart Poole Goode was one of the first women accused and executed for being a witch during the Salem Witch Trials.

Goode was born on July 11, 1653, into a wealthy Salem, Massachusetts, Puritan family. The family lost its fortune after her father committed suicide when Sarah was 17. She subsequently married a former indentured servant named Daniel Poole. After 10 years of marriage Poole died, leaving his wife with a sizable debt. Goode's second husband, William Goode, assumed the debt but was unable to improve their financial situation on his weaver's salary. Destitute and homeless, Goode and her husband were reduced to begging food on the streets. By this point, the 38-year-old woman had a reputation of scolding and cursing neighbors who refused to feed her.

An enslaved woman named Tituba, owned by Reverend Samuel Parris, accused Goode of being a witch. It was the reverend's daughter Elizabeth, also known as Betty, and her friend Abigail Williams whose strange behavior started the Salem Witch Trials. The pair of young girls had already accused Tituba of being a witch. Tituba confessed to being a witch and was sent to jail but did not have a trial. She earned her release by claiming that she was forced into witchcraft by Sarah Goode.

Seven people, including Goode's second husband William, testified against her. William stated that his wife had a strange wart (supposedly a mark of the Devil) on her body and was either a witch or soon to be one. Goode's four-year-old daughter Dorcas, who was also accused of being a witch and was tortured for nine months, testified against Goode. Dorcas insisted that her mother had three birds who acted as familiars, creatures that helped her perform witchcraft. In her defense, Goode repeatedly contended that she was falsely accused by her family and testified that Tituba and a fellow accused prisoner, Sarah Osburn, were the real witches.

Evidence was flimsy at Goode's trial. Abigail Williams, one of Sarah's accusers, lied and stated that she was afflicted by the older woman's witchcraft; Williams was counseled to stop lying, but her testimony was recorded as valid. Though in retrospect Goode's trial was a travesty of judicial process, the community was fully in the grips of a witch-hunt hysteria and demanded action. Salem's religious and legal leaders were happy to comply. Goode, who was pregnant with her second child, was condemned as a witch on June 30, 1692. She was kept in a Boston prison until she delivered her child, a daughter named Mercy. The baby died within three days of its birth. Within a month Goode was scheduled to hang at Salem's Gallows Hill on July 19, 1692. At her execution Reverend Nicholas Noyes commanded Goode to confess. She famously replied, "You are a liar. I am no more a witch than you are a wizard, and if you take away my life, G-d will give you blood to drink" (Norton 2002, 126).

Goode was executed with four other women convicted of witchcraft: Rebecca Nurse, Susannah Martin, Elizabeth Howe, and Sarah Wildes. Because witches were not allowed a proper church burial on consecrated ground, the women were buried in a temporary grave near the gallows. Several years later in 1710, William Goode petitioned the Massachusetts legislature for compensation. In spite of the fact that he had testified against his wife, he claimed that the political body destroyed his family. The Massachusetts government considered his plea and that of others who lost family members. In 1711 the Reversing the Attainders on Convicted Witches Act returned the rights to all who were convicted during the Salem Witch Trials of 1692.

Goode's husband received the largest amount of compensation of any petitioner for the loss of his wife. His daughter Dorcas, who had confessed to being a witch and was released from prison after her mother's hanging, never recovered from the months of being chained to the prison wall as a child. Twenty-five years after Goode's hanging, Reverend Noyes suffered internal bleeding from a blood embolism in his mouth; he died from choking on his own blood. Playwright Arthur Miller's *The Crucible* portrayed the character of Sarah Goode as a pitiful target of her accusers.

A. H. Forss

See also Protestant Women; Tituba; Witchcraft in New England; Witch Trials, Salem, Massachusetts

Further Reading

Norton, Mary Beth. 2002. *In the Devil's Snare.* New York: Knopf.

Pavlac, Brian Alexander. 2009. *Witch Hunts in the Western World: Persecution and Punishment from the Inquisition through the Salem Trials.* Westport, CT: Greenwood.

Great Awakening

The Great Awakening was a series of evangelical revivals that swept British colonial North American from 1730 to the 1740s. Evangelical men, preaching against Puritan theological tenets such as predestination, argued that both men and women had a right to choose their relationship with God and thus had a say in their own salvation. Women were particularly attracted to Great Awakening theology not only because it increased their religious responsibilities but also because the Great Awakening encouraged ideas about self-determination that appealed to relatively powerless women. Although men remained in control of the religious institutions before, during, and after the revivals, the ideas of the Great Awakening helped women create for themselves opportunities for public service and became the foundation for women's participation in a variety of reform movements in the following decades.

The Enlightenment, an intellectual movement that began in the late 1600s, challenged religious traditions and instead emphasized a reliance on free will, reason, and science. Many educated people adopted a scientific view (a heavy reliance on those things that could only be detected by the human senses) of life and dismissed matters of faith (a belief in the unseen) as illogical and irrational. As a consequence, some people felt themselves drifting away from spiritual matters. In this respect, the Great Awakening was a spiritual revival in direct response to the Enlightenment.

In spite of the Enlightenment, religion played an important role in British North American colonial culture in the 1600s and 1700s. According to the Puritan interpretation of the scriptures, women were required to submit to men's authority in both secular and religious matters. Puritan women were expected to remain silent in church and listen while men preached. Most women were devoutly religious and sought to obey church mandates, while others publicly or privately questioned their religion's approach to faith and gender roles. In fact, women greatly outnumbered men in both church membership and in Great Awakening revival attendance.

The "awakening" from spiritual slumber began in the Middle Colonies and spread to New England and then to the Southern Colonies. The Great Awakening was the largest popular movement in the colonies before the American Revolution (1775–1783). The religious movement began when traveling evangelists claimed that the official church ministers were lifeless, boring, emotionless, empty shells who lacked the ability to tend God's flock. The Holy Spirit, they insisted, was manifested through emotion, not reason or logic. They challenged church practices by preaching that salvation was not achieved by following articles of faith or engaging in specific rituals. Instead, they asserted, salvation was an on-the-spot event born of inner conviction. Born-again believers were called to be doers of the Word—not just hearers.

In 1739 George Whitefield (1714–1770), the most charismatic Great Awakening evangelist, arrived from England. Whitefield, who made several trips to the colonies, toured throughout the colonies proclaiming that the churches were lifeless just like the ministers who served them. Women in particular were attracted to Whitefield's style of preaching, which was designed to elicit emotions from the listeners. In this regard, Whitefield had no equal. On at least one occasion, he recalled that the crowd wept uncontrollably for half an hour after the sermon had concluded. Even the

The Great Awakening was a massive wave of evangelical Christian fervor that swept through the American colonies during the mid-18th century. Some believers marched in singing processions like this one, depicted in 1740. (North Wind Picture Archives)

scientifically minded Benjamin Franklin, who saw Whitefield in Philadelphia, uncharacteristically became so carried away with emotion that he put all his money in the collection plate.

Jonathan Edwards (1703–1758), perhaps the most famous evangelist of this time period, toured New England challenging believers to rededicate themselves to the service of God. In 1741, contradicting predestination doctrine (a belief that God had already decided who was saved and who was lost and that therefore there was nothing that believers could do to change that), Edwards delivered his most famous sermon, "Sinner in the Hands of an Angry God," in

which he told his listeners that they were bound for eternal torment in the fires of Hell unless they repented of their sins. Those in attendance were eager to repent. Women were perhaps more eager to do so than men, because however harsh Edwards's theology sounded, it did put salvation in the hands of the individual rather than the individual's husband, minister, or God.

During revival services, women reacted with outward displays of emotions. Women cried out during and after the preaching, and some had convulsions. In fact, evangelists targeted women during their sermons because they believed that women were more likely than men to display emotions. Revivalists equated the outpouring of emotions with the presence of the Holy Spirit, which validated their message. Thus, revivalists encouraged women to attend and speak at revivals. Many traditional church ministers criticized these evangelical practices. However, the fault they found with emotionalism was minor compared with their opposition to the evangelical practice of allowing women to speak during worship. Regardless of traditional mainstream ministers' objections to Great Awakening theologies, women continued to flock to revivals, often taking along the male members of their family.

In spite of the opposition, the Great Awakening had a lasting, although limited, influence on the role of women in religion and culture. The Quakers had a long-standing practice of allowing women to speak and preach, but after the Great Awakening Baptists and other Protestant denominations began giving women more leeway in the church by allowing them to participate in various facets of worship. Several women became exhorters (untrained preachers) who were allowed to preach to both women and men outside the church service. For example, in 1741 with her church's blessing, Bathsheba Kingsley rode on horseback across the countryside delivering the gospel message to her rural neighbors. Mary Reed's manifestations of the Holy Spirit impressed her minister so much that he allowed her to give her testimonial during the evening midweek church services for a couple of months.

Even though some church ministers were happy for women to take a more active role in services, men retained exclusive control over church governance. In truth, most women were not trying to change the religious establishment. They were merely enjoying the new opportunities that the Great Awakening had netted them. They did not fight for voting rights in the church or try to usurp men's authority. Instead, they sought areas available to women in which they could serve. First and foremost, many women assumed the role of religious guardians in their immediate families, gaining the power to dictate that their husbands and children attend church. Some women set up Female Societies to expand women's participation in religious life. One of the greatest effects of these organizations was the development of female leaders. For example, Sarah Osborn (1714–1796) ran a Female Society in her home in Rhode Island from the 1740s to the 1790s.

After Edwards's famous sermon in 1741, revivals continued for several more decades. Whitefield continued to evangelize, as did Edwards, but the decade-old sustained movement became increasingly sporadic after the 1750s. The Great Awakening had significant long-term effects. Numerous church divisions occurred as theologies clashed. As a consequence, several new denominations were born. The most affected by the turmoil were the Baptists, Congregationalists, Presbyterians, and the Anglican Church. Due to these and other religious controversies, both the established ministers and the revivalists recognized that their respective theologies would benefit from better religious training. Consequently, the older and wealthier people, "Old Lights," relied on Harvard and Yale to train their ministers, while the younger people, "New Lights" or "Awakeners," founded new colleges including Rutgers, Brown, Princeton, and Dartmouth. Religious revivals never completely disappeared. In fact, the fervor of the First Great Awakening reemerged in America in the early 1800s as the Second Great Awakening.

There were a handful of documented cases of born-again women who declared that they were willing to forsake their families if necessary to serve God. However, these women were the exception to the rule. Most "awakened" women continued to prioritize their family duties over religious concerns during and after the colonial period. However, the Great Awakening was the seed from which numerous female revivalists sprang during the antebellum era (1820–1860). Also, colonial Female Societies, which fostered a female culture of activism, were the forerunners of numerous female abolitionist societies (organizations that sought the end of slavery) and women's rights organizations in the 1800s.

Rolando Avila

See also Protestant Women; Quakers; *Vol. 2, Sec. 1:* Abolition/Antislavery Movement; African American Benevolent Societies; Anthony, Susan B.; *Vol. 2, Sec. 2:* American Equal Rights Association

Further Reading

Hall, Timothy D. 1994. *Contested Boundaries: Itinerancy and the Reshaping of the Colonial American Religious World.* Durham, NC: Duke University Press.

Juster, Susan. 1994. *Disorderly Women: Sexual Politics and Evangelicalism in Revolutionary New England.* Ithaca, NY: Cornell University Press.

Kidd, Thomas S. 2007. *The Great Awakening: The Roots of Evangelical Christianity in Colonial America.* New Haven, CT: Yale University Press.

Lambert, Frank. 1999. *Inventing the "Great Awakening."* Princeton, NJ: Princeton University Press.

Hall, Thomas/Thomasine (ca. 1600–Unknown)

Raised as a girl, Thomas/Thomasine Hall spent periods of time dressed and working as a man, at other times continuing feminine occupations. Hall seems to have lived as a male when it provided advantages such as greater mobility while reverting frequently to what was perhaps a more comfortable female role. Around 1627, Hall immigrated to the new colony of Virginia as an indentured servant. Hall's ambiguous and shifting gender performance soon attracted scrutiny from neighbors and officials who attempted to identify Hall's sex. Despite the lack of formal charges, the case wound up in the colony's highest court. The court agreed with Hall's self-identification as both a man and a woman but punished Hall by requiring Hall to wear clothing that was simultaneously male and female. Hall's case presents a fascinating opportunity to examine early modern constructions of sex and gender. Despite the apparent fluidity of gender indicated in Hall's choices and community responses, Hall's case underscores the importance of stable sex and gender categories in determining social relations and maintaining the early modern social order, particularly in a colonial society in flux. Moreover, because Hall's neighbors and acquaintances entered their opinions about Hall into court records, the case provides a rare view into ordinary people's views of sex and gender unmediated by elite medical discourses.

Thomas/Thomasine Hall was born around 1600 in England. She was christened and raised as a girl, first in Newcastle-upon-Tyne and then in London, where she went to live with her aunt around age 12. There she learned traditional female skills of needlework and lace making. In 1625 Hall's brother was pressed into the army, and soon Hall cut her hair and began to dress like a man to join the fight in France. After serving without incident, she returned to Plymouth in 1627 and resumed life as a woman. Soon, however, Hall heard about a ship leaving for Virginia and donned male clothing again to make the trip, likely finding passage as an indentured servant.

Hall arrived in Warrosquyoacke, Virginia, a small settlement near Jamestown. Founded in 1607 as the first English settlement, Jamestown was by the mid-1620s the center of political and social life in the royal colony. In contrast, nearby Warrosquyoacke consisted of two tobacco plantations and fewer than 200 people, most of them new arrivals. Within this tiny community, observers soon began to question Hall's sexual identity, perhaps because of her familiarity with "feminine" skills such as sewing or because she returned to female dress. In early 1629, a group of women inspected Hall's body and declared that Hall was a man, while Hall claimed during questioning to be both man and woman. The plantation commander, Captain Nathaniel Bass, however, decided that Hall was female. Ordered to dress as a woman, Hall was sold to a new master, this time as a maidservant. Still, questions about Hall's identity persisted. Groups of community members repeatedly examined Hall. A group of women inspected Hall again while she slept and then a third time while Hall was awake, and again concluded that he was a man. Next, a group of men forcibly searched Hall's body and decided that he was male.

At this point, the matter was complicated by rumors that Hall "did ly with a maid" known as "Great Besse" (Norton 1996, 187). Although fornication was common enough in the colony, the possibility that Hall was a woman introduced the specter of same-sex coupling. Hall's case became serious enough that local officials sent it to the General Court at Jamestown. Although there were no formal charges against Hall, the court heard witnesses and took conflicting testimony from Hall, from Hall's current and former masters, and from neighbors who had examined Hall's body.

In their decision, the court concurred with Hall's self-identification as both "a man and a woeman" (Norton 1996, 187). Rather than allow Hall to continue moving between male and female identities at will, however, their verdict marked Hall as abnormal.

They ordered Hall to wear men's clothing but also an apron and a woman's headdress, mandating a "permanent hybrid identity" for Hall (Brown 1995, 188). No records remain of Hall's life after this decision, but the court's verdict probably severely limited Hall's social and economic opportunities, since most colonial English social roles were strictly defined by gender. In refusing to allow Hall to present clearly as either male or female, the court rendered Hall an outsider.

Because of the limited sources in the case—the court record serves as almost the only remaining source of information about Hall—it is difficult to know how modern medical observers would have interpreted Hall's physical sex. The best analyses posit that Hall was probably intersex, looking female at birth but developing male genitalia during puberty. Yet the more important conclusions concern not facts about Hall's body but rather how contemporary observers interpreted what they saw. Apparently Hall's neighbors in colonial Virginia were confounded less by the appearance of Hall's genitalia than by the disjuncture between this genitalia and Hall's feminine behavior. The anomalies between Hall's body and behavior caused confusion and anxiety, since English colonists viewed sex as a primary factor in determining one's place and function in the community. Hall's neighbors in Virginia did not share modern notions of the dichotomy between biologically determined sex and culturally constructed gender. Quite simply, biology would have determined gender and gender roles. In the absence of a clear scientific framework, cultural behaviors helped them define sex, and gender distinctions were solidified through ordinary people's daily practices.

Anna L. Krome-Lukens

See also *Vol. 2, Sec. 3:* Hall, Murray

Further Reading
Brown, Kathleen. 1995. "'Changed . . . into the Fashion of a Man': The Politics of Sexual Difference in a Seventeenth-Century Anglo-American Settlement." *Journal of the History of Sexuality* 6(2): 171–193.

Norton, Mary Beth. 1996. "Searchers Againe Assembled." In *Founding Mothers and Fathers: Gendered Power and the Forming of American Society,* 183–202. New York: Knopf.

Reis, Elizabeth. 2005. "Impossible Hermaphrodites: Intersex in America, 1620–1960." *Journal of American History* 92(2): 411–441.

Joseph Dorman's "The Female Rake: Or, Modern Fine Lady" (1736)

Joseph Dorman's 1736 poem "The Female Rake: Or, Modern Fine Lady" suggests a morally flexible approach to female virtue. This view is not unlike that found in the excerpts from Martha Ballard's diary on premarital sex and childbirth, which are also found in this encyclopedia.

'Till Time had stol'n the Ligt'ning from her Eyes,
Sylvia, was never known to Moralize
She gave a Loose to ev'ry gay Desire,
And own'd the tender Flame she cou'd Inspire;
No priestly Doubts, cou'd on her Joys break in,
Imprudence only was a mortal Sin;
Conscience undisturb'd, she calmly slept,
and Virtue suffer'd nought—the Secret kept.

Think not that I from Virtue e'er will stray,
By chusing Fops, whose Vanities betray.
Virtue, we know, subsists in other's Thought,
And she is virtuous, who was never caught:
Our Virtue then, is Prudence in our Choice,
On that alone depends the publick Voice:
You, ever chaste, a Groupe of Youths enjoy'd,
But on Intrigue, *Mirtilla's* Fame destroy'd.
The World by Outside judges, and we see
Fame takes its Rise, from what we seem to be:
A Vestal thus, Imprudence shall undo,
While Caution make a Vestal—evn' of you.

Source: Joseph Dorman, *The Female Rake: Or, Modern Fine Lady: A Ballad Comedy* (London: Printed for J. Dorman, 1736).

Hibbins, Ann (d. 1656)

Notable for being the woman upon whom Nathaniel Hawthorne based his 1850 novel *The Scarlet Letter,* Ann Hibbins was a wealthy widow at the time Puritan authorities executed her as a witch. Her case and many others predate the Salem witchcraft cases but nonetheless suggest that much of the cultural motivation for Puritan persecution of women as witches was an attempt to maintain society's gender roles and even benefit financially from forfeit estates.

A belief in witchcraft was part of the ideology that the Puritans brought to New England from Europe. They believed in a spiritual warfare of sorts in which God and Satan competed for each human soul, and those who made a compact with Satan became witches. Women made up the bulk of suspected witches, but Puritans accused men of witchcraft as well. A putative witch could be brought to trial by the church or by secular authorities, though in Puritan communities the line between those two authorities was not definite.

Ann Hibbins (sometimes spelled Hibbens) was twice married and widowed. She and her second husband, William Hibbins, were wealthy and prominent in Massachusetts, so her status should have placed her above suspicion, but in 1640 she hired a carpenter to repair their house. Whether the carpenter and she had signed a contract is unclear, though it appears that a verbal agreement united them regarding what was to be repaired and its cost. Upon completion she judged the repairs inadequate and the price too high. She canvassed other carpenters, at least one of whom thought that the rate was double its true value. On these grounds, Hibbins apparently withheld payment.

Hibbins's actions troubled carpenter John Davis. Being a member of the same church as Hibbins, Davis sought guidance from the Puritan church elders, who examined both Mrs. and Mr. Hibbins in a church trial. At stake was whether the church would permit her to remain a congregant. The alternative was excommunication, or the removal of Hibbins from the church and thus her supposed removal from God's grace. The church elders, like Davis, found Hibbins problematic. She had apparently usurped the role of a man by negotiating a contract, written or verbal, with a man. Such action went beyond the scope of a woman's duties. She had in effect taken on the role of the husband, which was contrary to church teachings. Elders were, in fact, much more interested in Hibbins's active role in negotiations than in whether or not the carpenter's work had been inferior. Moreover, under examination she refused to admit that she had done anything wrong, instead insisting that she had not usurped her husband's role because he had given her permission to negotiate with the carpenter. The church elders appear to have been most offended at her refusal to bend to their will and community standards about appropriate female behavior. In this context the church trial may have been a formality for the elders to excommunicate her.

Excommunication in Hibbins's world would have been a serious punishment. Church members would have been forbidden to talk to Hibbins or in any way acknowledge her. At this juncture it is unknown whether Hibbins joined another church. She would have been a pariah, in the community but not of the community. Her husband, however, remained popular, and his presence appears to have protected his wife from further punishment.

The death of Hibbins's husband in 1654 left her both more powerful and more vulnerable. Because he had no children she inherited his estate, but his death left her at the mercy of church elders who did not like her. Just two years after her husband's death Hibbins stood trial for witchcraft before the Massachusetts General Court. She declared her innocence. Nonetheless, despite the absence of any evidence, the court convicted her. Because of her prominence, she knew a number of influential people who asked the court to set aside her verdict. The court complied with this request and then tried Hibbins a second time. Again there was no evidence of witchcraft, and again the court convicted her despite her declaration of innocence. Thereafter events moved swiftly. Massachusetts governor John Endicott (1601–1665) ordered her execution by hanging. On June 19, 1656, less than two months after her conviction, Massachusetts executed Hibbins for witchcraft. Her friend John Norton (1606–1663) later said that she was hanged for being smarter than her neighbors.

For some time historians were perplexed at Hibbins's execution, based on the notion that most women executed for witchcraft were people marginal to the community, such as Sarah Good (1653–1692) in Salem 40 years later. In reality, the witchcraft hysteria in Salem defies classification, lying outside the more general run of New England witchcraft cases. Historian Carol Karlsen, after an exhaustive examination of decades of witchcraft cases, found that almost 90 percent of all women executed as witches were women who stood to inherit because their husbands had no male heirs. In convicting and executing these women, patriarchal church authorities rid themselves of potentially powerful women while at the same time enriching church coffers by collecting executed women's estates.

In 1850 Nathaniel Hawthorne (1804–1864) published *The Scarlett Letter,* in which his main character, Hester Prynne, interacts with a Mistress Hibbins. Hawthorne's Hibbins attempts to sway Prynne into a contract with the devil. Hawthorne's novel, as a work of fiction, accepts the premise that witches did actually exist. In reality, Hibbins and all the other women executed for witchcraft in American were victims of the worst sort of gendered oppression.

Christopher Cumo

See also Goode, Sarah; Protestant Women; Tituba; Witchcraft in New England; Witch Trials, Salem, Massachusetts

Further Reading

Cott, Nancy F., Jeanne Boydston, Ann Braude, Lori D. Ginzberg, and Molly Ladd-Taylor. 1996. *Root of Bitterness: Documents on the Social History of American Women.* 2nd ed. Boston: Northeastern University Press.

Demos, John Putnam. 1982. *Entertaining Satan: Witchcraft and Culture in New England.* New York: Oxford University Press.

Karlsen, Carol F. 1998. *The Devil in the Shape of a Woman: Witchcraft in Colonial New England.* New York and London: Norton.

Hutchinson, Anne Marbury (1591–1643)

Puritan nonconformist Anne Hutchinson was a wife, mother, and midwife who lived in the Massachusetts Bay Colony and gained fame by challenging the

Anne Hutchinson led the first organized attack on the male-dominated Puritan religious establishment. Banished from the Massachusetts Bay Colony for her independent views, she has been hailed as one of America's earliest feminists. Illustration from *Harper's Monthly,* v. 102, 1901. (Library of Congress)

colony's leadership with her own interpretation of Puritan theology. She also threatened the social hierarchy by demonstrating her willingness and ability to operate outside traditional female cultural boundaries. Hutchinson's actions not only gained her notoriety in her own lifetime but also helped to transform the "Puritan Way" in the American colonies.

Born Anne Marbury in Alford, England, on July 17, 1591, Hutchinson was the third child of Francis Marbury and Bridget Dryden Marbury. A Cambridge-educated Anglican minister, Francis Marbury was himself no stranger to controversy; several times during his career as a clergyman and schoolmaster he was censured or imprisoned for his divergent interpretations of scripture and for challenging church hierarchy. Marbury took great interest in the proper schooling of his children, and Hutchinson was the recipient of both his knowledge and his religious views.

The education of females was a controversial issue, as they were considered intellectually weaker than males; the accepted role for women was in the home attending to domestic tasks. Anne Hutchinson's naturally high intellect coupled with her education, especially in her exceptional knowledge and understanding of the Bible, and her outspoken nature resulted in her ultimate confrontation with Massachusetts Bay leaders years later.

In 1612 Hutchinson married William Hutchinson, and the couple, who had known each other since childhood, moved to Alford to set up their household. The son of a prosperous textile merchant, William Hutchinson followed in his father's footsteps, a job that allowed him to travel to London to court Hutchinson, who had been living in London since 1605 when her father, now reconciled with the Anglican Church, had been assigned as vicar of the parish of Saint Martin in the Vintry. The Marbury and Hutchinson families held nonconformist beliefs, and William Hutchinson's family members were regular attendees at Reverend Marbury's sermons. Marbury had also been schoolmaster to William and his brothers.

The textile business was lucrative, and the Anne and William Hutchinson family grew in affluence and social status as well as size; their first child, Edward, was born within 10 months of his parents' marriage. The Hutchinsons added to their brood at the rate of one child approximately every year and a half thereafter. They became interested in the preaching of Reverend John Cotton, a Puritan who had begun to amass a following. Cotton's interpretation of the Puritan relationship between God's grace and human works as the basis for salvation held deep interest and relevance for the Hutchinsons, and they grew to see him as their spiritual mentor. As a nonconformist, however, Cotton often ran afoul of the Anglican Church and was soon summoned to appear before church leaders. Rather than confront his accusers and risk imprisonment as Reverend Marbury had done, Cotton accepted the invitation of John Winthrop, founder and governor

of the Massachusetts Bay Colony, to leave England and reside in America to exercise more religious freedom. In 1633 Cotton and his family sailed to their new home, leaving his congregation—and Anne and William Hutchinson—leaderless.

In 1634 the Hutchinson family, including 11 children, left England as well and reunited with Reverend Cotton as members of his Massachusetts Bay flock. As affluent, socially well-placed members of society, the Hutchinsons assumed a position of prominence within a community that was designed to operate within a strict, cohesive religious/social/governmental framework.

John Winthrop (1587–1649) brought the original group of Massachusetts Bay Colony settlers to America in 1630 on the ship *Arbella*. In an onboard sermon titled "A Modell of Christian Charity," Winthrop laid out his plan for a colonial government "both civill and ecclesiasticall" that would produce an exemplary "city on a hill" worthy of notice and emulation by the rest of the world. The key to the success of Winthrop's colony would be the maintenance of a covenanted society, the participants of which were all Puritans, an originally pejorative term used to describe their desire to "purify" the Church of England of its corruption and use of the elaborate rituals, vestments, images, and relics carried over from before its split with the Roman Catholic Church. Winthrop believed that his colony could serve as an example of how this cleansing could be accomplished, and if the English church could and would take notice, it could avoid the inevitable wrath that God would extend due to its unfaithfulness.

Two covenants formed the foundation of this society. First, the inhabitants pledged to support each other to achieve the goals of the colony. Second, they covenanted with God to make the colony work. The government of the colony would rest in the hands of a godly leadership composed of both clerical and secular men, all of whom were faithful members of the church. To this end, all members of the Puritan colony of Massachusetts Bay were expected to follow precisely the Puritan belief system as described by the local leadership. The success of the colony depended on observance of the covenants and strict adherence to the tenets of the covenanted society. No deviation from this order would be allowed.

However, Anne Hutchinson's divergent understanding of predestination became an issue of concern for the Puritan leadership of the Massachusetts Bay Colony, and it was certainly not the only one. Puritans believed in predestination, the understanding that God had determined from the beginning of time who would go to Heaven (the "elect") and who would not. In the Puritan belief system of Winthrop's followers, no amount of good deeds or faithfulness could get an unregenerate ("nonelect") person into Heaven; grace—or God's predetermination of one's election—was the only avenue. Only the elect were allowed to be full church members, and to join the church one must give a convincing argument for his or her election. One could never really know for sure if he or she was truly among the elect; the important factor was whether or not the candidate believed it and if the membership committee believed it. The Hutchinsons had no problem gaining acceptance as elect church members.

The confrontation with authorities began innocently enough. Soon after her arrival in the colony, Hutchinson began holding meetings in her home where women would gather to discuss the previous week's sermon. Hutchinson's deep knowledge and understanding of the Bible and its principles made the group extremely popular, and the size of the group grew rapidly. Meetings such as this were nothing new in Puritan communities, but as Hutchinson began to voice beliefs increasingly inconsistent with those of the local leadership, Winthrop and other influential members of the ruling elite began to sense a threat to their delicately balanced covenanted society. Eventually, Hutchinson further threatened the power structure by claiming that Reverend Cotton and her brother-in-law, Reverend John Wheelwright, were the only ministers in the colony who were among the elect.

More than one historian has observed that once Anne Hutchinson began to challenge the Puritan status quo and was brought before the local court, it was not a matter of if she would be convicted, only of which charges would bring her down. Winthrop and the panel of ministers who conducted the trial had an extremely difficult time gaining any leverage over their brilliant and well-educated defendant. Hutchinson, pregnant for the 15th time, effectively parried every attack of her accusers, responding with precise biblical quotes that confounded the challenges of the most expert ministers present.

Charges of heresy, acting outside her purview as a woman, and challenging authority and many other charges were hurled against Hutchinson, with little effect. However, whether from fatigue, frustration, or perhaps because of her true conviction, Hutchinson eventually caused her own undoing by stating before the court that she had received direct revelation from God.

On March 22, 1638, Anne Hutchinson was convicted of various errors by the Puritan court of the Massachusetts Bay Colony, excommunicated, and sentenced to banishment. The Hutchinson family first made their way to Rhode Island, and by 1642 the widowed mother of six remaining dependent children made her way to the Dutch settlement of New Amsterdam (New York). It was there in July 1643 that she and all but one of her children, Susan, were massacred by a Siwanoy Indian raiding party. Though English by birth, Anne Hutchinson remains one of the most important figures in American women's history for her intelligence and strength of conviction.

Lee Davis Smith

See also Dyer, Mary; Protestant Women

Further Reading

Battis, Emery. 1962. *Saints and Sectaries: Anne Hutchinson and the Antinomian Controversy of the Massachusetts Bay Colony.* Chapel Hill: University of North Carolina Press.

Bremer, Francis J., ed. 2003. *Anne Hutchinson: Troubler of the Puritan Zion.* New York: Krieger Publishing.

LaPlante, Eve. 2004. *American Jezebel: The Uncommon Life of Anne Hutchinson, the Woman Who Defied the Puritans.* New York: HarperCollins.

Morgan, Edmund S. 1937. "The Case against Anne Hutchinson." *New England Quarterly* 10: 635–649.

Trial of Anne Hutchinson before the General Court of Massachusetts Bay (1637)

The General Court was the highest court in authority in Massachusetts Bay Colony. It consisted of the governor, acting as chair of the court; the deputy governor; five assistants; and five deputies. Several other ministers were in attendance, including Reverend John Cotton, Mrs. Hutchinson's minister and the person who inspired her basic theological position. Hutchinson was accused of slandering ministers and troubling "the peace of the commonwealth and the churches." Meeting at Newton and presided over by Governor John Winthrop, the court examined Hutchinson on the charges and then sentenced her to banishment from the colony as "a woman not fit for our society."

Mr. [John] Winthrop, Governor: Mrs Hutchinson, you are called here as one of those that have troubled the peace of the commonwealth and the churches here; you are known to be a woman that hath had a great share in the promoting and divulging of those opinions that are the cause of this trouble, and to be nearly joined not only in affinity and affection with some of those the court had taken notice of and passed censure upon, but you have spoken divers things, as we have been informed, very prejudicial to the honour of the churches and ministers thereof, and you have maintained a meeting and an assembly in your house that hath been condemned by the general assembly as a thing not tolerable nor comely in the sight of God nor fitting for your sex, and notwithstanding that was cried down you have continued the same. Therefore we have thought good to send for you to understand how things are, that if you be in an erroneous way we may reduce you that so you may become a profitable member here among us. Otherwise if you be obstinate in your course that then the court may take such course that you may trouble us no further. Therefore I would intreat you to express whether you do assent and hold in practice to those opinions and factions that have been handled in court already, that is to say, whether you do not justify Mr. Wheelwright's sermon and the petition.

Mrs. Hutchinson: I am called here to answer before you but I hear no things laid to my charge.

Gov.: I have told you some already and more I can tell you.

Mrs. H.: Name one, Sir.

Gov.: Have I not named some already?

Mrs. H.: What have I said or done?

Gov.: Why for your doings, this you did harbor and countenance those that are parties in this faction that you have heard of.

Mrs. H.: That's matter of conscience, Sir.

Gov.: Your conscience you must keep, or it must be kept for you.

Mrs. H.: Must not I then entertain the saints because I must keep my conscience.

Gov.: Say that one brother should commit felony or treason and come to his brother's house, if he knows him guilty and conceals him he is guilty of the same. It is his conscience to entertain him, but if his conscience comes into act in giving countenance and entertainment to him that hath broken the law he is guilty too. So if you do countenance those that are transgressors of the law you are in the same fact.

Mrs. H.: What law do they transgress?

Gov.: The law of God and of the state.

Mrs. H.: In what particular?

Gov.: Why in this among the rest, whereas the Lord doth say honour thy father and thy mother.

Mrs. H.: Ey Sir in the Lord.

Gov.: This honour you have broke in giving countenance to them.

Mrs. H.: In entertaining those did I entertain them against any act (for there is the thing) or what God has appointed?

Gov.: You knew that Mr. Wheelwright did preach this sermon and those that countenance him in this do break a law.

Mrs. H.: What law have I broken?

Gov.: Why the fifth commandment.

Mrs. H.: I deny that for he [Mr. Wheelwright] saith in the Lord.

Gov.: You have joined with them in the faction.

Mrs. H.: In what faction have I joined with them?

Gov.: In presenting the petition.

Mrs. H.: Suppose I had set my hand to the petition. What then?

Gov.: You saw that case tried before.

Mrs. H.: But I had not my hand to [not signed] the petition.

Gov.: You have councelled them.

Mrs. H.: Wherein?

Gov.: Why in entertaining them.

Mrs. H.: What breach of law is that, Sir?

Gov.: Why dishonouring the commonwealth.

Mrs. H.: But put the case, Sir, that I do fear the Lord and my parents. May not I entertain them that fear the Lord because my parents will not give me leave?

Gov.: If they be the fathers of the commonwealth, and they of another religion, if you entertain them then you dishonour your parents and are justly punishable.

Mrs. H.: If I entertain them, as they have dishonoured their parents I do.

Gov.: No but you by countenancing them above others put honor upon them.

Mrs. H.: I may put honor upon them as the children of God and as they do honor the Lord.

Gov.: We do not mean to discourse with those of your sex but only this: you so adhere unto them and do endeavor to set forward this faction and so you do dishonour us.

Mrs. H.: I do acknowledge no such thing. Neither do I think that I ever put any dishonour upon you.

Gov.: Why do you keep such a meeting at your house as you do every week upon a set day?

Mrs. H.: It is lawful for me to do so, as it is all your practices, and can you find a warrant for yourself and condemn me for the same thing? The ground of my taking it up was, when I first came to this land because I did not go to such meetings as those were, it was presently reported that I did not allow of such meetings but held them unlawful and therefore in that regard they said I was proud and did despise all ordinances. Upon that a friend came unto me and told me of it and I to prevent such aspersions took it up, but it was in practice before I came. Therefore I was not the first.

Gov.: . . . By what warrant do you continue such a course?

Mrs. H.: I conceive there lies a clear rule in Titus that the elder women should instruct the younger and then I must have a time wherein I must do it.

Gov.: All this I grant you, I grant you a time for it, but what is this to the purpose that you Mrs. Hutchinson must call a company together from their callings to come to be taught of you? . . .

Mrs. H.: If you look upon the rule in Titus it is a rule to me. If you convince me that it is no rule I shall yield.

Gov.: You know that there is no rule that crosses another, but this rule crosses that in the Corinthians. But you must take it in this sense that elder women must instruct the younger about their business and to love their husbands and not to make them to clash. . . .

Mrs. H.: Will it please you to answer me this and to give me a rule for then I will willingly submit to any truth. If any come to my house to be instructed in the ways of God what rule have I to put them away? . . . Do you think it not lawful for me to teach women and why do you call me to teach the court?

Gov.: We do not call you to teach the court but to lay open yourself. . . .

[They continue to argue over what rule she had broken.]

Gov.: Your course is not to be suffered for. Besides that we find such a course as this to be greatly prejudicial to the state. Besides the occasion that it is to seduce many honest persons that are called to those meetings and your opinions and your opinions being known to be different from the word of God may seduce many simple souls that resort unto you. Besides that the occasion which hath come of late hath come from none but such as have frequented your meetings, so that now they are flown off from magistrates and ministers and since they have come to you. And besides that it will not well stand with the commonwealth that families should be neglected for so many neighbors and dames and so much time spent. We see no rule of God for this. We see not that any should have authority to set up any other exercises besides what authority hath already set up and so what hurt comes of this you will be guilty of and we for suffering you.

Mrs. H.: Sir, I do not believe that to be so.

Gov.: Well, we see how it is. We must therefore put it away from you or restrain you from maintaining this course.

Mrs H. If you have a rule for it from God's word you may.

Gov.: We are your judges, and not you ours and we must compel you to it.

Mrs. H.: If it please you by authority to put it down I will freely let you for I am subject to your authority. . . .

Deputy Governor, Thomas Dudley: I would go a little higher with Mrs. Hutchinson. About three years ago we were all in peace. Mrs Hutchinson, from that time she came hath made a disturbance, and some that came over with her in the ship did inform me what she was as soon as she was landed. I being then in place dealt with the pastor and teacher of Boston and desired them to enquire of her, and then I was satisfied that she held nothing different from us. But within half a year after, she had vented divers of her strange opinions and had made parties in the country, and at length it comes that Mr. Cotton and Mr. Vane were of her judgment, but Mr. Cotton had cleared himself that he was not of that mind. But now it appears by this woman's meeting that Mrs. Hutchinson hath so forestalled the minds of many by their resort to her meeting that now she hath a potent party in the country. Now if all these things have endangered us as from that foundation and if she in particular hath disparaged all our ministers in the land that they have preached a covenant of works, and only Mr. Cotton a covenant of grace, why this is not to be suffered, and therefore being driven to the foundation and it being found that Mrs. Hutchinson is she that hath depraved all the ministers and hath been the cause of what is fallen out, why we must take away the foundation and the building will fall.

Mrs. H.: I pray, Sir, prove it that I said they preached nothing but a covenant of works.

Dep. Gov.: Nothing but a covenant of works. Why a Jesuit may preach truth sometimes.

Mrs. H.: Did I ever say they preached a covenant of works then?

Dep. Gov.: If they do not preach a covenant of grace clearly, then they preach a covenant of works.

Mrs. H.: No, Sir. One may preach a covenant of grace more clearly than another, so I said. . . .

Dep. Gov.: When they do preach a covenant of works do they preach truth?

Mrs. H.: Yes, Sir. But when they preach a covenant of works for salvation, that is not truth.

Dep. Gov.: I do but ask you this: when the ministers do preach a covenant of works do they preach a way of salvation?

Mrs. H.: I did not come hither to answer questions of that sort.

Dep. Gov.: Because you will deny the thing.

Mrs. H.: Ey, but that is to be proved first.

Dep. Gov.: I will make it plain that you did say that the ministers did preach a covenant of works.

Mrs. H.: I deny that.

Dep. Gov.: And that you said they were not able ministers of the New Testament, but Mr. Cotton only.

Mrs. H.: If ever I spake that I proved it by God's word.

Court: Very well, very well.

Mrs. H.: If one shall come unto me in private, and desire me seriously to tell them what I thought of such an one, I must either speak false or true in my answer.

Dep. Gov.: Likewise I will prove this that you said the gospel in the letter and words holds forth nothing but a covenant of works and that all that do not hold as you do are in a covenant of works.

Mrs. H.: I deny this for if I should so say I should speak against my own judgment. . . .

Mr. Hugh Peters: That which concerns us to speak unto, as yet we are sparing in, unless the court command us to speak, then we shall answer to Mrs. Hutchinson notwithstanding our brethren are very unwilling to answer.

[The Governor says to do so. Six minsters then testify to the particular charges and that she was "not only difficult in her opinions, but also of an intemperate spirit."]

Mr Hugh Peters: . . . [I asked her] What difference do you conceive to be between your teacher and us? . . . Briefly, she told me there was a wide and broad difference. . . . He preaches the covenant of grace and you the covenant of works, and that you are not able ministers of the New Testament and know no more than the apostles did before the resurrection of Christ. I did then put it to her, What do you conceive of such a brother? She answered he had not the seal of the spirit.

Mrs. H.: If our pastor would shew his writings you should see what I said, and that many things are not so as is reported.

Mr. Wilson: . . . [W]hat is written [here now] I will avouch.

Mr. Weld: [agrees that Peters related Hutchinson's words accurately]

Mr. Phillips: [agrees that Peters related Hutchinson's words accurately and added] Then I asked her of myself (being she spake rashly of them all) because she never heard me at all. She likewise said that we were not able ministers of the New Testament and her reason was because we were not sealed.

Mr. Simmes: Agrees that Peters related Hutchinson's words accurately

Mr. Shephard: Also to Same.

Mr. Eliot: [agrees that Peters related Hutchinson's words accurately]

Dep. Gov.: I called these witnesses and you deny them. You see they have proved this and you deny this, but it is clear. You say they preached a covenant of works and that they were not able ministers of the New Testament; now there are two other things that you did affirm which were that the scriptures in the letter of them held forth nothing but a covenant of works and likewise that those that were under a covenant of works cannot be saved.

Mrs. H.: Prove that I said so.

Gov.: Did you say so?

Mrs. H.: No, Sir, it is your conclusion.

Dep. Gov.: What do I do charging of you if you deny what is so fully proved?

Gov.: Here are six undeniable ministers who say it is true and yet you deny that you did say that they preach a covenant of works and that they were not able ministers of the gospel, and it appears plainly that you have spoken it, and whereas you say that it was drawn from you in a way of friendship, you did profess then that it was out of conscience that you spake. . . .

Mrs. H.: . . . They thought that I did conceive there was a difference between them and Mr. Cotton. . . . I might say they might preach a covenant of works as did the apostles, but to preach a covenant of works and to be under a covenant of works is another business.

Dep. Gov.: There have been six witnesses to prove this and yet you deny it. [and then he mentions a seventh, Mr. Nathaniel Ward]

Mrs. H.: I acknowledge using the words of the apostle to the Corinthians unto him, [Mr. Ward] that they that were ministers of the letter and not the spirit did preach a covenant of works.

Gov.: Mrs. Hutchinson, the court you see hath laboured to bring you to acknowledge the error of your way that so you might be reduced, the time grows late, we shall therefore give you a little more time to consider of it and therefore desire that you attend the court again in the morning. [The next morning.]

Gov.: We proceeded . . . as far as we could. . . . There were divers things laid to her charge: her ordinary meetings about religious exercises, her speeches in derogation of the ministers among us, and the weakening of the hands and hearts of the people towards them. Here was sufficient proof made of that which she was accused of, in that point concerning the ministers and their ministry, as that they did preach a covenant of works when others did preach a covenant of grace, and that they were not able ministers

of the New Testament, and that they had not the seal of the spirit, and this was spoken not as was pretended out of private conference, but out of conscience and warrant from scripture alleged the fear of man is a snare and seeing God had given her a calling to it she would freely speak. Some other speeches she used, as that the letter of the scripture held forth a covenant of works, and this is offered to be proved by probable grounds. . . .

Controversy—should the witnesses should be recalled and made swear an oath, as Mrs. Hutchinson desired, is resolved against doing so

Gov.: I see no necessity of an oath in this thing seeing it is true and the substance of the matter confirmed by divers, yet that all may be satisfied, if the elders will take an oath they shall have it given them. . . .

Mrs. H.: After that they have taken an oath I will make good what I say.

Gov.: Let us state the case, and then we may know what to do. That which is laid to Mrs. Hutchinson charge is that, that she hath traduced the magistrates and ministers of this jurisdiction, that she hath said the ministers preached a covenant of works and Mr. Cotton a covenant of grace, and that they were not able ministers of the gospel, and she excuses it that she made it a private conference and with a promise of secrecy, &c. Now this is charged upon her, and they therefore sent for her seeing she made it her table talk, and then she said the fear of man was a snare and therefore she would not be affeared of them. . . .

Dep. Gov.: Let her witnesses be called.

Gov.: Who be they?

Mrs. H.: Mr. Leveret and our teacher and Mr. Coggeshall.

Gov.: Mr. Coggeshall was not present.

Mr. Coggeshall: Yes, but I was. Only I desired to be silent till I should be called.

Gov.: Will you, Mr. Coggeshall, say that she did not say so?

Mr. Coggeshall: Yes, I dare say that she did not say all that which they lay against her.

Mr. Peters: How dare you look into the court to say such a word?

Mr. Coggeshall: Mr. Peters takes upon him to forbid me. I shall be silent.

Mr. Stoughton [assistant of the Court]: Ey, but she intended this that they say.

Gov.: Well, Mr. Leveret, what were the words? I pray, speak.

Mr. Leveret: To my best remembrance when the elders did send for her, Mr. Peters did with much vehemency and intreaty urge her to tell what difference there was between Mr. Cotton and them, and upon his urging of her she said "The fear of man is a snare, but they that trust upon the Lord shall be safe." And being asked wherein the difference was, she answered that they did not preach a covenant of grace so clearly as Mr. Cotton did, and she gave this reason of it: because that as the apostles were for a time without the spirit so until they had received the witness of the spirit they could not preach a covenant of grace so clearly.

Gov.: Don't you remember that she said they were not able ministers of the New Testament?

Mrs. H.: Mr. Weld and I had an hour's discourse at the window and then I spake that, if I spake it. . . .

Gov.: Mr Cotton, the court desires that you declare what you do remember of the conference which was at the time and is now in question.

Mr. Cotton: I did not think I should be called to bear witness in this cause and therefore did not labor to call to remembrance what was done; but the greatest passage that took impression upon me was to this purpose. The elders spake that they had heard that she had spoken some condemning words of their ministry, and among other things they did first pray her to answer wherein she thought their ministry did differ from mine. How the comparison sprang I am ignorant, but sorry I was that any comparison should be between me and my brethren and uncomfortable it was. She told them to this purpose that they did not hold forth a covenant of grace as I did. But wherein did we differ? Why she said that they did not hold forth the seal of the spirit as he doth. Where is the difference there? Say they, why saith she, speaking to one or other of them, I know not to whom. You preach of the seal of the spirit upon a work and he upon free grace without a work or without respect to a work; he preaches the seal of the spirit upon free grace and you upon a work. I told her I was very sorry that she put comparisons between my ministry and theirs, for she had said more than I could myself, and rather I had that she had put us in fellowship with them and not have made that discrepancy. She said, she found the difference. . . .

This was the sum of the difference, nor did it seem to be so ill taken as it is and our brethren did say also that they would not so easily believe reports as they had done and withal mentioned that they would speak no more of it, some of them did; and afterwards some of them did say they were less satisfied than before. And I must say that I did not find her saying that they were under a covenant of works, nor that she said they did preach a covenant of works.

[More back and forth between Rev. John Cotton, trying to defend Mrs. Hutchinson, and Mr. Peters, about exactly what Mrs. Hutchinson said.]

Mrs. H.: If you please to give me leave I shall give you the ground of what I know to be true. Being much troubled to see the falseness of the constitution of the Church of England, I had like to have turned Separatist. Whereupon I kept a day of solemn humiliation and pondering of the thing; this scripture was brought unto me—he that denies Jesus Christ to be come in the flesh is antichrist. This I considered of and in considering found that the papists did not deny him to be come in the flesh, nor we did not deny him—who then was antichrist? Was the Turk antichrist only? The Lord knows that I could not open scripture; he must by his prophetical office open it unto me. So after that being unsatisfied in the thing, the Lord was pleased to bring this scripture out of the Hebrews. he that denies the testament denies the testator, and in this did open unto me and give me to see that those which did not teach the new covenant had the spirit of antichrist, and upon this he did discover the ministry unto me; and ever since, I bless the Lord, he hath let me see which was the clear ministry and which the wrong. Since that time I confess I have been more choice and he hath left me to distinguish between the voice of my beloved and the voice of Moses, the voice of John the Baptist and the voice of antichrist, for all those voices are spoken of in scripture. Now if you do condemn me for speaking what in my conscience I know to be truth I must commit myself unto the Lord.

Mr. Nowel [assistant to the Court]: How do you know that was the spirit?

Mrs. H.: How did Abraham know that it was God that bid him offer his son, being a breach of the sixth commandment?

Dep. Gov.: By an immediate voice.

Mrs. H.: So to me by an immediate revelation.

Dep. Gov.: How! an immediate revelation.

Mrs. H.: By the voice of his own spirit to my soul. I will give you another scripture, Jer[emiah] 46: 27–28—out of which the Lord showed me what he would do for me and the rest of his servants. But after he was pleased to reveal himself to me I did presently, like Abraham, run to Hagar. And after that he did let me see the atheism of my own heart, for which I begged of the Lord that it might not remain in my heart, and being thus, he did show me this (a twelvemonth after) which I told you of before. . . . Therefore, I desire you to look to it, for you see this scripture fulfilled this day and therefore I desire you as you tender the Lord and the church and commonwealth

to consider and look what you do. You have power over my body but the Lord Jesus hath power over my body and soul; and assure yourselves thus much, you do as much as in you lies to put the Lord Jesus Christ from you, and if you go on in this course you begin, you will bring a curse upon you and your posterity, and the mouth of the Lord hath spoken it.

Dep. Gov.: What is the scripture she brings?

Mr. Stoughton [assistant to the Court]: Behold I turn away from you.

Mrs. H.: But now having seen him which is invisible I fear not what man can do unto me.

Gov.: Daniel was delivered by miracle; do you think to be deliver'd so too?

Mrs. H.: I do here speak it before the court. I look that the Lord should deliver me by his providence . . . [because God had said to her] though I should meet with affliction, yet I am the same God that delivered Daniel out of the lion's den, I will also deliver thee.

Mr. Harlakenden [assistant to the Court]: I may read scripture and the most glorious hypocrite may read them and yet go down to hell.

Mrs. H.: It may be so. . . .

Gov.: I am persuaded that the revelation she brings forth is delusion.

[The trial text here reads:] All the court but some two or three ministers cry out, we all believe it—we all believe it. [Mrs. Hutchinson was found guilty]

Gov.: The court hath already declared themselves satisfied concerning the things you hear, and concerning the troublesomeness of her spirit and the danger of her course amongst us, which is not to be suffered. Therefore if it be the mind of the court that Mrs. Hutchinson for these things that appear before us is unfit for our society, and if it be the mind of the court that she shall be banished out of our liberties and imprisoned till she be sent away, let them hold up their hands.

[All but three did so.]

Gov.: Mrs. Hutchinson, the sentence of the court you hear is that you are banished from out of our jurisdiction as being a woman not fit for our society, and are to be imprisoned till the court shall send you away.

Mrs. H.: I desire to know wherefore I am banished?

Gov.: Say no more. The court knows wherefore and is satisfied.

Source: Thomas Hutchinson, *History of the Colony and Province of Massachusetts* (Boston, 1767), 336–384.

Indentured Servants

An estimated half to two-thirds of all Europeans who came to colonial North America, both male and female, arrived bound as indentured servants. In theory, poor English persons voluntarily traded their labor for a contractually agreed-upon time for eventual freedom and perhaps even landownership. In reality, indentured servitude functioned more as a kind of slavery. Indentured servants belonged to their employer or purchaser, who generally worked them long hours while providing minimal food and housing. As a result, the mortality rate for indentured servants was quite high. As a result of both high mortality rates and servant revolts, African slavery gradually replaced indentured servitude in the American colonies, though indentured servants could be found throughout the United States well into the 1800s.

Originally, to be indentured was to enter an apprenticeship—a system of learning a craft or trade from an experienced master in which the payment for the instruction was a given number of years of service. This form of being indentured originated with guilds that supervised apprentice programs in Europe, which provided a form of network building for artisans. Under the apprentice system, a master craftsman agreed to instruct a young indentured person as well as provide shelter, food, and clothing. In exchange, the apprentice (or indentured servant) worked for the master for a given length of time, after which the apprentice became a journeyman who would work for a master for a wage. Journeymen could become masters themselves.

In early colonial America, the process of indenturing was adapted to meet colonial landowners' desire for cheap labor. Between 1607 and 1700, North America experienced its first wave of immigration of English and Welsh settlement that was accompanied by a large influx of Africans. By the 1700s, personal debt, poverty, and unemployment in Europe compelled about 37,000 immigrants to come to North America, who arranged their travel as indentured servants. This pattern continued until the Revolutionary War began in 1775, with the addition of Germanic and Scotch-Irish indentured servants.

Agents working for ship captains in European ports recruited and made arrangements for those who bonded themselves, going to various destinations. They sought skilled workers in construction, agriculture, and the manufacture of clothing and shoes. In this legal contract, immigrants agreed to work for their masters for three to four years to pay back the costs of their Atlantic passage, living costs, and perhaps the freedom dues that came at the end of service. Beyond stipulating the length of service, the contracts offered little protection for servants unless they were minors who were assured of clothes, food, and board. These workers solved a problem for colonial landowners who found it increasingly difficult to hire free persons to do agricultural work, given the availability of affordable land, and allowed people to buy their own farms.

The majority of indentured servants were male. Men were typically between 16 and 20 years of age with agricultural backgrounds or little training in any trade. The high number of indentured men, along with unequal sex ratios in the colonies, impacted the lives of all colonial women because they became valuable commodities. Indentured men remained economically disadvantaged long after their contracts ended; prosperity sufficient for marriage was difficult to attain because these men left their indenture with few or no assets.

The indentured woman's experience significantly differed from that of her male counterpart. As early as

1609, ships arrived at the settlement at Jamestown carrying more than 100 women. Women were offered free land to come to the colonies, but women who accepted the offer delayed getting married, so the practice ended. By the 1630s, about 1 in 3 women arriving in the colonies was indentured. Women were in such short supply in the English colonies that men greeted ships eager to repay indentured women's fares in return for a woman they might marry. In this way indentured women helped equalize sex ratios. With unequal sex ratios, indentured single women had unprecedented opportunities for upward mobility in the mid-1600s, but as England's economic conditions improved, fewer women emigrated as indentured servants.

Native American women were also indentured, particularly if they were captured in military confrontations. Colonists attempted to indenture captive indigenous people, both male and female, to meet labor needs, but native people resisted the practice by running away. Also, high disease mortality rates among native people, who had little immunity to European diseases, discouraged their indenture.

The first black women were brought to Jamestown on ships in 1619 and were treated like white indentured servants. Individuals of African ancestry had hopes of earning eventual freedom, and some did until slavery was codified in Virginia law in the late 1640s. African slavery gradually replaced indentured servitude in most colonies.

An unwed bondwoman could expect to pay off her indenture in seven years unless she became pregnant during her time of service. A woman who gave birth to a child while indentured could expect to have time added to her term of service to make up for the labor her master lost while she was pregnant and caring for a small child. Unfortunately, indentured women had little control over their fertility because they were vulnerable to sexual abuse by their masters. Twenty percent of indentured female servants (forbidden to marry under contract terms) had illegitimate pregnancies, suggesting considerable sexual abuse. Masters doubly benefited because they had in their power a woman who had little recourse against sexual predation and a worker whose indenture contract could be extended if she became pregnant.

Some American colonists recognized indentured servitude as an abusive and oppressive practice. Quakers, with egalitarian sensibilities regarding the roles of women and men in society, vigorously opposed indentured servitude. Mennonites also strongly opposed indentured servitude and slavery. Indentured servants resisted their servitude by running away. Masters advertised in newspapers when indentured servants ran away, often issuing rewards for their capture and return, and runaway servants were expected to serve a longer term, usually extending their service to twice the time they were absent.

Tens of thousands of immigrants came to the colonies in the 17th and 18th centuries with the hope of greater opportunity. In reality, many indentured servants did not live to finish their contracts, victims of overwork and poor treatment. Some women and men, unable to support themselves when their contracts ended, renewed their indentures multiple times. In spite of the myth of upward mobility, these colonists never established themselves as freewomen or freemen but instead created a semipermanent class of poor white laborers.

Indentured servants, both male and female, remained relatively powerless through the 1700s. The American Revolution brought about a virtual end to the importation of indentured servants. The practice was already on the decline because a skilled labor force was in place, the population had increased, and there was an increasing number of African American slaves.

Nonetheless, small numbers of indentured servants continued in the new nation. During the American Revolution, wives and widows were forced to flee homes near battle sites and suffered hardship resulting from the fact that husbands, sons, and fathers were away at war. After the war, widows and destitute or orphaned children were indentured to pay debts or solve homelessness. Female Loyalists lost property for being on the losing side of the war and ended up indentured as well.

Servitude continued into the 1800s. After a financial panic in 1819, for example, when American jobs became seasonable and precarious and inflation was rampant, many women were forced to indenture themselves just to survive. Before labor laws were enacted during the 1930s, children were routinely exploited in work situations. "Poor laws" mandated that children from poor families could be indentured into service, where they received room, board, and clothes from a master in exchange for labor. The first child labor laws were enacted in Massachusetts during the 1830s and required minimal schooling for children under 15 years of age who worked in factories, and child labor was limited to 10 hours per day in 1842. During the early industrial revolution, children regularly worked in mines, glass factories, textile mills, and canneries and on farms. By the end of the 19th century, boys in urban areas worked as messengers, newsboys, bootblacks, and peddlers, many of them as indentured servants with no more freedoms or opportunities than 17th-century immigrants. The movement to end child labor, led by women such as Florence Kelley, Mary Harris "Mother" Jones, and Francis Perkins, also essentially ended indentured servitude in the United States.

Meredith Eliassen

See also Coverture; Slavery, African; *Vol. 1, Sec. 1:* Slavery, Native Americans; *Vol. 3, Sec. 1:* Jones, Mary Harris "Mother"; Kelley, Florence; *Vol. 3, Sec. 2:* Perkins, Frances

Further Reading

del Mar, David Peterson. 2011. *The American Family: From Obligation to Freedom.* New York: Palgrave Macmillan.

Hindman, Hugh. 2002. *Child Labor: An American History.* New York: M. E. Sharp.

Morgan, Edmund S. 2003. *American Slavery, American Freedom: The Ordeal of Colonial Virginia.* New York: Norton.

Ulrich, Laurel Thatcher. 1991. *Good Wives: Image and Reality in the Lives of Women in Northern New England, 1650–1750.* New York: Vintage Books.

"The Trappan'd Maiden: or, The Distressed Damsel" and "The Slave's Lament" (Mid-1600s)

Reproduced here are two versions of lyrics to an English ballad about the difficult life of a female indentured servant. The first version of the song is titled "The Trappan'd Maiden: or, The Distressed Damsel"; the second version is called "The Slave's Lament."

1. "THE TRAPPAN'D MAIDEN: OR THE DISTRESSED DAMSEL"

This Girl was cunningly Trappan'd, sent to Virginny from England, where she doth Hardship undergo, there is no Cure it must be so: But if she lives to cross the Main she vows she'll ne'r go there again.
Five years served I, under Master Guy,
In the land of Virginny-o
Which made me for to know sorrow, grief and woe,
When that I was weary, weary, weary-o.

When my dame says go, then I must do so,
In the land of Virginny-o,
When she sits at meat, then I have none to eat,

When that I was weary, weary, weary-o.

As soon as it is day, to work I must away,
In the land of Virginny-o
Then my dame she knocks, with her tinder box,
When that I was weary, weary, weary-o.

I have played my part, both at plow and cart,
In the land of Virginny-o
Billets from the wood upon my back they load,
When that I was weary, weary, weary-o.

A thousand woes beside, that I do here abide,
In the land of Virginny-o
In misery I spend my time that hath no end,
When that I was weary, weary, weary-o.

2. "THE SLAVE'S LAMENT"

It was in sweet Senegal where my foes did me enthrall
For the land of Virginia, Ginia-O

Torn from that lovely shore and must never see
  it more
And alas I am weary, weary-o
All on that lovely coast there's no bitter snow
  or frost
Like the land in Virginia, Ginia-O
There the streams forever flow and the flowers
  forever blow
And alas I am weary, weary-o
The burden I must bear while the cruel scurge
  I fear

In the land of Virginia, Ginia-O
And I think on friends most dear with a bitter,
  bitter tear
And alas I am weary, weary-o

Source: C. H. Firth, ed. "The Trappan'd Maiden: or, The Distressed Damsel," in *An American Garland: Being a Collection of Ballads Relating to America, 1563–1759* (Oxford: Oxford University Press, 1915), 251–253.

Letter of Elizabeth Sprigs to Her Father, John Sprigs (1756)

Elizabeth Sprigs, working as an indentured servant in Maryland, wrote to her father in London in 1756, thereby creating what is now a rare letter describing the life of an indentured servant in the 18th century.

Maryland, Sept'r 22'd 1756

Honored Father

My being for ever banished from your sight, will I hope pardon the Boldness I now take of troubling you with these, my long silence has been purely owning to my undutifullness to you, and well knowing I had offended in the highest Degree, put a tie to my tongue and pen, for fear I should be extinct from your good Graces and add a further Trouble to you, but too well knowing your care and tenderness for me so long as I retain'd my Duty to you, induced me once again to endeavor if possible, to kindle up that flame again. O Dear Father, believe what I am going to relate the words of truth and sincerity, and Balance my former bad Conduct my sufferings here, and then I am sure you'll pity your Destress Daughter, What we unfortunate English People suffer here is beyond the probability of you in England to Conceive, let it suffice that I one of the unhappy Number, am toiling almost Day and Night, and very often in the Horses drudgery, with only this comfort that you do not halfe enough, and then tied up and whipp'd to that Degree that you'd not serve an Animal, scarce any thing but Indian Corn and Salt to eat and that even begrudged nay many Negroes are better used, almost naked no shoes nor stockings to wear, and the comfort after slaving during Masters pleasure, what rest we can get is to rap ourselves up in a Blanket and ly upon the Ground, this is the deplorable Condition your poor Betty endures, and now I beg if you have any Bowels of Compassion left show it by sending me some Relief, Clothing is the principal thing wanting, which if you should condiscend to, may easily send them to me by any of the ships bound to Baltimore Town Patapsco River Maryland, and give me leave to conclude in Duty to you and Uncles and Aunts, and Respect to all Friends

Honored Father

Your undutifull and Disobedient Child

Elizabeth Sprigs

Source: Elizabeth Sprigs, "Letter to Mr. John Sprigs in White Cross Street near Cripple Gate, London, September 22, 1756," in *Colonial Captivities, Marches, and Journeys*, edited by Isabel Calder (New York: Macmillan, 1935), 151–152. Reprinted by permission of the National Society of the Colonial Dames of America in the State of Connecticut. Available at http://chnm.gmu.edu/fairfaxtah/lessons/documents/Elizabeth_Sprigs2.pdf.

Infanticide

Infanticide is the intentional killing of an infant by his or her parents. Historically, the reasons for infanticide include poverty, illegitimacy, and parental frustration. Whatever the reasons, Americans often attributed infanticide to satanic influence. Colonists brought the crime to colonial America from England, but the colonists found that Native Americans and other races practiced infanticide as well.

During the colonial period, most American women convicted of infanticide were unmarried and lower class. This demographic was also accused of other crimes, most notably witchcraft, more often than wealthier married women. During the late 1600s and early 1700s, Reverend John Hale, a key player during the Salem Witch Trials, linked infanticide to witchcraft. One of the more notable cases of infanticide and witchcraft can be found in Sarah Smith's trial in 1697. Records from Smith's trial suggest that people believed that the devil had told her to murder her own child. She was found guilty and executed.

Reverend Hale eventually applied "maleficium," a word that implied evil and cooperation with the devil, to infanticide cases; he believed that mothers literally bewitched their children to death. He could see no other reason why a mother would turn against what he and other Puritans believed was a woman's natural and inborn need to mother. Thus, a woman who killed her own offspring, to the colonial way of thinking, had to be influenced by Satan.

In reality, some mothers practiced infanticide because they found themselves unable to support their child. Many of the individuals guilty of the heinous crime of infanticide were poor. They hardly had enough resources to support themselves, and they lived in a world with few social services to help them. Oftentimes these women were unmarried, which compounded the problem.

Infanticide also occurred when the child was labeled a "bastard" child, meaning it was conceived outside of wedlock. Most colonial Americans considered bastardy shameful, though it was acceptable for a child to be born out of wedlock as long as the parents eventually married. Unmarried women with children faced immense negative social pressure. Finally, if a child was difficult in infancy, the frustration led some parents to intentionally harm the child.

Due to the link between witchcraft and infanticide, mothers who killed their children were viewed by Puritans as criminals who worked in unnatural or supernatural ways, not unlike the Puritan view of witches. Lawmakers decided that perpetrators of infanticide denied the religious and moral obligations of parenthood and deserved harsh punishment. Colonial America represented motherhood as a religious and moral duty necessary to the early foundation of the nation. Women who produced a child out of wedlock and also those who killed their babies were seen as in insult to the authority of both men and God.

Race changed the severity of the punishment for infanticide in the 1700s. The death of a nonwhite child, such as a Native American or an African American slave child, usually passed unpunished because colonial authorities did not view the child as important. However, a Native American or African American woman accused of killing a white child was typically punished more severely than white women.

An example of this double standard was the case of Patience Boston. Boston was a Native American servant who was convicted of murdering her own child. Because Native American children were seen as less than equal compared to white children, Boston was not executed. However, when Boston was convicted of murdering her master's child, she was executed. Crimes such as that of Patience Boston were used to prove the supposed inferiority of nonwhites. These crimes were also publicized to discourage marriage among races, specifically between whites and Native Americans. Publications included images and stories of Native Americans killing their own children by using stones to smash in their heads. Thus, these stories, like captivity stories, functioned to prove native savagery and inferiority when measured against white colonial stories. These stories were just that—stories—and had little to do with real Native Americans or their child-rearing practices as well as the cultural work they did.

Slaves, both Native American and African American, guilty of infanticide created a complex problem for the legal system. Lawmakers were generally eager to charge nonwhites for their crimes. However, their masters were often not as eager, for in the punishment masters lost valuable slaves. For example, a Native American slave named Maria was charged with infanticide in 1711. This was considered destruction of her master's property, and she was found guilty and sentenced to die. However, her master adamantly defended her, and Maria's life was spared. Her master did not want to lose Maria, thereby compounding the loss of his property. Several other cases dealt with the complex tug-of-war between race and infanticide because of the status of slaves as property. To admit that a slave could be held liable for a child murder was to admit that the slave was a sentient being, not merely property. Few slave-owning governments wanted to travel that sticky legal road.

As the century moved on, however, the punishment for infanticide lessened for a handful of reasons. Women who were convicted were no longer thrown in prison and executed, nor did authorities consider the hiding of a dead baby proof of murder. Punishments shifted from death to whippings and fines. Lawmakers did not condone infanticide, but as legal standards moved beyond "the devil did it," it became increasing difficult to tie the death of the child to the crime of the mother, which made the crime more difficult to punish. Also, lawmakers began to see infanticide as a result of the mother's environment and to feel pity for the woman.

B. C. Biggs

See also Bastardy; Indentured Servants; Protestant Women; Slavery, African; Witch Trials, Salem, Massachusetts

Further Reading

Dickeman, Mildred. 1975. "Demographic Consequences of Infanticide in Man." *Annual Review of Ecology and Systematics* 6: 107–137.

Harris, Sharon M. 1999. "Feminist Theories and Early American Studies." *Early American Literature* 34(1): 86–93.

Inheritance Laws

In colonial America, inheritance laws varied greatly depending on location. The British, Spanish, Dutch, and French colonies had legal systems based on sometimes dissimilar theories and origins that impacted inheritance laws for women in a variety of ways depending on time and place.

In the British colonies, which started with the first permanent settlement at Jamestown, Virginia, in 1607 and spanned the Atlantic coast of the present-day United States, inheritance and property laws limited women's ability to own property. When a woman married, she lost her separate legal status and became covered by her husband, becoming a *feme covert*. Coverture meant that a woman could not own property in marriage because she legally became her husband's property. Instead, a woman's husband owned the property. As a result, British inheritance practices favored sons rather than daughters. If a woman was widowed, she would inherit one-third of her husband's property. This is known as dower, or dower right. Dower rights ensured that women would have some property on which to live but prevented them from selling the property. Instead, the husband's will determined the path of the property after the wife's death, or law dictated that the property would pass on to legal heirs, generally children. Dower was meant to ensure that widows were cared for without violating the basic idea that men were property owners. Yet, there were exceptions. In England, separate estates developed that allowed the wealthy to place property in the hands of married women. This measure was enforced in equity courts instead of legal courts. In practice, colonists did not widely use separate estates, though the practice was more common in wealthy southern families. Even within the British colonies, there were variations as to how courts enforced the laws.

In colonial New Spain, which started with the settlement of St. Augustine, Florida, in 1565 and included colonies in Texas, New Mexico, Arizona, California, other parts of the Southwest, and even Louisiana for a period of time, Spanish law diverged from British law because it was based on Roman law, while British law was not. Under Spanish law, a married woman could own property. A woman could bring personal property other than a dowry, known as *bienes parafernales,* into marriage, and she retained ownership of these items, which often included clothing, jewelry, and other personal items. Additionally, wealthier women often brought dowries into marriage. Husbands could use dowries, but they could not sell or use the dowry property without the consent of the wife. Additionally, Spanish law had community property rights that declared that all property acquired during a marriage belonged equally to husband and wife. The Spanish did not intend for community property laws to divide property in cases of divorce. Instead, the community property laws ensured that when a spouse was widowed and remarried, the children of the first marriage would receive their proper share of the community property. The impact of these property laws on inheritance was drastically different than in the British colonies. Spanish inheritance laws said that all children, including daughters, would inherit property from parents fairly equally; no one child could inherit more than one-fifth to one-third of the estate. Thus, daughters tended to inherit the same amount of property as sons. Additionally, under Spanish law, illegitimacy was not necessarily a preclusion from inheritance. Parents could make some illegitimate children legal heirs through several processes, including simply naming them in their wills. Thus, Spanish inheritance laws tended to be significantly more generous to women in the Spanish colonies compared to women in the British colonies.

Like Spanish law, Dutch law was also based on Roman law, so the Dutch inheritance laws closely mirrored Spanish laws. Dutch women could own property and leave it in their will to their children, including their female children. In the Dutch colony of New York, which was founded in the early 1600s, some husbands and wives wrote mutual wills, meaning they wrote a will together. This practice seems to be particular to the Dutch. After the British invaded the Dutch colony of New Amsterdam and permanently took over in 1674, the property and inheritance laws began to change to British ones. Dutch colonial women lost property and inheritance rights and with them lost economic and social power.

Finally, French inheritance laws were similar to those of the Dutch. Women did not lose their separate legal identity in marriage as they did in English law. Also, both spouses had to sign civil contracts for the contract to be valid. Finally, widows received half the married estate upon a husband's death rather than the one-third dower rights required under English law. The other half of the estate went to children, including daughters. The French colonies were centered in Canada, along the Mississippi River, and in Louisiana. When the Spanish took over Louisiana as a result of the French loss to the British in the French and Indian War in 1763, the Spanish allowed Louisiana to keep its legal codes.

Thus, variations on inheritance laws among Euro-Americans meant that women from colony to colony experienced different opportunities and protections. Nonetheless, the overall trend was that women had less opportunity than men to inherit and accumulate property. The American Revolution as well as other wars and events that led to changes in governments, such as Texas independence, the Mexican American War, and the Louisiana Purchase, led to further changes in inheritance laws after the nation's colonial period. In many cases, these laws further disempowered women.

Amy M. Porter

See also Bastardy; Catholic Women; Coverture; Protestant Women; *Vol. 1, Sec. 1:* New France, Women in

Further Reading

Salmon, Marylynn. 1989. *Women and the Law of Property in Early America.* Chapel Hill: University of North Carolina Press.

Stuntz, Jean A. 2005. *Hers, His, & Theirs: Community and Property Law in Spain and Early Texas.* Lubbock: Texas Tech University Press.

Taylor, Alan. 2001. *American Colonies: The Settling of North America.* New York: Penguin.

Alice Bradford's Will (March 31, 1670/1671)

Historians have learned a lot about colonial American life by examining people's wills. Wills left by women are rare, but they provide insight into the material culture of the time and also suggest what was important to people and what was not. Note that Alice Bradford's wealth was in livestock but that she, like other colonial Americans, counted everything she owned in a will down to the chamber pots.

Plymouth Colony Wills 3:3–5
#P178
A true Inventory of the estate of mistris Allice Bradford senir: Late deceased aprised [by vs whose]
names are vnder written this 31th of March 1670 and
exhibited to the court of his [Majesty] held att New
Plymouth the seauenth day of Iune Anno: domine
one Thousand six hundred and seauenty; on the oath
of mistris Mary Carpenter;

Impr. 8 Cowes 20 00 00
Item 2 yearlings 01 10 00
Item a 2 yeare old steer 01 10 00
Item a steer of 4 yeare old 02 10 00
Item 1: 2 yeare old heiffer 01 10 00
Item 1 old horse and three mares 10 00 00
Item 17 sheep and 2 lambes 07 00 00
In the New Parlour Chamber
Item 1 bed a bolster and 2 pillowes 03 16 00
Item 1 green Rugg and 1 Couerlid & 2 blanketts 03
   00 00
Item a bedsteed & Crutaines and vallence 02 00
   00
Item 2 Chaires 00 15 00
Item 3 wrought stooles 00 11 00
Item one Table and Carpett 01 05 00
Item a Carued Chest 01 00 00
In the outward Parlour Chamber: a bedsteed and
   Curtaine and vallence and settle 01 10 00
In the old parlour Chamber; Item a smale bed 2 blan-
   ketts 1 Couerlid & a pillow 03 10 00
Item 1 old green Cloth Goune 00 10 00
Item 8 yards of hommade Cloth 01 04 00
Item 2 Chestes 00 10 00
Item 2 Iron beames 1 hogshed 1 barrell and other old
   lumber 01 05 00
In the studdy in bookes
Item mr Perkins two of them 01 00 00
Item 3 of docter Willetts on genises exodus & daniel:
   01 00 00
Item Quicksarraden 00 10 00
Item the history of the Church 00 08 00
Item Peter Martirs Comon places 00 15 00
Item Cartwright on Remise Testament 00 10 00
Item the history of the Netherlands 00 15 00
Item Peter Martir on the Romans 00 05 00
Item Moors workes on the New Testament 01 00 00
Item Cottons Concordance 00 08 00

Item Speeds history of the world 01 00 00
Item Weams Christian Sinnagogue & the
   protracture of the Image of God 00 08 00
Item the Meathod of Phisicke 00 02 00
Item Caluins harmony and his Coment on the artes
   00 08 00
Item downams 2cond parte of Christian warfare 00
   03 00
Item mr Cottons answare to mr Williams 00 02 00
Item Taylers libertie of Prophesye 00 01 06
Item Gouges domesticall dutyes 00 02 06
Item the Institutions or Reasons discused & obserua-
   tions diuine and morral the synode of dort and the
   Appollogye 00 06 00
Item mr Ainsworth workes the Counter poison & the
   tryall 00 02 00
Item mr Ainsworth on Genises exodus & liuitticus 00
   04 00
Item Caluin on Genises 00 02 06
Item dike on the decightfulnes of mans hart 00 01 06
Item Gifford Refuted 00 00 06
Item dod on the Comaundements and others of his
   00 03 00
Item 53 smale bookes 01 06 06
Item Caluin on the epistles in duch: and diuers other
   duch bookes 00 15 00
Item 2 bibles 01 00 00
Item the actes of the Church 00 05 00
Item 3 of mr Bridgg his workes 01 00 00
Item the Liues of the fathers 00 03 00
Item in a skin of buffe 00 15 00
[4] In the old Parlour
Item 1 feather bed 1 bolster 2 Ruggs and a blankett
   03 00 00
Item a bedsted & settle Curtaine and vallence 01 10
   00
Item a Court Cubbert 01 00 00
Item a Table and forme and 2 stooles 01 05 00
Item 1 great lether Chaire 00 08 00
Item 2 great wooden Chaires 00 06 00
Item 1 great wainscott Chist and a Cubbert 01 00 00
Item 2 boxes and a deske and a wrought stoole and
   an old Case of bottles 00 12 00
Item 2 guns and a paire of bandaleers 01 00 00
[in the margin] The plate
Item the great beer bowle 03 00 00
Item another beer bowle 02 00 00
Item a wine Cupp 01 00 00

Item a salt 02 15 00
Item a trencher salt & drame Cupp 00 15 00
Item 4 siluer spoones 02 09 00
Item a siluer dish 01 15 00

———

Item 2 blanketts 00 10 00
Item 1 diaper Table Cloth and a dozen of diaper Napkins 02 00 00
Item another diaper Table Cloth and 7 diaper napkins 01 10 00
Item 2 holland Tableclothes 00 15 00
Item 1 old Cubbert Cloth 00 03 00
Item 4 pillow beers 00 08 00
Item 5 towells 00 05 00
Item 3 holland sheets 01 10 00
Item 2 paire of Cotten and linnine sheets 01 05 00
Item 19 Cotton and linnine Napkins 00 15 00
Item a paire of pillowbears 00 02 06
Item 5 sheets 01 10 00
Item in shiftes and other wearing linnine 03 00 00
Item a dimycastor hatt 01 05 00
Item her wearing Clothes and a little peece of bayes 12 00 00
Item a wicker baskett; galley potts Y glasses & such smale thinges of Little vallue 00 05 00
[in the margin] in the great Parlour
Item 2 great Carued Chaires 01 04 00
Item a Table and forme and Carpett 01 05 00
Item 10 Cushens 01 00 00
Item a Causlett and hedpeece 01 10 00
Item 4 great lether Chaires 01 04 00
Item in glasses and earthen ware 00 04 00
Item in a Case and fiue kniues 00 05 00
Item a Rost & some other odde thinges 00 02 00

———

[in the margin] In the Kitchen
Item 24 pewter platters and a brim bason 07 00 00
Item 2 Flaggons: 2 quart potts & 2 pint potts 01 00 00
Item 6 smale pewter dishes and a smale bason 00 10 00
Item 7 porrengers 00 06 00
Item 6 pewter plates 00 09 00
Item 2 pewter Candlestickes & a salt seller 00 06 00
Item 3 Chamber potts and three smale sawcers and pewter funnell; 00 09 00
Item 2 pye plates 00 06 00
Item a tinning pan and 2 Couerings & a lanthorne 00 02 00

[5] Item 1 great Iugg and 5 smaller ones 4 earthen pans and 2 earthen potts 00 12 [00]
Item 2 French kettles 01 10 00
Item an old warming pan 00 03 00
Item 1 little French kettle 00 02 00
Item 2 brasse kettles 00 15 00
Item a duch pan 00 04 00
Item 3 brasse skilletts 00 04 00
Item 1 old brasse skimer and Ladle 00 01 00
Item 3 brasse Candle stickes and a brasse pestle and Mortor 00 09 00
Item a paire Andjrons 00 10 00
Item a Chafeing dish and a stew pan 00 10 00
Item 1 Iron skillett and an Iron Kettle 00 10 00
Item 2 Iron potts 00 16 00
Item 2 paire of pothangers and 2 parie of pott hookes 00 08 00
Item 2 paire of tonggs and 2 fier shouells 00 05 00
Item 2 spitts and a gridjron and an Iron driping pan 00 10 00
Item a paire of Iron Rakes 00 10 00
Item 4 dozen of trenchers 00 02 00
Item a box Iron 2 gallon glasse bottles and three pottle bottles 00 05 00
Item a spining wheele a bucking tubb 2 pailes 2 kimnells two bowles 4 smale wooden dishes 1 tray 2 Burchen trayes 00 16 00
Ite Scales & waightes with an Iron beame 00 07 00
Item 2 beer barrells 00 04 00
Item a parsell of sheepes woole 00 03 00
Item 2 male swine 00 10 00
Item in Mony 00 16 00
Item a siluer bodkin 00 04 00
Item in prouision 01 10 00
Item one halfe hogshed and a smale parsell of salt 00 03 00
Item one paire of oxen in Mr Ioseph Bradfords hand

———

sume totall 162 17 00

———

prised by
George Watson
Ephriam Morton
William harlow;
Captaine William Bradford and Mr Ioseph Bradford haueing the Cattle after named in theire Costody when the estate was prised; did giue in the number and kind of them vpon theire oathes as followeth;

Item 4 Cowes 2 Calues one oxe 4 yeare old one heiffer of two yeare old and 14 sheep besides lambes; were in Captaine Bradford Costody and hee was sworne to these Iune 1670

Item 2 oxen 4 Cowes 2 yearlinges one two yeare old steer 1 horse 2 mares 2 young Calues were in Mr Ioseph Bradfords Custody and hee was sworne to this Iune 1670

These were appertaineing to the estate and forenamed in the Inventory;

Alice Bradford

Source: "Alice Bradford," The Plymouth Colony Archive Project, http://www.histarch.illinois.edu/plymouth/P178.htm.

Jemison, Mary (ca. 1743–1833)

Mary Jemison (also known as Dehgewanus, Deh-he-wa-mis, and Dickewamis as well as "The White Woman of the Genesee") was a colonial American settler of Scotch-Irish descent. She was abducted by Shawnee Indians from her family's farm on the Pennsylvania frontier when she was a teenager and was later adopted into the Seneca tribe. Jemison became famous when an account of her captivity was published in 1824 by James E. Seaver. What particularly captured the public's attention was her refusal to return to white society. Rather, Jemison chose to stay with the Native Americans who had adopted her into their tribe.

Her parents, the Scotch-Irish Thomas and Jane Erwin Jemison, immigrated to America from what is today Northern Ireland. Their daughter Mary was born in 1742 or 1743 aboard the ship *William and Mary* on the Atlantic crossing. After a safe landing at Philadelphia, the family joined other Scotch-Irish immigrants in moving to Marsh Creek, about 10 miles north of today's Gettysburg, Pennsylvania. There they cleared land for a farm and built a house, though they did not have title to the land because it legally belonged to the Iroquois Confederacy. They and other nearby settlers occupied the land under the concept of squatters' rights in part because they, like other Euro-Americans, simply did not recognize that native people had any right to the land.

The French and Indian War, part of the Seven Years' War, was fought between the North American colonies of England and France between 1754 and 1763. Each side was allied with various Native American tribes.

Kidnapped as a teenager by members of the Seneca tribe, Mary Jemison became fully assimilated into her captors' culture and later chose to remain a Seneca rather than return to British colonial culture. (Vespasian/Alamy Stock Photo)

Mary Jemison's capture was just one small part of that war. According to Jemison, in 1755 (other sources say 1758) a raiding party of Shawnee warriors and several Frenchmen captured Jemison, most of her family, and a neighbor boy. The plan was to transport the captives to Fort Duquesne (present-day Pittsburgh), but with the large number of prisoners, the raiding party found that they would not be able to outrun the militia that was pursuing them. Mary Jemison and the neighbor boy were separated from the group. The raiding party killed and scalped the rest of the Jemison family. Mary later said that she saw the scalps the warriors were cleaning and recognized her mother's red hair. She could also clearly see which scalps belonged to her father and siblings.

Jemison was given moccasins and marched through the woods until the raiding party reached the fort. There she was given to two Seneca women, who took her with them to western New York. The Seneca people customarily adopted and acculturated captives into their society when they lost one of their own family members. In Jemison's case, her adopting Seneca family had lost a brother. Jemison later said that she was fortunate to fall into the hands of such kind and good-natured women.

The Senecas renamed Jemison. Some sources cite her name as Dickewamis, loosely translated as "two falling voices." Most others, including Seaver, who says it was Jemison's own translation, call it variants of Deh-he-wa-mis meaning a pretty girl or a pleasant, good thing.

Jemison was forbidden to speak English and learned much of the Seneca language in about a year. She was treated kindly by the Senecas, who accepted her as one of their tribe. Soon another tribe settled nearby, and she was told that she would marry a Delaware named Sheninjee, which she did in 1760. In her account, she said that Sheninjee treated her with great gentleness and consideration. Their first child died soon after birth, but a few years later she gave birth to a son whom she named Thomas after her father.

Jemison steadily acquired both the rights and responsibilities of Indian women. She learned the Seneca ways of cooking, baking, and sewing as well as tending fields. She also discovered that Seneca women were treated with respect, able to address the tribal council, and hold rights to the land they tended. Historians point out that with the Senecas, Jemison had rights possessed by few white or black women in colonial America. With the native people she found power and personhood that she would not have had in English colonial America.

Sheninjee went missing on a hunting trip and was eventually reported dead. When her son Thomas was three or four years old, Jemison married an older man named Hiokatoo. Though he was known as a fierce warrior, Jemison said that he was kind and tender to her. With this husband, Jemison had six more children. She named them for members of her lost European family: Jane, Betsey, Nancy, Polly, John, and Jesse.

During the American Revolutionary War (1776–1783), the Senecas were allies of the British who, they believed, would stanch the flow of white settlers onto Native American land and grant the Indians autonomy. With the victory of the American colonists, the flood of white settlers increased as they pushed their way westward onto land the Indians considered theirs, including that of the Senecas.

By the late 1780s Jemison had become a fully integrated member of the Seneca tribe, though she also made friends among nearby white settlers. According to tribal elders, she was free to live among the whites, but she refused partly due to her fear that her European relatives would not accept her Seneca children. The tribe celebrated her loyalty to the Senecas by giving her a gift of land. However, Seneca land was rapidly disappearing. Jemison aided the tribe in negotiations with the Americans and helped win more favorable terms for the tribe at the Treaty of Big Tree in 1797.

After 50 years of marriage Hiokatoo died, but Jemison continued her life as a respected widow in the Seneca tribe. When she was around 80 years of age, she went to the nearby town of Castile, New York, where she met Dr. James Everett Seaver, a local minister who was intrigued by her recollections. As she could no longer write English, Jemison allegedly dictated the story of her life to Seaver, who published it in 1824 as an original memoir titled *A Narrative of the Life of Mrs. Mary Jemison*.

The book became one of the most detailed captivity narratives of a white woman captured by Indians. Many scholars consider it to be reasonably accurate. Others question how much was really Jemison's and how much was slanted by Seaver to emphasize classic themes known to sell books, such as the damsel in distress and the ordeal of white women taken by nonwhite men. Some feel that Seaver, writing in his time, emphasized the tragedy of Jemison being taken against her will by "savages" and not the strength and resilience she showed to thrive. However, it diverged from the typical happy ending whereby the white woman or girl is removed or saved from the "savage" natives and returned to Anglo-Saxon society.

White Americans continued to push westward and absorb Native American land. Between 1823 and 1825, the Seneca tribe sold most of the remainder of the land to the settlers except for a two-acre tract reserved for Jemison and her daughters, who were permitted to stay. The rest of the Senecas moved onto a reservation. Jemison was well known to local whites as "The White Woman of the Genesee." Soon, however, she found that she missed the people among whom she had lived most of her life. She sold her land in 1831 and moved to the Indian reservation at Buffalo Creek, where she lived the remainder of her life with the Seneca people.

Jemison died on September 19, 1833, at around 90 years of age. She was buried on the Buffalo Creek Reservation. In 1874, her remains were reinterred at William Pryor Letchworth's Glen Iris Estate, currently Letchworth State Park in Castile, New York. A bronze statue marks her grave.

Historians find her tale fascinating, both for what it tells readers about life among the Seneca and what it reveals about the position of women among indigenous people such as the Senecas. Captivity narratives were popular in America, because among other things, they reinforced notions of Euro-American superiority, though Jemison's story suggests quite the opposite. The story of Eunice Williams (1696–1785), another captive who refused to return to her white family, echoes Jemison's in its embrace of native culture. Many white women such as Jemison preferred life among the Indians, in part because native women had considerably more cultural power and freedom than did Euro-American women.

Nancy Hendricks

See also Captives, English; Captivity Narratives; *Vol. 1, Sec. 3:* Williams, Eunice

Further Reading

Namias, June. 1993. *White Captives: Gender and Ethnicity on the American Frontier.* Chapel Hill: University of North Carolina Press.

Roop, Connie, and Peter Roop. 2000. *The Diary of Mary Jemison: Captured by the Indians (In My Own Words).* New York: Cavendish Square Publishing.

Seaver, James E. 2001 [1824]. *The Life of Mary Jemison: The White Woman of the Genesee.* Scituate, MA: Digital Scanning.

Mary Jemison's Account of Her Capture by Native Americans (1758)

Unlike Mary Rowlandson's captivity narrative from the 17th century, Mary Jemison's narrative of her captivity by Native Americans emphasizes the humanity of her captors and how well she adjusted to indigenous culture. Captured in 1758, Jemison dictated her story to James E. Seaver in 1824. What follows is the story of her capture and then her decision to remain among the Senecas rather than return to white society.

When we set off, an Indian in the forward canoe took the scalps of my former friends, strung them on a pole that he placed upon his shoulder, and in that manner carried them, standing in the stern of the canoe directly before us, as we sailed down the river. . . .

On the way we passed a Shawnee town, where I saw a number of heads, arms, legs, and other fragments of the bodies of some white people who had just been burned. . . .

All the prisoners that are taken in battle and carried to the encampment or town by the Indians are given to the bereaved families. . . . And unless the mourners have but just received the news of their bereavement, and are under the operation of a paroxysm of grief, anger, or revenge; or, unless the prisoner is very old, sickly, or homely, they generally save them, and treat them kindly. But . . . if their prisoner or prisoners do not meet their approbation, no torture, let it be ever so cruel, seems sufficient to make them satisfaction. It is family and not national sacrifices among the Indians, that has given them an indelible stamp as barbarians. . . .

It was my happy lot to be accepted for adoption. At the time of the ceremony I was received by the two squaws to supply the place of their brother in the family; and I was ever considered and treated by them as a real sister, the same as though I had been born of their mother. . . .

Soon after the close of the Revolutionary War, my Indian brother, Kau-jises-tau-ge-au (which being interpreted signifies Black Coals) offered me my liberty and told me that if it was my choice I might go to my friends [white society]. My son, Thomas, was anxious that I should go, and offered to go with me and assist me on the journey by taking care of the younger children and providing food as we travelled through the wilderness. But the Chiefs of our tribe, suspecting from his appearance, actions, and a few warlike exploits, that Thomas would be a great warrior or a good counsellor, refused to let him leave them on any account whatever.

To go myself and leave him was more than I felt able to do; for he had been kind to me and was one on whom I placed great dependence. The Chiefs refusing to let him go was one reason for my resolving to stay, but another, more powerful, if possible, was that I had got a large family of Indian children that I must take with me, and that if I should be so fortunate as to find my relatives, they would despise them, if not myself, and treat us as enemies or at least with a degree of cold indifference, which I thought I could not endure. . . .

Accordingly, after I had duly considered the matter, I told my brother that it was my choice to stay and spend the remainder of my days with my Indian friends, and live with my family as I had heretofore done. He appeared well pleased with my resolution and informed me, that as that was my choice, I should have a piece of land that I could call my own where I could live unmolested [unbothered] and have something at my decease to leave for the benefit of my children.

Source: James E. Seaver, *A Narrative of the Life of Mary Jemison,* 7th ed. (New York: Putnam, 1824). Available at Project Gutenburg, http://www.gutenberg.org/files/6960/6960-h/6960-h.htm.

Johnson, Arabella (d. 1630)

Lady Arabella Johnson was one of the earliest settlers of New England. With her husband Isaac Johnson, she arrived in what is now Salem, Massachusetts, in 1629. She died there the following year before the colonists were able to resettle in Boston and establish the Massachusetts Bay Colony. Isaac Johnson is considered by many to be the founder of the city of Boston.

Arabella Johnson was born in Nottinghamshire, England, and was the daughter of the third Earl of Lincoln. During this period in England the Puritans, a sect of English Protestants, unsuccessfully attempted to "purify" the Church of England. Puritans were also restricted in practicing their religion by England's religious laws. Many Puritans left England and immigrated to other countries, including the Netherlands and the American colonies. Both of Johnson's parents were sympathetic to the Puritans' desire to seek religious freedom elsewhere.

The Earl of Lincoln died in 1619, but before his death he gave his daughter Arabella permission to marry Isaac Johnson, a wealthy but untitled Puritan related to several noble families. They married in 1620 and in the spring of 1629 left England aboard the ship *Arabella,* which had been christened in Lady Arabella's honor. Also part of the little fleet were the *Talbot,* the *Ambrose,* and the *Jewel.* The trip was sponsored by the Massachusetts Bay Company, under the direction of Governor John Winthrop, Deputy Governor Thomas

Dudley, Isaac Johnson, and Richard Saltonstall. Arabella's sister Susan and her husband John Humfrey were supposed to accompany the group but were unable to sail with them.

On June 12 the Puritans arrived in Salem, Massachusetts (then called Naumkeag), which had been settled the previous year. They found the settlement in disarray. The original colonists had only two weeks' worth of food left and were suffering from disease and famine. Eighty colonists had died during the previous winter. The surviving colonists hoped to be resupplied by the *Arabella* fleet but were disappointed to find that the newly arrived ships carried little extra food. Some of the colonists left to find a more promising location for settlement. Many of them moved to Charlestown, near present-day Boston. Isaac Johnson was prevented from joining this group because his wife was gravely ill. Sources disagree on whether Lady Arabella was sick when she left England or whether she became ill on the voyage or after her arrival in America. Whatever the case, she died in Salem on August 31, 1630, of a severe fever.

Lady Arabella was buried in Salem. The remaining settlers, including Isaac Johnson, moved on to Charlestown. They found conditions there not much better than what they had left in Salem. There was no running water, and the colonists continued to suffer from disease and death. Isaac was instrumental in planning a permanent settlement in nearby Trimountain, which was renamed Boston, causing people to call him the founder of Boston. While some sources say that he died in 1630, most say that he was present when Trimountain was rechristened Boston on September 7, 1631, but died within a month. Arabella's sister Susan, who had married John Humfrey, arrived in Boston two years later, but the Humfreys remained in Massachusetts only eight or nine years before returning to England.

Lady Arabella's story did not die with her, however. During the 19th century there was a revival of interest in her, and such poets as Granville T. Sproat, Lucy Hooper, and Mrs. L. H. Sigourney wrote poems retelling the story as a tragic tale in which a grand lady sacrifices her life for religious principles. The Lady Arabella story was also recounted in poems and character sketches that appeared in such periodicals as *Godey's Lady's Book* (September 1842), the *Social Monitor and Orphan's Advocate* (May 1846), the *Lady's Repository* (August 1846), the *Southern Lady's Companion* (June 1848), and *Hours at Home* (November 1865). In addition, it was taught to young ladies in collections such as Ebenezer Bailey's *The Young Ladies' Class Book: A Selection of Lessons for Reading, in Prose and Verse* (1832), *The Hemans Reader for Female Schools* (1847), and *The Young Lady's Book of Elegant Prose* (1836). As such it served as a mythic American origin story, not unlike the Pocahontas story.

Nancy Snell Griffith

See also Dare, Eleanor and Virginia; *Vol. 1, Sec. 1:* Pocahontas

Further Reading
The Fathers of New England: A Chronicle of the Puritan Commonwealths. New England: Yale University Press, 1919.
Parker, H. F. *Discoverers and Pioneers of America.* New York: Derby and Jackson, 1860.

Johnston, Henrietta (1674–1729)

Henrietta de Beaulieu Dering Johnston was the first American artist of either sex to work in pastel and the first recorded professional American woman artist. Though she did her work in colonial South Carolina, Johnston was born in Rennes, France, to Francis and Suzanna de Beaulieu. Her parents were French Huguenots who migrated to London in 1687 because of religious persecution. Johnston settled in Ireland after her marriage to Robert Dering, the fifth son of Sir Edward Dering. Her interest in pastel portraits developed in Ireland after she came in contact with several Irish painters. The first pastel portraits she painted were of her in-laws, including the Earl of Barrymore and the Earl of Egmont.

In 1704 Johnston's first husband died, leaving her with two daughters to raise alone. A year later she married Gideon Johnston, the vicar of Castlemore, who had two sons and two daughters from his previous marriage. Gideon was in debt and decided to settle in South Carolina. The bishop of London had appointed the clergyman as his commissary, and with help from the Society for the Propagation of the Gospel, Johnston and Gideon and their children arrived in April 1708 at Charles Towne (now Charleston), a port and trading center for the Southern Colonies.

Johnston worked as her husband's secretary and managed the family with meager resources, as he did not receive regular pay. Here her passion for portrait painting was revived. Not only did she become the first pastel artist of America, but she also used her art to supplement the family income. Although in Europe pastel art was not uncommon, the art form was a new thing in colonial North America. In doing her artistic work, Johnston gradually depleted her stock of painting supplies. In 1711 when the Church needed to send important messages to the bishop of London by personal courier, she volunteered to go so she could purchase art supplies in London and return with them to South Carolina. Johnston also took Carolina rice to London to find buyers. Due to her precarious financial condition, she also took the time in England to appeal to the Society for the Propagation of the Gospel for more support for her husband's parish.

During her passage back to South Carolina, pirates attacked her vessel. She survived the attack, only to return to Charleston to face yet more problems. There were two hurricanes and the start of the Yamasee War between British colonists and several local Native American tribes. Johnston cared for hurricane and war refugees in the parsonage. In early 1716 when the Cherokees sided with the colonists against the Creeks, their traditional enemy, the war ended.

Johnston's husband, who had spent three years in England, died shortly after his return to North America in 1716, victim of a boating accident. Johnston continued her art during the rest of her life and thus supported herself and her family. Having gained some renown as an artist, she traveled to New York in 1725 to do portrait paintings of the elite of the city. Johnston died on March 9, 1729, in Charleston.

About three dozens portraits by Johnston still exist. The leading members of the Charleston society, members of Huguenot families, and elites of New York society form the subject matter of her paintings. The colonial elites commissioned their portraiture, reflecting the ethos of a well-off society. Her works dealt solely in pastel on 9-by-12-inch paper. Compared to her paintings done before leaving Ireland, Johnston's America works are lighter and smaller without deep lines. This is undoubtedly due to a shortage of painting materials, which she had to import at great cost. The large and oval eyes of the pastel portraits were directed toward the onlooker. Her portraits done in America were of bust length without details of dress and face. The female subjects of her paintings were pictured in chemises of delicate nature, whereas males were dressed in either armor or street attire. Johnston's works are exhibited in American museums such as the Gibbes Museum of Art in Greenville County, the Museum of Early Southern Decorative Arts, and the Metropolitan Museum of Art.

Patit Paban Mishra

See also Bradstreet, Anne; Protestant Women

Further Reading

Bodie, Idella. 1990. *South Carolina Women.* Orangeburg, SC: Sandlapper Publishing.

Middleton, Margaret Simons. 1966. *Henrietta Johnston of Charles Town, South Carolina: America's First Pastellist.* Columbia: University of South Carolina Press.

Perry, Lee Davis. 2009. *More Than Petticoats: Remarkable South Carolina Women.* Guilford, CT: Globe Pequot.

Kittamaquund, Mary (ca. 1634–ca. 1654)

Mary Kittamaquund (often spelled Kitomaquund), the daughter of a Piscataway chief, married Englishman Giles Brent, one of the first settlers of the Maryland colony. She may have been an intermediary between the Piscataway people and the colonial English. She and her husband later moved to Virginia, becoming that colony's first permanent English Catholic residents.

Little is known about Mary's life. The only child of Kittamaquund, the *tayac* (paramount chief) of the Piscataways, she was born around 1634. The Piscataway tribe, which was closely related to the Algonquins and Nanticokes, occupied land on the peninsula of lower Maryland between the Potomac River and the Chesapeake Bay. Their principal village was near the mouth of Piscataway Creek in present-day Prince Georges County. They also had 30 other settlements, including Yaocomoco, Potopaco, Patuxent, Mattapanient, Mattawoman, and Nancochtank (present-day Anacostia in the District of Columbia).

Until 1634, Kittamaquund's brother Wannas was the *tayac* of the Piscataways. The same year that Lord Baltimore's settlers, under the leadership of his brother, Lord Calvert, landed on Maryland's shores, Kittamaquund killed his brother and took over leadership of the tribe. He gave the English a former Piscataway settlement, which they named St. Mary's City in honor of their queen. Scholars assume that he did this in part to buffer the Piscataways against incursions by the Susquehannock from the north.

Under the leadership of the Jesuit missionary Andrew White, the English began attempting to convert the Piscataways to Catholicism. On July 5, 1640, Father White baptized Kittamaquund and his wife and gave them Christian names, Charles and Mary. Daughter Mary may have been baptized at this time or two years later. In 1641 Kittamaquund sent his daughter to St. Mary's City to be raised by Governor Calvert and Margaret Brent, who had come to Maryland in 1638. The Brents and Calverts were distant cousins going back several generations and may even have been related by marriage. Tayac Kittamaquund died in 1641, leaving Margaret Brent as Mary's guardian.

Giles Brent quickly gained prominence in the colony, occupying 60 acres in St. Mary's City and 2,000 acres elsewhere, 1,000 of these near Kent Fort. He was invited to join the Maryland Assembly in 1639. By 1642 he was lord of the manor of Kent Fort, which gave him considerable political, judicial, and military power. In 1643 Governor Calvert returned to England, leaving Giles Brent in charge as deputy governor of the colony. While Calvert was gone, Margaret Brent allowed Giles to marry Mary Kittamaquud, who was then only 10 or 11 years of age. This may have been done so that Giles could lay claim to the extensive lands ruled by Mary's late father, which he in fact did.

As civil war raged in England, the colonies had their own problems. While Calvert was out of the colony, a Protestant sea captain and merchant named Richard Ingle (possibly aided by Virginia fur trader William Claiborne) attacked St. Mary's City, burning the Catholic chapel and other buildings. Mirroring the conflict in England, Protestants attacked a number of colonial Catholic holdings. They also raided and burned the houses of Catholics on Kent and Palmer's Islands. In April 1645, Ingle sailed back to England with four prisoners: two Jesuit priests, the provincial secretary, and Giles Brent.

Governor Calvert returned to Virginia, and within two years he launched a campaign against the invaders and won back the Maryland colony. He died in St. Mary's City in 1647, leaving Margaret Brent as his executor. A freed Giles Brent returned to Maryland and attempted to claim all Piscataway lands as Mary's husband. This, however, was contrary to all Piscataway custom and also offended Calvert's brother Lord Baltimore because it violated the land grant on which his colony was founded. He was further offended when Margaret Brent sold some of his cattle to settle Governor Calvert's debts.

Out of favor with Lord Baltimore, the Brents, including Kittamaquud, began making plans to resettle in Virginia. Margaret, Giles, and Mary first moved to Chopawamsic (Chop) Island on the Virginia side of the Potomac River. They then relocated to the northern neck of Virginia, near present-day Aquia, where they established a plantation named Peace. Brent became interested in potential trade with the Native Americans of the upper Potomac Valley and began taking out patents on land upriver from Aquia. Sources indicate that after 1652, he and his sister Margaret were afraid to return to Maryland to manage their affairs there.

Little is known about Giles and Kittamaquund's family. They had at least two sons, Giles, born in 1652, and Richard, who apparently died young. They also had one daughter, Mary, born in 1654. Kittamaquud must have died or left Giles and returned to her indigenous family, because Giles remarried in 1654.

Kittamaquund's son Giles is perhaps best known for his involvement in Bacon's Rebellion (1676–1677), when he escaped hanging by changing sides. Daughter Mary married John Fitzherbert. She may have later divorced him and married Charles Beaven. Other sources indicate that there were additional children: a daughter, Katherine, born in 1649 who eventually married Richard Marsham, and a daughter and a son, Henry and Margaret, who both died young. Katherine, however, was more probably the daughter of Giles Brent's brother, Edmund.

The Brent family was prominent in Virginia for decades, becoming supporters of slavery and the Confederacy by the time of the American Civil War. Maryland named a resovoir after the Kittamquunds in 1966. Mary's life, both because it is largely lost to history and because she was used by both her native and English families, suggests some of the difficulties that indigenous women faced in colonial America.

Nancy Snell Griffith

See also Brent, Margaret; Catholic Women; *Vol. 1, Sec. 1:* Pocahontas

Further Reading

Land, Aubrey C. 1981. *Colonial Maryland: A History.* Milwood, NY: Kraus International Publishers.

Potter, Stephen. 1993. *Commoners, Tribute, and Chiefs: The Development of Algonquian Culture in the Potomac Valley.* Charlottesville: University of Virginia Press.

Knight, Sarah Kemble (1666–1727)

A Colonial New England businesswoman, Sarah Kemble Knight is primarily remembered today for a journal she authored that vividly describes her overland journey from Boston, Massachusetts, to New York City and back between October 1704 and March 1705. Her journal, first published in 1825, is one of the earliest examples of colonial women's narrative writing, notable for its focus on the secular world of travel, commerce, and social class.

Knight was born in Boston on April 18, 1666, to merchant Thomas Kemble (1622–1689) and Elizabeth Trerice Kemble (d. 1712). Her maternal grandfather, Nicholas Trerice, was a shipbuilder in Charlestown, Massachusetts, and while the historical record is unreliable, it is likely that Elizabeth Trerice and Thomas Kemble met through a business association between Trerice's father and her future husband. The couple

was living in Charlestown together when their first child, John, was born in 1656.

Sarah Kemble was the couple's second or third child and first daughter. Her childhood was spent in Boston's newly developed North End, where her father purchased land. The only child to outlive her parents, Knight eventually inherited the Moon Street property, where she remained until 1714. The neighborhood was prosperous, and the Kemble family rubbed elbows with members of such prominent colonial families as the Mathers, Cottons, and Reveres.

After relocating to Boston, Thomas and Elizabeth Kemble had three more children, two daughters and a son, before Thomas died in early 1689, when his eldest daughter was 22. Shortly before or after her father's death, Sarah Kemble married Richard Knight, a man about which little is known. Census records suggest that he was a woodworker and likely a generation older than his new wife, and their marriage may have been his second. The couple had one child, a daughter named Elizabeth, who was born shortly after their marriage on May 8, 1689. Richard Knight disappears from the historical record after October 1701, and by 1707 Sarah Kemble Knight was listed in a town census as a widow.

Over the winter of 1704–1705, Knight undertook a journey on horseback from Boston to New London, Connecticut, and then on to New York City, likely to assist in settling the legal affairs of her sister's late husband, Caleb Trowbridge, and her eldest brother, John, who died in New York City in 1699. During the trip she took notes regarding her travels and observations, and upon returning to Boston in March 1705 she wrote them up in the form of a diary that is one of the earliest examples of colonial American women's narrative record keeping. The account is particularly remarkable in its secular concerns and descriptive detail. Knight's diary is not an introspective record or religious confession but rather a series of entertaining stories punctuated with opinionated social commentary.

Knight never remarried after her husband's death. The Boston census of 1707 lists her as a shopkeeper and head of a household that included her elderly mother, Elizabeth Kemble; her unmarried daughter, Elizabeth Knight; her widowed sister, Mary Kemble

Trowbridge; Trowbridge's slave, described as an "Indian boy"; and several male boarders. Some historians have suggested that in addition to running a shop and keeping lodgers, Knight may also have supplemented the family income by teaching and copying and witnessing legal documents. Her name appears regularly as a witness on deeds. In a period when male literacy rates are estimated to have hovered around 60 percent of the population and women's at roughly half that figure, Knight's ability to read and write would have been valuable. She is described in official records as "Mistress Knight," an honorific marking her status in the community.

Knight's mother Elizabeth Kemble passed away in 1712. In 1713, Knight's daughter Elizabeth married John Livingston of New London, Connecticut, and the couple settled in New London. Knight followed her daughter south a year later, selling her house and relocating to Norwich, Connecticut, 15 miles up the Thames River from her daughter in New London.

There, Knight once again became a landowner and entrepreneur. Between 1714 and her death in 1727, she owned and rented farmland, ran an inn and tavern, managed a shop, and eventually accumulated an estate valued at roughly £2,000 at her death. Her daughter Elizabeth Livingston, by then also a widow, inherited her mother's property, which may have included several slaves. When Livingston herself died on March 17, 1735/1736, the inventory of her own estate documented two African American slaves, Rose and Pompey, and an Indian man, identified as John Nothing.

The manuscript that turned her mother into a notable literary figure was among Livingston's belongings when she died. The manuscript appears to have been kept by Livingston's executor until it came to the attention of author Theodore Dwight. A cousin of Aaron Burr, Dwight began his professional life as a lawyer but became involved in publishing when he founded the *New York Daily Advertiser*. He transcribed, edited, and published the first edition of the diary in 1825 under the title *The Journal of Madam Knight*. Nonetheless, the journal's authorship remained in dispute for over a quarter century thereafter.

In preparation for an 1858 edition of the narrative, William R. Deane conducted substantial background research and verified enough biographical details to satisfy himself and the scholarly community that Knight was indeed the author. Knight's journal remains an important primary source for colonial American historians because of its clear descriptions of people, customs, and places. That Kemble is a fascinating character and the journal is at times quite funny has also assisted in its longevity.

Anna J. Clutterbuck-Cook

See also *Vol. 1, Sec. 3:* Ballard, Martha; Murray, Judith Sargent; Rowson, Susannah Haswell; Sedgwick, Susan Anne Livingston Ridley

Further Reading

Keim, Billie Ewing. 1969. "Madam Sarah Kemble Knight: Eighteenth-Century American." Master's thesis, Texas Christian University.

Knight, Sarah Kemble. 1972. *The Journal of Madam Knight.* Boston: D. R. Godine.

Norton, Mary Beth. 2011. *Separated by Their Sex: Women in Public and Private in the Colonial Atlantic World.* Ithaca, NY: Cornell University Press.

Laydon, Anne Burras (1595–?)

Anne Burras Laydon secured a number of American firsts during her surprisingly uncelebrated life. She was the first English woman in the colonies to arrive unmarried, be married, and have the first child of English parents be born in Jamestown.

Nothing is known of her life before she was age 14 except that she lived in England and worked as a maid for Lucy Forrest. In 1608 Lucy, Anne, and Lucy's husband Thomas (listed as a gentleman on the ship's manifest) sailed for Jamestown. They arrived on the second supply ship of the year on September 30. They were the first two women to arrive at the Jamestown colony.

Lucy Forrest died almost immediately in 1608, leaving Laydon the only woman of English descent in the colony. By December she married John Laydon, a carpenter and laborer. Their union produced four living daughters by 1625. The eldest, Virginia (the others were Alice, Katherine, and Mary), was the first child of English descent to survive to adulthood in what would become the colonies. She has a grave marker preserved in Hampton, Virginia, that reads "We remember The First Surviving Child Born in Virginia to English Parents, Member of this Parish, Virginia Laydon was born about 1609, the first child of Anne Burras Laydon and John Laydon."

The family is attested in the muster roll of 1624–1625. The roll stated that John had two separate grants of 100 acres each as well as two houses, a palisade, and a musket. Anne was mentioned as 30 years of age. John received a headright grant of 250 acres in 1631 and is mentioned in the legal description of a neighbor's land in 1635. It has been suggested through land records that their daughter Alice married Thomas Willoughby around 1630.

Anne's lifetime spanned an incredible chapter in American history. She arrived in Jamestown nine months after a fire had destroyed what was a small collection of hovels behind a palisade, after a winter in which only 40 of the original 104 colonists survived (150 more had arrived before her). Her second winter there was during what was known as the Starving Time, when new arrivals of colonists and inadequate provisioning from arriving ships meant that desperate times were inevitable. No longer able to hold out, the 60 surviving colonists (including Anne and Thomas) of the 500 who began the winter had boarded a ship for England in July 1610 but turned around when they encountered supply ships two days later.

It would be another three years before a strain of the ideal cash crop for the region, tobacco, would be produced. In 1619, local representative governments began to meet in Jamestown. The next year would be the first year single women were shipped to the colony. Initially, there was no interest in providing single women for the men, who themselves were mostly young and single. It was not until 1619 with the advent of allotting private plots to the individuals (based on length of stay at Jamestown, prior to 1616) that it was recognized that women were necessary to form an economic unit and for heirs to inherit the land. The men asked that land also be allotted to their wives "because that in a newe plantation it is not knowen whether man or woman be the more necessary."

The year 1622 brought a serious Native American conflict, which claimed the lives of many upriver and living away from Jamestown; however, the Laydon family survived. By 1625, Anne and her daughters were 5 of the 53 females in the muster, compared to 124 males (with 9 others listed as "negroes").

Anne was among the first generation of those who became materially and socially successful in British America. Jamestown had gone from a precarious muddy camp belonging to a company to an established political, economic, and cultural center of the British Crown within the first decade and a half of her arrival. The transformations of the colony were paralleled in her own life. She had gone from maid to owner of an estate. A bronze monument commemorating the lives of 12 great Virginia women, including her, stands on the capitol square in Richmond.

Mark Anthony Phelps

See also *Vol. 1, Sec. 1:* Jamestown; Virginia Company

Further Reading
Kelso, William. 2006. *Jamestown, the Buried Truth.* Charlottesville: University of Virginia.
Smith, John. 1907. *The Generall Historie of Virginia, New England & The Summer Isles,* Vol. 1. Glasgow, UK: MacLehose.

Literacy

Women's literacy, or the right of women to read and write, has been historically controversial in many cultures and continues to be controversial in some parts of the world today. Much of North America was originally colonized by Protestants, so the American colonies and the new nation had relatively high literacy rates for girls and women.

Persons and institutions wishing to enforce the oppression of women have long understood that literate women can be problematic to sexist cultures. In 1667, for example, in what would become Mexico, Juana Ines de la Cruz joined a community of nuns. Well educated and startlingly intelligent, the teenage de la Cruz had already amassed a considerable library and published her own writing. Throughout her life she advocated for women's education until church officials threatened her with sanctions and ended her writing, if not reading, career.

The Protestant Reformation began as an attempt to reform the Catholic Church and encourage several new ideas, including literacy among the faithful. In 1517 Martin Luther published his Ninety-Five Theses, a document that condemned the Catholic Church for a host of theological abuses. Luther and other Protestants believed that Christians should all be able to read the Bible so as to discover God's word for themselves rather than allowing priests or church hierarchies to tell people what God wanted. Luther believed that women's literacy played a central role in the Reformation. He argued that women had to be literate so they could read and fully understand the Bible. The Reformation encouraged both literacy and the mass printing of books, because as more households were literate, more had books in the house, which in turn encouraged literacy.

Before conquest, indigenous American cultures were oral cultures. Because they had no tradition of the written word, literacy meant oral literacy, or the ability to hear, remember, and pass on folktales, history, and political traditions. Euro-American colonizers saw this difference as inferiority and in some cases attempted to teach natives to read. Also, many Euro-Americans believed that they had a responsibility to convert native people to Christianity, and this conversion often included literacy. In the 1800s white Americans used the boarding school system to force Native American children to learn to speak, read, and write English. Children who spoke their native language were often harshly punished at the schools and often went back to their families unable to communicate with non-English speakers and unaware of oral literacy traditions and thus ignorant of their own cultures.

Colonial North America had different literacy rates depending on region, class location, and race. The New England Colonies with Puritans or a legacy of Puritanism tended to be more literate than the Southern Colonies. The Massachusetts School Law of 1642 mandated that all children learn to read. Five years later Massachusetts passed the Old Deluder Satan Law, which reinforced reading laws by contending that Satan would have less influence over boys and girls who could read. Thus, Puritans sent both sexes to church-funded elementary schools, but few girls were allowed much education

beyond that stage. Only boys went to secondary schools and then only if they lived in towns large enough to support a private school. Nonetheless, by 1750, 9 out of 10 New England women and girls could read and write. There were no public schools to systematically teach literacy, nor were schools of any kind widely available to girls. Literacy rates were lower in the Southern Colonies. However, in New Orleans the Ursuline nuns founded an academy for girls in 1727 that became a model for female education.

By 1820 fully 80 percent of white American women could read. Moreover, they were reading, understanding, and writing about difficult texts such as the Bible, political and religious philosophers, and poetry. Elite- and middle-class girls and boys could attend dame schools, which were private and taught by women and often included room and board. Many of these schools had quite rigorous curriculums, teaching science, math, Latin, philosophy, and history.

In contrast, in 1820 only 20 percent of black Americans could read, and most of those were free blacks. It is difficult to know what percentage of literate blacks were women, but given that many women worked inside homes where lessons were given, they probably made up a considerable portion of literate black Americans. Poet Phillis Wheatley's work proves that she had considerable writing talents but also suggests that other black women must have as well.

Slave codes made reading illegal for blacks in bondage. North Carolina made reading and writing illegal for slaves in 1740, and Georgia did so in 1758. Slave owners understood that slaves who could read would be less likely to comply with their servitude and more likely to run away. Also, allowing slave literacy suggested that slaves had intellectual capacities equal to whites, which would undercut justifications for slavery. However, there were more literate slaves than the statistics suggest. Because slaveholders punished literate slaves, they had to pretend to be illiterate. Slaves, both female and male, could learn to read from their masters (or masters' children), from hiring out and working side by side with whites, and from black preachers.

America's founding generation identified literacy as one of the keys to the success of the United States. Literate citizens could better make enlightened and rational decisions about self-government. Ideologies such as republican motherhood held that literate women had a crucial role to play in influencing their children and husbands to become virtuous citizens of the American republic.

Peg A. Lamphier

See also Free Blacks, Colonial, Revolutionary War, and New Republic Periods; *Vol. 1, Sec. 3:* Republican Motherhood; Ursuline Nuns; Wheatley, Phillis; *Vol. 2, Sec. 3:* Boarding Schools, Native American

Further Reading

Cremin, Lawrence. 1970. *American Education: The Colonial Experience, 1607–1783.* New York: Harper and Row.

Monaghan, E. J. 2005. *Learning to Read and Write in Colonial America.* Boston: University of Massachusetts Press.

Perlmann, Joel, and Robert Margo. 2001. *Women's Work? American Schoolteachers, 1650–1920.* Chicago: University of Chicago Press.

Webber, Thomas. 1978. *Deep Like Rivers: Education in the Slave Quarter Community, 1831–1865.* New York: Norton.

Mestiza

The term "mestiza" denotes a mixed-race or mixed-blood woman. From the conditions of the 12th and 13th centuries, a period of Spanish conquest and wealth building, the concept of blood purity, or *limpieza de sangre,* developed as a way to maintain wealth and privilege for the Spanish elite and their descendants. Therefore, being of mixed blood carried a negative connotation. Also, the traditions of some of the many aboriginal societies in Africa and the Americas differed from the European traditions and were found wanting. Therefore, those who carried the blood of those philosophies were judged to be inferior.

In the early 1500s, Spanish military troops and missionaries reached North America and began producing offspring with aboriginal and African women both through intermarriage and consensual union but most often through the sex trade that was immediately established in the Caribbean beginning with Christopher Columbus and Bartolome de Las Casas. A few of the aboriginal leadership intermarried with Spanish men of high rank, thereby becoming a part of the new European elite. Most, however, were captured and distributed to military men as booty or sold elsewhere as slaves. Occasionally men who had acquired women by force grew to love their children and wives and freed them and/or bequeathed estates to their descendants.

By the 1600s, the aboriginal people of Spanish America had experienced a population decline of anywhere from 50 to 90 percent before they began to recover. As the population recovered, mestizas (*castas*) became an increasing percentage of the population, especially in the great Indian populations of Mexico, Guatemala, Ecuador, Peru, and Bolivia. As the Spanish established themselves and more Spanish women became available for marriage, unions between the indigenous peoples of the Americas and Africa became stigmatized. Through the early 1600s, the Crown imposed a policy of systematic segregation that led to an elaborate racial caste system.

Spanish law and opinion ranked mixed-race people in a descending order of worth and privilege. Europeans remained at the top of the spectrum with people of color below, while aboriginal and African people were placed at the bottom. Proof of descent was guarded and manufactured. Various races and racial mixtures were carefully distinguished and graded in a hierarchy of rank. A drop of African blood could deprive or restrict the rights of the individual from holding public office, entering professions, or being granted privileges enjoyed by the elite. The laws of the Indies assigned perfect legal equality to those of legitimate birth, but toward the end of the colonial period the charters of certain colonial guilds and schools excluded all mestizos without distinction.

Due to discriminatory policies and practices, many people, descendants of aboriginal and African peoples, became peons, vagabonds, and colonial militia. They were the farmers on rancheros or small farms and formed part of the lower middle class of artisans, overseers, and shopkeepers. Mestizos and Indios made up the coerced and exploited labor population as peons on the haciendas. Mestizas provided domestic labor and continued to be exploited sexually.

The idea of race was used successfully to divide people in the interest of the ruling class, but when it served the interests of the wealthy, identity was fluid and changing. A mestizo or mulatto son of a wealthy Spanish landowner or merchant, if acknowledged and made his legal heir, could pass into the colonial aristocracy. If traces of indigenous blood were too strong, the father might reach an understanding with the parish priest in charge of baptismal certificates and have the child's description on paper define him as white. A wealthy mulatto or mestizo could also purchase his legal whiteness from the Crown. Wealth continued to be a distinguishing characteristic of the colonial aristocracy. Mestizas might wed a wealthy man of privilege and therefore assume his status in society.

Prior to the idea of blood quantum or purity being imposed, community identity and belonging could be both cohesive and fluid. Both in Africa and the Americas, people who spoke different languages or dialects or were unique in other ways would not be considered inferior or superior to one group or another, nor would their differences necessarily exclude them from a group. The ideas of race, ethnicity, single identities, and blood purity are ideas imposed by colonial policies and divide families according to constructed heritages. In the English colonies, racial categories of privilege were fairly rigid and unpermeable. In both the French and Spanish colonies a person of mixed blood could pass from one category to another, depending on socioeconomic location, dress, language, and the type of work the person did. In the Spanish colonial West mestizas could, for example, transform themselves from "Mexican" or mixed blood to "Spanish" by attaining sufficient economic rank to enter the upper classes. In the contemporary American Southwest a woman who identifies herself as Spanish is making a claim about class status more than racial makeup. Self-identified mestizas, on the other hand, are no more or less likely to be mixed blood than a so-called Spanish person, but they are more likely to be working class. In 21st-century America the term "mestiza" also functions as a political identifier, signifying a rejection of majority culture oppression and identification sometimes identified with "Spanish."

Leleua Loupe

See also *Vol. 2, Sec. 1:* Miscegenation

Further Reading

Clayton, L., and M. L. Conniff. 2005. *A History of Modern Latin America.* Belmont, CA: Clark Baxter.

Keen, B., and K. Haynes. 2009. *A History of Latin America.* Boston: Houghton Mifflin Harcourt.

Van Deusen, N. 2012. "The Intimacies of Bondage: Female Indigenous Servants and Slaves and Their Spanish Masters, 1492–1555." *Journal of Women's History* 24(1): 13–43.

Midwives

Midwives are women of varying status, training, and skill who assist women with pregnancy and childbirth. Historically, midwives were also first-tier health care providers, particularly in the 1600 and 1700s when male doctors were scarce and poorly trained.

In early New England, female heath care providers were called midwives; in New Amsterdam *ziecken-troosters* and in Spanish colonies *curanderas, parteras,* or *matrons* conducted women's medicine. Among the Creole and Cajun communities of French Louisiana *sage femme* (wise woman) described someone of considerable respect in the community. Others responsible for childbirth include *vieille femme* (old woman), *chasse femme* (to expel), or *accoucheuse* (one who delivers). *Traiteurs* (treaters) specialized in treating certain illnesses. Healing traditions in the French South are rooted in West African, Native American, and Acadian traditions. In the predominately enslaved African American communities, the granny-midwife was the preeminent healer, and all Native American nations had women who specialized in women's medicine.

Some of these women addressed chronic illnesses, set bones, and provided minor surgery. In European communities they were often paid "nurses" or "doctresses." Jeanne Mance arrived from France as a trained nurse in 1606 and settled at Fort Ville-Marie (Montreal). There she established Hôtel-Dieu, the first hospital in New France. In most other communities female heath care providers were general practitioners, often in poorer communities. They earned considerable respect and gifts for their work.

Knowledge of pregnancy, birth, postpartum recovery, and herbal remedies passed from woman to woman over many generations. European midwives may have had access to birth manuals written during the 16th–18th centuries that illustrated the common belief that children kicked their way into the world. Some women kept recipe books that recorded knowledge passed down through the generations.

Women of African descent, first brought to the colonies by the Spanish in the early 1500s and the English in the early 1600s, brought centuries of knowledge and wisdom of West African and Central African women's medicine. Black midwives continued to pass their knowledge orally and through practice by apprenticing younger women. Like Native American healers, they were deeply spiritual and believed that they had been called on by God to the work, sometimes in a dream, vision, or special occurrence.

In economically well-off European communities, birth would take place in a borning room, partitioned off from other living areas. Some families used birthing stools or chairs to assist the process. For European women delivery was a social occasion, attended by women of the family and community. Postpartum care would last from two weeks to a month. Some Native American women gave birth in a women's house where they too might recover for up to a month. Enslaved African and poor Europeans often gave birth in their quarters and were likely expected to return to work soon after the birth.

Different healers had their own techniques for inducing labor, easing pain, delivering the placenta, cutting the umbilical cord, and coping with birth complications. Prayers were important to all women healers. Grannies might have placed a sharp ax or plow blade under the mattress or pillow of the laboring women to cut the pain. Salt was also thrown on the fire to ward away evil spirits, or they would be banished by having the woman kneel between two smoking fires, a tradition that dates back to tribal rites of Africa. European midwives offered cordials, red wine, or opium for relaxation or to ease pain; applied warm cloths to the stomach or administered an enema to dilate the birth passage; and administered snuff or white hellebore to make the mother sneeze to dislodge the birth. Belladonna served as an antispasmodic.

Skilled midwives from every region knew how to turn the child in the womb and had herbal recipes to give the mother strength or hasten labor. Often the herbs used to hasten labor were also used to bring on late menses or may have been used as abortaficients, such as juniper. European and African women learned additional remedies from Native American practitioners. Blue cohosh root, historically called squaw or papoose root, was known among people in the Northeast. Prepared as a tincture, it was said to increase the productivity of uterine contractions, decrease the duration of active labor and pushing, increase the efficiency of delivery, reduce maternal pain, and control postpartum hemorrhaging and pain. Grannies often buried the afterbirth in a culturally prescribed manner and sometimes brought the postpartum mother around the outside of the house, symbolizing a reintegration into the community.

In Euro-American communities midwives played important legal and political roles, and some were required to become licensed. Bishops policed midwives in the interest of the church and the state. By 1716, New York and Virginia required midwives to be licensed. Their legal role was as a servant of the state, a keeper of social and civil order, in that they testified as expert witnesses in cases concerning bastardy, paternity, rape, and infanticide. Elizabeth Phillips moved to Boston, licensed from the bishop of London, and practiced until 1759. In the Spanish colonies, prosecutors relied heavily on the testimonies of *matrons* and *parteras* to bolster their cases and base their sentences. Midwives performed medical examinations in cases of premarital sex, incest, adultery, and prostitution. Francisca Maria, a Native American woman from Huichapam, testified in an incest rape case in 1740; Gertrudis de Segura, a Spanish woman from San Pedro Jalostoc Ecatepec, testified in a rape and premarital sex case in 1748; and Josefa de Ocampo and Augutina de Najera, from Taxco, testified in a rape case in 1756.

New England communities provided a house or lot rent free to a midwife as long as she did not refuse callers, and in many non-English colonies, midwives were kept on the payroll. Communities in New Amsterdam provided salaries to female healers. The Dutch West India Company provided salaries to some healers and free houses in the city if they agreed to attend to the poor. French Louisiana paid midwives until

1756, with some review and oversight provided by physicians. Acadian midwife Marie Henriette LeJeune Ross practiced between 1786 and 1860 and is best known for quarantining smallpox patients in an epidemic of 1800 and inoculating those yet afflicted. Midwives in the South, usually enslaved women, were responsible for the birthing and aftercare of free and unfree, rural and urban, and European and African American families. Enslaved midwives were vital to maternity care in the South and were valuable slaves.

The general need for healers, while affording them high status and compensation not afforded to other women, did not protect women from persecution if they upset other social norms. Anne Hutchison was a well-respected upper-class Boston midwife in the 1640s. As a female intellectual and religious and political dissident, she also attracted the ire of the political and religious leaders of the Massachusetts Bay Company. Hutchison was found guilty of heresy and sedition, banished from the colony, and excommunicated her from the church. In addition, practices that went beyond what was acceptable and correlated with a patient's death were sometimes vulnerable to accusations of witchcraft, as was also the case for women who did not obey social norms.

Formal training and the approach to midwifery as a science first developed in Paris, France, in the early 16th century. Some women had the opportunity to train to become midwives, but most continued to rely on generational wisdom and experience. By 1700, French theories and practices of birth and the development of forceps in England led to the professionalization and masculinization of midwifery. By 1750, educated and wealthy European men began to return from medical schools to bring the new theories and practices to European colonies in America, legally replacing women in the practice by 1800. Male professionals claimed authority and expertise in the profession but often acquired much of their knowledge from the expertise of midwives. Because male medical professionals saw their role in childbirth as more about control and interference and because they had no knowledge of germ theory, they infected and/or killed many more mothers than did midwives. By 1850 the number of new mothers killed by puerperal fever, also known as childbed fever, had skyrocketed. As the medical profession expanded in the 1800s, women were often prevented from attending medical schools or obtaining medical licenses.

In 1813 the medical school in Philadelphia made midwifery instruction mandatory for its medical degree, which led to the establishment of an obstetrical department. The medical profession became an elite male practice as women healers lost prestige and patients to male physicians. In poor communities throughout America, midwives, *sage femme, curanderas,* old-grannies, and Native American healers continued to provide health care to poor and rural women throughout the 20th century.

Leleua Loupe

See also Hutchinson, Anne Marbury; *Vol. 1, Sec. 3:* Ballard, Martha; *Vol. 2, Sec. 1:* Blackwell, Elizabeth

Further Reading

Fontenot, Wonda L. 1994. *Secret Doctors: Ethnomedicine of African Americans.* Westport, CT: Bergin and Garvey.

Leavitt, Judith Walzer, ed. 1999. *Women and Health in America.* Madison: University of Wisconsin Press.

Tannenbaum, Rebecca J. 2002. *The Healer's Calling: Women and Medicine in Early New England.* Ithaca, NY: Cornell University Press.

Wertz, Richard W., and Dorothy C. Wertz. 1989. *Lying-In: A History of Childbirth in America.* New Haven, CT: Yale University Press.

Moody, Deborah (1586–1658/1659)

Taking her place beside other figures such as Anne Hutchinson and Mary Dyer, Lady Deborah Moody engaged in acts of civic and religious dissent during the colonial period in America. She also distinguished herself as a leader, becoming the first woman to establish a New York colonial settlement as well as to own land.

Born in London in 1586 to Walter and Deborah Dunch, Moody joined a well-established English family of radical Protestants. Her mother was a member of an outspoken family, particularly in matters of faith because her grandfather was a bishop. Her father was a lawyer and member of Parliament. As a youth,

Moody enjoyed the benefits accorded to young women of her station, including literacy.

In 1606 Moody married Henry Moody, who would go on to become a member of Parliament. When King James I knighted her husband, she became Lady Deborah Moody. Henry Moody died in 1629, leaving a still-young wife to make her way in the world as a widow.

Deborah Moody was a spirited and strong-minded individual, including in matters of state and religion. On several occasions, her expression of such views placed her at the center of controversy. For example, when she defied King Charles's order that members of the elite spend the majority of their time at their country estates rather than in London, she was prosecuted for that act of willfulness and commanded to return to the family estate of Garesdon.

Moody decided to flee the religious persecution she experienced in England, so she sailed with her son, Henry, to the New World. Once there, she acquired a 400-acre Massachusetts farm known as Swampscott and established a residence in Salem. In 1640, she joined the Salem church. Here as before, Moody's willingness to question authority caused conflict. Just two years after becoming a member of the church, Moody found herself charged by the Massachusetts Bay Colony for her expressions of doubt about the validity of infant baptism. She was accused of having Anabaptist beliefs for suggesting that adult baptism might be a more fitting practice, which could be said to reflect a more explicit act of choice on the part of the baptized person.

As the leader of a group of supporters, Moody left Massachusetts in 1643 to found the Gravesend Colony in the Dutch portion of Long Island, then known as New Netherland. As founder, Moody set in place the rules for Gravesend, banning such practices as slavery and the sale of alcohol to Indians. Conflicts and disputes among residents would be settled at town meetings. She even designed the settlement's configuration, including a central square and street grid that survive to this day.

On this basis, the Dutch granted Moody a charter for Gravesend, which helped afford area residents self-government and the freedom of religious belief, though not yet the right to practice those beliefs in public ways. She then took up residence at 27 Gravesend Road. As landowner, Moody became the first woman to cast a vote in the colonies in 1655. It is believed that she sheltered Quakers there, possibly even converting to Quakerism, and Gravesend became the site of the first organized Quaker meeting in North America. Moody's son, Henry, became New Netherland's ambassador to Virginia.

Gravesend remained largely farmland through the 1870s. At that time, commercial entertainments, including Coney Island and racetracks located in the vicinity, changed the character of the setting to a more urban, bustling environment. Gravesend was annexed by the city of Brooklyn in 1894.

Moody died in either late 1658 or early 1659 and may have been laid to rest in Old Gravesend Cemetery. A monument to Moody stands in the Gravesend town square in Brooklyn.

Over the course of her lifetime, Lady Deborah Moody demonstrated the power and importance of personal conviction. In so doing, she is remembered as a colonial-era town planner, leader, and advocate of civil liberties.

Linda S. Watts

See also Dyer, Mary; Hutchinson, Anne Marbury

Further Reading

Biemer, Linda. 1981. "Lady Deborah Moody and the Founding of Gravesend." *Journal of Long Island History* 17(2): 24–42.

Bremer, Francis J. 2012. *First Founders: American Puritans and Puritanism in an Atlantic World.* Lebanon: University of New Hampshire Press.

Cooper, Victor H. 1995. *A Dangerous Woman: New York's First Lady Liberty; The Life and Times of Lady Deborah Moody: Her Search for Freedom of Religion in Colonial America.* Bowie, MD: Heritage Books.

Koppelman, Lucille L. 1994. "Lady Deborah Moody and Gravesend, 1643–1659." *Halve Maen* 67(2) (Spring): 38–42.

Musgrove, Mary (ca. 1700–1763)

Mary Musgrove was born sometime around 1700 to an English trader and a Native American mother from the Creek tribe. At birth she was named Coosaponakeesa, although her father's relations knew her as Mary. Her Creek family must have been prominent, for she was allowed great influence among the Creeks throughout much of her lifetime. She spent time during her formative years with each of her parents, as she was comfortable in both native and white society and spoke both English and Muscogee. In either 1716 or 1717 she married John Musgrove, also a trader. Together they established a trading post on the Savannah River, where they remained until John Musgrove's death in 1735. Mary's unique upbringing and early life with Musgrove allowed her to become a significant cultural broker between the Creeks and colonial Georgia during the formative years of the colony.

James Oglethorpe and the first English settlers arrived in Georgia in 1733. Soon thereafter, Mary Musgrove became an interpreter and an adviser to Oglethorpe on how to work, live, and trade with the region's native populations. She continued this work even after she married Jacob Mathewes in 1737 and joined him at a trading post that they constructed on the Altamaha River.

One of the primary purposes for the establishment of Georgia was to prevent Spain from extending its influence north of Florida. Musgrove aided the English in this endeavor by encouraging her fellow Creek Indians to help protect Georgia's southern border. Her efforts proved critical to the colony when the War of Jenkins' Ear erupted in 1739, as she personally recruited Creek warriors for Oglethorpe. The conflict proved personally devastating for Musgrove, as she lost several kinsmen at the Battle of Fort Mose, including her brother.

In 1740, the English unsuccessfully besieged St. Augustine in Florida. In retaliation, the Spanish sent their Yamassee allies on a raiding expedition to Georgia. One of the targets razed by the Yamassees was the trading post constructed by Musgrove and her husband, Jacob. At the time the war ended in 1742, Musgrove was again a widow, as Jacob died in 1742 following a long illness. Her relationship with Oglethorpe strained due to his actions during the conflict, especially those related to Fort Mose. He assuaged her anger when he departed for England by awarding her a diamond ring and £200 for her service to Georgia with the promise of £2,000 more to come, though that was never received.

Musgrove continued her service as an intermediary between the Creeks and the English, although she increasingly became a controversial figure to both groups. Her problems with the English began in 1737 when she claimed that Yamacraw chief Tomochichi had granted her land in the vicinity of Savannah. England did not consider the gift valid, and the issue remained unaddressed for years. After Musgrove married Thomas Bosomworth in 1744, she claimed that they were gifted three islands, Ossabaw, Sapelo, and St. Catherine's, off the coast of Georgia by the Creek chief Malatche. Despite the claims of the Bosomworths, both the Creeks and Yamacraws believed that the land was never given away and thus still belonged to them. To complicate matters, the English coveted all the properties in question. In 1749, Musgrove and her husband led a contingent of Creeks loyal to Musgrove to Savannah to intimidate the English to rule in her favor but to no avail.

To further her cause with the English, Musgrove threatened to assist French emissaries who were in the region to secure the Creeks as allies, thereby removing the Creeks as buffers between England and its Spanish and French enemies. Musgrove also proclaimed herself "Queen of the Creeks." The latter point was especially questionable, as many Creek leaders, including Malatche, were actively repudiating her supposed influence on them. Unsuccessful in Georgia, the Bosomworths then went to England in 1754 to pursue their claims before the Board of Trade. That body referred them back to the Georgia courts. The matter was finally resolved in 1760 through a compromise proposed by Georgia's royal governor, Henry Ellis. The Bosomworths received St. Catherine's Island and an additional £2,100 for Ossabaw and Sapelo Islands. Mary Musgrove died on St. Catherine's Island in 1763.

John R. Burch Jr.

See also Kittamaquund, Mary; *Vol. 1, Sec. 1:* Malinche; *Vol. 1, Sec. 3:* Glory of the Morning

Further Reading
Green, Michael D. 2001. "Mary Musgrove: Creating a New World." In *Sifters: Native American Women's Lives,* edited by Theda Perdue, 29–47. New York: Oxford University Press.

Hahn, Steven C. 2012. *The Life and Times of Mary Musgrove.* Gainesville: University Press of Florida.

Protestant Women

There were diverse groups of Protestants living in colonial America. Puritans dominated the landscape of early New England, but the largest and most influential congregations during the colonial era were the Anglicans and the heirs of the Reformation such as the Congregationalists, Presbyterians, and Baptists. Although women were excluded from leadership positions within most Protestant denominations, religion offered women many opportunities to forge their own spiritual identity separate from that of their husbands or others. The Great Awakening of the mid-18th century accelerated this trend.

Nearly 20,000 Puritans arrived in New England during the Great Migration of 1630–1643. Most were interested in reforming, or "purifying," the Church of England and ridding it of its similarities to the Roman Catholic Church, such as emphases on elaborate rituals, the veneration of saints, and the recitation of set prayers. Puritan women were excluded from leadership positions within the church based on the Apostle Paul's biblical directive that women should hold no authority over men and should remain silent in church (1 Timothy 2:12). Puritan theology also encouraged its adherents to believe in the inherently sinful nature of women. Puritans did, however, believe that all souls were equal before God. Both men and women could testify to their conversion and become members of the church.

Plenty of women challenged the Puritan restrictions on women's authority in spiritual matters. Anne Hutchinson and her family arrived in Boston in 1634, where she soon began hosting spiritual discussions for as many as 60 women and men. In 1636, she accused Puritan ministers of preaching that salvation was dependent on good works rather than God's grace. She was tried for sedition and banished from the Massachusetts Bay Colony. Quakers posed additional challenges to Puritan authority. Quakers gave women freedom to speak in religious gatherings, and women served as missionaries and managed other women's activities within the church. In the 1650s, Mary Dyer was exiled from both the Massachusetts and Connecticut colonies, which had enacted laws banning Quakers. She was hanged for returning to Boston (to visit two friends who were jailed for their Quaker beliefs) on June 1, 1660. Both Dyer and Hutchinson settled in Rhode Island after their banishments, a colony whose policy of religious toleration contributed to the growth of dissenting sects such as the Quakers and the Baptists.

The Church of England arrived in colonial America with the settlers of Jamestown, Virginia, in 1607 and took root primarily in the Southern Colonies. Most Anglicans rejected the ideas of predestination and conversion, instead believing in an individual's capacity to earn salvation through good works. Sermons focused less on inner spiritualism and conversion and more on living a moral life. Although Anglican congregations welcomed men and women of different races and classes, the church maintained hierarchies of gender, class, and race. Women could not hold any formal offices, nor could they preach or perform sacraments (baptism, marriages, and communion, for example). Women did play an important role in the orchestration of such events, however, since they were typically held at home. Faith was a family affair for Anglicans, and women played an important role in perpetuating the faith at home through the recitation of family prayers and the continuation of religious education. Anglicans tolerated different religions and opinions more than Puritans, including the ideas and existence of Protestant dissenters. The traditional religious views of Native Americans and Africans, however, were deemed largely unacceptable, as they were in the Puritan theology.

In the 1730s and 1740s, America experienced an intense period of evangelical revivalism that crossed denominational boundaries. Many women found new spiritual and informal leadership opportunities within the religions that flourished during this Great Awakening. Central to revivalism was the idea that each individual had the authority to interpret the state of his or her soul without clerical interpretation or theological training. This belief had the potential to offer gender and racial equality among revivalists' congregations by asserting the supremacy of an individual's direct contact with God. Faith was affirmed on a personal level, and women were just as able as men to strengthen their relationship with God through personal prayer,

Bible study, and the performance of good works. Influential New Light revivalist ministers, including Jonathan Edwards and itinerant preacher George Whitefield, shared the message of salvation in dramatic and emotional sermons and encouraged similar outpourings of faith from listeners. Both women and men were known to shout, weep, sing, or even faint to express their feelings. Revivalism appealed to many African Americans, both free and enslaved, who soon converted to Christianity in substantial numbers, eventually leading to the establishment of the first black congregations and churches in the American colonies. While the Great Awakening offered women opportunities to experience salvation on their own terms, it failed to change women's political, social, or economic status within the community in any significant ways.

This fleeting renegotiation of women's roles in church and the relationship between clergy and their flock did not take place without question or criticism. Conservative Old Light clergymen complained about women's "disorderly behavior" during religious gatherings and condemned women and African Americans who shed their subordinate status and began to organize and speak out at religious gatherings and to found or

join reform movements. Baptist and Methodist congregations grew exponentially in the 17th century, while those men and women who disapproved of evangelical methods often joined Anglican or Quaker congregations. Some scholars argue that the Great Awakening fostered a spirit of contentious debate that ultimately contributed to a questioning of authority that sparked the American Revolution.

Kathleen Barker

See also Dyer, Mary; Great Awakening; Hutchinson, Anne Marbury; Quakers; Witchcraft in New England; Witch Trials, Salem, Massachusetts; *Vol. 1, Sec. 3:* Second Great Awakening

Further Reading

Brekus, Catherine. 2007. *The Religious History of American Women: Reimagining the Past.* Chapel Hill: University of North Carolina.

Demos, John. 1970. *A Little Commonwealth: Family Life in Plymouth Colony.* New York: Oxford University Press.

Juster, Susan. 1996. *Disorderly Women: Sexual Politics and Evangelicalism in Revolutionary New England.* Ithaca, NY: Cornell University Press.

Plymouth Colony Court Cases Involving Women (Mid-1600s)

Court orders involving women in colonial New England are relatively rare and often have to do with placing daughters into indentured service. Colonial families placed daughters as young as five into indentured service and formalized indenture contracts in the court. Colonial Americans also applied to the courts for matters we would today find trivial, such as the return of a daughter's clothing. Cases involving sexual misconduct were not uncommon, with women being either victims of some kind of sexual abuse or the perpetrators of sexual misconduct.

1. PLYMOUTH COLONY COURT ORDERS (1643–1670)

January 18, 1643/1644; vol. 2: 67

William Hoskine, of Plymouth, hath put Sarah, his daughter, to Thomas Whitney, and Winefride, his

wyfe, to dwell wth them vntill shee shall accomplish the age of twenty yeares, the said Thomas, and Winyfride, his wyfe, vseing her as their child, and being vnto her as father and mother, and to instruct her in learneing and soweing in reasonable manner, fynding vnto her meate, drink, and apparell [and] lodging during the said terme; and if it shall happen the said Sarah to marry before he shall haue accomplished the said age of twenty yeares, (she being six yeares of age the xvjth of September last past,) that then the sayd Thomas shall haue such satisfaction for her tyme then remayneing as shalbe adjudged reasonable [and] equall by two indifferent men.

May 5, 1646; vol. 2: 98

Vpon heareing of the cause betwixt Roger Shaundler and Kenelme Winslow, for his daughters cloathes, wch the said Kenelme detaineth vpon pretence of some further service wch he required of her, wherevnto the said Roger vtterly refused to consent, it is ordered by the Court, that the said Kenelme WInslowe shall deliuer the mayde her cloathes wthout any further delay.

March 2, 1651/1652; vol. 3: 4–5

Wheras John Willis, of Duxborrow, complained that his daughter in law, Rebeckah Palmer, was molested and hindered in performing faithfull service vnto her mr, viz, Samuall Mayo, of Barnstable by the wife of Trustrum Hull, of Barnstable aforsaid, the Court haue sent downe order by Roger Goodspeed, grand juryman, of Barnstable aforsaid, to wrarn the wife of ye said Trustrum Hull to desist from such practises any further, as shee or any other that shall soe doe will answare for her not appearing at this Court nor her attornie, to answare the suite comenced against her by the said John Willis.

Wee present Jonathan Couentrey, of the towne of Marshfeild, for makeing a mocion of marriage vnto Katheren Bradberey, servant vnto Mr Burne, of the same towne, without her masters consent, contrary to Court order.

June 8, 1655; vol. 3: 82

Imppr, we present Susanna, the wife of Robert Latham, for being in a great measure aguilty, with her said husband, in exercising creuelly towards theire late seruant, John walker, in not affording him convenient food, rayment, and lodging; especially in her husbands absence, in forceing him to bring a logg beyond his strength.

(Entry Struck from the Record)

Item, wee present Jane, the seruant of Wilam Swift, for an acte of fornification, by her owne confession vpon examination.

October 4, 1655; vol. 3: 91

And att this Court, Jane Powell, seruant to Willam Swift, of Sandwidge, appeered, haueing been presented for fornification, whoe, being examined, saith

that it was comitted with one David Ogillior, and Irish man, seruant to Edward Sturgis; shee saith shee was alured thervnto by him goeing for water one euening, hopeing to haue married him, beeing shee was in a sadd and miserable condition by hard seruice, wanting clothes and liuing discontentedly; and expressing great sorrow for her euell, shee was cleared for the present, and ordered to goe home againe.

June 1, 1658; vol. 3: 143

Wheras Susana Latham hath stood presented vnto this Court for sundry yeares for crewelty toawrd John Walker, seruant to Robert Latham, these are to signify, that accordingly as it was manifested in the Court, that if any will come in, they shall haue full and free libertie to procequte against her att the next October Court, or totherwise that then the said presentment shalbee raced out of the Court records.

[In the margins regarding the above entry:] At the Court held att Plymouth the fift of October, 1658, proclaimation was made three times in the Court, that if any would presecute Susanna Latham according to this order they should be heard; but none apeered in the case, and according to this order, her presentment was rased out of the records of the Court.

May 3, 1659; vol. 3: 160

Wheras complaint was mae against John williams, of Scittuate, for hard vsage of a daughter of John Barker, deceased, the Court hau4e ordered, that the said child shalbee and continew with Thomas Bird, of Scittuate, vntill the next Court; and that shee being weake and indeirme, the said tho Bird is to endeauor to procure meanes for her cure, and what expence hee shalbee att about the same, the Court engageth to take order that hee shalbe paid; and the said Thomas Bird is to appeer att the next Court to giue in what testimony hee can produce to cleare vp the case betwixt the said John Williams and his kinswoman, the said gerle.

March 7, 1659/1660; vol. 3: 180

Wheras complaint is made against, seruant of Leiftenant Peter Hunt, of Rehoboth, that hee, the said, hath attempted the chastity of an Indian woman, by offering violence to her, and that the complaint hath bine heard before Captaine Willett, and that there is great appeerance of truth in the said charge; the Court haue ordered that the said Capt Willett shall further examine the said youth, named, and incase hee shall find the accusation to bee true, that hee cause due correction to bee giuen him, and determine alsoe otherwise about the said fact as hee shall judge meet.

July 5, 1670; vol. 5: 43–44

Elizabeth Doxey, late seruant to Mr. Joseph Tilden, deceased, being deliuered of a child, and charging of Nathaniel Tilden to be the father of it, the said Nathaniel Tilden appeered att this Court to answare to it, and being examined, denyeth it; not withstanding, the Court saw cause to take cecuritie of him to saue the towne of Scittuate harmles from any damage that might acrew vnto them by the said child vntill another father appeereth; and a warrant was directed to the constables of Scittuate to cause her, the said Doxey, to bee sent as soon as shee is capable to Plymouth, to receiue punishment according to her demeritts.

Source: Nathaniel Shurtleff and Daniel Pulsifer, eds., *Records of the Colony of New Plymouth in New England,* 12 vols. (Boston: William White, 1856–1861). Available at Plymouth County Records, http://plymouthcolony.net /plymouthcounty/records.html#plycol.

2. CRIMINAL CASES INVOLVING NATIVE AMERICAN WOMEN IN PLYMOUTH COLONY COURT (1659, 1685)

The vast majority of criminal cases brought before the Plymouth Colony Court involving Native Americans describe crimes by men against men. The following are two rare cases involving women.

December 6, 1659; vol. 3: 180

Wheras complaint is made against, servant to Lieftenant Peter Hunt, of Rehoboth, that hee, the said, hath attempted the chastity of an Indian woman, by offering violence to her, and that the complaint hath bine heard before Captaine Willett, and that there is great appeerance of truth in the said charge; the Court haue ordered that the said Capt Willett shall further examine the said youth, named, and incase hee shall

find the accusation to bee true, that hee cause due correction to bee giuen him, and determine alsoe otherwise about the said fact as hee shall judge meet.

March 5, 1685; vol. 6: 153

Att his Court an Indian squa, named Betty, was indited for killing her husband, named Great Harry, with a stone; att the fist, being examined by the honored Mr John Walley, shee denyed it, but afterwards owned the fact, but said shee did not intend to kill him, but by throwing of a stone att a bottle of liquore and missing the bottle, shee hitt the said Indian, her husband, on the side of his head, wherof he died

The case being brought to the grand jury, they brought in billa very.

Source: Nathaniel Shurtleff and Daniel Pulsifer, eds., *Records of the Colony of New Plymouth in New England,* 12 vols. (Boston: William White, 1856–1861). Available at Plymouth County Records, http://plymouthcolony.net /plymouthcounty/records.html#plycol.

3. PLYMOUTH COLONY LAW REGARDING RUNAWAY NATIVE AMERICAN SLAVES OR "SERVANTS" (1682)

The following law lays out how to deal with a Native American—man or woman—who runs away from servitude.

July 7, 1682, PCR 11: 255:

It is enacted by the Court and the Authorities therof; that if an Indian whoe is a servant to the English shall run away amongst any Indians such Indians whither such a runaway Indian is come shall forthwith giue notice of the said Runaway to the Indian Constable whoe shall imediatley apprehend such Indian servant; and carry him or her before the Ouerseer or Next Magistrate whoe shall cause such servants to be whipt; and sent home by the Constable to his or her master whoe shall pay said Constable for his service therin according as the Majestrate or ouersser whoe sent such servant home shall Judge meet. . . .

Source: "Servants and Masters in the Plymouth Colony, Appendices I, II, and III on Plymouth Colony Laws, Court Orders, and Descriptive Statistics," Plymouth Colony Archive Project, http://www.histarch.illinois.edu/plymouth /Galleapp.html.

Quakers

Quaker women in America have nearly always enjoyed a greater amount of dignity, freedom, and equality with men than have women in other Christian communities. Early Quakers believed that God was working through every true follower of Christ to restore all creation to the state it was in before the fall of Adam and Eve. Against the gender hierarchies of this fallen world, the Quaker testimony of equality held that both men and women may be called by God and moved by the Spirit to preach the gospel message. Quakers (formally known as the Religious Society of Friends) have no set doctrine, no creeds, and no sacraments, and many meetings (churches) still worship mostly in silence and have no paid ministers. What all Quakers do have is a group of testimonies, or divine calls to action for building the kingdom of God on Earth. Possibly the two most radical of these have been peace—Quakers being famous, or infamous, for their pacifism—and equality. The latter testimony has afforded Quaker women their relatively high level of respect and autonomy.

Quakers became a distinctly recognizable group in England in the 1650s, though their founder, George Fox, had started to attract a following in the late 1640s. Religious persecution at the hands of the Puritans, together with the Quakers' desire to spread their message throughout the British Empire, led a handful of Friends (synonym for "Quakers") in the late 1650s to migrate to Rhode Island, where religious freedom allowed almost all persons to worship in peace, whatever their beliefs. From Rhode Island, Quakers of both sexes braved Puritan intolerance and preached their message in New England. Women preachers horrified many Puritans, who thought that women preaching in public to mixed audiences of both men and women violated Paul's command in the New Testament that women keep quiet in public worship, not to mention the Bible's seemingly clear hierarchy of genders, with men on top and women on the bottom. The literal quaking of Quaker women as the Spirit moved through their bodies suggested sexual impropriety to their opponents. That Quakers would let such women preach openly to men as well as women proved to most other Christians that Quakers were not Christians but infidels and should not be allowed to lead others astray. For instance, the Puritan authorities hanged Quaker evangelist Mary Dyer and two of her male companions on Boston Common in 1660.

Quaker women not only preached but also interpreted Scripture, for themselves and others—another typically male office. They also kept journals and wrote theological treatises, many of which they published. In these and many other ways they represented an early modern feminism. Yet not all was enlightened equality. Before the American Civil War, men and women in most Quaker meetings conducted their monthly business separately—the women charged with helping families who were poor and with seeing to it that the meeting's children were being raised properly—and the women's decisions usually had to be ratified by the men. Within the home, most Quaker families would almost certainly have followed their founder George Fox's advice that the man rule absolutely, though with charity toward his wifely "helpsmeet" and his entire household, including slaves (many Quakers were slaveholders until the late 1700s).

Many remarkable Quaker women worked within the confines of early American patriarchy to remake it. In the 1700s, Quaker women ministers preached and prophesied throughout the colonies and even crossed the Atlantic to minister to Friends in Great Britain. By the time of the American Revolution, they had carved out a public space that women in the new nation could occupy. One of these, Lucretia Coffin Mott, a Quaker, was the keynote speaker at the largely Quaker-organized Seneca Falls Convention in 1848, and she fought for abolition as a leader in the Female Anti-Slavery Society. (Quaker women in New York were also instrumental in the origins of Spiritualism.) Another, Sybil Jones, helped birth the Quaker missionary movement with her husband Eli. She took her first missionary journey in 1840, and just after the Civil War she and her husband established a school for girls in Palestine. Jones's nephew Rufus became one of the leading Quakers of his day in the late 19th and early 20th centuries. By then, the Victorian and evangelical gender mores of the wider culture had so permeated American society that the Quakers too began to limit women's public leadership. But the tradition of Quaker women's evangelism and activism, together with the

Quakers' testimony of equality, continued to nurture and validate women moved by the Spirit to redress the various injustices of their fallen patriarchal world.

Guy Aiken

See also Dyer, Mary

Further Reading

Bacon, Margaret Hope, ed. 1994. *'Wilt Thou Go on My Errand?': Journals of Three 18th Century Quaker Women Ministers.* Wallingford, PA: Pendle Hill Publications.

Doan, Petra L., and Elizabeth P. Kamphausen. "Quakers and Sexuality." In *The Oxford Handbook of Quaker Studies,* edited by Stephen W. Angell and Pink Dandelion, 445–457. New York: Oxford University Press.

Garman, Mary, Judith Applegate, Margaret Benefiel, and Dortha Meredith, eds. 1996. *Hidden in Plain Sight: Quaker Women's Writings, 1650–1700.* Wallingford, PA: Pendle Hill.

Garman, Mary Van Vleck. 2013. "Quaker Women's Lives and Spiritualities." In *The Oxford Handbook of Quaker Studies,* edited by Stephen W. Angell and Pink Dandelion, 232–244. New York: Oxford University Press.

Larson, Rebecca. 1999. *Daughters of Light: Quaker Women Preaching and Prophesying in the Colonies and Abroad, 1700–1775.* Chapel Hill: University of North Carolina Press.

Newman, Edwina. "Quakers and the Family." In *The Oxford Handbook of Quaker Studies,* edited by Stephen W. Angell and Pink Dandelion, 434–444. New York: Oxford University Press.

Tartar, Michele. 2001. "Quaking in the Light: The Politics of Quaker Women's Corporeal Prophecy in the Seventeenth-Century Transatlantic World." In *A Centre of Wonders: The Body in Early America,* edited by Janet Moore Lindman and Michele Lise Tartar, 145–162. Ithaca, NY: Cornell University Press.

Excerpts from a Declaration of the Quaker Women's Meeting of Lancashire (Late 1670s)

The Quakers were among the earliest proponents of equality for women in America. By the later 17th century, Quaker women were holding their own monthly and quarterly meetings both in England and the colonies. Reproduced here are excerpts of an epistle found in the archives of the Arch Street Meeting House in Philadelphia that was apparently sent to Quaker women in Philadelphia by the Lancashire (England) Women's Meeting in the late 1670s. The lengthy document provides Quaker women with instructions and guidelines for conducting meetings and for carrying out their duties and responsibilities, as they were envisioned by current Quaker thought on the role of women in the congregation.

From our Country Women's meeting in Lancashire to be Dispersed abroad, among the Women's meetings every where

. . . Soe all Dear friends and sisters, make full proofe of the gift of God that is in you, and neglect not, in this your day, and generation; but that you may be helps meet, in the Restoration, and Resurrection of the body of Christ, which is his Church, and that every one may know their place and calling therein as the Godly women under the law did. For all who were wise in heart, put their hands to the worke, about the tabernacle, and all the women whose hearts stirred them up in wisdom, had their several places to work in about the tabernacle as well as the men for all the Congregation of the Children of Israel every one both men and women whose spirits was made willing, they brought the Lord's offering to the works of the tabernacle: as you may see. Exod: 35.25–26.

And like wise Miriam the prophetess, the sister of Aaron tooke a Timbrell in her hand, and all the women went out after in triumph and singing prayse to the Lord, who by his mighty power had over-thrown pharaoh and his host, in the red sea. Exod: 15: 20.21.

And there was an assembly of women which as-sembled at the door of the tabernacle of the Congre-gation. Exod: 38.8. And like wise Hannah, when she had weaned her son Samuell, tooke him and went up to the house of the Lord, and took with her three bullocks, one Ephah, and a bottle of wine, and slew one bullock, and brought the child to Eli, and offered him up unto the Lord, and said for this child have I prayed, and the lord hath given me my portion, which I asked of him. And this child Samuell minis-tered unto the Lord, before Eli the priest, and Hannah prayed, and Oh! The gracious words, and prayer, that proceeded out of her mouth, by the powerful dem-onstration of the Eternall spirit, and the power of the almighty God in her. 1. Of Sam: 2. From 2 to 11. Which all the adversaries and gainsayers against women's meetings, and women's speaking, is not able to gainsay, nor resist; therefore let all the mouths be stopped, which would limit the Spirit of the Lord God, in male or female, which he hath not limited; but the Lord hath regard unto and takes notice of the women, and despises them not. . . .

And let us meet together, and keep our women's meetings, in the name and power, and fear of the lord Jesus, whose servants and handmaids we are, and in the good order of the Gospel meet.

1st And first, for the women of every . . . monthly meeting, when the men's monthly meetings is estab-lished, let the women likewise of every monthly meeting, meet together to wait upon the lord, and to hearken what the lord will say unto them, and to know his mind, and will, and be ready to obey, and answer him in every motion of his eternal spirit and power.

2ly And also, to make inquiry into all your severall particular meetings, that belongs to your monthly meetings, If there by any that walks disorderly, as doth not become the Gospell, or lightly, or wantonly, or that is not of good reporte: Then send to them, as you are ordered by the power of God in the meeting, (which is the authority of it) to Admonish, and exhort them, and to bring them to Judge, and Condemn, what hath been by them done or acted contrary to the truth.

3ly And if any transgression or Action that hath been done amongst women or maids, that hath been more publick, and that hath got into the world, or that hath been a publick offense among friends; then let them bring in a paper of condemnation, to be published as far, as the offense hath gone, and then to be recorded in a booke.

4ly And if there be any that goes out to Marry, with priests, or joineth in Marriage with the world, and does not obey the order of the Gospell as it is estab-lished amongst friends, then for the women's monthly meeting to send to them, to reprove them, and to bear their testimony against their acting Contrary to the truth, and if they come to repentance, and sorrow for their offense, and have a desire to come amongst friends again: before they can be received, they must bring in a paper of Condemnation, and repentance, and Judgment of their Action; which must be re-corded in Friends Booke: And also to carry that paper to the priest, that married them, and Judge, and Con-demn, and deny that Action, before him or any of the world before whome it shall come.

And dear sisters it is duely Incumbent upon us to look into our families, and to prevent our Children of running into the world for husbands, or for wives, and so to the priests: for you know before the wom-en's meetings were set up, Many have done so, which brought dishonor, both to God, and upon his truth and people.

Therefore it is our duty and care, to prevent such things in the power, and wisdom of God: and to see that our Children are trained up in the feare of God, in the new Covenant, for the Jews were to train their Children up in the old. For you know, that we are much in our families amongst our children, maids, and servants, and may see more into their inclina-tions; and so see that none indulge any to looseness and evill, but restraine it, for you see what became of Eli, and his familie, for not restraining his Children. . . .

Source: Milton D. Speizman and Jane C. Kronick, "A Seventeenth-Century Quaker Women's Declaration," *Signs* 1(1) (Autumn 1975): 235, 237, 241–242.

Queen Alliquippa (ca. 1680–1754)

Queen Alliquippa (Aliquippa) was a Native American leader in the Ohio River Valley during the 1700s. Her alliance with American colonists may have enabled the British to prevail in the French and Indian War (1756–1760). Though a woman of political influence and societal power, Alliquippa's full role in North American history has been lost to a historical record documented and interpreted by Euro-American elite men.

Alliquippa was born in present-day northern New York state, but her early life remains unknown. Conflicting accounts record her birth and affiliations; however, most sources agree that she belonged to the Seneca nation. or Onöndowa'ga (Great Hill People) of the Haudenosaunee or Iroquois Confederacy (a band of five nations—Mohawk, Oneida, Onondaga, Cayuga, and Seneca—politically united to preserve territorial peace in the northeastern woodlands). Prior to 1700, she migrated south to Pennsylvania with a splinter group identified as the Mingos or Mingo Senecas.

Historical documents suggest that Alliquippa, her husband, and a young child (possibly her son Kanuksusy) paid respects to province founder William Penn (1644–1718) before his 1701 return to England. Alliquippa or her husband must have held an elevated political position to meet with the pacifist Quaker leader. Interactions with the Quakers most likely influenced Alliquippa's lifelong affiliation with the British; unfortunately, no additional accounts exist from this period.

Queen Alliquippa led the Seneca people in the decades before the American Revolution. George Washington met with her in 1753, helping to assure that she and her people sided with the British against the French in the Seven Years War. (Universal History Archive/Getty Images)

Most sources suggest that Alliquippa's husband died soon after Penn's departure and imply that she inherited her leadership position from her deceased spouse or a prominent father. However, most Iroquois communities had high-ranking female leaders, or clan mothers. Descent among Iroquois peoples typically follows matrilineal lines, indicating that if Alliquippa inherited her social rank it was probably from her mother or maternal family, a reality that Euro-Americans would not have known or understood.

European fur trappers first documented "Aliquippa's Town"—four families on the Allegheny River in western Pennsylvania—in 1731. Over the next 20 years, the village relocated several times along the Allegheny, Ohio, and Monongahela Rivers but remained in the vicinity of modern-day Pittsburgh. As Britain and France skirmished over North America, Iroquois leadership in New York adhered to the 1701 treaty requiring aboriginal neutrality. Independent Senecas in the Allegheny–Ohio River Valley, however, followed local leadership under Alliquippa and allied with the British.

In 1748, British Indian agent Conrad Weiser (1696–1760) wrote that Alliquippa exercised supreme authority over a thriving community of 30 families. The British could only imagine that the elderly woman held her position by birthright like an English monarch rather than by merit, and they referred to her as Queen Alliquippa.

British Indian agent George Groghan (1720–1782) recorded his visit to the village and Alliquippa's inquiries about gunpowder and shot. The female leader had sent requests and payment to Philadelphia but received no supplies. The Seneca men were away aiding the British. Groghan had gunpowder in his possession but offered Alliquippa personal trinkets as tribute. When the female leader demanded the gunpowder, Groghan regarded her as a petulant child rather than a competent leader.

As Alliquippa's community grew, so did her regional influence. The Ohio Valley rivers provided transportation into the continental interior and were strategically important for colonization. Both European powers sought control over the rivers through alliance with Alliquippa. In 1749 while claiming territory for France, Pierre-Joseph Céleron stopped to meet with Alliquippa, but she denied him entrance to her village.

Maintaining good relations with the Seneca matriarch was of such importance that a young militia officer, George Washington (1732–1799), backtracked to Alliquippa's village when he heard that she was displeased. Six months later when Washington's missteps along the frontier escalated the conflict with the French, Alliquippa and her people faced retaliation. In hasty retreat, Washington built Fort Necessity. Alliquippa and Kanuksusy brought women and children to take shelter at the fort. The stockade, however, had inadequate resources; Washington sent the Senecas to Croghan's fortified post near Aughwick.

Washington surrendered at Fort Necessity on July 4, 1754, initiating the French and Indian War. The elderly Alliquippa died before the end of the year, but her son continued to negotiate all sides for peace until his untimely death from smallpox, under questionable circumstances, two years later. At his request, he was buried in a Quaker cemetery in Philadelphia.

Alliquippa's legacy can still be seen today throughout western Pennsylvania in the locations and landmarks that bear her name.

Keri Dearborn

See also Quakers; *Vol. 1, Sec. 1:* Clothing, Native American Women; Disease, Postconquest Impact on Native Americans; Food Production, Native American Women; Iroquois Confederacy; Matrilineal Descent; New France, Women in; *Vol. 1, Sec. 3:* Ursuline Nuns

Further Reading

Walton, Denver. 1992. "Aliquippa's Beginnings." *Milestones* 17(1): 32–39.

Slavery, African

Great Britain's quest for cheap labor to drive the labor-intensive North American colonial agricultural economy led Britain to originally rely on indentured servants (Europeans bound to work for several years in exchange for paid passage to America) and Native Americans. However, when neither servants nor natives were able to remedy the labor shortage for a variety of reasons, the British emulated the Spanish and turned to African slavery. The British passed laws to keep order and discourage slave revolts. These laws dehumanized the slaves and led to them being regarded as mere property. Therefore, legal protections that existed for British citizens did not apply to slaves. All slaves suffered within the slave system, though female slaves suffered the greatest degradation under the colonial slave laws.

In 1607 Britain established Jamestown, its first successful colony in North America. The primary purpose of the colony, and the other 12 added later, was to benefit England in some way. Unable to find gold as the Spanish had done a century earlier in the Americas, the British colonists set their sights on tobacco, which would prove to be a profitable crop. The British discovered that there were a variety of other valuable agricultural products that could be grown in the Southern Colonies, namely indigo and rice. All three of these crops were labor-intensive, but without a cheap labor supply, landowners could not make a profit growing them. By the 1640s, the British found themselves with a critical labor shortage. Indentured servants were not numerous enough to meet the need. Moreover, after Bacon's Rebellion in 1676, it became clear that poor whites would not be satisfied with the same conditions of poverty they had tolerated in England. Consequently, colonists attempted to enslave Native Americans. However, the experiment failed because natives could and did successfully run away. Also, indigenous people continued to die at relatively high rates from European diseases, making them an unstable workforce. In their search to end their labor supply problems, the English looked to Spain.

Immediately after Christopher Columbus sailed to the Bahamas in 1492, the Spanish began enslaving the inhabitants of the New World. Within a few years, the enslavement of the natives, along with disease and other cruelties associated with the enslavement, had resulted in genocide. Having decimated the native population, Spain turned to Africa for slaves. By 1502, Hispaniola (Haiti) served as an important port in the international slave trade. Thousands of African slaves were shipped to the Caribbean islands and the South American continent to work the sugarcane fields.

Spain's success convinced the British of the viability of using African slaves in North America. Also,

because indentured servants were bound to work for a limited time, they were only a temporary solution to the labor problem. On the other hand, slaves were bound to work for a lifetime and passed their enslaved condition to their children. Also, the indentured servitude system left colonists very little control over the supply of labor, because the supply of indentured servants was inconsistent. However, the African slave system allowed colonists the ability to increase or decrease their labor supply as they needed. And unlike native people, after being imported to the New World, Africans could not run away and go home. As a consequence, the British implemented African slavery in earnest after the mid-1600s. The number of slaves increased in the colonies, while the number of indentured servants decreased. Unlike many places in the New World, in North America the sex ratio between slave women and men became equal.

By the 1700s, slaves outnumbered whites in many but not most areas of the Southern Colonies, and the colonists were concerned about the possibility of slave rebellions. Their concerns were not unfounded. Numerous slave rebellions both minor and major occurred throughout the colonial period, including in 1663, 1687, 1712, 1720, 1739, and 1741. Following Spain's procedure, the British colonists passed laws designed to keep slaves in check. The specifics of the laws differed from colony to colony, but the main intent of the laws was the same: they were based on the notion that legally African slaves were property, not people. Perhaps this explained why in some colonies slaves were legally barred from having funerals. Nor were they allowed to marry, as legal scholars reasoned that the principle of coverture held that husbands essentially owned their wives, meaning legal slave marriages would deprive white masters of female slave ownership.

Slaves were forbidden to move about freely and barred from assembly so that they could not organize against their masters. They were barred from educational opportunities, because educated slaves would be more likely to question their state in life. Also, a slave who could read also had a better chance of escaping from captivity. Slaves were barred from drinking liquor due to concern that a drunken slave might dispense with inhibitions and challenge authority. Similarly, slaves were not allowed to raise a hand against a white even in self-defense. This stricture proved to be a problem for slave women, who were vulnerable to sexual predation by their white masters. Legally slave children followed the condition of their mother, making slaves of children with white fathers. Masters were more likely to free their slave children, and historians think that some slave women bargained their bodies in the hopes that their children would eventually be freed, not unlike Sally Hemings did with Thomas Jefferson.

Under these laws, masters reserved the right to punish their slaves in whatever way they deemed fit, including death. Since slaves were legally viewed as property, the killing of one's slave was not considered murder. Instead, it was seen as the destruction of one's own property. In like manner, if a white killed or maimed a slave owned by another colonist, it was the legal duty of the aggressor to pay the slave owner for property damages. It was also legal for a master to work his slaves for as many hours a day and as many days a week as he pleased.

Still, slaves were not entirely powerless under slavery. Some slaves, mostly men, ran away. Few women, Harriet Tubman and Sojourner Truth notable among them, could leave their children and escape. Punishments for attempting to escape were brutal and sometimes deadly. Women most often engaged in passive resistance, playing sick so as to deprive masters of their labor or purposefully breaking or losing things.

Slave women were expected to provide labor both inside and outside the home. In the home, female slaves worked as domestic servants (considered "women's work"). Outside the home, they did agricultural fieldwork (considered "men's work") alongside male slaves. Slave men and women engaged in unofficial marriage-type arrangements, but masters did not respect the conventions that marriage implied. Legally, slave women belonged to their masters and could be sold, raped, or handed over to another slave as a sexual partner. Some masters forced slave women to reproduce with men they did not choose. All of these realities destabilized the slave family structure, allowing slave women to achieve greater equality with slave men. However, with or without slave marriage, the slave family's instability meant that women became separated from their children, husbands, and close relatives. In some cases, slaves were sold several times during their lifetimes.

All slaves were subordinate to their masters due to their legal status. However, female slaves suffered greater degradation because of their gender. Besides the work in and outside the home, female slaves were also given a responsibility that was directly tied to sexuality. Sex between slaves was encouraged by slave masters, because women were expected to reproduce to increase slave numbers. Legally, both they and their offspring were their masters' property. In many cases, female slaves of various ages were expected to perform sexual duties for their masters. They had no choice and were sometimes beaten if they refused. The law protected the master while denying the female slave any legal protection. While some people considered the practice of sex between master and slave wrong because they opposed race mixing, most colonists either ignored or rationalized the practice. Also, sexual relations between masters and slaves were rarely viewed as rape by whites, then or now. Instead, the practice was seen by many as economically practical, because besides providing the masters with pleasure, it increased slave numbers. According to this rationalization, by breeding their own slaves personally, masters eliminated some of the costs associated with purchasing slaves. In truth, the practice was a well-known secret that most colonists, including religious groups and masters' wives, chose to remain silent about until the abolition movement began exposing the problem.

Rolando Avila

See also Indentured Servants; *Vol. 1, Sec. 1:* Slavery, Native Americans; *Vol. 1, Sec. 3:* Hemings, Sally

Further Reading

Adams, Catherine, and Elizabeth H. Pleck. 2009. *Love of Freedom: Black Women in Colonial and Revolutionary New England.* New York: Oxford University Press.

White, Deborah Gray. 1999. *Ar'n't I a Woman? Female Slaves in the Plantation South.* New York: Norton.

Wood, Betty. 2005. *Slavery in Colonial America, 1619–1776.* Lanham, MD: Rowman and Littlefield.

Wood, Peter H. 2003. *Strange New Land: Africans in Colonial America.* New York: Oxford University Press.

Virginia Slave Laws (1662, 1667)

In 1662, the Virginia colonial legislature solved the vexing question of the condition of children born of sex between masters and slaves—were they slave or free? Five years later the legislature also determined that the children of slave women could be baptized as Christians and remain slaves.

December 1662

Whereas some doubts have arisen whether children got by any Englishman upon a Negro woman should be slave or free, *be it therefore enacted and declared by this present Grand Assembly,* that all children born in this country shall be held bond or free only according to the condition of the mother; and that if any Christian shall commit fornication with a Negro man or woman, he or she so offending shall pay double the fines imposed by the former act.

September 1667

Whereas some doubts have risen whether children that are slaves by birth, and by the charity and piety of their owners made partakers of the blessed sacrament of baptism, should by virtue of their baptism be made free, *it is enacted and declared by this Grand Assembly, and the auhority thereof,* that the conferring of baptism does not alter the condition of the person as to his bondage or freedom; that diverse masters, freed from this doubt may more carefully endeavor the propagation of Christianity by permitting children, though slaves, or chose of greater growth if capable, to be admitted to that sacrament.

Source: William Waller Hening, *Statutes at Large: Being a Collection of All the Laws of Virginia,* Vol. 11 (Richmond, 1809–1823), 170, 260. Available at http://www.swarthmore.edu/SocSci/bdorsey1/41docs/24-sla.html.

Spinning Bees

Spinning bees were originally politically motivated demonstrations of colonial women spinning linen and wool to create colonial homespun cloth in the mid-1700s. The public activity gave women an economic space to show their influence on the practical, symbolic, and patriotic.

Unlike the Sons of Liberty, who operated as a secret activist organization, the ladies who organized these spinning bees, known as the Daughters of Liberty, were churchgoing women showing their Christian duty as virtuous women. They were providing cloth for their families while reinforcing their commitment to America prior to the American Revolution.

Once the colonies decided on the course of non-importation of British goods, women organized spinning bees to augment the shortage of available English textiles, such as silk and cotton. It was practical that women, the predominant spinners of thread, decided to make spinning a political public statement.

The first spinning bee took place in Providence, Rhode Island, on March 4, 1766. After that, there were 46 spinning bees in New England between 1766 and 1770. Each of these spinning parties averaged 47 women in attendance. Typically, the spinners were between the ages of 12 and 19. It was difficult for married and older women to participate in these public performances; they were too busy with daily chores and household duties. Predominantly, the spinning bees were held at the local minister's homes. Notices in newspapers advertised spinning bees, which were funded by churches.

The homespun skeins from the bees were given to the hosting minister to use for his own needs or to distribute to the poor. At the close of the spinning bees, participants stayed for a sermon or a group hymn sing-along. Thus, the spinning campaigns became an example of domesticated spirituality in which pious colonial women could properly express disdain against Britain's policies. Indeed, the bees were predominantly organized as a protest against the Townshend Acts of 1767. Charles Townshend, Great Britain's chancellor of the exchequer, created these acts as a moneymaking scheme for King George III of England. The spinning demonstrations were one way colonial women could

During the years leading up to the American Revolutionary War independence minded women would engage in spinning bees or contests as a form of public protest against British taxes and policies. Though spinning bees have garnered less historical notice than events like the Boston Tea Party, their number and popularity suggest they were an important tool in colonial resistance. (Eggleston, George Cary, *Life in the Eighteenth Century,* 1910)

protest. By making items they would have previously purchased, women took part in the successful boycott of British goods.

The spinning contests were in essence a ritualized gathering, a solitary activity made into a visual form of collective activism. These work sessions were a way for women to show patriotism. At the bees, the women participants proudly wore homespun, drank herbal tea, and ate produce grown in the colonies. It was a personal choice and a political commitment to the cause of American freedom. Participating in spinning bees became a badge of honor. The bees were

also a way of teaching younger generations, who had bought their cloth from England because it was cheaper to buy than to make it, how to produce their own cloth. The bee demonstrations taught women how to use the various types (cotton, wool, flax, etc.) of spindles. Instructions on how to spin one's own yarn became a unifying gendered activity.

Wealthy colonial women and most of those who resided in cities had lost the need to spin and therefore had forgotten how to make their own cloth. It was the local rural women, those who were still spinning to create the thread necessary for clothing and woolen blankets for their indigent families, who were the integral key to making the spinning bees successful. The spinning wheel, one of the few items owned by colonial women (women owning property was an anomaly), became a symbol of colonial feminism. Encouraged by the colonial support of the spinning bees, the Continental Congress passed a law in 1774 to boycott all British goods.

Once the American Revolution officially began in 1776, patriotic women organized additional spinning bees to create yarn for sewing soldiers' uniforms. Sarah Franklin Bache, daughter of statesman Benjamin Franklin, organized this second wave of spinning bees in Philadelphia. While women in America earned societal respect for their domesticity strategies and skills, womanhood became synonymous with civic domesticity; the feminine role of household activist, nurturer, and ethical protector created a new gendered title: republican mother.

A. H. Forss

See also *Vol. 1, Sec. 3:* Adams, Abigail; Adams, Louisa Catherine; Daughters of Liberty; Republican Motherhood; Washington, Martha

Further Reading

Berkin, Carol. 2005. *Revolutionary Mothers.* New York: Knopf.

Hoffman, Ronald, and Peter Albert, eds. 1989. *Women in the Age of the American Revolution.* Charlottesville: University of Virginia Press.

Norton, Mary Beth. 1980. *Liberty's Daughters.* Boston: Little, Brown, and Longman.

Tekakwitha, Kateri (1656–1680)

Mohawk woman and Catholic convert Kateri Tekakwitha spent her short life devoted to her faith. On her deathbed, the Jesuits recorded a miracle that soon made it into Catholic folklore, eventually leading to her canonization in 2012. Though the basic facts of her life remain few, Catholic Native Americans identify with her life and the parallels they see between her experience and their own history of oppression and marginalization.

Kateri Tekakwitha was born in the Mohawk village of Gahnaouagé, in what is now upstate New York. Her father was a religiously traditional Mohawk chief, while her Algonquin mother had been baptized as a Catholic before she was captured by the Mohawks, with whom her people were at war. While the Mohawks were matrilineal, tracing kinship and status through the mother's lineage, Tekakwitha was born into her father's clan because her mother was a captive. Tekakwitha's early childhood most likely included living in a longhouse, controlled by the family matron, and being socialized into tribal ways by the women of her clan. It is also likely that her mother had some influence on her later interest in Catholicism. The young girl's life changed dramatically in 1660 when a smallpox epidemic swept through the village, claiming the lives of all her immediate family members. Tekakwitha herself survived, but the disease left her health permanently impaired. In addition to general weakness, she was nearly blind, pockmarks scarred her face, and she remained sensitive to bright sunlight.

After the epidemic, Tekakwitha's paternal uncle and aunts adopted her, and they moved to a new village away from the contagion. The Jesuit accounts of Tekakwitha, the main source for the facts of her life, talk about her as a modest girl who avoided social gatherings and covered much of her head with a blanket because of the smallpox scars. They also claim that as an orphan, she was under the care of uninterested relatives. It is likely, though, that she learned traditional Mohawk women's skills, including how to make clothing and belts from animal skins; weave mats, baskets, and boxes from reeds and grasses; and prepare food and gather produce. She most likely also took part in the women's agricultural activities, growing corn, beans, and squashes. And she was expected to consider marriage. While her disfigurement undermined her appeal as a marriage partner, the family arranged a match. Tekakwitha refused the offer, an early sign of independence.

Growing up, Tekakwitha met Jesuit missionaries to the Mohawks and found their stories about Catholicism appealing. When Father Jacques de Lamberville visited her longhouse in 1676, he found her eager to learn more and, after a period of instruction, baptized her as Catherine. The baptism was a transformative event. Not only was Tekakwitha not married, but she also took on the French version of her name and followed Catholic practice, leading to harassment and ostracism from her own people. After 18 months of hardship, Tekakwitha ran away and settled at the Christian Mohawk community of Kahnawake at Sault Saint-Louis near Montreal, Canada.

At Kahnawake, Tekakwitha initially lived the rather ordinary life of a Mohawk woman, joining the activities expected of her as a member of a longhouse. But increasingly she found her calling in devout Catholicism, interrupting her daily labor with frequent visits to the church to attend Mass and receive communion. On Sundays and feast days she spent her time in the church, leaving only to take a meal. During the last year of her life, Tekakwitha modeled her behavior after the Catholic nuns and Jesuit priests she had encountered, performing numerous penances. She flogged herself before Confession, and she walked barefoot in the snow, fasted, slept on a bed of thorns, and burned herself with hot coals. At the Feast of the Annunciation on March 25, 1679, Tekakwitha completely committed her life to virginity, consecrating herself to Jesus Christ and Mary. This act earned her the name "Lily of the Mohawks" among Catholics.

This life of asceticism did include the pleasures of female companionship and the opportunity to instruct them about sacred themes while performing daily tasks together. Tekakwitha's virginity and chastity also appears to have attracted other women to Catholicism, and she served as their guide and teacher. Asceticism weakened Tekakwitha's frail constitution, and she fell ill. On April 17, 1680, she passed away at the mission of St. Xavier at Kahnawake, only 24 years old. Moments after her passing, according to the Jesuits present, the pockmark scars on her face disappeared, and her skin became fresh and youthful. This miracle and the witnesses of her life of dedication and service led to the devotional following for Tekakwitha throughout North America.

Tekakwitha became a candidate for sainthood as early as 1884. The Catholic Church declared her venerable in 1943, and in 1980, she was beatified. Pope Benedict XVI finally canonized her on October 21, 2012, making her the first Native American saint. Her life appeals especially to indigenous Catholics as reflective of their own history of desolation, marginalization, and survival against all odds. At an early age, Tekakwitha experienced profound sadness when she was separated from everything familiar to her. Her pockmarked face and her Catholicism led to misunderstanding, cruel treatment, and marginalization among her own people. Yet in the face of adversity, she endured and made a life for herself, combining elements of Native American upbringing and her devout Catholicism. What is particularly important about Tekakwitha is the fact that she was a Mohawk woman in an institution known for its patriarchal and paternalistic history. As such, she serves as a model for the convergence of native spiritual traditions and Catholicism.

Päivi H. Hoikkala

See also *Vol. 1, Sec. 3:* Sacagawea; Williams, Eunice

Further Reading

Bunson, Matthew, and Margaret Bunson. 2012. *St. Kateri: Lily of the Mohawks.* Huntington, IN: Our Sunday Visitor.

Cholonec, Fr. Pierre. 2012. *Kateri Tekawkitha, the Iroquois Saint.* Merchantville, NJ: ARX Publishing.

Tituba

Tituba was a slave most well known for her connections to the Salem Witch Trials of 1692. Through a series of false confessions and accusations, Tituba was able to save herself from execution. Her coerced testimonies, however, led to the arrests of 150 Salem residents and the execution of 19. Tituba spent 13 months in jail. She disappeared from the historical record after her release.

Often incorrectly identified as a Negro slave, Tituba was an Arawak Indian from a tribe in Guiana, South America, one of a small group kidnapped and transported from South America in 1674 and sold into slavery in Barbados. Barbadian records from 1676 indicate that Tituba was a child between the ages of 9 and 14 and was among 300 slaves on a sugar plantation in St. Thomas, Barbados. Owned by Samuel Thompson, she was the house servant and personal attendant of his mother, Elizabeth Pearsehouse.

Tituba remained the property of Thompson until 1680, when he became deathly ill and attempted to settle his debts and business affairs before his demise. Historians believe that Thompson's father was in business with Samuel Parris's (1653–1720) father. The younger Parris followed in his footsteps and served as a merchant in Barbados until 1680. Thompson may have sold Tituba to Samuel Parris or used her as a means of settling his debts. By 1680 when Parris returned to Boston, Massachusetts, he had two Indian slaves from Barbados: Tituba and a male slave, John Indian.

Tituba and John married in 1690 and are believed to have had a daughter named Violet. By this time, Parris had left Boston to become the minister of Salem Village. Tituba lived with the Parrises as a house slave. In late 1691, Parris's 9-year-old daughter Betty and his 11-year-old niece Abigail engaged in a fortune-telling custom of dropping the white of a raw egg into a glass of water to tell their futures. There is no evidence to support that Tituba participated in this game, which was an old custom derived in England and brought to the American colonies. Young Betty became ill shortly after the game, and by late February both Betty and Abigail were afflicted by inexplicable spontaneous fits.

Neighbor and parishioner Mary Sibley believed that the girls had been the target of a witch's spell. On February 25, 1691, Sibley went to Tituba and John to enlist their help in making a witchcake (a concoction of rye meal and urine, baked in ashes and fed to a dog to reveal the source of the spell), an Old English technique and form of countermagic that they believed would reveal the witch who had put the spell on the girls and ultimately cure their illness. Historians believe that Sibley went to Tituba and John based on the Puritan notion that Indians had more intimate knowledge of the occult and the spirit world. While Tituba's time in Barbados, with its large population of Africans, most likely exposed her to African religious and magical practices and made her familiar with African folklore, there is no documented evidence that she practiced the occult. Nonetheless, any practice of her native religion might have seemed occult to Puritans.

Reverend Parris discovered that Tituba aided in making a witchcake. In her 1692 testimony, Tituba claimed to have been introduced to this technique by her mistress in Barbados, Elizabeth Pearsehouse.

Reverend Parris believed that Tituba brought the devil into Salem and blamed her for the illness that had fallen upon his family. His beliefs were subsequently supported by Salem townspeople, and Tituba was arrested. During March 1–5, 1692, Tituba gave testimonies denying that she was a witch or that she had cast a spell to inflict harm on Betty and Abigail. Tituba continued to deny familiarity with the devil until fear of further punishment and torture from Reverend Parris spurred her to falsely confess. Her faked confession seemed to satisfy her accusers and allowed Tituba to gain a position of importance and authority in identifying other Salem "witches." By seemingly complying with the witch hunt, Tituba saved her life and placed the spotlight on others. Between March and October 1692, more than 150 people were arrested, 19 were hanged, 1 was pressed to death, and 4 died while in prison.

Tituba's confession was an act of slave resistance that not only played on the fears of the Puritans but also played upon their notions of confession and forgiveness. Tituba confessed her sin of consorting with the devil, detailed the ways in which such "partnership" harmed her, and begged for forgiveness, thus exhibiting a form of repentance. By March 1693, Tituba attempted to recant her confession. She admitted to lying to protect herself from execution and blamed Reverend Parris for forcing her into it, probably in an attempt to end the witch hunt hysteria that ended in so many deaths and caused so much destruction in the community. Although Salem residents did not believe her new confession, they blamed Parris for being overzealous.

By April 1693 Tituba, who was between the ages of 26 and 31, had spent 13 months in jail. Angered by her attempts to recant her testimony, Reverend Parris refused to pay her jail fees to have her released. An unknown person paid the fees of seven pounds and purchased Tituba and John Indian, who promptly disappeared from the historical record. Violet remained in the Parris household until his death, never to be reunited with her parents.

Sherri M. Arnold

See also Goode, Sarah; Hibbins, Ann; Protestant Women; Witchcraft in New England; Witch Trials, Salem, Massachusetts

Further Reading

Breslaw, Elaine. 1997. *Tituba, Reluctant Witch of Salem: Devilish Indians and Puritan Fantasies*. New York: New York University Press.

Hansen, Chadwick. 1974. "The Metamorphosis of Tituba, or Why American Intellectuals Can't Tell an Indian Witch from a Negro." *New England Quarterly* 47: 3–12.

Norton, Mary Beth. 2003. *In the Devil's Snare: The Salem Witchcraft Crisis of 1692*. New York: Vintage Books.

Wife Abuse, Colonial North America (1607–1754)

Recognized as a crime today, in colonial North America wife abuse was considered a proper tool for husbands to use to maintain order in a marriage. The most widely held view of marriage among Europeans in the early 17th century was that God imposed women's subordination as a punishment for Eve's fall from grace. Europeans imagined marriage as an institution that combined a man and a woman into one person, with the husband as the superior. Among the Spanish, patriarchal authority was also enforced to the point that Iberian law gave men the right to kill adulterous spouses. Under English common law, an unmarried woman could own and sell property, bequeath her property by will, make contracts, and sue and be sued. In marriage, under the system of coverture, she conferred many of these rights and responsibilities onto her husband, who held claim to his wife's productive labor and skills in running a household and all of the profits her labor generated.

Colonial governments did not consider wife beating a criminal offense and often encouraged the "rule of thumb," which allowed a husband to whip his wife as long as the switch was no larger in diameter than an average man's thumb. Church courts interpreted cruelty, strictly, as abuse sufficient to maim or threaten her life. The courts rarely intervened in domestic violence unless the woman was pregnant. And while a wife might get protection until she delivered, she would be expected to return to her husband's rule. While wife abuse was not considered a crime, between 1352 and 1828 a murderous wife, convicted of treason, carried a sentence of being burned at the stake.

As times changed, a network of informal surveillance discouraged husbands from abusing their power; those who most often intervened were other women. In New England justices fined spouses, imposed separations, and sometimes sentenced those found guilty of spouse abuse to whippings. Abusive wives were sentenced more often than abusive husbands. According to criminal records, Virginia may have been one of the most violent colonies, followed by Pennsylvania, New York, and North Carolina, and then by Massachusetts and Connecticut. Because cruelty was difficult to approve, many women whose names do not appear in court records were brought to the Philadelphia almshouse complaining of being beaten and abused by husbands.

For Africans and Native Americans, women experienced the colonial period as a decline in status, and more than likely the rate of domestic violence increased with prolonged war, enslavement, sexual exploitation, and genocide. For slaves, marriage was a relationship governed by custom and the community, not the law. West African traditions valued women, and prior to enslavement, gender relations tended to be more complementary. The community recognized a couple as husband and wife when they took certain responsibilities for each other. Both men and women could sever the marital bonds if their partners abandoned their responsibilities or experienced mistreatment. Iroquois and Algonquian tribes of New England were most often matrilineal and matrilocal. Recognition of several distinct types of marriage with flexible standards and easy divorce mitigated domestic violence.

Violence within Indian-French, Indian-Spanish, and Indian-African marriages differed depending on the circumstances. Women suffered less abuse when Europeans and Africans assimilated into native society but sustained more abuse when women, often through enslavement, were forced into unions. The Kaskaskias south of the Great Lakes and the Apalachees of the Southeast married inside their own nation and retained their gender complementary belief systems, likely reducing wife abuse. The Illinois who intermarried with the French maintained more female empowerment, while native peoples under Spanish colonization in Mexico experienced a severe decline in status and increase in domestic violence.

In the mid-18th century, a new ideal of the middle-class marriage emerged that discouraged domestic violence. Companionate marriage viewed the union as a partnership that stressed mutual affection, companionship, a single standard of sexual behavior, and complementary gender roles. Most people were beginning to rebel against the idea that any physical attack by a man was acceptable. Vermont (1787) and New Hampshire (1791) were the first states to sanction divorce on the grounds of domestic violence and to grant alimony to abused wives.

Leleua Loupe

See also Coverture

Further Reading

Daniels, Christine, and Michael V. Kennedy. 1999. *Over the Threshold: Intimate Violence in Early America.* New York: Routledge.

Dolan, Frances E. 2008. *Marriage and Violence: The Early Modern Legacy.* Philadelphia: University of Pennsylvania Press.

Plane, Ann Marie. 2000. *Colonial Intimacies: Indian Marriage in Early New England.* Ithaca, NY: Cornell University Press.

"About the Duties of Husbands and Wives" from Benjamin Wadsworth's *A Well-Ordered Family* (1712)

Benjamin Wadsworth (1670–1737), a Harvard-trained minister, published various collections of sermons and essays during his lifetime. He served as minister of the First Church in Boston and then as president of Harvard from 1725 until his death in 1737. In 1712 he published his essay in A Well-Ordered Family, *which gave a perhaps idealized view of family and marital relations in early 18th-century New England. The following excerpt describes the duties that spouses owed to one another.*

Concerning the duties of this relation we may assert a few things. It is their duty to dwell together with one another. Surely they should dwell together; if one house cannot hold them, surely they are not affected to each other as they should be. They should have a very great and tender love and affection to one another. This is plainly commanded by God. This duty of love is mutual; it should be performed by each, to each of them. When, therefore, they quarrel or disagree, then they do the Devil's work; he is pleased at it, glad of it. But such contention provokes God; it dishonors Him; it is a vile example before inferiors in the family; it tends to prevent family prayer.

As to outward things. If the one is sick, troubled, or distressed, the other should manifest care, tender-ness, pity, and compassion, and afford all possible relief and succor. They should likewise unite their prudent counsels and endeavors, comfortably to maintain themselves and the family under their joint care.

Husband and wife should be patient one toward another. If both are truly pious, yet neither of them is perfectly holy, in such cases a patient, forgiving, forbearing spirit is very needful. . . .

The husband's government ought to be gentle and easy, and the wife's obedience ready and cheerful. The husband is called the head of the woman. It belongs to the head to rule and govern. Wives are part of the house and family, and ought to be under the husband's government. Yet his government should not be with rigor, haughtiness, harshness, severity, but with the greatest love, gentleness, kindness, tenderness that may be. Though he governs her, he must not treat her as a servant, but as his own flesh; he must love her as himself.

Those husbands are much to blame who do not carry it lovingly and kindly to their wives. O man, if your wife is not so young, beautiful, healthy, well-tempered, and qualified as you would wish; if she did not bring a large estate to you, or cannot do so much for you, as some other women have done for their husbands; yet she is your wife, and the great

God commands you to love her, not be bitter, but kind to her. What can be more plain and expressive than that?

Those wives are much to blame who do not carry it lovingly and obediently to their own husbands. O woman, if your husband is not as young, beautiful, healthy, so well-tempered, and qualified as you could wish; if he has not such abilities, riches, honors, as some others have; yet he is your husband, and the great God commands you to love, honor, and obey him. Yea, though possibly you have greater abilities of mind than he has, was of some high birth, and he of a more common birth, or did bring more estate, yet since he is your husband, God has made him your head, and set him above you, and made it your duty to love and revere him.

Parents should act wisely and prudently in the matching of their children. They should endeavor that they may marry someone who is most proper for them, most likely to bring blessings to them.

Source: Benjamin Wadsworth, *A Well-Ordered Family* (Boston: B. Green, 1712). Available at Constitution Society, http://www.constitution.org/primarysources/marriage.html.

Wife Sales

Wife sales were exactly what they sound like they would be: the sale of wives by husbands. The sales were not a part of any legal government provision or any particular religion but have occurred around the world for centuries. The sales were an informal practice started among the people usually in open public areas such as the taverns or the marketplace. When a wife was auctioned, she was put into a halter, a rope, or strapped device used for leading or restraining cattle and stayed in that device throughout the sale. The use of the cattle implement was symbolic of the woman's position as property in the sale. Even if the wife agreed to the auction, it was all carried out within the husband's and buyer's power. The main reasons for the auctioning of wives were because of economic situations, adultery, or the lack of compatibility of the husband and wife.

The majority of wife sales in the United States trace back to England when divorces did exist but were practiced sparingly. Only middling- and elite-class people could afford divorces. Also, wife sales mainly took place in urban populations. Once the printing of newspapers became common, it was easier for wife sales to be posted (and for historians to trace them). Samuel Pyeatt Menefee looked at nearly 400 wife sales from the 11th century to the 1970s. During the industrial revolution (1785–1845) wife selling was at its highest peak. For English society, the peak was also a result of the American Revolution, the French Revolution, and the Napoleonic Wars and their aftermaths. The wars affected the economies, sometimes causing husbands to sell their wives to prevent the rest of the family from ending up in poor houses. Divorces during this time became only possible for those in the upper levels of society.

The most famous wife sale in British history is found in the fiction piece *The Mayor of Casterbridge* by Thomas Hardy. While inebriated, the protagonist sells his wife and child for five guineas at a carnival. He then goes on to become mayor but regrets his hasty decision regarding his family. Hardy's novel suggests that the wife complied with the sale and does not particularly condemn the practice.

Wife sales also took place in the United States. According to both colonial and U.S. law, when a woman married she legally became her husband's property. Called coverture or *feme covert,* women belonged first to their fathers and later to their husbands and had few legal controls over most aspects of their lives. Given the principles of coverture, some husbands did sell their wives, though the practice lost favor in the later decades of the 18th century. In 1878 one man sold his wife for two dollars and a dozen bowls of grogg. The sale was likely intended to circumvent the state's divorce ban and illustrates how commoners both ignored the law and created their own legal customs.

Some, though not most, Native Americans also participated in wife selling, generally as part of a debt transaction, though some peoples used a kind of ritual sale in lieu of divorce and remarriage. In the lands that would become the United States, there is a history of wife sales among some Native Americans as well as among the Japanese who populated the Hawaiian Islands before and after the annexation of 1898.

Finally, it should be noted that in the 200 years of American slavery many wives were sold away from their husbands and children. Masters did not generally recognize slave marriages as legal unions and did break up families through sale. Some of these sales of women of African descent would have been part of the concubinage trade, or the purposeful sale of a woman to a man for sexual use. Light-skinned slave women, such as Thomas Jefferson's slave Sally Hemings, were particularly prized on the slave market, and many of those sold would have been women who considered themselves married to a fellow slave. These sales did not officially end until the passage of the Thirteenth Amendment abolishing slavery in 1865.

Therese Torres

See also Coverture; *Vol. 1, Sec. 3:* Hemings, Sally

Further Reading

Cunningham, Hugh. 1983. "Wives for Sale: An Ethnographic Study of British Popular Divorce by Samuel Pyeatt Menefee." *American Historical Review* 88(1): 109–110.

Translation of the Marriage Contract of Brant Peelen and Marritje Pieters, Widow of Claes Sybrantsen (1643)

Reproduced here is a marriage contract between two individuals who are each entering into a second marriage before a magistrate in the Dutch colony of New Netherland in 1643. New Netherland passed under English control in the 1660s, becoming the colony of New York. The contract has been translated from Dutch to English.

In the year of our Lord and Saviour Jesus Christ, one thousand, six hundred and forty three, before me Cornelis van Tienhoven, admitted secretary in New Netherland for the General Incorporated West India Company, personally came and appeared Brant Peelen from Nykerk, widower of the late Lubbertje Wouters, and Marrietje Pieters, widow of the late Claes Sybrantsen, (with Jan Schepmoes her chosen guardian herein,) who declared that they intended to enter together into the holy state of matrimony, for which reasons and causes he, Brant Pelen, the present bridegroom, promises to pay from his first ready goods, means and effects immediately to his three children by his first wife, the sum of three thousand Carolus guilders, to wit: To his daughter Lysbet Brants, one thousand guilders; to Geert Brants, one thousand guilders, and to Gerritje Brants, a like thousand guilders. She, Marritje Pieters, present bride, promises to give and pay to each of her two children named Sybrant Claesen and Seltje Claes, as their paternal inheritance and property, the sum of Two hundred guilders; which aforesaid four hundred guilders he Brant Peelen shall be at liberty to use four consecutive years without interest, and if he Brant Peelen use the aforesaid money longer, he shall annually pay as interest of the hundred guilders five per cent, but on the express condition and stipulation that they, the bridegroom and bride, remain bound, with the help of God, to bring up Seltje Claes, the youngest child, to clothe her, to send her to school, to let her learn reading and writing and a good trade in such manner as honest parents ought and are bound to do, and as they can answer before God and men.

In this their marriage contract it is, with the will and pleasure of the bridegroom and bride, expressly agreed and stipulated by them, considering that there is nothing certain but death, and nothing more uncertain than the hour thereof, in order to provide against all such uncertainty of death by their joint will, they both, the bridegroom and the bride, declare that whenever Almighty God, the Creator of Heaven and Earth, whom they pray that it may be His holy will to bless them in this their marriage so as it shall be necessary for them here temporarily and hereafter eternally, Amen, shall call the first of them both out of this world, the longest liver of them shall remain in full occupation and possession of all the temporal goods that God hath granted, or shall grant, in this world jointly to them the bridegroom and bride; it being well understood that there should be no difference in regard to the property, but the property of both of them being common, it is computed of the same value, as no inventory is made on either side and it is assumed on both sides as of equal value, which is this concluded and contracted with their joint mature deliberation, wishing and requesting that this shall have full effect after the death of either of them.

It is further covenanted that whenever either of them dies, a proper inventory shall then be made of all the property that the both shall possess at the time, so that the lawful heirs may obtain pertinent [ ], and whenever the survivor shall have departed out of this sorrowful world, the lawful heirs on both sides shall then equally divide and each side receive a like portion of the estate; likewise, that the survivor shall be bound to manage the property as profitably as possible, expecting, with the help of God, only that it may not be squandered needlessly or improperly. If this occur, those whom it interests shall be at liberty to interfere, and that with cause and good reason.

Wherewith he, Brant Pelen, bridegroom and she Marritje Pieters, present bride, conclude their contract of marriage, and request that this may have effect and be valid before all Courts and judges, to this end renouncing all exceptions of what sort soever which may anywise contravene these presents, pledging themselves, in like manner under bond of all law for the payment of the sum of money promised to their children on either side. In testimony this is signed by them respectively, with Everardus Bogardus and Hendric Kip, witnesses hereunto invited, the 3d July AD 1643, in Fort Amsterdam, New Netherland.

Witnesses
Everardus Boghardus
Hendrick Hendricksen Kyp
Ian Iansen Scepmoes

This is the + mark of
Marritje Pieters
Brant Pelen

To my Knowledge, Cornelis van Tienhoven, Secretary.

Source: "Women's Rights in Early New York," New York State Archives, http://www.archives.nysed.gov/education/showcase/201001women/index.shtml.

Witchcraft in New England

During the mid-1600s in colonial North America, strong religious beliefs caused many people to believe in the supernatural. Demons, devils, and witches seemed all too real to the colonists in New England, particularly Puritans. Increasing religious intolerance and fervor among some Puritans created a level of paranoia that led to what must have been false accusations of witchcraft. In the past few decades, American historians have offered many reasons for colonial witchcraft beliefs, though not all have confronted the reality that most victims of witchcraft accusations were women.

Some historians speculate that accusations of witchcraft began as a way of explaining success in Puritan America. Puritans viewed prosperous individuals suspiciously and occasionally posited supernatural assistance to explain the economic differences between people. This theory does not take into account that women were more frequently accused of witchcraft than men and thus were more often executed. According to the principles of coverture, women did not own anything and were themselves property of their fathers or husbands. Only widowed women could accrue property and be considered economically successful. Out of the women convicted, most were married or widowed. Most were middle-aged, between the ages of 41 and 60. There was also a large group of women under 20 years old who were also convicted. Few of these women could be considered successful, though historian Carol Karlson has noted that an overwhelming number of women convicted and executed of witchcraft either had or would inherit family property because they had no alternative male heirs. In executing these women,

Puritan society rid itself of potentially powerful women and, if the women died without heirs, could convert their inheritances into church property.

Typically, younger girls accused middle-aged women of witchcraft. The young female accusers sometimes claimed that they had been bribed with money and clothes to renounce their Christian ideals and accept the devil. They also claimed to have been possessed by witches and forced to act out a number of inappropriate behaviors, some of them sexual in nature. Historians posit that as Puritan society matured, women lost status and power, a claim that can be substantiated by an examination of Puritan men's wills, and that younger women may have resented their loss of power. Given how dangerous it was in an intensely patriarchal society to take their resentment out on men, young women victimized older women who may have had opportunities to inherit that younger women no longer had. Moreover, in claiming to be the victim of an older female "witch," younger women won attention from the community and temporarily gained considerable power in witchcraft trials.

Puritans allowed boys and young men considerably more freedom and power, and as a result, it was rare for them to make claims of witch possession because they did not feel as much resentment. Although the type of people accused and the accusers followed a distinguishable trend, the types of witnesses did not. Witnesses and those who testified ranged in age from 20 to 60 years old, which implies that the general belief in witchcraft spanned generations.

Women most likely to be accused of witchcraft were not only likely to inherit but also were the kind of women who did not fit into Puritan society for a variety of reasons. Anne Hibbins, for example, was a verbally forthright woman who failed time and again to enact appropriately passive behavior. When her community executed her as a witch, they not only rid themselves of a woman they saw as troublesome but also benefited from the redistribution of her estate. Some convicted witches had been excommunicated from the church, as was also the case with Hibbins, and others were generally disliked by the townspeople. Anne Hutchinson, for example, irritated church authorities with her alternative theological views and narrowly escaped a witchcraft trial. Many accused women did not have sufficient evidence against them, but their notorious reputation or odd behavior made them vulnerable in communities that sought conformity above all else. Clearly, these women were not guilty of being witches and were often completely innocent of any crime.

The most well-documented cases of witchcraft come from Massachusetts and Connecticut colonies. The first legal trial regarding witchcraft for which a record survives occurred in Windsor, Connecticut, in 1647, but one of the more notable trials occurred in 1651. Hugh and Mary Parsons, a married couple from Springfield, Massachusetts, were both accused of witchcraft. They were considered middle class, and accusations against them came from people in both the lower and middle classes, showing that people from all walks of life fell prey to the supernatural hysteria that had seized colonial New England. Hugh was not well liked and was accused of extortion and constant bickering in his business. He was found innocent. Mary Parsons, however, had been driven nearly insane by the community's attacks on her family. During her trial she convinced herself that she was guilty of infanticide—the murder of her own child. The mental instability that Mary exhibited was a common symptom of those accused of witchcraft, though it is difficult to know if mental instability invited or resulted from witchcraft accusations.

The most famous witchcraft trials were in Salem, Massachusetts, in 1692. Over 150 people were arrested, but a fraction of those were executed. Although considerably fewer men were accused of witchcraft than women, men had more terrible punishments. For example, one man was crushed with heavy stones until he died because he refused to confess that he was a witch.

There are many theories regarding the cause of the mass accusations in Salem. Some historians theorize that the conservative religious views of colonial America led to mass hysteria regarding the supernatural. Disputes about cattle, land, debt, and more were common in colonial Massachusetts and led to a heightened sense of paranoia and mistrust. In some areas, tensions may have been high enough to cause witchcraft accusations. Fewer historians propose that those accused of witchcraft were victims of tainted poor-quality food—hallucinogens present in the food may have caused false visions that prompted the victims' odd behavior. This theory has the lure of science but leaves much unexplained. Another theory holds that the accusation of witchcraft was a form of social control. Those accused of witchcraft were considered odd, eccentric, and often antisocial. People who engaged in activities or behaviors that their community disproved of were likely to be accused of witchcraft. This prevented future odd behaviors by setting an example.

In Salem, Cotton Mather claimed that possession was the main cause of the girls' afflictions. Some claimed that it was because of contact with witches or because of antagonizing them. The girls verbally and physically attacked accusers, and they were prone to seizures and projections. Children who were considered possessed were not blamed. Puritans believed that the devil, working through a witch, caused the possessed to act against their families, neighbors, and clergy who were trying to help.

Most of the victims of possession exhibited aggressive and seemingly unexplainable behaviors. For example, Cotton Mather examined the servant girl Mercy Short and theorized that Mercy's problems were caused by spectral forces and prompted by the devil. In reality, Mercy was probably suffering from a kind of post-traumatic stress disorder from being taken captive by Indians when she was a child and seeing her family murdered. Mather, who played a significant role in the Salem witchcraft hysteria, was a Puritan minister who saw evil forces everywhere and defended the trials even after most people began to see them for what they were—mass hysteria.

Many colonists believed that witches took the form of animals to further deceive and spy on their victims. The witches were said to have ties to animal helpers, and it was said that they even suckled them. Eunice Cole, a girl from Salisbury, New Hampshire, was about to be whipped for witchcraft when her observers heard strange noises coming from under her shirt. They claimed that in removing her shirt, they exposed imp-like creatures suckling from her breasts. This phenomenon was seen during the Salem trials as well. People saw what they wanted to see. Colonists also believed that the witches held secret feasts where they shared beer or wine, bread, and meat with one another. Some reported that although the witches appeared to dance together, no sexual activity or nudity was reported.

During mass hysteria periods, many New England colonists chose to escape to neighboring colonies. Colonists Mary and Philip English and Nathaniel and Elizabeth Cary were accused of witchcraft during the Salem Witch Trials and fled to New York to escape execution. A Connecticut woman also went to New York to escape her false accusations and their resulting punishments. New York was eager to harbor the accused due to the state's poor relations with the other colonies. Historically, Dutch New Yorkers had a legacy of religious tolerance and looked askance at Puritan intolerance.

B. C. Biggs

See also Excommunication; Goode, Sarah; Hutchinson, Anne Marbury; Infanticide; Tituba; Witch Trials, Salem, Massachusetts

Further Reading

Karlson, Carol F. 1987. *The Devil in the Shape of a Woman: Witchcraft in Colonial New England.* New York: Random House.

Norton, Mary Beth. 2002. *In the Devil's Snare: The Salem Witchcraft Crisis of 1692.* New York: Knopf.

Ranlet, Philip. 2009. "A Safe Haven for Witches? Colonial New York's Politics and Relations with New England in the 1690s." *New York History* 90(1/2): 37–57.

Letter of Reverend Samuel Willard to Cotton Mather Regarding a Case of Witchcraft in Groton, Massachusetts (1671)

In the autumn of 1671 Elizabeth Knapp, the daughter of James and Elizabeth (Warren) Knapp of Groton, experienced a series of symptoms that led the minister of her town, Reverend Samuel Willard, to conclude that Elizabeth was the victim of witchcraft. Reproduced here is the letter the minister wrote about the incident to Cotton Mather that Willard titled "A Briefe Account of a Strange & Unusuall Providence of God

Befallen to Elizabeth Knap of Groton, By Me Samuel Willard." Mather later mentioned the incident, which apparently became widely known, in his Magnalia Christi Americana.

This poore & miserable object, about a fortnight before shee was taken, wee observed to carry herselfe in a strange & unwonted manner, sometimes shee would give sudden shriekes, & if wee enquired a Reason, would alwayes put it off with some excuse, & then would burst forth into immoderate & extravagant laughter, in such wise, as some times shee fell onto the ground with it: I my selfe observed oftentimes a strange change in here countenance, but could not suspect the true reason, but coneived shee might bee ill, & therefore divers times enquired how shee did, & shee always answered well; which made mee wonder: but the tragedye began to unfold itselfe upon Munday, Octob. 30. 71, after this manner (as I received by credible information, being that day my selfe gon from home).

In the evening, a little before shee went to bed, sitting by the fire, shee cryed out, oh my legs! & clapt her hand on them, immediately oh my breast! & removed her hands thither; & forthwith, oh I am strangled, & put her hands on her throat: those that observed her could not see what to make of it; whither shee was in earnest or dissembled, & in this manner they left her (excepting the person that lay with her) complaining of her breath being stopt: The next day shee was in a strange frame, (as was observed by divers) sometimes weeping, sometimes laughing, & many foolish & apish gestures. In the evening, going into the cellar, shee shrieked suddenly, & being enquired of the cause, shee answered, that shee saw 2 persons in the cellar; whereupon some went downe with her to search, but found none; shee also looking with them; at last shee turned her head, & looking one way stedfastly, used the expression, what cheere old man? which, they that were with her tooke for a fansye, & soe ceased; afterwards (the same evening,) the rest of the family being in bed, shee was (as one lying in the roome saw, & shee herselfe also afterwards related) suddenly throwne downe into the midst of the floore with violence, & taken with a violent fit, whereupon the whole family was raised, & with much adoe was

shee kept out of the fire from destroying herselfe after which time she was followed with fits from thence till the sabbath day; in which shee was violent in bodily motions, leapings, strainings & strange agitations, scarce to bee held in bounds by the strength of 3 or 4: violent alsoe in roarings & screamings, representing a dark resemblance of hellish torments, & frequently using in these fits divers words, sometimes crying out money, money, sometimes, sin & misery with other words.

On wednesday, being in the time of intermission questioned about the case shee was in, with reference to the cause or occasion of it, shee seemed to impeach one of the neighbors, a person (I doubt not) of sincere uprightnesse before God, as though either shee, or the devill in her likenesse & habit, particularly her riding hood, had come downe the chimney, stricken her that night shee was first taken violently, which was the occasion of her being cast into the floore; whereupon those about her sent to request the person to come to her, who coming unwittingly, was at the first assaulted by her stranglye, for though her eyes were (as it were) sealed up (as they were alwayes, or for the most part, in those fits, & soe continue in them all to this day) shee yet knew her very touch from any other, though no voice were uttered, & discovered it evidently by her gestures, soe powerfull were Satans suggestions in her, yet afterward God was pleased to vindicate the case & justifye the innocent, even to remove jealousyes from the spirits of the party concerned, & satisfaction of the by standers; for after shee had gon to prayer with her, shee confessed that she beleeved Satan had deluded her, & hath never since complained of any such apparition or disturbance from the person. These fits continuing, (though with intermission) divers, (when they had opportunity) pressed upon her to declare what might bee the true & real occasion of these amazing fits. Shee used many tergiversations & excuses, pretending shee would to this & that young person, who coming, she put it off to another, till at the last, on thursday night, shee brake forth into a large confession in the presence of many, the substance whereof amounted to thus much:

That the devill had oftentimes appeared to her, presenting the treaty of a Covenant, & preffering largely to her: viz, such things as suted her youthfull fancye, money, silkes, fine cloaths, ease from labor to show her the whole world, &c: that it had bin then 3 yeers since his first appearance, occasioned by her discontent: That at first his apparitions had bin more rare, but lately more frequent; yea those few weekes that shee had dwelt with us almost constant, that shee seldome went out of one roome into another, but hee appeared to her urging of her: & that hee had presented her a booke written with blood of covenants made by others with him, & told her such & such (of some wherof we hope better things) had a name there; that hee urged upon her constant temptations to murder her parents, her neighbors, our children, especially the youngest, tempting her to throw it into the fire, on the hearth, into the oven; & that once hee put a bill hooke into her hand, to murder my selfe, persuading her I was asleep, but coming about it, shee met me on the staires at which shee was affrighted, the time I remember well, & observd a strange frame in her countenance & saw she endeavered to hide something, but I knew not what, neither did I at all suspect any such matter; & that often he persuaded her to make away with herselfe & once she was going to drowne herselfe in the well, for, looking into it, shee saw such sights as allured her, & was gotten within the curbe, & was by God's providence prevented, many other like things shee related, too tedious to recollect: but being pressed to declare whither she had not consented to a covenant with the Devill, shee with solemne assertions denyed it, yea asserted that shee had never soe much as consented to discorse with him, nor had ever but once before that night used the expession, What cheere, old man? & this argument shee used, that the providence of God had ordered it soe, that all his apparitions had bin frightfull to her; yet this shee acknowledged, (which seemed contradictorye, viz:) that when shee came to our house to schoole, before such time as shee dwelt with us, shee delayed her going home in the evening, till it was darke, (which wee observed) upon his persuasion to have his company home, & that shee could not, when hee appeared, but goe to him; one evident testimony wherof wee can say somthing to, viz. the night before the Thanksgiving, Octob. 19. shee was with another maid that boarded in the house, where both of them saw the appearance of a mans head & shoulders, with a great white neckcloath, looking in at the window, at which they came up affrighted both into the chamber, where the rest of us were, they declaring the case, one of us went downe to see who it might bee, but shee ran immediately out of the doore before him, which shee hath since confessed, was the Devill coming to her; shee also acknowledged the reason of her former sudden shriekings, was from a sudden apparition, & that the devill put these excuses into her mouth, & bit her soe to say, & hurried her into those violent (but shee saith feigned & forced) laughters: shee then also complained against herselfe of many sins, disobedience to parents, neglect of attendance upon ordinances, attempts to murder herselfe & others; but this particular of a covenant shee utterly disclaimed: which relation seemed faire, especially in that it was attended with bitter teares, selfe condemnations, good counsells given to all about her, especially the youth then present, & an earnest desire of prayers: shee sent to Lancaster for Mr. Rowlandson, who came & prayed with her, & gave her serious counsells; but shee was still followed, all this notwithstanding, with these fits: & in this state (coming home on fryday) I found her; but could get nothing from her, whenever I came in presence shee fell into those fits, concerning which fits, I find this noteworthy, shee knew & understood what was spoken to her, but could not answer, nor use any other words but the forementioned, money, &c: as long as the fit continued, for when shee came out of it, shee could give a relation of all that had been spoken to her: shee was demanded a reason why shee used those words in her fits, & signifyed that the Devill presented her with such things, to tempt her, & with sin & miserye, to terrifye her; shee also declared that shee had seene the Devills in their hellish shapes, & more Devills then any one there ever saw men in the world. Many of these things I heard her declare on Saturday at night:

On the Sabbath the Physitian came, who judged a maine point of her distempr to be naturall, arising from the foulnesse of her stomacke, & corruptnesse of her blood, occasioning fumes in her braine, & strange fansyes; whereupon (in order to further tryall & administration) shee was removed home, & the succeeding weeke shee tooke physicke, & was not in such violence handled in her fits as before; but enjoyed an intermission, & gave some hopes of recovery; in which intermission shee was altogether sencelesse (as to our discoverye) of her state, held under securitye, & hardnesse of heart, professing shee had no trouble upon her spirits, shee cried satan had left her: A solemne day was kept with her, yet it had then, (as I apprehend,) little efficacy upon her; shee that day again expressed hopes that the Devill had left her, but there was little ground to thinke soe, because she remained under such extreame sencelessenesse of her owne estate: & thus shee continued, being exercised with some moderate fits, in which shee used none of the former expressions, but sometimes fainted away, sometimes used some struglings, yet not with extremitye, till the Wednesday following, which day was spent in prayer with her, when her fits something more encreased, & her tongue was for many houres together drawne into a semicircle up to the roofe of her mouth, & not to be remooved, for some tryed with the fingers to doe it: from thence till the sabbath seven night following: she continued alike, only shee added to former confessions, of her twise consenting to travell with the Devill in her company between Groton & Lancaster, who accompanied her in forme of a blacke dog with eyes in his backe, sometimes stopping her horse, sometimes leaping up behind, & keeping her (when she came home with company) 40 rod at least behind, leading her out of the way into a swampe, &c.: but still no conference would shee owne, but urged that the devills quarell with her was because shee would not seale a covenant with him, & that this was the ground of her first being taken. besides this nothing observable came from her, only one morning shee said God is a father, the next morning, God is my father, which words (it is to be feared) were words of presumption, put into her mouth by the adversary.

I suspecting the truth of her former storye, pressed, whether shee never verbally promised to covenant with him, which shee stoutly denied: only acknowledged that shee had had some thoughts soe to doe: but on the forenamed Nov. 26. shee was again with violence & extremity seized by her fits, in such wise that 6 persons could hardly hold her, but shee leaped & skipped about the house proforce roaring, & yelling extreamly, & fetching deadly sighs, as if her heartstrings would have broken, & looking wth a frightfull aspect, to the amazement & astonishment of all the beholders, of which I was an eye witnesse: The

Physitian being then agen with her consented that the distemper was Diabolicall, refused further to administer, advised to extraordinary fasting; whereupon some of Gods ministers were sent for: shee meane while continued extreamly tormented night & day, till Tuesday about noon; having this added on Munday & Tuesday morning that shee barked like a dog, & bleated like a calfe, in which her organs were visibly made use of: yea, (as was carefully observed) on Munday night, & Tuesday morning, when ever any came neere the house, though they within heard nothing at all, yet would shee barke till they were come into the house, on Tuesday, about 12 of the clocke, she came out of the fit, which had held her from Sabbath day about the same time, at least 48 howers, with little or no intermission, & then her speech was restored to her, & shee expressed a great seeming sence of her state: many bitter teares, sighings, sobbings, complainings shee uttered, bewailing of many sins fore mentioned, begging prayers, & in the houre of prayer expressing much affection: I then pressed if there were anything behind in reference to the dealings between her & Satan, when she agen professed that shee had related all: & declared that in those fits the devill had assaulted her many wayes, that hee came downe the chimney, & shee essayed to escape him, but was siezed upon by him, that hee sat upon her breast, & used many arguments with her, & that hee urged here at one time with persuasions & promises, of ease, & great matters, told her that shee had done enough in what shee had already confessed, shee might henceforth serve him more securely; anon told hir her time was past, & there was no hopes unlesse shee would serve him; & it was observed in the time of her extremity, once when a little moments respite was granted her of speech, shee advised us to make our peace with God, & use our time better then shee had done, the party advised her also to bethinke herselfe of making her peace, shee replyed, it is too late for me: the next day was solemnized, when we had the presence of Mr. Bulkley, Mr. Rowlandson, & Mr. Estabrooke, whither coming, we found her returned to a sottish & stupid kind of frame, much was prest upon her, but no affection at all discovered; though shee was little or nothing exercised with any fits, & her speech also continued: though a day or two after shee was melancholye & being enquired of a reason, shee complained that shee was grieved that so much pains were taken wth her, & did her no good, but this held her not long: & thus shee remained till Munday, when to some neighbors there present, shee related something more of he converse with the devill, viz. That it had bin 5 yeers or therabouts, since shee first saw him, & declared methodically the sundry apparitions from time to time, till shee was thus dreadfully assaulted, in which, the principall was, that after many assaults, shee had resolved to seale a covenant with Satan, thinking shee had better doe it, then be thus followed by him, that once, when shee lived at Lancaster, he presented himselfe, & desired of her blood, & shee would have done it, but wanted a knife, in the parley shee was prevented by the providence of God interposing my father; a 2nd time in the house hee met her, & presented her a knife, & as she was going about it my father stept in agen & prevented, that when shee sought & enquired for the knife, it was not to bee found, & that afterward shee saw it sticking in the top of the barne, & some other like passages shee agen owned an observable passage which shee also had confessed in her first declaration, but is not there inserted, viz. that the devill had often proffered her his service, but shee accepted not; & once in ptic: to bring her in chips for the fire, shee refused, but when shee came in shee saw them lye by the fire side, & was affraid, & this I remarke, I sitting by the fire spake to her to lay them on, & she turned away in an unwonted manner: she then also declared against herselfe her unprofitable life she had led, & how justly God had thus permitted Satan to handle her, telling them, they little knew what a sad case shee was in. I after asked her concerning these passages, & shee owned the truth of them, & declared that now shee hoped the devill had left her, but being prest whether there were not a covenant, she earnestly professed, that by Gods goodnesse shee had bin prevented from doing that, which shee of herselfe had been ready enough to assent to; & shee thanked God there was no such thing:

The same day shee was agen taken with a new kind of unwonted fitt in which after shee had bin awhile exercised with violence, shee got her a sticke, & went up and downe, thrusting, & pushing, here & there, & anon looking out at a window, & cryed out

of a witch appearing in a strange manner in forme of a dog downward, with a womans head, & declared the person, other whiles that shee appeard in her whole likenesse, & described her shape and habit: signifyed that shee went up the chimney & went her way: what impression wee reade in the clay of the chimney, in similitude of a dogs paw, by the operation of Satan, & in the form of a dogs going in the same place she tould of, I shall not conclude, though something there was, as I myselfe saw in the chimney in the same place where shee declared the foot was set to goe up:

In this manner was she handled that night, & the 2 next dayes, using strange gestures, complaining by signes, when shee could not speake explaining that shee was sometimes in the chamber, somet. in the chimney, & anon assaults her, sometimes scratching her breast, beating her sides, strangling her throat, & she did oftentimes seeme to our apprehension as if shee would forthwith bee strangled: She declared that if the party were apprehended shee should forthwith bee well, but never till then; whereupon her father went, & percured the coming of the woman impeached by her, who came downe to her on Thursday night, where (being desired to be present) I observed that she was violently handled, & lamentably tormented by the adversarye, & uttered unusual shriekes at the instant of the persons coming in, though her eyes were fast closed: but having experience of such former actings, wee made nothing of it, but waited the issue: God therefore was sought to, to signifye something. whereby the innocent might bee acquitted, or the guilty discovered, & 'hee Answered our prayers, for by 2 evident & cleere mistakes she was cleered, & then all prejudices ceased, & she never more to this day hath impeached her of any apparition: in the fore mentioned allegation of the person, shee also signifyed that somet. the devil alsoe in the likenesse of a little boy appeared together with the person: Fryday was a sad day with her, for shee was sorely handled with fits, which some perceiving pressed that there was something yet behind not discovered by her; & shee after a violent fit, holding her betweene two & 3 houres did first to one, & afterwards to many acknowledge that shee had given of her blood to the Devill, & made a covenant with him, whereupon I was sent for to her; & understanding how things had passed, I found that there was no roome for privacye, in another alredy made by her soe publicke, I therefore examined her concerning the matter; & found her not soe forward to confesse, as shee had bin to others, yet thus much I gathered from her confession:

That after shee came to dwell with us, one day as shee was alone in a lower roome, all the rest of us being in the chamber, she looked out at the window, & saw the devill in the habit of an old man, coming over a great meadow lying neere the house; & suspecting his designe, shee had thoughts to have gon away; yet at length resolved to tarry it out, & heare what hee had to say to her; when hee came hee demanded of her some of her blood, which shee forthwith consented to, & with a knife cut her finger, hee caught the blood in his hand, & then told her she must write her name in his booke, shee answered, shee could not Write, but hee told her he would direct her hand, & then took a little sharpened sticke, & dipt in the blood, & put it into her hand, & guided it, & shee wrote her name with his helpe: what was the matter shee set her hand to, I could not learne from her; but thus much shee confessed, that the terme of time agreed upon with him was for 7 yeers; one yeere shee was to be faithfull in his service, & then the other six hee would serve her, & make her a witch: shee also related, that the ground of contest between her & the devill which was the occasion of this sad providence, was this, that after her covenant made the devill showed her hell & the damned, & told her if shee were not faithfull to him, shee should goe thither, & bee tormented there; shee desired of him to show her heaven, but hee told her that heaven was an ougly place, & that none went thither but a company of base roagues whom he hated; but if shee would obey him, it should be well with her: but afterward shee considered with herselfe, that the terme of her covenant, was but short, & would soone bee at an end, & shee doubted (for all the devills promises) shee must at last come to the place hee had showne her, & withall, feared, if shee were a witch, shee should bee discovered, & brought to a shamefull end: which was many times a trouble on her spirits; this the Devill perceiving, urged upon her to give him more of her blood, & set her hand agen to his booke, which shee refused to doe,

but partly through promises, partly by threatnings, hee brought her at last to a promise that shee would sometime doe it: after which hee left not incessantly to urge her to the performance of it, once hee met her on the staires. & often elsewhere pressing her with vehemencye, but shee still put it off; till the first night shee was taken when the devill came to her, & told her he would not tarry any longer: shee told him shee would not doe it hee Answered shee had done it already, & what further damage would it bee to doe it agen, for shee was his sure enough: she rejoyned shee had done it already, & if shee were his sure enough, what need hee to desire any more of her: whereupon he strucke her the first night, agen more violently the 2nd as is above exprest:

This is the sum of the Relation I then had from her: which at that time seemed to bee methodicall: These things she uttered with great affection, overflowing of teares, & seeming bitternesse: I asked of the Reason of her weeping & bitternesse, shee complained of her sinns, & some in particular, profanation of the sabbath &c: but nothing of this sin of renouncing the goverment of God. & giving herselfe up to the devill: I therfore, (as God helped) applied it to her & asked her whether shee desired not prayers with & for her, shee assented with earnestnesse, & in prayer seemed to bewaile the sin as God helped, then in the aggravation of it, & afterward declared a desire to rely on the power & mercy of God in Christ: shee then also declared, that the Devill had deceived her concerning those persons impeached by her, that hee had in their likenesse or resemblance tormented her, persuading her that it was they, that they bare her a spleen, but he loved her, & would free her from them, & pressed on her to endeavor to bring them forth to the censure of the law.

In this case I left her; but (not being satisfied in some things) I promised to visit her agen the next day which accordingly I did, but coming to her, I found her (though her speech still remained) in a case sad enough, her teares dryed up, & sences stupifyed, & (as was observed) when I could get nothing from her, & therfore applyed myselfe in counsell to her, shee regarded it not, but fixed her eye steadfastly upon a place, as shee was wont when the Devill presented himselfe to her, which was a griefe to her parents, & brought mee to a stand; in the condition I left her:

The next day, being the Sabbath, whither upon any hint given her, or any advantage Satan tooke by it upon her, shee sent for mee in hast at noone, coming to her, shee immediately with teares told me that shee had belied the Devill, in saying shee had given him of her blood: &c: professed that the most of the apparitions shee had spoken of were but fansyes, as images represented in a dreame; earnestly entreated me to beleeve her, called God to witnesse to her assertion, I told her I would willingly hope the best, & beleeve what I had any good grounds to apprehend; if therefore shee would tell a more methodicall relation than the former, it would be well, but if otherwise, she must bee content that every one should censure according to their apprehension, shee promised soe to doe, & expressed a desire that all that would might heare her; that as they had heard soe many lyes & untruths, they might now heare the truth, & engaged that in the evening shee would doe it; I then repaired to her, & divers more then went; shee then declared thus much, that the Devill had sometimes appeared to her; that the occasion of it was her discontent, that her condition displeased her, her labor was burdensome to her, shee was neither content to bee at home nor abroad; & had oftentime strong persuasions to practice in witchcraft, had often wished the Devill would come to her at such & such times, & resolved that if hee would, shee would give herselfe up to him soule & body: but (though hee had oft times appeared to her, yet) at such times hee had not discovered himselfe, and therfore shee had bin preserved from such a thing: I declared a suspicion of the truth of the relation, & gave her some Reasons; but by Reason of the company did not say much, neither could anything further be gotten from her: but the next day I went to her, & opened my mind to her alone, & left it with her, declared (among other things) that shee had used preposterous courses, & therfore it was no marvell that shee had bin led into such contradictions, & tendered her all the helpe I could, if shee would make use of me, & more privately relate any weighty & serious case of Conscience to me, shee promised me shee would if shee knew any thing, but said that then shee knew nothing at all; but stood to the story shee had told the foregoing evening: & indeed what to make of these things I at present know not, but am waiting till God (if hee see meet) wind up the story, & make a more cleere discoverye.

It was not many dayes ere shee was hurried agen into violent fits after a different manner, being taken agen speechlesse, & using all endeavores to make away with herselfe, & doe mischiefe unto others; striking those that held her; spitting in their faces; & if at any time shee had done any harme or frightened them shee would laugh immediately; which fits held her sometimes longer, sometimes shorter, few occasions shee had of speech, but when shee could speake, shee complained of a hard heart, counselled some to beware of sin, for that had brought her to this, bewailed that soe many prayers had bin put up for her, & shee still so hard hearted, & no more good wrought upon her; but being asked whither shee were willing to repent, shaked her head, & said nothing. Thus shee continued till the next sabbath in the afternoone; on which day in the morning, being somthing better then at other times, shee had but little company tarryed with her in the afternoon; when the Devill began to make more full discoverye of himselfe:

It had bin a question before, whither shee might properly bee called a Demoniacke, or person possessed of the Devill, but it was then put out of Question: hee began (as the persons with her testifye) by drawing her tongue out of her mouth most frightfully to an extraordinary length & greatnesse, & many amazing postures of her bodye; & then by speaking, vocally in her, whereupon her father, & another neighbor were called from the meeting, on whom, (as soon as they came in,) he railed, calling them roagues, charging them for folly in going to heare a blacke roague, who told them nothing but a parcell of lyes, & deceived them, & many like expressions. after exercise I was called, but understood not the occasion, till I came, & heard the same voice, a grum, low, yet audible voice it was, the first salutation I had was, oh! you are a great roague, I was at the first somthing daunted & amazed, & many reluctances I had upon my spirits, which brought mee to a silence and amazement in my spirits, till at last God heard my groanes & gave me both refreshment in Christ, & courage: I then called for a light, to see whither it might not appeare a counterfiet, and observed not any of her organs to moove, the voice was hollow, as if it issued out of her throat; hee then agen called me great blacke roague, I challenged him to make it appear; but all the Answer was, you tell the people a company of lyes: I reflected on myselfe, & could not but magnifye the goodnesse of God not to suffer Satan to bespatter the names of his people, with those sins which hee himselfe hath pardoned in the blood of Christ.

I Answered, Satan, thou art a lyar, and a deceiver, & God will vindicate his owne truth one day: hee Answered nothing directly, but said, I am not Satan, I am a pretty blacke boy; this is my pretty girle; I have bin here a great while, I sat still, and Answered nothing to these expressions; but when hee directed himselfe to mee agen, oh! you blacke roague, I doe not love you: I replyed through God's grace, I hate thee; hee rejoyned, but you had better love mee; these manner of expressions filled some of the company there present with great consternation, others put on boldnesse to speake to him, at which I was displeased, & advised them to see their call cleere, fearing least by his policye, & many apish expressions hee used, hee might insinuate himselfe, & raise in them a fearlessenesse of spirit of him: I no sooner turned my backe to goe to the fire, but he called out agen, where is that blacke roague gon: I seeing little good to bee done by discorse, & questioning many things in my mind concerning it, I desired the company to joyne in prayer unto God; when wee went about that duty & were kneeled downe, with a voice louder then before something, hee cryed out, hold your tongue, hold your tongue, get you gon you blacke roague, what are you going to doe, you have nothing to doe with me, &c: but through Gods goodnesse was silenced, &, shee lay quiet during the time of prayer, but as soone as it was ended, began afresh, using the former expressions, at which some ventured to speake to him: Though I thinke imprudentlye: one told him, God had him in chaines, hee replyed, for all my chaine, I can knocke thee on the head when I please: hee said hee would carry her away that night. Another Answered, but God is stronger than thou, He presently rejoyned, that's a ly, I am stronger than God: at which blasphemy I agen advised them to bee wary of speaking, counselled them to get serious

parsons to watch with her, & left her, commending her to God:

On Tuesday following shee confessed that the Devill entred into her the 2nd night after her first taking, that when shee was going to bed, hee entred in (as shee conceived) at her mouth, & had bin in her ever since, & professed, that if there were ever a Devill in the world, there was one in her, but in what manner he spake in her she could not tell: On Wednesday night, shee must forthwith be carried downe to the bay in all hast, shee should never be well, till an assembly of ministers was met together to pray with & for her, & in particular Mr. Cobbet: her friends advised with me about it; I signifyed to them, that I apprehended, Satan never made any good motion, but it was out of season, & that it was not a thing now fiezable, the season being then extreame cold; & the snow deepe, that if shee had bin taken in the woods with her fits shee must needs perish: On friday in the evening shee was taken agen violently, & then the former voice (for the sound) was heard in her agen, not speaking, but imitating the crowing of a cocke, accompanied with many other gestures, some violent, some ridiculous, which occasioned my going to her, where by signes she signifyed that the Devill threatened to carry her away that night, God was agen then sought for her. & when in prayer, that expression was used, the God had prooved Satan a liar, in preserving her once when hee had threatned to carry her away that night, & was entreated soe to doe agen, the same voice, which had ceased 2 dayes before, was agen heard by the by-standers 5 times distinctly to cry out, oh you are a roague, and then ceased: but the whole time of prayer, sometimes by violence of fits sometimes by noises shee made, shee drouned her owne hearing from receiving our petition, as she afterwards confessed:

Since that time shee hath continued for the most part speechlesse, her fits coming upon her sometimes often, sometimes with greater intermission, & with great varietyes in the manner of them, sometimes by violence, sometimes by making her sicke, but (through Gods goodnesse) soe abated in violence, that now one person can as well rule her, as formerly 4 or 5: She is observed alwayes to fall into her fits when any strangers goe to visit her, & the more goe the more violent are her fits:

as to the frame of her spirits hee hath bin more averse lately to good counsell than heretofore, yet sometime shee signifyes a desire of the companye of ministers.

On Thursday last, in the evening, shee came a season to her speech, & (as I received from them with her) agen disouned a Covenant with the Devill, disouned that relation about the knife fore mentioned, declared the occasion of her fits to bee discontent, owned the temptations to murder; declared that though the devill had power of her body, shee hoped hee should not of her soule, that she had rather continue soe speechlesse, then have her speech, & make no better use of it then formerly shee had, expressed that shee was sometimes disposed to doe mischiefe, & was as if some had laid hold of her to enforce her to it, & had double strength to her owne, that shee knew not whither the devill were in her or no if hee were shee knew not when or how he entered; that when shee was taken speechlesse, she fared as if a string was tyed about the roots of her tongue, & reached doune into her vitalls & pulled her tongue downe, & then most when shee strove to speake:

On Fryday, in the evening shee was taken wth a passion of weeping, & sighing, which held her till late in the night, at length she sent for me; but then unseasonablenesse of the weather, & my owne bodily indisposednesse prevented: I went the next morning, when shee strove to speake somthing but could not, but was taken with her fits, which held her as long as I tarried, which was more then an houre, & I left her in them: & thus she continues speechlesse to this instant, Jan. 15. & followed with fits: concerning which state of hers I shall suspend my owne Judgment, & willingly leave it to the censure of those that are more learned, aged, & Judicious: only I shall leave my thoughts in resp. of 2 or 3 questions which have risen about her: viz.

1. Whither her distemper be reale or counterfiet: I shall say no more to that but this, the great strength appearing in them, & great weaknesse after them, will disclaime the contrary opinion: for tho a person may counterfiet much yet such a strength is beyond the force of dissimulation:

2. Whither her distemper bee naturall or Diabolicall, I suppose the premises will strongly enough

conclude the latter, yet I will adde these 2 further arguments:

1. the actings of convulsion, which these come nearest to, are (as parsons acquainted with them observe) in many, yea the most essentiall parts of them quite contrary to these actings:

2. Shee hath no wayes wasted in body, or strength by all these fits, though soe dreadfulle, but gathered flesh exceedinglye, & hath her naturall strength when her fits are off, for the most part:

3. Whither the Devill did really speake in her: to that point which some have much doubted of, thus much I will say to countermand this apprehension:

1. The manner of expression I diligently observed, & could not perceive any organ, any instrument of speech (which the philosopher makes mention of) to have any motion at all, yea her mouth was sometimes shut without opening sometimes open without shutting or moving, & then both I & others saw her tongue (as it used to bee when shee was in some fits, when speechlesse) turned up circularly to the roofe of her mouth.

2. the labial letters, divers of which were used by her, viz. B. M. P. which cannot bee naturally expressed without motion of the lips, which must needs come within our ken, if observed, were uttered without any such motion, shee had used only Lingualls, Gutturalls &c: the matter might have bin more suspicious:

3. the reviling termes then used, were such as shee never used before nor since, in all this time of her being thus taken: yea, hath bin alwayes observed to speake respectively concerning mee;

4. They were expressions which the devill (by her confession) aspersed mee, & others withall, in the houre of temptation, particularly shee had freely acknowledged that the Devill was wont to appear to her in the house of God & divert her mind, & charge her shee should not give eare to what the Blacke coated roage spake:

5. wee observed when the voice spake, her throat was swelled formidably as big at least as ones fist: These arguments I shall leave to the censure of the Judicious:

4. whither shee have covenanted with the Devill or noe: I thinke this is a case unanswerable, her declarations have been soe contradictorye, one to

another, that wee know not what to make of them & her condition is such as administers many doubts; charity would hope the best, love would alsoe feare the worst, but thus much is cleare, shee is an object of pitye, & I desire that all that heare of her would compassionate her forlorne state, Shee is (I question not) a subject of hope, & thererfore all meanes ought to bee used for her recoverye, Shee is a monument of divine severitye, & the Lord grant that all that see or heare, may feare & tremble: Amen.

S. W.

Source: Samuel A. Green, ed., *Groton in the Witchcraft Times* (Groton, MA: University Press, 1883), 7–21. Available at Hanover Historical Texts Project, http://history.hanover.edu/texts/Willard-Knap.html.

Excerpts from Cotton Mather's *Memorable Providences, Relating to Witchcrafts and Possessions* (1689)

Cotton Mather, the Puritan minister at the Old North Church in Boston, published Memorable Providences, Relating to Witchcrafts and Possessions *in 1689. In this excerpt, Mather discusses the supposed demonic possession of washerwoman Goody Glover, an Irishwoman who spoke English poorly and was eventually executed as a witch. Mather's book contained detailed descriptions of witch behavior and was read by many Puritan authorities, who used it in their own witch hunts. A copy of the book was owned by Samuel Parris, the minister in Salem in whose house occurred the events that initiated the Salem Witch Trials of 1692.*

Sect. VIII. It was not long before the Witch thus in the Trap, was brought upon her Tryal; at which, thro' the Efficacy of a Charm, I suppose, used upon her, by one or some of her Cruel the Court could receive Answers from her in one but the Irish, which was her Native Language; altho she under-stood the English very well, and had accustomed her whole Family to none but that Language in her former Conversation; and therefore the Communication between the Bench and the Bar,' was now cheefly convey'd by two honest and faithful men that were interpreters. It was long before she could with any direct Answers plead unto her Indictment and; when she did plead, it was with Confession rather than Denial of her Guilt. Order was given to search the old womans house, from whence there were brought into the Court, several small Im-

ages, or Puppets, or Babies, made of Raggs, and stuff't with Goat's hair, and other such Ingredients. When these were produced, the vile Woman acknowledged, that her way to torment the Objects of her malice, was by wetting of her Finger with her Spittle, and streaking of those little Images. The abused Children were then present, and the Woman still kept stooping and shrinking as one that was almost prest to Death with a mighty Weight upon her. But one of the Images being brought unto her, immediately she started up after an odd manner, and took it into her hand; but she had no sooner taken it, than one of the Children fell into sad Fits, before the whole Assembly.

Sect. XI. When this Witch was going to her Execution, she said, the Children should not be relieved by her Death, for others had a hand in it as well as she; and she named one among the rest, whom it might have been thought Natural Affection would have advised the Concealing of. It came to pass accordingly, That the Three children continued in their Furnace as before, and it grew rather Seven times hotter than it was. All their former Ails pursued them still, with an addition of (tis not easy to tell how many) more, but such as gave more sensible Demonstrations of an Enchantment growing very far towards a Possession by Evil spirits.

Source: Cotton Mather, *Memorable Providences, Relating to Witchcrafts and Possessions* (Boston: R. P., 1689). Available at http://law2.umkc.edu/faculty/projects/ftrials/salem/asa_math.htm.

Witch Trials, Salem, Massachusetts (1692)

The Salem Witch Trials began in 1692, lasted a year, and represented the most extensive witch-hunting episode in the history of Great Britain's North American colonies. Although the hysteria began in Salem Village, Massachusetts, it soon engulfed the entirety of Essex County. By the time the trials ended, 20 people had been executed (13 women and 7 men), and the local jails were filled with people awaiting trial after being accused of practicing witchcraft. Several people died before their cases could come to court.

The initial outbreak was centered in the home of Samuel Parris, Salem Village's minister. A group of girls ranging in age from 9 through 17, including Parris's daughter and niece, began suffering from fits and claimed to hear voices during early February 1692. A local doctor diagnosed them as being bewitched and launched a search for the witch or witches responsible. The girls initially accused three women, Sarah Goode, Sarah Osborne, and Tituba. Goode and Osborne were not well respected in the community, and Tituba was Parris's slave. Under intense interrogation, Tituba confessed to "hurting" the girls and implicated Goode and Osborne as her coconspirators. Osborne was sent to jail and died there on May 10, 1692. Goode was sentenced to hang, but her execution was delayed long enough for her to give birth to a child who died in prison. Her 6-year-old daughter Dorcas was also accused and imprisoned but was released when the panic ended.

Despite the identification of the supposed guilty parties, the girls continued to be afflicted with seizure-like fits and other odd behaviors. This prompted Puritan officials to level further accusations and enforce subsequent imprisonments, including prosperous women and

Though Puritan authorities portrayed witchcraft trials as a tool in their battle with Satan, in reality accusations, trials, and executions were used to control female behavior and thought. (Ridpath, John Clark, *Ridpath's History of the World,* 1901)

men who were influential within the community but were viewed as unsupportive of Parris's ministry, including tavern owner Bridget Bishop.

With Salem Village in obvious turmoil, Sir William Phips, governor of Massachusetts, established a special court in June to hear all of the cases. The court proved conflicted, as a judge resigned following the sentencing of Bishop to hang since she had been convicted on "spectral" evidence. This was essentially defined as the Devil working through the image of the accuser. The use of this questionable evidence led to the imprisonment of hundreds and the execution of 19 people between June and September 1692. After his wife Martha Corey was imprisoned on suspicion of witchcraft, elderly Giles Corey defended her. Then he too was imprisoned for five months, after which he was executed by being pressed to death with heavy rocks. Martha Corey was hanged three days later.

Within Massachusetts, many individuals were viewing the events in Salem Village with skepticism. In October 1692, Increase Mather and other prominent Puritan clergymen interceded in the trials. Their presence and actions provided the political support necessary for Phips to put a stop to the executions. This allowed for investigators to examine the motivations of some of the individuals tied to the victimized girls, such as Reverend Parris and Thomas Putnam, who were obviously benefiting from the process by seeing many of their critics imprisoned and thus having their reputations shattered. They were also economically benefiting from the process. Those accused of witchcraft had their property auctioned off, and those making the accusations had first bid on the auctions. The results of the scrutiny led to the release of the falsely imprisoned during the spring of 1693. The Massachusetts General Court essentially admitted in 1697 that the trials were unjust by declaring a day of atonement. This was followed in 1711 by reparations paid to some of the victims.

Although many theories have been posited about the causes of the Salem Witch Trials, there is no doubt that gender played a prominent role. The girls who made the initial accusations suddenly had a great amount of power in what was a patriarchal society. They wielded this power not on men in the main but instead on women vulnerable because of their economic or social status. This may explain why the first people accused were from the bottom rung of society, but as the accusations increased, the targets became people of better repute. When the respected male leaders of the colony interceded, that is when the girls returned to their subservient roles in society. Historian Carol Karlsen found that 9 of 10 executed women stood to inherit money or property because their families had no male heirs. In ridding itself of these women, Puritan authorities not only rid themselves of potentially economically powerful women but often availed themselves of their victims' inheritance.

The witch trials drew so much notoriety to the Puritans in Massachusetts that nobody else would ever again be tried for witchcraft in New England. Salem Village changed its name to Danvers to try to escape the ignominy of its history. Despite the shame invoked by the incidents, they continue to be brought to the fore through works such as Arthur Miller's *The Crucible* and Henry Wadsworth Longfellow's *Giles Corey of the Salem Farms*. On the 300th anniversary of the trials the city erected a permanent memorial composed of a series of stone benches, one for each of the executed people, circling a cemetery garden. Political activist and former Auschwitz prisoner Elie Wiesel spoke, as did playwright Arthur Miller. In more modern times the city of Salem embraced its connection to the trials and has become a favorite haunt for Halloween, with hotels booked years in advance.

John R. Burch Jr.

See also Bishop, Bridget; Goode, Sarah; Tituba; Witchcraft in New England

Further Reading

Demos, John. 2008. *The Enemy Within: 2,000 Years of Witch-Hunting in the Western World*. New York: Viking.

Karlsen, Carol. 1987. *Devil in the Shape of a Woman: Witchcraft in Colonial New England*. New York: Norton.

Norton, Mary Beth. 2002. *In the Devil's Snare: The Salem Witchcraft Crisis of 1692*. New York: Knopf.

Rosenthal, Bernard, ed. 2009. *Records of the Salem Witch-Hunt*. New York: Cambridge University Press.

Documents Relating to Ann Foster's Trial for Witchcraft in Salem, Massachusetts (1692)

In 1692 Ann Foster, a widow in her mid-70s living in Andover, Massachusetts, was accused of using witchcraft to sicken another Andover woman, Elizabeth Ballard. The accusation was based on the behavior of two Salem girls, Ann Putnam and Mary Wolcott, who upon being taken to Andover to uncover a possible witch, fell into fits at the sight of Foster. Urged to confess and put to torture, Foster refused to do so until her daughter, Mary Lacey, who was also accused, denounced her mother as a witch, likely in an attempt to save herself and her daughter. Foster was thus convicted of witchcraft and died in December 1692 while confined in the Salem jail. Reproduced here are depositions by Wolcott and others accusing Foster of witchcraft, a transcript of the examination of Foster, the indictment of Foster, an examination of Foster and her daughter and granddaughter, and a petition from Foster's son, Abraham Foster, asking that his late mother's name be cleared of what had by then become a discredited accusation.

1. MARY WALCOTT V. ANN FOSTER

Mary Walcot affirmed to the Jury of Inquest: that Ann Foster : of Andover: has afflicted her: both: before her examination: and at her examination & since: that time by biting pinching & choaking of her s'd Walcot also sayth she has:seen her s'd Foster afflict: Eliz Hubbert : at the time of her examination: by choaking & pinching of her: & #[that] she beleeved Foster is a witch: & that: she hath afflicted me & Eliz Hubbard by witchcraft #[Sept'r 13: 16] upon her oath

Sept'r 13: 1692

(Boston Public Library—Dept. of Rare Books and Manuscripts [1939 acquisition])

2. ELIZABETH HUBBARD V. ANN FOSTER

Eliz Hubbert. Affirmed to the Jury of Inquest: th't Ann Foster : both before: and at her examination & after hath afflicted her: she also affirmed: that she saw s'd Ann Foster or her apperition afflict Mary Walcot & Ann putnam : & she ses she verily beleeves: An

Foster is a witch & that she s'd Foster: did afflict her & the above named persons by witchcraft upon her oath: Sept't 13 1692

(Boston Public Library—Dept. of Rare Books and Manuscripts [1939 acquisition])

3. MARY WARREN V. ANN FOSTER

Mary Warin affirmed to the Jury of Inquest: that she saw Ann Foster or her Apperition: afflict: Mary Wallcot & Eliz Hubbert : & she also: afflicted me s'd Warin: before the Jury of Inquest: & I veryly believe s'd Foster is a witch & th't she—

Afflicted me & the persons mentioned: by Witchcraft upon her out Sept'r

(Boston Public Library—Dept. of Rare Books and Manuscripts [1939 acquisition])

4. EXAMINATIONS OF ANN FOSTER

The Examination and Confession of Ann Foster at Salem Vilage 15 July 1692 after a while Ann foster confessed that the divill apered to her in the shape of abird at several Times, such abird as she never saw the like before, & that she had had this gift (viz of striking the aflicted downe w'th her eye ever) since, & being ask't why she thought that bird was the divill she answred because he came white and vanished away black & that the divill told her that she should have this gift & that she must beleive him & told her she should have prosperity & #[that] she said that he had apeared to her three times & was always as a bird & the last time was about halfe a year since, & sat upon atable had two legs & great eyes & that it was the second time of his apearance that he promised her prosperity & that it was Cariers wife about three weeks agoe that came & perswaded her to hurt these people.

16. July. 1692. Ann Foster Examined conffesed that it was Goody Carier that made her a witch that she came to her in person about Six yeares agoe & told her if she would not be awitch the divill should tare

her in peices and Cary her away at w'ch. time she promised to Serve the divill, that she had bewitched a hog of John Lovjoyes to Death & that she had hurt Some persons in Salem Vilage that goody Carier came to her & would have her bewitch two children of Andrew Allins & that she had then two popets made and stuck pins in them to bewitch the said Children by which one of them dyed the other very sick, that she was at the meeting of the witches at Salem Villiage, that Goody Carier came & told her of the meeting & would have her goe, so they gat upon Sticks & went said Jorny & being ther did see mr Burroughs the minister who spake to them all, & this was about two months agoe that ther was then twenty five persons meet together, that she tyed a knot in a Rage & thre it into the fire to hurt [a woeman at Salem Village & that she was hurt by her & that her name is Goody Vibber] Timo. Swan & that she did hurt the rest that complayned of her by squesing popets like them & so almost choaked them.—

18 July 1692. Ann Foster Examined confesed that the devill in shape of a #[black] man apeared to her w'th Goody carier about six yeare since when they made her awitch & that she promised to serve the divill two yeares: upon w'ch the Divill promised her prosperity & many things but never performed it, that she & martha Carier did both ride on a stick or pole when they went to the witch meeting at Salem Village & that the stick broak: as they ware caried in the aire above the tops of the trees & they fell but she did hang fast about the neck of Goody Carier & ware presently at the vilage, that she was then much hurt of her Leg, she further saith that she hard some of the witches say that their was three hundred & five in the whole Country, & that they would ruin that place the Vilige, also saith ther was present at that metting two men besides mr Buroughs the minister & one of them had gray haire, she saith that she formerly frequented the publique metting to worship god. but the divill had such power over her that she could not profit there & that was her undoeing: she saith that above three or foure yeares agoe Martha Carier told her she would bewitch James Hobbs child to death & the child dyed in twenty four howers

21. July: 92. Ann. Foster Examined Owned her former conffesion being Read to her and further conffesed that the discourse amongst the witches at the meeting at Salem village was that they would afflict there to set up the Divills Kingdome This conffesion is true as wittnese my hand:

The marke of Ann: Foster

Ann Foster Signed & Owned the above Examination & conffesion before me

*John Higginson Just'e peace

Salem 10th September 1692
(Reverse) Ann Fosters Examination And Conffession (Essex County Archives, Salem—Witchcraft Vol. 2 Page 22)

5. INDICTMENT V. ANN FOSTER

Essex in the Province of the Massachuetts Bay in New England Anno R Rs & Reginae Gulielmi & Mariae Angliae &ca Quarto.Anno'qe Domini 1692

ss

The Juriors for our Sov'r Lord & Lady the King & Queen doe present that. Ann foster of Andivor In the County of Essex Widdow In & Upon the fifteenth Day of July In the year afores'd. and divers other days and times as well before as after Certaine Detestable arts called Witchcrafts and Sorceries wickedly and Mallitiously and felloniously hath used practised & Exercised at and in the Towne of Salem in the County of Essex-aforesaid in upon & against one Eliza Hobert of Salem in the County of Essex-aforesaid Single Woman by which Said wicked arts the Said Elizabeth Hobert the day & Yeare aforesaid and divers other days and times both before and after was and is Tortured aflicted Consumed Pined wasted and Tormented and also for sundry other acts of withcraft by the said Ann foster—Comitted and done before and Since that time against the peace of o'r Sov'r. Lord and Lady the King and Queen theire Crowne and Dignity and the forme of the Stattute in that Case made and Provided.

(Reverse) Indictm't Agst An foster for bewitching Eliza: Hobert Billa Vera

(Essex County Archives, Salem—Witchcraft Vol. 2 Page 21)

6. EXAMINATION OF ANN FOSTER, MARY LACEY SR., AND MARY LACEY JR., SECOND VERSION

21st July, 1692. Before Major Gidney, Mr. Hawthorne, Mr. Corwin and Capt. Higginson.

Q. Goody Foster you remember we have three times spoken with you, and do you now remember what you then confessed to us?—You have been engaged in very great wickedness, and some have been left to hardness of heart to deny; but it seems that God will give you more favour than others, inasmuch as you relent. But your daughter here hath confessed some things that you did not tell us of. Your daughter was with you and Goody Carrier, when you did ride upon the stick. A. I did not know it. Q. How long have you known your daughter to be engaged? A. I cannot tell, nor have I any knowledge of it at all. Q. Did you see your daughter at the meeting? A. No. Q. Your daughter said she was at the witches meeting, and that you yourself stood at a distance off and did not partake at that meeting; and you said so also; give us a relation from the beginning until now. A. I know none of their names that were there, but only Goody Carrier. Q. Would you know their faces if you saw them? A. I cannot tell. Q. Where there not two companies in the field at the same time? A. I remember no more.— Mary Warren, one of the afflicted, said that Goody Carrier's shape told her, that Goody Foster had made her daughter a witch.—Q. Do not you acknowledge that you did so about 13 years ago? A. No, and I know no more of my daughter's being a witch than what day I shall die upon. Q. Are you willing your daughter should make a full and free confession? A. Yes. Q. Are you willing to do so too? A. Yes. Q. You cannot expect peace of conscience without a free confession. A. If I knew any thing more, I would speak it to the utmost.—Goody Lacey, the daughter, called in, began thus; Oh mother how do you do? We have left Christ, and the devil hath gat hold of us. How shall I get rid of this evil one? I desire God to break my rocky heart that I may get the victory this time. Q. Goody Foster you cannot get rid of this snare, your heart and mouth is not open. A. I did not see the devil, I was praying to the Lord. Q. What Lord? A. To God. Q. What God do witches pray to? A. I cannot tell, the Lord help me. Q. Goody Lacey had you no discourse with your mother when riding? A. No, I think I had not a word. Q. Who rid foremost on that stick to the village? A. I suppose my mother.— Goody Foster said, that Goody Carrier was foremost—Q. Goody Lacey how many years ago since they were baptized? A. Three or four years ago, I suppose. Q. Who baptized them? A. The old serpent. Q. How did he do it? A. He dipped their heads in the water, saying, they were his and that he had power over them. Q. Where was this? A. At Fall's river. Q. How many were baptized that day? A. Some of the chief; I think they were six baptized. Q. Name them. A. I think they were of the higher powers.—Mary Lacey, the grand-daughter, was brought in, and Mary Warren fell into a violent fit. Q. How dare you come in here, and bring the devil with you to afflict these poor creatures?—Lacey laid her hand on Warren's arm, and she recovered from her fit.—Q. You are here accused of practising witchcraft upon Goody Ballard; which way do you do it? A. I cannot tell. Where is my mother that made me a witch, and I knew it not? Q. Can you look upon that maid Mary Warren, and not hurt her? Look upon her in a friendly way.—She, trying so to do, struck her down with her eyes. Q. Do you acknowledge now you are a witch? A. Yes. Q. How long have you been a witch? A. Not above a week. Q. Did the devil appear to you? A. Yes. Q. In what shape? A. In the shape of a horse. Q. What did he say to you? A. He bid me not to be afraid of any thing, and he would not bring me out, but he has proved a liar from the beginning. Q. When was this? A. I know not; above a week. Q. Did you set your hand to the book? A. No. Q. Did he bid you worship him? A. Yes, he bid me also afflict persons.—You are now in the way to obtain mercy if you will confess and repent. She said, the Lord help me. Q. Do not you desire to be saved by Christ? A. Yes.—Then you must confess freely what you know in this matter. She then proceeded.—I was in bed and the devil came to me and bid me obey him and I should want for nothing, and he would not bring me out. Q. But how long ago? A. A Little more than a year. Q. Was that the first time? A. Yes. Q. How long was you gone from your father, when you ran away? A. Two days. Q. Where had you your food? A. At John Stone's. Q. Did the Devil appear to you then, when you was abroad?

A. No, but he put such thoughts in my mind as not to obey my parents. Q. Who did the devil bid you afflict? A. Timothy Swan. Richard Carrier comes often a nights and has me to afflict persons. Q. Where do ye go? A. To Goody Ballard's sometimes. Q. How many of you were there at a time? A. Richard Carrier and his mother, and my mother and grandmother.

7. PETITION OF ABRAHAM FOSTER—CASE OF ANN FOSTER

The Honorable Committee now Sitting at Salem Sept. 13, 1710

Whereas my Mother Anne Foster of Andover suffered Imprisonment 21 weeks and upon her Tryall was condemned for Supposed witchcraft, upon such evidence as is now Generally thought Insufficient And died in Prison. I being well perswaded of my mothers

Innocency of the Crime for which she was condemned: Humbly desire that the Attainder may be taken off—

The Account of my charges and expences for my mother During her Imprisonment is as followeth

To money which I was forced to pay the keeper before I could have the dead body of my mother to bury. . . .

Money & provisions expended while she was in Prison

p'r *Abraham Foster the Son of the Deceased
(Reverse) Anne foster of Andover Condemned dyed in prison Confessor
(Mass. Archives Vol. 135 No. 159)

Source: "Transcripts of Proceedings Related to Ann Foster," University of Minnesota, http://www.tc.umn.edu/~austi012/ghtout/npr7.htm.

THEMATIC ISSUES ESSAY

The lives of women in colonial America (1607–1754) varied greatly depending on their ethnicity, freedom status, and the geographic area in which they lived. British and European settlers on the Atlantic seaboard and in the French and Spanish areas of the Gulf Coast and the Southwest brought their own similar yet subtly different cultural assumptions to the New World. Native American women's work ways and sociocultural realities often contrasted sharply with those of their European sisters, as did those of the African women who arrived in North America in the early 1600s. In the period of early colonial settlement, these differences were the most clear. However, over time many of these differences blended together as intercultural exchange—both voluntary and coerced—occurred. During the early colonial period some of the greatest influences on society were the religious or economic environments in which those colonies operated. In addition, adherence to the idea of a hierarchical society formed the basis upon which those societies were structured. These combined influences were the primary determinants of the role and status of women in the family and the community at large.

Religion played a critical part in the formation of cultural norms in the colonies, especially in the earliest period of settlement. While religious influence in the Chesapeake was not strong, it was one of the factors at the heart of gender expectations in New England. It is also important to note the increased emphasis that Quaker societies put on the participation of women in the church and community. In this case the mother, not the father, was the key link between the family and the church, and women exerted much more control of events outside the home environment. Quaker women's meetings were in charge of monitoring the family lives of other church members, mediating family disputes, and disciplining church members. They also administered poor relief and cooperated with men's meetings in the marriage approval process. This broader participation of Quaker women in society in effect took maternity public and made them mothers to their entire community, allowing them to exercise some of the same control over their neighbors as they would their own children.

The Great Awakening of the 1730s and 1740s resulted in increased male church involvement. The emphasis of heart religion, or a more personal, emotional religious experience, certainly appealed to women as well as men. At the same time, the movement broke up the existing tribalism by bringing droves of formerly unchurched people into the fold. The hold on the public significance of religion that was so prominent in the early years of colonization now began to relax, loosening the social control and church/state structure that had previously existed. As a result, the ties between many women's religious and familial roles were likewise loosened, marking the beginning of a change that extended into the Revolutionary era.

Gender Roles

The British settlers who arrived on the Atlantic coast of North America in the early 17th century brought a cultural understanding of properly ordered society that had been formed in England. The primary expectation for all white women, at least, was that of the "goodwife," or the obedient, honorable, competent, and accomplished woman of the house. Based on years of practice in England, the goodwife ultimately had to adapt to the realities of the American frontier, and between the first years of settlement and approximately 1750, ideologies regarding women and their roles in society passed through two transitional periods. The period of initial settlement extended to approximately 1660, at which time a period of transition began, ending roughly around 1750 when the advent of the American Revolution put an end to the colonial period and again initiated a change for American women.

Due to the patriarchal system in place and the isolation of the New World, the American colonial woman of the migration period found herself increasingly less an autonomous person and more a part of the familial system—an essential mechanical part, so to speak, of the organization that made the family unit function effectively. The accepted system placed her below her husband in the social hierarchy and above her children and any servants in her household. She was empowered to act on her husband's behalf as a deputy husband when the situation warranted and was in charge of running the household. However, with very few exceptions she acted at her husband's direction. Even when she performed as a deputy husband in cases where her husband was away or otherwise unavailable

to make decisions regarding the home or family, she had usually received his instructions in advance regarding issues she might face in his absence. Although she directed her household of children and servants regarding the daily operations of the parts of the homestead under her purview, it was her husband who prepared the budget, meted out punishment, and oversaw the running of the entire household. While she could have input and voice her opinions, her husband had the final say. They were, however, considered a unit. This is one of the reasons often given for the lack of voting rights for women in most colonies; the husband made decisions, often taking his wife's views into consideration, and society held that he cast his vote on her behalf as well as his own.

Historians suggest that the strict gender definitions and clear hierarchy within the early colonial family was a coping mechanism created in reaction to the uncertainty of life on the frontier. In a time and place of questionable survival rates, rigid hierarchical structure provided a road map for individual behavior that stabilized the family and at the same time exerted a measure of social control.

Education

Formal education for females was not considered a priority during the colonial era due to the perception of women's limited intellectual ability and the dominant ideology that the proper role of women was as wife, mother, and helpmeet. Indeed, it could be a dangerous thing; when a friend asked Massachusetts Bay Colony founder John Winthrop for advice concerning a marital issue, Winthrop replied that the problem was caused by his wife's habit of reading too much. Young women were educated but in different ways and to different degrees than young men, as befit their proper roles in colonial society.

While boys often attended schools and colleges, girls were usually taught at home. The curriculum included reading but not necessarily writing. Religious studies and instruction in common household tasks rounded out the education deemed necessary for the proper housewife. In addition to these basics, girls from elite families were often schooled in ornamental subjects such as dance, music, art, and fine needlework.

As the colonial period progressed, females of elite social status were encouraged to expand their knowledge to include natural philosophy, mathematics, and other subjects more common to the education of young men. This emphasis on more advanced education for women did not extend to a broader range of social classes until after the American Revolution, when ideology regarding the role of women in American society began to change.

Work, Waged and Unwaged

The image of the be-all, do-all colonial goodwife is primarily a myth. Lack of availability of even the most basic of household tools meant that colonial women were forced to improvise or swap work with their neighbors in order to feed and clothe their families. Early evidence shows that even by the mid-18th century fewer than 50 percent of households owned spinning wheels, cheese molds, or butter churns. The practice of swapping work allowed women to cooperate in the exchange of skills and raw materials in order to manufacture products for home use.

Most white women occupied a gendered domain of the dwelling and yards, which included the garden, milk house, kitchen, cellar, brew house, buttery, wash house, henhouse, and orchard. Women in the Chesapeake and other areas where slaves performed some household work were more likely to own more of the basic tools of the trade such as wheels, looms, and churns. In colonial cities and seaport towns of both regions women had more access to finished, imported goods. They also enjoyed more opportunity to self-support in these areas, as they were often the purveyors of homegrown or prepared foods or provided a service such as laundry or seamstress work. These goods and services were most often provided by widows or less affluent women, although there is evidence that some highly placed women engaged in commerce on a regular basis.

Clearly, life differed for these women depending on whether they lived in a town, in a rural area, or on the frontier. Farm dwellers placed intense importance on housewifery and its particular skills. In addition to keeping the home fire lit at all times, the farm wife was expected to engage in dairying, cheese making, slaughtering and processing of livestock, brewing of cider and beer, and bread making in addition to the other usual tasks of keeping a home clean and the family fed and clothed. These duties all required considerable skill, given the hit-or-miss nature of rising dough and fermenting beverages in a time devoid of packaged yeasts and starters.

City women lived in an environment of generally longer established families, had an earlier relationship with trade and manufacturing, and had greater access to household goods and tools. They were more likely to have larger inventories of equipment, supplies, and luxury items than their rural sisters. With more available finished goods, the city wife experienced far less pressure to do everything. Door-to-door hawkers brought foods for sale, and while few towns had retail trade centers, there were slaughterhouses, docks, and other venues that offered meats, fish, and other products. The daily bread making so critical to the rural goodwife may have even been dispensed with by city women who could purchase ready-made baked goods. Although the city goodwife enjoyed these conveniences, they came with a price. The daily collection of foodstuffs from vendors in different parts of the town was time-consuming. In addition, the model goodwife was expected to know who had the best-quality goods at the best price.

The frontier household resembled the rural home in many ways. However, frontier families were more likely to be less affluent than rural or urban families, their housing was usually smaller and more crude, and daily life was more dangerous. Access to equipment and manufactured goods was most limited in frontier homes.

For many women, the lack of availability of tools and materials necessary to perform household tasks often led to the sharing or bartering of work. Sharing work, in particular, offered the added bonus of visiting while the work was shared. The quilting bee is a prime example of such an exchange, but sharing work more often operated between only two or three women. With little hard currency available, barter became an important tool for colonial women. While similar to sharing work, this practice focused more on swapping off tasks or goods. For instance, a woman who needed stockings but had no sheep or spinning wheel might barter eggs from her chickens in order to obtain the wool. She might then offer part of it to someone who owned a spinning wheel and then would knit stockings from the wool yarn. This same process was repeated over and over again in almost infinite ways, allowing colonial housewives to obtain needed goods and services without owning all of the necessary production equipment or having access to cash.

Some women worked outside the home. Early on women farmed with their husbands, although the practice began to wane during the transition period. Women also often helped their shopkeeper husbands. Shops, taverns, and inns were often operated out of a home but perhaps in a separate room. Some of these businesses were gendered as well. Tailors were almost always men, while milliners and seamstresses were female. Women also might market surplus household products and services such as eggs, chickens, garden produce and herbs, knitting, spinning, sewing, or laundering. Acting as midwives and delivering babies was an essential and well-respected way for women to earn wages and be of service to their communities.

Some women worked for wages, which came nowhere near the same rate of pay as that of men. Female work consisted of household-type tasks such as spinning, knitting, and animal husbandry, but they were also employed in agricultural tasks such as hoeing, weeding, harvesting crops, and husking corn.

By the 1720s some enslaved women worked in plantation homes as cooks and maids, but the overwhelming majority of female slaves worked alongside enslaved men in the fields.

Legal and Political Power

Formal political power was practically a nonexistent commodity for women in the colonial period. The hierarchical, paternalistic environment of colonial America subsumed a woman's political power within that of her husband. In very few cases were women allowed to vote; with the family operating as a unit, the husband was considered to be casting the vote for himself as well as his wife.

Legal rights varied considerably from colony to colony and followed a trajectory of change that coincided with the transitions taking place in society as a whole. During the initial settlement period, the New England Colonies adhered to the civil and ecclesiastical model of jurisprudence, meaning that legal matters came before a court consisting of church leaders. The most common offenses concerned slander, fornication, and occasionally witchcraft. The 1638 blasphemy conviction of Anne Hutchinson proved the dedication of the Massachusetts Bay Colony to a uniform religious doctrine.

Female property ownership rights also varied widely from colony to colony. Generally, intestacy laws favored the eldest son over the mother and other siblings, while men exercised patriarchal control over family landholdings. Larger portions of estates usually went to the sons of the family, primarily because male siblings customarily received real property, while daughters received movable goods such as furniture, household goods, and sometimes livestock. This gendered division of property reinforced patriarchal ideals; men needed a home base in order to support a future family, while women were considered travelers from their father's homes to that of their husband's home. Widows usually received one-third of the estate as a dower right, which granted her the use, if not the ownership, of the family property. Widows were the most likely to own property outright and sometimes possessed the legal right to enter into contracts, unlike married women. The Dutch societies of New Amsterdam (later New York) adhered to a legal philosophy of marriage and property ownership that considered both the husband and the wife as equal partners, a status that diverged significantly from the English system.

The increase in the populace's general affluence that occurred after 1690 required some legal adjustment. Some courts recognized that women could have a personal estate, although they did not necessarily retain direct control of it. Other jurisdictions gave women a limited voice in land sale decisions. These changes led to increased freedoms, such as challenges to insufficient dower rights and the wrangling of sole control of their own estate or the equal sharing of responsibility for an estate held in common with a husband.

In a society where wives were highly valued, a young wealthy widow presented a tempting target for a single man in search of a suitable spouse. A husband could protect his property from a new husband who would become the owner and controller of the legacy once he married the widow by transferring property as either a fee simple or a life estate while he was still alive. These legal maneuvers kept the property safe for any children, as it would revert to them at the death of their mother regardless of her marital status. By the end of the transition period in the mid-1700s, large interlocking family networks were in place in the Chesapeake as well as some other areas, with Virginia possessing the most prominent of all.

Native Americans and African Americans interacted in varying degrees with colonists, often bringing with them cultural assumptions in direct opposition to the dominant culture. Native American gendered division of labor, for instance, contrasted sharply with English ideas of what was proper. In Indian cultures, women performed the agricultural tasks and men hunted. To colonists who considered most agriculture men's work and hunting often a leisure pursuit, Native American women appeared abused and overworked, while their men seemed lazy. Many Native American cultures were matrilineal in structure as well, a tradition that stood in direct opposition to Euro-American patriarchal society.

The first Africans are believed to have arrived in the colonies in 1619, and most historians agree that this initial group was treated as indentured servants, not slaves for life. As such, they would have had the same legal rights as the large number of white colonists. Indentured servants paid for their trip to the New World by selling the next five to seven years of their lives in servitude. There seems to have been very little social separation between black and white indentured servants in these early years, as numerous accounts exist of servants running away together, living together, and beginning families together. As the presence of Africans in the colonies increased and the availability of indentured servants began to dry up, distinctions between black and white servants appeared, with laws covering blacks becoming far harsher than those for whites. Eventually, slavery for life became the norm for African Americans in colonial America.

In the French and Spanish areas of North America, particularly in the Gulf Coast region, laws governing black individuals were often less harsh than in the British colonies. French and Spanish cultural ideology and race theory, while still resting firmly on the idea of patriarchy, contained a more malleable concept of race relations. During the period of French colonization of Louisiana, white women were scarcer than black women. Many of the French soldiers and administrators who were sent to Louisiana during this time formed long-term committed relationships with enslaved women of color. They often freed these women and their offspring and named them in their wills. While mixed relationships occurred in the British colonies as well, they appeared sooner and in much greater numbers in Louisiana and other Gulf Coast areas, resulting in the earliest and most affluent communities of free people of color on the continent.

Native American women and women of African descent could be enslaved or free and performed the same domestic, agricultural, and market-based chores as white women. Historically, African women dominated the marketplaces in their homeland, and they did the same in the marketplaces of some colonial cities. Their lives moved through the same cycles of work, marriage (or marriage-like) relationships, childbirth, and child rearing, with less fanfare and more difficulty than the average white woman of the time.

Immigration and Migration

The migration period of 1620–1660 and the transition (or middle) period of 1660–1750 had strong implications for women in colonial America. In the earliest period women came to the colonies in much smaller numbers than men. Some societies, such as the Puritans of New England and the Germans who populated the lower reaches of the Mississippi River during the French colonization of Louisiana, were more likely to come in family groups than other early immigrant groups. Considerably more women immigrated, either voluntarily or as slaves, in the transition period. The English represented the majority of immigrants in most North American seaboard colonies, followed by Germans and Scotch-Irish. Women who came to the colonies often arrived as indentured servants.

The earliest African women brought to British America came as indentured servants, but later they would be transported as slaves. While male Africans outnumbered women, by the 1700s male and female Africans experienced forced migration at about the same rates. Female slaves in the colonial period faced all the challenges and abuses that male slaves faced but were also victims of sexual violence. Most African women were enslaved and most slaves worked in agriculture, though small numbers of female slaves worked as domestics or cooks or in other domestic jobs.

The immigration of French women to colonial Louisiana ranged from Ursuline nuns to female criminals and prostitutes. The lack of marriageable women prompted the Crown to send a shipment of suitable women who became known as "casket girls" because of the small boxes of personal belongings they carried with them to the New World.

While Spain maintained colonies in North America, Spanish women arrived in much smaller numbers than did female immigrants to other areas of colonization, making Spanish men more likely to marry and reproduce with indigenous women.

Courtship, Marriage, and Divorce

Most colonial couples probably met during the course of their work or limited leisure time, at church, or through some orchestrated meeting. Age of marriage was approximately the early 20s for men and slightly younger for women; one limiting factor may have been the ability of a young husband to provide a home for his new wife. Once the couple had expressed their desire to marry and had obtained permission from their parents, they entered a betrothal period that firmly illustrated their intent to marry. This status placed the couple squarely between being single and married and carried with it its own specific set of legal and social obligations. However, a formal betrothal required fulfillment just as any other legal agreement did. Once betrothed, the issue of premarital intercourse became less fraught with social condemnation than it would have otherwise been.

Sexual intercourse outside of marriage was frowned upon and prosecuted as a legal offense. However, promiscuity carried a greater social burden than fornication between betrothed couples. The only proof of fornication outside of a third-party witness, however, was the birth of a child less than nine months

Though Puritans had held to strict gender roles, they were surprisingly tolerant with courting people. Couples were allowed private time together on the principle that if the woman became pregnant the couple would marry and all would be right in the sight of both the community and God. (Library of Congress)

after the wedding. This was not terribly unusual, given the socially modified status of betrothed couples. Rates of premarital pregnancies increased over the colonial period, from single digits in the early to mid-1600s to around 20 percent by the middle of the 18th century (Godbeer 2004, 10).

Following the betrothal came a period in which the banns, or announcement, of the intended marriage were posted. This process was intended to prevent unlawful marriages and to set the earliest date on which a couple could be married. Dowry negotiations were common, and the wedding—considered a civil affair and not a sacrament in Puritan societies—was usually held in the bride's home (Demos 1970, 152–164).

Variations in the way society developed—and subsequently in the way women experienced their daily lives—depended on the strength of this religious/hierarchical structure and the economic status of the colony. In both cases, however, life in the colonies differed significantly from life in England for women in terms of marriage age, widowhood, and daily labor pursuits; these were a few of the ways in which colonial women adapted to life in the colonies. In England, women tended to marry later and experience longer widowhood than women in the colonies. The value of the colonial goodwife, along with all the labor she represented, and the scarcity of women in geographic areas such as the Chesapeake meant that colonial women generally married younger and more frequently and were widowed later than women in England, all in the name of maintaining women's unwaged domestic work.

Colonial societies expected married couples to live together peacefully and productively. For this reason, communities and their magistrates paid close attention to the behavior of families, became involved in the reconciliation of marriage, and attempted to resolve problems short of divorce if at all possible. Divorce as we understand it today was a legal option in some places and not in others; sometimes the court allowed only a separation of bed and board, not a complete dissolution of the marriage with the opportunity for remarriage. Family turmoil, abandonment, and cruel punishment of a marriage partner were reasons for which divorce was allowed, as were infidelity and impotence; all of these represented potential sources of conflict or lack of fulfillment of the duties of marriage, both conditions that threatened the stability of the community as a whole. The issue of divorce was one part of the law always in flux and changed to reflect the changing realities of the colonial period.

Fertility and Fertility Control

The most important and highly respected function of the colonial woman was her role as a mother. The presence of many children in a household not only reflected well on her ability to adhere to the cultural standard of the life-giving mother but also created additional hands with which to make household work more manageable. In this regard, a woman's ability to bear children and raise them into strong adults was a primary goal and responsibility.

The issues of fertility and fecundity are closely related to the subject of childbirth and child rearing, as the spacing of births in the colonial household depended in many respects on the issue of breast-feeding and the beliefs and traditions surrounding them. Likewise, changes in birth patterns over time reflect changing attitudes regarding how long infants should remain at the breast. Given the desire for numerous children, few families intentionally practiced the most common methods of contraception, abstinence, and prolonged breast-feeding specifically to prevent additional births. These tactics were utilized primarily for the benefit of the infant.

Beliefs regarding issues such as breast-feeding and sexual abstinence during that period, although sometimes not firmly rooted in scientific understanding, focused foremost on what was in the best interest of the child. During the earliest periods of colonization, most women nursed their infants until they were between the age of one and two years, or until a full set of teeth appeared. More affluent women might hire a wet nurse or assign that job to an enslaved woman. In both cases, the issue of abstinence enters the equation, as the belief that sexual intercourse during this time would have a detrimental effect on the mother's ability to produce optimum-quality milk. Clearly, both of these circumstances contributed to spacing of births, which depended on the point at which the mother ceased nursing her child. As the 18th century approached, the age of weaning shortened dramatically to between 8 and 10 months, a change that may be related in some ways to the advent of the transition period, with its attendant social and economic changes.

Childbirth and Child Rearing

Childbirth was a social occasion for colonial women. Early labor, called "lying in," was accompanied by the presence of a midwife and/or a collection of friends and servants or slaves. The episode began as a party with the expectant mother as hostess, with the mood changing as labor began in earnest. Sometimes a birthing chair was used, and sometimes delivery occurred in a bed, often accompanied by linens reserved especially for that purpose.

The serious nature of childbirth is illustrated by stillbirth and infant mortality rates of the period. Of the three babies born to the three pregnant women on the *Mayflower*, one was stillborn, one lived less than a year, and one lived into his 80s; the mother of the stillborn infant died in childbirth. Between 1 and 1.5 percent of births ended in the death of the mother, while 10 to 30 percent of children died before the age of 5.

Religion played a significant part in the lives of colonial women, and as in other areas, differences existed between the North and the South where religion was concerned. In societies where people must make a choice in their religious affiliation, there is great interest in the spiritual upbringing of children. The early settlers of New England were Puritans who, in the words of John Winthrop of the Massachusetts Bay Colony, created governments "both civil and ecclesiastical," meaning that the church and the state were run by the same leaders. The Middle Colonies contained significant numbers of Quakers, while other denominations began to proliferate in both regions following the decline of Puritanism in the mid-17th century. Both Puritans and Quakers were obsessed with proper child rearing but in completely different ways; while Puritans were concerned with teaching their children the harsh realities of the world, Quakers were much more nurturing in their approach. However, both methods produced the child-oriented families typical of strongly religious societies.

Fathers took charge of directing the process of religious education within the home by their selection of literature and leading daily prayers, while mothers were in charge of implementing the father's plan. Indeed, mothers were in charge of all aspects of their children's education until the age of seven or eight, at which time children became the educational charges of their same-gender parent; fathers took over the education of their sons, and mothers continued the education of their daughters. It is important to remember, however, that the early moral education of all the children in the household was the responsibility of the mother.

Religion extended into the education of women and enhanced female literacy, since in order to properly carry out these duties, a colonial woman needed to be able to read the Bible. This became more important in the religion-centered New England and Middle Colonies than it was in the more economically driven Chesapeake and South, resulting in higher literacy rates in the former colonies.

Violence, Domestic and Sexual

Cultural ideologies about family in colonial America rested heavily upon the idea of a strict patriarchal and hierarchical society. For this reason, the domestic environment involved a complicated web of relationships ripe for conflict. While individuals often mistreated one another, many instances of domestic and sexual violence were not treated as crimes, in great part because the legal principle of coverture made wives the property of their husbands.

Nevertheless, such incidents were regularly identified and adjudicated by colonial courts, in part because Puritan society considered the family a "little commonwealth" that either threatened or strengthened the stability of the larger commonwealth. Therefore, the entire community had a stake in ensuring that families ran as smoothly as possible; neighbors and friends willingly reported domestic violence with little fear of social repercussion. A study of Plymouth Colony reveals that while rape and murder were both offenses that carried the death sentence, execution was virtually nonexistent. Instead, it appears that the courts imposed lesser sentences designed to maintain the harmony of the community. Violence by a master against his servant was often resolved by removing the servant from the household, either permanently or for a designated period of time. In these cases, the servant was usually placed with another family in the community, and the defendant was fined.

Husbands abused their spouses more frequently than did wives, although cases of husband abuse did occur. Resolution of abuse cases depended on the severity of the abuse. Sentences ranged from a judge's admonitions to the levying of small fines to the separation of bed and board, sometimes called a bed-and-board divorce.

Sexual abuses, including rape, were less commonly reported than domestic violence but still existed in colonial America. These cases were also handled with punishments such as fines and whipping, though the status of the victim and/or the perpetrator greatly affected the outcome of cases.

Fashion and Clothing

The early colonial period experienced limited economic participation and, as a result, limited shipments of imported goods. Not until the British mercantile system began to operate in the transition period of 1660–1750 did colonial women have access to a broad range of ready-made materials suitable for the production of fashion clothing. Prior to the mid-1600s, most components of wearable items such as textiles and leather goods would have been produced at home. Given the myriad tasks for which the colonial housewife was responsible, an extensive wardrobe was not common. As a broader array of wearable goods became more readily available, a woman's manner of dress became a clear indication of social status.

Clothing for women was modular, and the various components worn were chosen according to the social and economic status of the wearer. The first layer for all women was the shift, a loose garment usually made of white linen that functioned as a combination undergarment, blouse, and nightgown. Stockings came next. Women of yeoman status or above wore stays or corsets to give the body the proper shape and to provide support to the breasts and back. Petticoats, which resembled drawstring waist skirts, could be added in layers depending on the temperature and covered by a gown (dress) or an overpetticoat (skirt). Additional clothing options for women included a short gown (blouse), a stomacher (a dickey-like piece made to cover the front of the torso), and numerous variations of jackets. Hats, head scarves, neck scarves, buckled or laced shoes, and pockets (tie-on pockets used as a purse) completed the outfit. Maternity wear consisted of the same pieces of clothing, loosened in appropriate areas by way of existing drawstrings or laces.

The style, component parts, and materials from which garments were made indicated one's status. For example, a field slave might never wear stockings at all, while the most affluent women would only wear silk stockings; middling women would likely wear stockings made of cotton. Head coverings, textiles,

and parts of dress all combined to transmit social station and level of affluence.

Lee Davis Smith

Further Reading

Berkin, Carol. 1996. *First Generations: Women in Colonial America*. New York: Hill and Wang.

Demos, John. 1970. *A Little Commonwealth: Family Life in Plymouth Colony*. New York: Oxford University Press.

Godbeer, Richard. 2004. "Courtship and Sexual Freedom in Eighteenth-Century America." *OAH Magazine of History* 18: 9–13.

Hawke, David Freeman. 1989. *Everyday Life in Early America*. New York: Harper and Row.

Hofstadter, Richard. 1973. *America at 1750: A Social Portrait*. New York: Random House.

Main, Gloria L. 2006. "Rocking the Cradle: Downsizing the New England Family." *Journal of Interdisciplinary History* 37: 35–58.

Morgan, Edmund S. 1966. *The Puritan Family: Religion and Domestic Relations in Seventeenth Century New England*. New York: HarperCollins.

Norton, Mary Beth. 1984. "The Evolution of White Women's Experience in Early America." *American Historical Review* 89: 593–619.

Salmon, Marylynn. 1994. "The Cultural Significance of Breastfeeding and Infant Care in Early Modern England and America." *Journal of Social History* 28: 247–269.

Snyder, Terri L. 2012. "Marriage on the Margins: Free Wives, Enslaved Husbands, and the Law in Early Virginia." *Law and History Review* 30: 141–171.

Ulrich, Laurel Thatcher. 1980. "'A Friendly Neighbor': Social Dimensions of Daily Work in Northern Colonial New England." *Feminist Studies* 6: 392–405.

BIBLIOGRAPHY

Adams, Catherine, and Elizabeth H. Pleck. 2009. *Love of Freedom: Black Women in Colonial and Revolutionary New England*. New York: Oxford University Press.

Bacon, Margaret Hope, ed. 1994. *'Wilt Thou Go on My Errand?': Journals of Three 18th Century*

Quaker Women Ministers. Wallingford, PA: Pendle Hill Publications.

Battis, Emery. 1962. *Saints and Sectaries: Anne Hutchinson and the Antinomian Controversy of the Massachusetts Bay Colony.* Chapel Hill: University of North Carolina Press.

Bernhardt, Marie Frances. 1925. *Mistress Margaret Brent.* Richmond, VA: Catholic Women's Club.

Bodie, Idella. 1990. *South Carolina Women.* Orangeburg, SC: Sandlapper.

Bonomi, Patricia U. 2003. *Under the Cope of Heaven: Religion, Society, and Politics in Colonial America.* New York: Oxford University Press.

Bradstreet, Anne. 1981. *The Complete Works of Anne Bradstreet.* Edited by Joseph R. McElrath and Allan P. Robb. Boston: Twayne Publishers.

Breen, T. H., and Stephen Innes. 1980. *Myne Owne Ground: Race and Freedom on Virginia's Eastern Shore, 1640–1676.* Oxford: Oxford University Press.

Brekus, Catherine. 2007. *The Religious History of American Women: Reimagining the Past.* Chapel Hill: University of North Carolina.

Bremer, Francis J. 2012. *First Founders: American Puritans and Puritanism in an Atlantic World.* Lebanon: University of New Hampshire Press.

Bremer, Francis J., ed. 2003. *Anne Hutchinson, Troubler of the Puritan Zion.* New York: Krieger Publishing.

Chipman, Donald E., and Harriett Denise Joseph. 1999. *Notable Men and Women in Spanish Texas.* Austin: University of Texas Press.

Cholonec, Fr. Pierre. 2012. *Kateri Tekawkitha, the Iroquois Saint.* Merchantville, NJ: ARX Publishing.

Clark, Emily. 2007. *Masterless Mistresses: The New Orleans Ursulines and the Establishment of a New World Society, 1727–1834.* Chapel Hill: University of North Carolina Press.

Clark, Emily. 2013. *The Strange History of the American Quadroon: Free Women of Color in the Revolutionary Atlantic World.* Chapel Hill: University of North Carolina Press.

Cooper, Victor H. 1995. *A Dangerous Woman: New York's First Lady Liberty; The Life and Times of Lady Deborah Moody: Her Search for Freedom of Religion in Colonial America.* Bowie, MD: Heritage Books.

Cott, Nancy F. 1977. *Bonds of Womanhood: Woman's Sphere in New England, 1780–1835.* New Haven, CT: Yale University Press.

Cotton, Sallie Southall. 2010. *The White Doe: The Fate of Virginia Dare.* New York: FQ Books.

Cremin, Lawrence. 1970. *American Education: The Colonial Experience, 1607–1783.* New York: Harper and Row.

Curry, Leonard P. 1986. *The Free Black in Urban America, 1800–1850: The Shadow of a Dream.* Chicago: University of Chicago Press.

del Mar, David Peterson. 2011. *The American Family: From Obligation to Freedom.* New York: Palgrave Macmillan.

Demos, John. 1982. *Entertaining Satan: Witchcraft and Culture in New England.* New York: Oxford University Press.

Demos, John. 1995. *The Unredeemed Captive: A Family Story from Early America.* New York: Vintage.

Derounian-Stodola, Kathryn, and James Levernier. 1993. *The Indian Captivity Narrative, 1550–1900.* Twayne's United States Authors Series. New York: Macmillan.

Derounian-Stodola, Kathryn Zabelle, ed. 1998. *Women's Indian Captivity Narratives.* New York: Penguin Classics.

Dolan, Frances E. 2008. *Marriage and Violence: The Early Modern Legacy.* Philadelphia: University of Pennsylvania Press.

Drimmer, Frederick, ed. 1961. *Captured by the Indians: 15 Firsthand Accounts, 1750–1870.* New York: Dover.

Fontenot, Wonda L. 1994. *Secret Doctors: Ethnomedicine of African Americans.* Westport, CT: Bergin and Garvey.

Foulds, Diane E. 2010. *Death in Salem: The Private Lives behind the 1692 Witch Hunt.* Guilford, CT: Globe Pequot.

Gilfoyle, Timothy J. 1992. *City of Eros: New York City, Prostitution, and the Commercialization of Sex, 1790–1920.* New York: Norton.

Hall, David D. 1989. *Worlds of Wonder, Days of Judgment: Popular Religious Belief in Early New England.* New York: Knopf.

Hall, David D. 1991. *Witch-Hunting in Seventeenth-Century New England.* Boston: Northeastern University Press.

Hall, Timothy D. 1994. *Contested Boundaries: Itinerancy and the Reshaping of the Colonial American Religious World.* Durham, NC: Duke University Press.

Hemphill, C. Dollett. 1999. *Bowing to Necessities: A History of Manners in America, 1620–1860.* New York: Oxford University Press.

Horn, James. 2010. *A Kingdom Strange: The Brief and Tragic History of the Lost Colony of Roanoke.* New York: Basic Books.

Hudson, Marjorie. 2007. *Searching for Virginia Dare.* Winston-Salem, NC: Press 53 Books.

Juster, Susan. 1994. *Disorderly Women: Sexual Politics and Evangelicalism in Revolutionary New England.* Ithaca, NY: Cornell University Press.

Karlsen, Carol F. 1998. *The Devil in the Shape of a Woman: Witchcraft in Colonial New England.* New York and London: Norton.

Kelso, William. 2006. *Jamestown: The Buried Truth.* Charlottesville: University of Virginia, 2006.

Kenneally, James J. 1990. *The History of American Catholic Women.* New York: Crossroad.

Kessell, John L. 2002. *Spain in the Southwest: A Narrative History of Colonial New Mexico, Arizona, Texas, and California.* Norman: University of Oklahoma Press.

Kidd, Thomas S. 2007. *The Great Awakening: The Roots of Evangelical Christianity in Colonial America.* New Haven, CT: Yale University Press.

Knight, Sarah Kemble. 1972. *The Journal of Madam Knight.* Boston: D. R. Godine.

Lambert, Frank. 1999. *Inventing the "Great Awakening."* Princeton, NJ: Princeton University Press.

Land, Aubrey C. 1981. *Colonial Maryland: A History.* Millwood, NY: KTO Press.

LaPlante, Eve. 2004. *American Jezebel: The Uncommon Life of Anne Hutchinson, the Woman Who Defied the Puritans.* New York: HarperCollins.

Lasch, Christopher. 1997. *Women and the Common Life: Love, Marriage, and Feminism.* New York: Norton.

Lawton, Wendy. 2003. *Almost Home: A Story Based on the Life of the Mayflower's Mary Chilton.* Chicago: Moody Publishers.

Leavitt, Judith Walzer, ed. *Women and Health in America.* Madison: University of Wisconsin Press, 1999.

Mays, Dorothy A. 2004. *Women in Early America: Struggle, Survival, and Freedom in a New World.* Santa Barbara, CA: ABC-CLIO.

Middleton, Margaret Simons. 1966. *Henrietta Johnston of Charles Town, South Carolina, America's First Pastellist.* Columbia: University of South Carolina Press.

Monaghan, E. J. 2005. *Learning to Read and Write in Colonial America.* Boston: University of Massachusetts Press.

Morgan, Edmund S. 2003. *American Slavery, American Freedom: The Ordeal of Colonial Virginia.* New York: Norton.

Morison, Samuel M. 1991. *William Bradford, of Plymouth Plantation, 1620–1647.* New York: Knopf.

Myles, Anne G. 2001. "From Monster to Martyr: Re-Presenting Mary Dyer." *Early American Literature* 36: 1–30.

Namias, June. 1993. *White Captives: Gender and Ethnicity on the American Frontier.* Chapel Hill: University of North Carolina Press.

Norton, Mary Beth. 1996. *Founding Mothers and Fathers: Gendered Power and the Forming of American Society.* New York: Knopf.

Norton, Mary Beth. 2002. *In the Devil's Snare.* New York: Knopf.

Perlmann, Joel, and Robert Margo. 2001. *Women's Work? American Schoolteachers, 1650–1920.* Chicago: University of Chicago Press.

Perry, Lee Davis. 2009. *More Than Petticoats: Remarkable South Carolina Women.* Guilford, CT: Globe Pequot.

Philbrick, Nathaniel. 2006. *Mayflower.* New York: Penguin Group.

Plane, Ann Marie. 2000. *Colonial Intimacies: Indian Marriage in Early New England.* Ithaca, NY: Cornell University Press.

Plimpton, Ruth. 1994. *Mary Dyer: Biography of a Rebel Quaker.* Boston: Branden Publishing.

Roach, Marilynne K. 2013. *Six Women of Salem: The Untold Story of the Accused and Their Accusers in the Salem Witch Trials.* New York: Da Capo.

Roop, Connie, and Peter Roop. 2000. *The Diary of Mary Jemison: Captured by the Indians (In My*

Own Words). New York: Cavendish Square Publishing.

Rosenthal, Bernard, ed. 2009. *Records of the Salem Witch-Hunt.* New York: Cambridge University Press.

Salmon, Marylynn. 1989. *Women and the Law of Property in Early America.* Chapel Hill: University of North Carolina Press.

Schafer, Judith Kelleher. 2009. *Brothels, Depravity, and Abandoned Women: Illegal Sex in Antebellum New Orleans.* Baton Rouge: Louisiana State University Press.

Seaver, James E. 2001 [1877]. *The Life of Mary Jemison: The White Woman of the Genesee.* Scituate, MA: Digital Scanning.

Stone, Lawrence. 1977. *The Family, Sex and Marriage in England, 1500–1800.* New York: Harper and Row.

Strong, Paula Turner. 1999. *Captive Selves, Captivating Others: The Politics and Poetics of Colonial American Captivity Narratives.* Boulder, CO: Westview/Perseus Books.

Stuntz, Jean A. 2005. *Hers, His, & Theirs: Community and Property Law in Spain and Early Texas.* Lubbock: Texas Tech University Press.

Tannenbaum, Rebecca J. 2002. *The Healer's Calling: Women and Medicine in Early New England.* Ithaca, NY: Cornell University Press.

Taylor, Alan. 2001. *American Colonies: The Settling of North America.* New York: Penguin.

Thacher, James. 1991 [1835]. *History of the Town of Plymouth: From Its First Settlement in 1620, to the Year 1832.* Salem, MA: Higginson.

Ulrich, Laurel Thatcher. 1991. *Good Wives: Image and Reality in the Lives of Women in Northern New England, 1650–1750.* New York: Vintage Books.

Van Deusen, N. 2012. "The Intimacies of Bondage; Female Indigenous Servants and Slaves and Their Spanish Masters, 1492–1555." *Journal of Women's History* 24(1): 13–43.

Webber, Thomas. 1978. *Deep Like Rivers: Education in the Slave Quarter Community, 1831–1865.* New York: Norton.

Weber, David J. 1992. *The Spanish Frontier in North America.* New Haven, CT: Yale University Press.

Wertz, Richard W., and Dorothy C. Wertz. 1989. *Lying-In: A History of Childbirth in America.* New Haven, CT: Yale University Press.

White, Deborah Gray. 1999. *Ar'n't I a Woman: Female Slaves in the Plantation South.* New York: Norton.

Whiteaker, Larry. 1997. *Seduction, Prostitution, and Moral Reform in New York, 1830–1860.* New York: Garland Publishing.

Wood, Betty. 2005. *Slavery in Colonial America, 1619–1776.* Lanham, MD: Rowman and Littlefield.

Wood, Peter H. 2003. *Strange New Land: Africans in Colonial America.* New York: Oxford University Press.

3. Revolutionary America and the New Republic (1754–1819)

HISTORICAL OVERVIEW

From 1754 to 1819, the British North American colonies experienced changes that would result in the birth of a new nation and the early formation of the U.S. national identity. Profound political, social, cultural, and economic adjustments occurred during these six decades. While the world of this period was decidedly a masculine one, women played critical and sometimes surprising roles in the move toward independence and beyond. The ideologies that brought about the American Revolution influenced women's lives and the ways in which society viewed their purpose. Although beliefs surrounding women's function and activities evolved slowly and subtly, the effects of those changes were central in terms of their meaning for American society both in the Revolutionary and New Republic eras. The lives of women during this period were circumscribed by cultural ideas that tied them almost inextricably to their homes and families and in many ways depended on their socioeconomic and freedom status. However, women of the Revolutionary period—contrary to cultural norms governing gender, race, and status—often stepped outside their comfort zones and participated in the war as protesters, soldiers, spies, and camp followers. They impacted the economy and promoted the revolutionary cause by boycotting imported British goods and producing home manufactures to take their place. Following the American Revolutionary War, women of the New Republic became better educated and used their newly acquired political and ideological knowledge to more effectively teach their children to become productive American citizens. While it is difficult to gauge the degree to which this new ideology could be implemented

by women of the lower social classes, including servants and slaves, they no doubt were aware of the changes taking place in American society. While Native American women may have looked at this movement toward a new nation as a deeper threat, enslaved women likely hoped that it would lead to new opportunities for emancipation and an end to slavery.

The American Revolution was not only the revolution of American colonists against British rule but was also a cultural revolution that began decades before the first shots were fired at Lexington and Concord. In a letter to his friend Hezekiah Niles dated February 13, 1818, John Adams conveyed these dual meanings: "But what do we mean by the American Revolution? Do we mean the American war? The Revolution was effected before the war commenced. The Revolution was in the minds and hearts of the people. . . . This radical change in the principles, opinions, sentiments, and affections of the people, was the real American Revolution" (Adams 1856, 282). Adams's words testify to the understanding that it was more than political and economic disagreement that caused the American Revolution; a revolution in the cultural assumptions of American colonists was necessary before the revolution could occur. It was the change in the American way of thinking that Adams identified as "the real American Revolution." Adams's words referred to the gradual shaking off of hierarchical society, the rejection of monarchy and its related corruption, and a growing understanding that the American colonies could and should take care of themselves. This observation applied to society as a whole while women of this era remained subject to the hierarchical arrangement of the family; dependence on their husbands, fathers, or masters; and absolute masculine rule of their

During the American Revolution women worked as nurses, cooks, soldiers, spies, and more. Women made particularly effective spies and military intelligence gatherers during both the Revolutionary and Civil Wars. (Bettmann/Getty)

households and their government. The ways in which women's roles were fit into this equation do not reveal a lack of value for women of the period, however. Instead, they expose the critical nature of the tasks they performed.

The rumblings that would eventually lead to American independence began as early as the beginning of the French and Indian War (1754–1763) in North America, part of the Seven Years' War (1756–1763) in Europe. Both of these related conflicts involved the struggle for empire among the world's great powers. As the name suggests, the French and Indian War was fought between the British and French with help from Native Americans. American colonists, who considered themselves British as they were, in fact, primarily of British descent and a part of the British Empire, contributed both men and material fighting the French and Indian War alongside British regular troops. This familiarity, however, bred contempt that would be partially responsible for the American Revolution. Following the end of the war, standing troops remained in the colonies as a protective force, and it was tension with British soldiers stationed in Boston that was primarily responsible for the Boston Massacre of 1770.

The French and Indian War ended in 1763 with the first Treaty of Paris (a second Treaty of Paris, which was signed in 1783, ended the American Revolutionary War). King George III of England and his economic advisers now found themselves faced with the dilemma of how to pay for the costs of war. British citizens were already taxed to their limit, and visitors to the colonies had carried reports to England describing the apparent prosperity of American colonists. Colonists also enjoyed much lower taxes than British citizens, which encouraged legislators in the home country to view the colonies as a potential source of income.

The efforts of British legislators and administrators to resolve England's financial problems gave rise to legislation designed to regulate trade and ameliorate some economic issues. However, disagreement soon arose regarding the right of the Crown to tax for revenue purposes and not simply in order to regulate trade. Colonial responses to these perceived threats to liberty resulted in further retaliatory legislation, notably the Coercive Acts (known as the Intolerable Acts in the colonies) that, among other provisions, closed the port of Boston following the Boston Tea Party. While legislative efforts to control colonial dissent continued in England, revolutionary rhetoric continued to escalate in the colonies. Public interest in politics began to spread to all sectors of society, not just the governing class. The move toward independence from England went hand in hand with the idea of individual independence, as articulated in the concept of republicanism. Republican ideology advocated a society of landowning individuals who were free from

dependence on others and exercised civic virtue, or the willingness to place the good of society ahead of one's own interests. The message of the Enlightenment (an intellectual movement that placed emphasis on reason, science, and natural rights) encouraged colonists to press for independence. This initiative was slow to build, but the 1776 publication of *Common Sense* by Thomas Paine (1737–1809) articulated the argument for independence so clearly that it is largely credited for the change in hearts and minds that pushed colonists into agreement on the issue.

Both ideological and political changes during the period of the American Revolution and the early republic affected women in numerous and profound ways. During the earlier years of American colonization, ideological changes had occurred as a result of demographic and environmental factors. Now the shift in attitudes and behaviors would result from conscious efforts related to revolutionary rhetoric and later because of the needs of the new nation. As broad, public, and intentional as the majority of most changes were, the revolution that occurred among American women of the period nevertheless had to fit into a more circumscribed lifestyle considered appropriate for their status. As it had been in the colonial period, this was a world in which a woman's importance was inextricably attached to that of her husband. Her family was her primary concern, her home was her locus of power, and her sharing of responsibilities with her husband depended on the understanding that both had critical roles to play. Hers was private and subservient, while his was public and hegemonic. Still, many women of the Revolutionary and Early Republic eras found ways to impact their society directly while remaining inside the parameters of what was considered proper behavior for ladies of the time. Throughout this process, the cultural expectations of women were refined to reflect the dominant political beliefs of the time and the perceived needs of society. Free white women of all classes considered these changes and, as is true with all social changes, implemented them in ways that best suited their individual lives. As occupiers of the bottom rung in the hierarchical ladder, indentured servants and slaves may have ascribed to these beliefs just as their free sisters did but would have been primarily circumscribed by the conditions determined by their masters' households.

The world of these two eras was distinctly divided between male and female, with a gendered division of expectations, pursuits, and responsibilities for either sex. Men occupied the wider world, participating in business, politics, government, and society in general in an ideological concept known as republicanism. Republicanism carried with it certain requirements. The most important factor was property ownership, which ostensibly made the owner free by allowing him to support his family and live his life without obligations to a benefactor or patron. This idea contrasted sharply with the older feudal system of dependency wherein serfs lived and worked on the property of a large landowner in return for a part of the crop yield. In this arrangement, such dependents were also expected to do whatever the manor lord required of them, including going to battle on his behalf. The feudal arrangement therefore made the serf subject to the will of the landowner for whom he labored, thereby removing his political and economic freedom. Republicans saw this same sort of pattern in the behavior of corrupt politicians, patrons, and clients who operated in a continuous cycle of hegemony and dependency. Property ownership, republicans argued, produced men who were not beholden to anyone and were therefore free to think and act on their own behalf. Civic virtue, or the willingness to work for the good of the community by putting one's own desires behind the needs of the community, comprised another component of republicanism. Public service in the form of participation in government, public works, and other similar pursuits were considered the hallmark of proper civic virtue. Therefore, in the external public world, property-owning men were considered uniquely qualified to make decisions regarding business, government, and all other important matters.

How, then, did women fit into this equation? The proper place of women was in their homes, operating their domain in ways that would enhance their husbands' ability to accomplish their goals in the public world. Women's lives were decidedly private in scope. Coverture laws expressly reinforced this idea; women brought movable property into their marriages, property that was subsequently merged with the real property owned by her husband and therefore "covered" by him. This apparent lack of landownership coupled with the private domain in which she operated during this period rendered her effectively ineligible to be considered a republican except as an extension of her husband. Therefore, a woman's participation in the world outside her home and family was inextricably linked to that of her husband.

Women could and did make a difference in nontraditional ways, however. During the American Revolution in particular, many women of all stations in life used their stereotypical image of weakness and indifference to political matters in order to breach enemy lines as spies, transmit information, and even rescue prisoners of war. Some women worked within more traditional boundaries as the overseers of their households. Boycotting movements represent one important example of women's impact outside the home while remaining within their domestic sphere. Indeed, boycotting was one of the most effective strategies utilized by both men and women in efforts to gain the attention of the British Parliament, the governing body in charge of making laws for all parts of the British Empire. By refusing to purchase manufactured goods, colonists who launched effective boycotts managed to strike at the financial soft spot in the British mercantile system that prohibited American colonists from purchasing finished goods from other countries. As the persons primarily responsible for the purchase of household goods, Revolutionary-era women were in a prime position to make such boycotts work effectively. Additionally, it was women's spinning, sewing, and other household manufactures that took the place of imported goods, thereby strengthening their role in the protest. Stepping outside their traditionally private world, Revolutionary-era women formed associations of their own and signed nonconsumption agreements just as their men did. This is one area in which subservient women would have participated on a regular basis, regardless of their personal opinions about the conflict.

At the end of the Revolutionary War, Americans wrangled with important issues such as how to fashion the new government and what national identity would emerge. One response to both the uncertainty and the resolve of the nation was the concept of republican motherhood. This concept recognized the critical importance of the proper type of education and moral and political training of mothers in order that they might raise their children to be good American citizens. This was particularly important during the era of the New

Republic when all Americans struggled to understand what sort of nation the new United States would become. This need presented a new conundrum, however. If a woman's place was in the home, a broad education was unnecessary, and politics were out of her sphere of consciousness, how could she fulfill this new role? The answer came in the form of a new value system for women that allowed them more access to the tools of education and political consciousness.

Prior to the late 18th century, education and training of children had been accomplished in a gendered arrangement in which women were responsible for teaching their female children the skills necessary to run a household, while fathers trained their boys in ways that would prepare them for life in the wider world. The republican mother, however, was now considered the touchstone for training of good republican citizens, boys as well as girls. This new dynamic created a double-edged sword for the issue of women's education. The woman's primary purview was still that of her home, but now there was new emphasis placed on proper education in order to allow her to be the most effective republican mother possible. She must be educated enough to raise good little republican children but not so educated that she threatened the stability of her home and family by participating too much in the life of the mind. In the age of the Enlightenment, women were for the most part discouraged from reading the works of writers such as Montesquieu and John Locke. Rather, they were encouraged to concern themselves with literature that reinforced their understanding of moral issues. Religious writing and popular fiction that taught moral lessons were considered the most appropriate form of intellectual activity for women of this age. Heavy political discussions remained the domain of men and boys, but a solid foundation of moral and ideological belief systems prepared girls as well as boys to take their proper places in the new American nation.

Movements such as boycotting and republican motherhood gained their strength from the understanding that women's attachment to their homes and families was a natural state. Women did not gain any particular elevation of their status as a result of the American Revolution, nor did their role change significantly within the home. Still, these two examples prove that women could still have an impact on their wider world while occupying the culturally circumscribed space of the household.

The era of the American Revolution was arguably the most transformational in American history. At no time since the beginning of the Revolution in the mid-18th century has society experienced such drastic and widespread changes in culture, politics, and government. The ideology formed during this period set the American people on a path that led from their status as the colonial subjects of a British king to that of citizens of the most powerful nation in the world.

This transformation required much philosophical and political wrangling. The American Revolution affected the most obscure members of the "vulgar herd," the most prominent Founding Fathers, and every person between the two extremes. An understanding of the conditions of life in 18th-century colonial America and the structure of society renders a more clear understanding of the arguments for (or against) liberty presented by revolutionary participants. Religion, commerce, race, class, and other factors influenced the path of the revolution.

Even before the Revolutionary War ended, the work of forming a new nation began in earnest. The "American Scripture" of the founding documents not only established the laws and government for the new nation but also reflect the characteristics inherent in the American ethos. The transformation of a population from one that supported a monarchical, hierarchical society composed of people bound by obligation and separated by class and "parts" to one of an egalitarian society of virtuous, self-sufficient republican citizens is one that cannot be underestimated in terms of its importance to the pursuit of liberty for the American colonies. While the "softer sort" was not always front and center in this process, women filled critical positions and participated in initiatives and movements that did have significant impact on the success of the struggle.

Expansion of revolutionary ideas regarding freedom, liberty, equality, and virtue caused changes in the way the culture assessed women's roles in society. However, while the question of how revolutionary thought might affect the lives of slaves, no similar serious discussion regarding the rights of women ever emerged. Feminine roles allowed wives and mothers to expand their natural abilities in order to properly educate and inform their offspring of their responsibilities as good little republican children. To this end, education and some knowledge of the outside world became more important in the lives of women. Nevertheless, Revolutionary-era women negotiated a fine line between having enough education and political understanding in order to be effective republican mothers and having so much knowledge of the outside world that it threatened their femininity and subordinate role in society.

Moving into the early 19th century, ideas of the role of women in society changed again as the country began to form its national identity. At this time the participation of women outside the home as independent businesspeople actually began to constrict, and the meanings of words such as "virtue" began to change in meaning. Just as in the past, men and women were considered to have different purposes, but now those divisions had even stronger ramifications. The meaning of the term "virtue," for example, formerly connoted public virtue, or the practice of putting the needs of the government above one's own. While still important, the term now meant private virtue or personal moral constraint with women considered its primary keepers, a meaning more consistent with today's use of the word. These changes signify the transition of thought that clearly delineated between women's importance in domestic and private matters and men's concerns with politics, the economy, and other public matters.

Lee Davis Smith

Further Reading

Adams, Charles Francis. 1856. *The Works of John Adams, Second President of the United States: With a Life of the Author, Notes, and Illustrations, by His Grandson Charles Francis Adams.* Boston: Little, Brown.

Berkin, Carol. 1996. *First Generations: Women in Colonial America.* New York: Hill and Wang.

Berkin, Carol. 2005. *Revolutionary Mothers: Women in the Struggle for America's Independence.* New York: Vintage Books.

Breen, T. H. 2004. *The Marketplace of Revolution: How Consumer Politics Shaped American Independence.* New York: Oxford University Press.

Godbeer, Richard. 2004. "Courtship and Sexual Freedom in Eighteenth-Century America." *OAH Magazine of History* 18: 9–13.

Kerber, Linda K. 1980. *Women of the Republic: Intellect & Ideology in Revolutionary America.* New York: Norton.

Klepp, Susan E. 1998. "Revolutionary Bodies: Women and the Fertility Transition in the Mid-Atlantic Region, 1760–1820." *Journal of American History* 85: 910–945.

Lewis, Jan, and Kenneth A. Lockridge. 1988. "'Sally Has Been Sick': Pregnancy and Family Limitation among Virginia Gentry Women, 1780–1830." *Journal of Social History* 22: 5–19.

Main, Gloria L. 1994. "Gender, Work, and Wages in Colonial New England." *William and Mary Quarterly* 51: 39–66.

Main, Gloria L. 2006. "Rocking the Cradle: Downsizing the New England Family." *Journal of Interdisciplinary History* 37: 35–58.

Norton, Mary Beth. 1980. *Liberty's Daughters: The Revolutionary Experience of American Women, 1750–1800.* Boston: Little, Brown.

Norton, Mary Beth. 1984. "The Evolution of White Women's Experience in Early America." *American Historical Review* 89: 593–619.

Rothman, Ellen K. 1982. "Sex and Self-Control: Middle-Class Courtship in America, 1770–1870." *Journal of Social History* 15: 409–425.

Wood, Gordon S. 1991. *The Radicalism of the American Revolution.* New York: Vintage Books.

Wood, Gordon S. 1998. *The Creation of the American Republic, 1776–1787.* Chapel Hill: University of North Carolina Press.

Zagarri, Rosemarie. 1998. "The Rights of Men and Women in Post-Revolutionary America." *William and Mary Quarterly* 55: 203–230.

Adams, Abigail (1744–1818)

Gifted letter writer Abigail Adams was the wife of second president John Adams (1735–1826) and the mother of sixth president John Quincy Adams. Her letters provide a window into her life and important issues connected to the early development of the nation. She penned her most famous letter to her husband in 1776 in which she demanded more rights for wives. During the American Revolution and the years after, Adams served as her husband's assistant as she advised him and tended to their household.

Adams was born Abigail Smith on November 22, 1744, in Weymouth, Massachusetts, to Reverend William Smith and Elizabeth Quincy Smith. The clergy was highly regarded in early America, and Adams's father served as the minister of the First Congregational Church in Weymouth. As were most young girls at that time, Adams, one of four children, was educated at home. However, unlike most girls, Adams had access to a large library owned by her father. She had an insatiable curiosity and a sharp mind. In spite of not having a formal education, Adams managed to gain a store of knowledge superior to that of many colonial men and women. She studied history and mathematics, but she loved literature the most. She read books by various English writers including William Shakespeare, Alexander Pope, and James Thompson. She read world history and theology in English, French, Latin, and Greek. In fact, her self-education impressed her future husband, who confessed that he wished he could speak French as well as she did.

In 1764, 19-year-old Abigail Smith married John Adams, a Harvard graduate and promising attorney 10 years older than her. They had four children, Abigail, John Quincy, Charles, and Thomas Boylston, during the first decade of their marriage. Like her father, her husband had a large library, and Adams used it to continue her education during her adult years.

Because John traveled both before and after the Revolution, he and Abigail exchanged more than 1,000 letters throughout their marriage. Her forthright personality and his respect for her resulted in frank exchanges about family life and public politics. Abigail was a talented letter writer, often quoting from classical literature. Letters written during the American Revolutionary era reveal that she had a keen sense for developments on the home front. Taken as a whole, hundreds of letters chronicle the history of the United States from colonial times to the days of the early republic. Most of all, her letters reveal that she had a knack for analyzing important political issues and advising her husband throughout his political career.

First Lady Abigail Adams wrote many letters to her husband John across the long separations they endured during his career in politics. Most famous is her request that when founding their new country the members of the Continental Congress, "remember the ladies, and be more generous and favorable to them than your ancestors." (Bettmann/Getty)

In March 1776, Adams sent her husband the most famous letter she ever wrote, her "Remember the Ladies" letter. In the letter she told her husband that "In the new Code of Laws which I supposed will be necessary for you to make I desire you would Remember the Ladies, and be more generous and favorable to them than your ancestors." She warned that "If particular care and attention is not paid to the Ladies we are determined to foment a Rebellion, and will not hold ourselves bound by any Laws in which we have no voice, or Representation." To this her husband responded that "I cannot but laugh. . . . We know better than to repeal our Masculine systems." Then, in an attempt to appease her, he explained that in his opinion, within marriages men were masters only in "theory" but that wives were the masters in "practice." In spite of her rejected request, it should be noted that Adams never departed from the traditional role within her marriage either before or after she wrote the now-famous letter.

This letter and a handful of others form the basis of what some scholars have interpreted as colonial feminism. Other historians have denied such a claim and assert that the thoughts in the letter must be placed in proper context. During colonial times, a husband had complete legal control over his wife's body and property. Adams was ahead of her time in asking for legal action, which would ensure equality within the marriage relationship. However, she was not leading a public revolution for women. These were private thoughts expressed to her husband in confidence. Nonetheless, she had the ideas and wrote them to her husband. She may also have discussed ideas about female liberty with her family and friends. Certainly, she was not the only American woman in the Revolutionary period to imagine that expanding ideas about liberty might be applied to women.

During the American Revolution, Adams's husband left her at home while he went off to make revolution. Like many women, Adams stayed behind to manage her house and farm. Consulting with her husband whenever she could, she managed household expenses and two house servants. With little help from her husband, she bought and sold livestock and other items, actions usually reserved for men. Dealing with inflation and labor shortages, she managed to keep their investments secure. Whenever the fighting interrupted school, Adams took on the job of educating her children. In this sense, she was the epitome of a republican mother. Besides academic content, she also taught her children values. For example, she instructed her three sons that it was virtuous for men to undergo self-sacrifice in the service of others and their country. In like manner, she taught her daughter to be a good wife who would obey her husband and raise self-sacrificing, service-minded sons.

While the war was raging, revolutionary leaders became convinced that adroit diplomacy was needed to turn the war in their favor. After discussions, representatives chose a handful of men to serve in this important capacity. In 1777 while Adams was looking forward to her husband's homecoming, the Continental Congress appointed him ambassador to Europe along with Benjamin Franklin. John Adams accepted the appointment and departed in early 1778 with his son John Quincy. They went to Europe, visiting England, France, and Holland in search of support for the American Revolution. Separation was hard on the couple. Although she had a great fear of crossing the ocean, Adams set sail for Europe to join her husband and son in 1784. While in Europe, Adams was in charge of two large Adams homes: one in London and another in Paris. Each house had a staff of 8 to 10 servants, which was more than she was used to coordinating, but she managed. The Adams family returned to America in 1788.

After returning from Europe, John was elected the first vice president (1789–1797) and then the second president (1797–1801). During these executive years, Adams was often in poor health. She stayed at home in Quincy most of the time while her husband was away at the capital. They both agreed that the sacrifice of separation was justified because it was for a greater good. This dedication to service, in fact, was the foundation of her legacy as a founding mother.

Unfortunately, the couple's golden years were filled with grief. Their sorrow began in 1800 when their son Charles, who had been estranged from his father, died of ailments brought on by alcoholism. Then they were beset by political disaster. John was not reelected during the presidential contest of 1800. The couple felt rejected and hurt. They had invested their fortune and a lifetime of service to the country, and they felt that the country had turned its back on them. One of the most lasting effects of the political defeat was a rift that developed between the couple and newly elected president Thomas Jefferson. Interestingly, even though her husband reestablished a friendly correspondence with Jefferson later in life, Adams never did. She was her husband's most adamant defender, and after the election of 1800 she could not reconcile Jefferson's political views or his treatment of her husband. In 1813, the Adams's daughter Abigail (named after her mother) came home to die of cancer.

Five years later at the age of 74, Adams died of typhoid fever on October 28, 1818. She was survived by her husband and two children. She did not live to see the improvement of the Adams's family political fortunes, as her husband did one year before his death in 1826 with the election of her son, John Quincy Adams, to the presidency (1825–1829).

Though Abigail Adams lived a life of tremendous service to both her family and her country, she is best remembered for her letters to her husband. The couple never intended for their confidential exchanges to be made public, but the letters were published many years after their deaths. In their strength and intelligence, Abigail Adams's letters leave an indelible impression of a founding mother.

Rolando Avila

See also Republican Motherhood; Revolutionary War and Women

Further Reading

Gellis, Edith B. 1992. *Portia: The World of Abigail Adams.* Bloomington: Indiana University Press.

Holton, Woody. 2010. *Abigail Adams.* New York: Free Press.

Levin, Phyllis L. 1987. *Abigail Adams: A Biography.* New York: St. Martin's.

Withey, Lynne. 1981. *Dearest Friend: A Life of Abigail Adams.* New York: Free Press.

"Remember the Ladies" Letter Exchange between Abigail Adams and John Adams (1776)

In 1776 as her husband labored at the Continental Congress, Abigail Adams sent him her famous letter urging the members of the Congress to "remember the ladies." That letter follows along with John Adams's reply, Abigail Adams's comments on his reply to her friend Mercy Otis Warren, and Adams's reply to her husband.

1. ABIGAIL ADAMS TO JOHN ADAMS, MARCH 31, 1776

I long to hear that you have declared an independancy [sic]—and by the way in the new Code of Laws which I suppose it will be necessary for you to make I would desire you would Remember the Ladies, and be more generous and favourable to them than your ancestors. Do not put such unlimited power into the hands of the Husbands. Remember all men would be tyrants if they could. If perticuliar care and attention is not paid to the Ladies we are determined to foment a Rebelion, and will not hold ourselves bound by any Laws in which we have no voice, or Representation.

That your Sex are Naturally Tyrannical is a Truth so thoroughly established as to admit of no dispute, but such of you as wish to be happy willingly give up the harsh title of Master for the more tender and endearing one of Friend. Why then, not put it out of the power of the vicious and the Lawless to use us with cruelty and indignity with impunity. Men of Sense in all Ages abhor those customs which treat us only as the vassals of your Sex. Regard us then as Beings placed by providence under your protection and in immitation of the Supreem Being make use of that power only for our happiness.

2. JOHN ADAMS TO ABIGAIL ADAMS, APRIL 14, 1776

As to Declarations of Independency, be patient. Read our Privateering Laws, and our Commercial Laws. What signifies a Word.

As to your extraordinary Code of Laws, I cannot but laugh. We have been told that our Struggle has loosened the bands of Government every where. That Children and Apprentices were disobedient—that schools and Colledges were grown turbulent—that Indians slighted their Guardians and Negroes grew insolent to their Masters. But your Letter was the first Intimation that another Tribe more numerous and powerfull than all the rest were grown discontented.—This is rather too coarse a Compliment but you are so saucy, I wont blot it out.

Depend upon it, We know better than to repeal our Masculine systems. Altho they are in full Force, you know they are little more than Theory. We dare not exert our Power in its full Latitude. We are obliged to go fair, and softly, and in Practice you know We are the subjects. We have only the Name of Masters, and rather than give up this, which would compleatly subject Us to the Despotism of the Peticoat, I hope General Washington, and all our brave Heroes would fight.

3. ABIGAIL ADAMS TO MERCY OTIS WARREN, APRIL 27, 1776

Braintree April 27 1776

He is very saucy to me in return for a List of Female Grievances which I transmitted to him. I think I will get you to join me in a petition to Congress. I thought it was very probable our wise Statesmen would erect a New Government and form a new code of Laws. I ventured to speak a word on behalf of our Sex, who are rather hardly dealte with by the Laws of England which gives such unlimited power to the Husband to use his wife Ill.

I requested that our Legislators would consider our case and as all Men of Delicacy and Sentiment are adverse to Exercising the power they possess, yet as there is a natural propensity in Human Nature to domination, I thought the most generous plan was to put it out of the power of the Arbitrary and tyranick to injure us with impunity by Establishing some Laws in favour upon just and Liberal principals.

I believe I even threatened fomenting a Rebellion in case we were not considered and assured him we would not hold ourselves bound by any Laws in which we had neither a voice nor representation.

In return he tells me he cannot but Laugh at my extraordinary Code of Laws. That he had heard their Struggle had loosened the bands of Government, that children and apprentices were disobedient, that Schools and Colleges had grown turbulent, that Indians slighted their Guardians, and Negroes grew insolent to their Masters. But my Letter was the first intimation that another Tribe more numerous and powerful than all the rest were grown discontented. This is rather too coarse a complement, he adds, but that I am so saucy he wont blot it out.

So I have helped the Sex abundantly, but I will tell him I have only been making trial of the Disinterestedness of his Virtue, and when weigh'd in the balance have found it wanting.

It would be bad policy to grant us greater power say they since under all the disadvantages we Labour we have the ascendency over their Hearts.

And charm by accepting, by submitting sway.

4. ABIGAIL ADAMS TO JOHN ADAMS, MAY 7, 1776

I can not say that I think you very generous to the Ladies, for whilst you are proclaiming peace and good will to men, Emancipating all Nations, you insist upon retaining an absolute power over Wives. But you must remember that Arbitrary power is like most other things which are very hard, very liable to be broken and notwithstanding all your wise Laws and Maxims we have it in our power not only to free our selves but to subdue our Masters, and without violence throw both your natural and legal authority at our feet.

Source: L. H. Butterfield, ed., *The Adams Family Papers: Adams Family Correspondence*, Vol. 1 (Cambridge, MA: Belknap Press of Harvard University Press, 1963), 370–402. Copyright © 1963 by the Massachusetts Historical Society.

Adams, Hannah (1755–1831)

Author and historian Hannah Adams was the first American female to earn her living as a writer. She was the first female to obtain international acclaim as a religious historian and the first American writer to craft a full history of the Jewish people. Hannah was the first to give credit to other authors when using their sources, and she was a strong advocate for the 1790 U.S. copyright law. Adams was allowed access to the all-male Massachusetts Historical Society Library. Because of her voluminous work, she traveled among Boston's elite Federalist circles and received patronage from both men and women.

Born in 1755 in Medfield, Massachusetts, to Elizabeth and Thomas Adams, Hannah Adams was sickly and in poor health. She was homeschooled and had limited educational prospects. This lack only fueled her thirst for knowledge, and thanks to her father's expansive library, as she grew up she read voraciously.

Adams's father lost his wealth, so she sought ways to support herself. To make ends meet, her father took in boarders, one who schooled her in Latin and Greek, logic, and geography. A devout Universalist, Adams began to study different religions and differing sects of the Christian faiths. To earn money, she decided to compile her studies for print. She expanded her treatise to exegesis, defending Christian denominations she studied. Her *An Alphabetical Compendium of the Various Sects Which Have Appeared from the Beginning of the Christian Era to the Present Day* was published in 1784.

Looking to make more money from Adams's work, her publisher asked to print a new edition. To avoid having her work co-opted, Adams obtained legal copyright to her work under a new Massachusetts law and forbade its reprint. The publisher had no choice but to relinquish the manuscript.

In 1790 Adams sent a petition to Congress for passage of a countrywide copyright law, which was drafted into law that same year. She then traveled to Boston to find another printer for the new edition of *An Alphabetical Compendium.* A friend introduced her to King's Chapel pastor Reverend James Freeman, and he helped her contract printing services and assisted her in mounting a more remunerative second edition newly titled *A View of Religions.* Freeman was also instrumental in obtaining a long list of subscribers for this edition, which was published in 1791.

Demand for Adams's works occasioned additional printings in both England and the United States, and so she corresponded with clergy and religious scholars in distant places. In 1799 Adams published *A Summary History of New-England* as a compilation of historical information. The arduous reading took a toll on her vision, and she ceased work on the volumes for two years. She regained part of her vision and with the help of a secretary published the work.

Adams revised her third edition of *An Alphabetical Compendium of the Various Sects* and in 1801 took to the task of completing an abridged version of *A Summary History of New England* as a schoolbook. Historian and geographer Reverend Jedidiah Morse published his own *Compendious History of New England,* undercutting Adams's book. Adams waged a legal battle against Morse, seeking compensation for the financial losses she suffered. As a devout Congregationalist, Morse was disliked among the liberal religious families of New England. Many people provided Adams with legal services and financial support to wage the suit, which lasted for two years. Morse was required to apologize and pay damages, which he withheld until 1814.

In 1804 Adams published *The Truth and Excellence of the Christian Religion Exhibited.* She then embarked upon a *History of the Jews,* a two-volume first of its kind publication issued in 1812. In 1824 she published *Letters on the Gospels,* and in 1817 she published a final edition of her first work retitled *A Dictionary of All Religions and Religious Denominations.*

Hannah Adams died in 1831 and was buried in Mt. Auburn Cemetery in Cambridge. Her autobiography, *A Memoir of Miss Hannah Adams,* was published in 1832 one year after her death.

Jennifer Oliver O'Connell

See also Murray, Judith Sargent; Rowson, Susannah Haswell; Wheatley, Phillis; *Vol. 1, Sec. 2:* Bradstreet, Anne; Literacy

Further Reading

Adams, Hannah, and Hannah Farnham Sawyer Lee. 1832. *A Memoir of Miss Hannah Adams.* Boston: Gray and Bowen.

Curtiss, Elizabeth. 2002. "Hannah Adams." Dictionary of Unitarian & Universalist Biography, http://uudb.org/articles/hannahadams.html.

Schmidt, Gary D. 2004. *A Passionate Usefulness: The Life and Literary Labors of Hannah Adams.* Philadelphia: University of Pennsylvania Press.

Adams, Louisa Catherine (1775–1852)

Louisa Catherine Johnson Adams was married to the sixth president of the United States, John Quincy Adams (1767–1848). She served as first lady from 1825 to 1829. Born in England, she was America's only first lady born outside the United States. She was well educated, spoke several languages fluently, and was a favorite in the royal courts of Europe.

Louisa Catherine Johnson was born in London, England, on February 12, 1775. Though her mother, Catherine Nuth-Johnson, was a British citizen, Louisa's father was Joshua Johnson, an American merchant from Maryland who served as U.S. consul general in London. Louisa was the second of nine children, with seven sisters and one brother.

When Louisa was three years old the American colonies were at war with England, and Joshua Johnson moved his family to the safety of the French city of Nantes. It was there that the family entertained Americans, including John Adams and his 12-year-old son, John Quincy Adams. Louisa practiced Catholicism in France and the Anglican faith in England. She attended a convent school in Nantes and, upon their return to London, an English boarding school, where her teachers encouraged her to express her views openly. Later, Louisa wondered if this was not a mistake in an age when women were supposed to keep quiet in public.

In England, the 22-year-old Louisa again met John Quincy Adams, age 30. They were married in London on July 26, 1797. John Quincy Adams's father John Adams (1735–1826) was at this time president of the United States and objected to his son marrying someone born in another country, especially a country with which the United States had recently been at war. However, unlike his wife Abigail Adams (1744–1818), John Adams soon warmed to Louisa.

Suffering from ill health, migraines, fainting spells, and miscarriages, Louisa Adams had four children with her husband. However, three of the four died young, and only one, diplomat Charles Francis Adams, was still living at the time of her death.

Under President James Madison (1751–1836), Adams's husband was appointed minister to Russia in 1809. Though she was a favorite dancing partner of the czar, the dismal freezing winters, strange language, unusual customs, limited funds, and poor health took their toll on Adams. These were compounded by the death of her beloved daughter and namesake when the child was a year old.

One of the most remarkable episodes in Adams's life took place when her husband was called immediately to London in 1814. To join him, Adams, with her young son, was forced to make a terrifying six-week trek across Europe in winter during the Napoleonic Wars.

In 1817 when John Quincy Adams was appointed U.S. secretary of state under President James Monroe (1758–1831), the family moved to Washington, D.C. Louisa Adams became a noted hostess, welcoming diplomats and statesmen to her drawing room. She enhanced her Tuesday evening soirees by playing music on the harp. She developed a reputation for being politically astute as well as an outstanding hostess. Around this time, even her mother-in-law Abigail Adams expressed a new respect for Louisa.

Though she professed distaste for political life, Louisa Adams believed that her husband would make a good president. She quietly brought his name to the attention of influential people. She and her husband bought the former home of James and Dolley Madison, opening it to lavish entertainments. Adams's most famed party was an 1824 ball attended by about 1,000 guests honoring General Andrew Jackson (1767–1845). Later that year, Jackson became John Quincy Adams's political rival in the presidential election.

Jackson won the popular vote but not the required majority in the electoral college, so the U.S. House of Representatives decided the election. This involved an agreement that John Quincy Adams made with Congressman Henry Clay (1777–1852) that alienated political factions as well as Louisa Adams herself. She did not attend the 1825 inauguration.

In the White House, Adams wrote poems and plays that were often critical of her husband. She also found refuge from political unpleasantness by raising her own silkworms, harvesting her own silk, and using it in her sewing.

Adams served as first lady through 1829, leaving the White House at age 53. Her 4-year tenure was clouded by bitter political strife, ill health, a deteriorating relationship with her husband, and problems with her children such as alcoholism and sexual escapades. Adams and her husband became estranged, with him ignoring her when they were together and both of them spending summers apart.

John Quincy Adams did not win a second term as president, but instead of retiring he began 17 years of service in the U.S. House of Representatives in 1831. At this time, Louisa Adams helped raise two granddaughters after her son died. She joined her husband in the antislavery movement, which brought them closer together. She resumed political entertaining when her husband served in Congress and did so until his death in 1848.

Louisa Adams remained in Washington, living at the former residence of Dolley Madison. While Adams did not write a book about her life for publication, she created several autobiographical works: *Adventures of a Nobody; Record of a Life, or My Story;* and *Narrative of a Journey from Russia to France, 1815.* In 1852, she died of a heart attack at age 77. Both houses of Congress adjourned in mourning for Adams, the first woman whose death was so acknowledged. Along with John Adams, Abigail Adams, and John Quincy Adams, Louisa Adams is buried at the United First Parish Church in Quincy, Massachusetts.

Nancy Hendricks

See also Adams, Abigail; Eaton, Margaret "Peggy"; Jackson, Rachel Donelson; Parlor Politics

Further Reading

Allgor, Catherine. 2000. *Parlor Politics: In Which the Ladies of Washington Help Build a City and a Government.* Charlottesville: University Press of Virginia.

Nagel, Paul. 1987. *The Adams Women: Abigail and Louisa Adams, Their Sisters and Daughters.* New York: Oxford University Press.

O'Brien, Cormac. 2009. *Secret Lives of the First Ladies.* Philadelphia: Quirk Books.

Advice Literature

Eighteenth- and 19th-century advice literature includes etiquette books, conduct manuals, children-rearing advice books, and sometimes cookbooks and novels. Authors of advice literature often instructed young women and mothers about proper behavior, though how much of this advice women actually followed is almost impossible to know.

The advent of increasingly affordable printing presses in the 17th and 18th centuries meant that more and more people could set up shop as printers and publish books. More books meant that books became more affordable every decade. American advice literature proliferated during the colonial period, in part because families often lived far away from grandparents and other relatives as a result of both immigration and the fact that colonial Americans moved around more than their ancestors had. Thus, the oral traditions for advice giving lost their power, and many people sought advice from books. Advice literature ranged from books for young men that guided them through the perils of young manhood to child-rearing books. A great portion of advice literature was aimed at young women and mothers. In the late 18th century, advice literature branched out to include books on housekeeping and cooking.

In the 1600s, ministers and physicians generally wrote advice manuals. Authors often focused on child rearing, in part because Enlightenment ideals suggested that humans could be molded to good or bad behavior. In 1690, John Locke suggested that humans were born with a blank slate, or tabula rasa, and that parents had a responsibility not just to feed and house children but also to teach them moral values and behavior. Locke believed that childhood should be pleasant. Thus, he and others initiated a new way of thinking about child rearing that considered childhood a unique phase of human development that deserved particular attention. English colonists, including the Puritans, took these ideas about child rearing to the colonies along with books that advised parents, particularly mothers, on what to do, how to do it, and why.

The best-selling 18th-century child-rearing advice book was William Cadogan's *Essay on Nursing and the Management of Children,* which was first published in 1749 but was republished many times. Cadogan based his book on his experience with the orphans at the London Foundling Hospital and his observance of how animals treated their young. William Buchan's advice manual, published over 50 years after Cadogan's, also sold well in the colonies and echoed Cadogan's book in a number of ways. His *Advice to Mothers* (1804) told women how to wean, toilet train, feed, and correct children.

Historians of women have used child-rearing advice literature to track how colonial mothers behaved with their families but generally are skeptical about the absolute worth of advice literature. Advice literature is prescriptive in nature, not descriptive. Prescriptive literature describes how people should act, or how an author thought people should act. Advice books cannot tell historians how many women followed their advice, if they did so in whole or in part, or if they read the books and then ignored them. Advice literature describes the prescription for some behavior but does not describe mothers' or children's real behavior.

As many child-rearing advice manuals were written and purchased for mothers, just as many conduct manuals for young women circulated in colonial America. Conduct manuals for young ladies strictly followed gender ideals for women and thus changed their advice over time depending on what society imagined the perfect young lady should be. This genre of advice literature focused on virtue in young ladies and generally set a middle-class standard for young womanhood, a standard that poor women and women of color could not have hoped to attain.

Historians believe that the multiplicity of advice and conduct manuals for young women stems from a social anxiety about shifting power and hierarchies. Colonial Americans could move fairly quickly both up and down the social and economic ladder, in part because the economy followed a boom-and-bust cycle and because rapidly expanding frontiers, towns, and cities created a plethora of opportunities, both positive and negative. The seemingly ever-shifting social mobility made "correct" behavior, particularly for young women, all the more important for the stability it provided society. *The Lady's New Year's Gift* was one such manual. Written in 1688 by an English nobleman for his daughter, the book went through many reprintings and sold vigorously in the American colonies.

Novels also acted as a kind of conduct-based literature and became an important class of literature for middle-class white women. Novels often featured a virtuous young lady beset with problems, to which she had to respond correctly. Characters who responded incorrectly ended up "fallen," or unrespectable. The novels of Jane Austen, for example, which would have been read by American women, often contrasted virtuous and inappropriate behavior in young ladies. In Austen's world, young ladies who acted correctly and virtuously always lived happily ever after. Thus,

Austen's novels and a host of other novels sought not just to entertain but also to instruct or advise young women about how to act and think.

Early cookbooks could also function as a type of advice literature, though the advice in such books was generally less about virtue or morality and more about practical tips. Cookbooks often featured advice and recipes for treating illnesses as well as instructions in how to butcher animals, make cheese or sausage, and perform other tasks not in most modern cookbooks. The first American cookbook, Amelia Simmons's *American Cookery* (1796), contains advice on which foods were most nutritious, how to store food, and how to serve meals so that they were attractive, thereby suggesting that the American woman not only had to feed her family but do so in an artful manner.

Peg A. Lamphier

See also *American Cookery; The Lady's New-Years Gift: Or Advice to a Daughter*

Further Reading

Greven, Phillip. 1988. *The Protestant Temperament: Patterns of Child-Rearing, Religious Experience, and the Self in Early America*. Chicago: University of Chicago Press.

American Cookery (1796)

American Cookery was the first cookbook published by an American author in the United States. The book's author, Amelia Simmons, encouraged her readers to make use of American ingredients in their dishes and so it was the first instruction manual to merge English cooking traditions with American ingredients.

In the 17th and 18th centuries, women in the American colonies were more likely to receive cooking instruction from their mothers and other women in the household than through a cooking manual. Women might have exchanged an occasional handwritten "receipt," but most recipes were shared orally. Prior to the publication of *American Cookery*, the only books printed and used in the American colonies were of British origin. In 1742 William Parks published the first cookbook in America, a reprint of *The Compleat*

Housewife, a London manual written by Eliza Smith. English cookbooks functioned not just as cooking manuals but also as general household guides. Aimed at the gentry and upper-middle levels of society, they offered advice on preserving food, preparing home remedies, and managing a household economy. None of these British imprints included specifically American recipes, although they featured dishes that incorporated native products of the Americas such as sweet potatoes, chocolate, tomatoes, vanilla, and turkey.

American Cookery, or the Art of Dressing Viands, Fish, Poultry, and Vegetables, and the Best Modes of Making Pastes, Puffs, Pies, Tarts, Puddings, Custards, and Preserves, and All Kinds of Cakes, from the Imperial Plumb to Plain Cake: Adapted to This Country, and All Grades of Life was first published in Hartford, Connecticut, in 1796. The manual begins with instructions for roasting and preparing various meats, including turkey, wild fowl, and fish. Another section details the creation of custards, tarts, cookies, cakes, and puddings. The book closes with suggestions for preserving and pickling fruits and vegetables as well as instructions for making spruce beer. Unlike other cookbooks of the period, Simmons's work does not include medicinal recipes or tips on household management.

The recipes themselves were not particularly innovative; instead, the true innovation was Simmons's merging of English culinary traditions with American tastes and products. For example, Simmons included a recipe for Johny Cakes, a dish that had been served in the colonies for decades. Her instructions called for the use of maize instead of European grains. Another important innovation was Simmons's use of pearlash (or potash), an impure potassium carbonate obtained from wood ashes and a common household staple in the early American kitchen. She recommended pearlash as a leavening agent in dough, suggesting a forerunner of modern baking powder.

The book and its subsequent editions include patriotic recipes designed to be served at festive occasions, including particularly American events. *American Cookery* includes recipes for Election Cake and Independence Cake. Both recipes were clearly intended for large gatherings. The Election Cake recipe calls for 30 quarts of flour, 10 pounds of butter, and

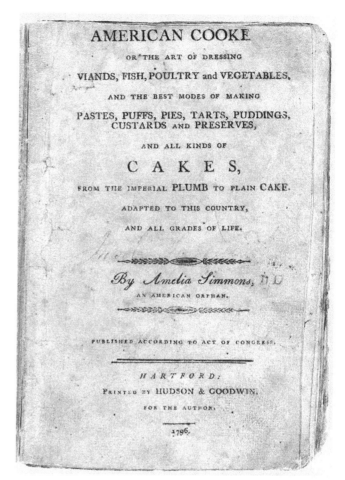

The first cookbook published by an American cook and author, *American Cookery* appeared in 1796. Though her work was a staple of colonial kitchens, almost no information survives about author Amelia Simmons. (Library of Congress)

14 pounds of sugar, while the Independence Day cake is to be frosted with loaf sugar and decorated with gold leaf.

Historians have suggested that Simmons, who labeled herself an "American Orphan" on the book's title page, was a domestic servant or cook in the New England or Hudson River Valley region. As described in the preface to her book, Simmons expected her audience to be women who were making their own way in the world, in particular those who worked in domestic service or lived in the households of friends and relatives. She did not discount the possibility that "ladies of fashion" (those unlikely to be cooking on a regular basis) might find the book entertaining as well.

American Cookery was so popular that it ran through four editions. While the book reflects cooking trends in New England and perhaps even the Middle Colonies, it does not reflect the cooking practices of the South, where dishes were heavily influenced by African traditions. By 1831, *American Cookery* had been surpassed in popularity and in sales by other cookbooks that incorporated emerging new technologies such as refrigeration and the cooking stove.

Kathleen Barker

See also *Vol. 4, Sec. 2:* Child, Julia; *Vol. 4, Sec. 3:* Waters, Alice Louise

Further Reading

Neuhaus, Jessamyn. 2012. *Manly Meals and Mom's Home Cooking: Cookbooks and Gender in Modern America.* Baltimore: Johns Hopkins University Press.

Simmons, Amelia. 1996. *American Cookery, or the Art of Dressing Viands, Fish, Poultry, and Vegetables, and the Best Modes of Making Pastes, Puffs, Pies, Tarts, Puddings, Custards, and Preserves, and All Kinds of Cakes, from the Imperial Plumb to Plain Cake: Adapted to This Country, and All Grades of Life.* 1796; reprint, n.p.: Createspace.

Colonial Recipes: Beverages and Foods (1750s, 1790s)

Published in Hartford, Connecticut, in 1796, Amelia Simmons's American Cookery *was the first American cookbook. Women who produced cookbooks before that date would have had their books published in London. The following are a number of colonial recipes from various sources. Note the casual approach to measuring and other details in these recipes.*

To Make Very Fine Syllabubs

Take a quart and a half a pint of cream, a pint of Rhenish, half a pint of sack, three lemons, near a pound of double refined sugar; beat and sift the sugar, and put it to your cream; grate off the rind of your three lemons, and put that in; squeeze the juice of the three lemons into your wine and put that to your cream, then beat altogether with a whisk just half an hour; then take it up altogether with a spoon and fill your glasses; it will keep good nine or ten days, and is best three or four days old; these are called the everlasting Syllabubs.

[from Eliza Smith, "The Complete Housewife," 1753]

King William's Possett

Take a quart of cream, and mix it with a pint of ale, then beat the yolks of ten eggs, and the whites of four; when they are well beaten, put them to the cream and ale; sweeten it to your taste, and slice some nutmeg in it; set it over the fire, and keep it stirring all the while; when it is thick, and before it boils, take it off, and pour it into the bason you serve it in to the table.

[from Eliza Smith, "The Compleat Housewife," 1758]

To Make English Katchup

Take a wide mouth'd bottle, put therein a pint of the best white-wine vinegar; then put in ten or twelve cloves of eschalot peeled and just bruised; then take a quarter of a pint of the best Langoon white wine, boil it a little, and put to it twelve or fourteen anchovies washed and shred, and dissolve them in the wine, and when cold put them in the bottle; then take a quarter of a pint more of white-wine, and put in it mace, ginger sliced, a few cloves, a spoonful of whole pepper just bruised, let them boil all a little; when near cold, slice in almost a whole nutmeg, and some lemon peel, and likewise put in two or three spoonfuls of horse-radish; then stop it close, and for a week shake it once or twice a day; then use it: 'Tis good to put into fish sauce, or any savoury dish of meat; you may add to it the clear liquor that comes from mushrooms.

[from Eliza Smith, "The Complete Housewife," 1758]

Soup Meagre

Take a half a pound of butter, put it into a deep stew pan, shake it about, and let it stand till it is done making a noise; then have ready six middling onions peeled and cut small, throw them in and shake them about; take a bunch of celery clean washed and picked, cut it into pieces half as long as your finger, a large handful of spinach clean washed and picked, good lettuce clean washed, if you have it, and cut small, a little bundle of parsley chopped fine; shake all this together well in the pan for a quarter of an hour, then shake in a little flour, stir altogether, and pour into the stew pan two quarts of boiling water; take a handful of hard dry crust, throw in a teaspoonful of beaten pepper, three blades of mace beat fine, stir altogether, and let it boil softly for half an hour; then take it off the fire, and beat up the yolks of two eggs and stir in, and one spoonful of vinegar; pour it into the soup dish and send it to table. If you have any green peas, boil half a pint in the soup for change.

[from Hannah Glasse, "The Art of Cookery Made Plain and Easy," 1796]

To Make Lamb and Rice

Take a neck or loin of lamb, half roast it, take it up, cut it into steaks, then take a half a pound of rice boiled in a quart of water ten minutes, put it into a quart of good gravy, with two or three blades of mace, and a little nutmeg. Do it over a stove or slow fire till the rice begins to be thick; then take it off, stir in a pound of butter, and when that is quite melted stir in the yolks of six eggs, first beat; then take a dish and butter it all over, take the steaks and put a little pepper and salt over them, dip them in a little melted butter, lay them into the dish, pour the gravy which comes out of them over them, and then the rice; beat the yolks of three eggs and pour all over, send it to the oven, and bake it better than half an hour.

[Hannah Glasse, "The Art of Cookery Made Plain and Easy," 1796]

A Hedgehog

This dish was called a "deceit" because it wasn't really a hedgehog, but a dessert made to look like a hedgehog.

Take two pounds of blanched almonds, beat them well in a mortar, with a little canary and orange-flower water, to keep them from oiling. Make them into stiff paste, then beat in the yolks of twelve eggs, leave out five of the whites, put to it a pint of cream sweetened with sugar, put in a half pound of sweet butter melted, set it on a furnace or slow fire, and keep it constantly stirring, till it is stiff enough to be made in the form of a hedgehog, then stick it full of blanched almonds, slit and stuck up like the bristles of a hedgehog, then put it into a dish; take a pint of cream, and the yolks of four eggs beat up, sweetened with sugar to your palate. Stir them together over a slow fire till it is quite hot; then pour it round the hedgehog in a dish, and let it stand till it is cold, and serve it up. Or a rich calf's-foot jelly made clear and good, poured into the dish round the hedgehog; when it is cold, it looks pretty, and makes a neat dish; or it looks pretty in the middle of a table for supper.

[Hannah Glasse, "The Art of Cookery Made Plain and Easy," 1796]

A Nice Indian Pudding

3 pints scaled milk, 7 spoons of fine Indian meal, stir together while hot, let stand till cooled; add 7 eggs, half pound of raisins, 4 ounces butter, spice and sugar; bake one and a half hour.

[Amelia Simmons, "American Cookery," 1796]

Source: "Syllabubs Three Ways," Colonial Williamsburg: History Is Served, http://recipes.history.org/2013/05/syllabubs-three-ways.

To Make an Apple Tansey

Take three pippins, slice them round in thin slices, and fry them with butter; then beat four eggs, with six spoonfuls of cream, a little rosewater, nutmeg, and sugar; stir them together, and pour it over the apples; let it fry a little, and turn it with a pye-plate. Garnish with lemon and sugar strew'd over it.

Source: E. Smith, *The Compleat Housewife: Or, Accomplished Gentlewoman's Companion* (London: J. and J. Pemberton, 1754). Available at Colonial Williamsburg, http://www.history.org/Almanack/life/food/appletansy.cfm.

Excerpts from Amelia Simmons's *American Cookery* (1796)

The following is the first section of Amelia Simmons's American Cookery, *the first American cookbook, published in Hartford, Connecticut, in 1796. Note the variety of foods she describes.*

AMERICAN COOKERY, OR THE ART OF DRESSING VIANDS, FISH, POULTRY and VEGETABLES, AND THE BEST MODES OF MAKING PASTES, PUFFS, PIES, TARTS, PUDDINGS, CUSTARDS AND PRESERVES, AND ALL KINDS OF CAKES, FROM THE IMPERIAL PLUMB TO PLAIN CAKE.

ADAPTED TO THIS COUNTRY, AND ALL GRADES OF LIFE.

By Amelia Simmons,
AN AMERICAN ORPHAN.

PUBLISHED ACCORDING TO ACT OF CONGRESS.
HARTFORD
PRINTED BY HUDSON & GOODWIN,
FOR THE AUTHOR. 1796

PREFACE.

As this treatise is calculated for the improvement of the rising generation of *Females* in America, the Lady of fashion and fortune will not be displeased, if many hints are suggested for the more general and universal knowledge of those females in this country, who by the loss of their parents, or other unfortunate circumstances, are reduced to the necessity of going into families in the line of domestics, or taking refuge with their friends or relations, and doing those things which are really essential to the perfecting them as good wives, and useful members of society. The orphan, tho' left to the care of virtuous guardians, will find it essentially necessary to have an opinion and determination of her own. The world, and the fashion thereof, is so variable, that old people cannot accommodate themselves to the various changes and fashions which daily occur; *they* will adhere to the fashion of *their* day, and will not surrender their attachments to the *good old way*—while the young and the gay, bend and conform readily to the taste of the times, and fancy of the hour. By having an opinion and determination, I would not be understood to mean an obstinate perseverance in trifles, which borders on obstinacy—by no means, but only an adherence to those rules and maxims which have flood the test of ages, and will forever establish the *female character,* a virtuous character—altho' they conform to the ruling taste of the age in cookery, dress, language, manners, &c.

It must ever remain a check upon the poor solitary orphan, that while those females who have parents, or brothers, or riches, to defend their indiscretions, that the orphan must depend solely upon *character.* How immensely important, therefore, that every action, every word, every thought, be regulated by the strictest purity, and that every movement meet the approbation of the good and wise.

The candor of the American Ladies is solicitously intreated by the Authoress, as she is circumscribed in her knowledge, this being an original work in this country. Should any future editions appear, she hopes to render it more valuable.

[Illustration]
DIRECTIONS for CATERING, or the procuring the best VIANDS, FISH, &c.

How to choose Flesh.

BEEF. The large stall fed ox beef is the best, it has a coarse open grain, and oily smoothness; dent it with your finger and it will immediately rise again; if old, it will be rough and spungy, and the dent remain.

Cow Beef is less boned, and generally more tender and juicy than the ox, in America, which is used to labor.

Of almost every species of Animals, Birds and Fishes, the female is the tenderest, the richest flavour'd, and among poultry the soonest fattened.

Mutton, grass-fed, is good two or three years old.

Lamb, if under six months is rich, and no danger of imposition; it may be known by its size, in distinguishing either.

Veal, is soon lost—great care therefore is necessary in purchasing. Veal bro't to market in panniers, or in carriages, is to be prefered to that bro't in bags, and flouncing on a sweaty horse.

Pork, is known by its size, and whether properly fattened by its appearance.

To make the best Bacon.

To each ham put one ounce saltpetre, one pint bay salt, one pint molasses, shake together 6 or 8 weeks, or when a large quantity is together, bast them with the liquor every day; when taken out to dry, smoke three weeks with cobs or malt fumes. To every ham may be added a cheek, if you stow away a barrel and not alter the composition, some add a shoulder. For transportation or exportation, double the period of smoaking.

Fish, how to choose the best in market.

Salmon, the noblest and richest fish taken in fresh water—the largest are the best. They are unlike almost every other fish, are ameliorated by being 3 or 4 days out of water, if kept from heat and the moon, which has much more injurious effect than the sun.

In all great fish-markets, great fish-mongers strictly examine the gills—if the bright redness is exchanged for a low brown, they are stale; but when live fish are bro't flouncing into market, you have only to elect the kind most agreeable to your palate and the season.

Shad, contrary to the generally received opinion are not so much richer flavored, as they are harder when first taken out of the water; opinions vary respecting them. I have tasted Shad thirty or forty miles from the place where caught, and really conceived that they had a richness of flavor, which did not appertain to those taken fresh and cooked immediately, and have proved both at the same table, and the truth may rest here, that a Shad 36 or 48 hours out of water, may not cook so hard and solid, and be esteemed so elegant, yet give a higher relished flavor to the taste.

Every species generally of *salt water Fish,* are best fresh from the water, tho' the *Hannah Hill, Black Fish, Lobster, Oyster, Flounder, Bass, Cod, Haddock,* and *Eel,* with many others, may be transported by land many miles, find a good market, and retain a good relish; but as generally, live ones are bought first, deceits are used to give them a freshness of appearance, such as peppering the gills, wetting the fins and tails, and even painting the gills, or wetting with animal blood. Experience and attention will dictate the choice of the best. Fresh gills, full bright eyes, moist fins and tails, are denotements of their being fresh caught; if they are soft, its certain they are stale, but if deceits are used, your smell must approve or denounce them, and be your safest guide.

Of all fresh water fish, there are none that require, or so well afford haste in cookery, as the *Salmon Trout,* they are best when caught under a fall or cateract—from what philosophical circumstance is yet unsettled, yet true it is, that at the foot of a fall the waters are much colder than at the head; Trout choose those waters; if taken from them and hurried into dress, they are genuinely good; and take rank in point of superiority of flavor, of most other fish.

Perch and Roach, are noble pan fish, the deeper the water from whence taken, the finer are their flavors; if taken from shallow water, with muddy bottoms, they are impregnated therewith, and are unsavory.

Eels, though taken from muddy bottoms, are best to jump in the pan.

Most white or soft fish are best bloated, which is done by salting, peppering, and drying in the sun, and in a chimney; after 30 or 40 hours drying, are best broiled, and moistened with butter, &c.

Poultry—how to choose.

Having before stated that the female in almost every instance, is preferable to the male, and peculiarly so in the *Peacock,* which, tho' beautifully plumaged, is tough, hard, stringy, and untasted, and even indelicious—while the *Pea Hen* is exactly otherwise, and the queen of all birds.

So also in a degree, *Turkey.*

Hen Turkey, is higher and richer flavor'd, easier fattened and plumper—they are no odds in market.

Dunghill Fowls, are from their frequent use, a tolerable proof of the former birds.

Chickens, of either kind are good, and the yellow leg'd the best, and their taste the sweetest.

Capons, if young are good, are known by short spurs and smooth legs.

All birds are known, whether fresh killed or stale, by a tight vent in the former, and a loose open vent if old or stale; their smell denotes their goodness;

speckled rough legs denote age, while smooth legs and combs prove them young.

A Goose, if young, the bill will be yellow, and will have but few hairs, the bones will crack easily; but if old, the contrary, the bill will be red, and the pads still redder; the joints stiff and difficultly disjointed; if young, otherwise; choose one not very fleshy on the breast, but fat in the rump.

Ducks, are similar to geese.

Wild Ducks, have redder pads, and smaller than the tame ones, otherwise are like the goose or tame duck, or to be chosen by the same rules.

Wood Cocks, ought to be thick, fat and flesh firm, the nose dry, and throat clear.

Snipes, if young and fat, have full veins under the wing, and are small in the veins, otherwise like the Woodcock.

Partridges, if young, will have black bills, yellowish legs; if old, the legs look bluish; if old or stale, it may be perceived by smelling at their mouths.

Pigeons, young, have light red legs, and the flesh of a colour, and prick easily—old have red legs, blackish in parts, more hairs, plumper and loose vents—so also of grey or green Plover, Blade Birds, Thrash, Lark, and wild Fowl in general.

Hares, are white flesh'd and flexible when new and fresh kill'd; if stale, their flesh will have a blackish hue, like old pigeons, if the cleft in her lip spread much, is wide and ragged, she is old; the contrary when young.

Leveret, is like the Hare in every respect, that some are obliged to search for the knob, or small bone on the fore leg or foot, to distinguish them.

Rabbits, the wild are the best, either are good and tender; if old there will be much yellowish fat about the kidneys, the claws long, wool rough, and mixed with grey hairs; if young the reverse. As to their being fresh, judge by the scent, they soon perish, if trap'd or shot, and left in pelt or undressed; their taint is quicker than veal, and the most sickish in nature; and will not, like beef or veal, be purged by fire.

The cultivation of Rabbits would be profitable in America, if the best methods were pursued—they are a very prolific and profitable animal—they are easily cultivated if properly attended, but not otherwise.—A Rabbit's borough, on which 3000 dollars may have been expended, might be very profitable; but on the small scale they would be well near market towns—easier bred, and more valuable.

Butter—Tight, waxy, yellow Butter is better than white or crumbly, which soon becomes rancid and frowy. Go into the centre of balls or rolls to prove and judge it; if in ferkin, the middle is to be preferred, as the sides are frequently distasted by the wood of the firkin—altho' oak and used for years. New pine tubs are ruinous to the butter. To have sweet butter in dog days, and thro' the vegetable seasons, send stone pots to honest, neat, and trusty dairy people, and procure it pack'd down in May, and let them be brought in the night, or cool rainy morning, covered with a clean cloth wet in cold water, and partake of no heat from the horse, and set the pots in the coldest part of your cellar, or in the ice house.—Some say that May butter thus preserved, will go into the winter use, better than fall made butter.

Cheese—The red smooth moist coated, and tight pressed, square edged Cheese, are better than white coat, hard rinded, or bilged; the inside should be yellow, and flavored to your taste. Old shelves which have only been wiped down for years, are preferable to scoured and washed shelves. Deceits are used by salt-petering the out side, or colouring with hemlock, cocumberries, or safron, infused into the milk; the taste of either supercedes every possible evasion.

Eggs—Clear, thin shell'd, longest oval and sharp ends are best; to ascertain whether new or stale—hold to the light, if the white is clear, the yolk regularly in the centre, they are good—but if otherwise, they are stale. The best possible method of ascertaining, is to put them into water, if they lye on their bilge, they are *good* and *fresh*—if they bob up an end they are stale, and if they rise they are addled, proved, and of no use.

We proceed to ROOTS and VEGETABLES—*and the best cook cannot alter the first quality, they must be good, or the cook will be disappointed.*

Potatoes, take rank for universal use, profit and easy acquirement. The smooth skin, known by the name of How's Potato, is the most mealy and richest flavor'd; the yellow rusticoat next best; the red, and red rusticoat are tolerable; and the yellow Spanish have their value—those cultivated from imported seed on sandy or dry loomy lands, are best for table use; tho' the red or either will produce more in rich, loomy, highly manured garden grounds; new lands and a sandy soil, afford the richest flavor'd; and most mealy Potato much depends on the ground on which they grow—more on the species of Potatoes planted—and still more from foreign seeds—and each may be known by attention to connoisseurs; for a good potato comes up in many branches of cookery, as herein after prescribed.—All potatoes should be dug before the rainy seasons in the fall, well dryed in the sun, kept from frost and dampness during the winter, in the spring removed from the cellar to a dry loft, and spread thin, and frequently stirred and dryed, or they will grow and be thereby injured for cookery.

A roast Potato is brought on with roast Beef, a Steake, a Chop, or Fricassee; good boiled with a boiled dish; make an excellent stuffing for a turkey, water or wild fowl; make a good pie, and a good starch for many uses. All potatoes run out, or depreciate in America; a fresh importation of the Spanish might restore them to table use.

It would swell this treatise too much to say every thing that is useful, to prepare a good table, but I may be pardoned by observing, that the Irish have preserved a genuine mealy rich Potato, for a century, which takes rank of any known in any other kingdom; and I have heard that they renew their seed by planting and cultivating the *Seed Ball,* which grows on the tine. The manner of their managing it to keep up the excellency of that root, would better suit a treatise on agriculture and gardening than this—and be inserted in a book which would be read by the farmer, instead of his amiable daughter. If no one treats on the subject, it may appear in the next edition.

Onions—The Madeira white is best in market, esteemed softer flavored, and not so fiery, but the high red, round hard onions are the best; if you consult cheapness, the largest are best; if you consult taste and softness, the very smallest are the most delicate, and used at the first tables. Onions grow in the richest, highest cultivated ground, and better and better year after year, on the same ground.

Beets, grow on any ground, but best on loom, or light gravel grounds; the *red* is the richest and best approved; the *white* has a sickish sweetness, which is disliked by many.

Parsnips, are a valuable root, cultivated best in rich old grounds, and doubly deep plowed, *late sown,* they grow thrifty, and are not so prongy; they may be kept any where and any how, so that they do not grow with heat, or are nipped with frost; if frosted, let them thaw in earth; they are richer flavored when plowed out of the ground in April, having stood out during the winter, tho' they will not last long after, and commonly more sticky and hard in the centre.

Carrots, are managed as it respects plowing and rich ground, similarly to Parsnips. The yellow are better than the orange or red; middling fiz'd, that is, a foot long and two inches thick at the top end, are better than over grown ones; they are cultivated best with onions, sowed very thin, and mixed with other seeds, while young or six weeks after sown, especially if with onions on true onion ground. They are good with veal cookery, rich in soups, excellent with hash, in May and June.

Garlicks, tho' used by the French, are better adapted to the uses of medicine than cookery.

Asparagus—The mode of cultivation belongs to gardening; your business is only to cut and dress, the largest is best, the growth of a day sufficient, six inches long, and cut just above the ground; many cut below the surface, under an idea of getting tender shoots, and preserving the bed; but it enfeebles the root: dig round it and it will be wet with the juices—but if cut above ground, and just as the dew is going off, the sun will either reduce the juice, or send it back to nourish the root—its an excellent vegetable.

Parsley, of the three kinds, the thickest and branchiest is the best, is sown among onions, or in a bed by itself, may be dryed for winter use; tho' a method which I have experienced, is much better—In September I dig my roots, procure an old thin stave dry cask, bore holes an inch diameter in every stave, 6 inches asunder round the cask, and up to the top—take first a half bushel of rich garden mold and put into the cask, then run the roots through the staves, leaving the branches outside, press the earth tight about the root within, and thus continue on thro' the respective stories, till the cask is full; it being filled, run an iron bar thro' the center of the dirt in the cask and fill with water, let stand on the south and east side of a building till frosty night, then remove it, (by slinging a rope round the cask) into the cellar; where, during the winter, I clip with my scissars the fresh parsley, which my neighbors or myself have occasion for; and in the spring transplant the roots in the bed in the garden, or in any unused corner—or let stand upon the wharf, or the wash shed. Its an useful mode of cultivation, and a pleasurably tasted herb, and much used in garnishing viands.

Raddish, Salmon coloured is the best, purple next best—white—turnip—each are produced from southern seeds, annually. They grow thriftiest sown among onions. The turnip Raddish will last well through the winter.

Artichokes—The Jerusalem is best, are cultivated like potatoes, (tho' their stocks grow 7 feet high) and may be preserved like the turnip raddish, or pickled—they like.

Horse Raddish, once in the garden, can scarcely ever be totally eradicated; plowing or digging them up with that view, seems at times rather to increase and spread them.

Cucumbers, are of many kinds; the prickly is best for pickles, but generally bitter; the white is difficult to raise and tender; choose the bright green, smooth and proper sized.

Melons—The Water Melons is cultivated on sandy soils only, above latitude 41 1/2, if a stratum of land be dug from a well, it will bring the first year good Water Melons; the red cored are highest flavored; a hard rine proves them ripe.

Muskmelons, are various, the rough skinned is best to eat; the short, round, fair skinn'd, is best for Mangoes.

Lettuce, is of various kinds; the purple spotted leaf is generally the tenderest, and free from bitter—Your taste must guide your market.

Cabbage, requires a page, they are so multifarious. Note, all Cabbages have a higher relish that grow on new unmatured grounds; if grown in an old town and on old gardens, they have a rankness, which at times, may be perceived by a fresh air traveller. This observation has been experienced for years—that Cabbages require new ground, more than Turnips.

The Low Dutch, only will do in old gardens.

The Early Yorkshire, must have rich soils, they will not answer for winter, they are easily cultivated, and frequently bro't to market in the fall, but will not last the winter.

The Green Savoy, with the richest crinkles, is fine and tender; and altho' they do not head like the Dutch or Yorkshire, yet the tenderness of the out leaves is a counterpoise, it will last thro' the winter, and are high flavored.

The Yellow Savoy, takes next rank, but will not last so long; all Cabbages will mix, and participate of other species, like Indian Corn; they are culled, best in plants; and a true gardener will, in the plant describe those which will head, and which will not. This is new, but a fact.

The gradations in the Savoy Cabbage are discerned by the leaf; the richest and most scollup'd, and crinkled, and thickest Green Savoy, falls little short of a Colliflour.

The red and redest small tight heads, are best for slaw, it will not boil well, comes out black or blue, and tinges, other things with which it is boiled.

BEANS.

The Clabboard Bean, is easiest cultivated and collected, are good for string beans, will shell—must be poled.

The Windsor Bean, is an earlier, good string, or shell Bean.

Crambury Bean, is rich, but not universally approved equal to the other two.

Frost Bean, is good only to shell.

Six Weeks Bean, is a yellowish Bean, and early bro't forward, and tolerable.

Lazy Bean, is tough, and needs no pole.

English Bean, what they denominate the Horse Bean, is mealy when young, is profitable, easily cultivated, and may be grown on worn out grounds; as they may be raised by boys, I cannot but recommend the more extensive cultivation of them.

The small White Bean, is best for winter use, and excellent.

Calivanse, are run out, a yellow small bush, a black speck or eye, are tough and tasteless, and little worth in cookery, and scarcely bear exportation.

Peas—Green Peas.

The Crown Imperial, takes rank in point of flavor, they blossom, purple and white on the top of the vines, will run, from three to five feet high, should be set in light sandy soil only, or they run too much to vines.

The Crown Pea, is second in richness of flavor.

The Rondeheval, is large and bitterish.

Early Carlton, is produced first in the season—good.

Marrow Fats, green, yellow, and is large, easily cultivated, not equal to others.

Sugar Pea, needs no bush, the pods are tender and good to eat, easily cultivated.

Spanish Manratto, is a rich Pea, requires a strong high bush.

All Peas should be picked *carefully* from the vines as soon as dew is off, shelled and cleaned without water, and boiled immediately; they are thus the richest flavored.

Herbs, useful in Cookery.

Thyme, is good in soups and stuffings.

Sweet Marjoram, is used in Turkeys.

Summer Savory, ditto, and in Sausages and salted Beef, and legs of Pork.

Sage, is used in Cheese and Pork, but not generally approved.

Parsley, good in *soups,* and to *garnish roast Beef,* excellent with bread and butter in the spring.

Penny Royal, is a high aromatic, altho' a spontaneous herb in old ploughed fields, yet might be more generally cultivated in gardens, and used in cookery and medicines.

Sweet Thyme, is most useful and best approved in cookery.

FRUITS.

Pears, There are many different kinds; but the large Bell Pear, sometimes called the Pound Pear, the yellowest is the best, and in the same town they differ essentially.

Hard Winter Pear, are innumerable in their qualities, are good in sauces, and baked.

Harvest and *Summer Pear* are a tolerable desert, are much improved in this country, as all other fruits are by grafting and innoculation.

Apples, are still more various, yet rigidly retain their own species, and are highly useful in families, and ought to be more universally cultivated, excepting in the compactest cities. There is not a single family but might set a tree in some otherwise useless spot, which might serve the two fold use of shade and fruit; on which 12 or 14 kinds of fruit trees might easily be engrafted, and essentially preserve the orchard from the intrusions of boys, &c. which is too common in America. If the boy who thus planted a tree, and guarded and protected it in a useless corner, and carefully engrafted different fruits, was to be indulged free access into orchards, whilst the neglectful boy was prohibited—how many millions of fruit trees would spring into growth—and what a saving to the union. The net saving would in time extinguish the public debt, and enrich our cookery.

Currants, are easily grown from shoots trimmed off from old bunches, and set carelessly in the ground; they flourish on all soils, and make good jellies—their cultivation ought to be encouraged.

Black Currants, may be cultivated—but until they can be dried, and until sugars are propagated, they are in a degree unprofitable.

Grapes, are natural to the climate; grow spontaneously in every state in the union, and ten degrees north of the line of the union. The *Madeira, Lisbon* and *Malaga* Grapes, are cultivated in gardens in this country, and are a rich treat or desert. Trifling attention only is necessary for their ample growth.

Having pointed out the *best methods of judging of the qualities of Viands, Poultry, Fish, Vegetables, &c.* We now present the best approved methods of DRESSING and COOKING them; and to suit all tastes, present the following.

Source: Amelia Simmons, *American Cookery* (Hartford, CT: Hudson and Goodwin, 1796), 17–24.

Arnold, Peggy (Margaret) Shippen (1760–1804)

Peggy (Margaret) Shippen Arnold, a Loyalist during the American Revolutionary War, was a major partner in her husband Benedict Arnold's conspiracy to turn over the military fort of West Point to the British.

Peggy Arnold was born on June 11, 1760, the fourth and youngest daughter of Philadelphia magistrate Edward Shippen IV and Margaret Francis, a prominent family who lived in the Society Hill district, where she was insulated by old money and privilege. Arnold was an exceptional beauty, with porcelain skin, blond hair, and blue-hazel eyes. Her father's favorite, she was treated to a quality education as well as training in culture and etiquette.

When the British occupied Philadelphia in 1777, the Loyalist-leaning Shippens freely entertained troops in their home. Arnold established and maintained an affectionate bond with Major John André, an officer under British general Sir William Howe. André drew flattering portraits of the young woman and gave her a lock of his hair, which she secreted in a locket. In 1778 when the British withdrew, André became an important part of the Arnolds' treasonous plot.

General Benedict Arnold took oversight of the city as commandant of the Philadelphia Continental Army. The Shippens hosted the 38-year-old Arnold in their home, where he met their then 17-year-old daughter. A courtship ensued, and the couple married in 1779. It was his second marriage.

The Shippens' refusal to choose sides in the war kept them under constant suspicion and scrutiny. Correspondence between Arnold and André through the ruse of requesting certain sewing supplies later proved instrumental in the plot to surrender an army base to the British. The "Millinery Letter" activated the subterfuge, and Arnold began trading information with André on troop movements and supplies. The Arnolds negotiated compensation of £20,000 if the deception succeeded and £6,000 should it fail, using Peggy Arnold's letters to André as cover.

West Point was a vital Continental Army stronghold on New York's Hudson River. A British overthrow would destroy the rebel forces and turn the tide of war. The Arnolds lobbied to install General Arnold at the fort to engineer the downfall. Peggy Arnold charmed Robert R. Livingston, a New York member of the Continental Congress, seeking his consideration of her husband for the post. Livingston was so taken with Peggy Arnold that he wrote to George Washington on her and her husband's behalf. Benedict Arnold took command of West Point in 1780.

Peggy Arnold stayed in Philadelphia to liquidate assets in preparation for their eventual escape while fielding correspondence between the British and her husband. She joined her husband in New York, and arrangements were made for him to meet André on the shores of the Hudson River, where he passed André documents and maps detailing West Point's fortifications.

André was subsequently captured and arrested, with the papers and maps still in his possession. Benedict Arnold received word of this on the same day that Washington was scheduled to meet with him at his home. Benedict first alerted Peggy and then fled to HMS *Vulture,* a British ship docked on the Hudson. Upon Washington's arrival, Peggy Arnold feigned hysterics, which gave her husband time to escape and convinced Washington that she had no knowledge of the plot.

Arnold returned to Philadelphia with her infant son Edward, feigning ignorance about her husband's whereabouts. Philadelphia authorities soon discovered the Millinery Letters between her and André. As a result, the Supreme Executive Council banished Arnold from Philadelphia. Edward Shippen escorted his daughter to the Jersey side of the Hudson, where she boarded a boat to New York. The Arnolds departed for England in 1781.

Both of the Arnolds were welcomed warmly in England and received an annuity from Queen Charlotte of £100 a year for the maintenance of their children, including those not yet born. King George III presented Peggy Arnold with £500, "obtained for her services, which were meritorious." The Arnolds had more children: James, Sophia, George, and William.

Peggy Arnold succumbed to uterine cancer on August 24, 1804, at the age of 44. She was buried next to her husband (who died in 1801) at St. Mary's Church in Battersea.

Jennifer Oliver O'Connell

See also Adams, Abigail; Loyalist Women; Washington, Martha

Further Reading

Jacob, Mark, and Stephen H. Case. 2012. *Treacherous Beauty: Peggy Shippen, the Woman behind Benedict Arnold's Plot to Betray America.* Guilford, CT: Lyons.

Rubin Stuart, Nancy. 2013. *Defiant Brides: The Untold Story of Two Revolutionary-Era Women and the Radical Men They Married.* Boston: Beacon.

Bailey, Anne Hennis (1742–1825)

A scout and courier during the American Revolutionary War and the Northwest Indian Wars, Anne Bailey was also a storyteller of incredible renown. Because of her eccentric behavior she is remembered both by colorful nicknames such as "Mad Anne" and for her acts of heroism and bravery.

Anne Hennis is said to have been born in 1742 in Liverpool, England, and was raised by parents who taught her to read and write. Her parents died around her 19th birthday, at which time she immigrated to the Shenandoah Valley in Virginia. She may have done so to be with relatives, but it is possible that she became an indentured servant to pay for passage to the American colonies.

Four years after arriving in colonial America, Bailey met and married her first husband, Richard Trotter, in 1765. They subsequently moved to Stauton, Virginia, in the Kanawha Valley and had one son, William. Because the area was popular with settlers, there was significant tension between the Native Americans already in the area and the Euro-American settlers. To address this, the governor of Virginia organized a militia. Trotter joined the militia and fought in the battle at Point Pleasant in Lord Dunsmore's War on October 10, 1774. Casualties were heavy for both sides, and Trotter lost his life.

When Bailey learned of her husband's death, she adopted men's clothing and vowed to avenge him in battle. Realizing that her son would not be safe alone, she left him with a neighbor. She then became a volunteer messenger and scout for the Virginia Militia in the Northwest Indian Wars and then later for the Revolutionary cause. She regularly traveled between Fort Savannah and Fort Randolph, about 160 miles, carrying messages. Furthermore, Bailey felt that it was her duty to help the war effort by urging men to join the militia, reasoning to them that in doing so they would help keep women and children safe. As a result, she knew the routes and wilderness very well and was highly respected by the region's settlers.

Bailey did not don men's clothing to pass herself off as a man but instead wore a combination of male and female clothing that served to mark her as a woman doing a man's job. She regularly dressed in a skirt and petticoat paired with a man's jacket. She was known to carry a tomahawk and a butcher knife in her belt and a rifle over her shoulder.

Bailey's adventures were the source of many of the thrilling stories she told in later life featuring both herself and her horse, Liverpool. She told several tales, but the most popular was about a time when she was forced to leave her horse behind and hide in a log when pursued by Shawnees, who sat on the very log she was hiding under. When they gave up the pursuit, she backtracked to their camp while they slept and took her horse back, whooping in delight as she raced away. The Native Americans thought that she was possessed and could not be touched by bullets or arrows. They left her alone and free from attack. In another story, she fell asleep in the snow while on a courier mission to acquire ammunition. Her horse walked back to the fort, alerting others to look for her and thus preventing her from freezing to death. In yet another adventure, Bailey was yelling at the gates of Fort Young. When the gates were opened she was bloody and haggard, holding two scalps from Indians she encountered on the trail. Because of her volatile temperament and her stories, Bailey was nickname "Mad Anne."

In 1785 Anne married John Bailey, a ranger and frontiersman. John was assigned to Fort Lee near Charleston, West Virginia, and they lived at nearby Clendenin's Settlement when hostilities broke out among settlers and Native Americans. Anne Bailey helped by riding around to settlers warning of impending attacks. When an impending attack by Native Americans was discovered in 1791, the officers at the fort realized that they did not have enough ammunition. The colonel asked for male volunteers to go to Fort Savannah, near Lewisburg, Virginia, to get supplies. When none came forward Bailey volunteered, setting off on the dangerous 100-mile trek and not stopping to eat or sleep along the way. When she arrived at Fort Savannah, she was given the gunpowder and an additional horse. She was also offered an escort on her return trip but refused. Her efforts saved the fort and the nearby settlement. She was treated as a hero, given whiskey and allowed to keep the horse. The Baileys remained at the fort until 1795, when the Treaty of Greenville ended the Northwest Indian Wars.

Records conflict about whether John Bailey died in 1794 or 1802. Nevertheless, after his death Anne Bailey retreated to the wilderness to live. She traveled a great deal, telling stories of her exploits as she carried messages and supplies to settlers. She made her last messenger trip to Charleston in 1817 at the age of 78. She reluctantly retired in 1818 and moved to Gallia, Ohio, to be with her son and his family. She remained independent until her death, living in a cabin that her son built for her. Bailey died there on November 22, 1825, and was interred in Gallia County, but later her remains were moved to Point Pleasant. Her dramatic life and heroic deeds are commemorated by the poem "Anne Bailey's Ride." She remains a model female adventurer and a woman who did not let social expectations or gender roles define her life.

Sarah Nation

See also Butterworth, Mary; Davis, Ann Simpson; Sampson, Deborah

Further Reading

Furbee, Mary. 2001. *Anne Bailey: Frontier Scout.* Greensboro, NC: Morgan Reynolds Publishing.

Lewis, Vergil. 2009. *The Life and Times of Anne Bailey: The Pioneer Heroine of the Great Kanawha Valley, 1742–1825.* n.p.: Create Space Independent Publishing Platform.

Ballard, Martha (1735–1812)

Martha Moore Ballard played a pivotal role in her community as a midwife and healer. Through her diary she has become a historically important female voice documenting social, economic, and religious change in rural postcolonial America.

Few women could write in the 18th century, and fewer still participated in public life, resulting in poor documentation of women's daily lives. Because women could not own property and seldom participated in legal matters, few details regarding individual women's lives appear in historical documents. For example, public record of Ballard's life is limited to her birth sometime in 1735, her 1754 marriage to Ephraim Ballard, and their children's birth dates. Ballard was a prominent figure in her community, yet without her journal the only thing we would know about her life would be a family story recounted by a famous grandniece, Clara Barton (1824–1912). Barton told the humorous tale of her grandmother and great-aunt (Ballard) hiding in a cellar to brew tea in defiance of family support of the prerevolutionary tea boycott. The girls claimed that the tea was for a sick neighbor. Providing medical care ran in the family; Ballard's uncle and two brothers-in-law (including Barton's grandfather) were physicians.

Ballard spent the first half of her life in the town of Oxford, Massachusetts. At the onset of the American Revolutionary War in 1777, Ballard and her husband relocated their family to a frontier settlement in Maine (then still part of Massachusetts). Hallowell was a remote community of approximately 100 families spread out along the Kennebec River.

On January 1, 1785, Ballard began writing daily entries in a hand-bound journal with a quill pen and ink. She was 50 years old, and for the next 27 years she documented her daily work providing medical care, her financial transactions and movement through the community, the textile work of her daughters, and the interactions of everyday people. Combined with maps of the area created by her husband, a surveyor, Ballard's journal weaves a history of an American frontier community.

Childbirth and Health Care

When Ballard began her journal she had been an active midwife for seven years. She was the mother of nine children, and her neighbors sought her assistance because of her skills, experience, and knowledge. Her diary documents the delivery of 816 babies, including 2 of her own grandchildren on the same day. While childbirth could be quite dangerous, Ballard lost very few mothers and babies in delivery, a reality that signifies her midwifery skill.

Despite depictions of Puritans as prudish, Ballard's journal reveals tolerant attitudes toward premarital sex. Over 30 percent of children in the postcolonial Northeast were born out of wedlock. An unmarried woman who became pregnant sued the alleged father for financial support. Marriage might follow, but the community's concern focused on the child's financial support. If the couple did not marry but financial support was supplied, neither party incurred shame.

Ballard chronicles her bachelor son being accused of paternity. As a midwife, Ballard represented the community and questioned women at the height of labor to identify the child's father. The society believed that a woman could not lie at that precise moment, and childbirth statements were legally binding.

Ballard also nursed the sick and documented the community's medical history, including physical injuries and disease. Daily entries follow the arc of a 1787 epidemic; a single sick child evolves into a community plagued by scarlet fever and fatalities. Infectious diseases swept through colonial America; Ballard herself lost three young daughters to diphtheria in 1769. Communicable diseases caused catastrophic consequence when transmitted to Native American populations.

Attitudes toward medicine were also changing. Ballard's knowledge of anatomy and physiology came from experience. Male physicians were increasingly educated from books.

Initially, two male physicians worked in Hallowell. Midwives treated minor illnesses and provided primary care to women and children. Most male doctors respected the midwives' expertise, and Ballard worked cooperatively with physicians. But in the later part of her career, young doctors were attending more births and pushing midwives out of the field. Ballard believed that some doctors recklessly prescribed opiate drugs to women in labor and endangered infants with unnecessary use of forceps during delivery.

The increasingly male-dominated medical field demeaned midwifery as unscientific, but Ballard records rare statistical evidence supporting midwifery. Ballard lost 5 mothers out of 998 career deliveries. In comparison, London hospitals at the time reported deaths of between 30 and 200 women per every 1,000 deliveries. Ballard also recorded fewer stillbirths and neonatal deaths than male counterparts. Some historians believe that the trend away from traditionally trained midwives and toward male physicians, considered to be more scientifically educated, negatively impacted women's health until the mid-20th century.

Economic Networks

Midwifery was Ballard's occupation, and she tracked payment of birth "fees" or "rewards" (Ulrich 1990, 89) in a specific column in her daily entries. She was also compensated for herbal remedies—salves, syrups, teas, and pills. As she traveled through the community, she detailed her economic interactions, including barter transactions between women, which are seldom historically documented.

The early years of the United States were economically unstable. Currency was unregulated and varied between states and regions. Dollars and cents replaced English shillings and pence, yet Ballard frequently received shillings and other foreign currency in payment.

Physical paper money and coins were frequently unavailable. Ballard was compensated for one delivery with 18 pounds of butter, $1 in currency, and $3 paid toward her account at a store in town. Supplies were also borrowed or purchased on account. Ballard's record of economic transactions reveals an interdependent community network.

The diary also details Ballard's daughters' economic enterprise—weaving. Ballard knitted and mended family clothing, but she was often away from home several days a week. The family grew flax, raised sheep for wool, and owned a loom. All of the Ballard women spun yarn and thread, but the girls wove textiles. Weaving had been a man's occupation, but as the process became more automated it provided less economic opportunity. Weaving gradually became part-time work for women in the late 18th and early 19th centuries. In families, homespun garments supplemented purchased manufactured clothing and fabrics. Women in the community specialized in different aspects of textile production and traded fibers or work. Ballard bartered a pair of leather shoes for 15 skeins of yarn. Another time, she traded flax to a seamstress who sewed dresses for the Ballard women.

The textile work documented in the journal chronicles a changing economy. The development of the cotton gin by Catherine Greene and Eli Whitney in 1793 enabled mass processing of cotton and marked cotton's emergence as an important American textile fiber. Ballard notes purchasing raw cotton for processing into fabric. Within a generation, however, this opportunity for women disappeared as industrialization made home textile production unsustainable as a trade.

Religion

The postcolonial period brought religious questioning and evolving Christian sects: freewill Methodists, Shakers, etc. Religious instability fragmented the Hallowell community. Ballard documented a mass murder and suicide committed by a neighbor as a tragic incident, but men in the community blamed the murderer's religious beliefs for his actions.

Disagreements over religious doctrine caused a young minister to be driven out of town. He left his wife behind, and several prominent men in town sexually assaulted her. Initially Ballard wrote nothing specific in her diary about the event, but her visits to the young woman reveal that she became pregnant, and Ballard was aware of the situation prior to the woman coming forward publicly. Charges were brought against the town's influential judge, who was also Ephraim Ballard's employer. Court records did not record testimonies, but Ballard wrote out her statement in her diary. The victim had confided in the midwife. Ballard had encouraged the woman to remain silent. She felt that exposing the situation would be more detrimental to the young woman.

The penalty for rape was death in this time period, but few men were ever found guilty. Puritan society regarded men as heads of households, with women beneath them. In most circumstances, a man's testimony was considered of greater value than a woman's. In Ballard's case, the judge who had raped her was acquit-

ted, and Ballard lost confidence in the town's male religious leaders. Interestingly, after the trial Ballard began referring to God as the "Great Parent of the Universe," a phrasing suggestive of her shifting religious beliefs.

Martha Ballard died in 1812 in Hallowell, Maine. Her family handed her diary down through the generations until her descendant Mary Hobart donated it to the Maine State Library in 1930. There it languished until historian Laurel Thatcher Ulrich began her work with it in the 1980s. In 1991 Ulrich's book based on the diary, *A Midwife's Tale,* won a number of prizes, culminating in a Pulitzer Prize. During a period of American history documented primarily from a male perspective, Ballard's diary offers a woman's point of view. She chronicled not only daily activities but also women interacting, creating an economic network, and participating in a culture that frequently overlooked their contributions.

Keri Dearborn

See also Boycotts, Tea and Textiles; Greene, Catharine Littlefield; Second Great Awakening; *Vol. 1, Sec. 1:* Clothing, Native American Women; Sexuality; *Vol. 1, Sec. 2:* Bastardy; Literacy; Midwives; Protestant Women; *Vol. 2, Sec. 1:* Shakers; *Vol. 2, Sec. 2:* Barton, Clara

Further Reading

McCausland, Robert R., and Cynthia MacAlman McCausland. 1992. *The Diary of Martha Ballard, 1785–1812.* Marco Island, FL: Picton.

Ulrich, Laurel Thatcher. 1990. *A Midwife's Tale: The Life of Martha Ballard Based on Her Diary, 1785–1812.* New York: Knopf.

Excerpts from the Diary of Martha Ballard (1788–1792)

Midwife Martha Ballard kept a journal for much of her life, the entries of which describe a world much different from today. Sally Pierce, who worked for the Ballards, was pregnant but not married. She confessed to fornication in a legal writ and swore that Ballard's son Jonathon was the father. Proof of her allegations was collected when in the middle of labor

Pierce swore to midwife Ballard that Jonathon was the child's father. Jonathon married Pierce soon after, but if he had not he would have been brought before the court and forced to provide economic support for the child. The community and the courts were far less concerned with premarital sex or immorality than they were with the practical realities of child support. Colonial Americans did not overly stigmatize women for premarital sex but did make every effort to force fathers to marry the mothers of their children. The stigma fell on the man, not the woman, if the couple did not marry.

November 6, 1788, Thursday

Clear & pleast. I have been at home, did house work & feel much fataugd. the Girls are gone to mr Crages. they are now returnd; informd that Hannah Fletcher has Sworn Shee is with Child by Joseph Fellers.

June 20, 1789, Saturday

a Clear morn. I was Calld at the riseing of ye Sun to Sarah White, Shee being in travil with her forth Child, & is yet unmarried. Shee remaind ill thro ye Day.

July 19, 1791, Tuesday

Cloudy part of ye Day. I went to mr Catons. Calld at mr Pollards, Jonses, Boltons, Voces & Densmores. Came home and went to mr Shuball Hinkleys. Capt Savages Lady Came home with me & Sleeps here. Shee informd me that Sally Peirce Swore a Child on my son Jon^a & he was taken with a warrent.

mr Abisha Cowen is his Bonds man for appearance at Coart

October 20, 1791, Sunday

Snowd & raind. I was Calld to See Sally Peirce at 9 h morn, the rideing very Bad. Doc^t Colman Calld me from there af^t noon to See his Lady. I was Calld from there to Sally before morn.

October 21, 1791, Monday

Clear. I was Calld from ye Docts to Sally, Shee was Safe Deld at 1 h pm of a fine Son. her illness very Severe but I left her Cleverly & returnd to ye Doc^ts about Sun Sett. Sally Declard that my Son Jon^a was the father of her Child.

February 29, 1792, Wednesday

Clear, a very Cold morn, Pleas^t Day. my Son Jonathan Brot his wife & little Son here. mr Ballard returnd from Pittst^n. I have been at home, finisht knitting Hannah a pair of hoes. mrs Welch here, Shee left her Dagt Jenny at mr Beemans.

Source: Martha Ballard's Diary Online, www.dohistory .org. Reprinted with permission.

Benevolent Associations

Benevolent associations emerged out of the need for marginalized groups to combat oppression and improve their lives. In the decades after the American Revolution, men and women joined a wide variety of benevolent associations. Women's participation in these philanthropic groups, both before and after the American Civil War (1861–1865), significantly affected American reform movements and prepared women for more sustained participation in public and partisan politics.

Benevolent societies supported specific needs with direct supportive services and acts to connect people along shared needs. Partially this tradition came out of the European concept of the almshouse,

houses owned by private charities for the support of aged or disabled people. William Penn, founder of Pennsylvania, also founded the first American almshouse, which was supported with state property taxes. Because government-funded almshouses were not widespread in the United States, benevolent societies generally developed out of the needs of different religious communities. Also called friendly societies, mutual aid societies, or fraternal organizations, these organizations provided services for the needy before the modern welfare state began to do so.

Early benevolent societies were voluntary associations established with ecumenical hopes of uniting different religions in the common cause of Christian unity, but they actually succeeded in strengthening denominational identity. Morality, or worthiness to receive support, had to be demonstrated. In urban areas, poor families received outdoor relief consisting of food, firewood, wool to spin, and money if they could demonstrate worthiness for assistance. By the late 1700s women began to not only join benevolent societies but also founded their own organizations.

During the American Revolution many women engaged in boycotts and public demonstrations of support for the cause of American independence. Women who had organizing experience in charitable work were able to effectively organize boycotts of British goods such as tea and textiles. Women also organized and participated in spinning bees, which promoted home production of textiles. Women's participation on public politics helped change gender ideology, giving rise to republican motherhood, an ideology that suggested that women had civic responsibilities. Women would use that ideology as well as their experience in the war to claim female moral authority, which in turn would expand women's activities in the public sphere, particularly in reform movements. Though it was not meant to do so, republican motherhood ideology transformed and expanded women's public reform work.

The reform impulses during the first half of the 19th century manifested themselves in five distinct areas that influenced women's activism: moral reform, the creation of utopian societies, institutional reform, the abolition movement, and the movement for women's rights. The New York Female Moral Reform Society (NYFMRS), for example, was established in 1834 to prevent prostitution. Rather than seeing prostitutes as morally lax women, the ladies of the NYFMRS believed that women turned to prostitution as an economic necessity, forced to do so by an economy that allowed women limited avenues of self-support. Female antislavery societies in Boston and Philadelphia, on the other hand, formed when all-male antislavery societies refused to admit women. These societies, which included both white and free black women, worked for the abolition of slavery in a variety of ways. By the mid-1800s the nation had scores of female benevolent and reform societies that worked on a variety of issues, including family poverty, custody rights, temperance, education, prison and mental health reform, abolition, and women's rights.

In the 19th-century West, freeborn Americans of African ancestry, along with Chinese, Jewish, German, and Italian immigrants, were systematically marginalized because they posed formidable competition for scarce resources in urban areas and in the gold fields. Women from each group respectively established benevolent societies and churches to address the particular needs of their community.

The largest slave market on the West Coast trafficked in Chinese women for the sex industry. At a time before Chinese immigration was tightly restricted, San Francisco fostered a well-organized slave market. Girls and women were sold as household servants and prostitutes. An organization called the Chinese Consolidated Benevolent Organization arranged a number of services for Chinese immigrants but did little about the sex trade. In 1874 Donaldina Cameron founded the San Francisco Presbyterian Mission Home to rescue Chinese girls and women from sex slavery.

In the 19th century an important but subtle shift of power occurred as states gradually allowed married women control over their property. Women increasingly established relief societies for other women in the public sector. By 1850 chapters of the Ladies Benevolent Society, run almost entirely by the wives of powerful men, provided support for poor widows and orphans. While oftentimes women from such organizations constrained their work to one or two philanthropic endeavors, such as widow relief, many women used these types of organizations as launching pads for women's rights organizations. Many women found private philanthropy limiting and came to believe that only with the right to vote would women be able to effect any meaningful change upon the nation. Thus, while women's benevolent work did much to address a plethora of social ills in the nation before the modern welfare state developed, it also prepared women for the demands of a more fully participatory political life. In doing so women expanded American democracy to not only include themselves but also to consider issues important to them.

Meredith Eliassen

See also *Vol. 1, Sec. 2:* Coverture; *Vol. 2, Sec. 1:* African American Benevolent Societies; Female

Antislavery Societies; Female Moral Authority and Sphere of Influence; New York Female Moral Reform Society; Temperance Movement

Further Reading

Attie, Jeanie. 1998. *Patriotic Toil: Northern Women and the American Civil War.* Ithaca, NY: Cornell University Press.

Giesberg, Judith Ann. 2000. *Civil War Sisterhood: The U.S. Sanitary Commission and Women's Politics in Transition.* Boston: Northeastern University Press.

Pasco, Peggy. 1992. *Relations of Rescue: The Search for Female Moral Authority in the West, 1874–1939.* New York: Oxford University Press.

Bonny, Anne (ca. 1700–1782)

Female pirate Anne Cormac Bonny (sometimes spelled Bonney) operated in the Caribbean Sea in the early 1700s. Though she never commanded her own ship, she became known for her ferocious fighting skills. She is often linked to another female pirate, Mary Read (1685–1721), who was Bonny's shipmate when they were captured by the authorities. Even when she was alive, Bonny became legendary as a free spirit who rejected the patriarchal system of her day, instead living an exciting life of relative freedom.

In the 17th and 18th centuries, treasure ships carried riches from the American colonies to their home ports in Europe via the Atlantic Ocean. They became ripe targets of pirates who stole their cargo and often killed their crews. Much of this piracy on the high seas had its origins in government-sanctioned plunder. As England, Spain, France, and other European countries continually fought wars against each other in the 1600s, they often sought to enrich themselves while crippling their enemies economically by taking command of other countries' ships. Governments called the government-sanctioned raids "privateering," as private sailors, rather than sanctioned navies, looted ships to enrich their sovereign. Rulers often rewarded successful privateers with rich bonuses and noble titles.

The Caribbean Sea was a particularly rich locale for this kind of plunder, especially for the English. Spanish

This 1725 engraving from *A General History of the Robberies and Murders of the Most Notorious Pyrates* shows Anne Bonny. Both her first and second husbands were pirates and she joined them in their exploits. (Bettmann/Getty)

galleons carried jewels and precious metals from their colonies on the western Gulf of Mexico, often called the Spanish Main, or mainland. The heavily laden treasure ships had to cross the Caribbean on their journey home, becoming tempting targets for privateers. However, when Spain and England signed treaties to end maritime attacks, privateers' livelihood became illegal and was called "piracy." Often, private ships and sailors had no other job prospects or found plundering ships too rewarding to give up. As a result, colorful tales of pirates and piracy abounded in the 1700s.

Into this atmosphere, Anne Bonny was born. Much of what is accepted about her life comes from a 1724 book titled *A General History of the Robberies and Murders of the Most Notorious Pyrates.* It was published under the name of Captain Charles Johnson, but many scholars believe it to be the work of English writer Daniel Defoe, author of the fantastical and fictional *Robinson Crusoe* and ribald *Moll Flanders*.

Bonny's birth is usually cited as somewhere between 1697 and 1702. She was born out of wedlock to a housemaid who worked in the home of her father, a married Irish attorney named Cormac. The scandal was such that her parents fled to today's Charleston, South Carolina. Bonny was 13 when her mother died. Cormac was able to make a comfortable living as a merchant and arranged a marriage between Bonny and a local man. She rebelled, instead marrying penniless sailor James Bonny in 1718. Her father promptly disowned her.

Anne and James Bonny left for New Providence in the Bahamas, where former privateer Woodes Rogers was royal governor. The island was a notorious hub of piracy, a career that James Bonny attempted unsuccessfully. In return for immunity, he became a paid informant for Rogers, gaining the trust of local pirates and then turning them in to the authorities.

Anne Bonny entirely rejected her father's respectability. She became involved with pirate John Rackham, called "Calico Jack" for his bright-colored clothing. Rackham was said to have originated the distinctive pirate flag that features a skull over two crossed daggers. Rackham offered to pay James Bonny to divorce Anne. Some stories say that Rackman was rebuffed by James; others say that Anne refused to be "sold like an animal."

Bonny and Rackham had a child together but left the baby in Cuba. In August 1720 Bonny and Rackham, with a crew of about a dozen men, attacked merchant ships around the coast of Jamaica. Having Bonny aboard was extremely unusual, because sailors generally considered women bad luck on a ship. Bonny was open about her gender and generally wore women's clothes. However, when attacking she changed into men's clothing and engaged in armed combat alongside her fellow pirates. They tended to treat her with respect, especially after an alleged incident when she stabbed a sailor through the heart for objecting to her presence.

Another infamous female pirate, Mary Read, joined Rackham's crew around this time. Read and Bonny became close friends. On November 15, 1720, the authorities captured Rackham's pirate ship when it was at anchor off the Jamaican coast. Most of the crew was belowdecks asleep or drunk. Bonny and Read battled fiercely but were taken prisoner. When they were tried on November 28, they were found guilty and sentenced to hang along with the men. However, both claimed to be pregnant, and under English common law their execution had to be delayed until after they gave birth. According to legend, Bonny was allowed to see Rackham before his execution, telling him, "Had you fought like a man, you need not have hanged like a dog."

Read is said to have died in prison. While there is no historical record of Bonny being hanged or released, some historians believe that she was ransomed by her father, with whom she reconciled. She is said to have been smuggled on a merchant ship back to Charleston, where she gave birth to Rackham's second child. In this version of the Bonny story, she married a local man with whom she lived a respectable life as a wife and mother of 10 children until her death on April 22, 1782. Others say that she escaped to a small Caribbean island, while still others say that she went to England, where she owned a tavern, regaling customers with tales of her past.

Nancy Hendricks

See also Butterworth, Mary

Further Reading

Cordingly, David. 2007. *Seafaring Women: Adventures of Pirate Queens, Female Stowaways, and Sailors' Wives.* New York: Random House.
Williams, Jeffrey S. 2007. *Pirate Spirit: The Adventures of Anne Bonney.* Lincoln, NE: iUniverse.

Boone, Jemima (1762–1829/1834)

In July 1776, Daniel Boone's daughter Jemima and two of her friends were kidnapped by Indians. Only a few days later, they were rescued by her father and other residents of Boonesborough. The oft-told story of the capture and the bold rescue served to embellish Daniel Boone's reputation as a daring and fearless leader. It is also illustrative of the common portrayal of the frontiersman as the strong male figure and the frontier woman as weak and dependent on him, a portrayal hardly rooted in reality.

Jemima Boone was born to Daniel Boone's wife Rachel Bryan Boone on October 4, 1762, in Rowan County, North Carolina. Daniel was away on an extended absence at the time, and some, including Daniel's own son Nathan, speculated that Jemima's father was actually Daniel's brother, Edward (Ned) Boone. After exploring the country on several previous trips, Daniel moved his family from North Carolina to Kentucky in 1775. There they established the fortified settlement of Boonesborough. Most settlers at this time lived in the southeastern part of Kentucky in Boonesborough, Harrodsburg, and Logan's Station. This was at the beginning of the American Revolutionary War, and there was increasing conflict between the settlers and the Native Americans, who were being supported by the British. The Shawnees, who lived north of the Ohio River, and the Cherokees, under their leader Dragging Canoe, frequently attacked settlers and hunters. By the late spring of 1776, only about 200 settlers remained in Kentucky.

On Sunday, July 14, 1776, Jemima Boone and her friends Elizabeth (Betsy) and Frances (Fanny) Callaway left Boonesborough to float in a canoe on the Kentucky River. According to later accounts, the girls were weary of being confined to the fort, and Jemima had an injured foot that she wanted to soak in the cool river. They had been warned to stay near the cabins and not to go near the opposite shore of the river, but they were caught in a current that carried them there.

Unbeknownst to the girls, there was a small war party watching the river. The group was made up of two Cherokee (one of whom was called Hanging Maw by the settlers) and three Shawnee warriors. They were part of a larger group of Native Americans who were returning to Ohio from a conference at the Cherokee town of Chota, located in present-day Tennessee. There they had planned a campaign against the settlers and had already murdered a nearby farmer.

As the canoe approached the north shore, one of the warriors grabbed it. One of the girls attacked a warrior with a paddle while the others screamed for help. Their screams alerted the settlement. The girls

were taken north toward the Ohio River, and Daniel Boone organized a rescue party of eight men to pursue them. Jemima and her friends made every attempt to slow the journey. Jemima made much of her injured foot, and the girls pretended to be hampered by their Sunday clothes. They also tried to mark their trail by breaking branches. Far from being powerless victims, the young women did everything in their power to resist their captors and encourage their rescue. When they stopped for the night, the warriors cut off their Sunday dresses at the knees, removed their shoes and stockings, and gave them moccasins to wear. They were then tied up for the night.

By the following afternoon they were 25 miles from Boonesborough. Sometime during their journey, the Indians came upon a stray horse and tried to get the girls to ride it to speed up their pace. But the girls, who were actually good riders, pretended that they could not ride at all, and this plan was abandoned. By the second morning, Boone and his men were only 10 miles behind the captives but making slow progress. Boone decided that the Indians were intending to cross the Licking River at the Upper Blue Licks and set off across country to intercept them. The third morning after their capture, the rescue party overtook the girls and their captors at Bald Eagle Creek near the present-day town of Sharpsburg, Kentucky, killing two of the Indians. The others fled, and the girls were returned home unharmed.

The following year Jemima married Flanders Callaway, one of her rescuers. They settled near Marthasville in Warren County, Missouri. They were to have six children. Several members of Jemima's family, including her parents, followed them there. Daniel Boone died in Jemima's home in 1820. According to different sources, Flanders Callaway died in either 1824 or 1829. Sources also differ as to the date of Jemima's death. Some indicate that she died in 1829, and others say that she died on August 30, 1834. She is buried in the Old Bryan Farm Cemetery near Marthasville.

Like other captivity narratives, the Boone story served to illustrate the savagery of the native people and the heroic power of white colonists. Captivity stories also emphasized female vulnerability to dangerous nonwhite men and as such were often tales of white women's sexual vulnerability. The dramatic story of Jemima's capture and subsequent rescue has been commemorated in numerous lithographs and paintings, including Charles Wimar's *The Abduction of Daniel Boone's Daughter by the Indians* (1853) and Howard Pyle's *The Capture of Elizabeth, Frances Callaway, and Jemima Boone* (1884). It is said that Jemima's kidnapping inspired the rescue of Cora and Alice Munro depicted by James Fenimore Cooper in *The Last of the Mohicans*. In more recent years, Jemima's story has been depicted in a one-woman show by L. Henry Dowell, *Jemima Boone, Daughter of the Frontier* (2011).

Nancy Snell Griffith

See also McCrea, Jane; Williams, Eunice; *Vol. 1, Sec. 2:* Captives, English; Captivity Narratives; Jemison, Mary

Further Reading

Draper, Lyman C. 1998. *The Life of Daniel Boone.* Mechanicsburg, PA: Stackpole Books.

Faragher, John Mack. 1992. *Daniel Boone: The Life and Legend of an American Pioneer.* New York: Holt.

Morgan, Robert. 2008. *Boone: A Biography.* Chapel Hill, NC: Algonquin Books.

Boycotts, Tea and Textiles

As tensions between the American colonies and the British government escalated in the years leading up to the American Revolutionary War, colonial women played a vital role in the success of numerous nonimportation efforts and boycotts of British goods. Many colonists became increasingly hostile to the various taxes imposed by British officials and saw nonimportation and boycott of British goods as a measured response. As the chief goods purchasers in colonial American families, women played an important role in boycotts.

In August 1764, Boston merchants began a boycott of British luxury items in response to the reviled Stamp Act, which required colonists to pay a tax on almost all official papers and documents. The British Parliament repealed the Stamp Act in 1766, and English goods were once again readily imported.

Colonists learned that boycotts could be effective ways to force the government to certain kinds of behavior. Just one year later Bostonians reinstated their boycott of luxury items from Britain as relations with the royal government worsened, and by mid-1769 merchants in Philadelphia and the House of Burgesses in Virginia had joined their effort. Colonial sentiment against the British practice of taxation without representation continued to grow, and in October 1774 the first Continental Congress formally adopted the Continental Association, by which delegates agreed to boycott all English imports and effect an embargo of exports to Britain. The movement became a litmus test for colonists, as Loyalists and revolutionary Patriots differed in their purchasing practices.

The success of all of these nonimportations, efforts and boycotts was largely due to the support and ingenuity of colonial women. In most colonial homes women were the managers of the household budget. Their everyday activities, such as buying clothes and food, made them an integral part of the colonial economy. Britain relied on colonial consumption of its imports for the success of its own economy. When colonial political leaders wanted to send a clear message to Britain of their unhappiness with new taxes, they attempted to affect the British economy by curbing consumption of imported goods. The support and cooperation of colonial women was essential to the success of such efforts and became a rallying cry for patriotism. Patriotic Daughters of Liberty, as they came to be known, were urged to give up or find local substitutes for articles traditionally imported from Britain. By 1774 the boycotts and import embargoes caused downright scarcity of some products, and the colonies relied on colonial women to develop feasible alternatives. While not all American women participated in the boycotts—like their male counterparts, some remained loyal to the British Crown—many others proudly shunned purchasing and consuming British goods and collectively worked to provide substitutes as needed by their families.

One British import that many colonial women actively subjected to boycott was tea. American women, as buyers for their households and some as merchants of imported goods, appealed for general abstention from buying or consuming British tea, a common staple of colonial households and taverns. As one example, Boston shopkeeper Elizabeth Murray encouraged colonial protestors to boycott British tea as a way to stand up for their valuable country against taxes that would only feed corrupt British leaders. Meanwhile, much farther south in Edenton, North Carolina, one of the richest women in the colony, Penelope Barker, hosted a tea party at which 50 other women signed a protest statement against the British practice of taxing the colonists without letting them have a say in the government. The petition, signed 10 months after the more famous Boston Tea Party, endorsed a boycott of tea and other British products. Barker sent the petition to a London newspaper, not afraid to publicly share the names of the women signees. While the British press lampooned the women as morally questionable and unfit mothers, many colonial Patriots praised the women for taking a stand. Indeed, women all over the colonies followed their lead and publicly committed to boycott British tea and other goods.

Women did more than merely refuse to buy British tea. They developed their own teas by growing and drying herbal substitutes. However insignificant this might sound, it would have taken considerable effort to gather seeds, plant herbal tea gardens, harvest flowers or greens, and dry and store them. Thus, women weighed in politically not only with their dollars but also with their labor.

Another target of many nonimportation efforts and colonial boycotts was British textiles. American women throughout the colonies, first as individuals at home and then as members of local sewing circles, produced so-called homespun cloth to replace British goods. Women had to spin yarn and weave fabric before they could make clothing, each step of which would have been tremendously labor-intensive. Spinning bees became popular not only as an entertainment where ladies could work their spinning wheels together but also as a form of public protest. Women would participate in public spinning demonstrations and competitions, all the while explicitly condemning British textiles.

While the early garments created of homespun fabric by American women were much coarser in texture and simpler in design than those imported from Britain, many colonists chose to wear the poorer-quality clothes as a symbol of patriotic pride and freedom. As more and more colonists began making their own clothes and the occurrence of spinning bees and sewing circles grew, homespun dresses and suits began to change. More decorations and embellishments were added to American clothes to replace the silk and linen traditionally found on British garments. Increasingly, antitaxation propagandists and colonial women themselves encouraging many homemakers to join the boycotts by connected the politics of nonimportation and nonconsumption to the security of the home and family. Spinning bees, sewing circles, and tea parties became social meetings where women could discuss political issues and bolster their sense of patriotism and political participation.

Kathleen Gronnerud

See also Daughters of Liberty; Revolutionary War and Women; *Vol. 1, Sec. 2:* Spinning Bees

Further Reading
Auslander, Leora. 2009. *Cultural Revolutions: Everyday Life and Politics in Britain, North America, and France.* Los Angeles: University of California Press.

Baumgarten, Linda. 2002. *What Clothes Reveal: The Language of Clothing in Colonial and Federal America.* New Haven, CT: Yale University Press.

Edenton Resolution: South Carolina Women Organize a Boycott (1774)

In response to the British Tea Act of 1773, 51 women in Edenton, South Carolina, drafted the Edenton Resolution on October 25, 1774. Inspired by revolutionary ideology, the women vowed to boycott British products, including tea.

As we cannot be indifferent on any occasion that appears nearly to affect the peace and happiness of our country, and as it has been thought necessary, for the public good, to enter into several particular resolves by a meeting of Members deputed from the whole

Province, it is a duty which we owe, not only to our near and dear connections who have concurred in them, but to ourselves who are essentially interested in their welfare, to do every thing as far as lies in our power to testify our sincere adherence to the same; and we do therefore accordingly subscribe this pa-

per, as a witness of our fixed intention and solemn determination to do so.

Source: "2.7 The Edenton 'Tea Party,'" *Morning Chronicle and London Advertiser,* January 31, 1775. Available at Learn NC, http://www.learnnc.org/lp/editions/nchist-revolution /4234.

Brant, Molly (1735/1736–1796)

A Mohawk Indian leader and tribal power, Molly Brant was part of the six nations of the Iroquois Confederacy. Iroquois society, unlike European society, was matrilineal, and Iroquois women were farmers. They did the work of planting, raising, harvesting, and preparing food. Because women did this work, they owned the food, which provided the basis for female power. In such a society Molly Brant rose to prominence as the chieftess of all Iroquois clan mothers. She kept most of the Iroquois nations loyal to Britain during the American Revolution. She was the common-law wife of Sir William Johnson, superintendent of Indians in the Mohawk River Valley, and after his death served as a cultural and political intermediary between her people and Euro-Americans.

Likely born in 1736, though some have proposed 1735, Molly Brant is sometimes given the name Mary, though she was known as Molly throughout her life. Historians know little about her childhood, a common occurrence for 18th-century people when records were seldom kept, particularly about marginalized people such as Native Americans and women. Brant, of course, was both. She was a British subject, though not a citizen, and was baptized in the Anglican Church. She lived briefly in Ohio in the 1740s, though her activities there are unknown. By age 15 Brant had lost her father and stepfather, one to disease and the other to warfare. Brant and her mother appear to have been poor during Brant's adolescence. Extended families were to help their poor relations, though one does not know what assistance Brant's kin provided, if any.

At about age 23, Brant entered the historical record as the domestic servant of William Johnson, though the two were apparently lovers from the outset. She bore Johnson nine children. Eight survived into

adulthood, a remarkable achievement in an era when diseases claimed about half of all children by age 5. Even though the couple did not marry, the Mohawks regarded the two as a married couple. Accordingly, Brant enjoyed high status among Native Americans.

Because the Mohawks accepted Johnson as one of their own, they were pleased that Brant was his spouse. As a result, the Mohawks more willingly dealt with English colonists with Johnson as their representative. Because of her prominence and that of her husband, Brant entertained numerous guests at her home. She also received delegations of various Native American nations, negotiating agreements of peace and trade with them. These negotiations were sometimes tense because Native American nations took a dim view of the British, who Johnson represented, and other Europeans for taking their land. Brant believed that Europeans should permit Native Americans to keep their land, though the reality was otherwise. As an elite woman, Brant owned four slaves. In this she was not alone. Many (but not all) Native Americans owned slaves, who could be other native people or people of African descent. That Brant owned slaves suggests her social class status as a woman of at least moderate means.

Upon Johnson's death, Brant opened a store that must have resembled a tavern in its sale of alcohol. Because of her prominence, the store was a gathering place for Native Americans. During the American Revolution, Brant joined the British cause as a spy. Like many contemporaries, she believed that Native Americans stood a better chance of keeping their land under British rule than in an independent America. George Washington knew and feared Brant as a spokeswoman for the Iroquois. In addition to her role as spy, Brant delivered ammunition to the British before the Battle of Oriskany in 1777. Revolutionary partisans retaliated by burning her home. After the Revolution, Brant left the nascent United States for Ontario, Canada, which had remained loyal to Britain. For her efforts during the Revolutionary War, Britain awarded Brant a pension and partially compensated her for the property she lost at the war's end. She died in 1796 at about 60 years old. Two hundred years after Brant's death, Canada issued a postage stamp with her image. Canada has also erected statues and plaques in her honor. She is less historically significant in the United States, in part because she did not support the colonial effort for independence from Britain.

Christopher Cumo

See also Loyalist Women; Sacagawea; *Vol. 1, Sec. 1:* Pocahontas; *Vol. 1, Sec. 2:* Kittamaquund, Mary

Further Reading

Earle, Thomas. 1996. *The Three Faces of Molly Brant.* Kingston, Ontario: Quarry.

Juettner, Bonnie. 2005. *100 Native Americans Who Changed American History.* Milwaukee: Almanac Library.

Butterworth, Mary (1686–1775)

One of the first counterfeiters of paper money in America, Mary Peck Butterworth was born on July 27, 1686, to Joseph Peck and Elizabeth Smart. Butterworth lived in the contested territory of Rehoboth, a border town in lands that were claimed by both the Plymouth and Massachusetts Bay Colonies. The first records of Butterworth appear at her marriage to John Butterworth Jr., a prominent house builder, in 1711.

Counterfeiters of the time used heavy copper plates to produce copied coins and bills and could not easily hide or dispose of these plates, so courts relied on the possession of copper plates as irrefutable evidence of counterfeiting. Butterworth invented a new method that could escape notice by the authorities. She placed a piece of starched muslin onto a genuine bill and pressed the bill onto paper using a hot iron. After successfully transferring the bill's imprint, she would burn or throw out the muslin. Then Butterworth would use crow quill pens to strengthen the image of the bill into an almost perfect duplicate. Using this method, she was able to create counterfeits of at least eight types of bills including those of Rhode Island, Connecticut, and Massachusetts.

By 1716, Butterworth was successfully running a counterfeiting ring from her kitchen. Her extended family joined in her trade, helping to both make and sell the bills for half their face value to trusted neighbors. The Peck-Butterworth counterfeit ring expanded to at least 12 known accomplices by the early 1720s, including 2 brothers, who made the quill pens; a sister-in-law, Hannah Peck, whose penmanship in detailing the bills rivaled Butterworth's; Nicholas Campe and his sister; and Daniel Hunt, a deputy sheriff in Rehoboth.

There were also several passers who would put the counterfeited bills into circulation, as Butterworth refused to do the task herself. One of the most notable passers was Daniel Smith, who served as town clerk and justice for the Bristol County Court of General Sessions. The involvement of notable county officials ensured that Butterworth's activities remained secretive and likely protected her family for quite some time.

Butterworth raised seven children while running her illegal operation. Historians estimate that her ring succeeded in producing and passing more than 1,000 pounds of forged bills in over seven years without being detected. Some of her profits are believed to have helped build Butterworth's new home in 1722. Authorities in Rhode Island grew suspicious of how the couple could afford such a large home. Additionally, several of the uninvolved justices of the Bristol County Court became suspicious of Daniel Smith's involvement in the ring. A court of quarter sessions issued a warrant to search for counterfeit plates in Smith's home in 1722. Butterworth's home was also searched, but no evidence was found to support the warrant. Apparently her ability to throw out the muslin evidence of her trade kept her safe.

In July 1723, Arthur Noble went to see the captured pirate ship *Ranger* at a gala in Newport with a supply of Butterworth's counterfeits on his person. Noble encountered three young women in Newport and enertained them using the counterfeit bills. Elizabeth Weir, the wife or employee of a local innkeeper, discovered the cheat at a tavern, and Noble was arrested. At about the same time, Nicholas Campe was interrogated by Governor Samuel Cranston of Rhode Island and revealed the story of Butterworth's operation to authorities. Cranston issued arrest warrants for Campe and several others involved in the ring. The case was brought to trial in Rhode Island, but a grand jury would not indict Campe.

Campe's deposition circulated in the colonies and caused the arrest and retrial of Butterworth and five others in Massachusetts. Unfortunately for the authorities, searches of the homes of Butterworth's ring members yielded no tangible evidence of the counterfeiting enterprise, and no one besides Campe confessed to the ring's existence. Thus, authorities had to drop charges against Butterworth and her accomplices.

Afterward, Butterworth closed her counterfeiting operation and retired on the gains made from her enterprise. No documentation of her exists after her 1723 trial except the birth records of her last two children. Protected by her family and friends, Butterworth lived the rest of her life in relative obscurity as a housewife. In 1771, her husband died at the age of 93. Butterworth died of old age in Rehoboth in 1775.

Tiffany Rhoades-Piotti

See also Bonny, Anne

Further Reading

Bowen, Richard LeBaron. 1946. *Early Rehoboth*, Vol. 2. Boston: Privately published.

Scott, Kenneth. 1957. *Counterfeiting in Colonial America*. Philadelphia: University of Pennsylvania Press.

Camp Followers

In most wars before the modern era armies marched with fighting men, but there were few or no men to fill auxiliary roles. Camp followers were women who followed armies to stay close to their loved ones, to earn a living providing services that armies did not provide for their soldiers, or both. Moreover, with their husbands, fathers, or brothers off to war, some women could not sustain their households. Women also followed armies because it was safer than staying home. The phrase "camp follower" has been used as a pejorative and stand-in for "prostitute," but in reality the majority of camp followers were crucial to the success of fighting forces.

During the American Revolutionary War (1775–1783), women followed both the Continental Army and the British Army. Women acted as cooks, laundresses, health care workers, seamstresses, food scavengers, sex workers, and sometimes even substitute soldiers. Oftentimes women undertook multiple roles, doing one job during periods of relative peace and another during battle. Nursing and water carrying became particularly important in the heat of military engagement. Because armies did not provide soldiers with cooked food or clean clothes, female camp followers stepped into the gap. Armies also made little or no provision for the wounded. Women played an important role in keeping some wounded men alive.

Famed camp follower Molly Pitcher may not have been a real person but rather a composite of women who heroically carried water to men in the midst of war. Or Molly Pitcher may have been Mary Ludwig Hays McCauley, a Pennsylvanian who joined Martha Washington and other women at Valley Forge to wash clothes and feed the troops. In 1778 McCauley, whose nickname may have been Molly, would help keep cannons cool by bringing pitchers of water to pour on the barrel. When the cannon barrel got too hot, or so the story goes, the men would call "Molly, Pitcher!"

It is difficult to know just how many women followed the two armies, but they often made up 3–5 percent of the total force, or up to 20,000 women. Continental Army regulations held that camp followers had to be married to a soldier and were entitled to a half ration. Children were awarded a quarter ration. Aside from rations, the camp followers were not paid from public funds. Individual soldiers paid women for their services. Most camp followers were poor women who had little choice but to follow the army in times of war. Sometimes elite women came to camp to help soldiers, as did Martha Washington occasionally, but they generally did so temporarily and not from economic necessity. Elite ladies also came to camps to show support for the troops, but many of them did little more than symbolic work.

Having decided to follow an army and make a living providing services to that army, camp followers often became passionate advocates for their army's cause and the soldiers with whom they served. Some even took up arms under fire. McCauley took over for her husband after he was injured manning a cannon. She swabbed and loaded the cannon for the rest of the battle. For her bravery, George Washington made her a noncommissioned officer.

Some of the camp followers did earn their living through sex work or prostitution. Army officers recognized that prostitutes were good for army morale and provided soldiers with a valuable service, though some of the leadership worried about sexually transmitted diseases among prostitutes. Nonetheless, prostitutes, who would have been among the poorest and most desperate of women, followed the armies during the American Revolutionary War as well as wars before and after. During the American Civil War, Major General Joseph Hooker became so famed for the number of prostitutes who followed his army that they became known as "Hooker's Brigade."

Civil War armies also had camp followers, but significantly fewer women and children traveled with the troops than during earlier wars. This statistic is due to the fact that organizations such as the United States Sanitary Commission provided considerable services once covered by camp followers. Also, army commands became better at providing auxiliary services to soldiers so that by the 20th century, camp followers disappeared in the United Sates.

Peg A. Lamphier

See also McCauley, Mary; Washington, Martha; *Vol. 2, Sec. 2:* United States Sanitary Commission

Further Reading

Berkin, Carol. 2006. *Revolutionary Mothers: Women in the Struggle for America's Independence.* New York: Vintage.

Norton, Mary Beth. 1996. *America's Daughters: The Revolutionary Experience of American Women, 1750–1800.* Ithaca, NY: Cornell University Press.

Colden, Jane (1724–1766)

The first female botanist in America, Jane Colden learned science from her father's father, Cadwallader Colden, who had a hobbyist interest in botany and trained her in the Linnaeus system of botanical classification. She studied flora in New York City, mainly along the Hudson River Valley. She was a well-known botanist in her time and was accepted among male botanists.

Jane Colden was born in the province of New York to Cadwallader and Alice (Christy) Colden. She was the 5th of 10 children. When her father learned of Colden's interest in botany, he wrote to a friend, "As it

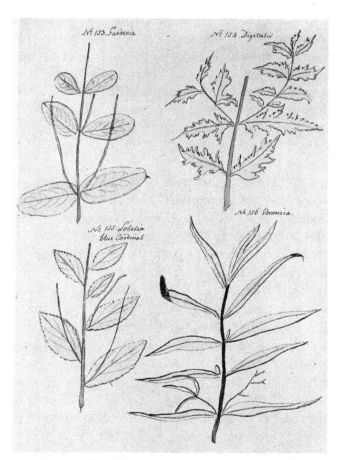

Drawing number 153 (1724–1766) comes from the work of botanist Jane Colden. She compiled specimens and information on more than 300 species of plants from the lower Hudson River Valley for her manuscript *Flora of New York.* (The Natural History Museum/ Alamy Stock Photo)

is not usual for woemen [*sic*] to take pleasure in Botany as a Science I shall do what I can to incourage [*sic*] her in this amusement which fills up her idle hours to much better purpose tha[n] the usual amusements eagerly pursued by others of her sex" (Colleen Beck-Kaplan 2010, 36). This attitude was common at the time. Science was considered a suitable course of study for women because people thought it was unchanging and thus taught obedience to order. Women were particularly encouraged to study botany and astronomy, while men were encouraged to study the classics or law. Maria Mitchell, for example, was the most famed and esteemed astronomer of the pre–Civil War (1861–1865) period but lost some ground after the war as society came to believe that science was a male-centered field of study. Science books in the 1700s were directed specifically toward women and emphasized that science was an undertaking that could improve the female mind and was preferable to other ways women could spend their time. The growing popularity of novel reading as a leisure activity for women as well as the increasing affordability of books also led to more scientific books being geared toward women, such as the 1865 *The Young Lady's Geography*.

By 1757, Colden had described and sketched more than 300 local plants. She was known by her contemporaries as an expert botanist regarding species indigenous to New York and her surrounding area. She was also an expert in the Linnaeus system of botanical classification. It is apparent from her writings and the writings of her peers that not only was she respected, but she was also secure in her place as a botanist. If her observations differed from other work in the field, she did not hesitate to say so in her writings. Nonetheless, her father often received the praise and acclaim that should have been directed toward Colden. One example is when Carl Linnaeus, the creator of the Linnaeus system, honored Cadwallader Colden, not his daughter, with the new generic name *Coldenia*.

During her time working as a botanist, Colden became a skillful plant illustrator and developed a technique for making ink impressions of leaves. She compiled information and illustrations for around 340 plants around the Hudson River Valley in New York City. She also joined the Natural History Circle, whose members consisted of both American and European botanists who shared seeds and plant samples with each other. In 1756 she discovered the Gardenia, which she named after botanist Alexander Garden. The scientific name was later changed because another plant had been assigned the scientific name Gardenia, but the group of flowering plants that Colden identified is still informally called gardenia.

Colden's scientific curiosity in her professional life also showed through to her domestic life. In 1756 she also maintained a log of her cheese making. The way that she recorded her cheese-making efforts reads much more like an experiment book than a recipe book. Colden married Dr. William Farquhar, a physician, on March 12, 1759. The marriage was short-lived because of her death in 1766. Like many women of her time, Colden died during the birth of their first child, who died within the week as well.

After Colden's death and during the American Revolutionary War, a Hessian captain found her drawings and plant descriptions. He returned to England with them, and now they are held at the British Museum. In 1963, the American Garden Clubs published a part of the manuscript. Colden's unnamed manuscript is still prized today for its artistry and accuracy.

Elliott Popel

See also *Vol. 2, Sec. 1:* Mitchell, Maria

Further Reading

Beck-Kaplan, Colleen. 2010. "Family of Science: Education, Gender, and Science in the Colden Family of New York 1720–1770." Electronic Theses, Treatises and Dissertations, Florida State University Libraries, http://diginole.lib.fsu.edu/islandora/object/fsu:175740/datastream/PDF/view.

Bonta, Marcia. 1991. *Women in the Field: America's Pioneering Women Naturalists.* College Station: Texas A&M University Press.

Robbins, Paula Ivaska. 2009. *Jane Colden: America's First Woman Botanist.* Fleischmanns, NY: Purple Mountain.

Corbin, Margaret (1751–1800)

Margaret Corbin fought in the American Revolutionary War and became the first woman in U.S. history to be granted a pension for military service. She earned her fame as a war hero when she took up her husband's place at his cannon after he died and continued firing until she herself was severely wounded. Corbin's cannon was the last one on the rebel's side to stop firing.

Corbin was born in 1751 in western Pennsylvania to Robert Cochran, a Scotch-Irish immigrant, and his wife Sarah, of whom little is known. Corbin was orphaned at a young age, five years old, when her parents were attacked and killed by Native Americans. She along with her brother were adopted by their uncle, with whom they had been staying at the time of the attack. In 1772 she married John Corbin, a farmer. When he decided to join the revolutionary militia three years later, she followed him to war. Like many wives and other camp followers, Margaret Corbin earned money by performing domestic duties for the soldiers such as cooking, laundry, and taking care of the wounded.

Corbin followed her husband to the battlefield during the Battle of Fort Washington on November 16, 1776. John was a matross, which meant that he loaded the cannon. When his partner was killed, John took over firing the cabin and Corbin acted as loader. When John was killed, Corbin continued loading and firing the cannon alone. Both Continental and British soldiers noticed the accuracy of her cannon fire. The British targeted her specifically with their own cannons. Though the British won the battle, Corbin remained at her post firing her cannon even after her arm, chest, and jaw were all hit by enemy fire. She and her fellow soldiers surrendered to British troops but were later released. She would never fully recover from these injuries and lost the use of her left arm for the rest of her life.

After her injury Corbin joined the Invalid Regiment at West Point, where she and other wounded soldiers would cook and do laundry for able troops. On June 26, 1776, the State of Pennsylvania gave Corbin an award of $30 in recognition of her bravery during the battle and to help with her expenses. Then on July 6, 1779, the Continental Congress granted her a lifelong pension. Though the pension was half the amount a man would have received, it was the first military pension granted to a woman. Corbin was included on military rolls until the end of the war. She was officially discharged from the Continental Army in 1783. After the war General Henry Knox and Quartermaster William Price helped Corbin by finding someone to help her bathe and dress.

After the war the Philadelphia Society of Women planned to erect a monument honoring Corbin. Disapproving of her manner and appearance when they met her, the ladies canceled the monument. Corbin, though a brave soldier, did not meet postwar standards of femininity or womanhood. She spent her free time smoking with other soldiers and talking with them, soldier to soldier.

Corbin died in Highland Falls, New York, on January 16, 1800, at the age of 48. Today there are three commemorative plaques celebrating Corbin's bravery near the Fort Washington battle site. In 1926 the Daughters of the American Revolution had her remains reinterred behind the Old Cadet Chapel at West Point, where a monument now stands for her. Only one other Revolutionary War hero is buried in the West Point cemetery. Corbin's battlefield experience and the acceptance she gained among soldiers belie modern arguments about the suitability of American women for military combat. Corbin and countless other American women fought bravely for their country, and the fact that many of these women, including Deborah Sampson, were granted pensions speaks to the fact that the government acknowledged their contributions on the field of battle.

Moriah Saldana

See also McCauley, Mary; Sampson, Deborah; Revolutionary War and Women

Further Reading
Berkin, Carol. 2005. *Revolutionary Mothers: Women in the Struggle for America's Independence.* New York: Knopf.

Daughters of Liberty

The Daughters of Liberty were colonial American women who banded together to help the cause of

American independence. Around 1766, colonial women began referring to themselves as Daughters of Liberty to support the cause of freedom. They aimed to show that women's political savvy could be vital to the struggle for American liberty from England. Successful efforts such as boycotting British goods and aiding the Continental Army led Samuel Adams, a Patriot, to say of the Daughters of Liberty that "With ladies on our side, we can make every Tory tremble." Although the Daughters of Liberty helped significantly during wartime, American women's legal and political rights remained limited after the American Revolutionary War was won.

Unrest against British rule grew in the American colonies in the late 1700s. Though taxation of the colonists and repressive laws against them were implemented, American colonists were not represented in the British Parliament. However, a British member of the House of Commons, Isaac Barré, spoke on behalf of the colonists against the proposed Stamp Act in 1765 and called them "sons of liberty." Subsequently, groups of discontented colonists came together and began referring to themselves as the Sons of Liberty. Shortly thereafter around 1766, groups of women were inspired to call themselves the Daughters of Liberty.

The women demonstrated their patriotism to the American cause by boycotting British goods, dealing a substantial loss to British merchants who depended on American buyers for their products. A significant blow was dealt to the British textile industry when the women boycotted imported cloth and made their own, which came to be known as homespun. Though they already labored from dawn to dark with myriad household tasks, they now took on the additional job of providing clothes for their families by weaving yarn and spinning wool into their own fabric.

However, they made the task as pleasant as possible while also calling attention to their patriotic endeavors. In a cooperative effort, they organized spinning bees to work together on their projects. Sometimes church groups held spinning contests on village squares, competitions that were entered by large numbers of women. Often for 12 hours at a time, they turned spinning wheels, producing hundreds of skeins of wool that would then be woven into cloth.

They made a point of wearing the rough homespun dresses to elegant social events. And they made sure colonial newspapers carried reports of their efforts, hoping to spotlight their patriotic work and inspire others to the cause.

At these spinning bees, many women were able to leave the restricted domestic sphere for the first time, enjoy each other's company while working (and therefore without guilt), and discuss topics such as politics about which they were usually expected to keep silent. Annoyed at the lack of patriotic support by some colonial merchants, who continued to deal in British-made goods, in 1768 a poem titled "The 20 Daughters of Liberty by Anonymous" (sometimes attributed to Hannah Griffitts) was published in the *Pennsylvania Gazette:*

> Since the men, from a party or fear of a frown,
> Are kept by a sugar-plum quietly down,
> . . . If the sons, so degenerate! the blessings
>   despise,
> Let the Daughters of Liberty nobly arise;
> And though we've no voice but a negative
>   here,
> The use of the taxables, let us forbear:—
> (Then merchants import till your stores are
>   all full,
> May the buyers be few, and your traffic be
>   dull!)
> . . . But a motive more worthy our patriot
>   pen,
> Thus acting—we point out their duty to men;
> And should the bound-pensioners tell us to
>   hush,
> We can throw back the satire, by biding them
>   blush.

To make recalcitrant merchants blush, public flyers were posted by the Daughters of Liberty, such as the following: *"It is desired that the Sons and Daughters of Liberty refuse to buy from* [name of merchant]." It is difficult to know how many store owners changed their policies as a result of women's efforts, but public pressure would have been effective in towns where everyone knew each other.

Throughout the colonies, Daughters of Liberty banded together. To further show their commitment to the American cause, they publicly opposed the Tea Act of 1773, which forced colonists to buy their tea from Britain's East India Company monopoly. More than 500 Boston women signed an agreement, printed in the newspaper, that they would not purchase or drink the mandated tea from England. The women invented substitutes for taxed items such as tea and sugar. Their brew, made with boiled herbs, flowers, and sometimes basil leaves, was called Liberty Tea. It allowed the colonists to support their patriotic cause while maintaining a cherished tradition.

Some Daughters of Liberty, such as Sarah Bradlee Fulton (1740–1835), took it further. Among other exploits, she was called the "Mother of the Boston Tea Party" for helping colonial men disguise themselves as Mohawk warriors when they dumped English tea into Boston Harbor in 1773, a loss to the shippers of about $1 million in today's money. Afterward she helped them remove the telltale war paint that would have identified them and subjected them all to arrest.

Some Daughters of Liberty also took it upon themselves as a mark of pride to restrict their gentlemen callers or those of their daughters only to men who espoused the patriotic cause. Again, it is difficult to know how many this strategy affected, but it does suggest the fervor that some women brought to the cause of liberty.

With the onset of the Revolutionary War (1775–1783), the Daughters of Liberty produced even more fabric and sewed uniforms for the soldiers of the Continental Army. They rolled bandages, made bullets, carried water, foraged for the soldiers' food, and nursed their wounds.

At least one leader of the Daughters of Liberty, Deborah Sampson (1760–1827), actually joined the Continental Army by disguising herself as a man. She fought bravely, was wounded twice, and, after petitioning, was later awarded a Revolutionary War soldier's pension, though less than that given to males.

One of the most legendary of these women was Molly Pitcher, thought to be Mary Ludwig Hays McCauley (1754–1832), who carried pitchers of water to the parched troops and poured some on the cannons to cool them before reloading. It was said that she received her nickname from the soldiers' cry of "Molly! Pitcher!" Though Molly Pitcher may have been a composite, several women were cited by eyewitness accounts for fighting amid the bullets on the front lines when their husbands fell.

One of these, Margaret Cochran Corbin (1751–1800), was a Daughter of Liberty from Philadelphia. She took her husband's place at the cannon after he was killed and kept firing until she was seriously wounded. In 1779, Corbin (nicknamed "Captain Molly") was awarded an annual pension of $50 by the State of Pennsylvania for heroism in battle, the first American woman to receive a military pension.

Other noted Daughters of Liberty included those who became national figures such as Abigail Smith Adams (1744–1818) and Martha Dandridge Custis Washington (1731–1802). As one of the Daughters of Liberty, Sarah Franklin Bache (1744–1808), whose father was Benjamin Franklin, raised money to finance the Continental Army and, with the women of Philadelphia, made more than 2,000 shirts for the Revolutionary soldiers quartered at Valley Forge. A 16-year-old girl, Sybil Ludington, was called the "female Paul Revere" for her daring 40-mile night ride to warn the American militia.

The names of most of the Daughters of Liberty will never be known. These were the women who labored quietly from dawn to dark over spinning wheels with one eye on their children. They held the home together when the men went away to fight, some never to return. These were the women who labored on the family farm so their men would not return home to ruin and bankruptcy. They repaired houses blasted by cannon fire. They shielded children from the roar of cannons while they themselves were in terror of British troops and foreign mercenaries on their land. They were forced to quarter enemy soldiers in their homes, to humbly serve them at best and suffer rape or death for treason at worst. They served the Continental Army as cooks, washerwomen, nurses, and spies.

One of the Daughters of Liberty, Abigail Adams, is famed for her admonition to her husband John to "Remember the Ladies." However, after the Revolution, despite the efforts of the Daughters of Liberty, women returned to being chattel with no legal rights to their property, earnings, or children. Still, like Rosie the Riveter during World War II, they knew they had contributed to victory. In the case of the Daughters of Liberty, they helped bring about the birth of a new nation.

Nancy Hendricks

See also Adams, Abigail; Corbin, Margaret; McCauley, Mary; Sampson, Deborah; Washington, Martha; *Vol. 1, Sec. 2:* Spinning Bees

Further Reading

Berkin, Carol. 2006 *Revolutionary Mothers: Women in the Struggle for America's Independence*. New York: Vintage Books.

Norton, Mary Beth. 1996. *Liberty's Daughters: The Revolutionary Experience of American Women, 1750–1800*. Ithaca, NY: Cornell University Press.

Roberts, Cokie. 2009. *Ladies of Liberty: The Women Who Shaped Our Nation*. New York: Harper Perennial.

Davis, Ann Simpson (1764–1851)

A spy for George Washington during the Pennsylvania campaigns, Ann Simpson Davis played a significant role in the American Revolutionary War.

Davis was born to Irish immigrants William Simpson and Nancy Hines Simpson in Buckingham Township, Pennsylvania, on December 29, 1764. This area of Pennsylvania was a hotbed for both sides of the debate over American independence. Simpson's neighbors included Tories (supporters of English rule) and Patriots (supporters of independence), resulting in various conflicts during the war years. Tory raids on Patriot storehouses and the reporting of military movements to British soldiers were common, endangering nearby Patriot troops. This mix of sympathies worked in Davis's favor when she became a spy. As an accomplished horsewoman, she was familiar with her neighbors, who were accustomed to seeing her riding along roads and through fields.

Davis's riding habits were crucial to her role in the Revolution. In 1780 at the age of 16, Davis was personally chosen by General George Washington as a courier to carry messages between him and his generals in eastern Pennsylvania. Her familiarity with the

area and to her neighbors as well as her young age and gender ensured that she was not often questioned about her rides through the countryside. Davis carried the messages in sacks of grain and vegetables or in her clothing, often meeting other couriers at mills around Philadelphia and Bucks County, Pennsylvania, to exchange correspondence. She was never caught, though she did swallow messages during at least one search of her person by British soldiers. Had the British caught Davis, she would have been charged with treason and sentenced to death by hanging.

Following her service, Davis received a letter of commendation from General Washington. The letter was loaned to family and eventually lost. Also, after the war the new government awarded Davis a land grant in the western territories similar to that given to male soldiers.

In June of 1783 Davis married her childhood friend, John Davis, who had been under the command of General Washington and was part of Washington's crossing of the Delaware on Christmas Eve of 1776. According to family legend, John is depicted as the man holding the American flag in Emanuel Gottlieb Leutze's (1816–1868) painting *Washington Crossing the Delaware* (1851). Davis settled into the life of a farmer's wife in Solebury, Pennsylvania, and gave birth to her first five children: Sarah, William, John, Nancy, and Samuel.

In 1795 Davis moved to Montgomery County, Maryland, near the Rock Creek Meeting House. Davis bore three more children during this time: Joshua, Joseph, and Elizabeth. The family again moved in 1816, this time to Ohio to claim the land that they had each received for their services during the Revolutionary War. Davis settled in Perry Township in Franklin County, Ohio (now part of Friendship Village). The family prospered, eventually building a brick house large enough to accommodate the family. John Davis died on January 25, 1832, five years after the house was finished.

Ann Davis died on June 6, 1851, at the age of 88, having led a relatively quiet life after her services to Washington. She was buried next to her husband in what is now the Davis Historical Cemetery on Riverside Drive on Route 33 in Ohio. The cemetery was later named after John and Ann Davis. Their gravestone is the largest monument in the cemetery, with an arch and urn over two pillars reading "Ann Davis was messenger and carried orders from General Washington to the other commanders in the Revolutionary War in 1779 and 1780." Davis also received several posthumous honors, including having two schools and a chapter of the Daughters of the American Revolution named after her. She is also remembered for her connection to General Ulysses S. Grant, who was the son of Davis's cousin, Hannah, and is believed to have visited her in Ohio, also his home state, in 1843.

However brief Davis's military service, she played a crucial role in the birth of the new nation. Her story suggests a world where battlefield and home front were not neatly divided spheres but rather overlapping areas where women could and did often play a crucial role.

Tiffany Rhoades-Piotti

See also Greene, Catharine Littlefield; Knox, Lucy Flucker; Revolutionary War and Women

Further Reading

Berkins, Carol. 2007. *Revolutionary Mothers: Women in the Struggle for America's Independence.* New York: Random House.

Diamont, Lincoln. 1998. *Revolutionary Women in the War for Independence: A One-Volume Revised Edition of Elizabeth Ellet's 1848 Landmark Series.* New York: Praeger.

Dower Rights

According to English common law, which was brought by the settlers to the American colonies, dower is the portion a widow receives from her deceased husband's estate should he die without making a will. Because the law mandated dower, wives were considered by the legal system to have dower rights.

In the 17th century, most women had almost no rights to buy, own, or sell property or to collect rents, make contracts, or bring lawsuits. A woman's property was managed by her father, and when she married it was managed by her husband. This system, known as coverture, recognized the husband and wife as one legal entity. Thus, after she married a woman was unable to own property in her own right, and her husband could dispose of her property without her permission.

The system of dower rights was established for the support of a woman and her children, should she have any, if her husband died without making a will. The law was intended not so much to give women rights but to minimize the burden that indigent widows placed on the culture. According to this system, a widow was entitled to one-third of her husband's estate. This dower existed only for her lifetime. It usually included an interest in only the husband's real estate, but later personal property was also included. She was not able to sell or bequeath the property because it did not belong to her, but she was entitled to collect rents and the income produced by crops grown on land. Until the 19th century, the widow's portion of the estate could not be used to settle her husband's debts, which meant that many estates went unsettled until the widow herself died.

Dower rights took effect only in the case of a legally recognized marriage. They were invalidated in cases of divorce or adultery. Some states did preserve these rights if a divorce or separation was the fault of the husband. If the husband made a will, his widow had the choice of taking her dower rights, or, in a process called a widow's election, accepting the terms of her husband's will, which might be more generous.

Beginning in the late 17th century, there were changes made to the system of dower rights. Some courts, abiding by prenuptial agreements, placed a woman's separate estate into a trust that was managed by a man other than her husband. In 1664, Maryland required that a married woman be interviewed privately by a judge before her husband could sell or trade any of her property. In 1771, New York enacted a law requiring a husband to obtain his wife's signature before he sold or transferred her property. This law also required that the wife meet privately with a judge to give her approval. In 1787, Massachusetts passed a law allowing women, in some cases, to be *feme sole* traders, able to execute contracts in their own right. Legal action was required, however, to establish the woman's legal separateness from her husband.

In 1809 Connecticut passed a law allowing women to execute wills, and in 1839 Mississippi granted women limited property rights, mostly in the matter of slave ownership. The Married Women's Property Act, passed by New York state in 1848, allowed a married woman to continue to own real estate that she brought into the marriage and to collect income from it. This property could not be disposed of by her husband or used to settle his debts. Women were also allowed to inherit or receive gifts of property and control them as if they were unmarried. This law was further expanded in 1860 and served as a model for laws in many other states. By 1900, married women in every state had gained substantial control over their own property.

A federal law passed in 1945 abolished dower in the United States. Most states, however, still have some sort of dower law in effect. Often, a widow automatically receives one-third of her husband's estate if he dies without a will. In some states a man is not allowed to leave his wife less than a one-third share unless there are special circumstances. In other states the widow receives half of the estate. And whatever property the woman receives she owns outright and not just during her lifetime.

Nancy Snell Griffith

See also *Vol. 1, Sec. 2:* Coverture

Further Reading

Salmon, Marylynn. 1986. *Women and the Law of Property in Early America.* Chapel Hill: University of North Carolina Press.

Draper, Mary (1719–1810)

During the American Revolution, Mary Draper worked hard to provide food, medical care, and even supplies to the newly formed Continental Army.

Born in 1719 in Massachusetts, Draper was twice married. Her first husband died, after which she married Moses Draper. The couple lived in Dedham, Massachusetts, and had five sons and one daughter. When the war began in 1775, the Continental Army consisted of volunteer members of the original 13 colonies. Because of the speed at which so many men had to leave their homes to join the Continental Army, soldiers were often without basic supplies. Their struggle inspired Mary Draper to take action.

When her husband and eldest son left to join the army, Draper enlisted the aid of her daughter. They designed a system for giving aid to soldiers who marched past the farm on their way to the front. Initially, Draper's help consisted of basic sustenance: the family farm was prosperous, and so Draper had abundant grain and dairy at her disposal as well as large ovens. She baked countless loaves of hearty brown bread, which she set out on long tables along the road that ran by her farm. She also provided pan after pan of fresh cheese produced by the family's dairy cows as well as apple cider made out of apples from the family's orchards.

Soldiers marching along the road on their way to confront the well-equipped British troops could now stop for a few minutes to rest and eat. This simple but filling repast served to replenish the hungry and exhausted troops, as did—one imagines—Draper's simple act of generosity and compassion. Draper was driven by a sense of urgency: not only did she perceive the hunger and need suffered by the soldiers, but she also seems to have understood that the war would be a long and costly endeavor. Draper also began providing the ill-equipped soldiers with basic medical care and articles of clothing.

Even after the members of the Continental Army had made their way past her farm, Draper felt called to help more. As a result of the Battle of Bunker Hill, a brutal, prolonged, and ultimately futile struggle by the Continental forces to prevent British forces from taking control of Boston Harbor (Ward 1995, 63–66), the Continental Army found itself running dangerously low on ammunition. At the time bullets were made of lead or pewter, a metal alloy that can be easily molded into a variety of shapes. During the 18th century pewter was a highly valued metal, not simply because of its usefulness as ammunition but also because it was used to create assorted housewares, including dishes, cutlery, and kettles. It was also used to create ornamental pieces such as candlesticks and sconces. Pewter pieces were far from common because pewter was expensive and thus restricted to the more affluent households. Thanks to many years of running a profitable farm, Draper had many pewter housewares. Upon learning of the Continental Army's need for ammunition, she gathered all of her pewter pieces and melted them down. She then cast bullets, using bullet molds that her husband had purchased before leaving to fight the British. Draper's willingness to sacrifice her valuable objects further highlights her determination to do everything she could to ensure the birth of the new nation.

Ironically, while the colonials fought the American Revolution with a mind toward reordering their society to create more egalitarian relationships, the reality was that in terms of gender relations, American society would remain largely unchanged for many decades to come. What the Revolution did signal was a sudden vast expansion of the power and influence available to women, because when men left to fight in battle, women were expected to fulfill new leadership roles within their families and communities. Draper demonstrated strength of character and perseverance. That she and women like her are not better known speaks to the absence of women in history and the inequality that ruled the country for so long.

Alberta M. Miranda

See also Boycotts, Tea and Textiles; Camp Followers; Corbin, Margaret; Davis, Ann Simpson; Knox, Lucy Flucker; McCauley, Mary; Reed, Esther; Revolutionary War and Women; Sampson, Deborah; Soldiers, Women Passing as Men, Revolutionary War

Further Reading

Ellet, E. F. 1998. *Revolutionary Women in the War for American Independence: A One-Volume Revised Edition of Elizabeth's Ellet's 1848 Landmark Series.* Edited by Lincoln Diamant. Westport, CT: Praeger.

Montgomery, Charles Franklin. 1973. *A History of American Pewter.* New York: Praeger.

Ward, Harry M. 1995. *The American Revolution: Nationhood Achieved 1763–1788.* New York: St. Martin's.

Drinker, Elizabeth (1734–1807)

Elizabeth Sandwith Drinker was an 18th-century Philadelphia Quaker and diarist. Writing in over three dozen volumes over the course of 50 years, Drinker recorded many of her life details as well as the events of the American Revolution and the New Republic as they impacted her family and friends.

Drinker was the eldest of two daughters born to William Sandwith and Sarah Jarvis. Her father was an Irish Quaker merchant and ship owner who had immigrated to America in the early 1700s. As upper-middle-class Quaker children, Drinker and her sister Mary received a formal education at Anthony Benezet's Friends' English School of Philadelphia.

In 1758, Drinker began keeping a diary and continued to do so until her death in 1807 at the age of 73. During the winter of 1758–1759, Drinker and her future husband, Henry Drinker (1734–1809), began courting. Henry was a widower and had been married to one of Drinker's friends. The couple married on January 13, 1761.

Henry was an ironmaster and a partner in the shipping firm of James and Drinker, and at one point he owned half a million acres of land. He was an active Quaker and served as the clerk for the Philadelphia Monthly Meeting. Henry traveled frequently on behalf of the shipping firm as well as on Quaker business, and in the early days of their marriage his wife frequently accompanied him.

On May 12, 1761, Sarah, the first of the Drinkers' nine children, was born. Only five of Elizabeth Drinker's children would survive into adulthood. Drinker's unmarried sister Mary lived with the family, which also included several servants. In spite of all the domestic work her children must have required, Drinker wrote copiously in her diaries during her husband's absences. Many entries focused on Drinker's role as caregiver and included her views on childbirth and vaccinations. As political instability increased in the English colonies, Drinker recorded events leading up to the American Revolutionary War. On December 24, 1761, she recorded an account of the Boston Tea Party. After the war began, she recorded events including the British occupation of Philadelphia. In January 1777, the Drinkers had American soldiers quartered in their home by order of the Council of Safety. As Quakers the Drinkers were pacifists, but nonetheless they were expected to provide blankets and other supplies to American soldiers. When they refused, Henry fell under suspicion of aiding and abetting the enemy and was taken prisoner in September 1777. He and a group of other Quakers became known as the "Virginia Exiles" when they were sentenced to exile in Virginia after refusing to swear an oath of loyalty to the new U.S. government.

With her husband gone, Elizabeth Drinker struggled to maintain her household and tried to prevent her home from becoming quarters for British soldiers. She recorded the rout of Washington's army and the flight of Congress and the townspeople from the encroaching British army. On September 26, 1777, Drinker reported that the British had arrived "in earnest," and on October 24 she wrote that she was asked to quarter British soldiers in her house. In December, Drinker allowed British major general John Crammond to take up residence in her household.

In April 1778, Drinker and three other Quaker women traveled to the provisional capital at Lancaster, Pennsylvania, to ask for the release of their husbands. Along the way, the women visited the American picket, where Drinker met George Washington (1732–1799) and his wife Martha (1731–1802). The women continued to Lancaster, where they were refused an official meeting, but they learned that their husbands would soon be returned to Pennsylvania. Drinker was reunited with Henry on April 25.

After the war, Drinker's diary entries became longer and more frequent. She read widely and recorded her thoughts on subjects as varied as race relations, Quaker meetings, and home crafts. Despite several gaps, Drinker's diary expanded into three dozen volumes and is a valuable source of information about the early years of the American republic. Drinker's health gradually declined, and she died in Philadelphia in 1807.

Karen S. Garvin

See also *Vol. 1, Sec. 2:* Quakers

Further Reading

Drinker, Elizabeth Sandwith. 1994. *The Diary of Elizabeth Drinker: The Life Cycle of an Eighteenth-Century Woman.* Edited by Elaine Forman Crane. Boston: Northeastern University Press.

Kerber, Linda K. 1980. *Women of the Republic: Intellect and Ideology in Revolutionary America.* Chapel Hill: University of North Carolina Press.

Norton, Mary Beth. 1980. *Liberty's Daughters: The Revolutionary Experience of American Women, 1750–1800.* New York: Little, Brown.

Eaton, Margaret "Peggy" (1799–1879)

Margaret O'Neale Eaton, better known as Peggy Eaton, is notable in American history for her role in the Petticoat Affair during Andrew Jackson's presidency. As a barmaid in her parents' hotel, a hotel in which many politicians frequented, she developed a reputation for

Rumors that Peggy Eaton had had an affair with her husband before they legally married created a rift among the other wives of Cabinet Secretaries in the administration of President Andrew Jackson. Dubbed the Petticoat Affair, it caused the president to reorganize the Cabinet and favor widowers when he could. (Library of Congress)

being vivacious and intelligent. After her marriage to a senator, she became embroiled in one of the most notorious scandals of her scandal-ridden times, the Petticoat Affair.

Eaton was the daughter of Rhoda Howell and William O'Neale, the owner of Franklin House, a popular Washington, D.C., hotel. To the patrons of her parents' hotel, Eaton was known as a daring young lady. Her father had to prevent her from undertaking multiple elopements and dissuade an array of suitors. In 1816 O'Neale allowed Eaton to marry John B. Timberlake, a 39-year-old purser in the U.S. Navy. They lived in a house across from the hotel. When Timberlake was at sea, Eaton continued to work in her parents' hotel. Together the couple had three children. It was during this time of her life that Eaton met Senator John Henry Eaton (1790–1856). Shortly after Timberlake died in 1828 during a 4-year voyage in the Mediterranean, Margaret O'Neale married Eaton. Timberlake committed suicide on the journey, and there were rumors that he did so because he was distraught after learning about an affair between the senator and his wife. There is no evidence for this story, and it may be just one of the rumors spread around Washington, D.C., society during Andrew Jackson's presidency.

When President Andrew Jackson appointed Senator Eaton to the position of secretary of war, Margaret Eaton was thrust into the political Cabinet social circle. During this era while husbands carried political power, wives governed the social aspect of Washington, D.C. Political wives and daughters also wielded considerable political power. In what was known as parlor politics, many women engaged in politics by orchestrating meetings and political deals at the social gatherings they conducted in their homes. Second Lady Floride Calhoun, the wife of Vice President John C. Calhoun, led the Washington ladies' efforts to socially ostracize Eaton, whom they saw as an outsider on account of her social class. The ladies, and by extension their husbands, also claimed to be shocked at the short interval between the death of Peggy Eaton's first husband and her remarriage. The ladies of the Cabinet would not answer social calls from Mrs. Eaton, would not address her at social gatherings, and spread gossip and rumors about the alleged affair be-

tween Mr. and Mrs. Eaton during her marriage to Timberlake. One of the only members of the Cabinet who remained loyal to the Eatons was Martin Van Buren, a widower who had no wife to pressure him into not speaking to Peggy Eaton.

President Jackson was sympathetic to the Eatons and thought that his political opponents, led by his vice president John Calhoun, unfairly fed the scandal so as to blacken the Jackson name. Thus, Jackson championed Peggy Eaton, whom he felt was being unfairly victimized. It is also possible that he was sympathetic to the Eatons because of the scandal involving his own late wife, Rachel Jackson, who had also been the subject of scorn because she had married Jackson before her previous marriage had been legally ended. President Jackson believed that it was the stress from such scandal that caused his wife's heart attack and death. In early 1831 Jackson purged his cabinet of Calhoun followers and replaced them with friends, generally referred to as the Kitchen Cabinet, a term that reflected their unofficial status in contrast to the official cabinet, or Parlor Cabinet. During President Jackson's reelection campaign he replaced Calhoun as his running mate with Van Buren.

Margaret Eaton was again the subject of controversy 3 years after the death of Senator Eaton when she married a 19-year-old Italian music and dancing teacher, Antonio Gabriele Buchignani. She was 59 years old at the time of the marriage. After 7 years of marriage, Buchignani left Eaton and took the bulk of her fortune as well as her 17-year-old granddaughter to Europe. Even though Eaton was able to obtain a divorce, she was unable to recover her finances. She died in poverty in Washington, D.C., on November 8, 1879, at age 80.

Moriah Saldana

See also Jackson, Rachel Donelson; Parlor Politics

Further Reading

Marszalek, John F. 1997. *The Petticoat Affair: Manners, Mutiny, and Sex in Andrew Jackson's White House.* New York: Free Press.

Meacham, Jon. 2008. *American Lion: Andrew Jackson in the White House.* New York: Random House.

Ferguson, Catherine (1774–1854)

Born a slave and illiterate all her life, Catherine "Katy" Ferguson devoted herself to the poor and neglected children of New York. She is remembered as the founder of what many believe was the first Sunday school in the city; Sunday was the only day that workers were not at work and able to attend public school, designed originally to teach literacy in a secular environment.

While some sources give Ferguson's birth date as 1779, Lewis Tappan's revised obituary of her, published in the *American Missionary* in August 1854, says that she was 80 years old when she died. This would mean that she was born in 1774. Ferguson, then named Katy Williams, was born while her mother was being transferred from Virginia to New York. They were owned by a Presbyterian elder whom Ferguson would only describe as "R.B." When Ferguson was 8 years old, her mother was sold to another owner; she would never see her mother again. Ferguson said in later interviews that this tragic separation resulted in her lifelong devotion to and compassion for children.

When Ferguson was 18 years old Isabella Graham, a widow who had recently arrived in New York from Scotland, bought her freedom for $200. Graham was a member of the Scotch Presbyterian Church, which was then part of the Associate Reformed Presbyterian Church. Katy originally agreed to repay her purchase price within six years, but the agreement was later modified. Under the new agreement, she worked as a servant (probably for Graham herself) for 11 months, which canceled $100 of her debt. Graham's son-in-law, merchant Divie Bethune, paid the remainder of the debt. Ferguson set herself up as a baker and became well known for her wedding and special occasion cakes. Around this same time she married and had two children, both of whom died in infancy. The marriage itself does not appear to have lasted very long.

At the turn of the century New York City was growing, fueled by an influx of immigrants from other parts of the United States as well as Europe. The city had significant urban poverty, as the city's poor worked long hours for low wages. The city teemed with illiterate children and adults. One of the methods used to combat this poverty was the establishment of schools that met on Sunday, the only day that workers were not at work and able to attend. At first these schools were secular, with an emphasis on teaching reading and writing, but later many of them became true Sabbath schools that concentrated on teaching the scriptures.

Although there is some confusion about just when Ferguson started her school, she most likely opened it in her home at 51 Warren Street in 1793. According to the Lewis Tappan obituary, she began collecting the neighborhood children, both black and white, into her home to give them a religious education. She taught them verses of scripture and hymns that she had memorized "and got suitable persons to come and hear them say their catechism, etc." In 1814 with the encouragement of Dr. John Mitchell Mason of the Associate Reformed Church, the classes were moved to a lecture room in the basement of his church on Murray Street. The school later became known as the Murray Street Sabbath School.

Ferguson did not limit her work to her Sabbath school. During her lifetime she took 48 children, 20 of them white, into her home, where she either raised them or kept them until she could find them a suitable home, essentially creating her own orphanage. For the last 40 years of her life she held a prayer meeting in her home every Friday evening for the poor children of her neighborhood and for those adults who did not attend church. For the last 5 years of her life, she held an additional meeting every Sunday afternoon.

Catherine "Katy" Ferguson died of cholera on July 11, 1854. According to Lewis Tappan, "The secret of Katy's usefulness was her fervent, uniform, and consistent piety. . . . The love of God was shed abroad in her heart, and it found expression in acts of benevolence to His children." Her life is a reminder of the good that one person, even one with few social or economic advantages, can accomplish.

Nancy Snell Griffith

See also *Vol. 1, Sec. 2:* Slavery, African; *Vol. 2, Sec. 1:* Abolition/Antislavery Movement; Slave Women

Further Reading

Hartvik, Allen. 1972. "Catherine Ferguson: Black Founder of a Sunday School." *Negro History*

Bulletin 35 (December): 176–177 (reprinted January–December 1996, pp. 1–3, 5–7).

"'Where Katy Lived, the Whole Aspect of the Neighborhood Was Changed': Lewis Tappan's Obituary for Catherine Ferguson (1854)." n.d. AARDOC, http://www3.amherst.edu/~aardoc/Ferguson.html.

Glory of the Morning (ca. 1711–ca. 1832)

Native American chief Glory of the Morning led the Winnebago/Ho-Chunk tribe during the 1700s in what is now Wisconsin.

While documentation is nonexistent, historians believe that Glory of the Morning, the generally accepted translation of her native name, Hopokoeau, was born around 1711. Her father was a chief, and she was born as a part of the Thunderbird Clan.

The Thunderbird Clan lived in a large village on Doty Island in the part of Wisconsin that is now Menash. Growing up in the area formed by the two branches of the Fox River flowing out from Lake Winnebago, Glory in the Morning was said to have impressed her community at an early age. She demonstrated a wisdom that set her apart from the other members of the tribe, including her brothers and other male elders. Consequently, despite her gender, when her father died when she was 18 years old, Glory in the Morning was named his successor as chief. Her elevation to chief split the tribe, with almost half of the members leaving and settling in a separate community. However, over time the rift partially healed, and many eventually returned.

Some historians believe that Glory in the Morning's ascension to chief was aided by her marriage to Joseph Sabrevoir DeCarrie (spelling is also reported as Descaris). DeCarrie is believed to have come to Wisconsin with the French Army in 1728. Captivated by the area and the young Ho-Chunk woman, he resigned his commission in 1729 and became a fur trader. He married Glory in the Morning and was adopted into her clan. The marriage may have enhanced her status as a prospective chief, with his abilities complementing hers. If true it would prove to be cruelly ironic, for as chief she felt an even greater responsibility to her people. After living with the tribe for about eight years,

DeCarrie decided to rejoin the army. Glory in the Morning resolved to stay with her tribe. DeCarrie took their daughter with him, while their two sons remained with their mother. The separation lasted for the rest of their lives, but the impact of the pair's emotional bonds was evident in many future actions.

During the 1730s and 1740s, Glory in the Morning witnessed a great deal of warfare between the Fox Indians and the French in the area that is now Michigan and Wisconsin. Likely due to her husband, Glory in the Morning aligned the Winnebagos with the French and played a pivotal role in achieving an end to the war in the late 1740s. However, the peace was short-lived, and when the British invaded the Midwest in the early days of what would become the French and Indian War, she again sided with the French. By then her husband had rejoined the French Army, but he died in 1760 of injuries suffered in the Battle of Ste. Foy, the last French victory of the war and one in which the French regained control of Quebec from the British.

Glory in the Morning is not referenced again in any surviving sources until 1832, when writer Julliette Kinzie visited the area. If estimates of her life's timeline are correct, Glory in the Morning would have been 121. Kinzie was sure it was the famed female chief but reported that she was so ancient and weak that she had to go around on all fours because she was unable to summon the strength to stand erect. Legend has it that not long after Kinzie's visit, Glory in the Morning was out in the woods when an owl, a creature whose presence was said to be an ill omen, spoke her name. That evening, wrapped snugly in furs and with a seemingly contented smile on her face, she died. Adding to the legend was the fact that on that night the village experienced a massive blizzard. Members of her tribe heard the rare sound of thunder, a sound they believed to be the gods of the clan calling Glory of the Morning home.

Glory of the Morning's legacy lived on, as she was the founding mother of the famed Decorah family, who produced numerous chiefs over the generations, many of whom played important roles in the various treaties signed between Native Americans and the U.S. government.

William H. Pruden III

See also Brant, Molly; Sacagawea; *Vol. 1, Sec. 1:* Malinche; Pocahontas; *Vol. 1, Sec. 2:* Kittamaquund, Mary; Queen Alliquippa; Tekakwitha, Kateri

Further Reading
Smith, David Lee. 1997. *Folklore of the Winnebago Tribe.* Norman: University of Oklahoma Press.

Greene, Catharine Littlefield (1755–1814)

The widow of American Revolutionary War hero Nathanael Greene, Catharine Littlefield Greene was also probably the coinventor of the cotton gin. Known as "Caty" to her friends, Greene demonstrated strength as a military wife, acumen as a businesswoman, and creativity as a contributor to the invention of the cotton gin. She is notable as an early American woman active in science and innovation.

Born in Block Island, Rhode Island, on February 17, 1755, Greene was the daughter of Phebe Ray, a descendant of the island's founders, and John Littlefield, a Rhode Island legislator. When Greene was 10 years old her mother died, and she entered the care of relatives in East Greenwich, Rhode Island. The aunt and uncle charged with Greene's care were socially and politically prominent. Her uncle, William Greene, later assumed the governorship of Rhode Island.

In 1772 Catharine Littlefield Greene met Nathanael Greene, a merchant and distant relation of her uncle. The two married in Greenwich, Rhode Island, on July 20, 1774. They made their first home in Coventry, Rhode Island. Together, they raised five children: George (b. 1776), Martha (b. 1777), Cornelia Lott (b. 1779), Nathanael Ray (b. 1780), and Louisa (b. 1783). A sixth child, Catherine (b. 1785), died as an infant.

When the American Revolution began, Nathanael became Rhode Island's brigadier general. Despite others' objections, Greene visited her husband in battle. When possible, she was accompanied in these travels by the couple's young children. The soldiers respected her fortitude in spending time at wartime encampments. Nathanael went on to serve with the Continental Army and command Washington's southern forces, attaining the rank of general.

After the war, Catharine and Nathanael Greene relocated to Georgia to develop land he received in recognition of his military leadership. The property, located in the vicinity of Savannah and known as Mulberry Grove, became the family's new home. Following Nathanael's death in 1786, a tutor charged with educating the Greene children stepped forward to assume additional duties, assisting Greene in managing the plantation.

At Mulberry Grove, Greene received notable visitors, including George Washington in 1791. Greene had sought for years to free her husband's estate from debts incurred during the Revolutionary War. Out of urgency, Nathanael had guaranteed the costs of acquiring sufficient clothing for his troops during a South Carolina campaign and gone into debt. By 1792, Washington forgave the sizable debt that had plagued the family's postwar finances.

Later that year when Eli Whitney arrived to tutor her neighbor's children, Greene persuaded him to modify his plans. She invited the recent Yale graduate to live at Mulberry Grove and serve as a handyman and mechanic. She also gave Whitney space for a makeshift laboratory for his scientific and mechanical experiments. During his stay at Mulberry Grove, Whitney learned from Greene about the challenges of de-seeding the cotton crop. In a year's time, the two shared conversations that resulted in the design and redesign of the cotton gin.

Questions surround the origin of this invention. While accounts vary, some historians contend that it was Greene who devised the cotton gin. Others suggest that the innovation was the result of collaboration in which Greene suggested the concept and revised the original design. Other people believe that Greene underwrote the costs of the prototype and its patent. In this era women were not permitted to hold patents, so Whitney could not have put her name on the patent even if he wanted to.

Greene's eldest son George died of accidental drowning in 1793. Initially, the 18-year-old was buried on the premises at Dungeness. In 1901, his remains were relocated and interred with his father's at a Savannah monument to the Revolutionary War hero.

In 1796 Greene married Phineas Miller, the tutor who had assumed management of Mulberry Grove.

Martha and George Washington served as witnesses to the marriage. When the family sold the property two years later, they relocated to Cumberland Island, Georgia, where they presided over another plantation, Dungeness. Greene remained there following Miller's death in 1803. She died in 1814 and was buried at Dungeness.

Linda S. Watts

See also *Vol. 2, Sec. 1:* Mitchell, Maria

Further Reading

Ogilvie, Marilyn Bailey. 1986. *Women in Science: Antiquity through the Nineteenth Century.* Boston: MIT Press.
Stegeman, John F., and Janet A. Stegeman. 1977. "President Washington at Mulberry Grove." *Georgia Historical Quarterly* 61(4) (Winter): 342–346.
Stegeman, John F., and Janet A. Stegeman. 1985. *Caty: A Biography of Catharine Littlefield Greene.* Athens, GA: Brown Thrasher Books.

Hemings, Sally (1773–1835)

Sally Hemings was an enslaved woman owned by Thomas Jefferson (1743–1826). The alleged sexual relationship between Hemings and Jefferson and his reported paternity of her children became a controversial public issue when it was initially reported in 1802 by journalist James Callender during Jefferson's first term as president of the United States. In 1998 one of Hemings's children, Eston Hemings, was linked by DNA evidence to a male Jefferson. While historical sources, circumstantial evidence, and Hemings family oral history have continued to fuel the discussion over the true nature of the relationship between Hemings and Jefferson, a research committee founded by the Thomas Jefferson Foundation found it likely that Jefferson had fathered all of Hemings's children.

Sally (given name probably Sarah) Hemings was born in 1773 at The Forest, Charles City County, Virginia, to Elizabeth (Betty) Hemings; Sally's father was John Wayles, owner of both the Forest plantation and the enslaved Betty. Wayles had taken Betty as his mistress following the death of his third wife, and they

had a total of six children together: Robert, James, Peter, Critta, Sally, and Thenia. Betty was herself the child of a white English sea captain and an enslaved African woman. Wayles's oldest surviving child (from his first marriage to Martha Eppes) was a daughter named Martha (1748–1782), who married Thomas Jefferson in 1772. Therefore, Sally Hemings was half sister to Martha Jefferson.

John Wayles died in 1773, and by 1776 the Hemings family was moved to the Jefferson home, Monticello. The Hemings family maintained favored status among the slaves owned by the Jeffersons. Sally, her mother, and her female siblings performed highly valued domestic chores, while her brothers were apprenticed to trades, including her brother James, who became a pastry chef. Later in life Sally was apparently employed as a seamstress and as Jefferson's chambermaid.

Little else is known about Sally Hemings's life prior to 1787. She had likely been a nursemaid to Maria Jefferson, who was six years younger than Hemings, and both were living at Eppington, the home of the now-deceased Martha Jefferson's aunt and uncle, when Thomas Jefferson—now ambassador to France—called for Maria to join him and her sister Martha in Paris. As her companion, 14-year-old Hemings accompanied Maria on the ocean voyage.

Hemings's exact place of residence while in France is unclear. Jefferson himself lived in the Hôtel de Langeac, a home located on the corner of the Champs-Elysées and the Rue de Berri in Paris, while his two daughters, Martha (called Patsy) and Maria (called Polly), resided primarily at the convent school Abbaye Royale de Panthemont, also in Paris. Hemings was now elevated from nursemaid to lady's maid and began training in sewing, laundering, and other skills necessary to maintain Martha's and Mary's wardrobes and lifestyle. In addition, Hemings may have received French lessons to help her better perform her duties.

As lady's maid to the Jefferson daughters, Hemings would have accompanied them to social engagements; Jefferson's receipt books show that he expended a significant amount of money on clothes for Hemings in Paris. While much less than what he spent on clothing for Maria and Martha, it was still certainly enough to properly outfit her for her new environment and duties as attendant to the Jefferson daughters. In addition, in 1788 Jefferson apparently began to pay monthly wages to both Hemings and her brother, James. Slavery was not allowed in France, and the Hemings siblings both knew that they had the option to remain free there rather than to resume their lives as Virginia slaves; the payment of wages may have been an effort on Jefferson's part to mollify them in some way by treating them as servants. Physical descriptions of Hemings are few, and no images have been found, but she was described as very beautiful with light skin and long, straight black hair and that she looked "very near white" (Gordon-Reed 1997, 134–135). Because of her relationship to Martha Wayles Jefferson, the two may have borne some resemblance to one another.

The Jefferson party returned to Virginia in 1789, and Hemings was allegedly pregnant at that time. However, this child did not live long. Hemings subsequently bore five additional children, four of whom lived to adulthood. While sources indicate that the rumored relationship between Hemings and Jefferson was known among his neighbors and some contemporaries, the affair did not become public knowledge until journalist James Callender began to publish sensationalized, incendiary articles describing Jefferson's "dusky Sally" and her alleged children by him. Jefferson was at this point in his first term as president, and it was Callender who had aided Jefferson's election by writing newspaper pieces less than complimentary to his Federalist opponents. For his efforts the hotheaded Callender had expected to be appointed to a lucrative job, but as president, Jefferson thought better of it and declined. Callender then turned on Jefferson with his scandalizing reports; the controversy over whether or not the stories were true has now roiled for well over 200 years.

In 1998, Dr. Eugene Foster and his associates published in the journal *Nature* the results of a DNA study conducted to end the controversy concerning Jefferson's paternity of Hemings's children. This study compared the Y-chromosome haplotypes of the Jefferson male bloodline with that of male descendants of Eston Hemings, Sally's youngest child and the only person for whom testable DNA was available. The scientists also tested Hemings's DNA against that of the Carr line. Jefferson's defenders had alleged that Jefferson cousins James and Peter Carr were the actual fathers of Hemings's children. The Y-chromosome haplotype of Thomas Woodson, a man who claimed to be the son of Thomas Jefferson and whose descendants had faithfully retained this information in their family history, was also tested. Results of the tests ruled out the Carr brothers and showed no similarity at all between the Woodson and Jefferson DNA. Eston's DNA did, however, match the Jefferson DNA.

Besides the DNA evidence, other information has been offered that supports Thomas Jefferson's paternity of the Hemings children. Chief of these are the calculations from Jefferson's travel records showings that he was present at Monticello at the time of each of Hemings's conceptions. Those acquainted with the children remarked that they bore a striking resemblance to Jefferson, and in fact, three of the four living children successfully passed into society as white, as did Hemings in her last years. Sources close to Jefferson believed that he was the father of Hemings's children, and in an 1873 newspaper interview Madison Hemings stated that he and his three siblings were Jefferson's children. In addition, the only nuclear family ever freed by Jefferson was the Hemings family. Beverley and Harriet were allowed to leave Monticello, apparently with Jefferson's blessing, and Madison and Eston were freed in Jefferson's will. While Sally Hemings was not manumitted in the will but passed to the heirs at his death, she was informally freed by Martha Jefferson Randolph soon after Jefferson died.

The Foster DNA study was evaluated by a specially appointed committee of the Thomas Jefferson Foundation in 2000 and, with the exception of one dissenting member, accepted the findings and concluded that "The DNA study, combined with multiple strands of currently available documentary and statistical evidence, indicates a high probability that Thomas Jefferson fathered Eston Hemings, and that he most likely was the father of all six of Sally Hemings's children appearing in Jefferson's records." ("Report of the Research Committee on Thomas Jefferson and Sally Hemings" 2000). The committee listed Hemings's children as Harriet (died as an infant), Beverly, another unnamed infant who died, Harriet, Madison, and Eston. The naming of an infant for a previously deceased sibling, as in the case of the two Harriet Hemings, was a common practice of the time. However, the Thomas Jefferson Foundation committee also acknowledged that there was much more to know about the case.

The controversy is in no way settled regarding the Hemings/Jefferson relationship, and many historians contend that there was no relationship between the two at all beyond that of slave and master. Numerous valid questions and concerns have been raised by Jefferson's defenders, many of which cannot be answered with currently available information. Principally, the DNA study only verified that Eston Hemings's father was a Jefferson but not necessarily Thomas Jefferson; the study did not determine paternity for any of the other Hemings children. Indeed, so many questions exist and the case is so complicated that the truth about the Hemings/Jefferson relationship may never be resolved.

Thomas Jefferson died on July 4, 1826, and according to his last will and testament, Madison and Eston Hemings were freed. They subsequently moved to Charlottesville, Virginia. Sally Hemings, still enslaved and a part of the Jefferson estate, was informally freed by Jefferson's daughter, Martha, and left Monticello to live with Madison and Eston. She died in 1835 and is presumably buried in Charlottesville, although the location of her grave is unknown.

Lee Davis Smith

See also *Vol. 2, Sec. 1:* Celia, a Slave; Mammy and Jezebel Stereotypes; Truth, Sojourner; Tubman, Harriet

Further Reading

Bay, Mia. 2006. "In Search of Sally Hemings in the Post-DNA Era." *Reviews in American History* 34: 407–426.

Brodie, Fawn. 1998. *Thomas Jefferson: An Intimate History.* New York: Norton.

Gordon-Reed, Annette. 1997. *Thomas Jefferson and Sally Hemings: An American Controversy.* Charlottesville: University Press of Virginia.

Hyland, William G. 2009. *In Defense of Thomas Jefferson: The Sally Hemings Sex Scandal.* New York: St. Martin's.

"Report of the Research Committee on Thomas Jefferson and Sally Hemings." 2000. Thomas Jefferson Foundation. http://www.monticello.org/site/plantation-and-slavery/vi-conclusions.

Hulton, Ann (?–?)

Ann Hulton was a colonist who lived in Massachusetts during the 18th century and gained fame because her letters contain eyewitness accounts of early events of the American Revolution. Hulton was a Loyalist, or an individual who did not support the idea that the 13 colonies of North America should declare independence from the British Crown in the 1770s. Hulton, the sister of Henry Hulton, lived in Boston with her brother's family, where the government employed him as the commissioner of customs. He had the unfortunate duty of collecting unpopular taxes and other fees owed to the British Crown during the age of the Imperial Crisis in the mid-1760s and early 1770s. Hulton wrote many of her letters to friends in England, primarily another woman named Elizabeth Lightbody. Hulton's letters offer firsthand accounts of famous events such as the Boston Tea Party and the Battles of Lexington and Concord. They remain an invaluable resource for scholars.

Hulton's exact date of birth is unknown. Her father was John Hulton, a merchant from Chester, England. Ann Hulton's brother Henry, a lifelong employee of the British Crown, received an appointment as the principal commissioner to the recently created Board of Customs in North America in September 1767. Not long after his marriage, he had to leave England for Boston, leaving his wife behind. Months later she gave birth to a son named Thomas, at which point either she or her husband decided that the family should join him in the colonies. Ann Hulton most likely accompanied her sister-in-law and infant nephew to Massachusetts. In an age when respectable women did not travel alone, Ann would have been considerable help to a young mother traveling with a baby. Hulton also hoped to make her own fortune as an independent merchant or planter, a revealing and unusual aspiration for a single woman. She arrived in Boston in early 1768 and lived with her brother's family for almost eight years.

Between 1767 and 1776, discord grew between the Loyalists and the Patriots. Patriots were colonists who wanted independence from the British Crown. At the time Hulton lived in Boston, political divisions ran deep. Approximately one-third of the colonial population considered themselves Loyalists, while another third identified themselves as staunch Patriots. This left the remaining population undecided as to which side they supported. The colonial struggle with the British Parliament over the issue of taxation without representation led to a series of taxes and fees that the Crown tasked Hulton's brother with collecting from citizens in Boston.

As a Loyalist among increasingly independence-minded Bostonians, Hulton faced many difficult experiences. Increasing public unrest resulted in mobs storming the offices and houses of government officials. On several occasions the unrest caused Ann and her family to take refuge at Castle William, a fort built on an island in the middle of Boston Harbor. Like many other Loyalist women, Ann had to decide if she would remain in the colonies and face future mob attacks, possible fines, confiscation of property, and arrest by local officials or leave her adopted home and return to England. In 1775, Hulton decided to return to England. Other Loyalist women, such as prominent merchant Elizabeth Murray Campbell Smith Inman, remained in Boston. Patriots seized her home in Cambridge during the Battle of Bunker Hill, and the Continental Army restricted her movements inside and outside the city of Boston during its siege. Another Loyalist woman, Flora MacDonald, accompanied Loyalist regiments in North Carolina after she arrived from Scotland in 1774. She comforted families who lost loved ones, either to capture or death, even after Patriot officials confiscated her family's plantation. Like many Loyalist women, she returned to Great Britain penniless and debt-ridden after the war ended.

Ann Hulton fared slightly better than some of her contemporaries. Although she never married or had any children, she remained an important member of her brother's family after they returned to England in mid-1776. Her letters, published in the early 20th century, remain an invaluable resource to those who study the experience of women and Loyalists in the American Revolution.

Deborah L. Bauer

See also Revolutionary War and Women

Further Reading

Allen, Thomas B. 2010. *Tories: Fighting for the King in America's First Civil War.* New York: Harper.

Hulton, Ann. 1927. *Letters of a Loyalist Lady: Being the Letters of Anne Hulton, Sister of Henry Hulton, Commissioner of Customs at Boston, 1767–1776.* Cambridge, MA: Harvard University Press.

Jackson, Rachel Donelson (1767–1828)

Rachel Donelson Robards Jackson was the wife of the seventh president of the United States, Andrew Jackson (1767–1845). Rachel Jackson saw her husband elected to the presidency but died before his inauguration, thus

Rachel Donelson Jackson took General Andrew Jackson as her second husband, unaware that her first had faked their divorce. This lead to accusations of bigamy during the presidential election of 1829. (Library of Congress)

never lived in the White House. She was at the center of vicious personal attacks, giving rise to the debate over what private information should be used in a political campaign.

Many sources place Rachel Jackson's birth date as June 15, 1767. She was born in the Virginia wilderness in either Halifax or Pittsylvania County. When she was 12 years old, she moved with her parents, seven brothers, and three sisters to Tennessee, where her father was cofounder of the present-day city of Nashville. The Donelsons were said to be the first white settlers in Tennessee and were one of its most prominent families. No record exists of a formal education for Rachel, though she could read and write. She was Presbyterian and was a devoted reader of the Bible.

In 1785 when Jackson was 18, she was married to landowner Lewis Robards. They lived in Kentucky until 1788. Claiming that Robards abused her, she fled to the home of her mother. Young circuit lawyer Andrew Jackson was boarding with the widowed Mrs. Donelson. When the family heard that Robards was coming to take Rachel back to Kentucky, she traveled to Natchez with a married couple. Jackson rode along as protector.

On the perilous journey, Rachel and Andrew fell in love. When a newspaper article appeared in 1791 stating that her divorce from Robards was final, she and Jackson were married. In reality the divorce had not actually been finalized, thus making Rachel technically a bigamist and the marriage invalid. After several years together, Rachel and Andrew discovered the trouble, ensured that the divorce was final, and remarried in Tennessee in 1794.

In 1804, the Jacksons bought a cotton farm. The Hermitage plantation grew from a humble log house. By 1821, it was an eight-room, two-story brick mansion surrounded by a 1,000-acre plantation. Jackson largely remained there during her husband's public career as soldier, businessman, and politician. She suffered greatly during his lengthy absences. Her time and energy were taken up by raising children in her care; the Jacksons had two adopted sons and were legal guardians for six boys and two girls, many from the large Donelson clan.

Andrew Jackson had become a national hero during the War of 1812 and was posted to political positions in Florida, New Orleans, and Washington, D.C. Rachel Jackson sometimes joined him, though she kept to herself except for attending religious services. Despite criticism of Jackson for her backwoods manners such as smoking a pipe, she was comfortable among the political figures they welcomed into their home. Even the sophisticated first lady, Elizabeth Monroe, liked her.

John Quincy Adams (1767–1848) defeated Andrew Jackson in the presidential election of 1824. When he ran again in 1828, supporters of Adams savaged Rachel viciously as an adulteress, bigamist, and divorcee. Andrew Jackson won by a landslide in 1828, but he never forgot the attacks on his wife.

Rachel purchased a white gown and slippers for the inaugural ball, signaling her intention to attend, but at the Hermitage on December 22, 1828, at age 61, she succumbed to a fatal heart attack. It is said that the horrified Andrew clung to her body, hoping she could be revived. Rachel was buried in Nashville in the garden of the Hermitage.

Newspapers that had savaged Rachel in life mourned her passing. About 10,000 people went to her funeral. Andrew never remarried and mourned Rachel for the rest of his life, wearing a locket with her picture close to his heart and keeping her portrait at his bedside. Though Rachel never lived in the White House as first lady, her presence was felt. Andrew sought to remove any federal workers suspected of circulating attacks against her. Most significantly, the Peggy Eaton Affair in which the wife of a cabinet member was vilified brought Jackson to Eaton's ardent defense. It resulted in the shake-up of the cabinet as well as the promotion of Martin Van Buren as Jackson's political heir apparent.

Nancy Hendricks

See also Eaton, Margaret "Peggy"

Further Reading

Brady, Patricia. 2011. *A Being So Gentle: The Frontier Love Story of Rachel and Andrew Jackson.* New York: Macmillan.

Meacham, Jon. 2009. *American Lion: Andrew Jackson in the White House.* New York: Random House.

Knox, Lucy Flucker (1756–1824)

Lucy Knox's prolific letters to her husband Henry Knox, who was a major general in the Continental Army, create a vivid record of life in Revolutionary America. Knox also followed her husband to numerous revolutionary outposts, raising children and serving as a hostess for military events.

Lucy Flucker Knox was born in 1756 to Thomas Flucker, the royal secretary of the province of Massachusetts Bay, and his wife, Hannah Waldo. As the daughter of a high-ranking government official, Knox enjoyed a privileged childhood. Her first glimpse of her future husband came in August 1773, when he was drilling on horseback with the Boston Grenadier Corps, a local militia, on Boston Common. Shortly thereafter she began visiting Knox at his bookstore, which had opened in 1771. She was soon in love with the largely self-educated and charming Knox. Henry's father died when he was just 12 years old, forcing Henry to leave school and become an apprentice to bookbinders in Boston to support his mother and younger brother before opening his own bookstore. Lucy's parents, however, disapproved of the match, believing that Henry was a common tradesman. That his parents were Irish immigrants did not help his case either, nor did the fact that he sympathized with the Patriot cause in Boston. In spite of her parents' disapproval, Lucy and Henry were married on June 16, 1774, at Boston's King's Chapel. Lucy's parents, staunch Loyalists, refused to attend the wedding.

Relations between the newly married couple and Lucy's parents remained tense, especially after fighting broke out in Lexington and Concord on April 19, 1775. Henry Knox was particularly interested in books on military strategy and artillery, and he often had conversations with the British military officers who browsed his bookstore. Since he was one of the few officers who had knowledge of military engineering and tactical artillery, George Washington, commander of the Continental Army, recognized Knox's skills and appointed him chief of artillery in October 1775. The Knoxes became frequent guests at Washington's Cambridge Headquarters.

In the winter of 1775–1776, Henry Knox led an expedition to Fort Ticonderoga and returned to Boston with 60 tons of artillery, which was maneuvered up Dorchester Heights. Astonished British generals realized that they had no choice but to evacuate Boston on March 17, 1776. In addition to this military victory, the Knoxes celebrated the birth of their first child, a girl named Lucy, on February 26, 1776. The celebration was muted, however, when the Knoxes learned that the Fluckers were among those who left Boston. During the war, Lucy Knox stayed with her husband in camp as often as he would allow, and she stayed with friends, including Martha Washington, when conditions made staying near her husband too difficult. Henry also discouraged his wife from staying at camp with him, believing that she had given up enough when she married him. Their many letters are from these periods when they were apart.

While her husband was in camp, Lucy Knox and her family would stay in private homes. She would visit the wives of other officers, host dinners for her husband's officer colleagues, and plan a variety of entertainments for the officer families. During the war Knox became known as a foremost hostess, a role she continued to play after the Revolution. Dangers came not just from battles but also from camp life in general. Knox was inoculated against smallpox, a controversial practice at the time. In the spring of 1779 she contracted infectious hepatitis, a common problem in campsites with poor sanitation and contaminated water. She had just given birth to her second child, daughter Julia, who died on July 2. During the course of their marriage Knox gave birth to 13 children, only 3 of whom survived into adulthood.

After the war the Continental Congress named Henry Knox secretary of war, a post he held until 1794. Throughout their lives the Knoxes were perpetually strapped for cash, but they continued to entertain lavishly in spite of Henry's meager salary. One potential source of income for the Knoxes was the 30-square-mile plot of land in Maine inherited by Lucy Knox. At the conclusion of the American Revolution in 1783, Henry Knox began to negotiate for his wife's inheritance of her share of the land.

In June 1795, the Knoxes and seven of their children moved to Thomaston, Maine, where they built an elaborate mansion they called Montpelier. On July 4, 1795, the family hosted a housewarming party for the residents of Thomaston. Guests included Native Americans, members of the Tarrantine tribe of coastal Maine who camped on the house's grounds. By 1798, the extravagant-spending Knoxes had to sell some of their land and mortgage their home to keep up with their debts.

In addition to their financial woes, Knox lost three of her children in 1796 and 1797. On April 23, 1796, 3-year-old Augusta and 18-month-old Marcus died of diphtheria. Six-year-old George Washington Knox recovered from diphtheria but died that winter. In January 1797, 14-year-old year old Julia died from consumption. At this point in her life, Knox had only three living children: her oldest, Lucy; her youngest, Caroline; and her son, Henry Jackson. On October 25, 1806, Henry died from an infection caused by swallowing a broken chicken bone. Knox continued to live in Montpelier, although she was forced to sell off many possessions and close up much of the house to pay off her husband's debts. She was devastated by her husband's death and became increasingly reclusive until her own death on June 20, 1824, at the age of 68.

Kathleen Barker

See also Adams, Abigail; Arnold, Peggy (Margaret) Shippen; Washington, Martha

Further Reading

Puls, Mark. 2010. *Henry Knox: Visionary General of the American Revolution.* London: Palgrave Macmillan.

Roberts, Cokie. 2004. *Founding Mothers: The Women Who Raised Our Nation.* New York: Harper.

Stuart, Nancy Rubin. 2012. *Defiant Brides: The Untold Story of Two Revolutionary-Era Women and the Radical Men They Married.* Boston: Beacon.

The Lady's New-Years Gift: Or Advice to a Daughter (1688)

George Savile, the first Marquess of Halifax (1633–1695), first published *The Lady's New-Years Gift: Or Advice to a Daughter* in 1688. This piece of didactic literature advised readers how to respond to different marital problems, how to conduct one's family and servants, and how to control one's vanity and pride, among other things. Lord Halifax shared beliefs common among men of his time period, arguing that husbands and wives were not equals but that each sex had key characteristics that the other one lacked. The work was published in London and gained a large readership in both England and the American colonies well into the 18th century.

Lord Halifax was an English political figure who served in both the House of Commons and the House of Lords during the 17th century. He wrote *The Lady's New-Years Gift* for his daughter, Elizabeth, who married the third Earl of Chesterfield. *The Lady's New-Years Gift* is split into nine sections: "Religion," "Husband," "House, Family, and Children," "Behavior and Conversation," "Friendships," "Censure," "Vanity and Affectation," "Pride," and "Diversions." Throughout the work, Lord Halifax emphasized that a wife's place is within the home, while her husband's duties lay outside it.

In "Husband," one of the most substantial sections, Lord Halifax justified the inferiority of women to men while also describing how men's and women's qualities complemented each other. He argued "That there is *Inequality* in the *Sexes,* and that for the better Oeconomy of the World, the *Men,* who were to be the Lawgivers, had the larger share of *Reason* bestow'd upon them; by which means your Sex is the better prepar'd for the *Compliance* that is necessary for the better performance of those *Duties* which seem to be most properly assign'd to it." He continued, stating that "We are made of differing *Tempers,* that our *Defects* may the better be mutually supplied: Your *Sex* wanteth our *Reason* for your *Conduct,* and our *Strength* for your *Protection:* Ours wanteth your *Gentleness* to soften, and to entertain us." Women lacked reason, but men provided it and benefited from the gentleness women offered them.

Lord Halifax's more practical advice on marital relations did not assume that his female reader would enter into a happy or well-functioning marriage. Women and men could both be involved in extramarital relations, and he freely admitted that women bore the brunt of the punishment for such dalliances (through pregnancy). However, he consoled his reader that the benefit of this inequality was that women held the honor of preserving the family. Lord Halifax enumerated some of the faults a woman might find in her husband: he could be a drunkard or could be ill-tempered, greedy, or weak and incompetent. In most of these situations, he advised that a wife could turn these faults to her advantage by learning how to diffuse a husband's temper and by avoiding comments and activities that aggravate poor behavior. Furthermore, he argued that a wife should be happy to marry a man with faults, because those faults make it more difficult for him to judge his companion. Overall, though, a woman should seek a husband who is a kind man and will be an able master.

In "House, Family, and Children," Halifax advised readers to embrace one's household duties because they provided a wife with worth and significance. A wife who ignored those duties and relied on her good looks would soon be disappointed to find that her looks had diminished with time and that she had little to contribute to the home. He further argued that a mother should employ kindness to cultivate obedience in her children: "Let them be more in awe of your *Kindess* than of your *Power.*"

The Lady's New-Years Gift was first published anonymously in 1688, and two "corrected" editions quickly came out later the same year. Readers encountered it in a variety of formats: 25 editions of the work itself appeared over almost a century, it was included along with Lord Halifax's other writings in multiple editions of his *Miscellanies,* and it was translated into French. Early American colonists imported Lord Halifax's advice, along with other conduct and etiquette books, into the colonies.

Amy Sopcak-Joseph

See also Advice Literature; *Vol. 2, Sec. 1:* Separation of Spheres

Further Reading

Newton, Sarah Emily. 1990. "Wise and Foolish Virgins: 'Usable Fiction' and the Early American Conduct Tradition." *Early American Literature* 25: 139–167.

Savile, George. 1912. *The Complete Works of George Savile, First Marquess of Halifax.* Edited by Walter Raleigh. Oxford, UK: Clarendon.

Lee, Mother Ann (1736–1784)

As founder of the Shakers, Mother Ann Lee was an innovative and powerful religious leader who, like her contemporary Jemima Wilkinson, challenged traditional church authorities in believing that women should be spiritual leaders. Mother Lee exhibited organizational skill that resulted in the establishment of Shaker settlements throughout New England and the Ohio River Valley that survived long after her death.

Much remains unknown about Lee's early life. Although her tombstone states that she was born on February 29, 1736, no official birth record exists. A baptismal record indicates that she was baptized on June 1, 1742, in Manchester, England. She married

Mother Ann Lee founded the Shakers, a religious sect that emerged from the First Great Awakening. She preached and led people at a time when very few women were allowed to even speak in church. (Mary Evans Picture Library/Alamy Stock Photo)

Abraham Standerin on January 5, 1762. Although Lee gave birth to four children, none survived to adulthood. These personal tragedies led her to a deeper involvement with a group she joined in 1758—the Shaking Quakers, led by Jane and James Wardley. Like the Quakers, the Wardleys' worship services involved expressive singing and bodily spasms, thus the group's moniker "Shakers." The Wardleys also encouraged adherents to follow the inner light, or conviction of God's grace, and taught that women could be spiritual leaders. Despite the similarities between Quakers and the Shaking Quakers, scholars have been unable to uncover any formal connection between the two groups.

Arrest records indicate that by the early 1770s Lee became one of the group's primary agitators in Manchester. She frequently appears in town records as a disturber of the peace and a disrupter of religious services. Increased persecution led her to immigrate to North America along with a small group of followers that included her husband and her brother William. Shaker tradition holds that the small band arrived in New York City on August 6, 1774, although the exact date of their arrival is unknown. Once in North America, the group dispersed. At some point after they arrived in New York, Lee's husband left her. According to her version of events, he could not accept her belief that the citizens of the Kingdom of God had to abstain from sexual intercourse. In 1779, Lee's group reunited outside of Albany, New York, on a farm owned by Shaker John Partington. This site became Niskayuna, the original Shaker settlement.

The Shakers maintained a low profile until wider events brought them public recognition. With suspicions heightened during the American Revolution, local authorities accused Shakers of disloyalty. Shakers had allegedly discouraged colonists from joining the military to support the Patriot cause. Suspicion continued throughout the war. Lee was arrested on July 24, 1780, and remained imprisoned until December 4, 1780. She returned to Niskayuna after New York authorities decided that she was not a threat to the revolutionary cause.

Sympathetic outsiders also began to notice the communal settlement. The Shakers labored to build a productive farm in the midst of swampland, and their industry attracted notice. Many Americans, such as the New Light Baptist Joseph Meacham, had been involved in the frequent evangelical revivals of the region that had been the Great Awakening and continued to look for a higher spiritual experience. Meacham and others found this experience at Niskayuna. Some people converted to Shakerism before returning to their farms in other parts of New England, while others stayed on at Niskayuna. Conversions also brought negative attention, as clergymen began to question Lee's authority as well as the community's strict policy on celibacy.

The spread of Shaker teaching led Lee, William Lee, and James Whittaker to tour New England between 1781 and 1783. This tour allowed them to consolidate their authority over other Shaker communities while also proselytizing. Lee shared authority with William and Whittaker, with the latter actually undertaking most of the public teaching. Although the three Shakers at times received a warm welcome, they also faced persecution. Hardship had adverse effects on their health. William died in the summer of 1784, and Lee died a few months later. Whittaker led the group until his death in 1787. Meacham took over as leader that same year but by 1790 called on Lucy Wright to join him as coleader. Wright held the position until her death in 1821.

Shakers honor Ann Lee with the title "Mother." Her precise role in Shaker teaching remains unclear, however. Because Lee was most likely illiterate and because her followers stressed divine revelation and the spoken word over written texts, the early Shakers left no written sources describing their distinctive doctrines. It is impossible to know how much historical truth the 1808 Lee biography by Benjamin S. Young contains or the oral accounts collected in the 1816 work *Testimonies*. The 1781 invective by a Shaker apostate and Baptist minister named Valentine Rathbun constitutes the earliest written source. Thus, reconstructing early Shaker beliefs regarding Lee remains difficult.

It appears that Shakers believed Lee to have a special relationship with God and an important part in inaugurating his kingdom. According to some early accounts, the Shakers believed Lee to be the second incarnation of Christ. Because Shakers seem to define

Christ as the spirit of goodness or the principle of wisdom rather than the historical Jesus of Nazareth, this claim does not appear as radical as it at first might seem. At other times, the Shakers described Lee as the woman of Revelation 12, the mother of the persecuted elect. Whatever Lee's specific role, sources indicate that early Shakers appear to have seen her as a motherly figure, instructing, disciplining, and comforting them and leading them into the restored Kingdom of God on Earth.

Nathan Saunders

See also *Vol. 1, Sec. 2:* Great Awakening; Quakers; *Vol. 2, Sec. 1:* Shakers

Further Reading

Foster, Lawrence. 1991. *Women, Family, and Utopia: Communal Experiments of the Shakers, the Oneida Community, and the Mormons.* Syracuse, NY: Syracuse University Press.

Humez, Jean M., ed. 1993. *Mother's First-Born Daughters: Early Shaker Writings on Women and Religion.* Bloomington: Indiana University Press.

Stein, Stephen J. 1992. *The Shaker Experience in America: A History of the United Society of Believers.* New Haven, CT: Yale University Press.

Loyalist Women

People who remained loyal to the British Crown and government during the American Revolution (1775–1783) were called Loyalists. Loyalists included white, Native American, and black women. Because they did not join the winning revolutionary cause, Loyalist women particularly suffered during and after the war.

With hindsight, it is easy for modern Americans to imagine that all colonials were in favor of the Revolution. Northern colonies that tended to be heavily for the Revolution were known as Patriots, while the Southern Colonies contained more Loyalists, or people who thought rebellion was a bad idea. Men had to declare for one side or the other, and this put many colonial American women in a difficult position. Regardless of their personal feelings, wives and daughters were seen as extensions of fathers and husbands

under the laws of coverture. Thus, women had little real political choice in their allegiance.

Individuals and mobs often victimized Loyalist women, who were vulnerable to rape and other assaults. Local governments were eager to identify Loyalists and confiscate their property. This caused many Loyalist families to move to either a friendlier town or colony or to Canada or England. Peggy Shippen, who married Patriot army officer Benedict Arnold, had to flee the colonies for London in 1781 when their plot to conspire with the British Army was discovered. Unlike most Loyalist women, Shippen arrived in London a rich and famous woman. She was celebrated for her change in loyalty, and the queen granted her a yearly annuity to pay for her children's education.

Most Loyalist women did not find themselves in such grand circumstances. Women who fled generally had children with them and left all or most of their belongings behind and had to start all over when they reached safety. Given these difficulties, many Loyalist women chose to stay in the colonies and resist the Patriots. Mary Morris, Margaret Inglis, and Susannah Robinson plotted unsuccessfully to kidnap the mayor of Albany, New York, after the Inglis house was ransacked in 1776. More women hid their husbands and sons from invading armies or helped British soldiers by feeding, housing, and nursing them. The active role that many women took in defending the Loyalist cause strongly suggests that they were more than victims of circumstance and were active agents of their own destiny.

Native Americans found themselves taking sides in the American Revolution as well, in great part because their destiny lay with whoever won the conflict. Colonists continued through the 1700s to expand into Native Americans' territory, bringing disease and violence with them. Some tribal groups allied with the British, believing that the Crown was the best way to protect their interests, while other groups allied with the Patriots on the principle that the British had not adequately protected them. The powerful Iroquois nation, for example, sided with the British, in part at least because Mohawk leader Molly Brant urged them to do so at a 1777 council meeting.

Patriot rhetoric about freedom and equality did not extend to black Americans, nor did the Continental government suggest that slavery might be antithetical to liberty. Most black colonials were slaves, so they had few choices during the war. Slave women would have had even fewer choices, in part because children anchored them to slavery. In 1775 Lord Dunsmore issued a proclamation in Virginia that offered freedom to any slaves who ran away from their masters and fought for the British. Over 30 percent of the slaves who did so were women, many of whom went to the British Army with their children in tow. In 1779 British general Sir Henry Clinton made slaves much the same offer in New York. As in Virginia, many of the slaves who ran away to the British Army were women with children. Clinton found himself inundated with slave refugees and eventually ordered some of them returned to their masters. About 3,000 of the black Loyalists were relocated to Nova Scotia and then to Sierra Leone and London.

Loyalist women, regardless of race or economic status, faced great difficulty during the American Revolution. Although many Americans celebrate the American Revolution as a triumph of liberty, colonists who remained loyal to the British government did not in general experience it as a positive.

Peg A. Lamphier

See also Arnold, Peggy (Margaret) Shippen; Brant, Molly; *Vol. 1, Sec. 2:* Coverture

Further Reading

Case, Stephen H., and Mark Jacob. 2012. *Treacherous Beauty: Peggy Shippen, the Woman behind Benedict Arnold's Plot to Betray America.* Guilford, CT: Lyons.

Potter-MacKinnon, Janice. 1995. *While the Women only Wept: Loyalist Refugee Women in Eastern Ontario.* Montreal: McGill Queens University Press.

Madison, Dolley (1768–1849)

A child of the American Revolution, Dolley Madison became perhaps the most celebrated woman of her generation. Her fame came from being more than a president's wife; she was also a skillfully practiced

First Lady Dolley Madison did much to support her husband's presidency, running a vital and informed political salon where political men could meet, collaborate, and compromise. Her political power in Washington continued until her death in 1849. (Perry-Castaneda Library)

political power. She virtually invented the first lady's role in Washington politics as an arbiter of parlor politics by influencing her husband and other men with regard to policy and was on equal terms with congressmen and diplomats.

Born Dolley Payne on May 20, 1768, and a Quaker by birth, she did not follow the Society of Friends policy in eschewing politics. Her parents John and Mary Coles Payne settled their family in Virginia, where, also contrary to Quaker teachings, they owned slaves. Her parents emerged as one of Virginia's largest landowners, grooming their daughter for life in elite society. Madison attended school and had private tutors, where she learned history, languages, and the literature of classical Greece and Rome. When she was about 15 years old her father freed the family's slaves and moved to Philadelphia. The city, like others in the Americas and throughout the world, was unhygenic by modern standards and rife with disease. Yellow fever probably killed one of Dolley's brothers. Her father perished several years later. At age 22 Dolley married Philadelphia attorney John Todd. The couple had two sons, John Payne and William. In 1793 John Todd, William, and John's parents all died from yellow fever.

James Madison (1751–1836), the architect of the U.S. Constitution, met and married the young widow in 1794. In many ways they seemed an odd match. He was 17 years older than her and considerably less cheerful. At five feet eight inches, Dolley towered over James, who stood at five feet three inches. Because James was not a Quaker, the Society of Friends expelled the new Mrs. Madison. Like her father, James was among the Virginia elite who owned slaves, a fact that did not seem to bother Madison at all. Later in her life, in spite of a directive in her husband's will not to do so, Madison separated slave families and sold slaves for profit.

Dolley Madison ascended the political ladder with her husband. President Thomas Jefferson's secretary of state, James became president in his own right in 1809. Madison practiced her political skills under the Jefferson administration, sometimes acting as the widowed Jefferson's hostess. At her husband's inauguration people remarked that Madison had the dignified appearance of a queen.

Styled as an aristocrat, Madison adorned herself in expensive French gowns. She opened the White House Wednesday evenings to discuss politics and literature. Men came in large numbers in hopes of talking with the first lady. Politicians and diplomats valued her as a discrete agent for people and issues. During the War of 1812 she gained fame for saving first U.S. president George Washington's portrait from a White House in flames. She had waited for her husband, who was at the battlefront, but when he did not appear she packed her carriages with White House valuables and fled just before the British advance. English officers arrived at the White House so soon after Madison's escape that they ate the meal she had ordered prepared for dinner. For her bravery Madison became a national hero.

After James's presidency the couple returned to Virginia. Madison's status as an elite political woman, however, did not ebb. James owned a 5,000-acre plantation in Virginia called Montpelier and another 1,000 acres in Kentucky.

James Madison, who outlived most of the founding fathers, died in 1836. His death left Dolley Madison bereft. She moved back to the nation's capital and supervised the publication of her husband's papers but burned documents she deemed too personal for public consumption. She also sold James's estate and its slaves to pay Payne's debts. Congress, eager to receive the former first lady, invited Madison to attend its deliberations whenever she wished, a privilege extended to no other woman of her time. In 1838 Congress purchased James's papers from Madison, providing her some relief from poverty. Dolley Madison died on July 12, 1849, and was buried in the Congressional Cemetery before being reinterred at Montpelier, where she now lies next to her husband James.

Christopher Cumo

See also Parlor Politics

Further Reading
Allgor, Catherine. 2013. *Dolley Madison: The Problem of National Unity.* Boulder, CO: Westview.
Roberts, Cokie. 2004. *Founding Mothers: The Women Who Raised Our Nation.* New York: HarperCollins.

Mathews, Mother Bernardina (1732–1800)

Mother Bernardina Mathews (sometimes spelled Mathews) founded the first American community of Catholic women in 1790. Mathews was prioress of a largely cloistered Carmelite community in Port Tobacco, Maryland, until her death in 1800.

Ann Mathews was born in Charles County, Maryland, in 1732, the daughter of Joseph Mathews and Susanna Croycroft. Her family was elite-class Marylanders and also faithful Catholics. Her father died when she was two years old, but her mother's inheritance and remarriage to Edward Clements secured the financial stability of the family. The colony of

Maryland was founded by Lord Baltimore as a place in which the rights of Catholics to practice their religion and conduct business without discrimination could be protected but was returned to Protestant royal control in 1692. The penal laws established against Catholics at this time included a prohibition on religious houses. Because Mathews wished to pursue a religious life, she was forced to go abroad, entering the Carmelite convent at Hoogstraten, located in the Lowlands in what is now Belgium. Three English-speaking convents could be found in Belgium at Antwerp, Liège, and Hoogstraten to accommodate the influx of Catholic women from Great Britain and its colonies. Mathews received the habit on September 30, 1754, taking the name Bernardina Teresa Xavier of Saint Joseph. She made her profession of faith on November 24, 1755, promising obedience, chastity, and poverty to God and the Blessed Virgin Mary of Mount Carmel.

The community at Hoogstraten recognized Mother Bernardina's religious conviction and leadership potential and appointed her mistress of novices at the completion of her own novitiate. Her studies included language, as she was able to read both her native English and the French spoken in the country surrounding the convent. She was elected prioress of the convent in 1771, serving in that capacity until her departure for Maryland. At the end of the American Revolution, Mother Bernardina received a letter from her brother, Ignatius Mathews, asking her to return to the new nation to found a convent.

The establishment of religious freedom that came with America's independence opened the door for the exiled religious women to return home, just as the French Revolution and other unrest in Europe made the nuns' future unclear. In fact, in 1794 the Hoogstraten convent relocated from Belgium to Dorset, England, under pressure from the French. John Carroll, the prefect of Baltimore, gave permission for the establishment of a convent in Maryland, welcoming the Carmelite sisters and their prayers to serve the Catholic population of the new country. At the time there were approximately 25,000 Catholics in the United States, with only 30 priests to serve them. Nearly 15,000 of these Catholics resided in Maryland. Mother Bernardina was among the 4 women who made the trek to the United States, taking with her 2 of her nieces who had joined her in religious life, Susanna and Ann Teresa Mathews, who adopted the names Mary Eleanora of Saint Francis Xavier and Mary Aloysia of the Blessed Trinity, respectively. Joining them were a British nun, Clare Joseph (Dickenson) of the Sacred Heart, and the convent's confessor, Father Charles Neale, a Jesuit priest and relative of the Mathews family. The party embarked from Holland on April 19, 1790, and arrived in New York, proceeding down the coast of Maryland to their destination, Charles County, on July 10, 1790. Mother Bernardina's brother Ignatius, who had sent the letter urging her to return to Maryland, died On May 11, 1790, while she was en route to America.

The nuns first established residence at Chandler's Hope, a property owned by the Neale family. After this property was deemed unsuitable for the needs of the convent, Father Neale acquired land at Port Tobacco, Maryland. This site included 800 acres of land. The religious community was dedicated on the feast day of Saint Teresa of Avila, October 15, 1790. This marked the founding of the first Catholic female religious order in the new United States. Mother Bernardina was named the first prioress of the Carmelite community, and Clare Joseph was named subprioress. Catholics in Maryland had become accustomed to sending their daughters abroad to join religious orders, so the convent was a welcomed addition to the new state.

The Carmelite order is a cloistered group, seeking God through prayer and remaining isolated from the outside world. John Carroll, who had granted permission for the women to return to America, discovered that he had a need for teachers in parochial schools. Much to Carroll's chagrin, the newly arrived nuns declined his pleas to alter their calling to fill the need for teachers. The sisters would eventually heed the call to teach but only for a short period of time before returning to cloister. This was in keeping with the Carmelite emphasis on contemplative prayer mixed with community action when necessary.

Mother Bernardina served as prioress of the Carmelite community at Port Tobacco until her death in 1800. Following Bernardina's death, Clare Joseph was promoted to prioress. By 1831 the convent was beset by lawsuits from neighbors and an economic downturn in the area. The City of Baltimore acquired the Port Tobacco convent that year. From 1790 to 2011, 136 women made professions and became members of the Carmelite community descended from the Port Tobacco Carmel and now located in Baltimore. It is estimated that two-thirds of the Carmelite monasteries in the United States can trace their origins to the convent established at Port Tobacco by Mother Bernardina. Carmelite nuns also have orders, including missions and enclosed monasteries, across the world.

Elizabeth Bass

See also *Vol. 1, Sec. 2:* Catholic Women

Further Reading

Currier, Charles. 2010. *Carmel in America: A Centenial History of the Displaced Carmelites in the United States.* Whitefish, MT: Kessinger Publishing.

FitzGerald, Constance, ed. 1990. *The Carmelite Adventure: Clare Joseph Dickinson's Journal of a Trip to America and Other Documents.* Baltimore: Carmelite Sisters.

McCauley, Mary (1754–1832)

Mary McCauley is likely the model for the composite character known as Molly Pitcher, a name given to women who assisted soldiers or performed other heroic acts during the American Revolution. McCauley served with her husband at the Battle of Monmouth (June 28, 1778) and served with the Continental Army until the end of the war. It was not until after her death that she became associated with the growing legend of Molly Pitcher.

A number of women carried water to troops during the American Revolution, inspiring the fictive name "Molly Pitcher." Mary Hays McCauley took up her husband's post at the Battle of Monmouth in 1778, making her the most famous "Molly Pitcher." (National Archives and Records Administration)

Mary Ludwig Hays McCauley was born to German immigrants in New Jersey on October 13, 1754. In 1768 she moved Carlisle, Pennsylvania, to serve in the household of Anna and Dr. William Irvine. That same year McCauley married William (some sources say John) Hays, a barber, and the couple settled in Carlisle, Pennsylvania. Hays joined the Continental Army as a gunner in 1776. He served in the 1st Pennsylvania Regiment of artillery, a unit commanded by Dr. Irvine. In 1777, Hays joined the 7th Pennsylvania Regiment. Like many other women, McCauley eventually followed her husband to war, likely serving with a support unit attached to the medical corps or the artillery. Among her jobs was the task of providing water (in pitchers) to the artillery corps.

The legend of Molly Pitcher was born during the Battle of Monmouth. McCauley and her husband were serving with Captain Francis Proctor's company in the Pennsylvania artillery regiment. Throughout the battle she supplied the tired and wounded men with drinking water and water to cool the cannon. When her husband collapsed from heat stroke (some sources say he was injured in battle), McCauley took his place at the cannon.

Returning home after the war, McCauley and her husband had one son, John Hays, born in 1780. McCauley apparently worked around town as a domestic servant. Her husband died in 1789 from wounds sustained during the war, and in 1793 she married George McCauley, a stone cutter, a Revolutionary War veteran, and a friend of her first husband's.

On February 18, 1822, Mary McCauley petitioned the Pennsylvania assembly for a pension. That same year the body passed "An Act for the Relief of Molly M'Kolly, for Her Service during the Revolutionary War" and awarded her an annual pension of $40. McCauley died on January 22, 1833, and is buried in Carlisle. There was no mention of her connection to the Molly Pitcher legend in her obituary. In 1856, however, her son's obituary claims that he was the son of the famous Molly Pitcher. By the centennial of the American Revolution, the town of Carlisle, Pennsylvania, agreed with this claim. On July 4, 1876, it erected a white marble statue over her grave, dedicated to "Molly Pitcher, the heroine of Monmouth."

Although there are many legends associated with the name Molly Pitcher, two elements remain essentially consistent across stories: the legendary Molly took her husband's place at cannon, and her actions took place in the Battle of Monmouth. In 1830 Freeman Current published *American Anecdotes,* which included the story of Molly Pitcher fulfilling her wifely duties by taking her fallen husband's place at the cannon. The 1835 *Cyclopedia of American History* presented Pitcher as a fierce Patriot who provided water to all the soldiers on the battlefield. Newspaper articles circulating in this period also presented Pitcher as an ardent Patriot who demanded to serve in her husband's stead.

Perhaps the most influential figure in the crafting of the Molly Pitcher legend was George Washington Parke Custis, George Washington's step grandson. In 1840, Custis began publishing serialized accounts of important moments of the American Revolution in the *National Intelligencer* under the title "Recollections and Private Memoirs of Washington." In his column describing the Battle of Monmouth, Custis described "Molly" as a brash camp follower who spoke with an Irish brogue and stopped the cannon after taking up the ramrod when several artillerymen had been killed. He claimed that Pitcher received the personal thanks of General Washington as well as a piece of gold for her service at the cannon. Custis added to the legend in 1843 when he described Pitcher as a camp follower who washed soldiers' clothing while wearing an artilleryman's uniform and hat.

McCauley herself left almost no records of her life aside from pension applications. Private Joseph Plumb Martin, whose memoir was first published in 1830, described a woman helping her husband fire artillery at Monmouth, a cannonball passing directly through her legs and tearing her petticoat. In 1927, William Stryker quoted the diary of Dr. Albigence Waldo in his work *The Battle of Monmouth.* Waldo claimed that a wounded officer had described a woman who allegedly took up a gun (or some sort of artillery) after her husband became incapacitated. Neither story mentions Mary McCauley or Molly Pitcher by name.

Further complicating the legend is the fact that two other women who served during the war have also occasionally been referred to as Molly Pitcher. One is

Deborah Sampson, a woman from Massachusetts who disguised herself in men's clothing and enlisted in the Continental Army under the name Robert Shurtleff. Another candidate for the legend of Molly Pitcher is Margaret Corbin, occasionally referred to as "Captain Molly." Corbin worked a cannon with her husband at Fort Washington in New York in 1776, and she was the first woman to receive a pension from the U.S. government for her service during the American Revolutionary War.

Kathleen Barker

See also Camp Followers; Corbin, Margaret; Sampson, Deborah

Further Reading

Butterfield, Emily Lewis. 2013. "'Lie There My Darling, While I Avenge Ye': Anecdotes, Collective Memory, and the Legend of Molly Pitcher." In *Remembering the Revolution: Memory, History, and Nation Making from Independence to the Civil War,* edited by Michael A. McDonnell et al., 198–213. Amherst: University of Massachusetts Press.

Raphael, Ray. 2004. *Founding Myths: Stories That Hide Our Patriotic Past.* New York: New Press.

Teipe, Emily J. 1999. "Will the Real Molly Pitcher Please Stand Up?" *Prologue: Quarterly of the National Archives and Records Administration* 31(2) (Summer): 118–126.

McCrea, Jane (1752–1777)

As a young woman engaged to a British soldier during the American Revolution, Jane McCrea, allegedly murdered in 1777 by Native Americans, fueled a propaganda war in the colonies and spawned debates over the use of Native American allies in war. Her story became a popular subject for artists and writers in the 19th century as a symbol of the predation of white women by men of color, or the supposed savage Other.

Jane McCrea was born in Bedminster (now Lamington), New Jersey, in 1752 to James McCrea and Mary Graham McCrea, both immigrants from Scotland. After her father's death in 1769, McCrea

lived with her eldest brother, John, and his family in the upper Hudson River Valley, not far from the remote British outpost of Fort Edward. At the outbreak of the American Revolution in 1775, McCrea's family divided their loyalties between the revolutionaries (or Patriots) and those remaining faithful to the British Crown, the Loyalists. Three of her brothers joined the Continental Army, but two others remained with the British military. In late 1776, McCrea became engaged to David Jones, a loyalist who joined the forces led by General John Burgoyne.

In the summer of 1777, Burgoyne launched his assault on the Hudson Valley region. Throughout the campaign he relied on Native Americans from the Iroquois Confederacy, a group of six tribes living across upper New York state. After Burgoyne's forces recaptured Fort Ticonderoga on July 6, 1777, most Patriots abandoned the Fort Edward area in anticipation of a British attack, but McCrea chose to remain behind in the hope of seeing her fiancé. On July 17, 1777, she traveled to Fort Edward to visit her friend Mrs. Sarah McNeil, who was packing to leave for Albany. The two women were discovered by a Native American scouting party under the command of Burgoyne. McNeil was eventually delivered to the British camp, but a second raiding party returned only with McCrea's scalp. Her dead body, which also bore a bullet wound, was found the next day near Fort Edward. There are conflicting accounts of McCrea's death. One version claims that her captors argued over who would take credit for seizing her, and therefore earn a reward for delivering her to her fiancé, and that she was murdered as they attempted to settle the dispute. A different account reports that McCrea was accidentally shot by Americans (aiming for the Native Americans) withdrawing from Fort Edward.

General Burgoyne faced a serious dilemma in the wake of McCrea's death. He knew that he could not punish the Native Americans involved without losing their support. However, his lack of action was perceived by Americans on both sides of the war as an unwillingness or inability to keep his Native American allies under control. George Washington and American commander Horatio Gates recognized the propaganda value of McCrea's death and used the incident to charge the British and their Native American allies with brutal treatment of noncombatants, particularly women. In a letter to Burgoyne in September 1777, Gates alleged that McCrea was murdered in her wedding dress, and he accused Burgoyne of employing murderers. Both Gates's letter and accounts of McCrea's murder were widely published in colonial newspapers, likely earning sympathy for the Patriot cause in upstate New York and New England. The story even reached London where, in the House of Commons, Edmund Burke used the example of McCrea's death to denounce the British policy of using Native American allies in warfare. The Continental Army likely used McCrea's death as a recruiting tactic for the remainder of the Revolution. Certainly Gates's ranks more than doubled after the American success at Ticonderoga and news of McCrea's murder.

Thousands of men, women, and children were captured or killed in the wars between colonists and Native Americans, yet McCrea continued to inspire popular culture for decades after her death. Most visual and textual representations perpetuated racial stereotypes of an innocent and unprotected American maiden gratuitously attacked by savage Native Americans. Examples include John Vanderlyn's painting *The Death of Jane McCrea*, exhibited in the Paris Salon of 1804. This was the first American *tableau d'histoire* ever to be accepted in that prestigious international art exposition. Joel Barlow commissioned the image to illustrate his 1807 epic poem *The Columbiad*, which celebrated American victory over the British. Both pieces emphasize McCrea's vulnerability at the hands of her stronger well-armed captors. McCrea inspired a number of additional paintings and lithographs in the 19th and 20th centuries. Asher B. Durand's *Murder of Miss McCrea* (1839) places her on horseback, watching a group of Native Americans engage in a heated argument with tomahawks raised. The other raiding party—or perhaps McCrea's potential rescuers—appear powerless in the distance. In 1900, McCrea made her first appearance on a calendar for Glen Falls Insurance Company. Based on a painting by F. C. Yohn titled *The Capture of Jane McCrea*, our heroine appears resigned to her fate, fully dressed in her wedding costume.

McCrea also appeared in numerous texts in the 19th century, each telling, or inventing, a different part of her story. In Michel René Hilliard-d'Auberteuil's

1784 novel *Miss McCrea: A Novel of the American Revolution*, McCrea is presented as a disobedient daughter who foolishly gave her heart to a Loyalist. In 19th-century works such as *The Life of Jane McCrea, with an Account of Burgoyne's Expedition in 1777*, published by David Wilson in 1853, McCrea is a romantic heroine driven by her heart rather than by reason. McCrea's death also served as an inspiration for similar events recounted by James Fenimore Cooper in his novel *The Last of the Mohicans*. In each work McCrea remains a victim and a martyr to American independence.

Kathleen Barker

See also Boone, Jemima; Rowlandson, Mary; *Vol. 1, Sec. 2:* Captives, English; Captivity Narratives

Further Reading
Edgerton, Samuel Y., Jr. 1965. "The Murder of Jane McCrea: The Tragedy of an American 'Tableau d'Histoire.'" *Art Bulletin* 47 (December): 481–492.
Namias, June. 1993. *White Captives: Gender and Ethnicity on the American Frontier.* Chapel Hill: University of North Carolina Press.

Mecom, Jane Franklin (1712–1794)

Jane Franklin Mecom was Benjamin Franklin's youngest and favorite sibling. Although lacking formal education, she carried on a lifelong correspondence with the brother who left home when she was only 11 years old. Their exchanges and their comparative lives offer insight into the role of gender in early American life as well as the challenges central to life in 18th-century North America.

Born on March 27, 1712, Jane Franklin was 1 of Josiah and Abiah Folger Franklin's 10 children (Josiah had 7 children with his first wife) and the only sibling younger than Benjamin. While colonial life tested most women, Jane had more than her share of challenges. As the youngest female child, she took care of her parents in their declining years. That burden was made no easier by her own family situation. At age 15 she married Edward Mecom, but he proved to be an erratic provider. She had 12 children within a span of

22 years, only 1 of whom was still alive at her death. One of her sons died fighting in the American Revolutionary War, and 2 suffered from mental illness. Other children suffered from poverty and struggled to stay out of debtors' prison. All of these domestic travails made Mecom's life one of hardship and heartache.

As the sister of two printers and the mother of another, Mecom read far more than the average colonial white woman and was considerably well versed in the events of her time. Mecom and her brother Benjamin had a special relationship. She was long touted as Franklin's favorite sibling, and their lifelong correspondence revealed much about their disparate lives. In fact, because the letters he wrote to his sister were more likely to include discussion of political issues than were letters sent even to his wife, the sibling exchanges have offered historians a distinctive look into Franklin's thinking. Franklin's letters also reveal a personal familial side. Upon hearing that his sister planned to marry, he wrote her to be sure that she understood that a good wife was both frugal and industrious. Franklin had considered sending a tea table for a wedding present, but he reconsidered, recognizing that such a gift ran counter to his more practical admonitions.

Meanwhile, their correspondence reveals at least one major difference in their worldview, as Mecom often bemoaned her brother's lack of religious faith. The contrast in their daily lives represented an even greater gap. While Franklin represented the colonies in Europe and was the most famous American in the world, Mecom embodied the experience of the white colonists whose lives were directly impacted, often to their detriment, by the developing conflict between the Crown and the colonies. For example, the Townshend Acts boycott forced Mecom to close her hat and bonnet making business because she used materials from England that Franklin had secured. Meanwhile, the exodus from Boston caused by the Crown's dissolution of the Massachusetts General Assembly caused Mecom to lose some of her best boarders.

In the aftermath of the Revolution as the United States struggled to make its new democratic experiment a success, Mecom witnessed the challenges that befell the young republic. She wrote about the sympathy she felt for the debtors whose cause was pursued by Daniel Shays and his comrades in the western part of Massachusetts. At the same time, she expressed great pride in the fact that her older brother continued to be among the leaders who sought to address the problems of governing a new young country.

When Franklin died, he bequeathed to Mecom the house in which she lived, assuring her security in old age. Jane Franklin Mecom died at home on May 7, 1794. Her home was later destroyed to make room for a monument to Paul Revere. She lived a full life, one that reflected the changing times in which she had lived, first as a British colonist and later as a citizen of the United States and the favorite sister of the nascent nation's most famous man.

William H. Pruden III

See also Arnold, Peggy (Margaret) Shippen; Revolutionary War and Women

Further Reading

Isaacson, Walter. 2003. *Benjamin Franklin: A Life.* New York: Simon and Schuster.

Lepore, Jill. 2013. *Book of Ages: The Life and Opinions of Jane Franklin.* New York: Knopf.

Van Doren, Karl, ed. 1950. *The Letters of Benjamin Franklin and Jane Mecom.* Philadelphia: American Philosophical Society.

Correspondence of Benjamin Franklin with Catherine Ray Greene (1755, 1775, 1776)

Benjamin Franklin maintained a friendship and a correspondence with Catherine Ray Greene, the wife of William Greene, from 1754 until his death in 1790. Although more than 100 letters between the two are extant, they only met in person five times, the last occasion being in Philadelphia in 1776. Catherine Greene was also close friends with Franklin's sister Jane Mecom, wife of Edward Mecom of Boston. When Boston was besieged by colonial forces in 1775, Jane Mecom fled the city and stayed with

Greene at her home in Warwick, Rhode Island. Some of the letters in the correspondence and reproduced here are from Mecom.

1. CATHARINE RAY AT BLOCK ISLAND (OFF RHODE ISLAND) TO FRANKLIN AT PHILADELPHIA (1755)

Block Island June ye 28th [1755]

Dear, Dear Sir

Excues my writeing when I tell you it is the great regard I have for you will not let me be Silent, for Absence rather increais than lesens my affections then, my not receiveing one line from you in answer to 3 of my last letters March ye 3d & 31st and April ye 28th gives me a Vast deal of uneasiness and occation'd many tears, for Suerly I have wrote too much and you are affronted with me or have not received my letters in which I have Said a thousand things that nothing Should have tempted me to [have] Said to any body els for I knew they wold be Safe with you—I'll only beg the favor of one line what is become of my letters tel me you are well and for give me & love me one thousandth Part So well as I do you and then I will be Contented and Promise an amendment, it is with the greatest reluctance I Shall finish my letter with out telling you of Some great alterations Since my last but you have my Promise So I will Pray God to Bless you with the Best of Blessings and Subcribe my Self Dear Sir

your most Sincere affectionate & obliged friend

C Ray

My Proper Respects to Mrs Franklin & Daugter
Pray take Care of your health and except the Sugar Plums they are every one Sweetn'd as you used to like

2. JANE (FRANKLIN) MECOM AND CATHARINE (RAY) GREENE AT WARWICK TO BENJAMIN FRANKLIN AT PHILADELPHIA (1775)

. . . but throw the Goodnes of God I am at last Got Saif Hear & kindly Reeved by Mr Green & His wife (who to my grate comfort when I had got Pac't up what I Expected to have liberty to carey out intending to Seek my fourtune with hundred others not knowing whither) Sent me an Invitation in a leter to Mrs Patridg of which I gladly acepted an the day I arived at Prove-dence had the unspeakable Pleasure of hearing my Dear Brother was Saif arived at His own home, Blessed be God for all His mercys to me an unworthy Creature, these People [the Greenes] Seem formed for Hospitality Apear to be Pleasd with the vast Adition to there famely which consists of old M r Gough [Gooch] & wife, there Sons wife & negro boy, Mr Thomas Leverett's wife 2 Children & a made, my Self an Grand Daughter [Jane Flagg] who I could not leve if I had it would have been her Death, & they Expect this Day 3 more of M r Leveretts chill,n young Mr Gouge, Suckey [Susannah Hubbard] & Mrs Pateridg & Daughter. & Seem as tho there harts were open to all the world. . . .

Dear Brother I am tould you will be joynd to the Congress & that they will Remove to conetecut [Connecticut] will you Premit me to come & See you there Mrs Green Says She will go with me—Jane

My Dear Dear Friend Welcom a Hundred times Welcom to our once happy Land, Are you in Health and allow me to ask you the old question over a gain if you are the Same good old Soul—Caty

3. JANE (FRANKLIN) MECOM AND CATHARINE (RAY) GREENE AT WARWICK TO BENJAMIN FRANKLIN AT PHILADELPHIA (1775)

Warwick July 14—1775

The Concern I knew my Ever Dear Brother would be in to know what was become of me made me take the first opertunity to write to him & twice Since, but did not reeve a line from you till the day befor yesterday when I reed yrs of the 17 June & this Day I have reed the first you wrot, it had been Returnd from Cambridg & had lane 3 weeks in Newport office, your care for me at this time Added to the Innumerable Instances of yr Goodnes to me gives me grat comfort under the Difeculties I feel with others but not in a grater Degree for I am in want of nothing haveing mony Suficent to Saport me Some time if I Should go to board (which however mrs Green will not Consent to) & I have with me most of the things I had to Sell & now & then Sell Som Small mater . . .

(Postscript by Catharine Greene)

My Dear Friend your letter which [I] had the Pleasure of Receiving gave me great Pleasure as it gave me a fresh Proff of your own Dear Self, & being once more on the Same Land with us, your Dear good Sister Grew Very impatient till She heard from you and began to fear you was not Come She was kind enough to Shew me her letter and you are fear full She will be trouble Some but be assurd that her Company Richly Pays as She goes a long and we are Very happy to gether and [I] Shall not Consent to Spare her to any body but her Dear Brother was he to Stay at home and Be Positive but if you are to Journey we must have her for She is my mama and friend and I tell her we are Rich that we have a lot here and another there and have 3 or 4 of them and we Divert one

4. JANE (FRANKLIN) MECOM AT PHILADELPHIA TO WILLIAM GREENE AT WARWICK BUT INTENDED FOR CATY GREENE (1776)

Philadelphia 8th may 1776

My Dear friend

you can't Imagin the Anxiety I have been in Since I reeved yr last, hearing then of yr famely being So Sick & not a word Since maks me fear Every thing, you can't Surely Sopose I Should think any thing of paying postage on any Extroydenary ocation I Sent won large paquet to Governer Cook without a word of Apolegy you must make it for me for it was by yr order, & I had not time to write a word. I have Sent a nother by yr Brother Wards Servant which I hope you will git Saif & Soon, ansure me quick I besech you by the post, but prehaps I may meet it for there has been a Alaram hear to Day which Almost Determins me to Sett out for NewEngland Directly & if I Should I Shall take Ray with me for He would Brake His hart if I Should Leave Him & I have promised I will not, I cannot hear whither my Daughters Goods are Gone as well as mine but Expect theye are, & I think there is but very litle Chance for her Husband to Escape being taken, She looks on her Self alredy as a Disconsolat widdow Intreets me to promis her I will Return that we may live to gather, what if I Should go & take yt House Mr Leverett had near Provedence do you think we could git a liveing in the way they began I am afraid Boston is not Sufficiently fortified yet. I thought not to tell you the circumstanc of the Alarm as you may hear it as quick & more perfict in the

News Papers but I will Just tell you that two Ships the Roebuck & a nother came up the River I forgit how many mils Distant from the City when a number of armed Gondelos & fier Ships went Down to Ingage them there was Grat fiering all Day till five o clock & there is an Expres come brings News they have Shatered them boath much & Drove the Roebuck on Shore the Same that was Ashore on Sunday week but go off again it is Expected She will be Taken, Ray Desiers me to Remember His Duty love & Respects where it is Due & pleas to Do the Same for your Affectionat friend

Jane Mecom

5. CATHARINE (RAY) GREENE AT WARWICK TO BENJAMIN FRANKLIN AT PHILADELPHIA (1776)

Warwick July ye 3d 1776

My Dearly belovd Friend

I Gladly once more Welcom you To your own home though I Lament the occation hope by this you have Recoverd your Health & the Pheteiuge of So Disagreeable a Tuor & have Resumd the Chearfull agreeable BENJAMIN FRANKLIN Pray God to Preserve you long a Blessing to your family Friends & Ingurd Country We have Disagreeable accounts from N-York and Quebeck But Still hope there Is Virtue & Stability enough in our friends to Send our Enemies a Shamd to there own homes, and be Simple Bread & Water the Portion of theire Cheifs and that in a Dungeon But I Reflect is not Such guilty Conciencionss Punishment enought He leave them to a Higer Power, And to our agreeable Corrispond which has been So long Bar,d I think your last favor is Jany 27th a long while indeed But you have been Sick and in a Strange Land do give Sister Some little account of it and She will give it me for She is a Dear good Woman and I know you have not time—In yours you wrote you had Put Ray to Lattin School which we was much Pleasd with as we Proposd giving him learning if his Capacity was good enough of which being Parents we did not think our Selves Judges Mr Greene was Just in Since my writeing and Designd to have wrote him Self to you but tis a Severe Drougth with us and has a Number of People makeing Hay So that is obligd to be with them But Desires his Kind Regards to you and Many thanks for your Care of his Boy and Says he hopes you will Call upon him for Money when ever you think fit for he does not love large Sums against him and would be Glad to know what Sum would Carry him throw Colledg and if you think tis Best for him to Come home this Vacancy whether he would be Willing to go again or not I Could Deny my Self any Pleasure for My Childrens advantage those at home with Jenny & the family are all well and Joyn in Respects to you I dont know but think Jenny is like to get one of our best Matches you are So good a friend to Matrimony that you will be Glad to hear of it I Could Run much farther but fear the Post will be gone So I bid you Day Day God Bless

your friend that loves you Dearly
Caty Greene

Brother Hubbart Desires his love to all

6. JANE (FRANKLIN) MECOM AT WARWICK TO SARAH (FRANKLIN) BACHE AT PHILADELPHIA (1776)

I have, as you suppose, heard of your ladies noble and generous subscription for the army, and honour them for it; and if a hearty good will in me would effect it would follow your example; but I fear what my influence would procure would be so diminutive we should be ashamed to offer it. I live in an obscure place, have but little acquaintance, and those not very rich; but, you may say, a mite has been accepted and may be again, but there was a time when there was more religion and less pride. I really believe our friend Mrs Greene would be forward to set the example here as any of your ladies, had she the power, but her family have suffered extremely in their fortune by the depreciation: several of their farms were let on lease, and had the paper money tendered to them, and could not help themselves: great part of their interest lay in Block Island, where they could get nothing, as the person has proved dishonest and poor, and a debt he had contracted in paper money, the creditor living in Newport, where he could not get at him to discharge it [because of the British occupation], and now the Britons have left it, insists on silver and the Gov r has paid it; I forget whether it was four thousand pound or four thousand dollars, but either is a great sum in silver at this day.

Source: William Greene Roelker, ed., *Benjamin Franklin and Catharine Ray Greene: Their Correspondence 1755–1790* (Philadelphia: American Philosophical Society, 1949). Reprinted with permission. Available at http://archive.org/stream/benjaminfranklin1949fran/benjaminfranklin1949fran_djvu.txt.

Morris, Mary (1749–1827)

A strong supporter of American independence from England and a celebrated hostess to the early leaders of the new country, Mary White Morris was born on April 13, 1749, in Philadelphia, Pennsylvania. She was the youngest child of Thomas and Esther White, who had settled in Maryland but later moved to Philadelphia, where the family prospered. As a prominent member of the Philadelphia social community Morris married wealthy shipping magnate Robert Morris on March 2, 1769, giving him three sons and two daughters in the course of the marriage. Their home, Hills, became a novelty at that time, with its tropical fruit, a fishpond, and an icehouse. Mary Morris's life and that of her family would be closely interwoven with the progress of the American Revolutionary War and the rise of the new

U.S. government, as Robert Morris would eventually work on and sign the Declaration of Independence, the Articles of Confederation, and the U.S. Constitution.

As a delegate to the assembly of Pennsylvania, Robert Morris was appointed to the Second Continental Congress and became a financier for the Continental Army of George Washington, while Mary's brother William was appointed chaplain to the Congress. In December 1776 as the British forces were advancing on Philadelphia, the Congress moved to Baltimore. Robert Morris stayed in the city to protect his holdings but sent his wife and children to safety in Baltimore, where she stayed with her parents. Similar to Abigail Adams, Mary Morris was in regular correspondence with her husband, sending him what war news she could along with updates on their parents, children, and friends.

In March 1777 Mary Morris returned to Philadelphia, but in December the British captured the city, and their home had to be abandoned for a time. The Congress moved to Lancaster and then York, Pennsylvania, but reassembled again in Philadelphia in July 1778. As the wife of a powerful member of Congress, Morris entertained political guests in her home in much the same way Dolley Madison would do for future presidents Thomas Jefferson and James Madison in later years. At Morris's events politics was the talk of the day, and many useful alliances were born. As the Morrises were supporters of the American Revolution, there were frequent visits by prominent French representatives to their house. The Prince de Broglie and the Chevalier de la Luzerne lavishly praised the housekeeping and hospitality during such a visit in 1782. Mary Morris's elegance, style, and sophisticated manners as a hostess made the elite of society feel at home in her house and helped convince the French to become allies of the new American government. George Washington was a close friend of the couple and often stayed in their house. He resided there in May 1787 when the Constitutional Convention opened in Independence Hall for the reworking of the Articles of Confederation.

After Robert was elected as a senator in October 1788, Morris accompanied Martha Washington to New York to see General Washington sworn in as the president on April 30, 1789. In the dinner parties given by the president, Morris and her husband were regular guests. When Philadelphia became the national capital, Morris and her husband rented their house for the sum of $1 per year to the new government to be used as the president's home.

With the ruin of the American land market in the late 1790s, Robert Morris incurred heavy losses from his involvement in land speculation. He was incarcerated for debts between February 1798 and August 1801 at Prune Street Prison in Philadelphia. Morris regularly visited her husband in prison. At this time Washington appealed to Morris and her daughter to stay in his home, but she remained with other family.

Robert Morris died in May 1806. Mary Morris received an annuity of $1,500 for the rest of her life from the Holland Land Company. In 1824, General Lafayette visited the city, and Morris was still prominent enough to attend the reception given in his honor on October 5. Morris died on January 16, 1827, and was buried in the family graveyard.

Patit Paban Mishra

See also Adams, Abigail; Revolutionary War and Women

Further Reading

Abbot, W. W. 1999. *The Papers of George Washington: Retirement Series,* Vol. 4. Charlottesville: University Press of Virginia.
Griswold, Rufus W. 1855. *The Republican Court: Or, American Society in the Days of Washington.* New York: D. Appleton.
Rappleye, Charles. 2010. *Robert Morris: Financier of the American Revolution.* New York: Simon and Schuster.

Murray, Judith Sargent (1751–1820)

Born May 1, 1751, in Gloucester, Massachusetts, Judith Sargent Murray was the eldest child of Winthrop and Judith Sargent. In the late 18th and early 19th centuries Murray was part of an international debate about the place of women in society, which she contributed to through writing. She believed that traditional gender roles should not deter women from achieving their ambitions and questioned why society put limits on even its most talented women. Throughout her life Murray wrote for several magazines and completed three plays, often under assumed names such as Constantia or the male name Mr. Vigilius, nicknamed "The Gleaner."

In 1769, Murray married ship captain John Stevens. She and her family became followers of the Universalist faith in 1770 and befriended a traveling minister, John Murray, who became her mentor. Her family donated land for him to build America's first Universalist/Unitarian meetinghouse. Because of the American Revolution, Murray's husband went bankrupt, forcing them to flee to the West Indies to avoid creditors. There she turned to writing as a means of income. She had been a prolific correspondent and had already begun to keep copies of all her letters before mailing them, similar to the habit of Thomas Jefferson.

Murray published works to promote Unitarian beliefs and her belief in the equality of the sexes, such as "Desultory Thoughts upon the Utility of Encouraging a Degree of Self-Complacency, Especially in Female Bosoms" (1784).

After Stevens died in 1786, Murray returned to the United States and in 1788 married John Murray. In 1792, Judith Murray started writing a column for *Massachusetts Magazine,* her first use of "The Gleaner" as pseudonym. In 1795 she became the first woman to have a play produced in Boston, *The Medium or Virtue Triumphant.* While its lead character, Eliza Clairville, desires a marriage of equals and refuses marriage until she achieves her own financial security, it too was written under a pseudonym, "A Citizen of the United States." In 1798, again in financial difficulties caused by her husband, Murray published *The Gleaner,* three volumes of plays, poetry, and prose popular among the Founding Fathers. George Washington and John Adams wrote endorsements to help her solicit subscribers for early purchase.

Murray's feminist ideology came forth in an essay she wrote and kept in her files but did not publish titled "On the Equality of the Sexes" in 1779. Had she published it and done it under her own name, scholars might have ranked Murray among the earliest feminists along with the English writer Mary Wollstonecraft (1759–1797), who published *A Vindication of the Rights of Woman* in 1792. Murray's arguments are still being repeated today: "Will it be said that the judgment of a male of two years old, is more sage than that of a female's of the same age? I believe the reverse is generally observed to be true. But from that period what partiality! How is the one exalted, and the other depressed, by the contrary modes of education which are adopted! The one is taught to aspire, and the other is early confined and limited. As their years increase, the sister must be wholly domesticated, while the brother is led by the hand through all the flowery paths of science. Grant that their minds are by nature equal, yet who shall wonder at the *apparent* superiority, if indeed custom becomes *second nature.*"

With that attitude, Murray helped found a female academy south of Boston in 1802 to teach women. Then when her second husband died in 1815, she finished his autobiography and moved to Natchez, Mississippi, where her one surviving child lived. Murray died there on June 9, 1820.

In the 1990s Unitarian minister Gordon Gibson journeyed to Murray's last residence, where he found Murray's papers intact. These letters and other memorabilia revealed Murray to have been an ambitious writer, one who sought both to be taken seriously by scholars and critics and to be popular with the masses.

Christopher Cumo

See also *A Vindication of the Rights of Woman*

Further Reading

Murray, Judith Sargent, with an introductory essay by Nina Baym. 1992. *The Gleaner.* Schenectady, NY: Union College Press.

Schloesser, Pauline. 2002. *The Fair Sex: White Women and Racial Patriarchy in the Early American Republic.* New York: New York University Press.

Skemp, Sheila L. 1998. *Judith Sargent Murray: A Brief Biography with Documents.* Boston: Bedford Books.

Skemp, Sheila L. 2009. *First Lady of Letters: Judith Sargent Murray and the Struggle for Female Independence.* Philadelphia: University of Pennsylvania Press.

Part 1 of Judith Sargent Murray's "On the Equality of the Sexes" (1790)

Judith Sargent Murray's (1751–1820) essay "On the Equality of the Sexes" predates Mary Wollstonecraft's much more famous A Vindication of the Rights of Woman *by two years. Like Wollstonecraft, Murray argues that women have as much intellectual capacity as men. Here is the first part of Murray's two-part essay.*

TO THE EDITORS OF THE MASSACHUSETTS MAGAZINE,

GENTLEMEN,

The following ESSAY *is yielded to the patronage of Candour.—If it hath been anticipated, the testimony of many respectable persons, who saw it in manuscripts as early as the year 1779, can obviate the imputation of plagiarism.*

THAT minds are not alike, full well I know,
This truth each day's experience will show;
To heights surprising some great spirits soar,
With inborn strength mysterious depths
    explore;
Their eager gaze surveys the path of light,
Confest it stood to Newton's piercing sight.
    Deep science, like a bashful maid retires,
And but the *ardent* breast her worth inspires;
By perseverance the coy fair is won.
And Genius, led by Study, wears the crown.
    But some there are who wish not to
        improve
Who never can the path of knowledge love,
Whose souls almost with the dull body one,
With anxious care each mental pleasure
    shun;
Weak is the level'd, enervated mind,
And but while here to vegetate design'd.
The torpid spirit mingling with its clod,
Can scarcely boast its origin from God;
Stupidly dull—they move progressing on—
They eat, and drink, and all their work is done.
While others, emulous of sweet applause,
Industrious seek for each event a cause,
Tracing the hidden springs whence knowledge
    flows,
Which nature all in beauteous order shows.
    Yet cannot I their sentiments imbibe,
Who this distinction to the sex ascribe,
As if a woman's form must needs enrol,
A weak, a servile, an inferiour soul;
And that the guise of man must still proclaim,
Greatness of mind, and him, to be the same:
Yet as the hours revolve fair proofs arise,
Which the bright wreath of growing fame
    supplies;
And in past times some men have *sunk*
    so *low,*
That female records nothing *less* can show.
But imbecility is still confin'd,

And by the lordly sex to us consign'd;
They rob us of the power t'improve,
And then declare we only trifles love;
Yet haste the era, when the world shall know,
That such distinctions only dwell below;
The soul unfetter'd, to no sex confin'd,
Was for the abodes of cloudless day design'd.
    Mean time we emulate their manly fires,
Though erudition all their thoughts inspires,
Yet nature with *equality* imparts
And *noble passions,* swell e'en *female hearts.*

Is it upon mature consideration we adopt the idea, that nature is thus partial in her distributions? Is it indeed a fact, that she hath yielded to one half of the human species so unquestionable a mental superiority? I know that to both sexes elevated understandings, and the reverse, are common. But, suffer me to ask, in what the minds of females are so notoriously deficient, or unequal. May not the intellectual powers be ranged under these four heads—imagination, reason, memory and judgment. The province of imagination hath long since been surrendered to us, and we have been crowned and undoubted sovereigns of the regions of fancy. Invention is perhaps the most arduous effort of the mind; this branch of imagination hath been particularly ceded to us, and we have been time out of mind invested with that creative faculty. Observe the variety of fashions (here I bar the contemptuous smile) which distinguish and adorn the female world: how continually are they changing, insomuch that they almost render the wise man's assertion problematical, and we are ready to say, *there is something new under the sun.* Now what a playfulness, what an exuberance of fancy, what strength of inventine imagination, doth this continual variation discover? Again, it hath been observed, that if the turpitude of the conduct of our sex, hath been ever so enormous, so extremely ready are we, that the very first thought presents us with an apology, so plausible, as to produce our actions even in an amiable light. Another instance of our creative powers, is our talent for slander; how ingenious are we at inventive scandal? what a formidable story can we in a moment fabricate merely from the force of a prolifick imagination? how many reputations, in the fertile brain of a female, have been utterly despoiled? how industrious are we at improving a hint? suspicion how easily do we convert into conviction, and conviction, embellished by the power of eloquence, stalks abroad to the surprise and confusion of unsuspecting innocence. Perhaps it will be asked if I furnish these facts as instances of excellency in our sex. Certainly not; but as proofs of a creative faculty, of a lively imagination. Assuredly great activity of mind is thereby discovered, and was this activity properly directed, what beneficial effects would follow. Is the needle and kitchen sufficient to employ the operations of a soul thus organized? I should conceive not, Nay, it is a truth that those very departments leave the intelligent principle vacant, and at liberty for speculation. Are we deficient in reason? we can only reason from what we know, and if an opportunity of acquiring knowledge hath been denied us, the inferiority of our sex cannot fairly be deduced from thence. Memory, I believe, will be allowed us in common, since everyone's experience must testify, that a loquacious old woman is as frequently met with, as a communicative man; their subjects are alike drawn from the fund of other times, and the transactions of their youth, or of maturer life, entertain, or perhaps fatigue you, in the evening of their lives.

"But our judgment is not so strong—we do not distinguish so well."—Yet it may be questioned, from what doth this superiority, in this determining faculty of the soul, proceed. May we not trace its source in the difference of education, and continued advantages? Will it be said that the judgment of a male of two years old, is more sage than that of a female's of the same age? I believe the reverse is generally observed to be true. But from that period what partiality! how is the one exalted, and the other depressed, by the contrary modes of education which are adopted! the one is taught to aspire, and the other is early confined and limited. As their years increase, the sister must be wholly domesticated, while the brother is led by the hand through all the flowery paths of science. Grant that their minds are by nature equal, yet who shall wonder at the *apparent* superiority, if indeed custom becomes *second nature;* nay if it taketh place of nature, and that it doth the experience of each day will evince. At length arrived at womanhood, the uncultivated fair one feels a void, which the employments allotted her are by no means capable of filling. What can she do? to books she may not apply; or if she doth, *to those only of the*

novel kind, lest she merit the appellation of a *learned lady;* and what ideas have been affixed to this term, the observation of many can testify. Fashion, scandal, and sometimes what is still more reprehensible, are then called in to her relief; and who can say to what lengths the liberties she takes may proceed. Meantimes she herself is most unhappy; she feels the want of a cultivated mind. Is she single, she in vain seeks to fill up time from sexual employments or amusements. Is she united to a person whose soul nature made equal to her own, education hath set him so far above her, that in those entertainments which are productive of such rational felicity, she is not qualified to accompany him. She experiences a mortifying consciousness of inferiority, which embitters every enjoyment. Doth the person to whom her adverse fate hath consigned her, possess a mind incapable of improvement, she is equally wretched, in being so closely connected with an individual whom she cannot but despise. Now, was she permitted the same instructors as her brother, (with an eye however to their particular departments) for the employment of a rational mind an ample field would be opened. In astronomy she might catch a glimpse of the immensity of the Deity, and thence she would form amazing conceptions of the august and supreme Intelligence. In geography she would admire Jehovah in the midst of his benevolence; thus adapting this globe to the various wants and amusements of its inhabitants. In natural philosophy she would adore the infinite majesty of heaven, clothed in condescension; and as she traversed the reptile world, she would hail the goodness of a creating God. A mind, thus filled, would have little room for the trifles with which our sex are, with too much justice, accused of amusing themselves, and they would thus be rendered fit companions for those, who should one day wear them as their crown. Fashions, in their variety, would then give place to conjectures, which might perhaps conduce to the improvements of the literary world; and there would be no leisure for slander or detraction. Reputation would not then be blasted, but serious speculations would occupy the lively imaginations of the sex. Unnecessary visits would only be indulged by way of relaxation, or to answer the demands of consanguinity and friendship. Females would become discreet, their judgments would be invigorated, and their partners for life being circumspectly chosen, an unhappy Hymen would then be as rare, as is now the reverse.

Will it be urged that those acquirements would supersede our domestick duties. I answer that every requisite in female economy is easily attained; and, with truth I can add, that when once attained, they require no further *mental attention*. Nay, while we are pursuing the needle, or the superintendency of the family, I repeat, that our minds are at full liberty for reflection; that imagination may exert itself in full vigor; and that if a just foundation is early laid, our ideas will then be worthy of rational beings. If we were industrious we might easily find time to arrange them upon paper, or should avocations press too hard for such an indulgence, the hours allotted for conversation would at least become more refined and rational. Should it still be vociferated, "Your domestick employments are sufficient"—I would calmly ask, is it reasonable, that a candidate for immortality, for the joys of heaven, an intelligent being, who is to spend an eternity in contemplating the works of the Deity, should at present be so degraded, as to be allowed no other ideas, than those which are suggested by the mechanism of a pudding, or the sewing the seams of a garment? Pity that all such censurers of female improvement do not go one step further, and deny their future existence; to be consistent they surely ought.

Yes, ye lordly, ye haughty sex, our souls are by nature *equal* to yours; the same breath of God animates, enlivens, and invigorates us; and that we are not fallen lower than yourselves, let those witness who have greatly towered above the various discouragements by which they have been so heavily oppressed; and though I am unacquainted with the list of celebrated characters on either side, yet from the observations I have made in the contracted circle in which I have moved, I dare confidently believe, that from the commencement of time to the present day, there hath been as many females, as males, who, by the *mere force of natural powers*, have merited the crown of applause; who, *thus unassisted*, have seized the wreath of fame. I know there are who assert, that as the animal power of the one sex are superiour, of course their mental faculties also must be stronger; thus attributing strength of mind to the transient organization of this earth born tenement. But if this reasoning is just, man must be content to yield the palm to many of the brute creation, since by not a few of his brethren of the field, he is far surpassed in bodily strength. Moreover, was this argument admitted, it would prove too much, for occular demonstration evinceth, that there are many robust masculine ladies, and effeminate gentlemen. Yet I fancy that Mr. Pope, though clogged with an enervated body, and distinguished by a diminutive stature, could nevertheless lay claim to greatness of soul; and perhaps there are many other instances which might be adduced to combat so unphilosophical an opinion. Do we not often see, that when the clay built tabernacle is well nigh dissolved, when it is just ready to mingle with the parent soil, the immortal inhabitant aspires to, and even attaineth heights the most sublime, and which were before wholly unexplored. Besides, were we to grant that animal strength proved any thing, taking into consideration the accustomed impartiality of nature, we should be induced to imagine, that she had invested the female mind with superiour strength as an equivalent for the bodily powers of man. But waving this however palpable advantage, for *equality only*, we wish to contend.

[*To be concluded next month.*]

Source: *The Massachusetts Magazine, or, Monthly Museum Concerning the Literature, History, Politics, Arts, Manners, Amusements of the Age*, Vol. 2, *1790* (Boston: Printed by I. Thomas and E. T. Andrews, 1790). Available at University of Pennsylvania, http://digital.library.upenn.edu/women/murray/equality/equality.html.

Observations on the Real Rights of Women (1818)

Written by Hannah Mather Crocker (1752–1829) and published in 1818, *Observations on the Real Rights of Women: With Their Appropriate Duties Agreeable to Scripture, Reason, and Common Sense* was the only book arguing for women's rights to appear in America between 1800 and 1820. In an age of postrevolutionary political and social conservatism, *Observations* made a forceful, if pragmatically limited, case for the recognition of women's abilities as equal to those of men.

Crocker was a prominent Bostonian and well-known writer. Born on June 27, 1752, to Reverend Samuel Mather and Hannah Hutchinson and the youngest of seven children, she could trace her New England roots back to the first families of New England: she was the granddaughter of Cotton Mather and a descendant of religious dissident Anne Hutchinson. At the age of 26 Hannah married Joseph Crocker, an American Revolutionary War veteran and local shopkeeper. She gave birth to 10 children between 1780 and 1795. Throughout their marriage the Crockers lived with her parents in the Mather family home, where Hannah Crocker managed a household of three generations. When her husband died in 1797, Crocker had trouble supporting her large family, surviving through the sale of ancestral property and charitable funds from the Society of the Cincinnati.

Although *Observations* is Crocker's best-known work, when it appeared she had already established herself as one of Boston's public intellectuals. Crocker published at least five poems in Boston newspapers. She also explored theology through both unpublished writing and sermons, and she published treatises on freemasonry and temperance. While not explicitly addressing the question of women's rights, both *A Series of Letters on Freemasonry* (1815) and *School of Reform: Or Seaman's Safe Pilot to the Cape of Good Hope* (1816) articulate an important place for women in the social and political fabric of the new nation. Crocker also invested in the intellectual pursuits and education of other women: she was one of a group of women who founded St. Ann's Lodge, a Masonic lodge for women, in 1778 and organized the School of Industry for impoverished girls in Boston's North End in 1813.

In *Observations,* Crocker grounded her argument for women's equality in theological and historical examples of exceptional women, making a case for women's place alongside men in the American republic. She displayed her wide-ranging knowledge of previous works on women's rights, drawing on the writing of women such as Mary Wollstonecraft (1759–1797) and Mercy Otis Warren's (1728–1814) *History of the Rise, Progress, and Termination of the American Revolution* (1805). While pragmatically accepting the emerging division of public and private labor along gender lines, Crocker nevertheless argued for women's moral equality with men and the importance of women's access to education and their leadership in certain socially acceptable contexts, such as benevolent societies and social clubs. In this the book contributed to an ideology that historians call republican motherhood, which argued that the new American nation required educated women to sustain democracy. *Observations* attracted considerable attention, both positive and negative, upon its release.

Observations has continued to challenge its readers in the almost 200 years since its first appearance, with later generations of women's rights and feminist activists holding it in ambivalent regard. During the late 19th century, for example, suffrage leaders Harriet Robinson (1825–1911), Elizabeth Cady Stanton (1815–1902), and Matilda Gage (1826–1898) dismissed Crocker's articulation of women's role as too limited. Lack of access to Crocker's writing, since her work was largely out of print or in manuscript form, generally led 20th-century scholars and activists to perpetuate this view. When mentioned, Crocker's contribution to the literature on women's rights was generally critiqued as insufficient in its radicalism. More recently, scholars Eileen Botting and Sarah Houser have challenged this view, arguing that *Observations* is an astute articulation of the tension between an egalitarian ideal and the lived realities of an imperfect social, economic, and political system. That Crocker's work continues to be debated so many years after its publication is an indication of the complexity of its political philosophy and the enduring relevance of its subject.

Anna J. Clutterbuck-Cook

See also Republican Motherhood; Warren, Mercy Otis

Further Reading

Botting, Eileen Hunt, and Sarah L. Houser. 2006. "'Drawing the Line of Equality': Hannah Mather Crocker on Women's Rights." *American Political Science Review* 100(2): 265–278.

Crocker, Hannah Mather. 2011. *Observations on the Real Rights of Women and Other Writings*. Edited with an introduction by Constance J. Post. Lincoln: University of Nebraska Press.

Parlor Politics

"Parlor politics" is a phrase used by historians of women to describe the ways in which public politics function outside official halls of government. In the earliest decades of the United States, politicians often exercised power in the city's parlors and dining rooms rather than in public governmental buildings. Wives, sisters, and daughters of politicians played a significant role in the exercise of such private-sphere political machinations while also establishing the social rules of the new government.

When Great Britain signed the Treaty of Paris in the fall of 1783, the United States officially became a nation. The newly minted United States was also very much defined by what it was not: a monarchy. Creating a new government that functioned differently from a monarchy was a complicated undertaking. Not only did the United States require founding documents that set up governments, courts, and laws, but it also needed to determine how the government would function and what it would look like. In 1790 Congress approved a new capital to be built on the Potomac River at the confluence of Maryland and Virginia. In November 1800 Congress had its first session in the city, officially making it a functioning national capital. Among the important questions asked in the new capital was whether people could run a government in the absence of a monarchical court. The ladies of Washington helped to answer this question as they worked out how politics would work in the private sphere (their homes).

Widower Thomas Jefferson was the first president to take up residence in Washington. Dolley Madison, the wife of Jefferson's vice president, became his hostess at state functions. In virtually inventing the job of first lady, Madison also became the prime mover in Washington's parlor politics. She and other Washington ladies established the tradition of morning calls, or ladies visiting each other's houses for short daytime visits. A lady would have an at-home day when she would receive callers in her parlor, and on other days she would visit ladies on their at-home days.

While this might appear to be frivolous time-wasting by elite-class women with not enough to do, in fact the calling ritual played an important role in establishing political hierarchies and creating bridges between political factions. The round of calls laid the groundwork for a social network into which men could step when they were not in the public sphere conducting official government business. Men began to make calls as well, particularly on Sunday, finding that meetings in parlors, where their wives had cultivated relationships, allowed deals to be struck that had not seemed possible in more official milieus.

Politicking happened at private dinners as well, both in the socializing that happened before and after dinner and at the dining room table. Washington ladies would organize dinners, pick the attendees to fit a particular political purpose, and then orchestrate who sat with and spoke to whom. Women could ensure the success of a husband's political career with astute dinner party planning.

Women also engaged in politics themselves, doing more than putting men together or making friends with other men's wives. Women advocated for reforms, issues, and candidates on their own. Some women did so particularly effectively. In the early 1800s, Dolley Madison was the undisputed champion of political management. Sometimes called "the Republican Queen" (referring to the political principles of republican democracy and not the modern political party), Madison set the standard for home decoration, dress, and manners. She was stately but approachable and dignified but kind to everyone, from the lowliest political functionaries to ambassadors and senators. Having established herself as a society leader, she made herself a political leader, modeling how Washingtonians behaved and thought in a democratic manner. She then used her power to ensure her husband's election to the presidency and to convince others to follow his policies.

Madison was neither the first nor the last woman to use her social position and the private sphere to practice political power. Nor were parlor politics confined to the nation's first decades. During the American Civil War and Reconstruction years, Kate Chase Sprague used her considerable social and political acumen to further her father's political life. As President Abraham Lincoln's secretary of the treasury and a prominent antislavery advocate, Salmon P. Chase worked to create new ways to fund the Civil War and to encourage Northern politicians to consider ending slavery and moving into a new era of racial equality. In these great matters his daughter helped him considerably, paying calls and establishing a political salon at his home where politicians could meet to discuss differences. Chase Sprague also had a hand in her father's presidential aspirations. In 1868, she left her father's parlor behind and set up camp in a New York hotel so she could manage his bid for the nomination from her hotel room. Since ladies were not allowed on the convention floor, she invited men to her room and wrote directions, which she expected to be followed.

Dolley Madison, Kate Chase Sprague, and a host of other American women skillfully operated at the center of the nation's political life and did so without being able to vote or run for office by engaging in parlor politics. The importance of this type of political participation has long been overlooked, though today women continue to operate politically within the private sphere, reminding us that not all politics are public.

Peg A. Lamphier

See also Madison, Dolley

Further Reading

Allgor, Katherine. 2002. *Parlor Politics: In Which the Ladies of Washington Help Build a City and a Government.* Charlottesville: University of Richmond Press.

Allgor, Katherine. 2007. *A Perfect Union: Dolley Madison and the Creation of the American Nation.* New York: Holt.

Lamphier, Peg. 2003. *Kate Chase and William Sprague: Politics and Gender in a Civil War Marriage.* Lincoln: University of Nebraska Press.

Philipse, Mary (1730–1825)

Mary Philipse was the daughter of Frederick Philipse III, a wealthy landowner and politician. Although she is best known for having momentarily been the object of affection for a young George Washington, Philipse's life was defined by courage and personal sacrifice.

Philipse was born on July 3, 1730, the heiress to a great fortune. Her family owned a massive tract of land that spanned 22 miles along the Hudson River near what is now Yonkers, New York. The land had been in the Philipse family since the mid-1600s. In 1658 Fredryk Felypse, a Dutch man from Bolswaert, Holland, arrived in what was then called New Amsterdam. By 1682 he had amassed a fortune, which allowed him to begin construction on what was to become Philipsborough, the massive manor located on the Philipse estate in Yonkers. The manor was so large that 50 servants were required to run and maintain it.

Mary Philipse married Roger Morris, a colonel in the British Army during the French and Indian War, after being courted by George Washington. She was an important member of the Loyalist community during the American Revolutionary War. (Chaiba Media)

When George Washington (1732–1799), then a young colonel of only 24 years of age, met Philipse through family friends, he seemed immediately drawn to her, and they courted over the course of several months. Philipse ended the courtship and married Major Roger Morris, an officer of the British military forces, on January 19, 1758. Her decision was in keeping with her character, for Philipse was known for being headstrong and deeply independent; this latter trait was evident in her choice to not marry until she was 28, which in the 18th century was considered very late in life.

The first 10 years of Philipse's marriage to Morris were relatively peaceful. Despite owning the family estate in Yonkers, the couple built a luxurious mansion in Harlem Heights, New York, then a heavily wooded area. They called the property Mount Morris and enjoyed a life of ease. Unfortunately, Philipse's marriage to Morris had severe consequences after the outbreak of hostilities between the colonies and the British Empire, for not only was Morris an Englishman, but he was also a Loyalist. The Loyalists were persons who resided in the colonies while remaining loyal to Britain. Loyalists were considered figures of suspicion by many Americans, as their allegiances were ultimately not to the colonies but to Britain, and specifically the British military. Once conflicts a rose between the colonies and Britain, Philipse urged her husband to go to England until the tensions abated. He complied, leaving for England on May 5, 1775. Philipse stayed behind with their four children, in large part so she could protect the family's extensive landholdings from the increasingly hostile Patriots.

Terrible trials followed Morris's departure. To the surprise of many British Loyalists, tensions between America and Britain did not die down; instead, anger grew and spread as the colonies mobilized to fight for their independence from Britain. Philipse tried to stay in Mount Morris, but American forces began to close in on New York, and in early 1776 she was forced to flee to the Philipse estate in Yonkers. In the meantime, the American forces led by General George Washington confiscated Morris Manor and used the former family home as an army headquarters.

In late 1777, Morris returned from Great Britain to reunite with his family. He found the situation for British Loyalists increasingly dangerous. Legislation passed condemning the Loyalists to death. and the remaining Philipse lands were confiscated by the American government as punishment for the family's Loyalist ties. Despite Philipse's determination to protect her family's properties, it was clear that leaving America was the only way to ensure her family's survival. Soon, the family left for Great Britain.

Despite the many hardships that she endured, Philipse apparently never considered abandoning her commitment to her Loyalist husband. Although her story might be interpreted as characterized by loss—loss of property, loss of wealth, and loss of social standing—it can also be seen as a story of determination. Philipse was far more than simply a youthful George Washington's romantic interest: she was a woman who knew her own mind and followed it, whether it told her to reject Washington's romantic overtures or to remain true to her husband and her country, Great Britain.

Alberta M. Miranda

See also Adams, Abigail; Eaton, Margaret "Peggy"; Washington, Martha; *Vol. 1, Sec. 2:* Bradstreet, Anne

Further Reading

Desmond, Alice Curtis. 1947. "Mary Philipse: Heiress." *New York History* 28(1): 22–32.

Ellet, E. F. 1998. *Revolutionary Women in the War for American Independence: A One-Volume Revised Edition of Elizabeth's Ellet's 1848 Landmark Series.* Edited by Lincoln Diamant. Westport, CT: Praeger.

Pinckney, Eliza Lucas (1722–1793)

Eliza Lucas Pinckney was an agricultural innovator at a time when men typically took charge of their farms. Eliza established a reputation as an expert in the cultivation of indigo, and in the years before the American Revolutionary War, she almost single-handedly made it an important crop in coastal South Carolina.

Pinckney was born Eliza Lucas on December 28, 1722, to well-to-do parents. Her father, George Lucas, did not want his daughter to be only ornamental, so he arranged for her to be educated in England at a time when few daughters received any formal education at all. Once out of school Pinckney settled with her family in coastal South Carolina, where her family owned three sugar plantations. The Lucas estate had a large library, from which Pinckney read copiously.

When Pinckney was 17, her father left South Carolina to join the British Army, in which he was a colonel. He entrusted his three plantations to his daughter. As with her father, Pinckney's work largely consisted of slave management. She planted rice and later indigo as her staples, experimented with other crops, and raised pigs. She described her workload as heavy and fatiguing. This characterization must have been more true for her slaves. She did not query her father for advice but instead undertook all aspects of the plantations, hiring and firing overseers, corresponding with factors in London, and buying and selling land and livestock. Pinckney viewed the profits from the plantations as hers rather than her father's even though the land belonged to him.

Pinckney is best known as a pioneer in the growing of indigo in South Carolina. In the early 18th century rice was the main staple crop of South Carolina, and slaves were more numerous than whites. A decline in rice consumption in Europe in the 1740s convinced Pinckney that indigo was the crop of the future, though it was used as a dye rather than food. In 1739, her father sent her indigo seeds from the Caribbean. Along with indigo and rice, Pinckney grew ginger, cotton, alfalfa, and perhaps cassava, almost surely as a subsistence crop for the plantation's slaves.

Success was not immediate. Frost killed the first indigo planting. The next year the harvest was small with two more lean years to follow. Pinckney sought advice from a man of African descent who had expertise in indigo growing. She probably also sought advice and help from her slaves, many of whom were from West Africa and were familiar with indigo cultivation.

Only in 1744 was the harvest bountiful. Pinckney hired a dye maker to process the leaves into dye cakes.

She sent 17 pounds of dye cakes to London, whose merchants thought it as good as anything the French sold them. Rather than keep the market to herself, Pinckney shared indigo culture with friends in the hopes of persuading them to try the crop. One year she took seeds from an entire crop and sent them to every farmer she knew in South Carolina. Because of her efforts, by 1747 South Carolina exported 138,000 pounds of indigo.

In 1744 Pinckney married the widower Charles Pinckney, though he was more than twice her age. She had four children, one of whom died in infancy, in the first six years of marriage. Pinckney's duties to her husband and children did not prevent her from running her plantations as she had when she was single. In 1752, Pinckney and her husband moved temporarily to England to educate their children, returning to their South Carolina plantations in 1758. Their daughter Harriott came with them. Two sons remained in England to continue their education. On July 12, 1758, Charles died from malaria. Pinckney mourned him, pouring out her grief in letters to friends. Her sons returned to South Carolina and became politically influential Federalists. Pinckney was especially close to her daughter Harriott, who married a South Carolina planter. The armies of the Revolutionary War destroyed much of her lands, though Pinckney supervised their rebuilding after the war. She died of cancer in 1793. President George Washington acted as one of her pallbearers. In 1989, Pinckney was the first woman inducted into the South Carolina Business Hall of Fame.

Christopher Cumo

See also Revolutionary War and Women; Washington, Martha

Further Reading

Jepson, Jill. 2009. *Women's Concerns: Twelve Women Entrepreneurs of the Eighteenth and Nineteenth Centuries.* New York: Peter Lang.

Spruill, Marjorie Julian, Valinda W. Littlefield, and Joan Marie Johnson, eds. 2009. *South Carolina Women: Their Lives and Times.* Athens: University of Georgia Press.

Pitcher, Molly. *See* McCauley, Mary

Reed, Esther (1746–1780)

Esther de Berdt Reed was a British-born American Patriot best remembered for organizing women's support of the American Revolution in her adopted home of Philadelphia.

Reed was born in London on October 22, 1746, the daughter of merchant Dennis de Berdt. Because of her father's business and his contacts with the American colonies, she saw firsthand how the increasingly volatile political situation affected British merchants who depended on exporting goods. She and Joseph Reed, an American lawyer who had studied law in London, courted throughout the 1760s. They delayed marriage because they wanted to wait until a time when Joseph could settle in London with his bride. After he dealt with the business troubles of both his father and wife, it became clear that they would never be able to live in London. The couple married in 1770 and promptly moved to Philadelphia, where he set up a successful law practice and, by 1775, she had become both a mother and an American.

After the battle at Lexington and Concord in April 1775, Joseph was called to serve with George Washington as his secretary and aide-de-camp. Reed was left to move her young children around the countryside during the war because Philadelphia was a city deeply divided between Patriots and Loyalists and thus not a safe place for young children. In 1778, Joseph was elected president of the Executive Council, a position akin to governor, of Pennsylvania. In her position as the governor's wife, Reed published "The Sentiments of an American Woman" in June 1780 to articulate why and how American women could contribute to the war effort. Her work first appeared in Philadelphia as a one-page sheet but was later reprinted in various newspapers.

Despite a societal belief in women's natural weakness and inferiority to men, Reed appealed to what she clearly imagined to be her female audience: "Our ambition is kindled by the same of those heroines of antiquity, who have rendered their sex illustrious, and have proved to the universe, that, if the weakness of our Constitution, if opinion and manners did not forbid us to march to glory by the same paths as the Men, we should at least equal, and sometimes surpass them in our love for the public good" (Reed 1790, 1).

Reed's pamphlet was published five years into the war, when Americans needed to reinvigorate the enthusiasm that launched them into the conflict. She urged her female readers to revisit their initial enthusiasm for rebellion, recommit to tea boycotts, and renounce "superfluities" for handmade and homemade goods such as textiles. She urged women to spin and weave flax for soldiers' garments, an act that would doubly support the American Revolution by supporting soldiers and taking money out of the hands of merchants who sold English-made goods. In an addendum to her first pamphlet, Reed laid out a plan for collecting funds from American women to support American soldiers. She thought that the women in each county should choose a "Treasuress" who would collect money from women and girls and carefully record the sums in a book before moving those funds to the Continental Army. Reed followed her pamphlet writing by forming the Ladies' Association of Philadelphia, which coordinated the fund-raising in that city.

With the plans that Reed laid out for them, the women of Philadelphia began to collect money. Not content to simply contribute their own money, they also went door-to-door soliciting contributions. Money poured in from a wide range of women, despite the fact that some people did not approve of the idea of genteel women asking for money. The Marchioness de Lafayette, wife of the famous French general, donated the largest amount, but far more modest sums came in from housemaids and elderly widows who wanted to show their support. In total, the Ladies' Association of Philadelphia collected $300,000 in paper money, an astonishing act given the wartime economy. The association also inspired women in other colonies, such as New Jersey, Maryland, and Virginia, to undertake similar campaigns.

Reed originally intended for the funds to go directly to the soldiers as a reward above and beyond what the army would supply them. She believed that subsistence items, such as food and clothing, should be provided by the government. However, George Washington expressed concern about giving $2 of hard specie (gold or silver coins) to his troops, as Reed suggested. He feared that his soldiers would turn the hard money into hard liquor. Thus, funds would encourage drunkenness, not patriotism. He urged her to use the funds for clothing instead, which the soldiers needed badly.

A few weeks after Reed had settled upon making linen shirts as the women's offering to the soldiers, she fell ill with dysentery and died on September 18, 1780, at the age of 33. Sarah Franklin Bache, the daughter of Benjamin Franklin, oversaw the women's next project: purchasing linen and assigning shirt making to individuals. The ladies provided 2,200 shirts to the army, and each seamstress, whether married or unmarried, embroidered her name on each shirt she made. Washington thanked Bache and her committee: "The Army ought not to regret its sacrifices or its sufferings when they meet with so flattering a reward as in the sympathy of your sex; nor can it fear that its interests will be neglected, while espoused by advocates as powerful as they are amiable" (Roberts 2004, 130). As Reed had articulated, American women may not have been expected to pick up arms alongside their men, but certainly their enthusiasm and energy benefited the Continental Army all the same.

Amy Sopcak-Joseph

See also Revolutionary War and Women; *Vol. 2, Sec. 2:* Ladies' Aid Societies/Soldiers' Aid Societies

Further Reading

Berkin, Carol. 2005. *Revolutionary Mothers: Women in the Struggle for America's Independence.* New York: Knopf.

Reed, Esther de Berdt. 1790. *The Sentiments of an American Woman.* Philadelphia: John Dunlap.

Roberts, Cokie. 2004. *Founding Mothers: The Women Who Raised Our Nation.* New York: HarperCollins.

Republican Motherhood

The term "republican motherhood," coined by historian Linda Kerber, describes a set of gender ideologies that developed in the colonies and the new nation around the time of the American Revolution (1775–

1783). The term "republican" refers not to the modern political party but rather to what historians call small-r republicanism, or the set of political ideas that underwrote the Revolution. Thus, a woman who was familiar with the ideals of the Revolution and passed them on to her family both by deeds and words was one who embraced republican motherhood. These ideologies of womanhood both empowered and limited women in the late 18th and early 19th centuries.

The American Revolution created opportunities for women to expand their public and domestic roles. Before the war women participated in resistance to British power by boycotting English trade goods such as tea, coffee, and textiles. Prewar spinning bees, where young women competed to see who could spin the most thread or yarn in a given amount of time, were also demonstrations against the British government. American women, both Patriot and Loyalist, also undertook a number of extraordinary roles during the war. Women such as Abigail Adams, Martha Washington, and many less famous women kept the family farms, plantations, and businesses going while the men went off to war or to found a new government. Poor women became camp followers, traveling with armies and providing fighting men with valuable services, working as cooks, laundresses, scavengers, nurses, and water carriers. Other women used their homes to nurse or hide soldiers.

Both during and after the war the founding generation was conscious of American women's contributions to the Revolution. Nonetheless, laws and customs continued to constrain women, keeping them from formal schools and most jobs and businesses and outside any official role in public life, including voting and running for office. The ideas that made up republican motherhood arose from the dissonance between the importance of women and their oppression. Rather than encourage women to join in the promise of equality and liberty, the founding generation embraced ideas that said that women's power could be found in the home, as guardians of civic virtue and educators of young citizens.

The downside of republican motherhood, insofar as the independence of women is concerned, was that it served to further confine women to the domestic sphere. Women were to be wives and mothers and thus engaged in the domestic work of housekeeping, childbearing, and child rearing. They were not meant to be equal to men, particularly with regard to the rights of citizenship. The upside was that if American women were to be virtuous republican wives and mothers who understood the ideals of the Revolution and ensured that their families did as well, women had to be literate and educated. Also, republican motherhood imbued domestic work with political meaning, making the work more powerful to the society than it had been. Thus, American women could use the ideology of republican motherhood to wield power, however limited, both inside and outside the home.

Perhaps the most significant benefit of ideology of republican motherhood lay in its promotion of education for women. If women were to guide husbands and teach children American values, then women had to be educated enough to do so. Towns and cities funded schools that allowed for the education of both boys and girls. The schools encouraged girls to learn literature, languages, science, and philosophy. Few girls were allowed to go on to higher education, and indeed few institutions of higher education took female students until the mid-1800s, such as Oberlin College.

While republican motherhood ideologies were aimed at all American women, they were most influential with middle-class white women. Poor working women, who could not afford education and had less time to nurture children (who may have been doing agricultural or factory work themselves), could not always fulfill the premise of the ideology. Nor could slave women, who had little control over their families and little to no opportunity for education. Thus, the ideas of republican motherhood proved impossible for poor women or women of color to enact. Furthermore, because republican motherhood was a normative gender ideology, or an idea about how "normal" women thought and behaved, any woman or group of women who could not conform to the ideology could be classified by society as outside of respectable womanhood.

By the early 19th century, the idea of republican motherhood was endemic in America. Katharine Sedgwick promoted republican motherhood in her novels by creating feisty main characters who refused to express patriotism through domestic values. Harriet Beecher Stowe did much the same in *Uncle Tom's Cabin* but emphasized women's role in guiding Americans to

antislavery values. Poet Lydia Sigourney promoted republican motherhood both in her poems and in conduct books she wrote for young ladies, emphasizing that a lady's virtue had to be modeled to those around her. Antebellum reformers such as Elizabeth Cady Stanton used the ideals of republican motherhood to argue that women had a moral authority that men did not have and thus a special responsibility to reform the nation.

Eventually republican motherhood ideologies gave way to ideas encapsulated as the cult of true womanhood, which put particular emphasis on women's supposedly natural domesticity and purity. Nonetheless, the ideas found in republican motherhood continued to influence American women throughout the 19th century and can still be found in America today.

Peg A. Lamphier

See also Adams, Abigail; Camp Followers; Washington, Martha; *Vol. 1, Sec. 2:* Literacy; Spinning Bees; *Vol. 2, Sec. 1:* Cult of True Womanhood; Female Moral Authority and Sphere of Influence; Oberlin College; Sigourney, Lydia Howard Huntley; Stanton, Elizabeth Cady; Stowe, Harriet Beecher

Further Reading
Kerber, Linda. 1980. *Women of the Republic: Intellect and Ideology in Revolutionary America.* Chapel Hill: University of North Carolina Press.
Kerber, Linda. 1997. *Towards an Intellectual History of Women: Essays by Linda K. Kerber.* Chapel Hill: University of North Carolina Press.
Wood, Gordon. 2009. *Empire of Liberty: A History of the Early Republic, 1789–1815.* New York: Oxford University Press.

Revolutionary War and Women

Because of the realities of war, women took over all duties of their husbands, fathers, brothers, and sons who left to serve in the American Revolutionary War. Women physically and financially supported their families in the absence of male heads of family. They also supported soldiers through a variety of means and sometimes even directly participated in the war as nurses, laundresses, and soldiers.

Because there was more work than workers in colonial America, women found that they could engage in a variety of roles, regardless of their gender. Aside from the domestic labor associated with bearing and raising children and managing a household, women often made extra goods that they sold for additional income. It was not uncommon for a woman to take over a deceased husband's business or farm.

Colonial women divided their loyalties, with some women supporting the revolutionary or Patriot cause and others remaining loyal to the British Crown. As men prepared for military battle and political engagement, women did too. Most famously, Abigail Adams's lifelong management of the family farm allowed her husband John Adams the economic space to become a founding father. While he was serving in the Continental Congress between 1774 and 1778, she assumed management of the household. When John was in France in 1778, Abigail expanded her role by renting the farm to tenants and starting a private import business that sold various household goods. Abigail Adams also wrote letters that served as eyewitness accounts of the home front during the Revolution. She encouraged friends such as Mercy Otis Warren to start their own businesses as well as reminded her husband to remember the rights of women in the formation of the new nation.

Women were willing to help the revolutionary effort through political and economic means. In June 1770 the Sons and Daughters of Liberty urged the boycotting of British goods. In the same month 300 Boston women pledged to boycott tea. In 1774 in North Carolina, 51 women pledged to do everything in their power to support nonimportation. Women began spinning their own cloth to achieve this pledge. In 1778, a Boston coffee merchant refused to sell beans to the women of the city. Infuriated and refusing to back down, they stormed the warehouse, overwhelmed the merchant, and loaded the goods on their handcarts.

Women were also effective fund-raisers for the war effort. The first organization of women in America was established by Esther Reed (1746–1780) in Philadelphia in 1780. As the wife of the president of Pennsylvania, she was able raise $3,000 for the Revolution and the Continental Army. She wanted to give cash directly to the soldiers; Washington, fearing that they would spend it on alcohol, suggested that she buy linen and sew shirts instead. When Reed died, Sarah Franklin Bache (1744–1808) took up her efforts.

Poor women helped the war effort by becoming camp followers. Women followed army units and provided valuable services, including cooking, sewing, and nursing. Prostitutes also followed armies and in times of need helped with nursing and other crucial work. Women known as "Molly Pitchers," such as Mary Ludwig Hays McCauley (1754–1832), were on the battlefield giving their husbands water and other aid.

Women were also known to fight in battles either when their husbands were injured or through voluntary enlistment. Most famously, in 1781 Deborah Sampson Gannett dressed as a man and then enlisted to fight, earning a pension for her bravery in the war. Bravery and opportunity collided in war hero Nancy Hart of Georgia. She and her family lived in the unsettled low country. When British soldiers approached her cabin and demanded lodging, she distracted them with food, alerted neighbors of their presence, and then killed two with their own muskets and hanged three more.

On the other side of the conflict were the Loyalists or Tories, who refused to renounce their loyalty to the king. Loyalists faced considerable difficulties in some regions of the colonies. Many times husbands and fathers were in hiding or exile, leaving wives and children alone, subject to vigilantes and looting mobs. Many women chose to leave their community, often without their possessions. Leaving may have also meant having to relinquish their dower property, further diminishing their personal wealth. The most heartbreaking consequence of retreating may have been leaving sons over the age of 12 to fight in the Patriot army.

Some Loyalist women created a resistance movement to fight against the revolutionaries. Women refused loyalty oaths to the new government and hid husbands and sons, and some collected information for the British to use against the Patriots. Elizabeth Lichtenstein, daughter and wife of Loyalist officers, chronicled the Tory cause and served as a solidifying element in social circles. Peggy Shippen, married to

Benedict Arnold, was from a Loyalist family in Philadelphia who were prominent politicians and judges. Her treasonous correspondence and Arnold's implication resulted in their exile.

Native American women played a part in the American Revolution as well. Most indigenous peoples sided with the British in the war because they believed that their chances of having their land rights respected were greater under British rule than they would be under the colonists' independent nation. Native American women served as cultural intermediaries, as support systems for fighting men, and sometimes as soldiers or spies. Mohawk Molly Brant is perhaps the best known of these women.

African American women's position in Revolutionary America was just as chaotic. Most black women in America were slaves doing various types of domestic work, though sometimes they were used in building and repairing fortifications, as in the siege of Savannah. Recognizing slavery as one of the greatest weaknesses of the colonists, in 1775 Lord Dunmore's Proclamation declared martial law in Virginia and promised freedom to slaves who ran away from their masters and joined the British Army. Though Dunmore left the colony only a year later, effectively freeing very few slaves, a 1779 proclamation offered freedom to slaves whether they fought for the British or not.

Many slave women were unwilling or unable to run away because they had small children. Other women stayed within British lines during the war and were able to marry and have children with little interference from masters. The British subsequently put slaves to work in personal service duties such as valets or agricultural work instead of battle, as promised. When the war ended, these former slaves left with the British to Nova Scotia and the Caribbean. Over the course of the war approximately 100,000 slaves ran away from their masters to seek freedom with the British Army, resulting in the largest emancipation effort in American history until the American Civil War.

One voice that uniquely exemplified the restrictions of blacks in America was Phillis Wheatley (1753–1784). She had been born in Africa and brought to America as an eight-year-old slave. Her extraordinary literary aptitude eventually earned her freedom, but while America fought for independence, she was writing poetry that was full of double meaning. Her work supported the Revolution while pointing out the difference between the rhetoric of liberty and the pro-slavery reality of the new nation.

When the war for American independence ended, women were not any freer than they had been before the war. They were still under the rule of fathers and husbands, and in some places limited rights such as voting and jury service were revoked. Employment and educational opportunities were further restricted. Slavery was slowly abolished in northern states, but slave numbers gradually increased in southern states.

Nevertheless, seeds for future abolition and suffrage movements had been sown with the ideas of revolution and independence, particularly as women embraced the ideas of republican motherhood. Through the war many American women came to understand their crucial role in the outcome of the Revolution. They understood that they had important skills and knowledge to pass on to the next generation. Republican motherhood encompassed a set of ideas that found power in the domestic sphere, turning motherhood into a civic duty. Women used these ideas to push for greater educational opportunities, arguing that literate and informed women would be better mothers to future citizens. Historians point out that these ideas both confined women in the domestic sphere and empowered women's work within the domestic sphere. In the latter, women would find the impetus to join a number of 19th-century reform movements and in doing so significantly expand their own liberty.

Sarah Nation

See also Adams, Abigail; Arnold, Peggy (Margaret) Shippen; Boycotts, Tea and Textiles; Brant, Molly; Camp Followers; Reed, Esther; Republican Motherhood; Sampson, Deborah; Soldiers, Women Passing as Men, Revolutionary War; Warren, Mercy Otis; Wheatley, Phillis

Further Reading
Berkin, Carol. 2006. *Revolutionary Mothers: Women in the Struggle for America's Independence.* New York: Vintage.

Buel, Joy Day, and Richard Buel Jr. 1984. *The Way of Duty: A Woman and Her Family in Revolutionary America.* New York: Norton.

Kerber, Linda K. 1980. *Women of the Republic: Intellect and Ideology in Revolutionary America.* Chapel Hill: University of North Carolina Press.

Ross, Betsy (1752–1836)

The story of Betsy Ross's design and sewing of the first American flag during the American Revolution has remained a well-entrenched American myth since its introduction to the public approximately a century after the alleged events took place. Even the name of the main character of the story, "Betsy Ross," is misleading, since Betsy was her nickname and Ross was the first of her three married names. However, the American public has clung to the Betsy Ross story in spite of its inaccuracy, suggesting that the story is culturally important regarding popular understanding of women's roles in the Revolution.

Elizabeth Griscom was born on January 1, 1752, into a Quaker family in Philadelphia. She married John Ross, who was not a Quaker, in 1773. She was expelled from the Quakers as a result. She and her husband began an upholstery business in Philadelphia, which included making flags for the Royal Navy. Ross was one of many women who sewed flags for the military. After her husband died in 1776, she married

Betsy Ross is widely credited with making the first American flag for George Washington. The Ross story illustrates several of the problems with American women's history. It has no basis in fact and celebrates a woman's domestic talents and ignores the multitude of women who made real contributions to the Revolutionary War. (National Archives)

Joseph Ashburn in 1777. He died in 1782, and she married John Claypoole a year later. In 1817, she became a widow for the third and last time. She had seven children. Ross died on January 30, 1836, at the age of 84. Compared to other women of her time, Elizabeth Griscom Ross Ashburn Claypoole was far less extraordinary than her story suggests.

In 1870 William J. Canby, Ross's grandson, presented a paper before the Historical Society of Pennsylvania in which he related a family oral tradition. According to Canby, in June 1776 Commander in Chief George Washington (1732–1799) and two Continental Congress members visited his grandparents' upholstery shop in Philadelphia. Washington handed Ross a rough sketch of a flag they had in mind with stripes and a straight row of 13 six-pointed stars set in a blue field. From a design standpoint, Ross pointed out that five-pointed stars would work best. According to Canby's story, his grandmother took a piece of paper, folded it into triangles, clipped the folded paper once with a pair of scissors, and then unfolded the paper to reveal a perfect five-pointed star. She also suggested that the stars would look better against the blue field if they were set in a circle. The men accepted her advice, and she created the first American flag within days after the men left her shop.

Since Canby's paper, Americans have embraced the story as the truth. The story conveys patriotism and a sense of American enterprising ingenuity. These were traits that appealed to Americans especially after the American Civil War (1860–1865), when territorial expansion and new technological developments seemed to imply unlimited possibilities on the horizon. At its core, the Betsy Ross flag tale is the story of a woman's contribution in the fight for independence. Perhaps the fact that early American women were largely denied the promise of the American Revolution makes the story particularly powerful because it makes invisible the second-class status of women. Nonetheless, from its inception serious historians have contended that the Betsy Ross story is no more than a folktale.

First, neither Canby, who relied on affidavits, nor any other historian has been able to find any written documentation to support the story. There is no contemporary written record of Washington's visit or flag order. Second, the story is plagued with important chronological errors. Congress did not approve of an official flag design until 1777, one year after the events were said to have taken place. Third, a single first flag never existed. There were several first flags. Also, in 1779 Charles Wilson Peale painted a famous portrait of Washington standing in front of the official flag, which had six-pointed stars. In 1778, Benjamin Franklin (1706–1790) and John Adams (1735–1826) described the official flag as having 13 stripes alternating in red, white, and blue. In fact, flag sheets from as late as the 1790s show American flags striped in these three colors with four-, six-, and eight-pointed stars. Thus, the "first flags" did not have five-pointed stars or just red and white stripes.

The Betsy Ross story functions for Americans as a kind of creation myth. And while Betsy Ross was a real woman, her story is larger than her life, transforming her into an all-purpose Founding Mother.

Rolando Avila

See also Revolutionary War and Women

Further Reading

Harker, John Balderston. 2005. *Betsy Ross's Five Pointed Star.* Titusville, FL: Canmore.

Miller, Marla R. 2010. *Betsy Ross and the Making of America.* New York: Henry Holt.

Rowlandson, Mary (1637–1711)

Mary White Rowlandson was an English Puritan living in southeastern New England. She was captured by Native Americans during Metacom's War (1675–1676) and held for 11 weeks before being ransomed. Upon surviving her captivity, she wrote about her experiences and published them in a book, *The Sovereignty and Goodness of God* (1682). She is known for writing not only what is believed to be the first Indian captivity narrative but also the first published book by a North American woman.

Not much is known about Mary Rowlandson prior to the publication of her book, but according to Robert K. Diebold, she was probably born in South Petherton in Somerset, England. Her father, John

White, immigrated to Salem, Massachusetts, before the rest of the family joined him a year later. The family moved to Lancaster by 1653, where her father enjoyed his position as a wealthy landowner. Rowlandson married Joseph Rowlandson, who served as the town's first minister in 1656. They had four children, but one died in infancy before the Indian raid. (Diebold 1983, 1245–1246). In February 1676 when the Indians raided the small town of Lancaster in Massachusetts, they captured Rowlandson along with her 3 children and 19 of their neighbors.

The raid was due to the conflicts between the colonists and the Native Americans. As more English settlers immigrated to the New World, tensions between the two parties grew. The result was a declaration of war by Metacomet (1639–1676), the leader of the Wampanoag tribe, against what the Indians perceived as those who were invading their territory. The war was hence named Metacom's War or Metacomet's War after the Indian leader's name. However, because the colonists referred to Metacomet as King Philip, the war is also commonly known as King Philip's War. The reason for this nickname comes from religious differences between England and Spain. When the Pilgrims had left England to escape persecution for their Puritan beliefs, England was still at war with Spain. Since King Philip II of Spain was Catholic and therefore perceived as an enemy to the English Puritans, these same Puritans projected his name onto Metacomet, whom they perceived as another godless heathen.

Nearly 30 narratives on King Philip's War had been composed between 1675 and 1682, but Rowlandson's narrative stands out as the only one to have been written by a woman. Her narrative alone made the genre of the captivity narrative popular due to her vivid and provocative descriptions of the tribulations that she suffered during her captivity. Furthermore, Rowlandson creatively structured her narrative into 20 different removes (or various departures after settling in one area for some time), illustrating with biblical verses the trials she had undergone. While these poignant allusions to biblical references may seem excessive to modern readers, Rowlandson's contemporaries mostly came from Puritanical roots and appreciated her zeal for Christianity.

Within the first paragraph of the narrative, Rowlandson describes the chaos around her in graphic detail. Bullets fly, bowels are split open, and Indians "knock [people] on the head" during the initial raid (Rowlandson 1997, 69). Rowlandson also captures the victims' emotions, vividly describing her elder sister pleading to the lord to "let me dy with them" upon finding out her son had been killed, only to join him moments later (Rowlandson 1997, 69). Rowlandson constantly reports her reflections upon each scene of the Indians' attack. She admits that she would tell herself that she would rather have the Indians kill her if they were ever to attack, but when the time came, she decided to allow them to take her alive because she felt that these tribulations were God's way of testing her. In this way, she assumes the role of the messenger who undergoes great trials and, having survived them, experiences a life-changing transformation. For this reason, *Sovereignty* not only serves as a historical documentation of one of the Indian raids during King Philip's War but also as an opportunity to tell a story of a miracle someone lived through and encourage deeply religious Protestants to renew their faith in God for having read about his miracle.

While Rowlandson's contemporaries probably found the religious aspect of her narrative the most relevant, it serves as an important historical document of the interactions between two different cultures during the colonial period. Rowlandson shockingly recounts the savage behavior of the Indian race, oftentimes comparing them to wild animals. Before the Indians lead her and her neighbors away from Lancaster, Rowlandson surveys the damage, evaluating that many Christians were lying in a pool of their own blood "like a company of sheep torn by wolves" (Rowlandson 1997, 70). Even though the Native Americans perceived the New England colonists as the invaders who tried to steal their territory, Rowlandson treats the colonists as the victims who were hunted by barbaric natives.

Rowlandson also writes about how different the Indians' living styles are from those of the colonists. During the sixth remove, they took her to a village that she refers to as "a great Indian town" before retracting her statement and referring to their homes as "nests." While the depictions of her Indian captors were heightened for dramatic effect, these descriptions served as models for later American authors who wrote about interactions between Indians and Americans in their works.

After Rowlandson's release the family moved to Wethersfield, Connecticut, where they lived until her husband's death in 1678. Then she and her children moved to Boston, where she wrote and published her captivity narrative. Rowlandson died there on January 5, 1711.

Maryellen Diotte

See also McCrea, Jane; Williams, Eunice; *Vol. 1, Sec. 2:* Captives, English; Captivity Narratives; Jemison, Mary

Further Reading

Diebold, Robert K. 1983. "Mary Rowlandson." In *American Writers before 1800: A Biographical and Critical Dictionary,* edited by James A. Lervernier and Douglas R. Wilmes, 1245–1247. Westport, CT: Greenwood.

Lepore, Jill. 1998. *The Name of War: King Philip's War and the Origins of American Identity.* New York: Random House.

Rowlandson, Mary. 1997. *The Sovereignty and Goodness of God.* Edited by Neal Salisbury. Boston: Bedford/St. Martin's.

Excerpts from Mary Rowlandson's Account of Her Capture by Indians (1682)

Native Americans captured Mary Rowlandson in 1676 during King Philip's War, when they attacked and burned the town of Lancaster, Massachusetts. Rowlandson was held for one week until ransomed by money raised by several women of Boston. She published The Sovereignty and Goodness of God: Being a Narrative of the Captivity and Restoration of Mrs. Mary Rowlandson *only weeks after her release. The book became an immediate best seller, in part because it reaffirmed Euro-American notions of native people as heathen savages. This excerpt is taken from the 1682 printing.*

Mary Rowlandson Some of Her Experiences.

I HAD often before this said, that if the Indians should come, I should choose rather to be killed by them than taken alive, but when it came to the trial, my mind changed; their glittering weapons so daunted my spirit, that I chose rather to go along with those (as I may say) ravenous bears, than that moment to end my days. And that I may the better declare what happened to me during that grievous captivity, I shall particularly speak of the several Removes we had up and down the wilderness.

The First Remove

Now away we must go with those barbarous creatures, with our bodies wounded and bleeding, and our hearts no less than our bodies. About a mile we went that night, up upon a hill, within sight of the town, where we intended to lodge. There was hard by a vacant house (deserted by the English before, for fear of the Indians); I asked them whether I might not lodge in the house that night? to which they answered, "What, will you love Englishmen still?" This was the dolefulest night that ever my eyes saw. Oh, the roaring and singing, and dancing, and yelling of those black creatures in the night, which made the place a lively resemblance of hell. And miserable was the waste that was there made, of horses, cattle, sheep, swine, calves, lambs, roasting pigs, and fowls (which they had plundered in the town), some roasting, some lying and burning, and some boiling, to feed our merciless enemies; who were joyful enough, though we were disconsolate. To add to the dolefulness of the former day, and the dismalness of the present night, my thoughts ran upon my losses and sad, bereaved condition. All was gone, my husband gone (at least separated from me, he being in the Bay; and to add to my grief, the Indians told me they would kill him as he came homeward), my children gone, my relations and friends gone, our house and home, and all our comforts within door and without, all was gone (except my life), and I knew not but the next moment that might go too.

There remained nothing to me but one poor, wounded babe, and it seemed at present worse than death, that it was in such a pitiful condition, bespeaking compassion, and I had no refreshing for it, nor suitable things to revive it. Little do many think, what is the savageness and brutishness of this barbarous enemy, those even that seem to profess more than others among them, when the English have fallen into their hands. . . .

The Second Remove

But now (the next morning) I must turn my back upon the town, and travel with them into the vast and desolate wilderness, I know not whither. It is not my tongue or pen can express the sorrows of my heart, and bitterness of my spirit, that I had at this departure; but God was with me in a wonderful manner, carrying me along and bearing up my spirit, that it did not quite fail. One of the Indians carried my poor wounded babe upon a horse; it went moaning all along: "I shall die, I shall die." I went on foot after it, with sorrow that cannot be expressed. At length I took it off the horse, and carried it in my arms, till my strength failed and I fell down with it. Then they set me upon a horse with my wounded child in my lap, and there being no furniture on the horse's back, as we were going down a steep hill, we both fell over the horse's head, at which they, like inhuman creatures, laughed, and rejoiced to see it, though I thought we should there have ended our days, overcome with so many difficulties. But the Lord renewed my strength still, and carried me along, that I might see more of his power, yea so much that I could never have thought of, had I not experienced it. . . .

Her Return

. . . About the sun's going down, Mr. Hoar, myself, and the two Indians, came to Lancaster, and a solemn sight it was to me. There had I lived many comfortable years among my relations and neighbors; and now not one Christian to be seen, or one house left standing. We went on to a farm house that was yet standing, where we lay all night; and a comfortable lodging we had, though nothing but straw to lie on. The Lord preserved us in safety that night, and raised us up again in the morning, and carried us along, that before noon we came to Concord. Now was I full of joy and yet not without sorrow: joy, to see such a lovely sight, so many Christians together, and some of them my neighbors. There I met with my brother, and brother-in-law, who asked me if I knew where his wife was. Poor heart! he had helped to bury her and knew it not; she, being shot down by the house, was partly burned, so that those who were at Boston at the desolation of the town, came back afterward and buried the dead, did not know her. Yet I was not without sorrow, to think how many were looking and longing, and my own children among the rest, to enjoy that deliverance that I had now received; and I did not know whether ever I should see them again. Being recruited with food and raiment, we went to Boston that day, where I met with my dear husband; but the thoughts of our dear children, one being dead, and the other we could not tell where, abated our comfort in each other. . . .

Source: Mary Rowlandson, *A True History of the Captivity and Restoration of Mrs. Mary Rowlandson* (New England, 1682). Available at Bartleby, http://www.bartleby.com/163/213.html.

Rowson, Susannah Haswell (1762–1824)

British-born actress and teacher Susannah Rowson was also a best-selling American novelist, poet, and playwright in the 18th century. Her 1791 novel *Charlotte Temple* was the best-selling book, aside from the Bible, in America until Harriet Beecher Stowe's *Uncle Tom's Cabin.*

Rowson was born Susannah Haswell in Portsmouth, England, to Lieutenant William Haswell and Susannah Musgrave Haswell. Her mother died during childbirth. Early in her life, the Royal Navy sent Rowson's father to Massachusetts. A nurse in England raised Rowson for four years until her father, who had remarried, sent for her. She joined him at Nantucket in January 1767. Rowson would later recall her journey to America in her novel *Rebecca, or the Fille de Chambre* (1792), which described how her ship arrived in Boston Harbor during a snowstorm.

Rowson was educated at home. She became well read, familiar with works by Virgil, Homer, Shakespeare, and Spencer, and was often tutored by James Otis, a family friend and pamphleteer for the revolutionary cause. In October 1775 her family moved to Hingham when American revolutionaries confiscated their property during the American Revolution. The family subsequently lived on charity, since Rowson's father was unwilling to side with the Americans, until they were sent to England in 1778 in exchange for prisoners of war.

In England, Rowson secured a position as a governess. She traveled with her employer to France. In 1786 she married William Rowson, an actor and singer. Susannah Rowson's employment became the couple's primary source of income throughout their married life. That same year she published her first novel, *Victoria,* which she dedicated to the socialite and author Georgia Cavendish, the duchess of Devonshire. Over the next four years, Rowson published several other novels.

The most notable of these novels was *Charlotte Temple; or, A Tale of Truth,* published in 1790, that became an American best seller. The novel featured nine separate passages in which Rowson spoke to her readers, offering authoritative advice to women about how to make the most important decision of their lives: marriage. The most striking point about the audience of this book is that it was quite clearly intended to be female. In her preface Rowson explicitly states that she is writing to "the fair sex," specifically to the "young and thoughtless" among them, and in the asides in which she comments on the story, she addresses her readers as "my dear girls." The novel also focused on the themes of seduction and betrayal and was one of the first novels to use the American Revolution as a setting. The novel became so popular that a grave site was erected to the fictional protagonist in Trinity Churchyard in New York City that became a shrine and tourist destination. However, Rowson did not own the copyright to the novel and so made very little money from it despite its best-seller status.

A year later Rowson published *Mentoria,* a collection of 10 letters, three short stories, and an essay for women who did not read novels. *Mentoria* centered on Helena Askam, a governess to the four Winworth daughters, who sent the grown girls letters signed "Mentoria." The collection focused on the false allure of social ambition and the importance of female friendships.

In 1792, Rowson and her husband went bankrupt. They joined Rowson's half sister, Charlotte, as actors in Edinburgh. Their career led them to immigrate to America in 1793, where they opened a play by Thomas Wignell at the Chestnut Street Theater in Philadelphia. Rowson continued to write novels and plays, often performing in the plays she wrote. Her first play, *Slaves in Algiers, or A Struggle for Freedom* (1793), dramatized Americans held captive in North Africa. Rowson utilized the existence of white slavery to celebrate the freedoms of the recently constituted United States. Her play also featured feminist rhetoric, with Rowson's characters delivering statements about women having as much spirit as the bravest men. Conservatives criticized the liberal nature of the play. English journalist William Cobbett called her "Our American Sappho." A Greek lyric poet from Lesbos, "Sappho" by the late 1800s was understood as a code word for a lesbian or "unnatural" woman. In the introduction of her next book Rowson wrote that he was a "loathsome reptile."

Rowson also wrote *Americans in England; or, Lessons for Daughters* and appeared in the comic opera *Farmer* in Boston at the Federal Street Theater. In 1797, Rowson left her career as an actress to begin the Young Ladies Academy for girls in Boston. Six years later, she moved the school to Medford. In 1811, Rowson and her husband—now working as a clerk in a customhouse—moved to a house on Hollis Street in Medford. The couple never had children, but Rowson raised her husband's son by another woman and two adopted daughters. She also supported her brother's widow and children. The Young Ladies Academy closed when Rowson retired in 1822.

Rowson continued writing and worked as an editor for the *Boston Weekly Magazine* until her death on March 2, 1824. Her last novel was published posthumously in 1828 as *Charlotte's Daughter; or, The Three*

Orphans as the sequel to *Charlotte Temple.* Rowson had published nine novels, four volumes of poetry, and six textbooks for young women; wrote and starred in six dramas; and produced several songs.

Tiffany Rhoades-Piotti

See also Loyalist Women; *Vol. 1, Sec. 2:* Bradstreet, Anne; *Vol. 2, Sec. 1:* Domestic and Sentimental Fiction; Harper, Frances; Stowe, Harriet Beecher

Further Reading

Rowson, Susannah. 2010. *Charlotte Temple.* Bibliolife.

Rust, Marion, 2008. *Prodigal Daughters: Susanna Rowson's Early American Women.* Chapel Hill: University of North Carolina Press.

Showalter, Elaine. 2009. *A Jury of Her Peers: American Women Writers from Anne Bradstreet to Annie Proulx.* New York: Knopf.

Showalter, Elaine. 2011. *The Vintage Book of American Women Writers.* New York: Vintage.

Sacagawea (ca. 1788–1812/1884)

Shoshone Indian Sacagawea accompanied the Lewis and Clark expedition as the only woman from the Missouri River over the Continental Divide on to the Pacific coast. The wife of the expedition's Canadian French interpreter Toussaint Charbonneau, Sacagawea has been memorialized as the indispensable guide for Meriwether Lewis and William Clark. She captured the romantic imagination of the nation, becoming the symbol of both the contributions of Native Americans to American history and their fate at the hand of American settlers. While her role as a guide has been exaggerated, Sacagawea's services as an interpreter and her knowledge of native food resources greatly contributed to the success of the expedition. As such, she served an important role as a cultural broker between the Indian and American worlds.

Sacagawea was born in a Northern Shoshone village near the Lemhi River Valley in present-day Idaho, likely a member of the Agaiduka, or Salmon Eater, band of the tribe. Around 1800 when the band was on a hunting or war expedition east of their home territory in present-day Montana, Sacagawea was captured

Though often described as the Native American woman who accompanied Lewis and Clark on their epic 1804–1806 expedition to the Pacific, Sacagawea actually led the party for a significant portion of the trip. She traversed as many miles as the men in the party but with a growing baby strapped to her back. (Library of Congress)

by the Hidatsa Indians from what is now North Dakota. In 1804, French fur trader Charbonneau purchased her from the Hidatsas and claimed her as his wife. Lewis and Clark encountered the two while wintering among the Mandans in 1804–1805 and hired Charbonneau as their interpreter. When they embarked upon their journey west in April 1805, Sacagawea accompanied the expedition together with the couple's two-month-old son, strapped to a cradle board on her back.

When Sacagawea became part of the expedition, she did not control her life. She was a teenager with a young infant, bound to a man who apparently had a liking for young Indian women (at the time, he had another young Indian wife). In his journals, Lewis commented on her cheerful, cooperative attitude, one that he interpreted as different from the indifference that set primitive people apart from civilized people. Lewis was to change his mind later, not just about Sacagawea but to some extent about Indian people in general, and come to see her as a full human being.

There was a clear advantage to having Sacagawea and the young infant along: their presence signaled to possibly hostile Indians along the way that the expedition was not a war party. But there was more to her role in the success of the endeavor than her mere passive presence. Although not accredited in the roster as an equal partner with the interpreters George Drouillard and Charbonneau, she performed crucial translation tasks from the very beginning of the trek west. Often it was Sacagawea who communicated with the Indians and translated what they were saying to Charbonneau, who then delivered the message to Lewis and Clark. When Sacagawea became seriously ill in early June, Lewis himself acknowledged the significance of her role as not just interpreter but also a cultural mediator, noting in his journal that they depended on her for friendly relations with the Native Americans who provided the expedition with horses along the route from the Missouri to the Columbia River.

When the expedition finally came across the Shoshones, it became apparent that they were Sacagawea's people. She was immediately recognized by a woman who had also been a captive of the Hidatsas, and general rejoicing at her return followed. An even more emotional reunion took place when Sacagawea sat down to interpret the meeting between Lewis and Clark and the Shoshone leader, Cameahwait. Looking up at the chief, she realized that he was her brother. In their *History of the Expedition,* the two explorers noted that she instantly embraced him, weeping profusely. Negotiations for buying the horses for the overland journey went on for two weeks. In the end, while she could have rejoined her people, Sacagawea carried on with Lewis and Clark, clearly identifying her own best interests with the expedition and maybe even enjoying the adventure of exploration.

Sacagawea's most critical contribution to the expedition came in helping alleviate the greatest threat to its success: perpetual hunger. While the men all hunted

and fished, they were not consistently successful. Sacagawea had grown up learning the female indigenous skills of collecting roots and berries; she could locate and prepare edible plants unknown to the men in the expedition. She also understood their medicinal properties. In addition, she was able to trace the underground food caches of small animals and merely dug them up to feed the men. She cracked small animal bones to extract the nourishing marrow and prepared the meat and other meals. Clark was impressed with Sacagawea's service as well as her strength in the harsh conditions, nicknaming her Janey in his journals. He also became attached to her son, Jean Baptiste, whom he fondly called Pomp, and assumed responsibility for his education.

After wintering among the coastal Indians, the expedition began its return trip to St. Louis, retracing its route over the first mountain range. At that point, the group decided to split. Lewis took a few men to explore a short northern route back to the falls of the Missouri, while Clark and the rest of the expedition retraced the route they had taken west the previous summer, then cut across to the Yellowstone River and followed it back up to the Missouri. On this trek Sacagawea came into her own as a guide, leading the expedition through her childhood surroundings.

When the two groups met, the expedition was over. They cruised down the Missouri, greeted by Indians who had seen them off the previous year. Since his services as interpreter were no longer necessary, Charbonneau asked to be paid and released from service. On August 17, 1806, Lewis noted in his journal the services that Charbonneau had provided. Furthermore, he wrote, "his wife was particularly useful among Shoshones. Indeed, she has borne with a patience truly admirable the fatigues of so long a route, encumbered with the charge of an infant, who is even now only 19 months old" (Karttunen 1994, 42). Charbonneau received his wages of $500.33, while Sacagawea received nothing, reflective of notions about women and their rights, or lack thereof. According to the legal practice of the time, a woman at marriage became a *feme covert,* meaning that her legal identity was absorbed into that of her husband. It did not even occur to Lewis and Clark to compensate Sacagawea because she was a married woman. Additionally, regardless of the respect they had for her, she was an Indian.

Sacagawea's life after the expedition remains shrouded in mystery. Traditional historical records suggest that Sacagawea, her son Jean Baptiste, and Charbonneau went to St. Louis around 1810 to accept Clark's offer of 320 acres of land and additional pay as well as to finance the education of their son. Sacagawea and Charbonneau returned to the upper Missouri River country to work for the Missouri Fur Company trader Manuel Lisa. Jean Baptiste appears to have stayed behind to begin his education under the patronage of Clark. Most historians believe that Sacagawea herself died at Fort Manuel on the Missouri River of "putrid fever" on December 20, 1812.

The alternative version of Sacagawea's life persists among the Shoshones, Comanches, Mandans/Hidatsas, and Gros Ventres and other Indian nations. Their oral traditions maintain that Sacagawea left Charbonneau and wandered from tribe to tribe until marrying and having children among the Comanches. When her Comanche husband died, she reunited with her firstborn son and adopted nephew and helped her Wind River Shoshone people in their transition to life on their newly created reservation. In this version of her life, she died and was buried on her Wyoming reservation on April 9, 1884.

Sacagawea continues to capture the imaginations of both Indians and non-Indians alike. Arguably, there are more monuments, memorials, rivers, lakes, and other natural markers named after her than any other American woman. Her life, both real and fictional, has been resurrected numerous times by historians, novelists, anthropologists, and feminists. In 1998, the Dollar Coin Design Advisory Committee recommended that Sacagawea be depicted on the new dollar coin, first minted in 2000. The most authentic picture of this extraordinary young woman emerges from the journals of Lewis and Clark, but it is a picture seen through the eyes and prejudices of American men. The real Sacagawea remains elusive.

Päivi H. Hoikkala

See also *Vol. 1, Sec. 1:* Pocahontas; *Vol. 1, Sec. 2:* Coverture; Kittamaquund, Mary; Tekakwitha, Kateri; *Vol. 4, Sec. 2:* Women of All Red Nations

Further Reading

Hunsaker, Joyce Badgley. 2001. *Sacagawea Speaks: Beyond the Shining Mountains with Lewis and Clark.* Guilford, CT: Globe Pequot.

Karttunen, Frances. 1994. "Over the Continental Divide: Sacajawea (ca. 1790–1812 or 1884)." In *Between Worlds: Interpreters, Guides, Survivors,* 23–45. New Brunswick, NJ: Rutgers University Press.

Kessler, Donna J. 1996. *The Making of Sacagawea: A Euro-American Legend.* Tuscaloosa: University of Alabama Press.

Sampson, Deborah (1760–1827)

Deborah Sampson was a Massachusetts woman who disguised herself as a man and served as a soldier in the Continental Army during the American Revolution. She became a celebrated figure in her own lifetime, in part because of the publication of her memoir in 1797 and a lecture tour in 1802 and 1803. Like other veterans, Sampson petitioned the federal government for military benefits after the war. She spent nearly 30 years fighting for a federal pension, and when it was finally granted she also won official recognition that she had served her country as a soldier.

Sampson was born in Plympton, Massachusetts, on December 17, 1760, to Jonathan Samson and Deborah Bradford. (The family spelled its name "Samson"—without the "p"—but on her lecture tour and in her biography, her name is spelled Sampson.) Although descended from founders of Plymouth Colony, Sampson's family struggled to make ends meet throughout her childhood. In the mid-1760s, her father abandoned the family and moved to Maine. Her mother, unable to care for Sampson and her six brothers and sisters, sent the children to live with neighbors and relatives. Sampson lived in various households before being placed with the family of Jeremiah and Susannah Thomas of Middleborough at the age of 10. Here Sampson learned a variety of domestic skills while also honing her agricultural skills. Although she was not necessarily an indentured servant (no such contract has been discovered), Sampson was likely not paid for her work.

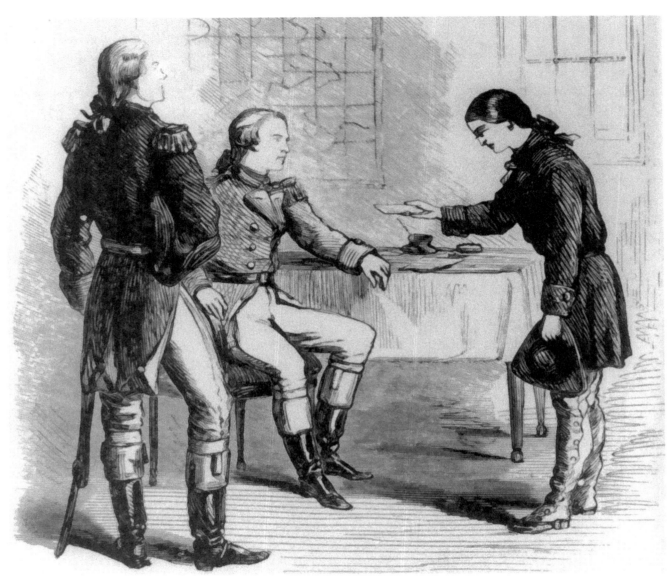

Deborah Sampson Gannett served in the Continental Army for seventeen months during the Revolutionary War as Robert Shurtleff. She and hundreds of other women belied the notion that women could not serve in combat by disguising themselves as men and fighting. (Library of Congress)

Freed from service at age 18, Sampson worked as a weaver to support herself. She also spent two summers teaching school, which likely involved instructing young women to read. Despite the fact that Sampson's own educational prospects were limited, her few surviving letters and diary reveal a curious, well-read mind. On November 12, 1780, Sampson was admitted to the Third Baptist Church in Middleborough at a time when Baptist membership was booming in New England. According to church records, however, Sampson's

membership was suspended on September 3, 1782, when she was accused of dressing in men's clothing and enlisting in the army.

Although British major general George Cornwallis had surrendered 8,000 troops at Yorktown in October 1781, the American Revolutionary War was not over. More than 26,000 British troops remained in America, including 13,000 in New York City. George Washington, commander of the American Continental Army, decided to maintain an army in the Hudson

Valley in 1782 to contain the British troops in the region. In March 1782, Massachusetts issued a call for troops to serve for three years or the duration of the war. Sampson first tried to enlist in Middleborough in March or April under the name "Timothy Thayer." When she was recognized, she tried again. She successfully enlisted in Uxbridge, Massachusetts (about 45 miles away), on May 20, 1782. Binding her breasts, disguising herself in men's clothing, and using the name "Robert Shurtleff" (also spelled Shurtlieff), Sampson was mustered into the Light Infantry Company of the 4th Massachusetts Regiment in Worcester, Massachusetts, on May 23. She received a payment of £60 for her enlistment. Sampson then marched to West Point, New York, with about 50 other recruits, where she received a loosely tailored uniform, which would easily have hidden her female figure.

Light infantry companies were the most active military units in the Hudson Valley in the winter of 1782–1783. According to Sampson's six pension applications as well as others' accounts of military action during this period, she first saw action in late June or early July 1782. Her company was sent on a scouting mission south from the army's winter quarters in Newburgh, New York, toward the British encampments in New York City. On their return to camp, the company was fired upon by a corps of Loyalists. In a second skirmish near Tarrytown, Sampson received a flesh wound to the head as well as a musket ball injury. (The site of this second injury remains a mystery, although historian Alfred Young suspects that Sampson was shot in the shoulder or upper body.) Beginning in the winter or spring of 1783, Sampson served as a waiter (an officer's servant or orderly) to General John Paterson, a position in which she would remain until the fall.

News of the Treaty of Paris, which officially ended the American Revolution, reached Washington's camp in the spring of 1783, and most soldiers were furloughed. On June 24, however, Washington received a request from the president of the Continental Congress asking him to send troops to Philadelphia to suppress a potential mutiny among soldiers who were protesting their lack of pay. Washington sent 1,500 troops, including Sampson, to Philadelphia. While there she contracted some sort of fever (malaria and smallpox

were both rampant in the city at the time). Her true identity was discovered as she recovered in a hospital. When released she returned to Washington's headquarters where, her fellow soldiers celebrated her— as Deborah Sampson—for her brave exploits during the war.

Sampson was discharged from the Continental Army on October 25, 1783. She returned to her aunt and uncle's farm in Sharon, Massachusetts, where she married Benjamin Gannett on April 7, 1785. Gannett, a farmer with limited education, was the oldest son of one of the most prosperous men in Sharon. This family connection, however, would not keep Sampson and her family from suffering financial hardships. She and Gannett would eventually have three children: Earl Bradford (b. 1785), Polly (b. 1787), and Patience (b. 1790).

In the 1790s Sampson collaborated with Herman Mann, a schoolteacher and later printer in Dedham, on a memoir. In 1797, he published *Female Review: Or, Memoirs of an American Young Lady*. The book brought widespread attention to Sampson's exploits as a soldier. Although Mann met with Sampson many times while preparing the biography, it is far from an accurate portrayal of her life. The work is representative of the heroic novels of the time, full of dramatic embellishments and romantic subplots. Although Mann's biography leaves readers with a questionable sense of Sampson's past, it did provide future generations with the only surviving portrait of her. Mann commissioned an image of Sampson for the frontispiece of the book. The image, taken from an oil painting by Joseph Stone of Framingham, depicts Sampson as a tall woman with long hair and wearing a fashionable dress. The frame around her portrait combines feminine flowers with a musket, a sword, and other symbols of Sampson's military career.

In 1802 Sampson embarked on a speaking tour, a very unusual career path for a woman in the late 18th century. The tour began at Boston's Federal Street Theater and continued in locales such as Worcester, Providence, and Albany. At each engagement Sampson would deliver an oration written primarily by Mann. At many events she also dressed in her uniform, armed herself with a musket, and performed maneuvers from the soldiers' manual on the exercise of arms.

In a fragmentary diary of her tour, Sampson wrote that she was generally well received by her audiences, and she was often pleased by the "respectable" nature of the crowds that came to see her performance.

On January 11, 1792, Sampson successfully petitioned the Massachusetts government for back pay. To support her request, she acquired letters of reference from officers under whom she served, including Colonel Henry Jackson (who testified that Sampson had served in his regiment and received an honorable discharge) and Captain Eliphalet Thorp (who confirmed that it was Mrs. Deborah Sampson Gannett who had enlisted as a soldier). She was awarded £34. In 1804 Sampson petitioned the U.S. government for an invalid pension, available to soldiers injured during the Revolution. Among those who supported her claim were John Paterson, a congressman from New York, and industrialist Paul Revere. Congress approved Sampson's request on March 11, 1805. She was granted a pension of $4 per month, to begin retroactively with January 1, 1803. In March 1818 Congress passed the first general pension act, and Sampson petitioned for hers in September. After months of wrangling and more letters of support as well a personal inventory of her assets and net worth (proving her need for the pension), Sampson began receiving her general pension payments from the federal government in 1821.

Sampson died on April 29, 1827. Her husband continued to petition the government for support, but it was not until after his death that a special act of Congress provided Sampson's daughters with a more generous pension. Her family was awarded $80 per year, prorated to cover the period from March 4, 1831, to Benjamin's death in January 1837, for a grand total of $466.66.

Kathleen Barker

See also Corbin, Margaret; Davis, Ann Simpson; Greene, Catharine Littlefield; McCauley, Mary; Soldiers, Women Passing as Men, Revolutionary War; *Vol. 2, Sec. 2:* Edmonds, Sarah Emma; Velazquez, Loreta Janeta

Further Reading
Mann, Herman. 1797. *The Female Review: Life of Deborah Sampson, the Female Soldier in the War of Revolution.* New York: Arno.

Young, Alfred F. 2004. *Masquerade: The Life and Times of Deborah Sampson, Continental Soldier.* New York: Knopf.

Schools for Girls and Women

Initially, the American colonial educational system was based on religious and philosophical ideas that settlers brought with them from Europe. The educational experience of the New England Colonies, Middle Colonies, and Southern Colonies differed to some degree, but they had one significant thing in common: for the most part, females were permitted limited educational opportunities compared to males. In spite of the limitations that women faced as both students and teachers, women played an important role in the development of informal American schools. After the American Revolution and into the era of the early republic, Americans began to forge their own unique educational identity. Over time, Americans began to see the value in universal education, and with the introduction of common and public schools, women gained greater formal educational opportunities.

Two educational tracks were set up for colonial American students. Lower-class students generally learned basic skills such as reading, writing, math, and religion. Male students from wealthy families were taught the basics but also a variety of other classes, such as Latin and Greek, to prepare them for college. Since colleges were in short supply in the colonies, most well-to-do parents sent their sons to colleges in Europe. In 1636, Boston-based Harvard in Massachusetts became the first North American college. More than half a century later in 1693, the College of William and Mary was founded in Williamsburg, Virginia. Both colleges were originally created to train clergymen. Most colonials saw no reason to educate women beyond the basic skills.

In New England, the Puritans were strongly guided by reformation ideas, which stressed the supremacy of the scriptures. Instead of trusting church traditions, European Protestant reformers argued that the faithful should be able to read the Bible. Consequently, Puritan schools taught a number of subjects, most blended with religion, but they considered reading as the most important educational skill.

In contrast, the population of the Middle Colonies was much more varied than in the North. Besides the English, the area included Dutch, Irish, Scottish, and German settlers. Each of these settlers set up schools, which promoted their own particular beliefs. The Quakers uniquely believed in setting up schools to educate both boys and girls. Puritans persecuted Quakers for their beliefs, including their practice of allowing women to become spiritual leaders.

The colonies in the South had the most rigid class system. Southerners believed that only males from wealthy families should be educated beyond the basic skills. Slaves were generally excluded entirely from any sort of education.

In all three regions, the earliest schools were home schools. Parents, usually the mother, taught their children basic skills at home. If parents could afford the small tuition fee, they would sometimes send their children to dame schools, a European concept. As the name suggests, dame schools were taught by women in their homes. For obvious reasons, the level of instruction in dame schools depended on the knowledge of the dame. Both boys and girls ideally received lessons in basic academic as well as homemaking-type skills. However, sometimes children learned only numbers and letters, and other times dames provided no more than a babysitting service. Unfortunately, most colonial girls only received home and dame school educations, because most of them were excluded from formal schools even after the passage of early compulsory education laws. For example, the Massachusetts School Laws in 1642, 1647, and 1648, which inspired other areas of the colonies to adopt similar laws, required communities with more than 50 families to build a grammar school to prepare male students for college.

Some women received more than a basic skills education. For example, Benjamin Franklin's and Thomas Jefferson's daughters received a better education than most men in the colonies. Self-educated Abigail Adams gave herself a better education than that of John Adams, her college-educated husband and future president. Other women, educated in either America or Europe, made a living as teachers. Like Adams, many women found informal ways to educate themselves and turned their skills to teaching.

Although opportunities were limited, some orphaned girls and girls from lower-class families were accepted into various apprenticeships, where they learned academic skills as well as crafts. Parents would sometimes send their young daughters to boarding school to live with a widow or unmarried woman who would educate the young ladies in the arts (drawing, painting, and music) as well as manners and literature. Evening (or night) schools were private schools created to supplement women's education after they mastered skills learned at home or at dame schools. Some evening schools taught a variety of subjects that went far beyond the basic skills, including foreign languages, accounting, drawing, geography, algebra, geometry, trigonometry, ethics, logic, and philosophy.

In spite of these efforts, most colonial and Revolutionary-era women remained less educated than men. Over time and especially after the American Revolution and into the era of the early republic, Americans gradually disassociated themselves from European models and began to forge their own unique educational identity. Textbooks, known as spellers, which taught students the American way of spelling English words, became the underpinning of all schoolhouses across the country. By the early 1800s, American education had moved away from a major focus on religion and began to focus on teaching skills that were good for commerce, such as math. Education was also fashioned into a tool to promote American democracy, patriotism, good citizenship, and moral values. By the mid-1800s, women gained greater educational opportunities in formal schooling with Horace Mann's (1796–1859) introduction of the idea of public secondary schools for all children.

Rolando Avila

See also Adams, Abigail; *Vol. 1, Sec. 2:* Dyer, Mary; Literacy

Further Reading

Jennings, Wagoner, Jr., and Wayne J. Urban. 2008. *American Education: A History*. New York: Routledge.

Kendall, Elaine. 1999. "Beyond Mother's Knee: The Struggle to Educate Women." In *Portrait of America*, Vol. 1, *To 1877*, edited by Stephen B. Oates, 163–174. Boston: Houghton Mifflin.

Sugg, Redding S., Jr. 1978. *Motherteacher: The Feminization of American Education.* Charlottesville: University Press of Virginia.

Second Great Awakening

The Second Great Awakening was a mass religious movement in America and the second of its kind. Notably, the evangelical impulse that began in 1790 and lasted through the 1840s emphasized the individual's role in universal salvation. In a time when many Americans frowned on women's work outside the home, the religious nature of the movement legitimized women's activities in the public sphere, empowering women to take up a variety of secular causes in an effort to reform society.

In the 1730s and 1740s both Jonathan Edwards and George Whitefield, two of the leading First Great Awakening preachers, laid the groundwork for a faith that emphasized the role of individuals in seeking their own salvation based on personal revelation. Nonetheless, many Protestants theologians held fast to the doctrine of predestination, a belief that God had chosen only a few people to be saved and that there was nothing a person could do to change their eternal destiny.

In the late 1700s, a number of influential revivalists sought to reestablish personal choice as a doctrine in salvation and in so doing created the Second Great Awakening. Evangelists like Charles Grandison Finney taught that God offered an opportunity for salvation to all people. Black, white, young, old, rich,

While much has been written about the male preachers and religious ideology of the Second Great Awakening, approximately two-thirds of revival goers were women. Women attended these revivals, absorbed their message of the perfectibility of the human spirit, and gave birth to a wave of social justice crusades that define the early nineteenth century. (Library of Congress)

poor, men, and women had access to salvation—not just a privileged few. In this new faith, it was up to believers to make a freewill choice to seek out and accept the gift of salvation from God.

The mass religious movement swept through both cities and the countryside. In the country, camp revival meetings became common as early as 1800. Hundreds of people from various denominations flocked to hear sermons preached by rotating charismatic ministers. The net effect was that visitors listened to sermons all day long. In some cases, religious services went on for several days. Many preachers adopted the practice of placing prospective converts in the "anxious box" so that they could preach directly to them hour after hour until they accepted salvation. Often, converts displayed overtly dramatic responses by falling on the ground and shaking widely, creating a lively and entertaining revival atmosphere. In the cities, the fiery messages that preachers delivered were said to awaken believers from spiritual slumber by igniting a spiritual fire inside their hearts. In New York state, for example, some areas were nicknamed "burnt-over districts." According to some estimates, in 1839 Finney converted more than 100,000 people in New York, and oftentimes the majority of converts were women.

The universal nature of the new faith particularly attracted women. Since colonial times, traditional Protestants had viewed women as the weaker sex. In contrast, evangelicals, who believed that all people could be saved, placed women in a state of spiritual equality with men. In fact, in some ways women were regarded as spiritually superior to men because more women than men heeded the call to salvation. Some evangelists capitalized on the state of affairs by empowering women to tend to the salvation of the rest of their households. Many women responded by bringing their husbands and children to the faith. Others became evangelists and spiritual hymn writers, spreading the message to the world.

The universal nature of the new faith resulted in a more democratic approach to religion. In short, the Second Great Awakening empowered women as individuals and as a group. It changed the way Americans saw women's role in religion and society, and this new view encouraged women to engage in reform movements based on the notion that if women were uniquely able to reform their own households they might also be best suited for national reforms due to "female moral authority." Some of the most notable female reform movements included temperance, abolition, suffrage, and utopian ventures.

Ultimately, leadership roles in the new faith equipped some women to take on new leadership roles in society. Many women joined activist clubs. Some of the most famous activists included Sojourner Truth, an advocate of abolition and women's rights; Harriet Tubman, an abolitionist and the chief conductor of the Underground Railroad; and Susan B. Anthony, a proponent of temperance, abolition, and suffrage, who was arrested for voting illegally in a presidential election and proclaimed at her trial that "Resistance to tyranny is obedience to God."

Rolando Avila

See also *Vol. 1, Sec. 2:* Great Awakening; *Vol. 2, Sec. 1:* Abolition/Antislavery Movement; Anthony, Susan B.; Female Moral Authority and Sphere of Influence; Temperance Movement; Truth, Sojourner; Tubman, Harriet; Women's Rights Movement

Further Reading

Hatch, Nathan O. 1989. *The Democratization of American Christianity.* New Haven, CT: Yale University Press.

Sedgwick, Susan Anne Livingston Ridley (1788–1867)

A member of an illustrious and literary family, Susan Anne Livingston Ridley Sedgwick published works for young readers during the first half of the 19th century.

Born Susan Anne Livingston Ridley, on May 24, 1788, in Stockbridge, Massachusetts, Sedgwick was the first of two daughters of Matthew and Catherine Livingston. Her sister Matilda Frances Sherbourne Ridley, born in 1789, married Robert Watts and lived until 1862. Sedgwick's family was politically active and socially prominent. Her maternal grandfather was New Jersey governor William Livingston (1723–1790).

Sedgwick married Theodore Sedgwick Jr. on November 28, 1808. Her husband was born in Sheffield, Massachusetts, on December 31, 1781, the eldest son of Pamela Dwight and Theodore Sedgwick, a delegate to the Continental Congress who also went on to become a politician and state supreme court judge. Sedgwick Jr. graduated from Yale College in 1798, studied law, and practiced in Albany, New York, from 1801 to 1821.

Following his years of practicing law in Albany, Sedgwick Jr. relocated to Stockbridge, Massachusetts, where he engaged in farming and became president of the county agricultural society. As a Democrat and active opponent of slavery, Sedgwick Jr. also entered politics. He served in the state legislature (1824, 1825, and 1827) and made several unsuccessful attempts at becoming elected as the lieutenant governor of Massachusetts. In addition, he published several volumes, among which were *Hints to My Countrymen* (1826) and *Public and Private Economy* (1838). He died of apoplexy in Pittsfield, Massachusetts, on November 7, 1839.

The Sedgwicks had one son, born in Albany, New York, in 1811 and named Theodore after his father. The son graduated from Columbia College in 1829 and was admitted to the bar in 1833. Like both his father and his grandfather, he practiced law. He went on to become a U.S. district attorney and also published various writings, including *Memoir of Governor William Livingston* (1833) and *Treatise on the Measure of Damages* (1847).

Susan Sedgwick devoted her energies to a different form of writing than her husband or son pursued and did not begin publishing until her son had grown up and moved away. She chose juvenile fiction. Her works include *The Morals of Pleasure* (1829), *The Children's Week* (1830), *Allen Prescott: Or, The Fortunes of a New England Boy* (1834), *The Young Emigrants: A Tale Designed for Young Persons* (1836), *Alida: Or, Town and Country* (1844), and *Walter Thornley, or A Peep at the Past* (1859).

As some of the titles of Sedgwick's novels suggest, her writings shared the characteristic interest of 19th-century authors, especially women, in using the power of fiction as a vehicle to deliver lessons in morals, manners, and the proper conduct of life. Many writers believed that such didactic volumes could reach readers unlikely to seek such advice through the means of nonfiction, such as advice literature and moral essays. In this respect, numerous works of American fiction from this era in U.S. history represent efforts both to inform and uplift readers, particularly the young, immigrants, and members of the working class. Rather than functioning as works chiefly intended for leisure and enjoyment, such novels aspired to the audience's personal, social, and spiritual improvement.

Two of Sedgwick's published works, *Allen Prescott* and *Alida,* took shape from her recollections of remarks by her maternal aunt, Susan Livingston Symmes, who had witnessed the American Revolution firsthand and spoke to the harsh realities of war not just for soldiers but also for entire communities. Sedgwick's novels both paid tribute to her aunt and served to dramatize the lasting effects of the American Revolutionary War (1775–1783) on American society.

Few published critiques of Sedgwick's work are available. The exception is an 1844 review of *Alida* published in the *North American Review.* Introducing excerpts from the novel, the reviewer praises her characters and compares Sedgwick's work to that of Jane Austen. The commentary is not entirely laudatory, suggesting that Sedgwick is still honing her craft. Still, the fact that she received notice in this way indicates that she was regarded as an author of considerable promise.

There was, however, another woman in the Sedgwick family who achieved even greater literary notice than did Sedgwick. Her classmate and later her sister-in-law, Catharine Maria Sedgwick, was widely known as an author in a genre then classified by the diminutive term commonly applied to works by women, domestic fiction. Catharine Sedgwick's published novels include *Hope Leslie* (1827) and *The Linwoods* (1835). Her work was often compared to that of author Susan Warner. Like her sister-in-law, Catharine Sedgwick also composed some work targeted to young readers.

Susan Sedwick died in Stockbridge, Massachusetts, in 1867. She was buried in the Sedgwick family plot, Sedgwick Pie, in Stockbridge Cemetery.

Sedgwick earned a reputation as an American author, taking particular interest in presenting fiction directed to the distinctive needs and interests of youthful readers during the 19th century.

Linda S. Watts

See also Advice Literature

Further Reading

Dewey, Mary. 1871. *Life and Letters of Catharine M. Sedgwick.* New York: Harper and Brothers.

Kenslea, Timothy. 2006. *The Sedgwicks in Love: Courtship, Engagement, and Marriage in the Early Republic.* Boston: Northeastern University Press.

Sedgwick, John. 2007. *In My Blood: Six Generations of Madness and Desire in an American Family.* New York: HarperCollins.

Seton, Elizabeth Ann (1774–1821)

The first Catholic saint born in the United States and the founder of the Sisters of Charity of St. Joseph's, Ann Bayley Seton was born on August 28, 1774, to Dr. Richard Bayley (1744–1801) and Catherine Charlton (d. 1777). After her mother's death, Seton's father married Charlotte Amelia Barclay (1759–1805), and Seton spent some of her childhood and teen years living with Bayley relatives in New Rochelle, New York. On January 25, 1794, she married William Magee Seton (1768–1803), the son of a prominent New York merchant. The couple had five children. Although she devoted a considerable amount of time to her family responsibilities, Elizabeth Seton enjoyed participating in the New York social scene.

As a founding member of New York's Society for the Relief of Poor Widows, Seton also engaged in charitable work by collecting money and visiting families in need. In 1798 after the death of her husband's father, Seton and her husband moved into the Seton family home on Stone Street and cared for his younger brothers and sisters, including 7-year-old Cecilia and 10-year-old Harriet, who remained close to Seton throughout their lives. Unfortunately, the disruption caused by the elder Seton's death and William Magee's struggle with tuberculosis led the family's business into bankruptcy, placing the Setons in a precarious financial position.

In an effort to restore his health, Seton and her family traveled to Leghorn (Livorno), Italy, in October 1803. Italian officials quarantined the passengers on arrival, fearing the spread of yellow fever, which was then raging in New York. Both parents and their eight-year-old daughter Anna Maria spent the next month in a damp, drafty cell, a dangerous situation for someone in the final stages of tuberculosis. Although released on December 19, William Magee Seton did not recover, dying on December 27, 1803. In February and March 1804, Anna Maria and Elizabeth Seton contracted a form of scarlet fever, and mother and daughter did not return to New York until June. However, Seton's Italian sojourn proved fortuitous for her spiritual development. As an Episcopalian, Seton was unfamiliar with the doctrines of the Roman Catholic Church.

While in Italy, Seton visited historic sites and attended Catholic worship services with her friends, Antonio (1764–1847) and Amabilia Filicchi (1773–1853). The Filicchi family fostered Seton's interest in Catholicism, sharing art, religious literature, and their personal convictions. Although attracted to Catholicism, Seton did not join the Church in Italy. She continued to study and pray, convinced that God would guide her in her religious search. Despite opposition from family and friends, Seton experienced a conversion when she returned from Italy and made her profession of faith in Roman Catholicism at St. Peter's Church in New York City on March 14, 1805. In doing so she joined an oppressed minority in a 19th-century America, where Protestants held almost all positions of social, economic, and political power. Indeed, Catholics were so despised that most both the temperance movement and the anti-immigrant nativist movements were anti-Catholic movements in a thin disguise.

The next few years were trying ones, as Seton faced the task of providing for her five children. Reverend Louis Dubourg (1766–1833) proposed that Seton move to Baltimore, and he persuaded her to start a school. In 1808 Seton rented a house on Paca Street, adjoining St. Mary's Seminary and College. The school remained small, but during her stay in Baltimore, Seton's interest in religious life grew, and along with the Sulpician priests who advised her, she began investigating the possibility of starting a community of religious women in Maryland. After Reverend

Pierre Babade recruited two young women to join her, Seton began planning a community of nuns. With a donation from Samuel Sutherland Cooper, Seton secured some property near Emmitsburg, Maryland. There she founded the Sisters of Charity of St. Joseph's, the first new Catholic community of religious women in the United States.

The nascent community continued to develop and regularize its rules between 1809 and 1812. The Sulpicians initially proposed that the sisters join with the Daughters of Charity in Paris, but Seton opted for her community to remain independent. The priests made no further efforts to unite with the French religious community until the 1840s. In 1810, Bishop Benedict Flaget delivered a copy of the *Common Rules* of the Daughters of Charity to Emmitsburg, which he had received on a journey to France. With minor adaptations necessitated by American social conditions, the Sisters of Charity of St. Joseph's adopted these rules in 1812. By the time Seton died, the community operated the school in Emmitsburg, staffed the infirmary and managed domestic operations at Mount St. Mary's College, and administered orphanages in Philadelphia and New York City.

Seaton spent the years after the establishment of her community working to expand their charitable activities. She succumbed to tuberculosis in 1821 when she was 46 years old. Two of her daughters preceded her in death. Seton's example, writings, and the ministries that the Sisters of Charity established have influenced the faith, education, and well-being of thousands of individuals throughout the United States. The original community of five women has grown into six foundations and their branches, now united in the Sisters of Charity Federation. On September 14, 1975, Pope Paul VI canonized Elizabeth Ann Seton. She was the first American-born person, male or female, to be made a saint and remains an important symbol for American Catholics.

Kristine Ashton Gunnell

See also *Vol. 1, Sec. 2:* Catholic Women; *Vol. 2, Sec. 1:* Daughters of Charity

Further Reading

Bechtle, Regina, S.C., and Judith Metz, S.C., eds. 2000–2006. *Elizabeth Bayley Seton Collected Writings.* 3 vols. Ellin M. Kelly, mss. ed. New York: New City Press, http://via.library.depaul.edu/vincentian_ebooks/.

Melville, Annabelle M., and Betty Ann McNeil, DC. 2009. *Elizabeth Bayley Seton, 1774–1821.* Hanover, PA: Sheridan.

Soldiers, Women Passing as Men, Revolutionary War

Early American history provides significant evidence of women's desires to participate in the battle for freedom. The American Revolutionary War (1775–1783) is one of the first conflicts with documented evidence of women disguising their gender in an attempt to fight on the battlefield. While there are fewer documented cases of women passing for men in the Revolutionary War, by the time of the American Civil War (1861–1865) there are accounts of hundreds of women cutting their hair, adopting male aliases, and binding their breasts to serve alongside their male counterparts. These women challenged society's gender roles that only allowed women to serve as nurses, cooks, laundresses, and spies by pushing such gender boundaries and gathering up arms to fight.

In the years before the American Revolution, there were women soldiers on the frontier. One of the most renowned is Anne Hennis Trotter Bailey (1742–1825) of Virginia, who vowed revenge when Native Americans killed her husband. In 1774, she dressed in male buckskin attire and gained a reputation for being absolutely fearless. During the American Revolution, she became a courier and scout. She received regular army pay and rations and gained the respect of her male comrades.

Since boys as young as 12 were said to have joined the American ranks during the Revolutionary War, a soldier with a high voice and no facial hair was not cause for alarm. Sometimes women soldiers cut their hair short and rubbed dirt on their faces to simulate the growth of a beard. With the soldiers sleeping and often bathing in their clothes, the women's guise could be carried out under layered bulky attire. In both the Revolutionary War and the Civil War, modesty prevailed for all soldiers when handling bodily functions, allowing women the privacy necessary to pass as a man.

During the American Revolutionary War, this gender ruse allowed women to live lives beyond the confines of the home and move into roles other than wife and mother. Many women who decided to disguise their gender were concerned with more than adventure. Most were poor, unmarried, and young and wished to go to war so as to collect a soldier's paycheck. One of the more well-known women who served in the Revolutionary War was Deborah Sampson (1760–1827) of Plympton, Massachusetts. Noted to have been a direct descendant of William Bradford (1590–1657), the former governor of Plymouth Plantation, Sampson enlisted in the 4th Massachusetts Regiment in 1782 under her deceased brother's name, Robert Shurtliff. She fought in New York until 1783, when she was wounded in battle and her true gender was discovered by the attending physician. The doctor did not reveal her secret, and after a year and a half of serving with her regiment, Sampson was honorably discharged.

In 1777, Ann (or Nancy) Bailey of Boston adopted the name Samuel Gay and enlisted in the 1st Massachusetts Regiment. While there are few details about her short time in service, there are accounts that confirm that she was promoted to the rank of corporal, the highest rank of any woman who served during the Revolutionary War. After a few weeks of service, Bailey left the 1st Massachusetts Regiment. It is believed that her abrupt departure may have been linked to the discovery that she was a female. Her true gender identity discovered, Bailey was fined and imprisoned for impersonating a man.

Sally St. Claire, a Creole woman from South Carolina, joined a South Carolina regiment during the Revolutionary War to remain close to her lover. Little is known of St. Claire's early life or her time in service. Records indicate that she enlisted in 1778 and fought in the Battle of Savannah, where both she and her lover were killed in battle. It was not until her death that she was discovered to be a woman.

While the numbers were lower for women who served in the Revolutionary War, historians note that by the American Civil War, there were upwards of 400 women who served under the guise of being men. These women came from diverse and varied backgrounds—rich and poor, literate and illiterate, city dwellers and rural denizens. Their reasons for service were varied. Many women enlisted to remain close to their husbands, lovers, or brothers. Others enlisted for adventure. Some women enlisted to avoid being married off to unsuitable men or to free themselves from unbearable family situations. Enlistment in the army allowed women to make their own money, and many were able to relieve the financial burdens of their families back home. Other women enlisted because they deeply believed in the cause for either the Confederate or Union side and desired to play a more active role in the war effort.

Even after the Revolutionary War, women continued to serve their country disguised as male soldiers. Some sources cite one "Lucy Brewer," who was alleged in an "autobiography" to have secretly fought as a marine aboard USS *Constitution* during the War of 1812. However, many historians feel that the legend was a tactic to sell "her" book, *The Female Marine,* which was probably written by a male.

There are reports that in the Mexican-American War (1846–1848), Elizabeth Newcom (b. ca. 1825) joined the Missouri infantry as "Bill Newcom." Though she marched 600 miles to camp in Colorado, she was discovered to be female and summarily discharged.

For decades after both the Revolutionary War and the Civil War, military officials denied the existence of women soldiers. Diaries, letters, and narratives were dismissed as hoaxes. Proven women soldiers were scorned as prostitutes, lesbians, or crazy women. Officials denied that the women could have gone undetected at induction, though for much of American history the induction exams given to prospective soldiers were cursory at best. The conscripts were asked to walk to make sure they were not too lame to march, and their mouths were examined to make sure they had at least three teeth to tear open cartridge packets. They were not asked to undress.

It is impossible to know just how many women went to war disguised as men, because the only ones known to history are the ones who, for one reason of another, were caught and made public. We can know that women have served in combat for the entirety of American history and did so with bravery and honor.

Sherri M. Arnold

See also Corbin, Margaret; Davis, Ann Simpson; Knox, Lucy Flucker; Revolutionary War and Women; Sampson, Deborah; *Vol. 2, Sec. 2:* Boyd, Isabella Marie "Belle"; Cushman, Pauline; Edmonds, Sarah Emma; Velazquez, Loreta Janeta

Further Reading

Blanton, De Anne, and Lauren Cook. 2002. *They Fought Like Demons: Women Soldiers in the American Civil War.* Baton Rouge: Louisiana State University Press.

Leonard, Elizabeth D. 1999. *All the Daring of the Soldier: Women of the Civil War Armies.* New York: Norton.

Silvey, Anita. 2008. *I'll Pass for Your Comrade: Women Soldiers in the Civil War.* New York: Clarion Books.

Young, Alfred F. 2004. *Masquerade: The Life and Service of Deborah Sampson, Continental Soldier.* New York: Vintage Books.

Toypurina (1760–1799)

Toypurina, a Kumi-Vit (or Tongva) woman from the village of Javachit in today's San Gabriel Valley, California, was born nine years before the Spanish began colonizing southern California. The Spanish would have identified her as a Gabrielino, a term that identified all native people who were relocated to San Gabriel Mission (est. 1771) and baptized. A leader of an insurrection against the San Gabriel Mission in 1785, she continues to be a symbol of resistance to Spanish colonization. After the foiled campaign and years of imprisonment, she was baptized and later married a presidio soldier. Therefore, she also represents the process of accommodation in the face of overwhelming threat and coercion. Toypurina was a doctor, a wise woman, and a leader of her community. She earned respect among the leadership and populations of at least seven villages. Toypurina is a reminder of the value and status of women recognized in the traditional Kumi-Vit worldview. She experienced the impact of Spanish patriarchal order and the disruptive culture imposed through the establishment of 21 missions in Alta California.

Javachit was one of many independent Kumi-Vit villages whose territory embraced the Los Angeles, Santa Ana, San Gabriel, and Rio Hondo Rivers. Before the Spanish came the Kumi-Vit people numbered 5,000 and were distributed among 1,500 square miles of territory into 50 politically independent villages. Some of the villages competed for resources, while others were bound to each other through economic, social, and religious ties. Coastal villages tended to compete with those in the foothills and mountains.

The Kumi-Vits thrived on a hunting and harvesting subsistence economy. They also participated in an intertribal trade network that included the Serrano, Cahuilla, Chemehuevi, and Mojave peoples. Men hunted, and women were responsible for the managing, harvesting, preparing, and cooking of foods (acorn and pinon) central to the Kumi-Vit diet. Toypurina spoke at least one of the four dialects of the Takic language family (Uto-Aztecan language group). Kumi-Vit religious cosmology taught people to be stewards of the land and negotiate land-use rights rather than to see themselves as the center of the universe and owner or conqueror over all other life forms. Kumi-Vit leadership included the dominant lineage leader of his or her village. The shamans also comprised the leadership, although under their own authority.

Kumi-Vit women enjoyed marked freedom, respect, and independence, particularly when compared to Euro-American women. Women were valued in their role as mothers, and children were prized and nurtured. In addition to doing the life-sustaining work of the population, women produced clothing and participated in tribal ceremonies and mourning rituals. Spiritual women such as Toypurina were responsible for the elaborate mourning ceremonies and for distribution of food following communal hunts. They controlled dances, studied astronomy, and kept time, important for seasonal planting, harvesting, and ceremony. Such tribal members also cured physical, emotional, and spiritual ailments.

Toypurina was a young woman on September 8, 1771, when the Franciscans established Mission San Gabriel near the Rio Hondo River, the fourth mission of Alta California. The acquisition of native women by soldiers often began with chasing and lassoing them, followed by rape and then the murder of Kumi-Vit men when they attempted to protect the women. "Men, women and children would be whipped, tied up and driven to the mission. There a ritual of submission was required from men and boys . . . [and] women and children were used as leverage to secure baptisms" (Castillo 1994, 71–72). The sexual violence that accompanied the conquest did not help the Church's efforts to convert natives, but Church officials could do little to curb the military's behavior.

By relocating members of rival and more distance villages to the mission, the Spanish conquest also increased competition for land and resources. Beginning with a failed insurrection in 1771 and through the early 1780s, Kumi-Vit leaders resisted colonization. Continued sexual assaults, floggings, theft of children, acute loss of resources, and increased mortality led many women to accept baptism. The pressure applied to the most vulnerable women and children probably led the men to accept baptism, as they did what was necessary to stay close to their loved ones. Once baptized, neophytes (trainees) were confined to the mission to labor in the fields and industries of the mission, making them little more than slaves. The introduction of systematic labor exploitation, sexual abuse, and violence quickly brought free native women under the patriarchal authority of the missions.

Mission authorities began confining girls by the age of six or seven to *monjeros* (barracks) to be isolated from male contact until married. Women were confined again following the death of a husband. *Monjeros,* which were little more than prisons, lacked sewage and ventilation and contributed to the proliferation of disease and high mortality. Birthrates declined partially because women practiced birth control and infanticide to avoid the birth of children who were the product of rape. Some chose not to bring children into a world that they experienced as harsh and that was under rapid, unwanted change. Women who attempted to escape were brutally whipped and sometimes put in shackles. Thus, in all ways mission Indian life denied women's power and the opportunity for respect and positions of leadership that Kumi-Vit society honored.

By 1785, Toypurina had become a formidable doctor and had witnessed the devastating impacts of Spanish influence that undermined the recognition of

women's value and status. As a doctor, a ceremonial leader, and a wise woman, she had both influence and kinship connection. Nicolas Jose (1748–ca. 1790), the first *alcalde* (Indian supervisor) and the third adult male to have been baptized at Mission San Gabriel, approached Toypurina to assist him in destroying the mission. He may have had considerable influence inside and outside the mission, balancing his leadership role between two worlds. He brought beads and other things to Toypurina as compensation for her services.

Nicholas organized resistance from within the mission while counting on Toypurina's influence among the free Kumi-Vits. She expected to be paid in mission cattle following a successful uprising. She recruited *tumia r* Temejavaguichi of Juvit Rancheria, Aliyivit of Jajamovit Rancheria, the *tumia r* of Jachivit Rancheria, the population of Azucavit, and others. Seven villages agreed to join forces in an effort to eject the Spanish from their territory. Traditionally, war parties were led by both men and women such as Toypurina and Jose. Unfortunately for the free natives, the plot was discovered. Nicolas, Toypurina, and at least 20 others were imprisoned at the Presidio to await trial and sentencing. Nicolas testified that he was motivated to rebel due to oppression of native culture and ceremony. Toypurina testified that she participated in the insurrection in an effort to end Spanish occupation of Kumi-Vit territory.

In 1777 after being held for two and a half years, Nicolas was exiled and condemned to six years of hard labor in irons. Toypurina was exiled to Mission San Carlos in Monterey and spent 16 months in solitary confinement. Upon release she faced retribution from 20 followers and 2 chiefs who had sworn revenge on her for the failed campaign. Perhaps because of the threat from her own people, Toypurina chose to convert. In 1787 at the age of 27, she was baptized Regina Josepha at Mission San Gabriel, the 29th baptism. It is also possible that her baptism was not consensual. She may also have been forced to be baptized while in prison and in shackles. Two years later she married Presidio soldier Manuel Montero and bore at least three children. Her son, Cesario, and daughter, Juana de Dios Montero, were born at San Luis Obispo Mission. Maria Clementina, their last known child, was born at San Carlos Borromeo Mission in November

1794. Toypurina lived with her family at various missions until she died on May 22, 1799, and was buried at the age of 39 at Mission San Juan Bautista.

Toypurina was born prior to the Spanish conquest at a time and in a society that valued women and their contributions. Kumi-Vit women were equals among men even if oftentimes the labor they performed was different than that of their male counterparts. Toypurina survived apocalyptic changes throughout her life when most indigenous people did not. She learned to adapt to survive. However unsuccessful her revolt was, she stands as an icon of native female agency and serves as a reminder that California missions were not the beneficent agents of indigenous transformation from savages to civilized people. Rather, the mission system did great damage to indigenous culture and indigenous women.

Leleua Loupe

See also *Vol. 1, Sec. 1:* Hunter-Gatherers; Slavery, Native Americans; *Vol. 1, Sec. 2:* Mestiza

Further Reading

Bauer, William. 2006. "Toypurina." *News From Native California* 19(3): 34–36.

Castillo, Edward D. 1994. "Gender Status Decline, Resistance, and Accommodation among Female Neophytes in the Missions of California: A San Gabriel Case Study." *American Indian Culture and Research Journal* 18(1): 67–93.

Hackel, Steven W. 2003. "Sources of Rebellion: Indian Testimony and the Mission San Gabriel Uprising of 1785." *Ethnohistory* 50(4): 644–688.

Ursuline Nuns

Ursuline nuns educated girls across North America and elevated women's participation in colonizing New France, becoming the first teaching order of women within the Catholic Church. They influenced Native American textile art and promulgated a positive image of native peoples that impacted ideals of personal freedom and European political theory, potentially contributing to the American Revolution and the French Revolution.

The Company of St. Ursula was a response to the poverty, illiteracy, and subsequent exploitation of women endemic throughout Europe in the 16th century. Angela Merici (1474–1540) organized the first Ursulines in Brescia, Italy, in 1535. Her innovation was unprecedented within the Catholic Church. Merici envisioned women working within a community to educate and empower other women rather than nuns cloistered away from the public.

The first Ursulines resided in private homes, met regularly with a community of sisters, and operated under all-female governance headed by a mother superior. This structure empowered the women, but their independence unnerved Church hierarchy, resulting in an initial refusal to ordain the order. Still, Ursuline companies established schools for girls throughout Europe, especially in France and Germany. French women maintained personal wealth through direct inheritance and property ownership. Religious-minded women with financial independence, such as young widows of the upper class, were drawn to the Ursulines.

Merici died before the company was officially recognized in 1546; she was canonized as a saint in 1807. In 1639 Mother Marie de l'Incarnation, Marie Guyard (1599–1672), two other French Ursuline sisters, and three Augustinian nursing sisters sailed to the remote outpost of Quebec, the capital of New France. They were the first Catholic nuns in North America. Under Guyard's leadership, the Ursulines and their benefactress, Marie-Madeleine de Chauvigny de la Peltrie (1603–1671), built North America's first convent and school for girls and founded an orphanage.

Guyard felt spiritually called to minister to Native Americans. She learned the local native languages, trained her nuns, and wrote the first dictionary, grammar references, and Christian books in Huron, Algonquian, Montagnais, and Iroquois.

The Ursulines taught preteen women literacy in preparation to receive communion, developed elocution and language skills through staged theatricals, and celebrated faith in the study of music. Cultural art appreciation would later inspire founding mothers of growing American cities to support opera, music, and theater.

The sisters educated students in math and elementary science, empowering female involvement in trade and industry. They also offered trade skills—spinning, sewing, knitting, and fine embroidery.

Across New France, the French merchant class sent their daughters to Ursuline boarding schools, but the sisters also provided classes for Native American, African, Hispanic, and mixed-race girls (métis). Schools were established at Trois Riviéres (1697), Montreal (1670), and New Orleans (1727). By 1731, 12 Ursuline schools were educating women to influence colonization, trade, and even diplomacy. Female colonists managed half of the property in New France. Native American and mixed-race woman became influential translators during tribal negotiations with Europeans.

Esther Wheelwright (1696–1780), a New England captive among the Abenakis, was ransomed by a French Jesuit priest and joined the Ursulines. She became their mother superior in 1760 following the British invasion of Quebec. While the British expelled the Jesuits, Wheelwright, an English speaker, negotiated to keep Ursuline schools, convents, and Catholic churches open.

Philanthropic women in France and New France funded the sisters' endeavors, and business acumen enabled them to support themselves. Ursuline sisters brought gold-gilding technology to New France. Thin gold foil was applied to wooden objects—frames, religious altars, and artifacts—to brighten up dreary chapels and to produce saleable items for other religious institutions.

As upper-class French women, many Ursulines, including Guyard, Peltrie, and Parisian sister Marie Lemaire des Anges (1641–1717), were skilled at needlework. They created embroidery masterworks to decorate altar frontals, liturgical ornaments, and religious vestments.

Native American women traditionally decorated garments with dyed tufts of animal hair or porcupine quills in geometric designs. The Ursulines taught European needlework to their students. Native American students returning to tribal cultures incorporated new floral themes, pictorial elements, and embroidery techniques into traditional textiles, creating new forms of Native American art.

Similarly, the Ursulines absorbed native and métis women into their ranks and adopted their ethnic crafts. Wheelwright, having learned birch bark techniques as

a captive, encouraged production of birch bark boxes and moose hair embroidery. Exotic curios were presented to visiting dignitaries and patrons and were sold in France to fund schools and hospitals. Native American dolls and miniature birch bark canoes that benignly depicted unfamiliar people were made specifically for European markets. Some scholars believe that these scenic depictions shaped 18th-century European political philosophy by suggesting the ideal of *le bon sauvage,* "the good wild man" (individuals with innate goodness free of the corrupting influence of society).

Jean-Jacques Rousseau (1712–1778) spent his young adult years in France as a Catholic convert, where he may have encountered Ursuline curios. His writings on individual freedom and equality as a natural state, juxtaposed against the corrupting influence of complex society, influenced the political beliefs of Thomas Jefferson and others involved in the American Revolution and the French Revolution.

In 1900, Pope Leo XIII called all Ursuline sisters to come together under the Ursulines of the Roman Union with an administrative representative in Rome. Some groups, however, remained independent under the original Company of St. Ursula. All Ursuline sisters remained dedicated to education and empowering women to reach their full potential.

Keri Dearborn

See also Dower Rights; *Vol. 1, Sec. 1:* Clothing, Native American Women; Cultural Interaction; New France, Women in; *Vol. 1, Sec. 2:* Captives, English; Catholic Women; Inheritance Laws; Mestiza

Further Reading
Maison Générale des Ursulines, Quebec. 2007. "Les Ursulines." http://www.ursulines-ur.org/index.php?option=com_content&view=article&id=30&Itemid=33&lang=en.

Phillips, Ruth Bliss. 1998. *Trading Identities: The Souvenir in Native North American Art from the Northeast, 1700–1900.* Seattle: University of Washington Press.

Sister Mary of Jesus. 1948. "Ursulines." In *The Encyclopedia of Canada,* Vol. 6, edited by W. Stewart Wallace, 221–224. Toronto: University Associates of Canada.

Vaillande Douvillier, Suzanne (1778–1826)

Suzanne Théodore Vaillande Douvillier was the first ballerina to perform in the United States. The French-born Vaillande also left her mark on the American stage as the first female choreographer in addition to contributing to set designs. Vaillande contributed to American theatrical arts on multiple levels—a feat that had not been previously accomplished by a woman in the United States.

Born in France in 1778, Vaillande was raised by her mother, who does not appear to have ever married. Records from this time period are incomplete, particularly for the working-class French, so historians know little of Vaillande's early life. She studied dance at the Paris Opéra, marking her as a classically trained ballerina. Ballet opera, which contained both dancing and singing, was popular in 18th-century France. Ballet, as an art form for continual dance rather than dance interspersed with singing or talking, developed in midcentury. By the time Vaillande trained as a ballerina, dancers were wearing no-heeled dancing shoes and clothing that allowed for natural movement. The young Vaillande excelled at this new art form. She developed a swift and successful career as a ballerina in France with regular performances at the Nicolet's Théâtre des Grands Danseurs du Roi under the stage name Mademoiselle Théodore.

When Vaillande was a teenager, both France and its colonies faced political turmoil. During the French Revolution she traveled to Santo Domingo, where she met Alexandre Placide, a French entertainer skilled in acrobatics, gymnastics, and dance with whom she had a professional and probably romantic relationship. However, the colony faced a revolt in 1791, which may have convinced Placide and Vaillande to relocate once more. The two moved to the United States, where they launched a lucrative career.

Ballet itself was relatively new to New York when Vaillande and Placide arrived in 1792. Vaillande first performed in America under her stage name Madame Placide, though she was not married to Placide at the time. Her appearance at New York's John Street Theatre in *The Bird Catcher,* one of the first traditionally choreographed French ballets, was the first ballet performance in the state. Vaillande was the featured ballerina for the majority of the ballets and pantomimes that Placide would go on to stage for the New York Theater that season. She also performed ballet and pantomimes around the country, including Pennsylvania, Massachusetts, and Rhode Island, before settling in South Carolina. In addition to being recognized as a talented performer with many leading roles, Vaillande became the first female choreographer in the United States when she worked on the ballet *Echo and Narcissus* in 1796.

During Vaillande's career as a dancer, both Placide and Louis Douvillier, a singer and dancer who joined the troupe while they toured in Boston, courted Vaillande. Although not legally married to her, Placide was jealous of Douvillier's affection for Vaillande; he challenged the singer to a duel for the ballerina's hand. Though Douvillier lost the duel with a minor injury, he asked Vaillande to marry him. She accepted, and in late 1796 Vaillande's stage name changed to Madame Douvillier. She performed with her husband in New Orleans and began to hone her choreography skills.

Vaillande continued to push the boundaries of theatrical work throughout her life. She was the first female performer to play a male character onstage in the United States, though the American theater had a long tradition of men playing female roles. She also contributed to set design, though she was rarely credited for her work. Because she was reportedly disfigured in her later years, Vaillande wore a mask during her final performance as Donna Anna in *Don Juan.* Vaillande died at age 48 a few years after her late husband and was buried in the St. Louis Cemetery. Throughout her career, Vaillande expanded her role in professional dance as a student, performer, choreography, and set designer. Though major American cities now all have ballet companies, American formal dance culture was in its very infancy when Vaillande performed, and though she is relatively unknown today, she should be considered a pioneer of American dance culture.

Cynthia M. Zavala

See also *Vol. 3, Sec. 1:* Baker, Sara Josephine; Duncan, Isadora; *Vol. 3, Sec. 2:* Graham, Martha

Further Reading

Homans, Jennifer. 2010. *Apollo's Angels: A History of Ballet.* New York: Random House.

Lee, Carol. 2002. *Ballet in Western Culture: A History of its Origin and Evolution.* New York: Routledge.

A Vindication of the Rights of Woman (1792)

A Vindication of the Rights of Woman, written by British feminist Mary Wollstonecraft in 1792, addresses several issues regarding the repression of women advocated by philosophers who believed that women should not receive an education. Wollstonecraft extended the argument she initiated in *A Vindication of the Rights of Man* (1790), in which she rejected monarchies and the aristocracy in favor of republicanism. In her magnum opus of women's rights, she challenges the systematic subjugation of uneducated women. Although both the author and text received negative criticism at the time, Wollstonecraft's *Vindication* was an important founding document for American women's rights.

After Edmund Burke (1729–1797) published *Reflections on the French Revolution,* arguing that social upheaval would set a dangerous precedent for the future of monarchies, Wollstonecraft provided one of the first published rebuttals via *A Vindication of the Rights of Man.* In addition to challenging Burke's defense of the aristocracy, Wollstonecraft criticizes the rhetoric he employed, believing that it reinforced problematic gender dynamics. She would later expand these arguments in *A Vindication of the Rights of Woman.*

As political discussions in response to the French Revolution spread in England, they often included arguments about the education of women. In response to Charles Maurice de Talleyrand-Périgord's pamphlet *Rapport sur l'instruction publique,* Wollstonecraft argued that women had a right to education. Influenced by intellectuals such as Dr. Richard Price (1723–1791) and Thomas Paine (1737–1809), Wollstonecraft argued for an end to the social restrictions women faced, including access to education, on the grounds of ethics and reason.

Throughout *A Vindication of the Rights of Woman,* Wollstonecraft grappled with the failure of contemporary philosophers to include women as part of the revolution for rights. She criticized the accepted belief that women were naturally weaker, both physically and intellectually, and therefore were incapable of rational thought. Furthermore, she targeted the systematic subjugation of women through the institution of marriage, religious doctrine, and domesticity. To provide women with a better opportunity to contribute positively to society, Wollstonecraft argued that rational education was necessary.

In the first chapters, Wollstonecraft establishes that virtue is obtained by men through reason; as a result, denying access to rational education would prevent women from obtaining virtue, a necessary attribute of modern citizenship. She also emphasizes that while men are educated to become professionals and contributors to society, women are groomed for outward aesthetics and marriageability. Wollstonecraft reasons that it would be undesirable and unethical to deny women the rights granted to men. To bolster her argument in later sections, she examines how it is unethical to withhold education from women by examining the path to marriage and duties of wives and mothers to challenge the imbalance of power between men and women.

In 1798 William Godwin (1756–1836), Wollstonecraft's widower, published *Memoirs of the Author of a Vindication of the Rights of Woman.* His unconventional approach in providing an intimate account of Wollstonecraft's career and affairs was not well received and contributed to the negative criticism against her work. Wollstonecraft and Godwin, for example, though married, lived in separate adjoined houses. The couple also married only once they discovered that Wollstonecraft was pregnant. Their daughter Mary was also an unconventional woman, famous chiefly for writing *Frankenstein: Or, The Modern Prometheus* (1818).

Although the rights of women did not change immediately after its publication, *A Vindication of the Rights of Woman* would serve as inspiration for women's rights activists by the turn of the century. Both literary and political figures—from George Eliot and Virginia Woolf to Millicent Garrett Fawcett—attempted to rehabilitate Wollstonecraft's memory. Prominently published throughout the 1800s, *Rights of Woman* garnered a wide readership in the United

States. Among these readers were activists Lucretia Mott, Elizabeth Cady Stanton, and Susan B. Anthony. Despite the initial rejection of Wollstonecraft as radical and unorthodox in her philosophy on women's education and in the personal choices she made during her lifetime, *A Vindication of the Rights of Woman* remains one of the earliest important documents of the feminist movement.

Cynthia M. Zavala

See also *Observations on the Real Rights of Women; Vol. 2, Sec. 1:* Anthony, Susan B.; Mott, Lucretia Coffin; Stanton, Elizabeth Cady; Women's Rights Movement

Further Reading

Godwin, William. 2001 ed. *Memoirs of the Author of a Vindication of the Rights of Woman.* Ontario, Canada: Broadview Literary Texts.

Gordon, Lyndall. 2005. *Vindication: A Life of Mary Wollstonecraft.* New York: Harper.

Wollstonecraft, Mary. 1992. *A Vindication of the Rights of Woman.* Edited by Miriam Brody. New York: Penguin.

Excerpt from Mary Wollstonecraft's *A Vindication of the Rights of Woman* (1792)

Although Mary Wollstonecraft was an English writer, her A Vindication of the Rights of Woman *would have been available to American women. The book, excerpted here, is often credited with being a founding document in the 19th-century women's rights movement.*

The most perfect education, in my opinion, is such an exercise of the understanding as is best calculated to strengthen the body and form the heart. Or, in other words, to enable the individual to attain such habits of virtue as will render it independent. In fact, it is a farce to call any being virtuous whose virtues do not result from the exercise of its own reason. This was Rousseau's opinion respecting men: I extend it to women, and confidently assert that they have been drawn out of their sphere by false refinement, and not by an endeavor to acquire masculine qualities. Still the regal homage which they receive is so intoxicating, that till the manners of the times are changed, and formed on more reasonable principles, it may be impossible to convince them that the illegitimate power, which they obtain, by degrading themselves, is a curse, and that they must return to nature and equality, if they wish to secure the placid satisfaction that unsophisticated affections impart. But for this epoch we must wait—wait, perhaps, till kings and nobles, enlightened by reason, and, preferring the real dignity of man to childish state, throw off their gaudy hereditary trappings: and if then women do not resign the arbitrary power of beauty—they will prove that they have *less* mind than man.

I may be accused of arrogance; still I must declare what I firmly believe, that all writers who have written on the subject of female education and manners, from Rousseau to Dr. Gregory, have contributed to render women more artificial, weak characters, than they would otherwise have been; and consequently, more useless members of society. I might have expressed concern on a lower key; but I am afraid it would have been the whine of affectation, and not the faithful expression of my feelings, of the clear result which experience and reflection have led me to draw. . . .

Though, to reason on Rousseau's ground, if man did attain a degree of perfection of mind when his body arrived at maturity, it might be proper, in order to make a man and his wife *one,* that she should rely entirely on his understanding; and the graceful ivy, clasping the oak that supported it, would form a whole in which strength and beauty would be equally conspicuous. But, alas! husbands, as well as their helpmates, are often only overgrown children; nay, thanks to early debauchery, scarcely men in their outward form—and if the blind lead the blind, one need not come from heaven to tell us the consequence.

* * *

Rousseau declares that a woman should never, for a moment, feel herself independent, that she should be governed by fear to exercise her *natural* cunning, and made a coquettish slave in order to render her a more alluring object of desire, a *sweeter* companion to man, whenever he chooses to relax himself. He carries the arguments, which he pretends to draw from the indications of nature, still further, and insinuates that truth and fortitude, the corner stones of all human virtue, should be cultivated with certain restrictions, because, with respect to the female character, obedience is the grand lesson which ought to be impressed with unrelenting rigour.

What nonsense! when will a great man arise with sufficient strength of mind to puff away the fumes which pride and sensuality have thus spread over the subject! If women are by nature inferior to men, their virtues must be the same in quality, if not in degree, or virtue is a relative idea; consequently, their conduct should be founded on the same principles, and have the same aim.

Source: Mary Wollstonecraft, *A Vindication of the Rights of Woman with Strictures on Political and Moral Subjects* (London: Joseph Johnson, 1792). Available at http://womhist .alexanderstreet.com/awrm/doc1.htm.

Wall, Rachel (1760–1789)

As the first American-born female pirate, Rachel Wall collaborated with her husband and other sailors to capture and loot ships at sea.

Wall was born in Carlisle, Pennsylvania, in 1760 and raised on a farm by a conventional Presbyterian family. When Wall was a child, her father gathered the family for morning and evening prayer. Every Sabbath, he quizzed his children on the Holy Scripture and on other holy books he would read to them. Longing to live by the waterfront, Wall ran away from home at a young age. She shortly returned and lived with her family for 2 years before leaving home again at age 16. She never saw her family again.

During a visit to a harbor near Harrisburg, Pennsylvania, Wall was attacked by a group of girls. A sailor named George Wall saved her. The two fell in love and eloped. The couple traveled together to New York and Boston, where George left Wall to work on a fishing schooner. Wall took a job as a servant with a prominent home in Beacon Hill.

After two months, Wall's husband came back with five of his shipmates to convince her to leave her life of servitude and join them at sea. George proposed that he, his wife, and his shipmates become pirates. Wall's husband and his friends served aboard privateers during the American Revolutionary War and hardly saw the moral disconnect in taking the step to full piracy when they had been paid by the government to do much the same.

In early 1781, the crew began their life of piracy. Wall's husband decided to use her as bait. When the weather was good, the crew would work on the schooner as simple fishermen. After a storm, Wall and the crew would make the ship appear battered, and Wall would scream for help as other ships approached. The unsuspecting captain and crew would board Wall's ship to rescue her, and the crew on Wall's ship would murder and rob them. Once the pirates plundered and pillaged the vessel of all loot, they would throw the bodies overboard and sink the ship. Upon returning to shore the crew would blame the deaths and loss of a ship on bad weather.

For about a year the crew continued this ruse. Within a year, the crew was $6,000 richer from the 12 ships they plundered and sank. The lucrative business came to an end when Wall's husband mistook the eye of a hurricane as the end of the storm and died at sea. A New York ship offered Wall and the remaining crew help and brought them to shore. Another account claims that Wall's husband was murdered during a fight on another ship and that in her mourning she decided to quit the life of piracy.

Once in Boston, Wall returned to her former job as a maid for the Beacon Hill home. After a year of piracy, she found her income as a servant inadequate and supplemented her earnings by petty theft and prostitution. She was ultimately caught for the theft of another woman's bonnet in 1789. Wall was charged with highway theft, a crime punishable by hanging. She was also a suspect in a waterfront murder. In

Wall's confession she denied being guilty of the crime for which she was charged. She did confess to piracy, although she said that she never committed murder.

Rachel Wall was hanged on October 8, 1789, along with two men for highway robbery. She was the last woman to be hanged in the state of Massachusetts. She remains one of a relatively small number of 18th-century female pirates. Anne Bonny and Mary Read worked together with famed pirate "Calico Jack" Rackham in the Caribbean in the 1700s, while Mary and Thomas Harvey worked the Carolina Sea Islands at about the same time. The most powerful female pirate of all time was undoubtedly Ching Shih, famed for her portrayal in the third *Pirates of the Caribbean* movie, who commanded over 300 ships and as many as 40,000 pirates.

Adrienne Harwell

See also Butterworth, Mary

Further Reading

Jensen, Vickie. 2012. *Women Criminals: An Encyclopedia of People and Issues,* Vol. 1. Santa Barbara, CA: ABC-CLIO, 2012.

Sharp, Anne Wallace. 2002. *Daring Pirate Women.* Minneapolis: Lerner Publications.

Yolen, Jane, and Christine Joy Pratt. 2008. *Sea Queens: Women Pirates around the World.* Watertown, MA: Charlesbridge.

Warren, Mercy Otis (1728–1814)

Born into a prominent New England family, author and political philosopher Mercy Otis Warren was close friends with public figures such as Abigail (1744–1818) and John Adams (1735–1826), Elbridge Gerry, Thomas Jefferson (1743–1826), and George Washington (1732–1799). Warren served as a key intellectual figure during the American Revolution and Early Republic periods.

Born in West Barnstable, Massachusetts, on September 14, 1728, Warren was the 3rd child and 1st daughter of 13 children born to Judge James Otis Sr. and Mary Allyne. The Otis family was well established in the Massachusetts colony: Warren's grandfather John Otis served in the Massachusetts House of Representatives, and her father was a lawyer and judge who served as attorney general of the province. During Warren's childhood, the Otis household included at least 1 black slave as well as indentured servants. Despite her support for the American Revolution, some of Warren's later writing reflects a sense of disappointment and loss in a world in which her family's position of power was unquestioned within their community.

Warren was particularly close with her father and eldest brother, James Otis Jr., and was encouraged by both of them to read widely and practice her skill with the pen. Along with James, she studied Greek and Latin classics in translation as well as work by William Shakespeare, Alexander Pope, John Dryden, John Milton, and Sir Walter Raleigh. The support and encouragement by men in pursuit of intellectual endeavors was a recurring pattern in Warren's life, one that gave her license to step outside the bounds of colonial and early republican womanhood.

On November 14, 1754, Mercy Otis married James Warren (1726–1808), a lawyer practicing in Plymouth, Massachusetts. Between 1757 and 1766, Mercy Otis Warren gave birth to five sons: James, Winslow, Charles, Henry, and George, all of whom lived to adulthood. Their 54-year marriage was a strong partnership, and both husband and wife chafed against the often necessary separations of the American Revolutionary period. The couple seemed most content when living together on the Warren family estate, Eel River, in Plymouth, Massachusetts. During the years leading up to the American Revolution, the Warren home became a site for political debates and organizing. James Warren supported his wife in her role as a revolutionary polemicist. After the Revolution when both Warrens suffered personal and political disappointments, Eel River served as their refuge.

Warren began writing poetry during the 1760s, though none of her early poems were published during her lifetime. Her first published work, written at the encouragement of her fellow revolutionaries, was *The Adulateur,* a satirical play in blank verse. Written as a critique of Governor Thomas Hutchinson's role in the Boston Massacre, it appeared serially in the *Massachusetts Spy* during March and April 1772. This was followed by *The Defeat,* published in the *Boston*

Historian and playwright Mercy Otis Warren is remembered for her insightful commentary on American politics. Though largely forgotten by historians, she wrote the first history of the American Revolution. (Cirker, Hayward and Blanche Cirker, eds., *Dictionary of American Portraits*, 1967)

Gazette in May and July 1773, and *The Group,* published in pamphlet form in April 1775. All three of these works appeared anonymously, though their authorship was an open secret among friends and family. At this point in her career, Warren was ambivalent about her role in the political realm, and in private letters she expressed anxiety and uncertainty about women's role in the public sphere.

The period following the American Revolutionary War was a difficult one for the Warrens, both politically and personally. They were uncomfortable with the social instability and rowdy nature of early republican politics, and the rise of new players in the political scene frustrated James Warren's political ambitions. As a result, he withdrew from public life in 1778, a decision that drew criticism from many family friends. Domestically, the couple faced the convalescence of their son James, who had lost a leg during the war and suffered from mental health problems that today might be described as post-traumatic stress disorder.

During the tumultuous constitutional debates of 1787, James and Mercy Warren reentered politics on the side of the anti-Federalists, expressing a strong distrust of centralized government. Mercy Warren, writing as "a Columbian Patriot," published a pamphlet in February 1788, widely circulated throughout the new nation, that was a passionate defense of decentralized government. The Warrenses' anti-Federalist position led to a falling out with John and Abigail Adams, who were already bitter about James's earlier withdrawal from public life and saw James and Mercy Warren as undermining the efforts to build a new nation.

As she entered her 60s, Warren published her first book, which was the first work to appear under her own name: *Poems, Dramatic and Miscellaneous* (1790). Fifteen years later, she followed this up with one of the earliest histories of the American Revolution: the three-volume *History of the Rise, Progress, and Termination of the American Revolution: Interspersed with Biographical, Political, and Moral Observations* (1805). Warren's narrative wove together factual information about people and events with a passionate defense of classical republican ideals of public virtue and obligation. *History of the Rise, Progress, and Termination of the American Revolution* also incorporates the perspective and experience of

women more fully than her previous political work, making a strong case for the importance of women's participation in the creation of the new nation. To Warren's disappointment, her history met with little critical attention and weak sales.

The publication of *History of the Rise, Progress, and Termination of the American Revolution* brought Warren's career to a close. During the final decade of her life, she lived at Eel River with her husband and son James, who had moved in with his aging parents in 1800. Their son Henry, his wife, and nine grandchildren lived nearby. On November 28, 1808, James Warren passed away at the age of 82. Warren died 6 years later on October 19, 1814, after a short and sudden illness. She was 86 years old.

Anna J. Clutterbuck-Cook

See also Adams, Abigail; *Observations on the Real Rights of Women;* Republican Motherhood

Further Reading
Davies, Kate. 2005. *Catharine Macaulay and Mercy Otis Warren: The Revolutionary Atlantic and the Politics of Gender.* New York: Oxford University Press.
Stuart, Nancy Rubin. 2008. *The Muse of the Revolution: The Secret Pen of Mercy Otis Warren and the Founding of a Nation.* Boston: Beacon.
Zagarri, Rosemarie. 1995. *A Woman's Dilemma: Mercy Otis Warren and the American Revolution.* Wheeling, IL: Harlan Davidson.

Washington, Martha (1731–1802)

Martha Dandridge Custis Washington was a private family-oriented woman who endured personal tragedy and provided extraordinary support and stability to others, including the Continental Army of the Revolutionary War. As the wife of the first president of the United States, George Washington (1732–1799), she originated the role of first lady, creating an ideal for successors.

Washington was born the eldest of eight children to John and Frances Dandridge, middle-class landowners descended from the Virginia Colony's founding families. Her father owned a medium-sized tobacco plantation, where the Dandridge women prepared the family's food, spun their own yarn, and sewed most of their everyday garments assisted by one or two house slaves.

While some historians describe Washington as educated only in domestic matters, plantation-class women typically were literate and handled legal documents. They were also taught strong arithmetic skills to maintain household financial records. As the oldest daughter, Washington helped raise her younger siblings and throughout her life was happiest when surrounded by family, especially children.

The petite five-foot-tall Washington, with dark brunette hair, was an accomplished equestrian and had an interest in textiles. Just prior to her 19th birthday, she married Daniel Parke Custis, a man 20 years her senior and one of Virginia's wealthiest planters. The couple had four children, but their first son died of malaria at age 2. Further tragedy struck in 1757 when Washington's 4-year-old daughter and husband died.

At age 26, Washington was a widow with 2 children under age 4. This early experience taught her "that the greater part of our happiness or misery depends upon our dispositions, not upon our circumstances" (Fields 1994, 224). Rather than despair, she took on the management of her plantations.

When Custis died without a will, his estate—including 18,000 acres of farmland, multiple homes, and 300 African slaves—fell under English inheritance law. Dower rights entitled Washington to manage the properties in trust for her two living children—John "Jack" Parke Custis (1754–1781) and Martha Parke Custis (1756–1773).

Washington was the wealthiest widow in Virginia, a position offering independence not afforded most colonial women. She could manage her own affairs, including whether or not she remarried. Despite proposals from wealthy widowers, Washington eventually chose an indebted bachelor six months her junior: George Washington. A distinguished military officer from the French and Indian War (1754–1763), he shared her frugal nature and love of the land. They were married on January 6, 1759, and moved to his family home at Mount Vernon, Virginia.

Their marriage was a loving partnership. George Washington oversaw the management of her properties, but documents reveal that she maintained active involvement in business matters. They never had any children, but George helped raise Jack and young Martha. Unfortunately, Washington's daughter developed epilepsy, and despite investigation into various medical treatments, the girl died of a seizure at age 17.

Though Martha Washington publicly claimed no interest in politics, political activists gathered at Mount Vernon. When unpopular taxes were placed on English imports, the Washington household participated in the various tea and textile boycotts. As George was leaving to represent Virginia at the First Continental Congress, Washington admonished one of his corepresentatives to stand firm with her husband on independence from England.

During the eight years of the American Revolutionary War while George acted as general of the Continental Army, Washington managed the plantation during the summer and followed the army to its encampment each winter. She acted as nurse, mother, and confidante to the men under her husband's command. Mercy Otis Warren (1728–1814) noted how Washington brought unusual kindness and comfort to the war-weary soldiers and the general.

Washington also supplied much-needed food and clothing (made by her textile workers at Mount Vernon) after she saw how the Continental Congress had failed to provision the soldiers. When support for the war waned, Washington invited local women to come and call on her and her circle of officers' wives, including Lucy Knox and Catherine "Kitty" Greene. When the visitors arrived, they were put to work knitting socks and sewing shirts for the soldiers.

Even the end of the war came with a personal price; Washington's remaining son contracted typhus at Yorktown and died. He left a young widow with four small children. Washington and her husband adopted and raised the two youngest grandchildren.

Washington hoped that the war's end would bring a return to a private life, but George accepted election to the presidency in 1789. Throughout her husband's eight years in office, Washington used her friendly nature to moderate political advisories, charm foreign dignitaries, and champion the military veterans who had served under her husband. She was a thoughtful hostess tasked with delicately balancing open social events reflecting democratic ideals and weekly official dinners highlighting cultured hospitality to engender the respect of European allies. Abigail Adams (1744–1818), the wife of Vice President John Adams, became a close friend of Washington's and noted the universal respect and admiration paid to the first lady.

Exposure to a wider world in New York and Philadelphia during the presidency impacted Washington, and she became a supporter of increased education for women, sending her granddaughter to one of the newly established schools for girls.

Throughout their lives, when separated the Washingtons wrote weekly. Upon her husband's death, Washington burned 41 years' worth of their private letters. She preserved the privacy they had so often given up for the public good. Many modern scholars feel that Washington's full influence as a founding American figure is unknown because of the lack of primary documents revealing her interaction with her husband, the first president of the United States. Martha Washington died on May 22, 1802 at Mount Vernon.

Keri Dearborn

See also Adams, Abigail; Boycotts, Tea and Textiles; Dower Rights; Greene, Catharine Littlefield; Knox, Lucy Flucker; Revolutionary War and Women; Warren, Mercy Otis; *Vol. 1, Sec. 2:* Inheritance Laws; Slavery, African

Further Reading

Brady, Patricia. 2005. *Martha Washington: An American Life.* New York: Viking Penguin.

Fields, Joseph E. 1994. *Worthy Partner: The Papers of Martha Washington.* Westport, CT: Greenwood.

Roberts, Cokie. 2004. *Founding Mothers: The Women Who Raised Our Nation.* New York: HarperCollins.

Wheatley, Phillis (1753–1784)

Poet Phillis Wheatley was born in West Africa, sold into slavery, and eventually freed. She wrote poems at a time when many people argued that people of African descent were so inferior to Euro-Americans as to be fit only for slavery. She is remembered as a preeminent poet of the American Revolutionary period.

Wheatley was born in Gambia around 1753 but was sold into slavery and shipped to the United States when she was 7 or 8 years old aboard the *Phillis,* a slave ship that landed in Boston, Massachusetts. Purchased by John Wheatley, a wealthy Boston merchant, as a domestic servant for his wife and teenage children, he named her Phillis after the slave ship that brought her to America. Unlike most slaves, Wheatley had an opportunity to demonstrate an intellectual talent that her masters were willing to develop. As a result, she received a rather extensive education for the time—something rather rare for any woman, let alone a slave. Under the guidance of 18-year-old Mary Wheatley, the enslaved girl quickly grasped the English language, eventually engaging in in-depth studies of literature as well as a wide array of subjects that included Latin, Greek, and religious studies. For Wheatley, these studies ultimately became the inspiration for her poetry and the basis for her most highly anthologized poetic works.

Encouraged by Mary to use her education to write, Wheatley published her first poem, "On Messrs. Hussey and Coffey," on December 2, 1767, in the *Newport Mercury* newspaper, marking the beginning of what would prove a short-lived yet influential literary career. Laden with allusions to the classical works and Christianity, in which she was educated, her poetry reflected the values instilled in Wheatley during her time in slavery. These themes proved popular with many American readers, particularly in the developing colonies where the First Great Awakening of the 1730s and 1740s swept a spirit of Christian revitalization throughout the Northeast. At the same time, Wheatley often incorporated a larger social message in these works, as in her poem "On Being Brought from Africa to America," where she reminds the Christian masses that the enslaved black race should not solely be condemned, for much like herself, they could also be refined.

Wheatley's emphasis on Christian values also aided in the acceptance and appreciation of her work by local white audiences, foregrounding her humanity in stark contrast to the prevailing stereotypes of slaves as inferior that were prominent in racial discourse from the antebellum South to the industry-driven North. In fact, because of her intellectual skill, Wheatley was often cited in abolitionist talks and literature as evidence of the humanity and talents of the growing free black population. Her works, after all, demonstrated, at least to the circle of white families and supporters all around her, that blacks were not in fact the brute and unintelligent beasts solely bred for labor that many proslavery proponents claimed them to be.

Wheatley, through her literary example and frequent exposure to white society, illustrated to Americans in the New Republic that blacks could be educated if allowed to escape the dehumanizing effects of slavery. While there is certainly an element of racist thinking among Wheatley's admirers, who assumed that black Americans achieved a pinnacle of humanity only in emulating whites, she nonetheless offered an important role model for people who believed that slavery was wrong.

After the publication of several poems in newspapers and periodicals, Wheatley gained wider recognition with her 1768 poem titled "To the King's Most Excellent Majesty," a poem that celebrated the repeal of the Stamp Act. Her tendency to record significant historical events later became a dominant thread across her literary works. Eventually Wheatley was able to gain even greater attention at home and abroad with the publication of a funeral elegy that she composed for Selina Hastings, the countess of Huntingdon, in response to the death of George Whitefield, her chaplain and one of the founders of Methodism. The poem was published in both London and Boston in 1771, which drew Wheatley international attention. The following year the publication of her poem "Recollection" in the *London Magazine* brought her further fame.

In time, Wheatley amassed enough poetry to compile a full-length collection titled *Poems on Various Subjects: Religious and Moral.* Unable to find a publisher in Boston due to the rising racial prejudice, she published the collection in London in 1773, guided by the support of Selina Hastings. This collection demonstrated an artistic and intellectual skill that was relatively unheard of from a slave.

Prior to the publication of the collection, however, Wheatley returned to Boston to nurse her sickly mistress and was soon after granted her freedom. In 1774 Wheatley's poetry collection was also published in the colonies, establishing her as one of just a few American women at the time, Anne Bradstreet included, to have their work appear in print for a public audience.

The 46 poems in the book were written according to European standards of poetry, modeled after the work of Alexander Pope and composed in traditional form, much like the works she read as a teenager under the tutelage of Mary Wheatley. Reflecting on key historical events and dedicated to influential figures, Phillis Wheatley's poetry not only portrayed her thoughts on life in Boston but also demonstrated the cultural literacy she was afforded by the family that once owned her.

Racial prejudice of the era, however, worked against the success of these early poems, as many American readers and critics frequently denied that she was the author of these works. Many Americans simply refused to believe that a black woman could write poetry. As Wheatley moved forward in her literary career, she had to convince a panel of Boston's literary and political elite of her authorship. To combat the potential racial prejudice that would threaten its later success at home, *Poems* thus contained a letter from John Wheatley assuring the readers that Wheatley had written the poems as well as an "Attestation" from New England's literary leaders. This same tradition was later prominent in the slave narratives of the antebellum period as black authors continued to have to prove the legitimacy of their authorship. Thus, published letters of support by well-known white figures in the community became a tradition in black American literature.

Though Wheatley continued writing poetry, eventually compiling enough work for a second proposed collection, her literary career essentially ended not long after the publication of her first book. In October 1775 Wheatley wrote a poem honoring General George Washington, which captured his attention and resulted in an invitation to his headquarters in Cambridge early the following year. On April 1, 1778, however, she married John Peters—a decision that proved disastrous for Wheatley's literary endeavors.

Peters's failure to maintain employment and financial instability left the family in abject poverty. During this time Wheatley gave birth to three children, all of whom died at a very young age. Under these conditions she found it difficult to write. When Peters was imprisoned for outstanding debts, Wheatley found herself unable to adequately provide for herself.

Sickly throughout her life, Wheatley died in relative obscurity and poverty on December 5, 1784, shortly after giving birth to her third child. Though unable to find a publisher in her lifetime for her second collection of poetry, she remains a significant figure in American poetry today. Able to merge classical forms with religious themes and a pious spirit, she challenged the dominant misconceptions of blacks as unintelligent, bestial creatures. She was promoted instead as a rare talent of her day and age.

Certainly much of Phillis Wheatley's success can be attributed to the unprecedented support that she received from the Wheatley family, but her talent was her own. She was vital to the growth of African American literature during the 19th and 20th centuries. She was one of the first voices of the steadily growing canon of American poets. Her poems, considered raceless by some and for others coded with a larger sociocultural message, paved the way for other women writers of color, writers such as Alice Walker who have recognized the vital role that her literary foremothers like Wheatley and Zora Neale Hurston have played in forging a place for women of color within the once exclusive canon of American literature.

Christopher Allen Varlack

See also *Vol. 1, Sec. 2:* Great Awakening; Slavery, African; *Vol. 2, Sec. 2:* Freedwomen; *Vol. 3, Sec. 2:* Hurston, Zora Neale; *Vol. 4, Sec. 2:* Walker, Alice

Further Reading

Brawley, Benjamin Griffith, ed. 1935. *Early Negro American Writers: Selections with Biographical and Critical Introductions.* Chapel Hill: University of North Carolina Press.

Carretta, Vincent. 2011. *Phillis Wheatley: Biography of a Genius in Bondage.* Athens: University of Georgia Press.

Foster, Frances Smith. 1993. *Written by Herself: Literary Production by African American Women, 1746–1892.* Bloomington: Indiana University Press.

Gates, Henry Louis. 2003. *The Trials of Phillis Wheatley: America's First Black Poet and Her Encounters with the Founding Fathers.* New York: Basic Civitas Books.

Poems of Phillis Wheatley

Phillis Wheatley (ca. 1753–1784) was a significant Revolutionary-era American poet. Though critics disagree about the quality of her poems, the fact that she wrote poetry at all while enslaved in a culture that evaluated her as inferior and even subhuman provided powerful proof of African American female agency. In the first of her poems reproduced here, "On Being Brought from Africa to America," Wheatley begins the poem by suggesting that she is grateful for slavery but ends in a subtle rebuke of the institution.

The vast majority of Wheatley's poems do not address slavery but instead are written to some important person on some notable occasion, such as the second poem here, written to George Washington. Washington praised her work in 1773 and corresponded with her. Poems such as those here provide an interesting window into Revolutionary-era culture.

On Being Brought from Africa to America

'TWAS mercy brought me from my Pagan
   land,
Taught my benighted soul to understand
That there's a God, that there's a Saviour too:
Once I redemption neither sought nor knew,
Some view our sable race with scornful eye,
"Their colour is a diabolic die."

Remember, Christians, Negroes, black as Cain,
May be refin'd, and join th' angelic train.

His Excellency General Washington

Celestial choir! enthron'd in realms of light,
Columbia's scenes of glorious toils I write.
While freedom's cause her anxious breast
  alarms,
She flashes dreadful in refulgent arms.
See mother earth her offspring's fate bemoan,
And nations gaze at scenes before unknown!
See the bright beams of heaven's revolving
  light
Involved in sorrows and the veil of night!

The Goddess comes, she moves divinely fair,
Olive and laurel binds Her golden hair:
Wherever shines this native of the skies,
Unnumber'd charms and recent graces rise.

Muse! Bow propitious while my pen relates
How pour her armies through a thousand
  gates,
As when Eolus heaven's fair face deforms,
Enwrapp'd in tempest and a night of storms;
Astonish'd ocean feels the wild uproar,
The refluent surges beat the sounding shore;
Or think as leaves in Autumn's golden reign,
Such, and so many, moves the warrior's train.

In bright array they seek the work of war,
Where high unfurl'd the ensign waves in air.
Shall I to Washington their praise recite?
Enough thou know'st them in the fields of
  fight.
Thee, first in peace and honors—we demand
The grace and glory of thy martial band.
Fam'd for thy valour, for thy virtues more,
Hear every tongue thy guardian aid implore!

One century scarce perform'd its destined
  round,
When Gallic powers Columbia's fury found;
And so may you, whoever dares disgrace
The land of freedom's heaven-defended race!
Fix'd are the eyes of nations on the scales,
For in their hopes Columbia's arm prevails.
Anon Britannia droops the pensive head,
While round increase the rising hills of dead.
Ah! Cruel blindness to Columbia's state!
Lament thy thirst of boundless power too late.

Proceed, great chief, with virtue on thy side,
Thy ev'ry action let the Goddess guide.
A crown, a mansion, and a throne that shine,
With gold unfading, WASHINGTON! Be
  thine.

Source: Basker, James G. 2002 *Amazing Grace: An Anthology of Poems about Slavery.* New Haven: Yale University, 293.

Phillis Wheatley's Letter to Reverend Samson Occom Containing a Strong Antislavery Statement (February 11, 1774)

In 1761 John Wheatley, a Boston merchant, purchased a slave girl of about 8 years of age for his wife, who wanted a companion and household servant. Mrs. Wheatley taught Phillis how to read and write, and by the age of 14 Phillis was writing poetry. Although Phillis was treated like a daughter in the Wheatley family, she was an anomaly, an educated black slave, and so she never fit comfortably into any group, either black or white, in Boston society. The following is a letter she wrote in 1774, when *she was about 21 years old. The letter contains the strongest antislavery statement that we have from Phillis Wheatley.*

Reverend and honoured Sir,
   I have this day received your obliging kind epistle, and am greatly satisfied with your reasons respecting the negroes, and think highly reasonable what you offer in vindication of their natural rights: Those that invade them cannot be insensible that the divine

light is chasing away the thick darkness which broods over the land of Africa; and the chaos which has reigned so long, is converting into beautiful order, and reveals more and more clearly the glorious dispensation of civil and religious liberty, which are so inseparably united, that there is little or no enjoyment of one without the other: Otherwise, perhaps, the Israelites had been less solicitous for their freedom from Egyptian slavery; I do not say they would have been contented without it, by no means; for in every human breast God has implanted a principle, which we call love Freedom; it is impatient of oppression, and pants for deliverance; and by the leave of our modern Egyptians I will assert, that the same principle lives in us. God grant deliverance in his own way and time, and get him honour upon all those whose avarice impels them to countenance and help forward the calamities of their fellow creatures. This I desire not for their hurt, but to convince them of the strange absurdity of their conduct, whose words and actions are so diametrically opposite. How well the cry for liberty, and the reverse disposition for the exercise of oppressive power over others agree—I humbly think it does not require the penetration of a philosopher to determine.

Source: *Connecticut Gazette,* March 11, 1774. Available at Perspective in Literature, http://www.csustan.edu/english /reuben/pal/chap2/wheatley.html.

Wilkinson, Jemima (1752–1819)

Evangelist Jemima Wilkinson, as part of the religious fervor of the Great Awakening, preached sexual abstinence and acceptance of all people. Believing that she was God's holy vessel, she was the first American woman to establish a utopian religious community. Wilkinson established Jerusalem in western New York in 1794.

Born on November 19, 1752, in what was then the colony of Rhode Island, Jemima Wilkinson was the 8th of 12 children of Quakers Jeremiah and Amey Whipple Wilkinson. They named her Jemima because it had been the name of one of Job's daughters in the Old Testament. Lacking a formal education, Wilkinson was self-taught and read the Bible as her primary source of information about the world. Born in poverty, she would rely on elite patrons for her economic support for most of her life.

Strong and athletic, Wilkinson was an adept horse rider from her youth. In adulthood she was strong enough to fell trees for her settlement in western New York. Because she had been raised a Quaker, Wilkinson believed that women could be religious leaders. Wilkinson's memory allowed her to quote long passages from the Bible. The First Great Awakening led her to deepen her faith. In her 20s she became ill, possibly with typhus, and experienced what she believed to be a vision of two archangels. Wilkinson believed that her old self had died and that God had resurrected her with a new soul. Acting in everything as she believed God had commanded her, she held revival meetings in her home and traveled about New England preaching. She recruited four sisters and one brother to her ministry. She preached to American and British troops during the American Revolution and began to call herself the Publick Universal Friend and the Friend of Sinners.

General Horatio Gates attended one of Wilkinson's meetings and thought that she believed herself to be the second coming of Jesus in female form. Wilkinson never made a clear claim of divinity. In fairness, it is difficult to reconstruct what she believed because she was a mystic and spoke ambiguously. She stressed morality and the universality of biblical stories. Her mature beliefs meshed with the Quakerism of her childhood, though the Quakers abjured her beliefs.

In 1788 Wilkinson believed that God was calling her to preach in Britain, but in the midst of war the Royal Navy would not let her cross the Atlantic. Filled with the Holy Spirit, she attempted to cure the sick as Jesus is said to have done, but these efforts were unsuccessful. In one case a woman died in her arms. In the 1780s Rhode Island recognized Wilkinson's ministry as a denomination, though she protested that she had no ties with any denomination. Her ties were to Jesus alone. Nonetheless, her religious group was called the Society of Universal Friends. That decade

Wilkinson expanded her ministry beyond New England to Pennsylvania. In 1782 she arrived in Philadelphia, where she made both converts and enemies.

Tiring of the urban bustle, Wilkinson came to believe that God called her into the wilderness to worship in relative solitude. For Wilkinson the wilderness meant western New York, where in 1788 she made her first attempt at establishing a utopian community. The Shaker communities in Pennsylvania may have been her inspiration. Her initial attempt was unsuccessful because the community could not afford to buy the land, but in 1794 Wilkinson and her followers established Jerusalem, New York. Visitors were welcome in the community, which stressed friendship and kindness. People who broke the community's rules on absolute sexual abstinence were asked to leave.

Spiritual matters consumed Wilkinson, so she entrusted the leadership of the community to her closest confidante, Sarah Friend. Because Wilkinson and her followers were the first community of white people in a region populated by Seneca people, she claimed herself a Seneca chief, though there is no evidence that the Senecas agreed to her title. Wilkinson died on July 1, 1819, and was buried in an unmarked grave, apparently in accord with her wishes. After her death rumors arose that she had risen from the dead, and her followers attributed miracles to her. Her utopian community dissolved after 1800.

Christopher Cumo

See also *Vol. 1, Sec. 2:* Great Awakening; Quakers; *Vol. 2, Sec. 1:* Shakers; Utopian Movement

Further Reading

Wisbey, Herbert A. 1964. *Pioneer Prophetess: Jemima Wilkinson, the Publick Universal Friend.* Ithaca, NY: Cornell University Press.

Williams, Eunice (1696–1785)

The life story of Eunice Williams, captured by Native Americans in 1704, resisted standard captivity narratives, which were designed to demonstrate the horrors of what could happen to God-fearing Puritans who fell into the hands of "heathen savages." Williams actually found her life among the native people to be empowering and rejected her English family's efforts to return her to colonial English society.

Williams was born on September 17, 1696, in Deerfield, Massachusetts, to Reverend John Williams and Eunice Mather Williams. On the morning of February 29, 1704, when Eunice Williams was seven years old, a combined force of Frenchmen, Abenakis, Hurons, Mohawks, and Pennacooks attacked Deerfield. They killed 48 people, including Williams's 2 youngest siblings. Among the 112 of the town's residents who were captured were the surviving members of the Williams family. The raiding party forced their captives to march to Canada. Many of them did not survive the trek, including Williams's mother.

Once in Canada, the surviving Williamses were dispersed among the various Native American groups. Williams was adopted into a Mohawk family to replace a female who had died of smallpox. By 1707, most of the Williams family had been released by their captors and had returned to New England. Soon thereafter, her father John Williams authored *The Redeemed Captive Returning to Zion,* which included his version of the family's experiences at the hands of both the Iroquois and the French. Throughout the text, it was obvious that he was especially distressed by his daughter's conversion by French Jesuits to Catholicism, which he discovered from her in one of the few conversations they had while both were in Canada.

John Williams's narrative suggested that his freedom and that of most of his children was proof of God's love for Puritans. The narrative also emphasized the inferiority of native people, particularly when compared to Puritan Christians. Religious leaders of the day, most notably Cotton and Increase Mather, used captivity narratives to fortify the religious and political beliefs of their followers. Due to the popularity of *The Redeemed Captive Returning to Zion,* Eunice Williams's continued captivity became problematic over time for both the Williams and Mather families. Her continued existence among Catholic native people begged the question that if God truly favored the Puritans, then how could a member of two of the most prominent families of ministers in New England choose to embrace Catholicism and a Mohawk way of life?

Little is documented from Williams's life among the Mohawks. She lived in Kahnawake, near Montreal, Canada, where she learned Iroquois culture and customs. She would have lived in a family unit and village where women were seen as equal to but different from men. While learning to speak Iroquois, she forgot her native tongue. The Jesuits gave her the name Margaret when she was baptized. As an adult among the Iroquois, she was known as A'ongote. She married Arosen, and they had three children together. Native child-rearing practices would have been significantly more relaxed and emotion-based than the practices of the Puritans, who viewed children as sinful and in need of physical correction.

Although Williams remained with the Mohawks for the rest of her life, she retained a connection with her original family through her surname. Because the Iroquois were matrilineal, her children used Williams as their last name. Despite what her Puritan relatives believed, Williams was not a captive of the Mohawks; she one of them. She consciously rebuffed efforts to be "freed," as she preferred to stay in Kahnawake with her husband, children, and extended native family.

Williams periodically gathered information about her English family. She was aware that her father had gone back to minister to the people of Deerfield and had remarried. She cited his marriage as the reason that she was not willing to visit him. Once John Williams died, his son Stephen continued to encourage Eunice Williams to return to New England. Although she never returned to live with her white family, she visited them in 1740, 1741, 1743, and 1760. On those trips, she was accompanied by Mohawk relatives and an interpreter.

Williams died at Kahnawake on November 26, 1785. Her great-grandson Eleazer Williams produced a captivity narrative in 1842 titled *A History of the Life and Captivity of Miss Eunice Williams* that celebrated Williams's life as a Catholic Kahnawake Mohawk. Although intended to counter John Williams's views toward Catholic Indians in *The Redeemed Captive Returning to Zion,* Eleazer's book wasn't published until 2006.

Today Williams's life story stands in direct conflict with standard captivity narratives and some historical approaches to native people. Captivity narratives

such as Mary Rowlandson's were designed to illustrate the superiority of Euro-Americans and savagery of Native Americans. Other captivity tales, such as Jane McCrea's, were used as prowar, procolonist propaganda. In these narratives women are unwilling victims of barbaric Indians. Williams, like a number of other Euro-American women, did not regret her "captivity" and indeed was not actually a captive but a willing member of the Iroquois people, finding in that life greater power and freedom than she would have as a Puritan.

John R. Burch Jr.

See also McCrea, Jane; Rowlandson, Mary; *Vol. 1, Sec. 1:* Iroquois Confederacy; Matrilineal Descent; *Vol. 1, Sec. 2:* Captives, English; Captivity Narratives; Protestant Women

Further Reading

Demos, John. 1994. *The Unredeemed Captive: A Family Story from Early America.* New York: Knopf.

Haefeli, Evan, and Kevin Sweeney. 2003. *Captors and Captives: The 1704 French and Indian Raid on Deerfield.* Amherst: University of Massachusetts Press.

Haefeli, Evan, and Kevin Sweeney, eds. 2006. *Captive Histories: English, French, and Native Narratives of the 1704 Deerfield Raid.* Amherst: University of Massachusetts Press.

Simpson, Audra. 2009. "Captivating Eunice: Membership, Colonialism, and Gendered Citizenships of Grief." *Wicazo Sa Review* 24(2) (Fall): 105–129.

THEMATIC ISSUES ESSAY

Middle- and upper-class women in the Revolutionary and New Republic periods (1754–1819) built upon the customs and culture of their colonial-era predecessors. Just as the American colonies moved from a society based on hierarchy and deference toward one of liberty and self-sufficiency, women's lives moved in tandem, albeit on a much more gradual and limited basis. Meanwhile, the lives of African American and Native American women were not governed by the same social and cultural schema reserved for white women. In general, they were considered to have even less intellectual ability and potential for leadership than white women; though many such women proved that they could possess formidable attitudes and intellectual skills, most nonwhite women were governed by different codes of conduct that more closely reflected society's assessment of them as slaves or other outsiders, and society ascribed its assumptions to them accordingly.

Key to the revolution against British rule was the shift in colonial ideology that focused on the value of liberty not only as a political change but also as a way of life, a concept known as republicanism. Strongly influenced by the Enlightenment, a philosophical movement of the 17th and 18th centuries that emphasized the use of reason and the rejection of tradition based on the works of John Locke (1632–1704), Isaac Newton (1643–1727), and others, republicanism evolved from the concept of natural rights, among them life, liberty, and property. Self-sufficient property ownership and public virtue, or the willingness to sacrifice one's own personal interests for the benefit of the greater good, were key components in republican ideology.

Gender Roles

As revolutionary rhetoric expanded, white women's lives and the ways in which they negotiated the expectations imposed upon them became more nuanced as they assimilated revolutionary ideals. These new ideologies were reflected in almost all areas of the feminine experience, and once the American Revolutionary War ended, the task of building the new nation encouraged women to further refine their activities and belief systems in order to more effectively negotiate the changing world around them. When Benjamin Franklin (1706–1790) deliberated on the choice of a spinning wheel or a tea table as a wedding gift for his sister Jane, he chose the spinning wheel—better to encourage his sister to be practical and industrious rather than merely decorative. This image is a fitting metaphor for the expectations for such women in the Revolutionary and Early Republic eras.

The white women of the Revolutionary and New Republic had been raised in a society in which social and cultural norms tied them inextricably to their husbands in virtually all matters of their daily lives. The hardworking housewives of the prewar 18th century became the bastions of republican motherhood in the late 18th and early 19th centuries. While Revolutionary-era women did not emerge from America's fight for liberty with much more freedom or rights of their own—which they did not actively pursue—they did gain a new purpose. As republican mothers they were deemed responsible for instilling in their children an understanding and appreciation for the republican way of life—a necessity in the ever-evolving world of the New Republic.

The boundaries of the circumscribed life were frequently tested, however, by women who found opportunities to take part in the political, intellectual, economic, and cultural world outside their usual purview. While most women of the late 18th and early 19th centuries were expected to be helpmeets to their husbands and caretakers of their homes and families above all else, their actions beyond the home and hearth distinguished them as much more than simply "notable housewives" or "pretty gentlewomen." These two terms described the ultimate goals to which women were expected to aspire. To be notable required dedicated attention to every aspect of work in the home, and to be referred to as notable was among the highest of compliments. If 18th-century commentators are to be believed, the women of the time never stopped moving in order to fulfill this feminine ideal. Nothing took the place of what went on inside her home, and she was expected to excel—even revel—in the perfect completion of every task.

While differing in the types of women to which they referred, both terms carried with them the central theme of devotion to home and family and the binary division of responsibilities between male and female. In the commonly accepted assessment of the time, women were considered to be physically and intellectually weaker than men, which rendered them unsuitable for life in the public sphere. This was not considered to be a shortcoming but rather an indication of the precise suitability of women for particular important tasks for which men were specifically unsuited. This, above all, was a woman's purpose: to defer to her husband's judgment, which due to his own natural makeup and purpose was considered superior to hers. It was her duty and obligation to defer to his decisions and his will. Too much education was considered unnecessary and even dangerous. As a person whose purpose in life required her to be perfectly attuned to the needs of her own household, interest in public affairs was unnecessary. Although women were considered the weaker sex, this weakness was a natural and necessary condition that perfectly completed the whole when combined with her husband's abilities.

While this was the dominant ideology in place, it was not always strictly adhered to by the women it claimed to define. During the Revolutionary period, women participated in boycotts of British goods, raised funds for the support of the Continental Army, and served as camp followers, spies, and even soldiers. Bold, well-educated elite women such as Mercy Otis Warren (1728–1814) wrote literary works that bolstered the Patriot cause. Ordinary women, including slaves and servants, hid information in the folds of their skirts and passed it across enemy lines. The vast majority of women participating in these activities did so while also managing a household and family, which was itself an all-consuming task. Clearly, while custom and propriety dictated that women of the time served best while within the confines of hearth and home, the women themselves did not always see it that way.

Education

Formal education for females was not considered a priority during the colonial era due to the perception of women's limited intellectual ability and the dominant ideology that the proper role of women was as wife, mother, and helpmeet. Indeed, it could be a dangerous thing; when a friend asked Massachusetts Bay Colony founder John Winthrop for advice concerning a marital issue, Winthrop replied that the problem was caused by his wife's habit of reading too much. Young women were educated but in different ways and to different degrees than young men as befit their proper roles in colonial society. The ideology of republican motherhood convinced some men to educate women so that as mothers they could contribute to the early education of their sons.

While boys often attended schools and colleges in order to obtain the broadest education possible, girls were usually taught at home. The curriculum included reading but not necessarily writing; religious studies and instruction in common household tasks rounded out the education deemed necessary for the proper housewife. In addition to these basics, girls from elite families were often schooled in ornamental subjects such as dance, music, art, and fine needlework. As the colonial period progressed, females of elite social status were encouraged to expand their knowledge to include natural philosophy, mathematics, and other subjects more common to the education of young men. This emphasis on more advanced education for women did not extend to a broader range of social classes until after the American Revolution, when ideology regarding the role of women in American society began to change.

Work, Waged and Unwaged

Rural women achieved notability for the level of perfection they attained in the keeping of their home, an endeavor that included not only housework but also dairying and other forms of farm labor typically reserved for women. Their notability also carried with it the responsibility for home manufactures, primarily the fabrication of clothing and the production of foodstuffs. Such a list of daily chores was not only repetitive but was also physically draining, particularly when considering that there were almost always children underfoot who also required attention. For southern women on plantations, enslaved women performed this manual work, with slave-owning females acting as supervisors and managers. This often created uncomfortable connections between enslaved biracial women who were the children of the husbands of the women who owned them.

Middle- and upper-class women who lived in cities had far more access to finished goods than their countrified sisters and therefore were spared some of the heavy work associated with rural life. While this did give them more time and opportunity for leisure, much of it spent receiving and calling on friends, it did not absolve urban women from the responsibility to be notable. While notable housewives in the country complained about their inability to keep things clean, city women used the time not spent on producing home goods to do exactly that. What "pretty gentle-women" lacked in cupboards full of home-produced cheese and textiles they made up for in sparkling floors and highly polished tabletops. The urban woman's list of daily tasks was no less exhausting than that of her counterpart in the country, as urban women still tended kitchen gardens, did laundry, cooked, and performed all the other duties necessary in order to keep an urban home in notable condition, all the while minding her children as well. Even women with servants or slaves often remarked that management of these assistants often took as much time and effort as doing the tasks themselves. The servants and slaves themselves, whether in rural or urban settings, spent their days performing the same household tasks that would have occupied their mistresses without the option of delegating their work to someone else. In addition, they were just as likely to perform agricultural work alongside male laborers.

Females became aware of the gendered arrangement of public and private spheres at a very early age; girls were trained by their mothers in the household arts, which included not only such tasks as sewing, cooking, and cleaning but also spinning, candle making, gardening, beer making, dairy management, and any number of additional crafts necessary in order to properly operate a home. Urban women had more access to finished goods than did rural women, and some women had more help from servants, but all were involved to one degree or another in the use of these skills in order to fulfill the functions of a proper wife and mother. Women and girls often exchanged work with their friends and neighbors in order to maximize individual talents. For example, an especially competent knitter who was not particularly good at spinning (or who did not own a spinning wheel) might offer to knit for a friend who was the better spinner. The most prevalent income-producing activity was the barter or sale of surplus household production, such as eggs and wool.

Studies of women's nonwaged work reflect an overwhelming status of women as home keepers. However, women did sometimes work outside the home, either as wage earners or as employees in family businesses. While scant evidence exists of wage-earning women during the colonial period, by the time of the American Revolution women's participation in the paid workforce becomes apparent. It must also be noted that lack of written evidence does not mean that women did not earn money outside the home. Many women likely marketed foodstuffs and participated in the marketplace but kept no written records of their business pursuits due to widespread female illiteracy. A gendered division of labor dictated which jobs were appropriate for women and which were acceptable for men. For example, men primarily tailored garments, and while some women tailors can be identified, women generally sewed gowns, shirts, and similar apparel.

Legal and Political Power

In legal matters, single women wielded more power than married women. The *feme sole* (single female) had broader legal rights and privileges, particularly those related to property ownership, than a married woman, or *feme covert* (covered female). The exception to this was the "deputy husband" function performed by married women when their husbands were away and the legal matters of the home or business fell to the wives. Under these circumstances, decisions normally reserved for the husband were legally made by the wife. This concept obviously contained contradictions; while the husband was present, the wife was considered to be unequipped in terms of intellect or experience to make crucial decisions, but while he was away, her ability to function in his stead was legally recognized as possible and appropriate.

The major political question for women of the Revolutionary era was on which side their sympathies might lie. This question is both easier and more difficult to answer than one might expect. First of all, a woman's political alliances were, by definition, the same as her husband's. That said, while the disagreement over taxes, tea, and so many other issues involved colonists and England and while most colonists were indeed British, many were not. Those who were not had little interest in arguing over the subtleties of British rights. Regardless of their sympathies or lack thereof, many found themselves just as embroiled in the conflict. At the least, they fell subject to both colonial and British policies that impacted their daily lives. As household managers, women of all backgrounds found themselves negotiating the difficult issue of providing clothing, provisions, and supplies for their families.

Much of this hardship came about due to the boycotting and nonimportation of British manufactured goods. As one of the most successful tactics employed by American colonists over the course of the Revolution, boycotting and nonimportation agreements were economic measures in which women could participate in revolutionary activity. The agreements signed by women pledging to boycott the purchase of imported British products were political statements of their support for the American cause and an expression of their potential political power.

By refusing to purchase tea and other similar imported goods, women of this period exerted significant economic pressure on the British mercantile system already reeling from the debt incurred in the French and Indian War. The mercantile system was the model for economic success at the heart of England's struggle for empire in the New World. The mercantile plan required the American colonies to send raw materials to England, which would in turn send finished goods to the colonies. By refusing to purchase imported goods from the mother country, women—responsible for nearly all the purchasing of household goods, especially in urban areas where most revolutionary fervor occurred—could exert their own form of power and influence. By further producing comparable home-manufactured goods, women sustained such movements and reinforced revolutionary assertions that the colonies could support themselves without British interference. Boycotting played a crucial role in the chain of events leading to the American Revolution in that it was not only an effective form of protest against unpopular British policies but also struck at the vulnerable economic nucleus of England's New World strategy. Without the involvement of revolutionary women, the nonimportation and boycotting movements so instrumental in the success of the American Revolution would not have been possible.

The women who signed boycotting agreements and abided by them were clearly protesting on two separate levels. On its face, these agreements mirrored the complaints of the male sector of revolutionary society. However, by vowing to forgo the purchase of imported British goods, many of them luxury items, American women protested any allusion to the perceived weakness in their feminine constitutions that made such items attractive to them in the first place. Indeed, this protest could be quite laden with meaning. During the Stamp Act Crisis (1765), the British government required certain items, among them all colonial legal documents, to be produced on official stamped paper. In protest, some young women refused to obtain marriage licenses until they could be legally procured on unstamped paper.

Once the Revolutionary War began in earnest, women participated on numerous levels. From the beginning of the war, women of all socioeconomic levels became camp followers. Women attached themselves to military units for any number of reasons, and the conditions they experienced varied widely. Officers' wives, for instance, would often arrive en masse at the winter encampments. Their presence ushered in a social season that lifted morale for their husbands and enlisted men as well. Beginning with no less than Martha Washington herself, these women were afforded comfortable lodgings and venues for festivities. Some women sought out work as nurses, cooks, and laundresses, which brought with them wages paid by the army. This was a precarious position, however, as they were often subject to sexual harassment by unruly troops. Some worked for individual soldiers, providing cooking, sewing, and laundry services. There were other career camp followers as well. Sutlers (traveling merchants) and prostitutes were regular fixtures on an army's march, and women figured prominently among them. Perhaps the most pathetic of the camp followers were the women who were forced to travel with the army in order to be with their husbands because they had nowhere else to go. These women frequently had their children in tow as well, for without close proximity to their husbands these women had neither the personal safety nor the financial wherewithal to take care of their families alone.

Among the most courageous female participants in the American Revolution were the women who directly participated in the war as spies, soldiers, and emissaries and worked shoulder-to-shoulder with their husbands. Indeed, women were so ubiquitous on the battlefield that the mythical figure of Molly Pitcher, one of the best-known revolutionary heroines, emerged as a composite symbol of all the women who carried water to cool the cannons and refresh the troops. Deborah Sampson Gannett, who enlisted under the name Robert Shurtleff, was one of the many women who donned men's clothes and enlisted in the Continental Army. She served approximately 18 months before an army surgeon discovered her secret during the course of medical treatment. Other women followed suit. Besides Gannett, Ann Bailey, Anne Smith, Sally St. Clair, and Anna Maria Lane, who enlisted alongside her husband, are some of the women who are known to have disguised themselves as men in order to fight on the front lines. There were likely many more whose contributions have not been discovered.

Responses to these women's tactics were varied. Gannett was honorably discharged and received a soldier's pension. She later traveled on a lecture tour, giving her wartime experiences to packed houses. Margaret Corbin received a pension as a disabled war veteran. For her efforts, Bailey was discharged, fined, and jailed, and Smith was also jailed and fined. St. Clair paid the ultimate price in battle in 1782.

Immigration and Migration

From the earliest period of migration, women came to the colonies in much smaller numbers than men. Some societies, such as the Puritans of New England and the Germans who populated the lower reaches of the Mississippi River during the French colonization of Louisiana, were more likely to come in family groups than the early immigrants to other colonies. However, in Virginia, for example, very few women immigrated with the initial wave of settlement; between 1620 and 1622, only 147 women were transported to that colony. The resulting low ratio of females to males did not begin to reconcile in earnest until after the 1660s, first in New England and later in other colonies. The English represented the majority of immigrants in most North American seaboard colonies, followed by Germans and Scotch-Irish.

Women who came to the colonies alone usually arrived as indentured servants in the earlier years. It is believed that the earliest African women brought to British America came as indentured servants. But soon, all African women would arrive as slaves and be identified as property rather than people.

Other colonial immigration patterns differed from those of British North America. The immigration of French women to colonial Louisiana ranged from Ursuline nuns to female criminals and prostitutes. The severe lack of marriageable women in the colony eventually prompted the Crown to send a shipment of suitable women who became known as "casket girls" because of the small boxes of personal belongings they carried with them to the New World. While Spain maintained colonies in North America, Spanish women arrived in much smaller numbers than did female immigrants to other areas of colonization.

Courtship, Marriage, and Divorce

Arranged marriages were not uncommon, especially among the higher ranks of society. Couples entering into matrimony did not expect to be in love with one another on their wedding day, but may have expected to grow to love one another in the future. High on the list of desirable attributes was the social and financial suitability of the bride or groom not only to the intended spouse but also to the family in general; upper-crust marriages forged alliances between families and strengthened social standing. Marrying up to a slightly higher rung on the social ladder was usually desirable, assuming that the proper mate could be found. Indentured servants often had to wait until their term of indenture was up before they could marry, unless their intended could afford to buy out their contract. The ability of slaves to marry depended on their location; they would be subject to receipt of their master's permission, and their marriages were never considered legal.

Not all marriages were arranged, of course, but even in those that were, courtship could begin with simple meetings at church services, dances, parties, and similar social functions. During courtship, young couples often exchanged love letters and tokens of affection. Betrothal, or the intention of marriage, represented a gray area in the relationship somewhere between single status and matrimony, and it appears that the rules regarding sexual interaction were relaxed following betrothal. Young men often visited their sweethearts' homes, and in situations that included sometimes great distances between houses, the young man might even be invited to spend the night.

Once married, wives continued the pattern of family hierarchy they had known all their lives. Previously considered to be under the protection of her father, a wife now prepared to spend her life under the protection of another male authority figure—her husband. Like the greater world around it, the family operated within a hierarchy all its own. Husbands enjoyed the highest status due to their assumed superiority in terms of physical and intellectual ability and their position as providers, decision makers, and actors in the larger community. Wives came next followed by children, with the oldest male in the lead position. In a gendered division of responsibilities, women took care of the home and the general needs of the children, with specific attention to the training of girls in household tasks, which could range from embroidery to animal husbandry. Fathers made decisions that affected the household and prepared their sons for work and civic life. In the case of bonded women, legal marriage was not allowed. Masters sometimes did allow religious ceremonies between enslaved peoples in order to encourage family bonding in hopes that it would make attempts to run away much harder. But enslaved wives never legally belonged to such husbands and could be sold away at any time, as could any children they shared. Other owners did not allow even the pretense of marriage, instead assigning male and female slaves to live together based on preferred physical characteristics in order to breed new generations of healthy slaves.

As the 17th century turned into the 18th century, death of family patriarchs caused the breakup of family properties, necessitating the division of estates into smaller parts in order to compensate heirs. Inheritance customs dictated that sons received land, while daughters received movable property such as furniture and livestock. Most families had numerous children among whom to divide the estate. Likewise, a widow was entitled to a certain percentage of her husband's property, known as her dower right. Therefore, by the first half of the 18th century, each beneficiary of an estate usually received a very small part of the whole. This reality removed much of the need for children to remain unconditionally obedient to their parents in order to preserve a large inheritance and often required them to become more financially independent. Increased Enlightenment emphasis on happiness and reduced emphasis on tradition and duty, coupled with new opinions on the rights of the individual, caused younger people to be less concerned with sexual continence as a social norm and more interested in exercising their own freedoms, ostensibly less constrained by obligations to their families.

Fertility and Fertility Control

Historians have observed a steep increase in the rate of premarital pregnancy among couples who wed in the last quarter of the 18th century. While the levels of sexual freedom in play during this period may seem surprisingly high, the permissiveness of parents was not so much different from earlier generations in the colonial era, who experienced a much lower premarital pregnancy rate. The major difference was the way in which Revolutionary parents attempted to handle the issue of potentially sexually active youths and the very real possibility of premarital pregnancy. Pragmatism played a major role in the way parents and interested third parties dealt with this issue. The serious implications for women concerning this steep rise in pregnancies and its particular relationship to the Revolutionary period merit attention and explanation.

Prior to the middle of the 18th century, bridal pregnancy rates ranged below 20 percent; in the late 17th century, that statistic had been in the single digits. However, by the 1770s and 1780s the percentage of young women who were pregnant on their wedding day had risen dramatically, to over 30 percent (Godbeer 2004, 10). It is important to note that this rise was not necessarily due to an increase in general promiscuity but instead reflects the number of couples who delivered infants early enough to indicate that the brides were pregnant before they married. This rise in the obvious evidence of premarital sexuality begs two questions: (1) What conditions led to this rapid increase in premarital pregnancies? (2) How did parents react to and handle this situation?

The changes depended on a number of factors, among them demographics, place of residence, the influence of Enlightenment ideology, and the rhetoric of freedom and liberty in operation at the time. As in many other factors in the lives of Revolutionary women, the ways in which people internalized these concepts and worked within these conditions impacted the society in which they lived in large and small ways alike. Revolutionary couples also inherited a cultural mind-set that viewed pregnancy out of wedlock as an issue that, unless it was reconciled by the child's father's financial support, represented an economic threat to society more than it did a moral one.

Premarital sexual relations and pregnancies had not been unusual during the colonial period. The impetus for this situation arose from the Puritan understanding of the meaning of betrothal. Consensus dictated that formal betrothal was closely akin to marriage, and therefore the difference between the two was of no great concern in terms of sexual activity. Additionally, the greatest concern of the community was the question of whether or not the young woman and her baby would be supported by the father or if they would become a public burden. In the minds of early colonials, abandonment by the father was a much larger threat to the community than the pregnancy itself. The testimony of a mother regarding paternity was sufficient in order to determine the identity and culpability of the father. Ideally, it was his willingness to support the child that made the community whole again.

So, how to deal with this apparently unfettered access to opportunities for premarital sex? The responses to the problem depended as well on whether the couple lived in an urban or rural setting. In rural locations, pragmatism dictated that parents accept the inevitable and condone overnight stays and unchaperoned visits in order to exert at least some oversight of the relationship. A custom known as bundling allowed courting couples to sleep in the same bed with the requirement that they remained clothed. Sometimes a bundling board, or divider, was used to remind the sweethearts of the separation they must keep. It was also not unusual for parents to adopt a liberal policy concerning the terms of unchaperoned visits as long as said visits were approved and the identity of the suitor known.

Given the increase in bridal pregnancies during the fourth quarter of the 18th century, clearly these methods were not effective in preventing sexual activity. However, they did serve an important purpose in efforts to maintain social stability. By this time, courts had become less concerned with moral issues and more involved in legal matters regarding issues of economics in general. In contrast to previous practice, the word of the mother alone was no longer adequate in order to hold a party responsible for a premarital pregnancy. By condoning sexual activity within the home in the form of unchaperoned visits or overnight stays, parents could more easily ascribe accountability to the specific male in question. Accepting the reality that betrothed couples were probably going to engage in sexual relations anyway, pragmatic allowance of more sexual freedom provided leverage to a young woman's parents should her beloved attempt to dodge responsibility for her condition.

The somewhat ineffective methods of preventing premarital pregnancy among courting couples has already been described. Among married couples, the most commonly used method of controlling family size was breast-feeding. By postponing the weaning of an infant for as long as possible, most women managed to fall into a pattern of one pregnancy every two years. While certainly not a foolproof method, it gave spouses some modicum of control over family size while keeping the birthrate high enough to overcome high infant mortality rates, which virtually guaranteed the loss of one or more children within the first few years of life. Chemical and herbal abortifacients (compounds that caused abortion) were included in medical reference books and were in common use by white women as well as enslaved women, who feared bringing more children into a life of slavery.

Not all marriages resulted in wedded bliss or lasted until the inevitable parting brought by death. Obviously, not all couples adhered to the culturally prescribed strategy of the well-ordered household governed by a decisive father who was assisted by a deferential, competent, notable housewife. Divorces did occur and probably would have been more common if they had been more widely available. Only in New England was marriage considered a civil contract that could be dissolved, and individual colonies varied greatly in their interpretations of the scope of the contract. Most other colonies were governed by laws based on ecclesiastical rules that effectively placed a high burden of proof on the party requesting a divorce.

Childbirth and Child Rearing

By the early 1800s following a period of exceptionally high bridal pregnancy rates and low infant mortality rates, American society changed the focus of pregnancy from one of duty to a more personal experience that celebrated the child. The movement encouraged women to shorten their period of childbearing from the traditional every two years pattern to one of less children over fewer years. This attitude coincided well with the demands of republican motherhood, which necessitated the careful attention to the minds and spirits of children rather than their importance as units of labor or products of feminine duty.

Children were a valuable resource in terms of the potential labor they could provide. Large families increased the productivity of the family, particularly in rural areas where more hands were needed to perform daily tasks. Daughters were particularly important in the operation of the household, and while they learned a variety of tasks, some jobs were considered most suitable for young women. Girls learned to spin at an early age and from that point were tasked with most of the fiber and textile production in the household. This activity was so ubiquitous that the term "spinster" became synonymous with unmarried women, while the expression "the distaff side" (a term referring to a part of the spinning wheel) described women in general. A mother's primary responsibility to her daughters was to teach them everything she knew about the effective operation of a household, an education that included not only how to do laundry and milk cows but also how she would fit into the family structure in relation to her husband.

Violence, Domestic and Sexual

Laws in Revolutionary-era America based in coverture assumed that daughters belonged to their fathers and that wives belonged to their husbands. Thus, the law held that a man had the right to do with his wife what he wished, up to and including beating her. Moreover, gender ideologies and social custom encouraged both men and women to think that wives owed their husbands obedience. As a result, women victimized by family violence were left with few or no resources.

Sexual violence, both within and outside of the family, was probably as widespread in this time period as any other in American history. Unfortunately, because the law did not recognize marital rape or encourage rape accusations outside of marriage, incidents of rape are difficult to track. Some women successfully prosecuted rape cases, but the numbers are low.

African American slave women had no recourse against rape. Masters legally owned slave women and were allowed to have sex with them, even without consent. Moreover, notions of consent were muddied by both masters' property rights and racist ideologies that held that slave women were sexually libidinous and thus eager for all sexual contact. Slave women did take steps to avoid unwanted sexual contact with masters and other men but often did so unsuccessfully.

Clothing and Fashion

Women's clothing styles changed quite a bit in this period. As the American Revolution began, women continued to wear multiple layers of skirts and petticoats, reinforced by relatively rigid corsetry. Upper-class women wore finer fabrics and adorned their dresses with lace and satin ribbons, while lower-class women wore plain cloth, often hemp or wool based. Slave women and poor white women would have owned only one dress of rough material and often gone shoeless. For the upper-classes, shoes often had heels but were not differentiated by right and left foot. Married women wore hats or caps, much as they had since the Renaissance, while unmarried women and girls could wear their hair down.

As the turn of the century approached, women's clothing took on a simplicity not seen in decades. Heavy skirts and petticoats began to fall out of style for simple shift dresses, often worn without elaborate corsetry. The empire waist came into vogue for dresses, and for upper-class women feathered headdresses became highly desirable. Poor and slave women continued to dress simply, in great part because they could not afford to do otherwise.

Lee Davis Smith

Further Reading

Adams, Charles Francis. 1856. *The Works of John Adams, Second President of the United States: With a Life of the Author, Notes, and Illustrations, by His Grandson Charles Francis Adams.* Boston: Little, Brown.

Berkin, Carol. 1996. *First Generations: Women in Colonial America.* New York: Hill and Wang.

Berkin, Carol. 2005. *Revolutionary Mothers: Women in the Struggle for America's Independence.* New York: Vintage Books.

Breen, T. H. 2004. *The Marketplace of Revolution: How Consumer Politics Shaped American Independence.* New York: Oxford University Press.

Godbeer, Richard. 2004. "Courtship and Sexual Freedom in Eighteenth-Century America." *OAH Magazine of History* 18: 9–13.

Kerber, Linda K. 1980. *Women of the Republic: Intellect & Ideology in Revolutionary America.* New York: Norton.

Klepp, Susan E. 1998. "Revolutionary Bodies: Women and the Fertility Transition in the Mid-Atlantic Region, 1760–1820." *Journal of American History* 85: 910–945.

Lewis, Jan, and Kenneth A. Lockridge. 1988. "'Sally Has Been Sick': Pregnancy and Family Limitation among Virginia Gentry Women, 1780–1830." *Journal of Social History* 22: 5–19.

Main, Gloria L. 1994. "Gender, Work, and Wages in Colonial New England." *William and Mary Quarterly* 51: 39–66.

Main, Gloria L. 2006. "Rocking the Cradle: Downsizing the New England Family." *Journal of Interdisciplinary History* 37: 35–58.

Norton, Mary Beth. 1980. *Liberty's Daughters: The Revolutionary Experience of American Women, 1750–1800.* Boston: Little, Brown.

Norton, Mary Beth. 1984. "The Evolution of White Women's Experience in Early America." *American Historical Review* 89: 593–619.

Rothman, Ellen K. 1982. "Sex and Self-Control: Middle-Class Courtship in America, 1770–1870." *Journal of Social History* 15: 409–425.

Wood, Gordon S. 1991. *The Radicalism of the American Revolution.* New York: Vintage Books.

Wood, Gordon S. 1998. *The Creation of the American Republic, 1776–1787.* Chapel Hill: University of North Carolina Press.

Zagarri, Rosemarie. 1998. "The Rights of Men and Women in Post-Revolutionary America." *William and Mary Quarterly* 55: 203–230.

BIBLIOGRAPHY

Allen, Thomas B. 2010. *Tories: Fighting for the King in America's First Civil War.* New York: Harper.

Allgor, Catherine. 2000. *Parlor Politics: In Which the Ladies of Washington Help Build a City and a Government.* Charlottesville: University Press of Virginia.

Allgor, Catherine. 2013. *Dolley Madison: The Problem of National Unity.* Boulder, CO: Westview.

Attie, Jeanie. 1998. *Patriotic Toil: Northern Women and the American Civil War.* Ithaca, NY: Cornell University Press.

Auslander, Leora. 2009. *Cultural Revolutions: Everyday Life and Politics in Britain, North America, and France.* Los Angeles: University of California Press.

Baumgarten, Linda. 2002. *What Clothes Reveal: The Language of Clothing in Colonial and Federal America.* New Haven, CT: Yale University Press.

Berkin, Carol. 2006 ed. *Revolutionary Mothers: Women in the Struggle for America's Independence.* New York: Vintage.

Bradstreet, Anne. 1981. *The Complete Works of Anne Bradstreet.* Edited by Joseph R. McElrath and Allan P. Robb. Boston: Twayne Publishers.

Brady, Patricia. 2005. *Martha Washington: An American Life.* New York: Viking Penguin

Brady, Patricia. 2011. *A Being So Gentle: The Frontier Love Story of Rachel and Andrew Jackson.* New York: Macmillan.

Case, Stephen H., and Mark Jacob. 2012. *Treacherous Beauty: Peggy Shippen, the Woman behind Bene-*

dict Arnold's Plot to Betray America. Guilford, CT: Lyons.

Castillo, Edward D. 1994. "Gender Status Decline, Resistance, and Accommodation among Female Neophytes in the Missions of California: A San Gabriel Case Study." *American Indian Culture and Research Journal* 18(1): 67–93.

Cordingly, David. 2007. *Seafaring Women: Adventures of Pirate Queens, Female Stowaways, and Sailors' Wives.* New York: Random House.

Demos, John. 1994. *The Unredeemed Captive: A Family Story from Early America.* New York: Knopf.

Dewey, Mary. 1871. *Life and Letters of Catharine M. Sedgwick.* New York: Harper and Brothers.

Diamont, Lincoln. 1998. *Revolutionary Women in the War for Independence: A One-Volume Revised Edition of Elizabeth Ellet's 1848 Landmark Series.* New York: Praeger.

Drinker, Elizabeth Sandwich. 1994. *The Diary of Elizabeth Drinker: The Life Cycle of an Eighteenth-Century Woman.* Edited by Elaine Forman Crane. Boston: Northeastern University Press.

Ellet, E. F. 1998. *Revolutionary Women in the War for American Independence: A One-Volume Revised Edition of Elizabeth's Ellet's 1848 Landmark Series.* Edited by Lincoln Diamant. Westport, CT: Praeger.

Fields, Joseph E. 1994. *Worthy Partner: The Papers of Martha Washington.* Westport, CT: Greenwood.

Furbee, Mary. 2001. *Anne Bailey: Frontier Scout.* Greensboro, NC: Morgan Reynolds Publishing.

Furey, Constance. 2012. "Relational Virtue: Anne Bradstreet, Edward Taylor, and Puritan Marriage." *Journal of Medieval and Early Modern Studies* 42(1): 201–224.

Gellis, Edith B. 1992. *Portia: The World of Abigail Adams.* Bloomington: Indiana University Press.

Godwin, William. 2001 ed. *Memoirs of the Author of A Vindication of the Rights of Woman.* Ontario, Canada: Broadview Literary Texts.

Gordon, Lyndall. 2005. *Vindication: A Life of Mary Wollstonecraft.* New York: Harper.

Gordon-Reed, Annette. 1997. *Thomas Jefferson and Sally Hemings: An American Controversy.* Charlottesville: University Press of Virginia.

Greven, Phillip. 1988. *The Protestant Temperament: Patterns of Child-Rearing, Religious Experience, and the Self in Early America.* Chicago: University of Chicago Press.

Hackel, Steven W. 2003. "Sources of Rebellion: Indian Testimony and the Mission San Gabriel Uprising of 1785." *Ethnohistory* 50(4): 644–688.

Haefeli, Evan, and Kevin Sweeney. 2003. *Captors and Captives: The 1704 French and Indian Raid on Deerfield.* Amherst: University of Massachusetts Press.

Haefeli, Evan, and Kevin Sweeney, eds. 2006. *Captive Histories: English, French, and Native Narratives of the 1704 Deerfield Raid.* Amherst: University of Massachusetts Press.

Hatch, Nathan O. 1989. *The Democratization of American Christianity.* New Haven, CT: Yale University Press.

Holton, Woody. 2010. *Abigail Adams.* New York: Free Press.

Hulton, Ann. 1927. *Letters of a Loyalist Lady: Being the Letters of Anne Hulton, Sister of Henry Hulton, Commissioner of Customs at Boston, 1767–1776.* Cambridge, MA: Harvard University Press.

Hunsaker, Joyce Badgley. 2001. *Sacagawea Speaks: Beyond the Shining Mountains with Lewis and Clark.* Guilford, CT: Globe Pequot.

Hyland, William G. 2009. *In Defense of Thomas Jefferson: The Sally Hemings Sex Scandal.* New York: St. Martin's.

Jennings, Wagoner, Jr., and Wayne J. Urban. 2008. *American Education: A History.* New York: Routledge.

Jensen, Vickie. *Women Criminals: An Encyclopedia of People and Issues,* Vol. 1. Santa Barbara, CA: ABC-CLIO, 2012.

Juettner, Bonnie. 2005. *100 Native Americans Who Changed American History.* Milwaukee: Almanac Library.

Kendall, Elaine. 1999. "Beyond Mother's Knee: The Struggle to Educate Women." In *Portrait of America,* Vol. 1, *To 1877,* edited by Stephen B. Oates, 163–174. Boston: Houghton Mifflin.

Kenslea, Timothy. 2006. *The Sedgwicks in Love: Courtship, Engagement, and Marriage in the Early Republic.* Boston: Northeastern University Press.

Kerber, Linda K. 1980. *Women of the Republic: Intellect and Ideology in Revolutionary America.* Chapel Hill: University of North Carolina Press.

Kessler, Donna J. 1996. *The Making of Sacagawea: A Euro-American Legend.* Tuscaloosa: University of Alabama Press.

Lee, Carol. 2002. *Ballet in Western Culture: A History of its Origin and Evolution.* New York: Routledge.

Levin, Phyllis L. 1987. *Abigail Adams: A Biography.* New York: St. Martin's.

Lewis, Vergil. 2009. *The Life and Times of Anne Bailey: The Pioneer Heroine of the Great Kanawha Valley, 1742–1825.* n.p.: Create Space Independent Publishing Platform.

Mann, Herman. 1972. *The Female Review: Life of Deborah Sampson, the Female Soldier in the War of Revolution.* New York: Arno.

Marszalek, John F. 1997. *The Petticoat Affair: Manners, Mutiny, and Sex in Andrew Jackson's White House.* New York: Free Press.

McCausland, Robert R., and Cynthia MacAlman McCausland. 1992. *The Diary of Martha Ballard, 1785–1812.* Marco Island, FL: Picton.

Meacham, Jon. 2009. *American Lion: Andrew Jackson in the White House.* New York: Random House.

Nagel, Paul. 1987. *The Adams Women: Abigail and Louisa Adams, Their Sisters and Daughters.* New York: Oxford University Press USA.

Neuhaus, Jessamyn. 2012. *Manly Meals and Mom's Home Cooking: Cookbooks and Gender in Modern America.* Baltimore: Johns Hopkins University Press.

Norton, Mary Beth. 1996 ed. *Liberty's Daughters: The Revolutionary Experience of American Women, 1750–1800.* Ithaca, NY: Cornell University Press.

O'Brien, Cormac. 2009. *Secret Lives of the First Ladies.* Philadelphia: Quirk Books.

Phillips, Ruth Bliss. 1998. *Trading Identities: The Souvenir in Native North American Art from the Northeast, 1700–1900.* Seattle: University of Washington Press.

Potter-MacKinnon, Janice. 1995. *While the Women Only Wept: Loyalist Refugee Women in Eastern Ontario.* Montreal: McGill Queens University Press.

Puls, Mark. 2010. *Henry Knox: Visionary General of the American Revolution.* London: Palgrave Macmillan.

Raphael, Ray. 2004. *Founding Myths: Stories That Hide Our Patriotic Past.* New York: New Press.

Robbins, Paula Ivaska. 2009. *Jane Colden: America's First Woman Botanist.* Fleischmanns, NY: Purple Mountain.

Roberts, Cokie. 2004. *Founding Mothers: The Women Who Raised Our Nation.* New York: Harper.

Roberts, Cokie. 2009. *Ladies of Liberty: The Women Who Shaped Our Nation.* New York: Harper Perennial.

Salmon, Marylynn. 1986. *Women and the Law of Property in Early America.* Chapel Hill: University of North Carolina Press.

Scott, Kenneth. 1957. *Counterfeiting in Colonial America.* Philadelphia: University of Pennsylvania Press.

Sharp, Anne Wallace. 2002. *Daring Pirate Women.* Minneapolis: Lerner Publications.

Simmons, Amelia. 1996. *American Cookery, or the Art of Dressing Viands, Fish, Poultry, and Vegetables, and the Best Modes of Making Pastes, Puffs, Pies, Tarts, Puddings, Custards, and Preserves, and All Kinds of Cakes, from the Imperial Plum to Plain Cake: Adapted to this Country, and All Grades of Life.* Introduction by Karen Hess. 1796; reprint, n.p.: Createspace, 2014.

Smith, David Lee. 1997. *Folklore of the Winnebago Tribe.* Norman: University of Oklahoma Press.

Stegeman, John F., and Janet A. Stegeman. 1985. *Caty: A Biography of Catharine Littlefield Greene.* Athens, GA: Brown Thrasher Books.

Stuart, Nancy Rubin. 2012. *Defiant Brides: The Untold Story of Two Revolutionary-Era Women and the Radical Men They Married.* Boston: Beacon.

Sugg, Redding S., Jr. 1978. *Motherteacher: The Feminization of American Education.* Charlottesville: University Press of Virginia.

Teipe, Emily J. 1999. "Will the Real Molly Pitcher Please Stand Up?" *Prologue: Quarterly of the National Archives and Records Administration* 31(2) (Summer): 118–126.

Thomas, Earle. 1996. *The Three Faces of Molly Brant.* Kingston, Ontario: Quarry Press.

Ulrich, Laurel Thatcher. 1990. *A Midwife's Tale: The Life of Martha Ballard Based on Her Diary, 1785–1812*. New York: Knopf.

Ward, Harry M. 1995. *The American Revolution: Nationhood Achieved 1763–1788*. New York: St. Martin's.

Williams, Jeffrey S. 2007. *Pirate Spirit: The Adventures of Anne Bonney*. Lincoln, NE: iUniverse.

Wisbey, Herbert A. 1964. *Pioneer Prophetess: Jemima Wilkinson, the Publick Universal Friend*. Ithaca, NY: Cornell University Press.

Withey, Lynne. 1981. *Dearest Friend: A Life of Abigail Adams*. New York: Free Press.

Wollstonecraft, Mary. 1992. *A Vindication of the Rights of Woman*. Edited by Miriam Brody. New York: Penguin.

Yolen, Jane, and Christine Joy Pratt. 2008. *Sea Queens: Women Pirates around the World*. Watertown, MA: Charlesbridge.

Young, Alfred. 2005. *Masquerade: The Life and Times of Deborah Sampson, Continental Soldier*. New York: Vintage Books.

Editors and Contributors

Editors

Peg A. Lamphier, PhD, teaches in an interdisciplinary program at California State Polytechnic at Pomona in southern California and American history at Mount San Antonio College. An American historian specializing in American Civil War and women's history, she has also authored *Kate Chase and William Sprague: Politics and Gender in a Civil War Marriage* and *Spur Up Your Pegasus: Family Letters of Salmon, Kate, and Nettie Chase, 1844–1873*.

Rosanne Welch, PhD, teaches humanities courses for California State Polytechnic University, Pomona, and MFA screen writing programs at California State University, Fullerton, and Stephens College, Missouri. A film and television historian, Welch has published chapters in *Torchwood Declassified: Investigating Mainstream Cult Television* and *Doctor Who and Race: An Anthology* and has edited *Three Ring Circus: How Real Couples Balance Marriage, Work, and Family* and *The Encyclopedia of Women in Aviation and Space* (ABC-CLIO, 1998).

Contributors

Guy Aiken
University of Virginia

Ellen M. Anstey
Tsongas Industrial History Center
Lowell, MA

Sherri M. Arnold
Morgan State University
Baltimore, MD

Rolando Avila
University of Texas–Rio Grande Valley

Kathleen Barker
Massachusetts Historical Society

Elizabeth Bass
Oklahoma Historical Society
Oklahoma City, OK

Deborah L. Bauer
University of South Florida
Tampa, FL

Stephanie Bayless
Butler Center for Arkansas Studies
Little Rock, AR

Nancy Beach
Independent Scholar
Hillsborough, NC

Roshunda L. Belton
Grambling State University
Grambling, LA

Deena Benjamin
Independent Scholar
Claremont, CA

B. C. Biggs
California State University, Fullerton

Wendy Braun
University of Tennessee–Knoxville

Susan Roth Breitzer
Independent Scholar
Fayetteville, NC

Linda Briley-Webb
Independent Scholar
Scottsdale, AZ

John R. Burch Jr.
Campbellsville University
Campbellville, KY

Leo J. Burke
Independent Scholar
Davis, CA

John Cappucci
University of Windsor
Windsor, Ontario, Canada

Rhonda J. Chadwick
Independent Scholar
North Providence, RI

Denisa Chatman-Riley
California State Polytechnic, Pomona

Sutapa Chaudhuri
Kanailal Bhattacharyya College
India

Anna J. Clutterbuck-Cook
Massachusetts Historical Society
Boston, MA

L. E. Colmenero-Chilberg
Black Hills State University
Spearfish, SD

Christopher Cumo
Independent Scholar
Massillon, OH

Deborah L. Daughetee
Independent Scholar
Las Vegas, NV

Andrew Davis
California State Polytechnic, Pomona

Keri Dearborn
Independent Scholar
Woodland Hills, CA

Maryellen Diotte
University of Kansas
Lawrence, KS

John A. Drobnicki
York College/CUNY

Meredith Eliassen
San Francisco State University

A. K. Estores-Pacheco
Independent Scholar
Lake Forest, CA

Wanda Little Fenimore
Hampden-Sydney College
Farmville, VA

A. H. Forss
Metropolitan Community College
Omaha, NE

Dustin Gann
Arizona State University
Tempe, AZ

Karen S. Garvin
Independent Scholar
College Park, MD

Devora Geller
Brooklyn College-CUNY

Nilanjana Ghosal
Indian Institute of Technology, Hyderbad
India

Charles N. Giberti
University of Cincinnati

Melanie Beals Goan
University of Kentucky
Lexington, KY

Nancy Snell Griffith
Independent Scholar
Davidson, NC

Kathleen Gronnerud
Independent Scholar
Cot De Caza, CA

Kristine Ashton Gunnell
UCLA Center for the Study of Women
Los Angeles, CA

Karin Gutman
Independent Scholar
Marina del Rey, CA

Adrienne Harwell
Independent Scholar
Pomona, CA

Nancy Hendricks
Independent Scholar
Hot Springs, AR

Päivi H. Hoikkala
California State Polytechnic, Pomona

Julie Holcomb
Baylor University
Waco, TX

Marilyn K. Howard
Independent Scholar
Columbus, OK

Rebecca Kohn
San Jose State University

Swathi Krishna S
Indian Institute of Technology Hyderabad
India

Anna L. Krome-Lukens
University of North Carolina
Chapel Hill, NC

Rachel Levy
Harvey Mudd College
Claremont, CA

Leleua Loupe
Mount San Antonio Community College

Eric G. Lovik
College of the Albemarle
Elizabeth City, NC

Mariana Magaña
Independent Scholar
Porterville, CA

Stephanie McKinney
California State Polytechnic, Pomona

Chelsea Medlock
Oklahoma State University

Alberta M. Miranda
Independent Scholar
Victorville, CA

Patit Paban Mishra
Sambalpur University
India

Linda F. Mollno
California State Polytechnic, Pomona

Sean Morton
Independent Scholar
Simcoe, Ontario, Canada

Meghana Muppidi
Independent Scholar
Pomona, CA

Sarah Nation
Independent Scholar
Claremont, CA

Kristin O'Brassill-Kulfan
University of Leicester
United Kingdom

Jennifer Oliver O'Connell
Independent Scholar
Los Angeles, CA

Kathleen M. O'Donnell
California State University
Monterey Bay, CA

Meghan O'Donnell
California State University
Monterey Bay, CA

Valerie Palmer-Mehta
Oakland University
Rochester, MI

Lauren Palmor
University of Washington
Seattle, WA

Cynthia J. Parker
Independent Scholar
Los Angeles, CA

Mark Anthony Phelps
Ozarks Technical Community College
Springfield, MO

Laura J. Ping
The Graduate Center, City University of New York
New York, NY

Elliott Popel
Independent Scholar
Pomona, CA

Amy M. Porter
Texas A&M University–San Antonio

Robin Potter
Brooklyn College

William H. Pruden III
Ravenscroft School
Raleigh, NC

Kimberley Reilly
University of Wisconsin–Green Bay
Green Bay, WI

Christina L. Reitz
Western Carolina University
Cullowhee, NC

Tiffany Rhoades-Piotti
Independent Scholar
New York

Moriah Saldana
Independent Scholar
San Diego, CA

Nathan Saunders
University of South Carolina
Columbia, SC

Allison Elizabeth Schottenstein
University of Texas at Austin
Austin, TX

Lee Davis Smith
Tulane University School of Continuing Studies
New Orleans, LA

Amy Sopcak-Joseph
University of Connecticut
Storrs, CT

Robert L. Thornton
Westfield State University
Westfield, MA

Lynda C. Titterington
Independent Scholar
Columbus, OH

Tabatha Toney
Oklahoma Historical Society

Therese Torres
California State University, Fullerton

Christopher Allen Varlack
Morgan State University
Baltimore, MD

Linda S. Watts
University of Washington, Bothell
Bothell, WA

Rachel Webb
Independent Scholar
Scottsdale, AZ

V. C. Woods
Independent Scholar
Los Angeles, CA

James A. Wren
San Jose State University
San Jose, CA

Cynthia M. Zavala
Independent Scholar
La Puente, CA

Index

2:94–95; Mott, Lucretia Coffin (1793–1880), 2:95–97; Mott, Lucretia Coffin (1793–1880): *Discourse on Woman* (1850), 2:97–99; New York Female Moral Reform Society (NYFMRS), 2:99–100; Nichols, Mary Gove (1810–1884), 2:100–101; Oberlin College, 2:101–102; Oberlin College documents (1836, 1841, 1845, 1860), 2:102–104; Oneida Community (1836–1881), 2:104–105; Peabody, Elizabeth Palmer (1804–1894), 2:105–106; Philadelphia Female Anti-Slavery Society (PFASS), 2:107–108; Post, Amy (1802–1889), 2:108–209; quilts/quilting, 2:109–110; Rose, Ernestine (1810–1892), 2:110–112; Seneca Falls Convention (1848), 2:112–113; separation of spheres, 2:113–115; Shakers (1747–present), 2:115–116; Sigourney, Lydia Howard Huntley (1791–1865), 2:116–117; slave women, 2:117–118; Spiritualism, 2:118–120; Stanton, Elizabeth Cady (1815–1902), 2:120–122; Stanton, Elizabeth Cady (1815–1902): Waterloo, New York, Speech (1848), 2:122–123; Stewart, Maria (1803–1879), 2:123–124; Stewart, Maria (1803–1879): "Religion and the Pure Principles of Morality" speech (1831), 2:125; Stone, Lucy (1818–1893), 2:125–127; Stowe, Harriet Beecher (1811–1896), 2:127–128; Stowe, Harriet Beecher (1811–1896): letter to Frederick Douglass (1851), 2:128–129; suffrage movement, 2:130–132; suffrage movement: Amanda Bloomer's petition for relief of taxation or relief of political disabilities (1878), 2:132; temperance movement, 2:132–134; temperance movement: temperance pledge (1834), 2:135; Ten-Hour Movement, 2:135–136; Ten-Hour Movement: editorial from *Factory Tracts* arguing for a 10-hour workday (1845), 2:136–137; thematic issues essay, 2:160; thematic issues essay: childbirth in child rearing, 2:164; thematic issues essay: courtship, marriage, and divorce, 2:160–161; thematic issues essay: education, 2:165–166; thematic issues essay: fashion and clothing, 2:166; thematic issues essay: fertility and fertility control, 2:163–164; thematic issues essay: gender roles, 2:161–163; thematic issues essay: immigration and migration, 2:161; thematic issues essay: overview, 2:160; thematic issues essay: violence, domestic and sexual, 2:161; thematic issues essay: work, waged and unwaged, 2:164–165; Truth, Sojourner (ca. 1797–1883), 2:137–139; Truth, Sojourner (ca. 1797–1883): certificates of character testifying to Sojourner Truth's trustworthiness as an author (1850), 2:139; Truth, Sojourner (ca. 1797–1883): "Ain't I a Woman?" speech (1851), 2:139–140; Tubman, Harriet (ca. 1820–1913), 2:140–141; Tubman, Harriet (ca. 1820–1913): her account of the rescue of Charles Nalle (1886), 2:141–142; *Uncle Tom's Cabin* (1852), 2:142–143; Underground Railroad, 2:143–146; Utopian Movement, 2:146–147; *The Voice of Industry* (1845–1848), 2:147–148; *The Voice of Industry* (1845–1848) article on worker recruitment practices (1846), 2:148–149; Willard, Emma (1787–1870), 2:149–150; Willard, Emma (1787–1870): excerpt from her *Plan of Female Education* (1819), 2:150–152; Women's

Prison Association (WPA), 2:152–153; women's rights movement, 2:153–155; women's rights movement: divorce complaint of Susan Forster (1826), 2:155–157; women's suffrage associations (1869–1890), 2:157–158; Wright, Frances (1795–1852), 2:158–160. *See also specific entries*

Antheil, George (1900–1959), 3:325
Anthony, Susan B. (1820–1906): American Woman Suffrage Association (AWSA), 2:13; antislavery movement and, 2:13; arrest of, 121; constitutional amendments and, 2:7, 2:14; date and place of birth, 2:13; death of, 2:14; full name of, 2:13; her career as a professional activist, 2:13; *History of Woman Suffrage*, 2:14; Married Women's Property Act, 2:13; National Woman Suffrage Association (NWSA), 2:13; New York State Women's Temperance Party, 2:13; Nineteenth Amendment, 3:120; overview of, 2:12–14; parents of, 2:13; primary document: her remarks at her trial for voting illegally (1873), 2:14–16; in Rochester, 2:13; significance of, 2:12; Stanton, Elizabeth Cady, 2:12, 13; temperance movement, 2:133; Underground Railroad, 2:145; U.S. coinage and, 2:14; Women's Education and Industrial Union (WEIU), 2:371; women's rights and, 2:13; work of, 2:12
antiabortion activism, 4:190
anticommunist women's organizations: American Women Against Communism, 4:8, 9; characteristics of, 4:8; communism and gender, 4:8; House Committee on Un-American Activities (HUAC), 4:8; Minute Women of the U.S.A., 4:8, 9; notable clubs, 4:9; overview of, 4:8–9; the Red Scare, 4:8; against UNESCO, 4:9
antilynching reform, 3:191
Anti-Saloon League (ASL): Association Against the Prohibition Amendment (AAPA), 3:13, 14; date founded, 2:133; Eighteenth Amendment, 3:14; Food and Fuel Control Act (1917), 3:14; overview of, 3:13–14; primary document: "Belated Guests" by Mary Waddell (1921), 3:14–15; Prohibition Bureau, 3:14; publishing house of, 3:14; Russell, Howard Hyde, 3:14; success of, 3:14; support for, 3:14
antislavery fairs: Boston Female Anti-Slavery Society Fair, 2:16; donations, 2:16; importance of, 2:16–17; overview of, 2:16–17; Philadelphia Female Anti-Slavery Society, 2:16, 17; purpose of, 2:16; Townsend, Hannah, 2:16; Weston, Maria, 2:16; Weston, Maria and Anne, 2:16
antistalking legislation: basic model offered by the federal government, 4:280; categories of state law involving, 4:280; federal stalking law, 4:280; first state law, 4:280; Interstate Stalking Act (1996), 4:280; overview of, 4:280–281; significance of, 4:280; state approaches to, 4:280; Violence Against Women Act, 4:280; Violent Crime Control and Law Enforcement Act, 4:280
antisuffrage movement: American conservatism and, 2:284; beliefs of, 2:284; Goldman, Emma, 2:284; New York State Association Opposed to Women's Suffrage, 2:284; overview of, 2:283–284; primary document: antisuffrage

Howe, Julia Ward (1819–1910): her "Battle-Hymn of the Republic" (1861), 2:222–223; Jacobi, Mary Putnam (1842–1906), 2:223–224; Keckley, Elizabeth (1818–1907), 2:224–225; Keckley, Elizabeth (1818–1907): excerpts from her memoir *Behind the Scenes* (1868), 2:225–226; Ladies' Aid Societies/Soldiers' Aid Societies, 2:226–227; Lincoln, Mary Todd (1818–1882), 2:227–229; Lincoln, Mary Todd (1818–1882): two letters of (1862, 1870), 2:229–230; Livermore, Mary Ashton Rice (1820–1905), 2:231–232; *Minor v. Happersett* (1875), 2:232–233; *Minor v. Happersett* (1875): on the constitutionality of denying votes to women (1875), 2:233–234; Mo-nah-se-tah (ca. 1851–1922), 2:234–235; Nightingale Plan, 2:235–236; Nightingale Plan: excerpts from Florence Nightingale's *Notes on Nursing* (1859), 2: 236–237; nurses, Civil War, 2:238–239; nurses, Civil War: excerpts from the diary of Kate Cumming (1866), 2:239–240; Pinkerton Detective Agency, 2:240–242; Port Royal Experiment, 2:242–243; Port Royal Experiment: letters relating to the Port Royal experiment (1862), 2:244–245; Richmond Bread Riot (1863), 2:245–247; soldiers, women passing as men, civil war, 2:247–249; spies, 2:249–251; Starr, Belle (1848–1889), 2:252–253; Surratt, Mary (ca. 1823–1865), 2:253–254; thematic issues essay, 2:263–264; thematic issues essay: childbirth and child rearing, 2:270–271; thematic issues essay: clothing and fashion, 2:271; thematic issues essay: courtship, marriage, and divorce, 2:269–270; thematic issues essay: education, 2:265–266; thematic issues essay: fertility and fertility control, 2:270; thematic issues essay: gender roles, 2:264–265; thematic issues essay: immigration and migration, 2:268–269; thematic issues essay: legal and political power, 2:267–268; thematic issues essay: violence, domestic and sexual, 2:271; thematic issues essay: work, waged an unwaged, 2:266–267; Tompkins, Sally (1833–1916), 2:255–256; United States Sanitary Commission (USCC), 2:256–257; Van Lew, Elizabeth (1810–1900), 2:257–258; Vaughn, Hester (ca. 1860s), 2:259; Velazquez, Loreta Janeta (1842–1902), 2:260–261; Walker, Mary (1832–1919), 2:261–262; Willard, Frances (1839–1898), 2:262–263. *See also specific entries*

Clackum, Fannie Mae, 4:24

Clark, Joseph B., 4:221

Clayton, Fay, 4:204–205, 4:320

Clinical Research Bureau (CRB), 3:10, 3:262

Clinton, Bill, 3:281, 4:285, 286, 290, 297

Clinton, Henry, 1:269

Clinton, Hillary (1947–): on Bill Clinton's romantic liaisons, 4:285; candidacy for president of the United States, 4:285, 286; Children's Defense Fund, 4:285; Clinton, Bill, and, 4:285; daughter of, 4:285; early activism of, 4:284; education of, 4:284–285; father of, 4:284; in Fayetteville, Arkansas, 4:285; as First Lady of the United States, 4:285; first woman nominated for the presidency, 4:286; *Hard Choices*, 4:286; her husband's gubernatorial contests, 4:285; impeachment of Richard Nixon, 4:285; *An Invitation to the White House: At Home with History*, 4:285; *It Takes a Village—And Other Lessons Children Teach Us*, 4:285; in Little Rock, Arkansas, 4:285; *Living History*, 4:285; marriage of, 4:285; memoir of, 4:285; Monica Lewinsky scandal and, 4:285; mother of, 4:284; "The 100 Most Influential Lawyers in America" and, 4:285; opposition to the Vietnam War, 4:284; overview of, 4:284–285; President's Task Force on Health Care Reform and, 4:285; at the Rose Law Firm, 4:285; as secretary of state, 4:285; significance of, 4:284; support of civil rights, 4:284; as U.S. Senator, 4:285; Wellesley commencement address, 4:285; Whitewater land development deal, 4:285; at Yale Law School, 4:285

Clisby, Harriet, 2:371

clothing, Native American women: in California, 1:11; clothing lamentation, 1:11; cultural status of women, 1:11; European contact and, 1:11; fringe, 1:10; Great Plains cultures, 1:11; headdresses, 1:10; hides, uses of, 1:10; Mississippian Culture, 1:11; overview of, 1:10–11; ownership of skins, 1:11; in the Southwest, 1:11; tanning animal skins, 1:10; tunic-shaped silhouettes for shirts and dresses, 1:10

Coalition of Hispanic Women's Organization, 4:310

Coast Miwoks, 1:60

Coates, Dorothy Love, 4:153

Cobb, Laura (1892–1981): awards and honors to, 3:309; date and place of birth, 3:308; death of, 3:309; effects of vitamin deficiency, 3:309; overview of, 3:308–309; in the Philippines, 3:309; as prisoner of war, 3:309; significance of, 3:308; as a teacher, 3:308; at the U.S. Naval Hospital at Guam, 3:309; at the U.S. Navy Hospital in Canacao, Philippine Islands, 3:309

Cochran, Jacqueline (1906–1980): Aviation Hall of Fame, 3:311; Bendix cross-country air race, 3:310; birthplace of, 3:310; breaking the sound barrier, 3:309, 311; British Air Transport Auxiliary (ATA), 3:311; date of birth, 3:310; early childhood, 3:309–310; Federation Aeronautique Internationale Gold Medal, 3:311; flight records of, 3:310–311; Harmon Trophy to, 3:310, 311; Jacqueline Cochran Cosmetics Company, 3:310; Lovelace, Randolph, 3:311; marriage of, 3:310; Ninety Nines and, 3:311; original interest in flying, 3:310; overview of, 3:309–311; photograph of, 3:310; Pilot of the Decade, 3:311; primary document: her final report on Women Air Force Service Pilots Program (1945), 3:312–314; significance of, 3:309; Women's Airforce Service Pilots (WASP), 3:311, 346

Cochrane, Elizabeth Jane (1864–1922). See Bly, Nellie (1864–1922)

Cohen, Ruth Schwartz, 2:165

Coit, Stanton, 2:351

Colden, Jane (1724–1766): current status of her work, 1:246; death of, 1:246; drawing number 153 (1724–1766) of, 1:245; education of, 1:245; her drawings and plant

(1666–1727), **1**:148–149; law clarifying property rights in the Colony of New York (1710), **1**:104–105; Laydon, Anne Burras (1595–?), **1**:149–150; literacy, **1**:150–152; mestiza, **1**:152–153; midwives, **1**:153–155; Moody, Deborah (1586–1658/1659), **1**:155–156; Musgrove, Mary (ca. 1700–1763), **1**:156–158; Protestant women, **1**:158–161; Protestant women: Plymouth Colony court cases involving women (mid-1600s), **1**:159–161; Quakers, **1**:162–163; Quakers: excerpts from a declaration of the Quaker women's meeting of Lancashire (late 1670s), **1**:163–164; Queen Alliquippa (ca. 1680–1754), **1**:165–166; slavery, African, **1**:166–168; slavery: Virginia Slave Laws (1662, 1667), **1**:169; spinning bees, **1**:169–171; Tekakwitha, Kateri (1656–1680), **1**:171–172; thematic issues essay, **1**:195–196; thematic issues essay: childbirth and child rearing, **1**:201–202; thematic issues essay: courtship, marriage, and divorce, **1**:200–201; thematic issues essay: education, **1**:196–197; thematic issues essay: fashion and clothing, **1**:203; thematic issues essay: fertility and fertility control, **1**:201; thematic issues essay: gender roles, **1**:196; thematic issues essay: immigration and migration, **1**:199–200; thematic issues essay: legal and political power, **1**:198–199; thematic issues essay: violence, domestic and sexual, **1**:202–203; thematic issues essay: work, waged and unwaged, **1**:197–198; Tituba, **1**:172–174; wife abuse, Colonial North America (1607–1754), **1**:174–175; wife abuse, Colonial North America (1607–1754): "About the Duties of Husbands and Wives" from Benjamin Wadsworth's *A Well-Ordered Family* (1712), **1**:175–176; wife sales, **1**:176–177; wife sales: marriage contract: translation of the marriage contract of Brant Peelen and Marritje Pieters, widow of Claes Sybrantsen (1643), **1**:177–178; witchcraft in New England, **1**:178–180; witchcraft in New England: letter of Reverend Samuel Willard to Cotton Mather regarding a case of witchcraft in Groton, Massachusetts (1671), **1**:180–189; witchcraft in New England: excerpts from Cotton Mather's *Memorable Providences, Relating to Witchcrafts and Possessions* (1689), **1**:189; witch trials, Salem, Massachusetts (1692), **1**:190–91; witch trials, Salem, Massachusetts (1692): documents relating to Ann Forster's trial for witchcraft in Salem, Massachusetts (1692), **1**:192–195. *See also specific entries*
colonial recipes: beverages and foods (1750s, 1790s), **1**:222–223
Colored Female Free Produce Society (CFFPS): Bethel African Methodist Episcopal Church, **2**:27; Forten family, **2**:28; free produce fares, **2**:28; gender-based slogans, **2**:28; Harper, Frances Ellen Watkins (1825–1911), **2**:28; Lewis, Alice Jackson, **2**:28; overview of, **2**:27–28; Philadelphia Female Anti-Slavery Society, **2**:27; promotion of merchants, **2**:28; purpose of, **2**:27; White, Lydia, **2**:28; women's rights movement and, **2**:28
Colored Women's League, **2**:332
Combahee River Collective (CRC), **4**:191

Commission on the Status of Women, **2**:154
communism and gender, **4**:8
Comprehensive Child Development Act (1971), **4**:268
compulsory education laws, **2**:381
Comstock Laws: as both progressive social changes and conservative reactions, **3**:9; Comstock, Anthony, **2**:198; Comstock Act (1873), challenges to, **2**:198–199; *Crane* decision, **2**:198; definition of, **2**:198; *Griswold v. Connecticut*, **2**:199; "little Comstock Laws," **2**:198; overview of, **2**:198–199; purpose of, **2**:198; Sanger, Margaret, **2**:198; *United States v. One Package*, **2**:198–199, **3**:277–278
Congressional Union (CU), **3**:112
Connecticut Woman Suffrage Association (CWSA), **2**:76
conservation and recycling: canning, **3**:315; conservation propaganda effort, **3**:314–315; conservation slogan, **3**:314; fat and grease conservation, **3**:315; gas rationing, **3**:315; homefront resources, goals of, **3**:314; overview of, **3**:314–315; and patriotism, **3**:315; primary document: recipes to help women cook during wartime rationing (1943), **3**:315–318; shortage of goods, **3**:314; stamp-based rationing system, **3**:315; victory gardens, **3**:315; voluntary rationing, **3**:314–315
consumer culture: advertising, **4**:18–19; advertising and women, **4**:19; after World War II, **4**:19; the automobile, **4**:19; the baby boom, **4**:19; celebrity endorsements, **4**:19; consumerism, **4**:18; credit/credit cards, **4**:19; industrialization and, **4**:19; materialism, **4**:18, 19; overview of, **4**:18–20; social status and, **4**:19
Contraband Relief Association, **2**:225
Cooper, Anna J. (1858–1964): American Negro Academy, **3**:39; birth name of, **3**:39; "Colored Women as Wage Earners," **3**:39; death of, **3**:40; dissertation of, **3**:40; as editor, **3**:39; education of, **3**:39, 40; organizations founded by, **3**:39; overview of, **3**:39–40; parents of, **3**:39; as president of Frelinghuysen University, **3**:40; significance of, **3**:39; teaching career of, **3**:39; *A Voice from the South: By a Woman from the South*, **3**:39
Corbin, Margaret (1751–1800): burial of, **1**:247; date and place of birth, **1**:247; Daughters of Liberty, **1**:249; death of, **1**:247; legend of Molly Pitcher, **1**:274; military action of, **1**:247; military service pension, **1**:247; overview of, **1**:247; parents of, **1**:247; pension to, **1**:247; wounding of, **1**:247
Cori, Gerty (1896–1957): Cori, Carl, **4**:20; the Cori ester, **4**:20; date and place of birth, **4**:20; death of, **4**:20; education of, **4**:20; gender discrimination and, **4**:20; marriage of, **4**:20; memberships in, **4**:20–21; Nobel Prize, **4**:20; overview of, **4**:20–21; parents of, **4**:20; religion and, **4**:20; research of, **4**:20; significance of, **4**:20; Washington University and, **4**:20
Corn Mother: Cherokees, **1**:12; commonality in legend of, **1**:13; definition of, **1**:11; Eastern Woodland peoples, **1**:12; geographical differences in the legend, **1**:12; Hopi Katchina Doll, photograph of, **1**:12; overview of, **1**:11–13; Pawnee

work, waged and unwaged, **3**:286–287; Thompson, Dorothy (1894–1961), **3**:271–273; Toklas, Alice (1877–1967), **3**:273–274; Toklas, Alice (1877–1967): her letter to friends (1946), **3**:274; United Cannery, Agricultural, Packing, and Allied Workers of America (UCAPAWA), **3**:274–275; United Cannery, Agricultural, Packing, and Allied Workers of America (UCAPAWA): Aubrey Williams's address to (1937), **3**:276–277; *United States v. One Package* (1936), **3**:277–278; *United States v. One Package* (1936) document, **3**:279–280; United States Women's Bureau (1920–), **3**:280–281; Velez, Lupe (1908–1944), **3**:281–283; Wong, Anna May (1905–1961), **3**:283–284. *See also specific entries*

Great Plains culture: Apaches, migration of, **1**:24; bison, **1**:24, 25; Comanches, **1**:24; community power of women, **1**:24–25; environmental changes, **1**:24; horses, **1**:25; Indian wars, **1**:25; Lakotas, **1**:24; life expectancy of women, **1**:25; location of the Great Plains, **1**:23; Mandans, Omahas, Osages, and Pawnees, **1**:24; matriarchal and/or matrilineal tribal practices, **1**:23; migration, **1**:24; overview of, **1**:23–25; Paleo-Indians and, **1**:23; precipitation at, **1**:23, 24; reservations, **1**:25; responsibilities of women, **1**:24; vegetation and fauna of, **1**:23

Greeley, Horace, **2**:20, 180

Green, Hetty (1834–1916): children of, **2**:309; date and place of birth, **2**:308; death of, **2**:309; estate of, **2**:309; inheritances of, **2**:308; investments of, **2**:309; marriage of, **2**:309; miserly nature of, **2**:309; nickname of, **2**:308; overview of, **2**:308–309; parents of, **2**:308; portrait of, **2**:309; prenuptial agreement, **2**:308–309; *Robinson V. Mandell* (1868), **2**:308; significance of, **2**:308

Greene, Catharine Littlefield (1755–1814): burial place of, **1**:259; the cotton gin, **1**:258; date and place of birth, **1**:258; death of, **1**:259; family of, **1**:258; Greene, Nathaniel, **1**:258; marriages of, **1**:258; at Mulberry Grove, **1**:258; overview of, **1**:258–259; parents of, **1**:258; Revolutionary War debts, **1**:258; Whitney, Eli, **1**:258

Greene, Catherine Ray: correspondence of Benjamin Franklin (1755, 1775, 1776), **1**:276–279

Greenebaum, Michael, **3**:153

Greenglass, David, **4**:60

Greenhow, Rose (1814–1864): burial of, **2**:216; date and place of birth, **2**:215; death of, **2**:216; espionage work of, **2**:215, 216; house arrest and imprisonment of, **2**:216; marriage of, **2**:215; memoir of, **2**:216; overview of, **2**:210, 215–216; photograph of, **2**:215; primary document: letter of Confederate spy Rose Greenhow to Secretary of State William H. Seward (1861), **2**:216–218; as a proslavery enthusiast, **2**:215–216; as a symbol to white Americans, **2**:216; Wilson, Henry, **2**:216

Grenville, Richard, **1**:61

Grimké, Archibald, **2**:71

Grimké, Francis, **2**:71

Grimké, Sarah (1792–1873) and Angelina (1805–1879): activism of, **2**:54; antislavery petition, **2**:71; *Appeal to the*

Christian Women of the South, **2**:71; attempt to vote, **2**:71; childhood of, **2**:71; children of Angelina, **2**:71; date and place of births, **2**:71; deaths of, **2**:71; dress controversy, **2**:71; female antislavery societies, **2**:54; Letters on the Equality of the Sexes," **2**:71; marriage of Angelina, **2**:71; National Association for the Advancement of Colored People, **2**:71; nephews of, **2**:71; overview of, **2**:70–71; primary document: Angelina Grimké's *Appeal to the Christian Women of the South* (1836), **2**:72–73; prominence of, **2**:71; Quakerism and, **2**:54, 72; significance of, **2**:72–73; speaking tour of, **2**:71

Griswold, Estelle, **4**:221

Griswold v. Connecticut, **2**:199, **3**:30, **4**:84, **4**:221–222

Groghan, George (1720–1782), **1**:165

Gulovich, Maria (1921–2009), **3**:338

Guyard, Marie (1599–1672), **1**:316

Guy-Sheftall, Beverly, **4**:111

Hakluyt, Richard, **1**:59

Hale, John, **1**:136

Hale, Ruth, **2**:127

Hale, Sarah Josepha, **2**:69, 70

Hall, Murray (d. 1901): adopted daughter, **2**:310; bail bonds business, **2**:310; breast cancer, **2**:310; characteristics of, **2**:310; death of, **2**:310; Iroquois Club, **2**:310; library of, **2**:310; New York politics and, **2**:310; overview of, **2**:310–311; sex of, **2**:310; significance of, **2**:310; women of, **2**:310

Hall, Thomas/Thomasine (ca. 1600–unknown): childhood of, **1**:119; court rulings on, **1**:119–120; date and place of birth, **1**:119; gender performance of, **1**:119; military service of, **1**:119; overview of, **1**:119–120; primary document: Joseph Dorman's "The Female Rake: or, Modern Fine Lady" (1736), **1**:120; sexual identity of, **1**:119; significance of, **1**:120; in Warrosquyoacke, Virginia, **1**:119

Hall, Virginia (1906–1982), **3**:337

Hallelujah Lasses, **2**:347

Hamilton, Alice, **2**:314

Hamilton, Alice (1869–1970): date and place of birth, **3**:65; death of, **3**:66; education of, **3**:65–66; at Harvard Medical School, **3**:66; Health Committee for the League of Nations and, **3**:66; her interest in public health, **3**:66; at Hull House, **3**:66; Illinois Occupation Disease Commission, **3**:66; on industrial accidents, **3**:66; Occupational Safety and Health Act (OSHA), **3**:65; overview of, **3**:65–66; photograph of, **3**:65; significance of, **3**:65

Hancock, Joy Bright, **3**:343

Handler, Ruth, **4**:10–11

Handsome Lake, **1**:29

Hanna, Kathleen, photograph of, **4**:348

Hanson, Elizabeth, **1**:100

Hardin, Garrett, **4**:190

Harding, Warren G., **3**:151

Hardy, Sheila, **4**:33

Harlan II, John Marshall, **4**:221

purpose of, **2**:84; reaction to, **2**:85; right to name, **2**:85; Stone, Lucy, **2**:85

Married Women's Property Act (1848): Banking Panic of 1837, **2**:87; benefits of, **2**:87; consequences of, **2**:86, 87; coverture, **2**:86; first limited Married Women's Property Act, **2**:87; limited acts prior to, **2**:87; overview of, **2**:13, 86–87; primary document: Married Women's Property Act (1848), **2**:87–88; purpose of, **2**:86; reactions to, **2**:87; Section 1 of, **2**:86; Section 2 of, **2**:86–87; Section 3 of, **2**:87; Section 4 of, **2**:87

Married Women's Property Act (1860), **2**:121, 153

Marshall, Thurgood, **4**:45, 75

Marston, Elizabeth, **3**:351

Marston, William Moulton, **3**:350

Martin, Del, **4**:21

Mason, Lucy Randolph, **2**:335

maternal feminism, **4**:99

Maternity Center Association (MCA), **3**:291

Mather, Cotton (1663–1728): primary document: excerpts from Cotton Mather's *Memorable Providences, Relating to Witchcrafts and Possessions* (1689), **1**:189; primary document: letter of Reverend Samuel Willard to Cotton Mather regarding a case of witchcraft in Groton, Massachusetts (1671), **1**:180–189; Rowlandson, Mary, **1**:99; witchcraft in New England, **1**:180; witch-hunting and, **1**:113

Mathews, Mother Bernardina (1732–1800): alternative spelling, **1**:270; in Baltimore, Maryland, **1**:271; as Bernardina Teresa Xavier of Saint Joseph, **1**:271; birth name, **1**:270; Carmelite convent at Hoogstraten, **1**:271; Carmelite order and, **1**:272; Catholicism and, **1**:271; at Chandler's Hope, **1**:271; date and place of birth, **1**:270; family of, **1**:270; overview of, **1**:270–272; Port Tobacco convent, **1**:271–272; significance of, **1**:270

Mathews, Robert, **2**:147

matrilineal descent: Choctaws, **1**:40; definition of, **1**:39; fictive kinship, **1**:40; Hopis, **1**:40; Iroquois Confederacy, **1**:40; matrilocality, **1**:39; Native American tribes, **1**:39–40; options for determining lineage, **1**:39; overview of, **1**:39–41; and the status for women, **1**:39; Toypurina, **1**:40

Matthews, Charles (1776–1835), **2**:89

Matthews, Victoria Earle, **2**:335

Maybeck, Bernard (1862–1957), **3**:102–103

McAfee, Mildred, **3**:344

McCall's, **4**:137

McCarthy, Catherine, **3**:110

McCauley, Mary (1754–1832): *American Anecdotes*, **1**:273; Battle of Monmouth and, **1**:273; birth name of, **1**:273; Carlisle, Pennsylvania and, **1**:273; Custis, George Washington Parke, **1**:273; *Cyclopedia of American History* (1835), **1**:273; date and place of birth, **1**:273; death of, **1**:273; depiction of, **1**:272; fame of, **1**:273; legend of Molly Pitcher, **1**:244, 249, 267, 272, 273–274; marriages of,

1:273; military pension, **1**:273; overview of, **1**:272–274; parents of, **1**:273; son of, **1**:273; war stories about, **1**:273

McClintock, Barbara (1902–1992): date and place of birth, **4**:46; death of, **4**:47; education of, **4**:46–47; genetics and, **4**:47; Nobel Prize, **4**:47; overview of, **4**:46–47; parents of, **4**:46; significance of, **4**:46; on women and science, **4**:47

McClure's Magazine, **3**:32

McCormick, Katherine, **4**:77

McCrea, Jane (1752–1777): art concerning, **1**:275; date and place of birth, **1**:274; death of, **1**:274, **1**:274–275; as English female captive, **1**:97–98, 274; Gates, Horatio, **1**:274–275; literature concerning, **1**:275; overview of, **1**:274–275; in popular culture, **1**:275; propaganda value of, **1**:274–275; significance of, **1**:274

McDaniel, Hattie (1893–1952): awards and honors to, **3**:249; criticism of, **3**:248; date and place of birth, **3**:247; death of, **3**:249; father of, **3**:247; film appearances, **2**:84, **3**:248, 249; on the minstrel circuit, **3**:248; mother of, **3**:247; overview of, **3**:247–249; photograph of, **3**:248; primary document: her Oscar acceptance speech (1939), **3**:2:49; quoted on playing a maid, **3**:249; on radio, **3**:248, **3**:249; significance of, **3**:247; during World War II, **3**:248

McDonald, Audra Ann (1970–): Broadway Impact and, **4**:321; criticism of, **4**:321; daughter of, **4**:321; early performance career of, **4**:320; education of, **4**:320–321; on hyperactivity, **4**:321; marriages of, **4**:321; overview of, **4**:320–321; parents of, **4**:320; photograph of, **4**:320; *The Secret Garden* musical, **4**:321; significance of, **4**:320; Tony Award performances, **4**:321

McDowall, John R., **2**:99

McDowell, Mary, **4**:292

McWhirter, Martha, **2**:147

Meacham, Joseph, **1**:267

Mead, Margaret (1901–1978): at the American Museum of Natural History, **4**:176; awards and honors to, **4**:176; Benedict, Ruth, and, **3**:218–19; bisexuality, **4**:176; books published, number of, **4**:176; child of, **4**:176; *Coming of Age in Samoa*, **4**:176; date and place of birth, **4**:175; death of, **4**:176; education of, **4**:175–176; influence on American culture, **4**:176; marriage of, **4**:176; Native American study, **4**:176; New Guinea study, **4**:176; overview of, **4**:175–176; parents of, **4**:175; popularity of, **4**:175; *Redbook* column of, **4**:175; religion and, **4**:175; Samoan study, **4**:176; significance of, **4**:175; teaching positions, **4**:176; during World War II, **4**:176

Mecom, Jane Franklin (1712–1794): children of, **1**:275–276; date of birth, **1**:275; death of, **1**:275; her brother Benjamin, **1**:275; letters of, **1**:275; marriage of, **1**:275; overview of, **1**:275–276; parents of, **1**:275; primary document: correspondence of Benjamin Franklin with Catherine Ray Greene (1755, 1775, 1776), **1**:276–279; significance of, **1**:275

"Me" decade, **4**:83, 84–85

Megan's Law: civil rights activists on, **4**:322; constitutionality of, **4**:322; criticism of, **4**:322; definition of, **4**:321;